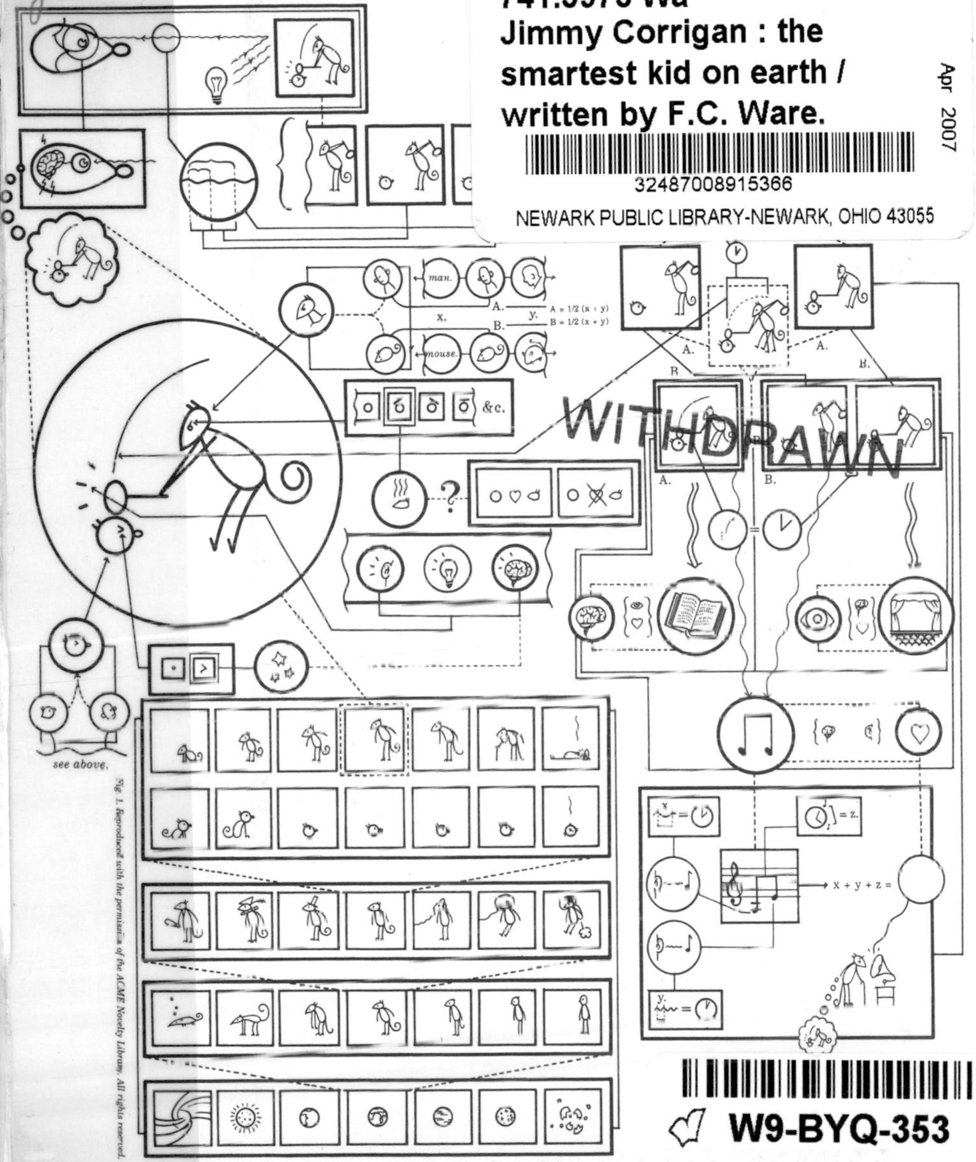
man.
mouse.
x.
y.
A.
B.
A = 1/2 (x + y)
B = 1/2 (x − y)
&c.
A.
B.
see above.
= z.
x + y + z =

Fig. 1. Reproduced with the permission of the ACME Novelty Library. All rights reserved.

New Pictorial Language Makes Marks.

Good for Showing Stuff, Leaving out Big Words.

Article reproduced with the permission of The Journal of Liberal Arts Degrees.

It is the natural inclination of children to describe events common to their lives through sequences of simple pictograms and images, for such "picture stories" serve to "make sense" and "order" the exciting and sometimes confusing new world which accosts them. However, with the onset of early education, social conditioning, and class circumstance, this congenital skill has been traditionally left to atrophy, kept alive only by the occasional prick to attention by the various "napkin gags" and "refrigerator clippings" which commonly litter the back pages of our newsdailies. Such an unfortunate cultural situation serves only to associate an otherwise potentially effective language with such juvenilia as lawn games, pony races, and gaily-costumed musclemen, thus greatly compromising both the maturity of material available for consumption and the happiness of those willing to submit to a life of companionless mockery in blind pursuit of its production. Despite these obstacles, a variegated loam for exciting stories and thrilling adventures has long lain untilled, yet now the seeds are being sewn, encouraged by a startling and seemingly unstoppable rise in illiteracy, and an accompanying dive in the general intelligence of the populace.

With the many recent technological breakthroughs in pictorial linguistics (as exemplified by airline safety cards, battery diagrams, and feminine protection directions), such heretofore-dormant skills of Comic Strip Apprehension (or CSA) are being reawakened in the adult mind, paving the way for the explosion of more complicated literature which almost certainly looms within the next decade. "CSA is here to stay," remarks a well-known and highly decorated researcher of popular culture, "and all we can do is get ready. People can hardly form sentences that make any sense anymore; they're making nouns into verbs, and acronyming words out of the first letters of a lot of other words, and using words wrong all the time to mean things that they don't. So I guess little pictures are about the only way we're going to be able to tell stuff in the future, since most anybody can understand them. I think it'll be good, because people like looking at pictures, and I think words have had their day, anyway. It's a media-saturated world where media saturates everything and you can't think about anything except media saturation all the time." This same researcher added that adaptation of popular motion pictures, game shows, and installation art to this new language would also appear an inevitability. "I can see the whole of human culture being converted to CS – it's convenient, and saleable. Besides, people are getting less smart every day everywhere. It's a real world movement."

Certain publishing houses are experimenting with this new form of expression, test-marketing carefully demographed entertainments, and then strategically aiming them at a less-educated and/or intellectually blunted segment of the consumer pool. The results, thus far, are encouraging. "Dumb people are eating it up," says our researcher. "They love it. Especially people who buy a lot of stuff. This could be big." When queried as to the literary content of many of these projected releases, however, he is less forthcoming: "Uh, I dunno. Stories about people that people'll want to read. Fantasy stuff – y'know. Pretty girls, cars. We figure that'll take care of itself. We're working with a lot of content providers at the moment and so most of it's hush-hush. We're polling. You want to fill out a survey?"

Regardless, this "visual language" has secretly been in use by the military for many years, for its humorous, cross-cultural appeal to a wide variety of the ignorant made it the perfect means by which to explicate the mechanics of weaponry and killing. "It's like a movie, except without the popcorn," one articulate private offered. "I like it. Especially when there's naked chicks and stuff. It's like you're really there, except you're not."

It is expected that the earliest examples of such literature will appear in target economic regions later in the year, with a general release in the fall.

Additional copies of this article may be procured by writing to the publisher, address below.

Popular Press Easily Duped.

Quotations regarding the hardcover edition, selected as an aid to purchasing confidence.

Here included as a shameless and offensive last-minute effort to fill up this space (which reproduces an uncomfortably-sized, yet indispensible, Appendix originally included with the hardcover editions of this book) with something.

"In exchange for your efforts, this haunting and unshakable book will change the way you look at your world." – *Time.*

"*Jimmy Corrigan* pushes the form of comics into unexpected formal and emotional territory." – *The Chicago Tribune.*

"Ware's exquisite graphic narratives bring a nifty surprise. What looks like an extended nostalgia trip turns out, on more thorough examination, to be a satisfyingly maudlin rejection of retromania that's been taking a lot of his hipster peers on a ride to nowhere new." – *The Village Voice Literary Supplement.*

"Ware exploits the medium in ways that have never been explored." – *The Onion.*

"Third best book of the year." – *Entertainment Weekly.*

"Ware's work is among the very best graphic, comic, illustrative, and fine artwork being produced in the world right now." – *Mother Jones.*

"Stupendous." – *Matt Groening.*

"Dilbertesque." – *The Boston Herald.*

"Thunderous, heartbreaking." – *The Detroit Free Press.*

"One of the best comics in the world." – *Wired.*

"Slowly builds a portrait of lonely, empty lives with a bleakness that belies the artist's brilliant visual images." – *The Arkansas Democrat Gazette.*

"Reshap[es} and elevat[es] comic-book storytelling." – *The Hartford Courant.*

"May simply be the most moving, entertaining, and original graphic novel ever made." – *The Virginia Pilot.*

"Its plot, its characters, its artwork, its delineation between thought and reality are the work of quiet, complex genius." – *The Madison Daily Cardinal.*

"A cult classic among aficionados of beautifully crafted, inventively ironic adult comics." – *The Dallas Morning News.*

"Steeped in the devastating loneliness of contemporary life and in the petty cruelties that man inflicts upon his own kind." – *The Nashville Scene.*

"A wise tale, a poignant and poetic story, sharply written, ingenious in its conception, brilliantly executed." – *The Minneapolis Star Tribune.*

"Weighed down by its ambition." – *The Seattle Stranger.*

"Uses comics as a tool for confession and self-expression." – *The Silicon Valley Metro.*

"A tangled simulation of consciousness and memory." – *The Washington City Paper.*

"Mr. Ware's style, a blend of simplified body forms and overly detailed layouts, may make the strip a daunting read for newcomers to the comics medium, much the way the dense language of *Ulysses* challenged readers. The joys of the two works are the same, however: of being swept away by the dense poetry of an exciting and powerful work of art." – *The Wall Street Journal.*

Our braggadocio continues at right.

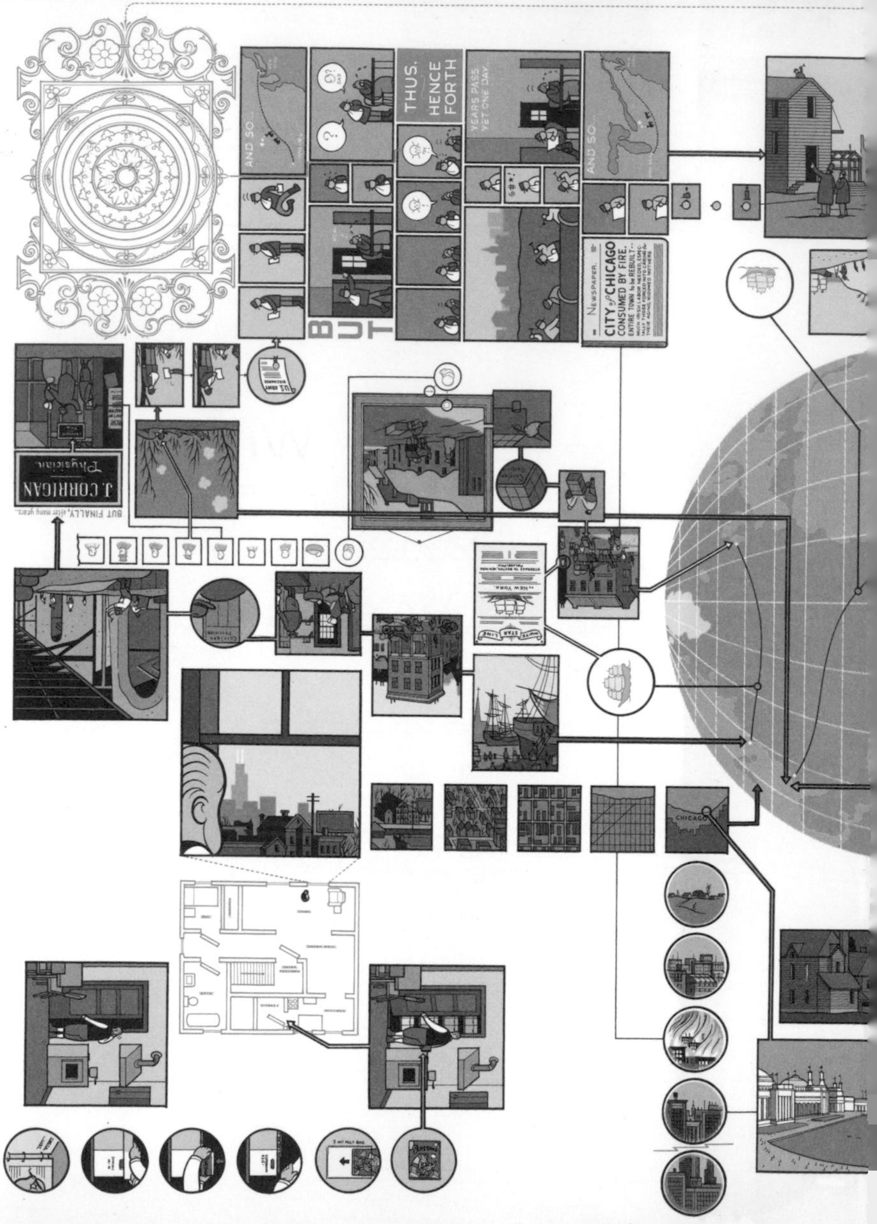
AND SO...
THUS. HENCE FORTH
YEARS PASS YET ONE DAY...
AND SO...
BUT
NEWSPAPER.
CITY of CHICAGO
CONSUMED BY FIRE.
ENTIRE TOWN to be REBUILT
J. CORRIGAN
Physician
BUT FINALLY, after many years...
CHICAGO

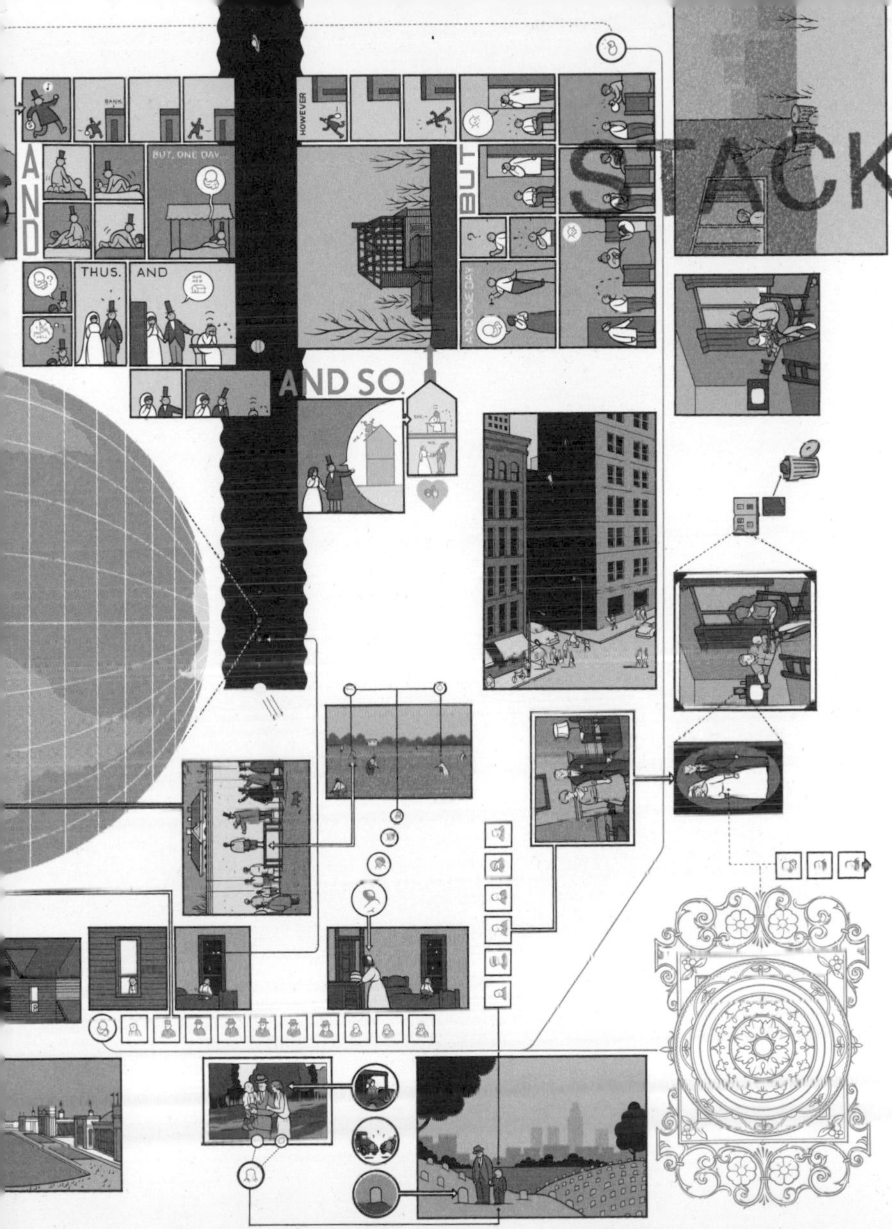
BANK
AND
BUT, ONE DAY...
THUS.
AND
HOWEVER
BUT
AND ONE DAY
AND SO

"Ware's work is the comic equivalent of Joyce's *Ulysses* – no one's ever read it, and those who have know that it sucks, but it sure looks great on your bookshelf." – *Ted Rall, slate.com.*

"Patiently lulls readers into awkward silences, childhood reveries and pained family interactions." – *The Washington Post.*

"In early July (2000) I was visiting my parents in Florida, and late one night on C-Span, I caught an episode of *Booktalk* or whatever they call their show about books, and the entire show, which aired late at night, presented a representative from some publisher pitching books from their Fall schedule to various managers from some Washington D.C. bookstore.

One of those books was the *Jimmy Corrigan* book, and it was somewhat dispiriting to see the stony faces of the bookstore managers as they debated whether their customers would willingly pay nearly $30.00 "for a comic book." They passed the dummy of the book around, looking at it with various degrees of incomprehension. Perhaps even more unnerving was the book rep's attempt to hype the book with comments that Ware was currently a "hip" and "hot"cartoonist in his field.

Ware had apparently also done the cover for the publisher's Fall catalog, and one of the managers dismissed the cover as being confusing and incomprehensible to her, or words to that effect. They quickly moved on the the next book being pitched, and I went to bed." – *Robert Cook, The Comics Journal Message Board, 8/8/2000.*

"Perceptive, poetic and sometimes profound."
– *The London Independent.*

"A work of genius." – *Zadie Smith, author,* White Teeth.

"Arguably the greatest achievement of the form, ever."
– *Dave Eggers, author,* A Heartbreaking Work of Staggering Genius.

"So real and awkward, it almost feels wrong to read it. I think Chris Ware must be a genius."
– *David Sedaris, author,* Me Talk Pretty One Day.

"Ware has a hyper, self-effacing streak that will be familiar to anyone who's Dave Eggers." – *San Jose Mercury News.*

"Ware attended Brownell-Talbot School through the 10th grade and spent part of one semester at Omaha Central High School before he moved to Texas and graduated from high school and the University of Texas at Austin." – *The Omaha World-Herald.*

"An excruciatingly desolate yet wonderfully nuanced portrait of loneliness." – *The New York Times.*

"Beautiful, poignant, and at times utterly heartbreaking, this multilayered coming-of-age story may be one of the finest sympathetic portraits of a loser we have in literature."
– *The Boston Sunday Globe.*

"Nearly impossible to read." – *The L.A. Times Book Review.*

"A meticulous record of the minutiae of nothing happening: eating, waiting, being disappointed." – *The London Review of Books.*

"On the cutting edge of any visual medium (including film)."
– *The Johns Hopkins News-Letter.*

"Demanding, disturbing, funny and exciting. Oh yes, and essential."
– *Time Out.*

"It is unlike any comic book you have ever seen ... skim a page and you'll miss a tiny delight – a Thumbelina landscape; a postage-stamp still-life; an entire treatise, in Lilliputian letters, on vinyl siding as a metaphor for life." – *CNN.*

"The colours are dreadful, it's like looking at a bottle of Domestos or Harpic or Ajax. Awful bleak colours, revolting to look at; it's on its way to the Oxfam shop. Disgusting look to it. Really horrible."
– *poet Tom Paulin, BBC Newsnight, December 8th, 2001.*

Selected as one of the "best" books of the year by *The Village Voice Literary Supplement* and *Time Out;* also awarded a 2000 *American Book Award,* and included in the *2002 Whitney Biennial of American Art.*

As well, Anglophiles may be interested to note that it was inexplicably accorded the *Guardian First Book Award, 2001.*

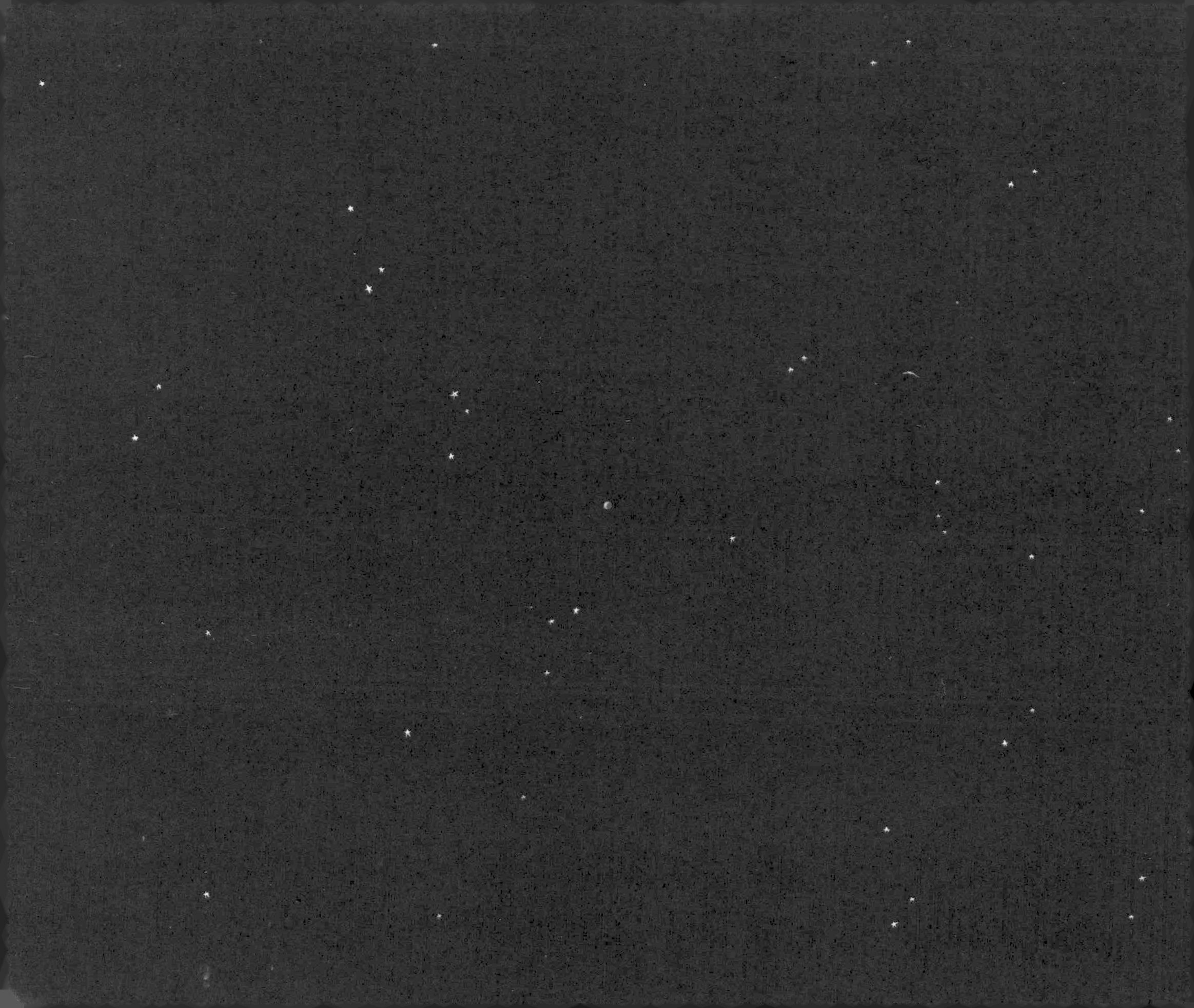

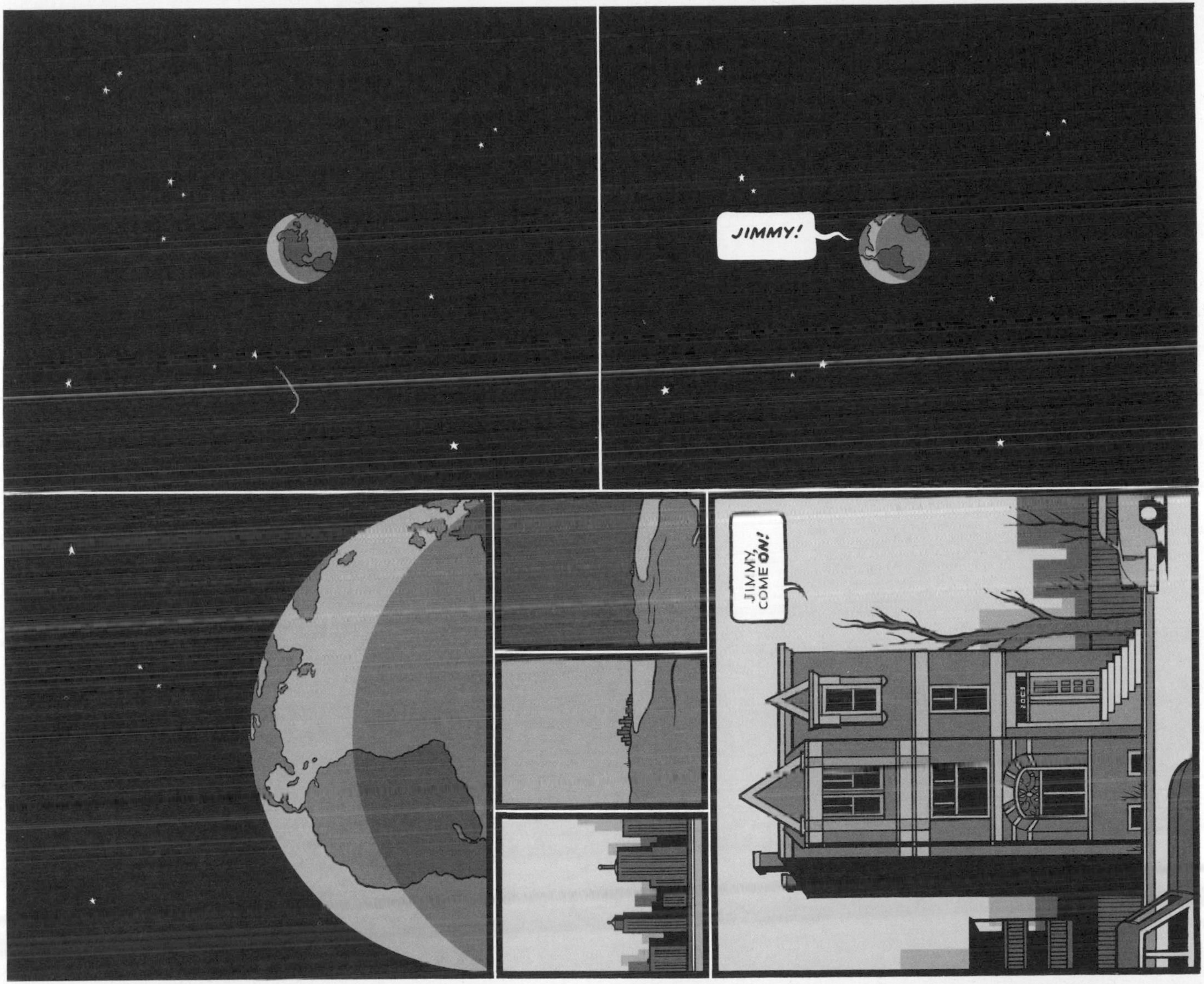
JIMMY!
JIMMY, COME ON!

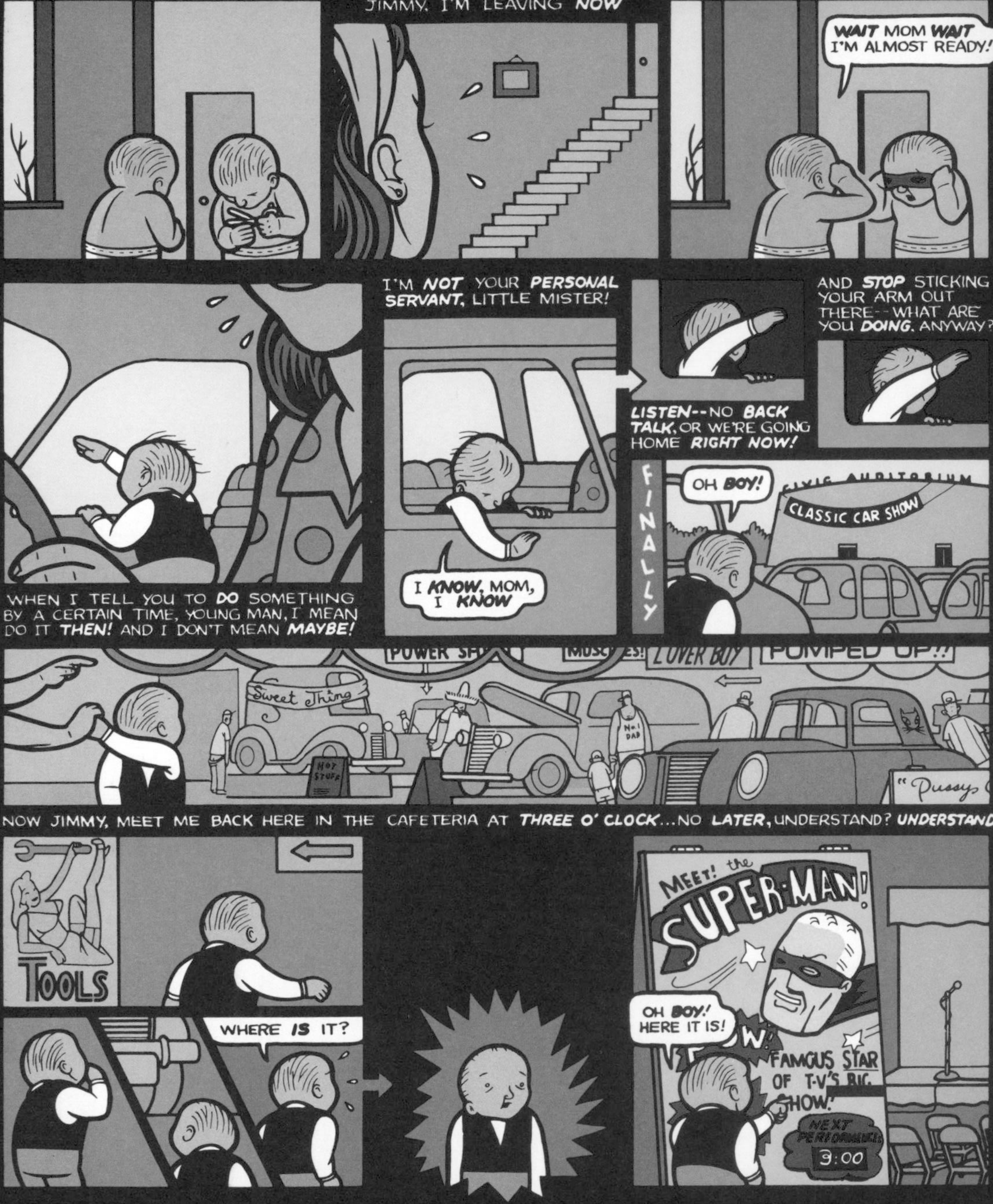
JIMMY, I'M LEAVING NOW
WAIT MOM WAIT I'M ALMOST READY!
WHEN I TELL YOU TO DO SOMETHING BY A CERTAIN TIME, YOUNG MAN, I MEAN DO IT THEN! AND I DON'T MEAN MAYBE!
I'M NOT YOUR PERSONAL SERVANT, LITTLE MISTER!
I KNOW, MOM, I KNOW
LISTEN--NO BACK TALK, OR WE'RE GOING HOME RIGHT NOW!
AND STOP STICKING YOUR ARM OUT THERE--WHAT ARE YOU DOING, ANYWAY?
FINALLY
OH BOY!
CLASSIC CAR SHOW
POWER SH
LOVER BOY
PUMPED UP!!
Sweet Thing
HOT STUFF
No.1 DAD
"Pussys
NOW JIMMY, MEET ME BACK HERE IN THE CAFETERIA AT THREE O' CLOCK...NO LATER, UNDERSTAND? UNDERSTAND?
TOOLS
WHERE IS IT?
OH BOY! HERE IT IS!
MEET! the SUPER-MAN!
POW!
FAMOUS STAR OF T-V'S BIG SHOW!
NEXT PERFORMANCE
3:00

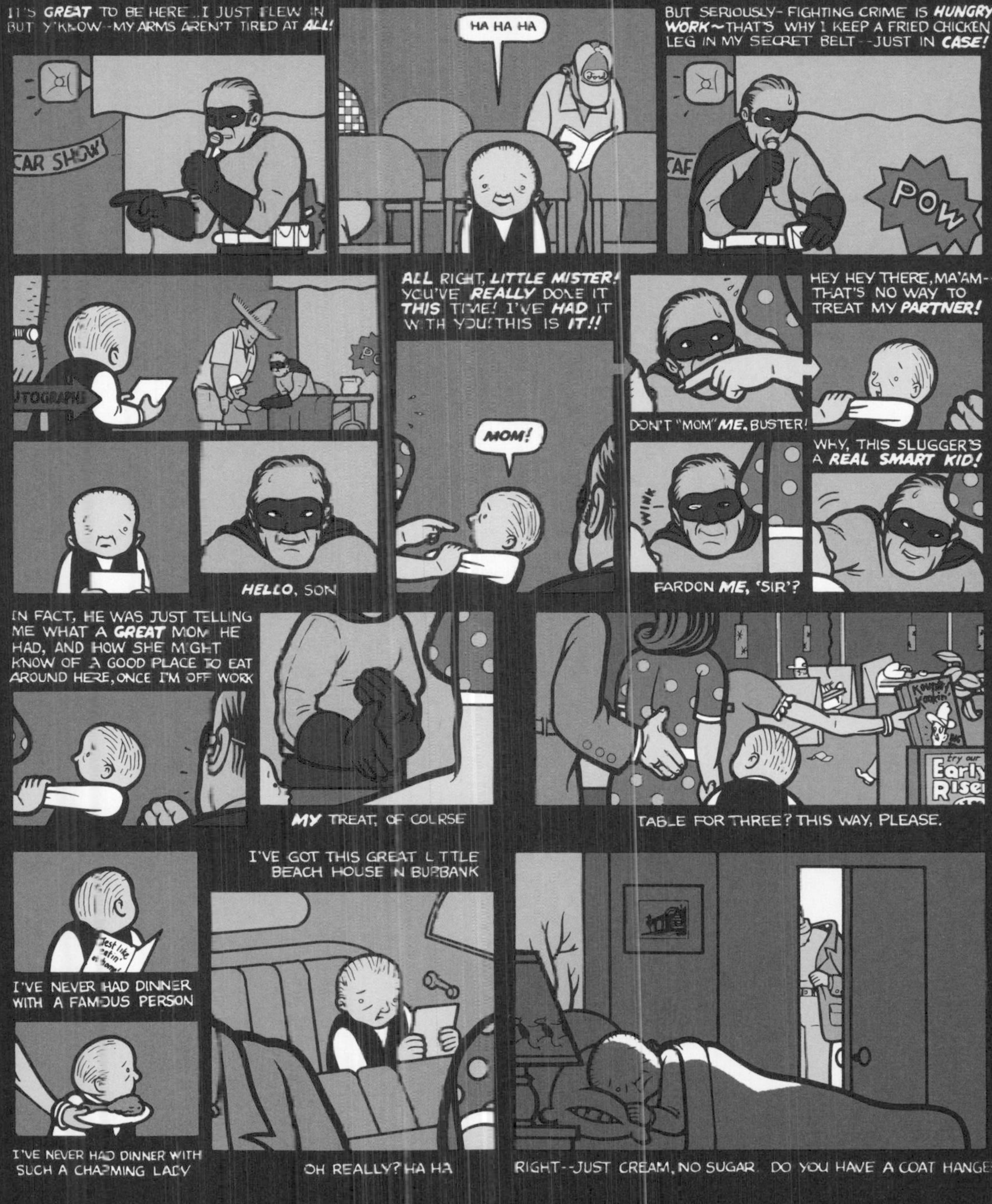
IT'S **GREAT** TO BE HERE...I JUST FLEW IN
BUT Y'KNOW--MY ARMS AREN'T TIRED AT **ALL!**
CAR SHOW
HA HA HA
BUT SERIOUSLY- FIGHTING CRIME IS **HUNGRY WORK**~THAT'S WHY I KEEP A FRIED CHICKEN LEG IN MY SECRET BELT--JUST IN **CASE!**
POW
AUTOGRAPHS
ALL RIGHT, **LITTLE MISTER!** YOU'VE **REALLY** DONE IT **THIS** TIME! I'VE **HAD** IT WITH YOU! THIS IS **IT!!**
HEY HEY THERE, MA'AM--THAT'S NO WAY TO TREAT MY **PARTNER!**
DON'T "MOM" **ME**, BUSTER!
MOM!
HELLO, SON
WINK
WHY, THIS SLUGGER'S A **REAL SMART KID!**
PARDON **ME**, 'SIR'?
IN FACT, HE WAS JUST TELLING ME WHAT A **GREAT** MOM HE HAD, AND HOW SHE MIGHT KNOW OF A GOOD PLACE TO EAT AROUND HERE, ONCE I'M OFF WORK
MY TREAT, OF COURSE
TABLE FOR THREE? THIS WAY, PLEASE.
try our Early Riser
I'VE NEVER HAD DINNER WITH A FAMOUS PERSON
I'VE GOT THIS GREAT LITTLE BEACH HOUSE IN BURBANK
I'VE NEVER HAD DINNER WITH SUCH A CHARMING LADY
OH REALLY? HA HA
RIGHT--JUST CREAM, NO SUGAR. DO YOU HAVE A COAT HANGER?

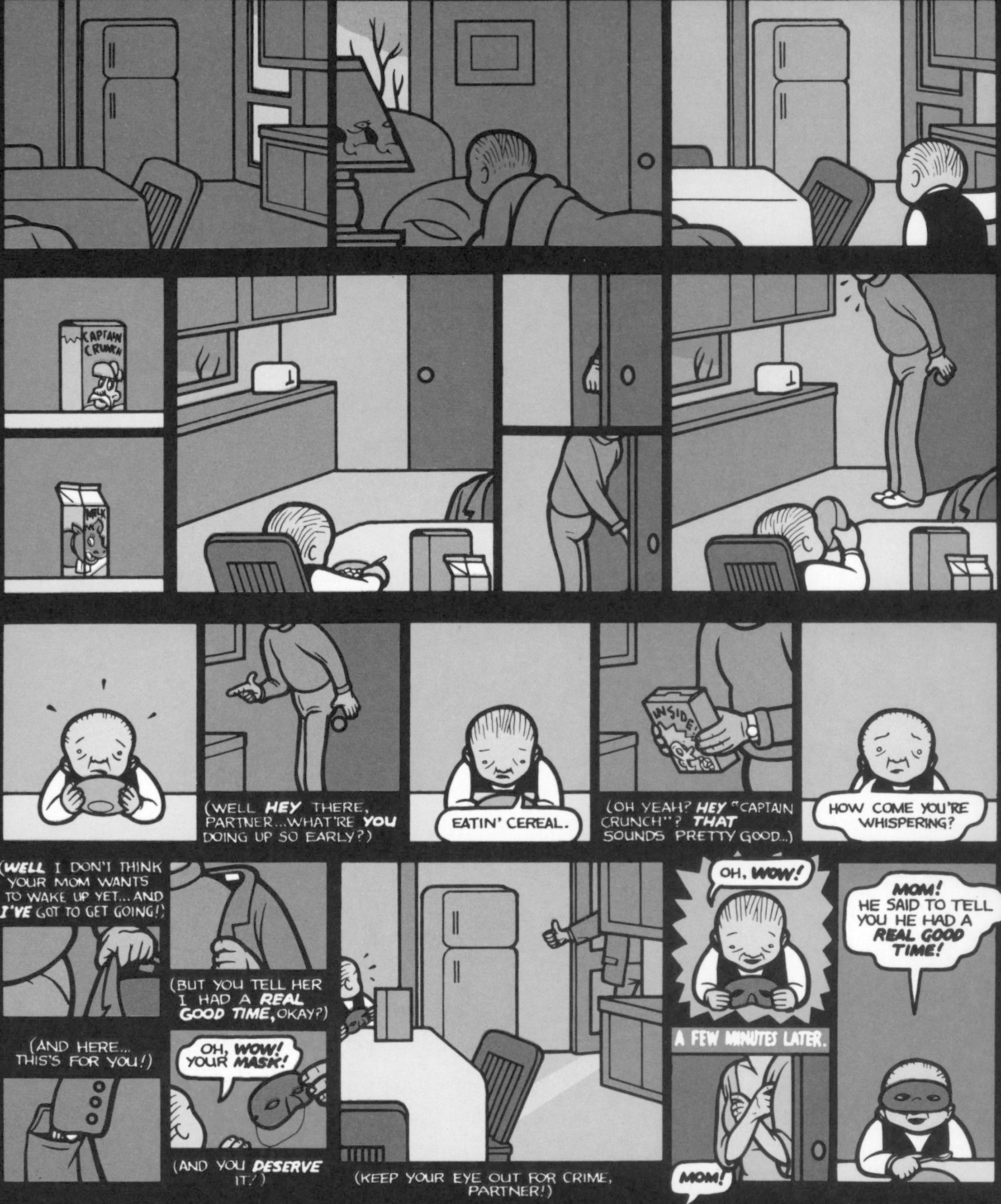
CAPTAIN CRUNCH
MILK
(WELL HEY THERE, PARTNER...WHAT'RE YOU DOING UP SO EARLY?)
EATIN' CEREAL.
INSIDE!
(OH YEAH? HEY "CAPTAIN CRUNCH"? THAT SOUNDS PRETTY GOOD...)
HOW COME YOU'RE WHISPERING?
(WELL I DON'T THINK YOUR MOM WANTS TO WAKE UP YET... AND I'VE GOT TO GET GOING!)
(BUT YOU TELL HER I HAD A REAL GOOD TIME, OKAY?)
(AND HERE... THIS'S FOR YOU!)
OH, WOW! YOUR MASK!
(AND YOU DESERVE IT!)
(KEEP YOUR EYE OUT FOR CRIME, PARTNER!)
OH, WOW!
A FEW MINUTES LATER.
MOM!
MOM! HE SAID TO TELL YOU HE HAD A REAL GOOD TIME!

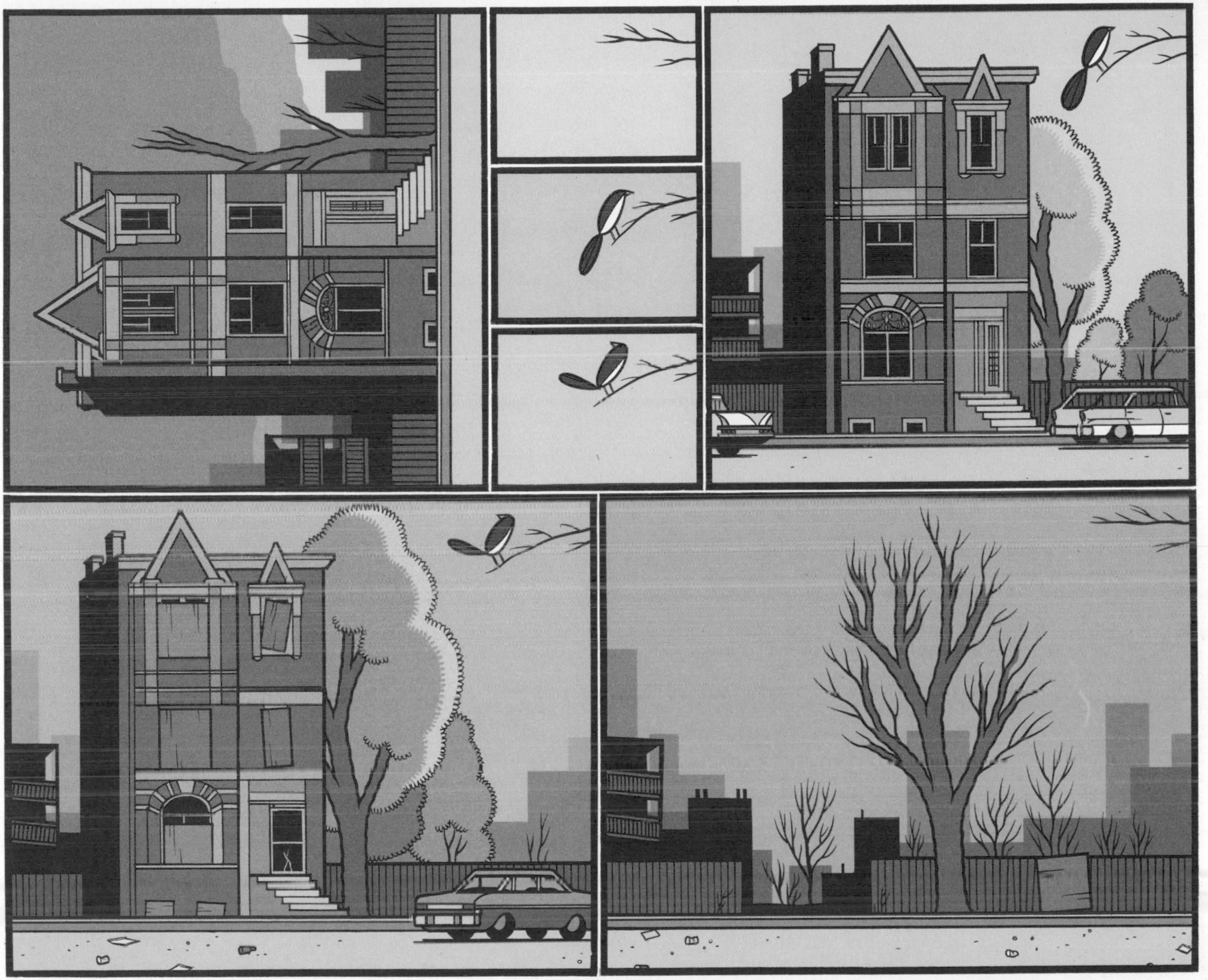

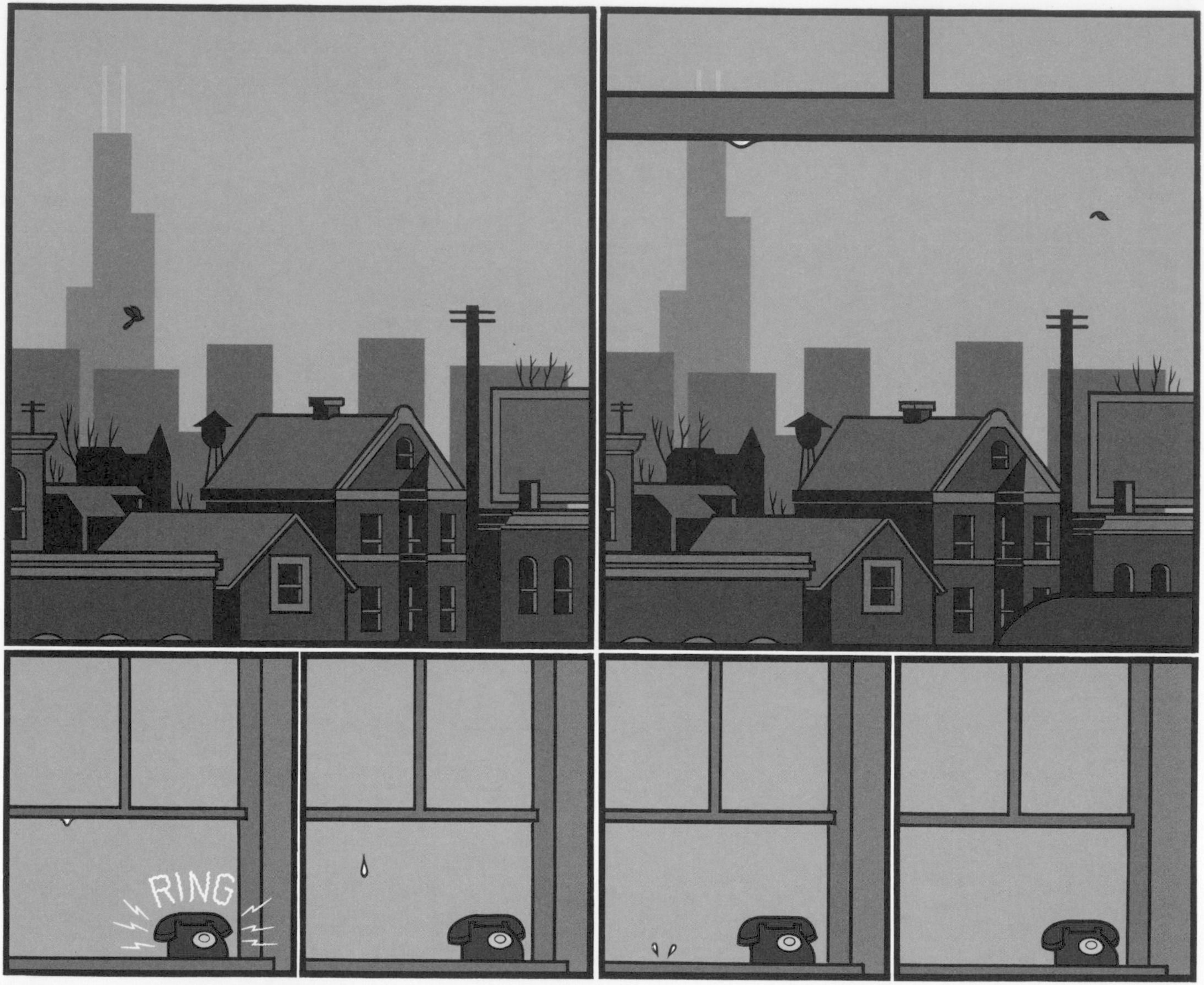
RING

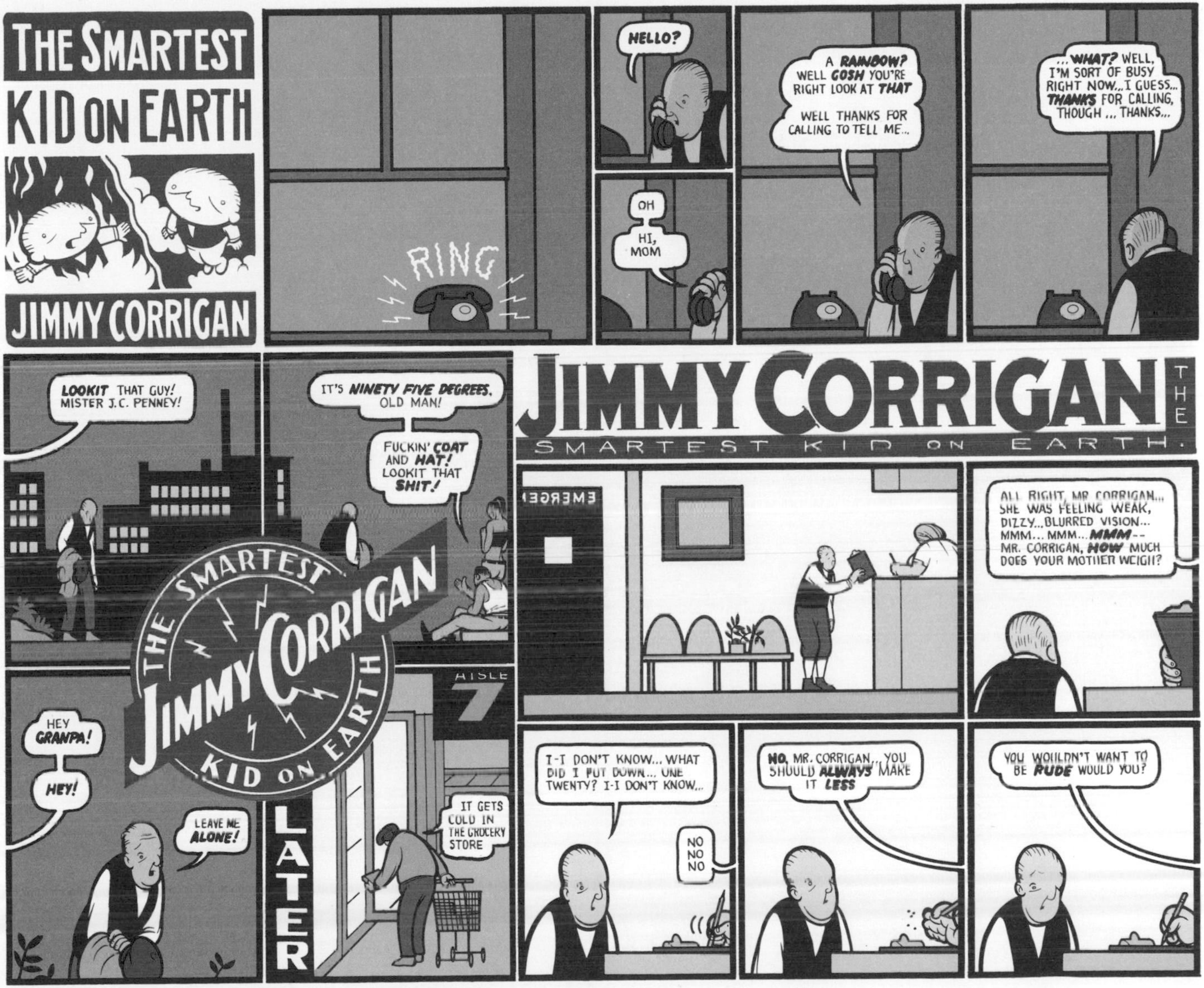
THE SMARTEST KID ON EARTH
JIMMY CORRIGAN
RING
HELLO?
OH
HI, MOM
A RAINBOW? WELL GOSH YOU'RE RIGHT LOOK AT THAT
WELL THANKS FOR CALLING TO TELL ME...
...WHAT? WELL, I'M SORT OF BUSY RIGHT NOW... I GUESS... THANKS FOR CALLING, THOUGH ... THANKS...
LOOKIT THAT GUY! MISTER J.C. PENNEY!
IT'S NINETY FIVE DEGREES, OLD MAN!
FUCKIN' COAT AND HAT! LOOKIT THAT SHIT!
THE SMARTEST JIMMY CORRIGAN KID ON EARTH
HEY GRANPA!
HEY!
LEAVE ME ALONE!
LATER
AISLE 7
IT GETS COLD IN THE GROCERY STORE
JIMMY CORRIGAN THE SMARTEST KID ON EARTH.
EMERGE
ALL RIGHT, MR CORRIGAN... SHE WAS FEELING WEAK, DIZZY... BLURRED VISION... MMM... MMM... MMM -- MR. CORRIGAN, HOW MUCH DOES YOUR MOTHER WEIGH?
I-I DON'T KNOW... WHAT DID I PUT DOWN... ONE TWENTY? I-I DON'T KNOW...
NO NO NO
NO, MR. CORRIGAN... YOU SHOULD ALWAYS MAKE IT LESS
YOU WOULDN'T WANT TO BE RUDE WOULD YOU?

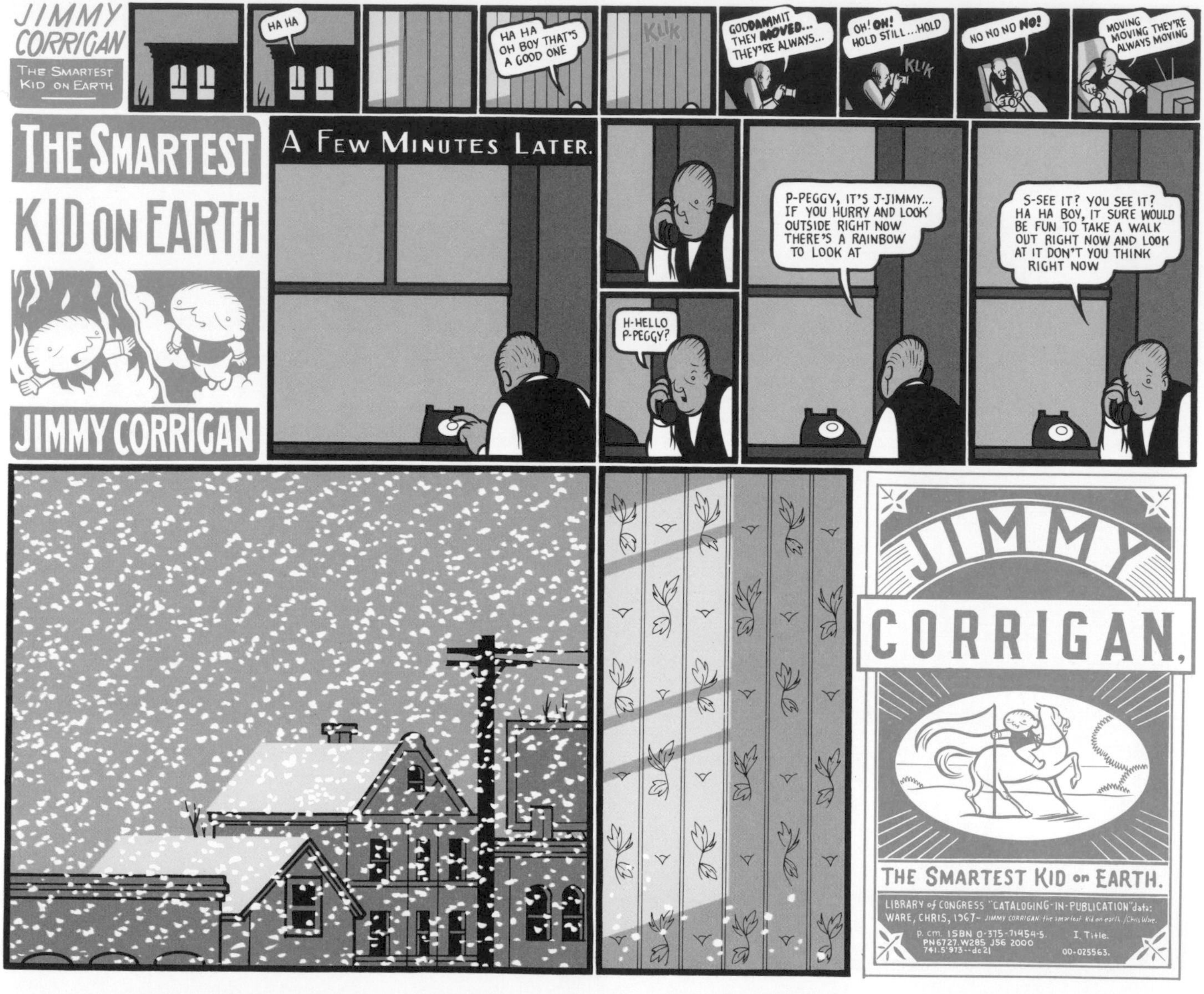
JIMMY CORRIGAN
THE SMARTEST KID ON EARTH
HA HA
HA HA OH BOY THAT'S A GOOD ONE
KLIK
GODDAMMIT THEY **MOVED**... THEY'RE ALWAYS...
OH! **OH!** HOLD STILL...HOLD
KLIK
NO NO NO **NO!**
MOVING MOVING THEY'RE ALWAYS MOVING
THE SMARTEST KID ON EARTH
JIMMY CORRIGAN
A FEW MINUTES LATER.
H-HELLO P-PEGGY?
P-PEGGY, IT'S J-JIMMY... IF YOU HURRY AND LOOK OUTSIDE RIGHT NOW THERE'S A RAINBOW TO LOOK AT
S-SEE IT? YOU SEE IT? HA HA BOY, IT SURE WOULD BE FUN TO TAKE A WALK OUT RIGHT NOW AND LOOK AT IT DON'T YOU THINK RIGHT NOW
JIMMY CORRIGAN,
THE SMARTEST KID on EARTH.
LIBRARY of CONGRESS "CATALOGING-IN-PUBLICATION" data:
WARE, CHRIS, 1967- JIMMY CORRIGAN: the smartest kid on earth. / Chris Ware.
p. cm. ISBN 0-375-71454-5. I. Title.
PN6727.W285 J56 2000
741.5'973--dc21 00-025563.

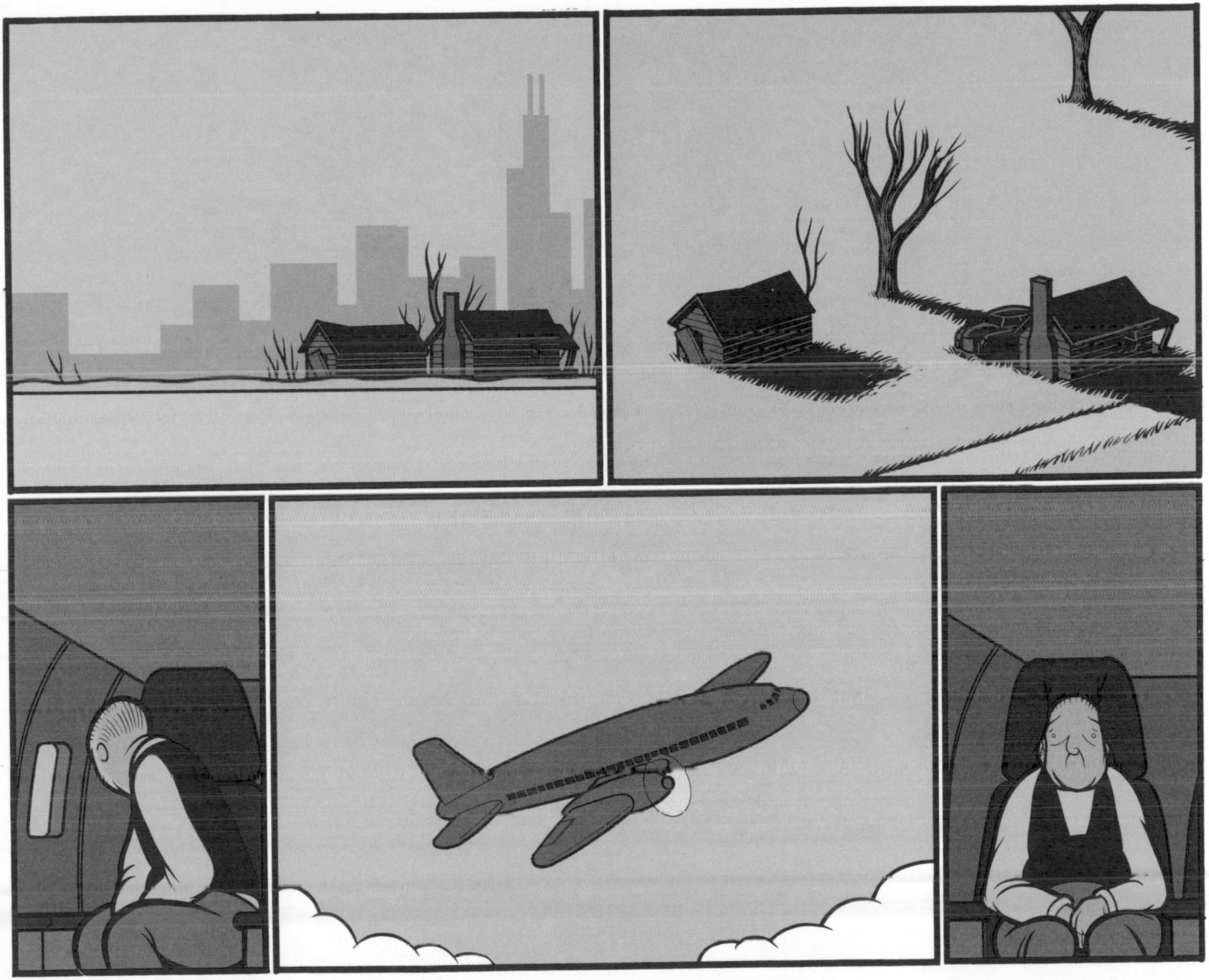

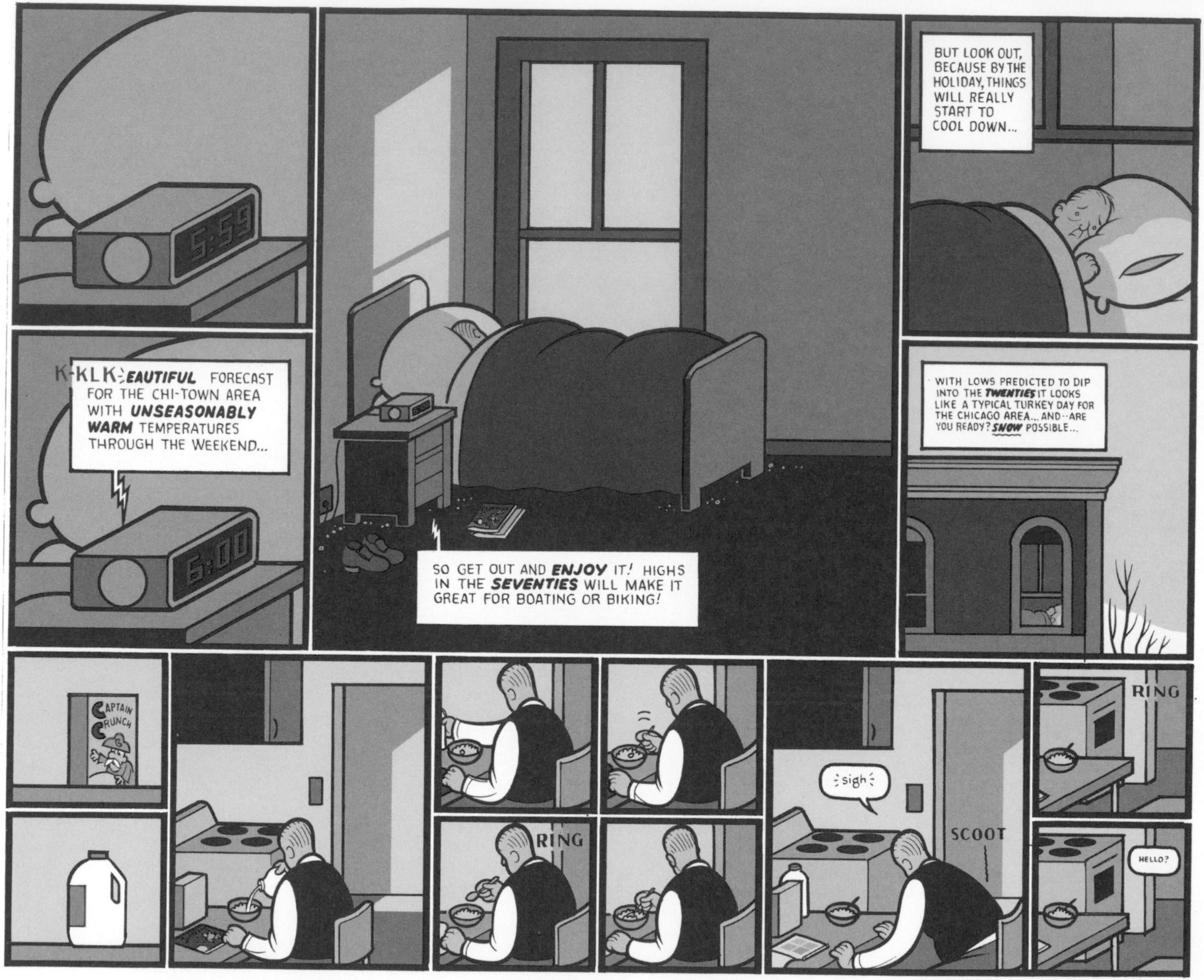

K-KLK-EAUTIFUL FORECAST FOR THE CHI-TOWN AREA WITH UNSEASONABLY WARM TEMPERATURES THROUGH THE WEEKEND...
SO GET OUT AND ENJOY IT! HIGHS IN THE SEVENTIES WILL MAKE IT GREAT FOR BOATING OR BIKING!
BUT LOOK OUT, BECAUSE BY THE HOLIDAY, THINGS WILL REALLY START TO COOL DOWN...
WITH LOWS PREDICTED TO DIP INTO THE TWENTIES IT LOOKS LIKE A TYPICAL TURKEY DAY FOR THE CHICAGO AREA... AND--ARE YOU READY? SNOW POSSIBLE...
CAPTAIN CRUNCH
RING
sigh
SCOOT
RING
HELLO?

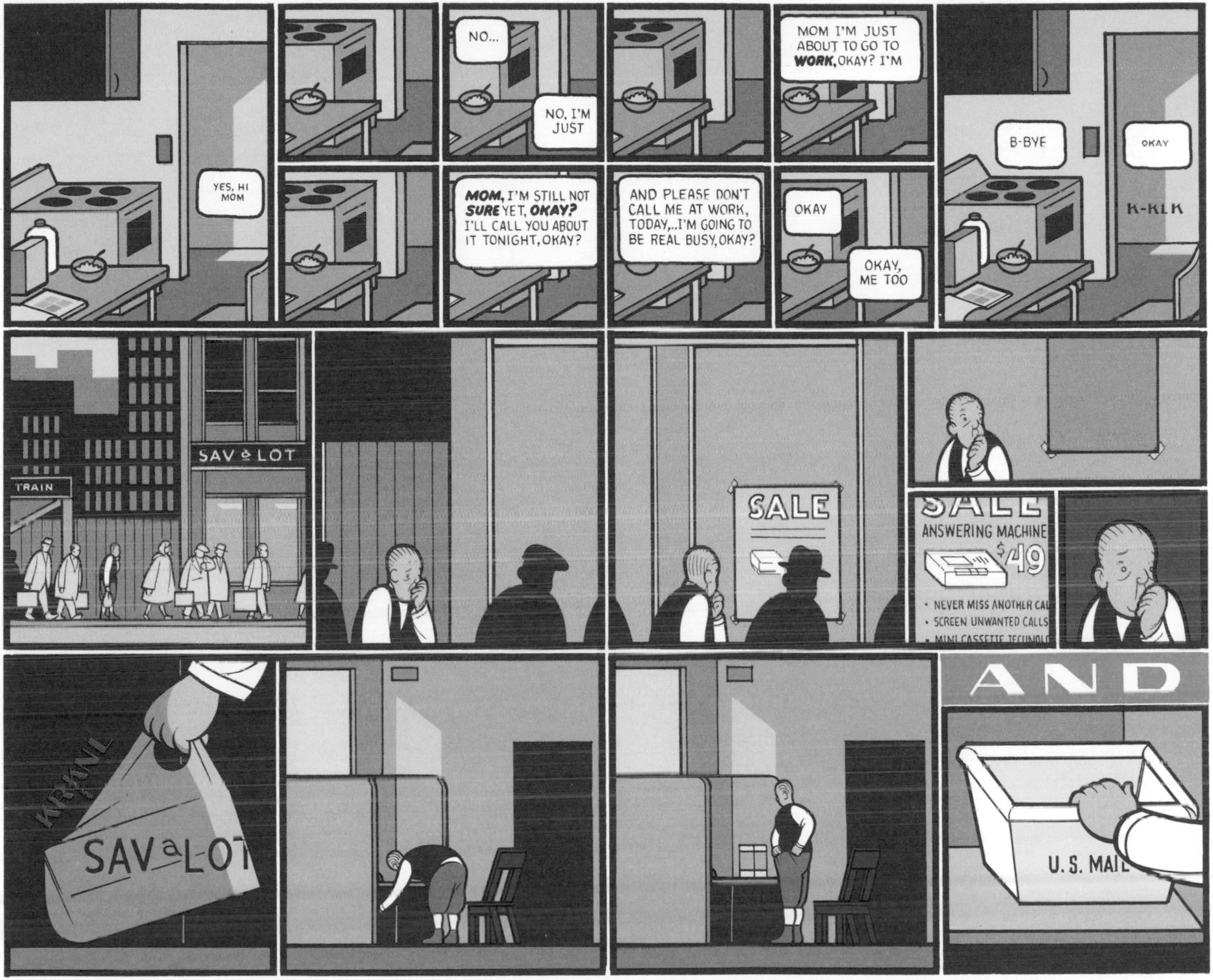

YES, HI MOM
NO...
NO, I'M JUST
MOM I'M JUST ABOUT TO GO TO WORK, OKAY? I'M
MOM, I'M STILL NOT SURE YET, OKAY? I'LL CALL YOU ABOUT IT TONIGHT, OKAY?
AND PLEASE DON'T CALL ME AT WORK, TODAY,..I'M GOING TO BE REAL BUSY, OKAY?
OKAY
OKAY, ME TOO
B-BYE
OKAY
K-KLK
TRAIN
SAV a LOT
SALE
SALE
ANSWERING MACHINE
$49
• NEVER MISS ANOTHER CAL
• SCREEN UNWANTED CALLS
KRNKL
SAV a LOT
AND
U.S. MAIL

HA HA

YOU KNOW, PEGGY, LET'S PLANT THAT PEACH GROVE TOMORROW

HA HA OH, *JIMMY*

JIMMY!

JIMMY!! TAKE YOUR MAIL AND GET *OUT* OF HERE! I'VE GOT *WORK* TO DO!

O-OKAY, PEGGY... I-I'M SORRY...

Dear Son,

I think its about time we fellas get to know each other, what do you say?

I'm not real good at letters, lets get together, I think we'd have a lot to talk about!

Let me know what you think. I hope this finds you well...Please think about it!

your friend, Dad
(really!)

"DAD"?

BUT I DON'T HAVE A

RING

HELLO?

JIMMY?

MOM? MOM I THOUGHT I TOLD YOU *NOT* TO *CALL* ME AT

I KNOW, I *KNOW,* JIMMY... I JUST WANTED TO MAKE SURE YOU GOT THE LETTER I SENT.

L-L-LETTER?

YES...I SENT IT YESTERDAY

I WANTED TO MAKE SURE THAT YOU GOT IT. IT'S GOT SOMETHING IN IT.

I-IT DOES?

YES IT'S A JOKE LETTER A FUNNY JOKE LETTER TO CHEER YOU UP

A-A FUNNY *JOKE*...?

YES... YOU'LL KNOW IT WHEN YOU SEE IT

BUT

...BUT I COULDN'T FIND AN ENVELOPE THAT WAS BIG ENOUGH.

Love, Mom

HA HA THAT *IS* A FUNNY JOKE!

I-I GUESS I GOT IT, THEN

OH *GOODY*... I'M *GLAD*... IT'S *FUNNY*, ISN'T IT?

Y-YES HA HA I GUESS IT IS

OKAY... I JUST WANTED TO MAKE SURE. YOU HAVE A GOOD DAY NOW, OKAY?

O-OKAY B-BYE

GOODBYE

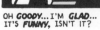

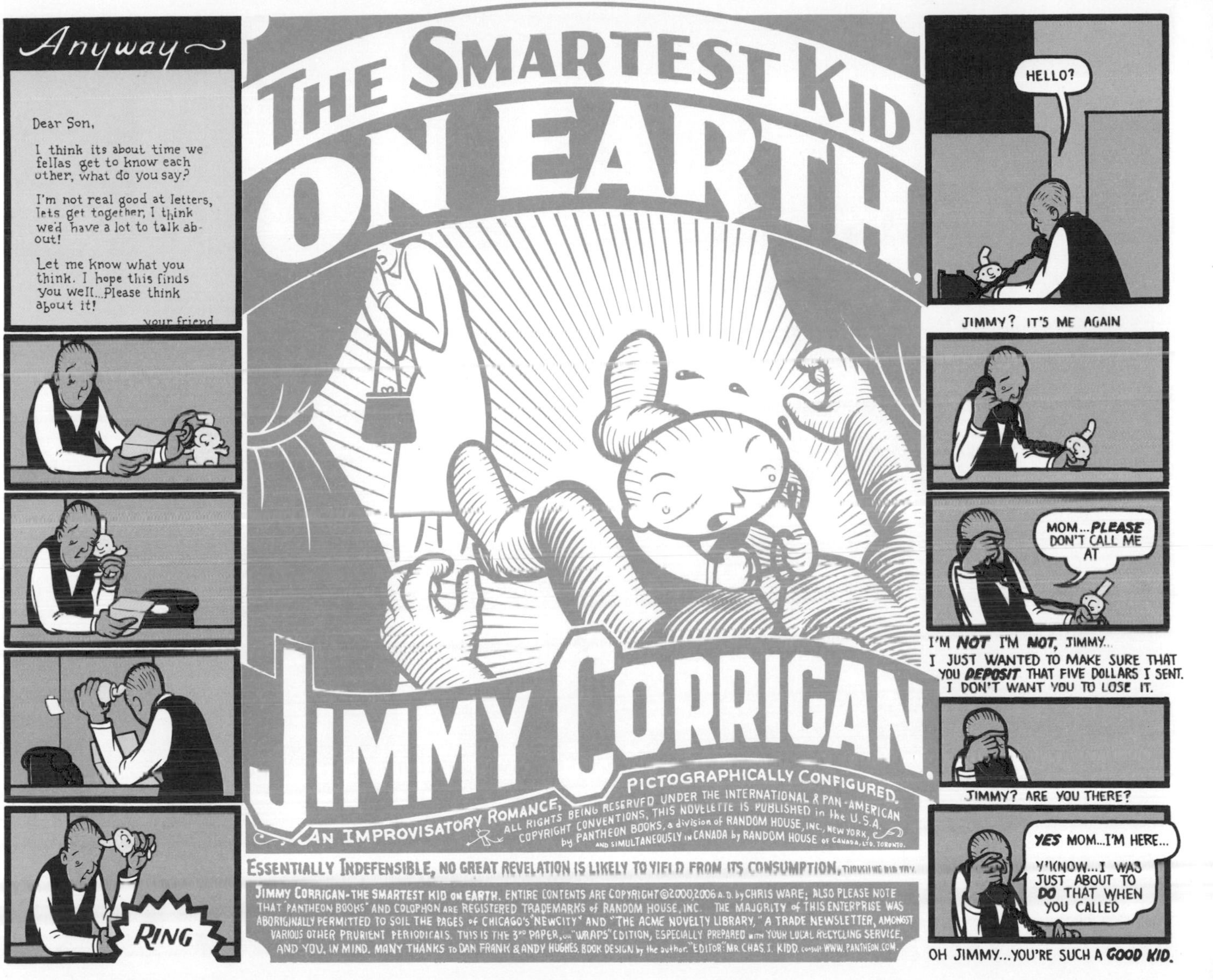

Anyway
Dear Son,
I think its about time we fellas get to know each other, what do you say?
I'm not real good at letters, lets get together, I think we'd have a lot to talk about!
Let me know what you think. I hope this finds you well...Please think about it!
your friend
RING
THE SMARTEST KID ON EARTH.
JIMMY CORRIGAN.
AN IMPROVISATORY ROMANCE, PICTOGRAPHICALLY CONFIGURED.
ALL RIGHTS BEING RESERVED UNDER THE INTERNATIONAL & PAN-AMERICAN COPYRIGHT CONVENTIONS, THIS NOVELETTE IS PUBLISHED in the U.S.A. by PANTHEON BOOKS, a division of RANDOM HOUSE, INC., NEW YORK, AND SIMULTANEOUSLY IN CANADA by RANDOM HOUSE OF CANADA, LTD. TORONTO.
ESSENTIALLY INDEFENSIBLE, NO GREAT REVELATION IS LIKELY TO YIELD FROM ITS CONSUMPTION, THOUGH WE DID TRY.
JIMMY CORRIGAN - THE SMARTEST KID ON EARTH. ENTIRE CONTENTS ARE COPYRIGHT ©2000,2006 A.D. by CHRIS WARE; ALSO PLEASE NOTE THAT "PANTHEON BOOKS" AND COLOPHON ARE REGISTERED TRADEMARKS of RANDOM HOUSE, INC. THE MAJORITY of THIS ENTERPRISE WAS ABORIGINALLY PERMITTED TO SOIL THE PAGES of CHICAGO'S "NEWCITY" AND "THE ACME NOVELTY LIBRARY," A TRADE NEWSLETTER, AMONGST VARIOUS OTHER PRURIENT PERIODICALS. THIS IS THE 3RD PAPER, or "WRAPS" EDITION, ESPECIALLY PREPARED with YOUR LOCAL RECYCLING SERVICE, AND YOU, IN MIND. MANY THANKS to DAN FRANK & ANDY HUGHES. BOOK DESIGN by the author. "EDITOR": MR. CHAS. I. KIDD. consult WWW.PANTHEON.COM.
HELLO?
JIMMY? IT'S ME AGAIN
MOM...PLEASE DON'T CALL ME AT
I'M NOT I'M NOT, JIMMY...
I JUST WANTED TO MAKE SURE THAT YOU DEPOSIT THAT FIVE DOLLARS I SENT. I DON'T WANT YOU TO LOSE IT.
JIMMY? ARE YOU THERE?
YES MOM...I'M HERE...
Y'KNOW...I WAS JUST ABOUT TO DO THAT WHEN YOU CALLED
OH JIMMY...YOU'RE SUCH A GOOD KID.

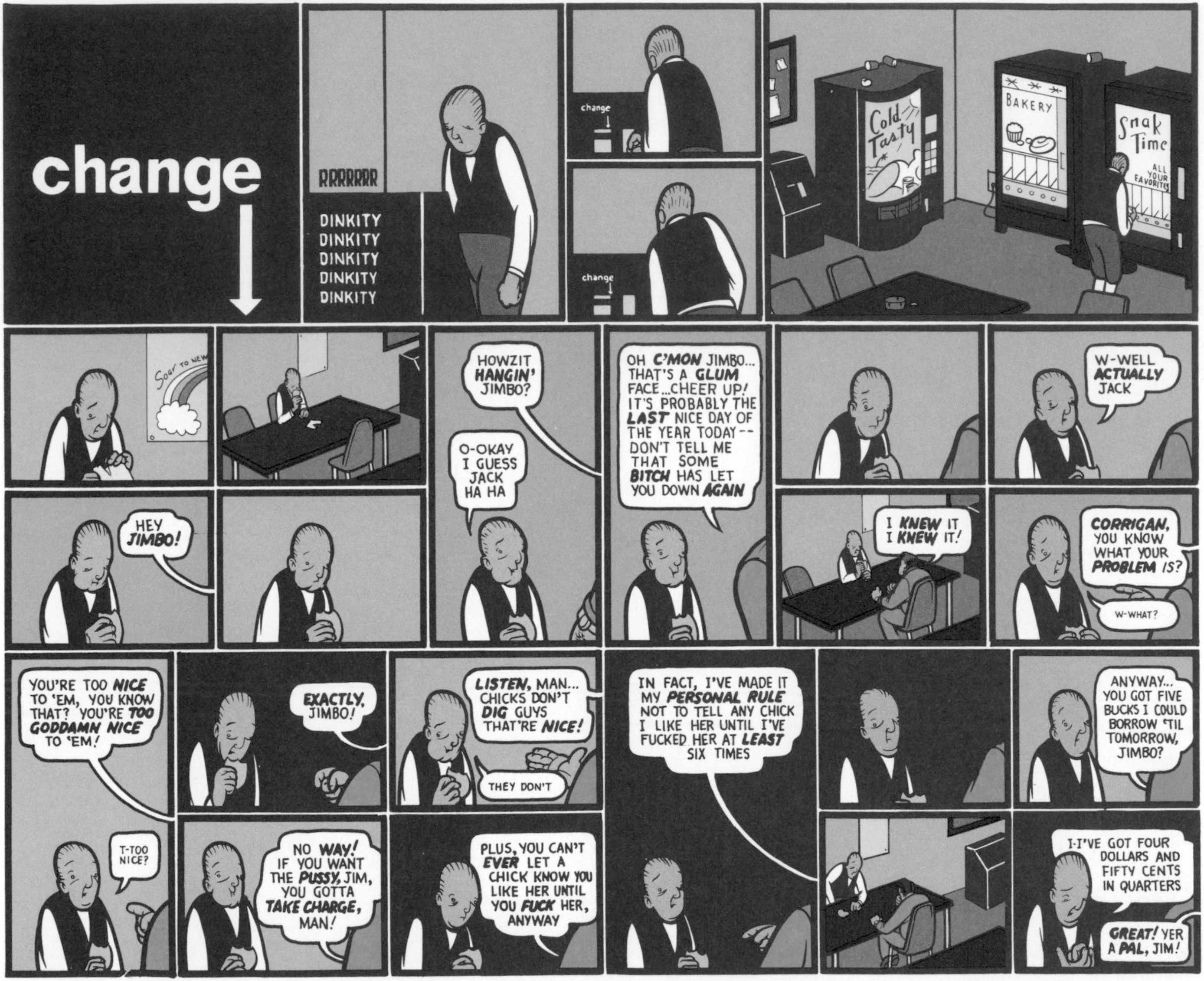

change
RRRRRRR
DINKITY DINKITY DINKITY DINKITY DINKITY
change
change
Cold Tasty
BAKERY
Snak Time
ALL YOUR FAVORITES
Soar TO NEW
HEY JIMBO!
HOWZIT HANGIN' JIMBO?
O-OKAY I GUESS JACK HA HA
OH C'MON JIMBO... THAT'S A GLUM FACE...CHEER UP! IT'S PROBABLY THE LAST NICE DAY OF THE YEAR TODAY-- DON'T TELL ME THAT SOME BITCH HAS LET YOU DOWN AGAIN
W-WELL ACTUALLY JACK
I KNEW IT, I KNEW IT!
CORRIGAN, YOU KNOW WHAT YOUR PROBLEM IS?
W-WHAT?
YOU'RE TOO NICE TO 'EM, YOU KNOW THAT? YOU'RE TOO GODDAMN NICE TO 'EM!
T-TOO NICE?
EXACTLY, JIMBO!
NO WAY! IF YOU WANT THE PUSSY, JIM, YOU GOTTA TAKE CHARGE, MAN!
LISTEN, MAN... CHICKS DON'T DIG GUYS THAT'RE NICE!
THEY DON'T
PLUS, YOU CAN'T EVER LET A CHICK KNOW YOU LIKE HER UNTIL YOU FUCK HER, ANYWAY
IN FACT, I'VE MADE IT MY PERSONAL RULE NOT TO TELL ANY CHICK I LIKE HER UNTIL I'VE FUCKED HER AT LEAST SIX TIMES
ANYWAY... YOU GOT FIVE BUCKS I COULD BORROW 'TIL TOMORROW, JIMBO?
I-I'VE GOT FOUR DOLLARS AND FIFTY CENTS IN QUARTERS
GREAT! YER A PAL, JIM!

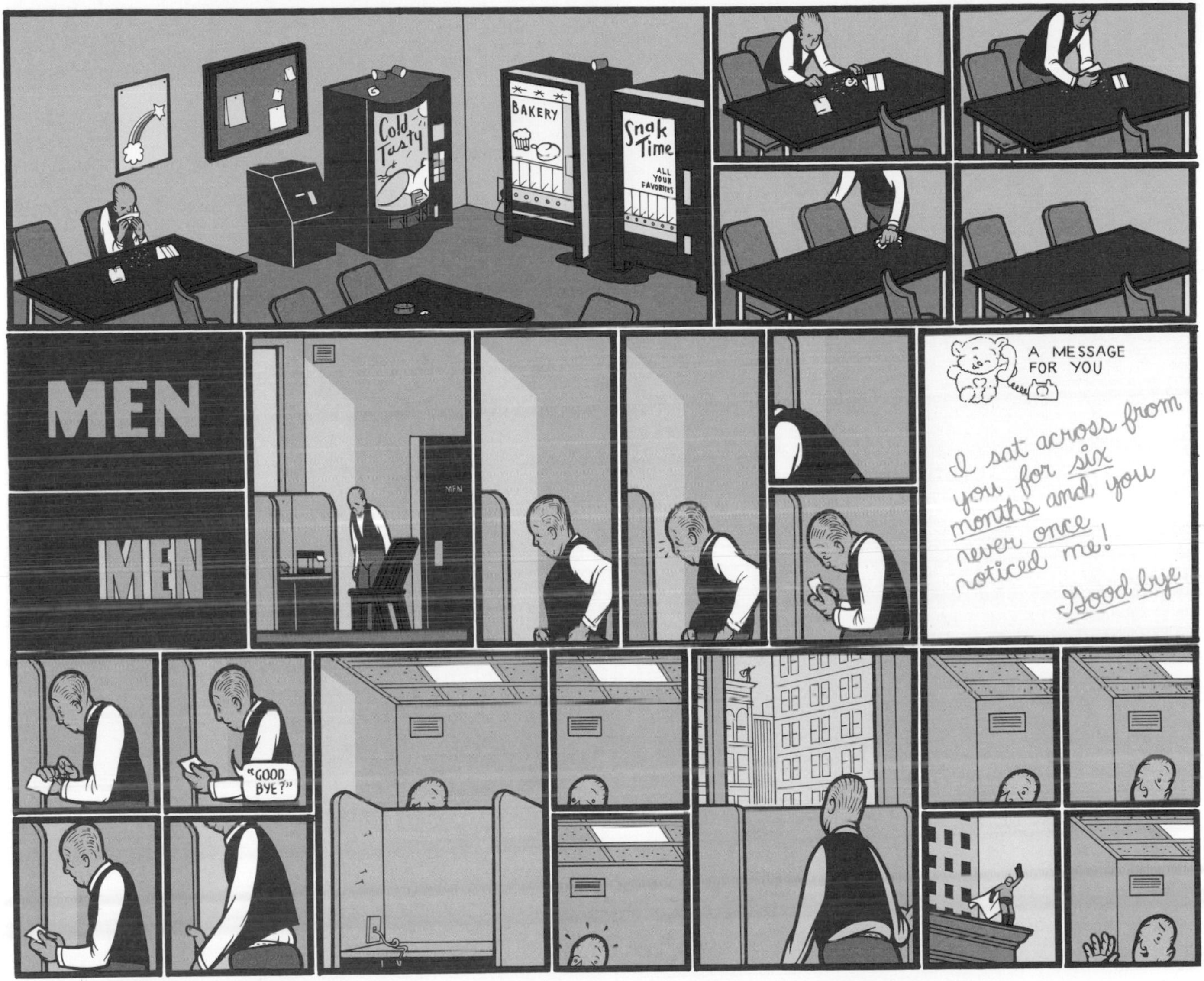
Cold Tasty
BAKERY
Snak Time
ALL YOUR FAVORITES
MEN
MEN
A MESSAGE FOR YOU
I sat across from you for six months and you never once noticed me!
Good bye
"GOOD BYE?"

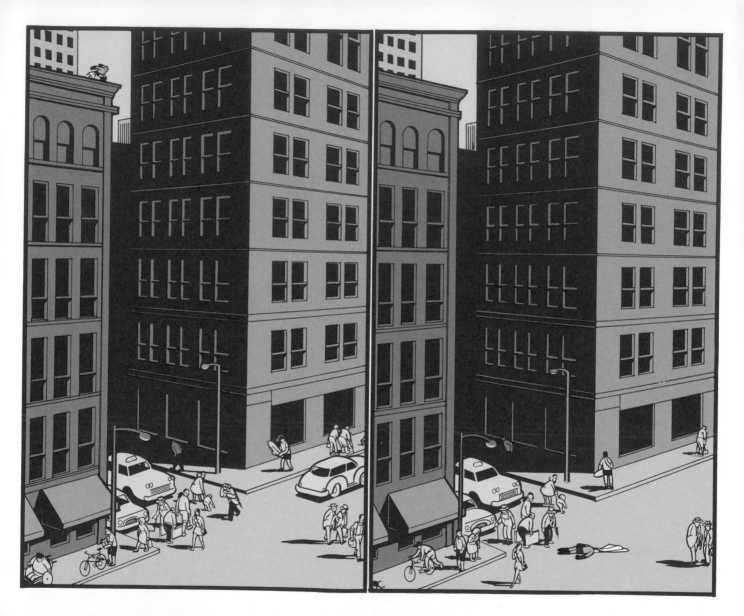

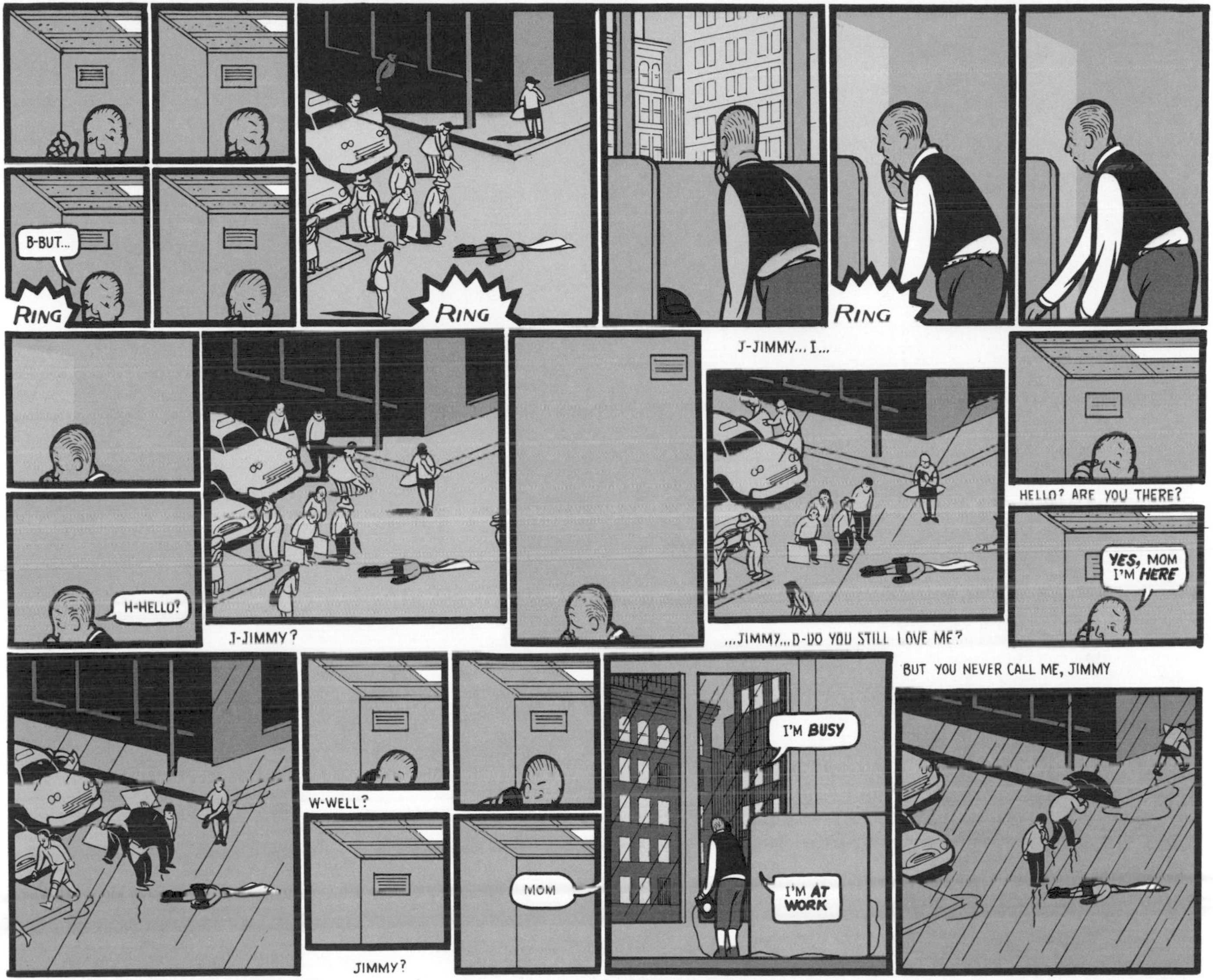

B-BUT...
RING
RING
RING
J-JIMMY... I...
HELLO? ARE YOU THERE?
H-HELLO?
J-JIMMY?
...JIMMY... D-DO YOU STILL LOVE ME?
YES, MOM I'M HERE
BUT YOU NEVER CALL ME, JIMMY
W-WELL?
JIMMY?
MOM
I'M BUSY
I'M AT WORK

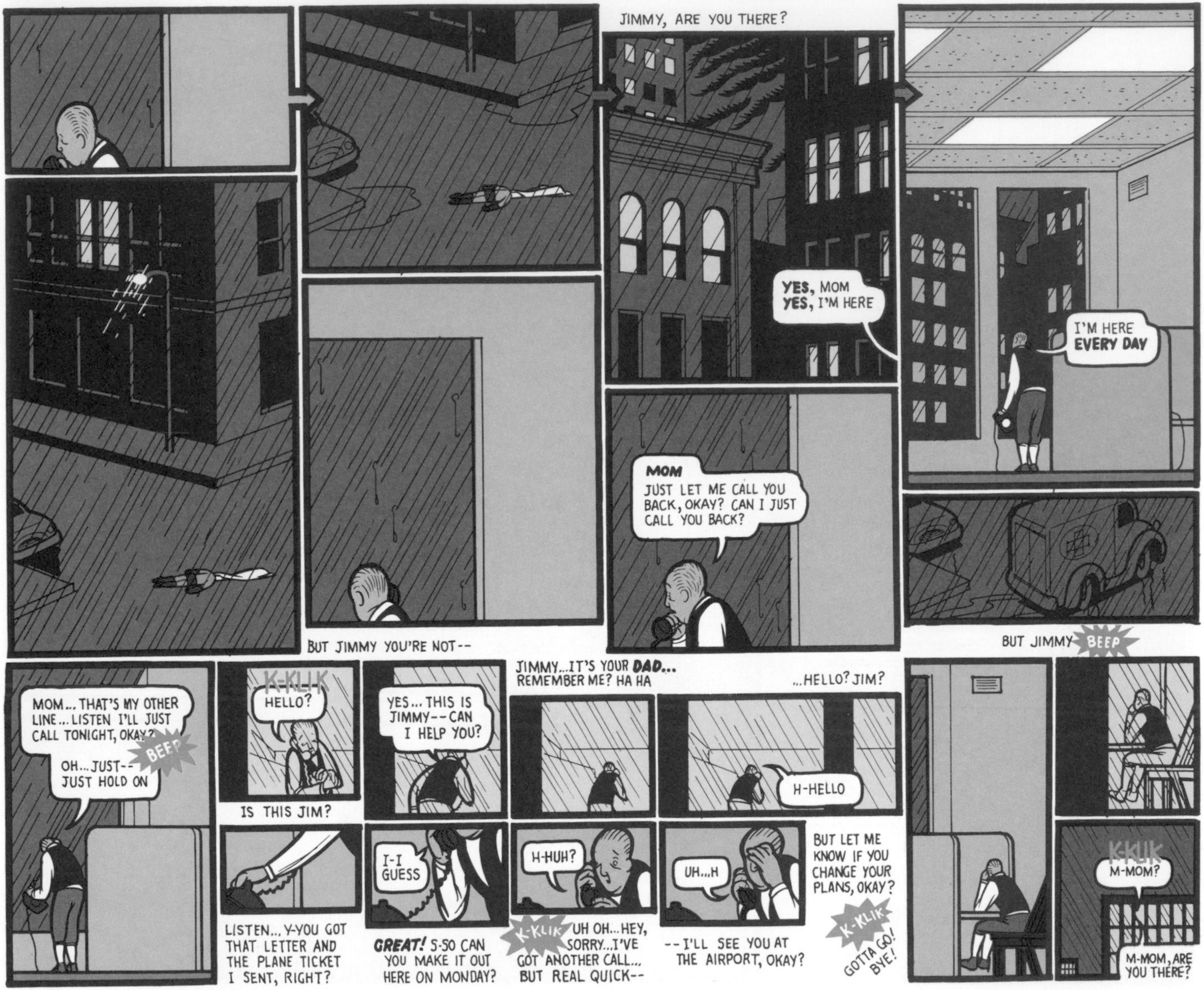
JIMMY, ARE YOU THERE?
YES, MOM
YES, I'M HERE
I'M HERE EVERY DAY
MOM
JUST LET ME CALL YOU BACK, OKAY? CAN I JUST CALL YOU BACK?
BUT JIMMY YOU'RE NOT--
BUT JIMMY
BEEP
MOM... THAT'S MY OTHER LINE... LISTEN I'LL JUST CALL TONIGHT, OKAY?
BEEP
OH... JUST-- JUST HOLD ON
K-KLIK
HELLO?
IS THIS JIM?
YES... THIS IS JIMMY-- CAN I HELP YOU?
JIMMY... IT'S YOUR DAD... REMEMBER ME? HA HA
...HELLO? JIM?
H-HELLO
LISTEN... Y-YOU GOT THAT LETTER AND THE PLANE TICKET I SENT, RIGHT?
I-I GUESS
GREAT! S-SO CAN YOU MAKE IT OUT HERE ON MONDAY?
H-HUH?
K-KLIK
UH OH... HEY, SORRY... I'VE GOT ANOTHER CALL... BUT REAL QUICK--
UH...H
--I'LL SEE YOU AT THE AIRPORT, OKAY?
BUT LET ME KNOW IF YOU CHANGE YOUR PLANS, OKAY?
K-KLIK
GOTTA GO! BYE!
K-KLIK
M-MOM?
M-MOM, ARE YOU THERE?

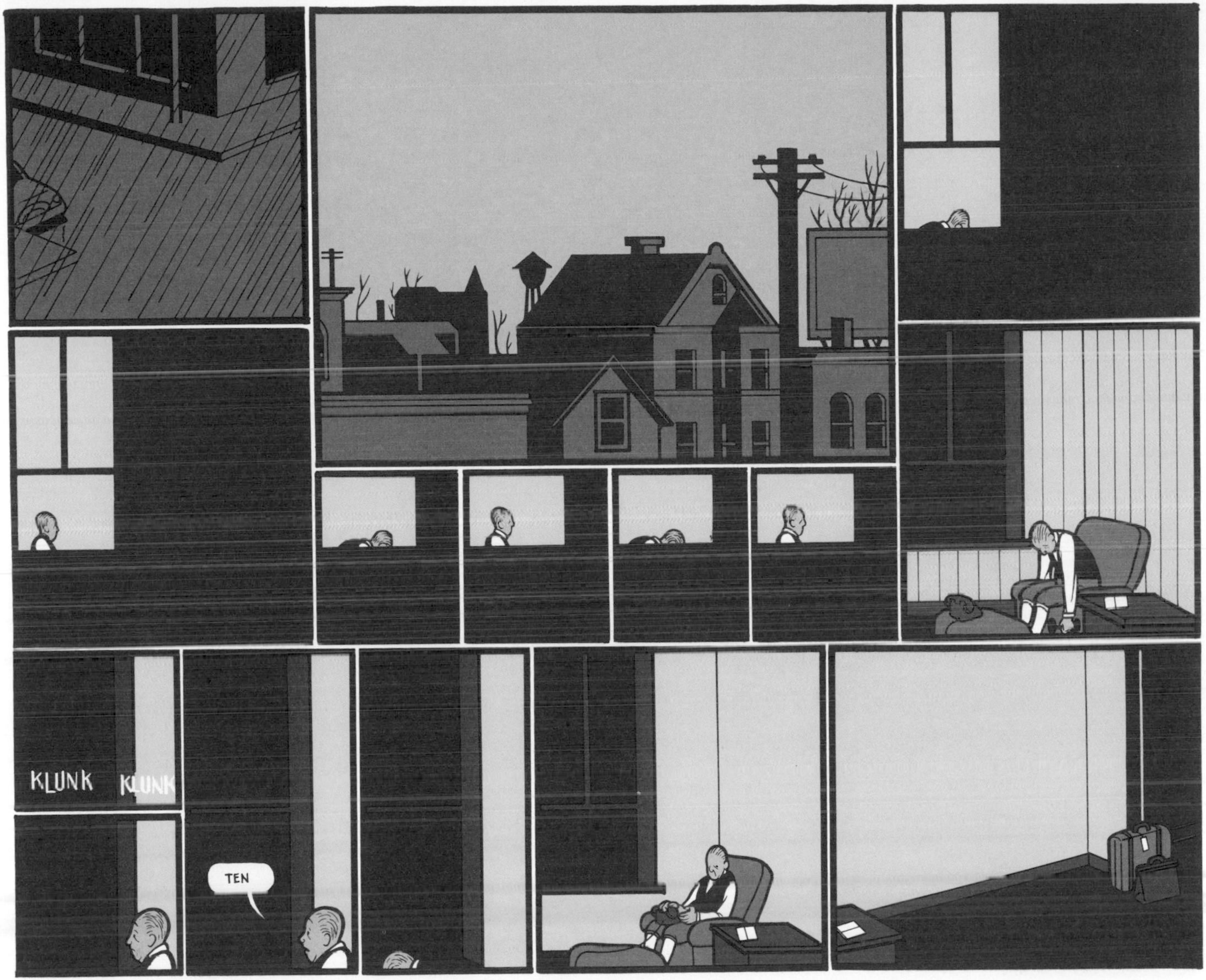
KLUNK
KLUNK
TEN

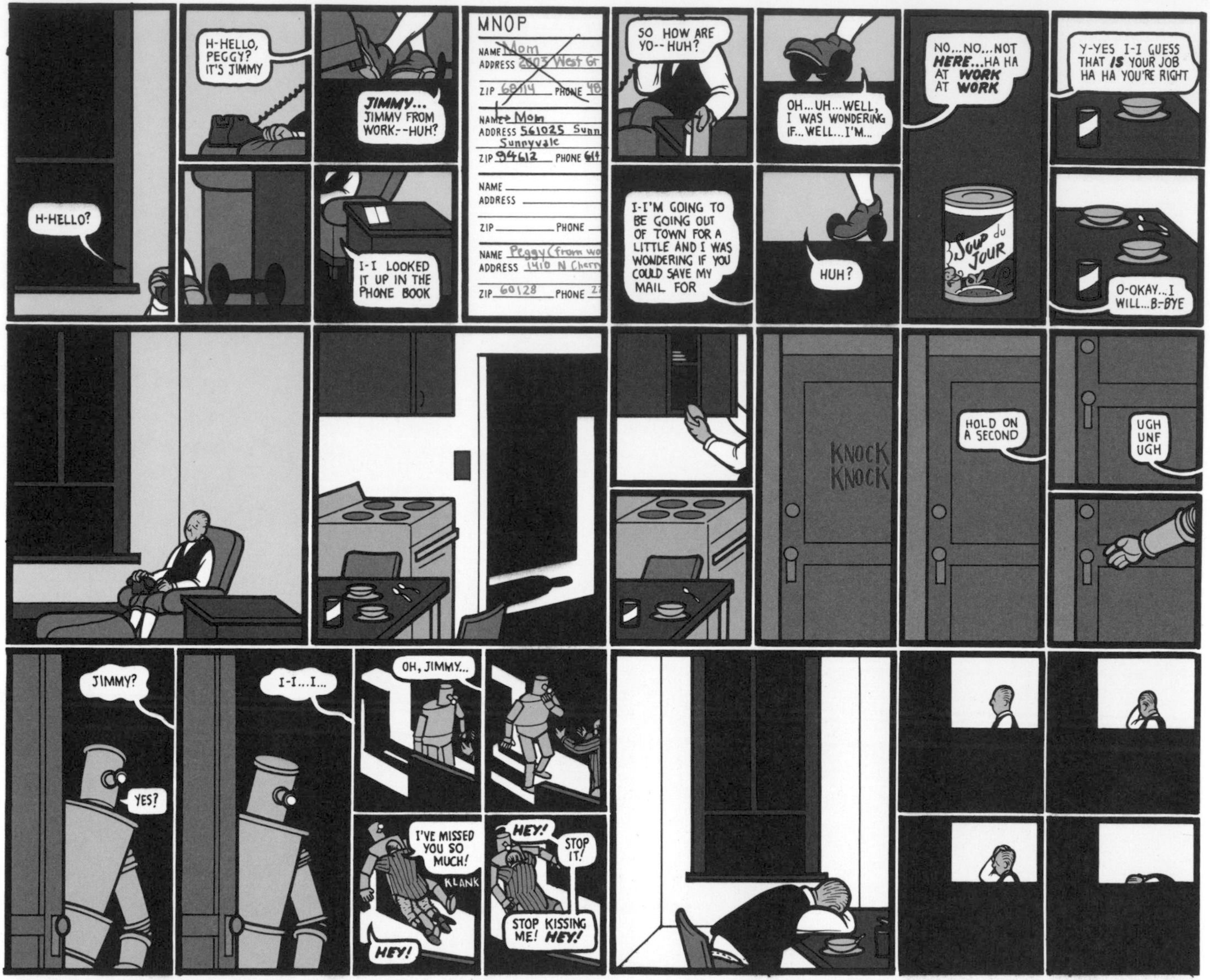
H-HELLO?
H-HELLO, PEGGY? IT'S JIMMY
JIMMY... JIMMY FROM WORK.--HUH?
I-I LOOKED IT UP IN THE PHONE BOOK
MNOP
NAME Mom
ADDRESS 2003 West Gr
ZIP 68114 PHONE
NAME Mom
ADDRESS 561025 Sunn
Sunnyvale
ZIP 94612 PHONE
NAME
ADDRESS
ZIP PHONE
NAME Peggy (from wo
ADDRESS 1410 N Cherr
ZIP 60128 PHONE
SO HOW ARE YO-- HUH?
I-I'M GOING TO BE GOING OUT OF TOWN FOR A LITTLE AND I WAS WONDERING IF YOU COULD SAVE MY MAIL FOR
OH...UH...WELL, I WAS WONDERING IF...WELL...I'M...
HUH?
NO...NO...NOT HERE...HA HA AT WORK AT WORK
Soup du Jour
Y-YES I-I GUESS THAT IS YOUR JOB HA HA YOU'RE RIGHT
O-OKAY...I WILL...B-BYE
KNOCK KNOCK
HOLD ON A SECOND
UGH UNF UGH
JIMMY?
YES?
I-I...I...
OH, JIMMY...
I'VE MISSED YOU SO MUCH!
KLANK
HEY!
HEY!
STOP IT!
STOP KISSING ME! HEY!

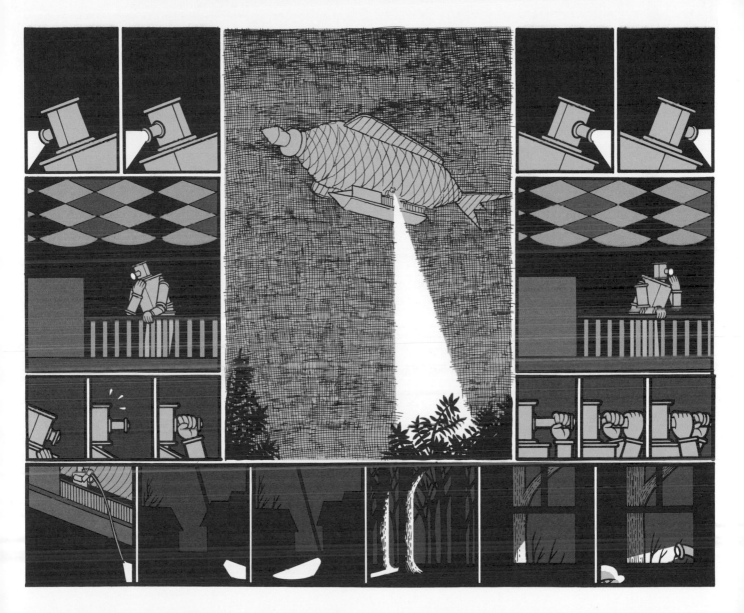

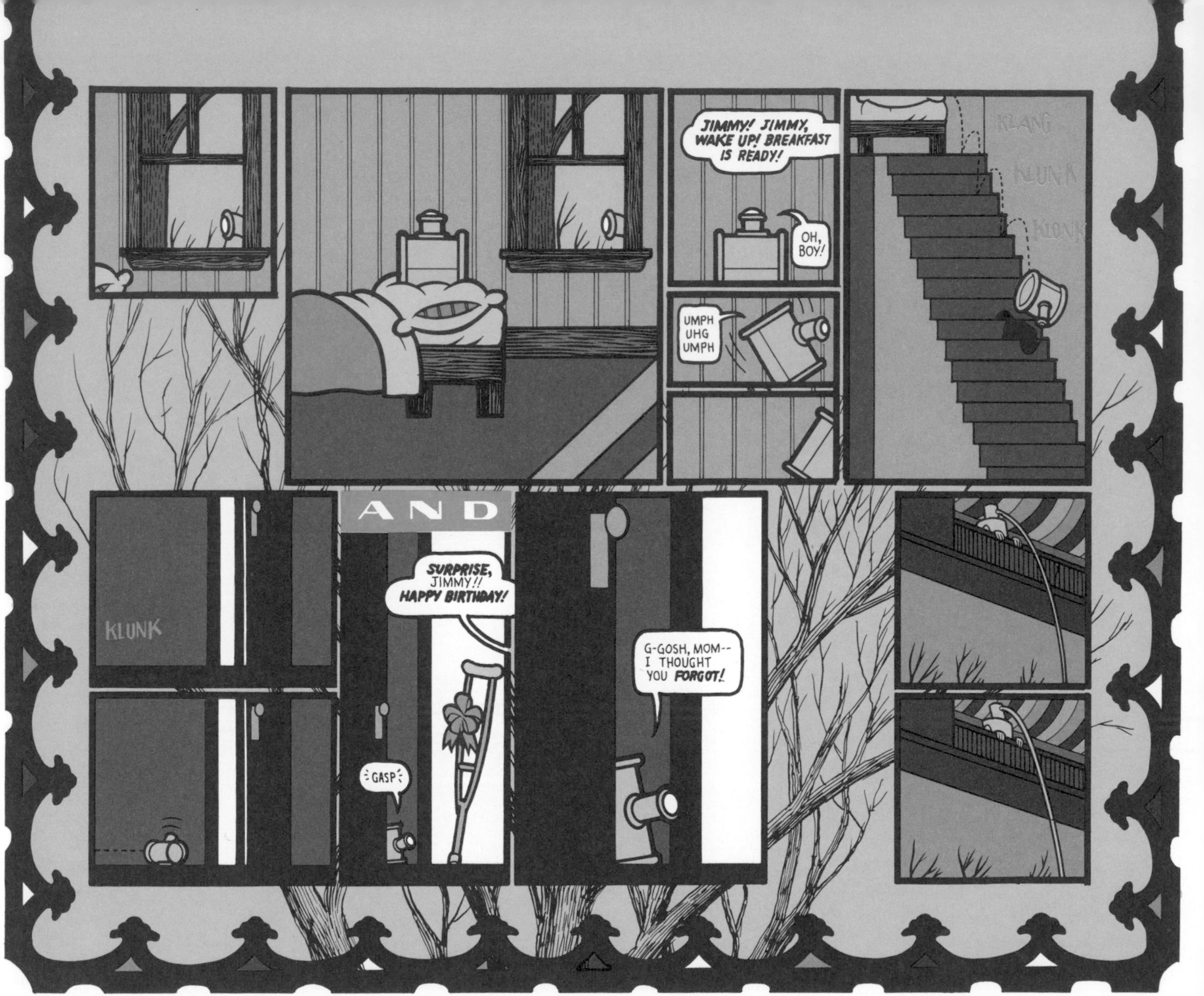
JIMMY! JIMMY, WAKE UP! BREAKFAST IS READY!
OH, BOY!
UMPH UHG UMPH
KLANG
KLUNK
KLONK
KLUNK
AND
SURPRISE, JIMMY!! HAPPY BIRTHDAY!
GASP
G-GOSH, MOM-- I THOUGHT YOU FORGOT!

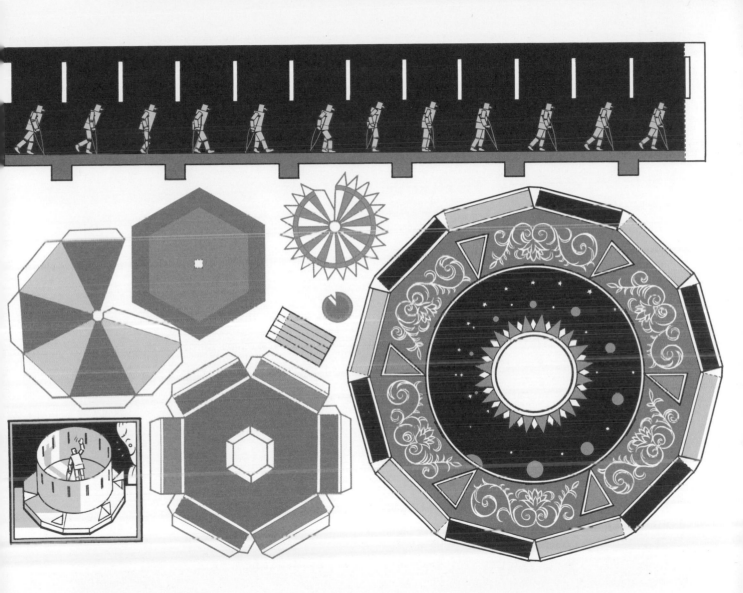

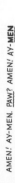

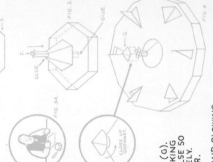

MEMORIZE ALL INSTRUCTIONS BEFORE WAKING UP THE PIECES ON OTHER SIDE.

● WELL HERE'S A FUN THING WHICH IS SURE TO APPEAL TO THE YOUNG BOY, GIRL, OR AIRSHIP PASSENGER IN ALL OF US. IT BEGS ONLY A SMALL AMOUNT OF EFFORT TO CONSTRUCT, AND THE ATTENTIVE STUDENT WILL BE REWARDED WITH A CONVINCING MODEL OF LIFE IN WHICH HE OR SHE MAY FIND SOME POETIC SYMPATHY. ALL THAT IS REQUIRED IS A SHARP HOBBY KNIFE, A METAL STRAIGHT EDGE, COMMON HORSE GLUE, AND THE SORT OF FREE LEISURE TIME THAT AIRPLANE PASSENGERS COMMONLY ENJOY. AS ALWAYS, GREAT PATIENCE AND A CLEAN WORK AREA ARE REQUIRED FOR FULFILLMENT OF THIS DIVERSION, AND IT SHOULD NOT BE ATTEMPTED IF EITHER ARE COMPROMISED.

● *GENERAL GUIDELINES* - CUT OUT ALL PIECES ALONG HEAVY BLACK LINES, AND USE A BLUNT OBJECT SUCH AS THE SEAT POCKET CARD TO SCORE ALONG ALL FOLDS. DON'T USE ANY MORE GLUE THAN IS ABSOLUTELY NECESSARY, AND KEEP YOUR HANDS AND CLOTHING CLEAN. DON'T TOUCH THE PERSON NEXT TO YOU, OR YOURSELF, OR MOM. *NO!* PAY CLOSE ATTENTION TO THE WOMAN'S INSTRUCTIONING -- BACK TO BUSINESS. CLASS PASSENGERS -- CUT OUT -- CUT OUT OF PAPER LIKE BEFORE. *COME ON!* BACK TO BUSINESS. FIRST CLASS -- TELL YOU WHAT TO DO, AND HOW TO DO IT. THANK YOU. OKAY-- BACK TO BUCKLING PAPER -- IT BUCKLES WITH GLUE AND SO NOW YOU CAN START AND CONCENTRATE, FINALLY. WHERE WAS IT? YES! NOW...NOW:

1. *FIG 1.* ASSEMBLE THE WHEEL FUNDAMENT (A). CUT OUT CENTER CIRCLE, AND FOLD UP ALL SIX FLAG TABS WHICH CIRCLE IT. FOLD DOWN AND GLUE ALL TWELVE SIDES.
2. CURL UP AND GLUE CENTER CONE (B) AND AFFIX THROUGH BOTTOM OF WHEEL FUNDAMENT.

3. *FIG. 2.* FOLD UP BASE TOP (C). GLUE ALL SIX SIDES, AND FOLD DOWN CENTER TABS. ASSEMBLE SUPPORT CONE (D). GLUE SUPPORT CONE UP THROUGH BASE TOP, AFFIXING TABS TO EDGES OF CONE. GLUE THIS ASSEMBLY TO BASE (E). LET DRY AGAIN.

4. *FIG. 3.* GLUE FOUR-SIDED SUPPORT ROD (F) TOGETHER. INSURE THAT IT INSERTS CLEANLY INTO THE SUPPORT CONE. IF NOT, SLIGHTLY ENLARGE THE OPENING OF THE CONE WITH A PENCIL.
5. PUT GLUE ON THE END OF THE SUPPORT ROD AND INSERT IT INTO THE SUPPORT CONE AS STRAIGHT AS POSSIBLE SO THAT IT SLIDES INTO THE BASE.
6. ADD GLUE WHERE THE ROD ENTERS THE CONE; ABOUT 1/8" SHOULD PROTRUDE FROM THE TOP. IF NOT, REMOVE, MAKE AN APPROPRIATELY-SIZED REPLACEMENT OUT OF SCRAP PAPER, AND WRITE AN ANGRY LETTER TO THE FATHER. *(FIG. 3A.)* LET DRY THOROUGHLY. DEAR DAD. STOP!

7. *FIG. 4.* CURL UP AND GLUE GROMMET CONE (G). GINGERLY GLUE TO SUPPORT ROD TABS, TAKING CARE NOT TO SPREAD GLUE ANYWHERE ELSE SO THAT THE WHEEL FUNDAMENT MOVES FREELY. LET DRY FOR ONE FULL WEEK TO THE LETTER.

8. ONCE DRY, TEST BY HOLDING BASE IN HAND AND BLOWING AGAINST DAD. DEAR DAD. I DON'T EVEN KNOW DAD. DON'T KNOW, DON'T KNOW, DON'T KNOW. DON'T KNOW IF HE HATES ME -- DON'T WANT ME? AM I DONE NOW? DON'T KNOW!

9. NO -- NOW I KNOW... REMEMBER ALL ALONG NOW! DUMB -- RIGHT THERE ALL ALONG -- GET ALONG -- GET ALONG LITTLE DOGGIES, GET ALONG! HAW!

10. HAW! PAW I GET ALONG, PAW! IN THE PAW PAW PATCH, PAW. PLAYIN IN THE PAW PAW PATCH WITH PAW. DON'T -- HAW! GET ALONG PAW! TIME FOR DINNER -- *SUPPER.* ← WHAT THEY SAY, PAW ... SAY AMEN -- A-MEN, PAW!

AMEN! AY-MEN. PAW? AMEN! AY-**MEN**

A.
FIG. 1.
B.
GLUE TABS TO UNDERSIDE OF 'A.'
C.
FIG. 2.
D.
E.
F.
GLUE.
FIG. 3A.
FIG. 3.
GLUE.
CLOSE UP GROMMET.
G.
FIG. 4.
H.
FIG. 5.

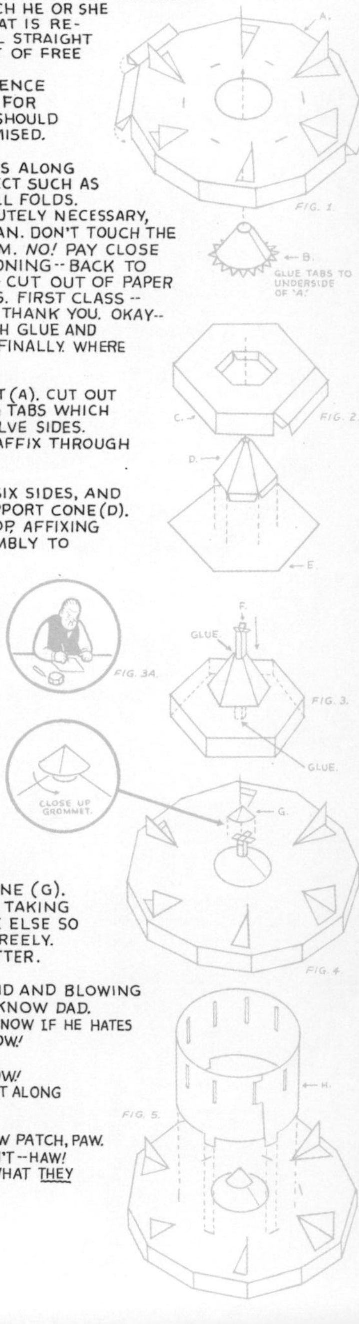

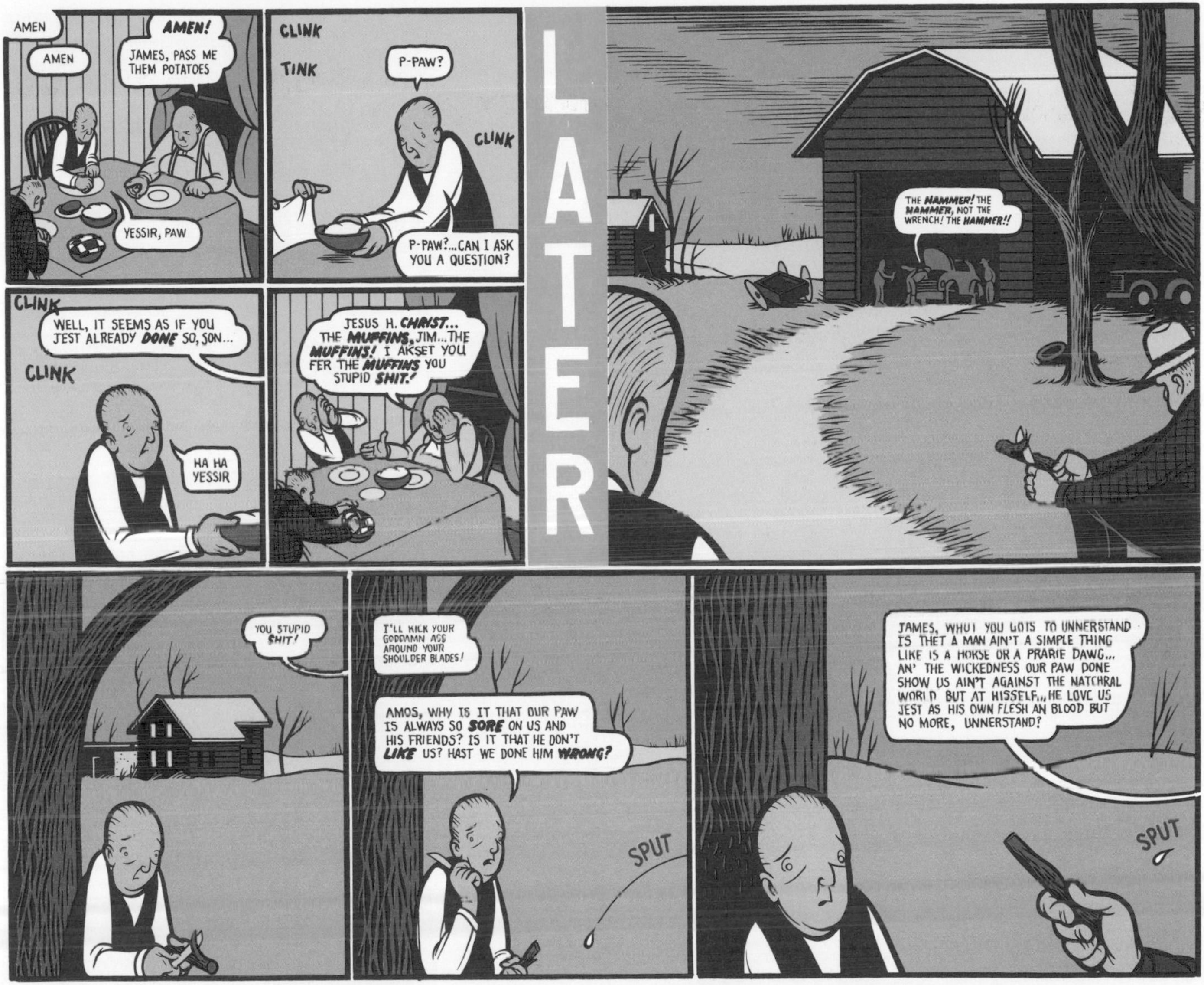
AMEN
AMEN
AMEN!
JAMES, PASS ME THEM POTATOES
YESSIR, PAW
CLINK
TINK
P-PAW?
CLINK
P-PAW?...CAN I ASK YOU A QUESTION?
CLINK
WELL, IT SEEMS AS IF YOU JEST ALREADY DONE SO, SON...
CLINK
HA HA YESSIR
JESUS H. CHRIST... THE MUFFINS, JIM...THE MUFFINS! I AKSET YOU FER THE MUFFINS YOU STUPID SHIT!
LATER
THE HAMMER! THE HAMMER, NOT THE WRENCH! THE HAMMER!!
YOU STUPID SHIT!
I'LL KICK YOUR GODDAMN ASS AROUND YOUR SHOULDER BLADES!
AMOS, WHY IS IT THAT OUR PAW IS ALWAYS SO SORE ON US AND HIS FRIENDS? IS IT THAT HE DON'T LIKE US? HAST WE DONE HIM WRONG?
SPUT
JAMES, WHUT YOU GOTS TO UNNERSTAND IS THET A MAN AIN'T A SIMPLE THING LIKE IS A HORSE OR A PRARIE DAWG... AN' THE WICKEDNESS OUR PAW DONE SHOW US AIN'T AGAINST THE NATCHRAL WORLD BUT AT HISSELF... HE LOVE US JEST AS HIS OWN FLESH AN BLOOD BUT NO MORE, UNNERSTAND?
SPUT

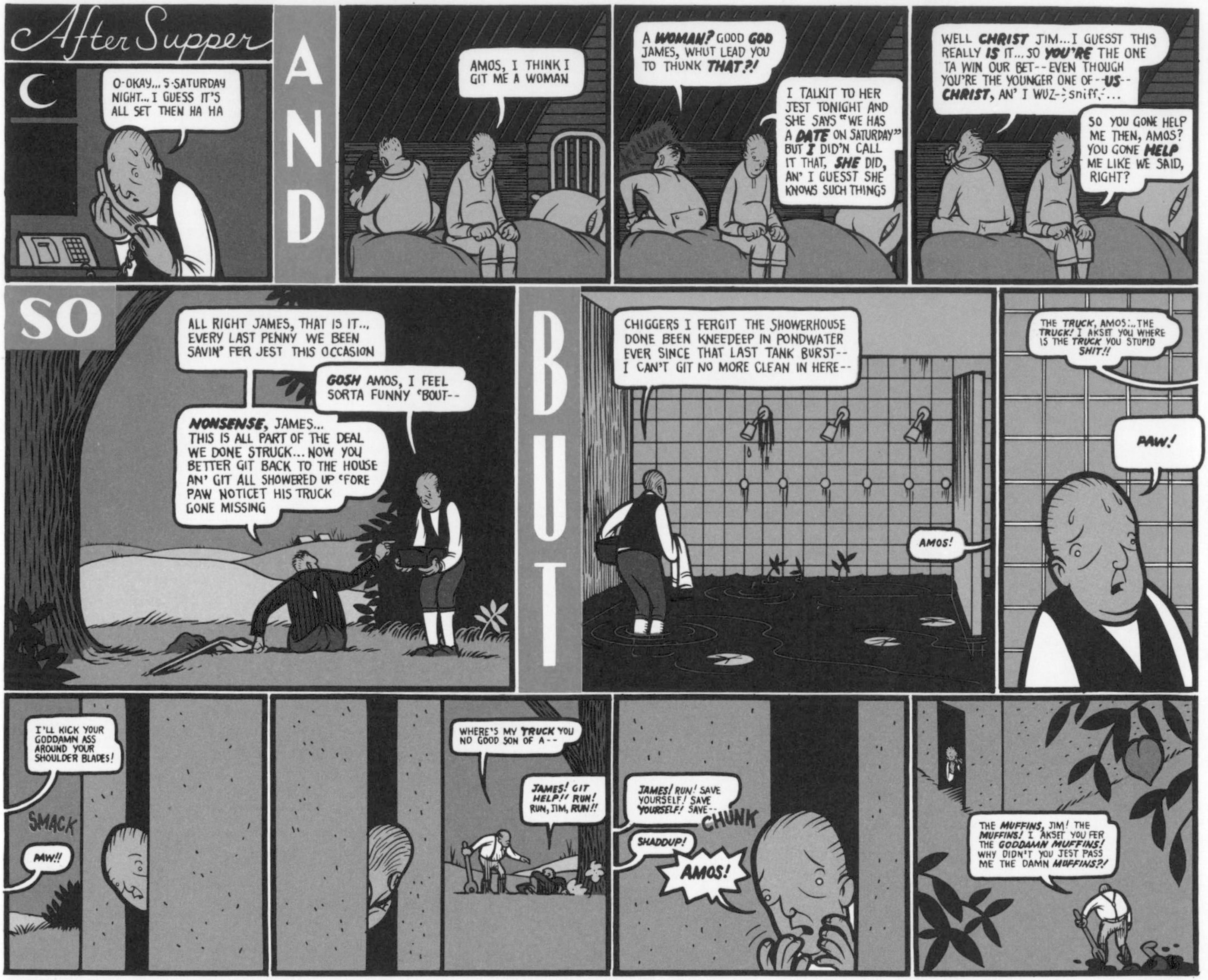
After Supper
O-OKAY... S-SATURDAY NIGHT... I GUESS IT'S ALL SET THEN HA HA
AND
AMOS, I THINK I GIT ME A WOMAN
A WOMAN? GOOD GOD JAMES, WHUT LEAD YOU TO THUNK THAT?!
KLUNK
I TALKIT TO HER JEST TONIGHT AND SHE SAYS "WE HAS A DATE ON SATURDAY" BUT I DID'N CALL IT THAT, SHE DID, AN' I GUESST SHE KNOWS SUCH THINGS
WELL CHRIST JIM... I GUESST THIS REALLY IS IT... SO YOU'RE THE ONE TA WIN OUR BET-- EVEN THOUGH YOU'RE THE YOUNGER ONE OF--US-- CHRIST, AN' I WUZ--sniff--...
SO YOU GONE HELP ME THEN, AMOS? YOU GONE HELP ME LIKE WE SAID, RIGHT?
SO
ALL RIGHT JAMES, THAT IS IT... EVERY LAST PENNY WE BEEN SAVIN' FER JEST THIS OCCASION
GOSH AMOS, I FEEL SORTA FUNNY 'BOUT--
NONSENSE, JAMES... THIS IS ALL PART OF THE DEAL WE DONE STRUCK... NOW YOU BETTER GIT BACK TO THE HOUSE AN' GIT ALL SHOWERED UP 'FORE PAW NOTICET HIS TRUCK GONE MISSING
BUT
CHIGGERS I FERGIT THE SHOWERHOUSE DONE BEEN KNEEDEEP IN PONDWATER EVER SINCE THAT LAST TANK BURST-- I CAN'T GIT NO MORE CLEAN IN HERE--
AMOS!
THE TRUCK, AMOS!... THE TRUCK! I AKSET YOU WHERE IS THE TRUCK YOU STUPID SHIT!!
PAW!
I'LL KICK YOUR GODDAMN ASS AROUND YOUR SHOULDER BLADES!
SMACK
PAW!!
WHERE'S MY TRUCK YOU NO GOOD SON OF A--
JAMES! GIT HELP!! RUN! RUN, JIM, RUN!!
JAMES! RUN! SAVE YOURSELF! SAVE YOURSELF! SAVE--
CHUNK
SHADDUP!
AMOS!
THE MUFFINS, JIM! THE MUFFINS! I AKSET YOU FER THE GODDAMN MUFFINS! WHY DIDN'T YOU JEST PASS ME THE DAMN MUFFINS?!

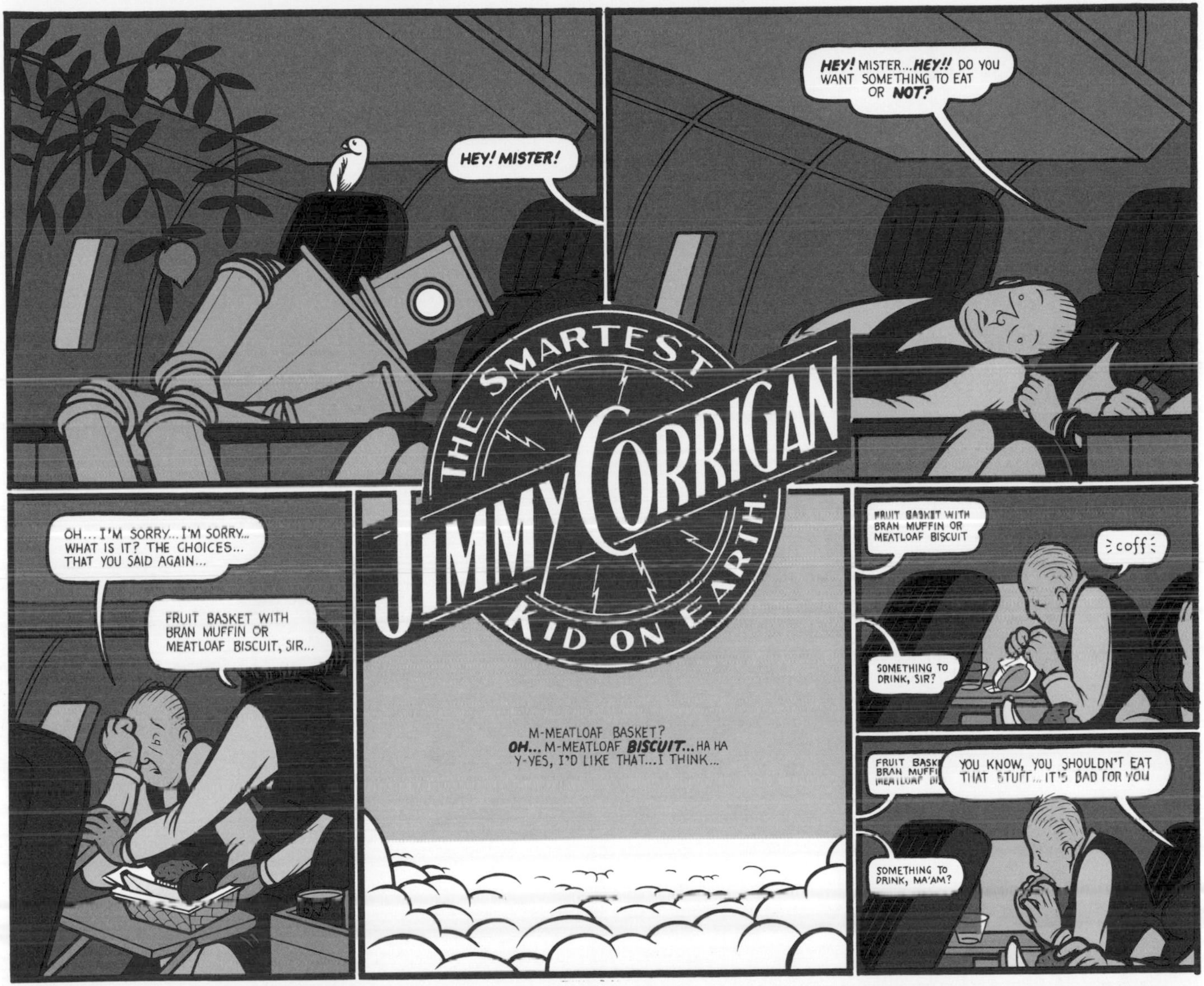
THE SMARTEST
JIMMY CORRIGAN
KID ON EARTH.
HEY! MISTER!
HEY! MISTER... HEY!! DO YOU WANT SOMETHING TO EAT OR NOT?
OH... I'M SORRY... I'M SORRY... WHAT IS IT? THE CHOICES... THAT YOU SAID AGAIN...
FRUIT BASKET WITH BRAN MUFFIN OR MEATLOAF BISCUIT, SIR...
M-MEATLOAF BASKET?
OH... M-MEATLOAF BISCUIT... HA HA
Y-YES, I'D LIKE THAT... I THINK...
FRUIT BASKET WITH BRAN MUFFIN OR MEATLOAF BISCUIT
coff
SOMETHING TO DRINK, SIR?
YOU KNOW, YOU SHOULDN'T EAT THAT STUFF... IT'S BAD FOR YOU
SOMETHING TO DRINK, MA'AM?

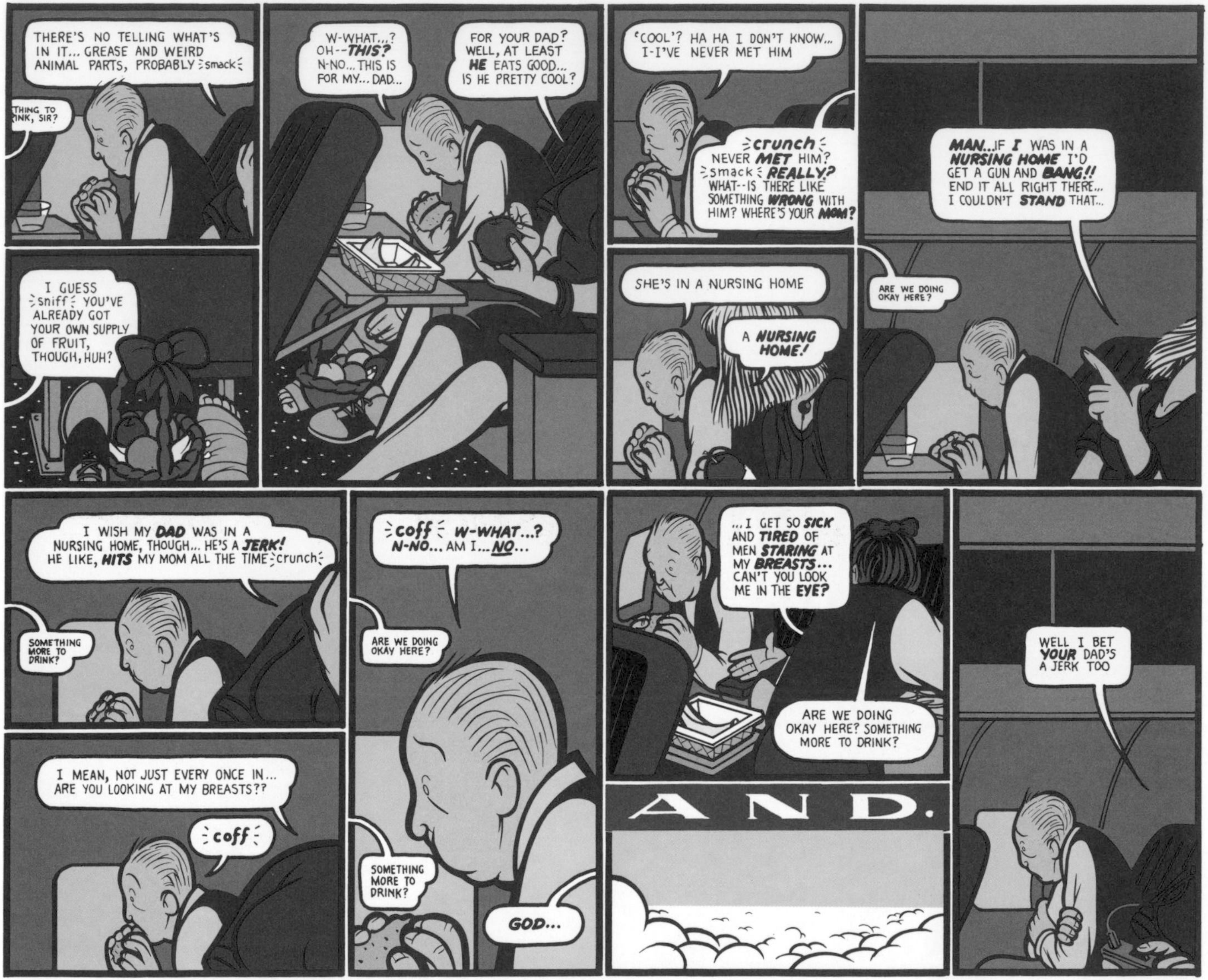
THERE'S NO TELLING WHAT'S IN IT... GREASE AND WEIRD ANIMAL PARTS, PROBABLY smack
THING TO RINK, SIR?
I GUESS sniff YOU'VE ALREADY GOT YOUR OWN SUPPLY OF FRUIT, THOUGH, HUH?
W-WHAT...? OH--THIS? N-NO... THIS IS FOR MY... DAD...
FOR YOUR DAD? WELL, AT LEAST HE EATS GOOD... IS HE PRETTY COOL?
'COOL'? HA HA I DON'T KNOW... I-I'VE NEVER MET HIM
crunch NEVER MET HIM? smack REALLY? WHAT--IS THERE LIKE SOMETHING WRONG WITH HIM? WHERE'S YOUR MOM?
SHE'S IN A NURSING HOME
A NURSING HOME!
MAN... IF I WAS IN A NURSING HOME I'D GET A GUN AND BANG!! END IT ALL RIGHT THERE... I COULDN'T STAND THAT...
ARE WE DOING OKAY HERE?
I WISH MY DAD WAS IN A NURSING HOME, THOUGH... HE'S A JERK! HE LIKE, HITS MY MOM ALL THE TIME crunch
SOMETHING MORE TO DRINK?
I MEAN, NOT JUST EVERY ONCE IN... ARE YOU LOOKING AT MY BREASTS??
coff
coff W-WHAT...? N-NO... AM I... NO...
ARE WE DOING OKAY HERE?
SOMETHING MORE TO DRINK?
GOD...
...I GET SO SICK AND TIRED OF MEN STARING AT MY BREASTS... CAN'T YOU LOOK ME IN THE EYE?
ARE WE DOING OKAY HERE? SOMETHING MORE TO DRINK?
AND.
WELL I BET YOUR DAD'S A JERK TOO

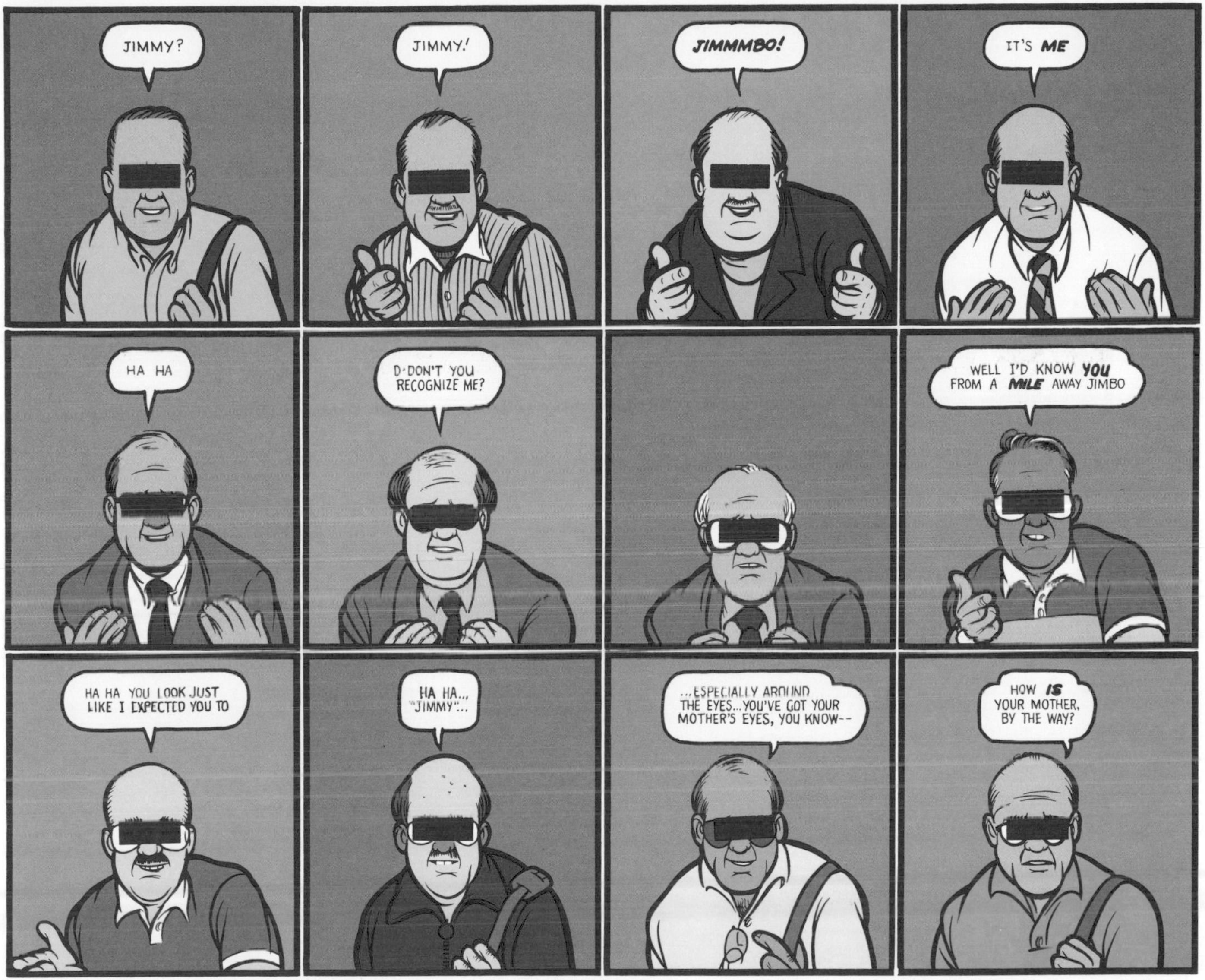
JIMMY?
JIMMY!
JIMMMBO!
IT'S **ME**
HA HA
D-DON'T YOU RECOGNIZE ME?
WELL I'D KNOW **YOU** FROM A **MILE** AWAY JIMBO
HA HA YOU LOOK JUST LIKE I EXPECTED YOU TO
HA HA.., "JIMMY"...
...ESPECIALLY AROUND THE EYES...YOU'VE GOT YOUR MOTHER'S EYES, YOU KNOW--
HOW **IS** YOUR MOTHER, BY THE WAY?

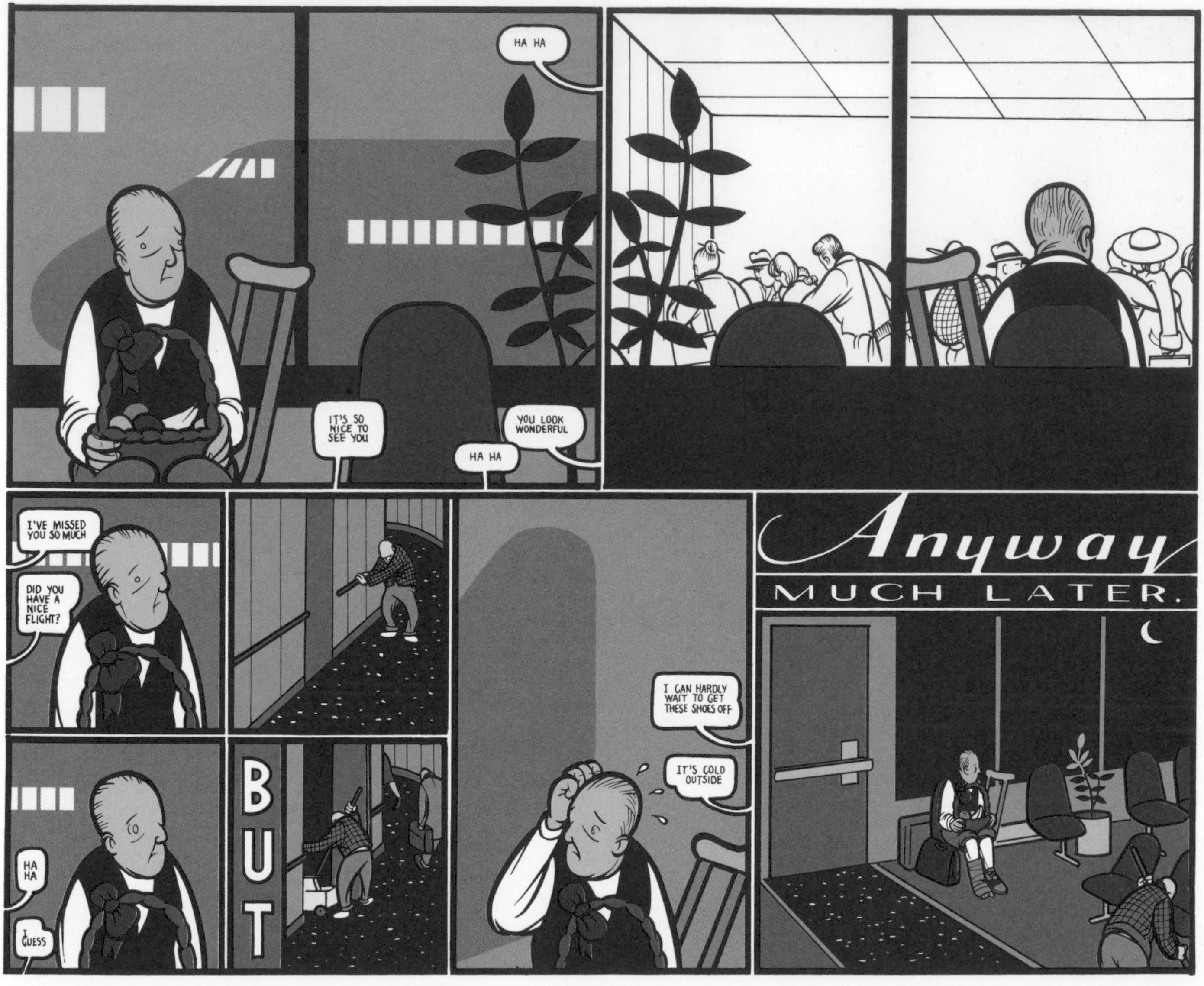

HA HA
IT'S SO NICE TO SEE YOU
HA HA
YOU LOOK WONDERFUL
I'VE MISSED YOU SO MUCH
DID YOU HAVE A NICE FLIGHT?
HA HA
I GUESS
BUT
I CAN HARDLY WAIT TO GET THESE SHOES OFF
IT'S COLD OUTSIDE
Anyway
MUCH LATER.

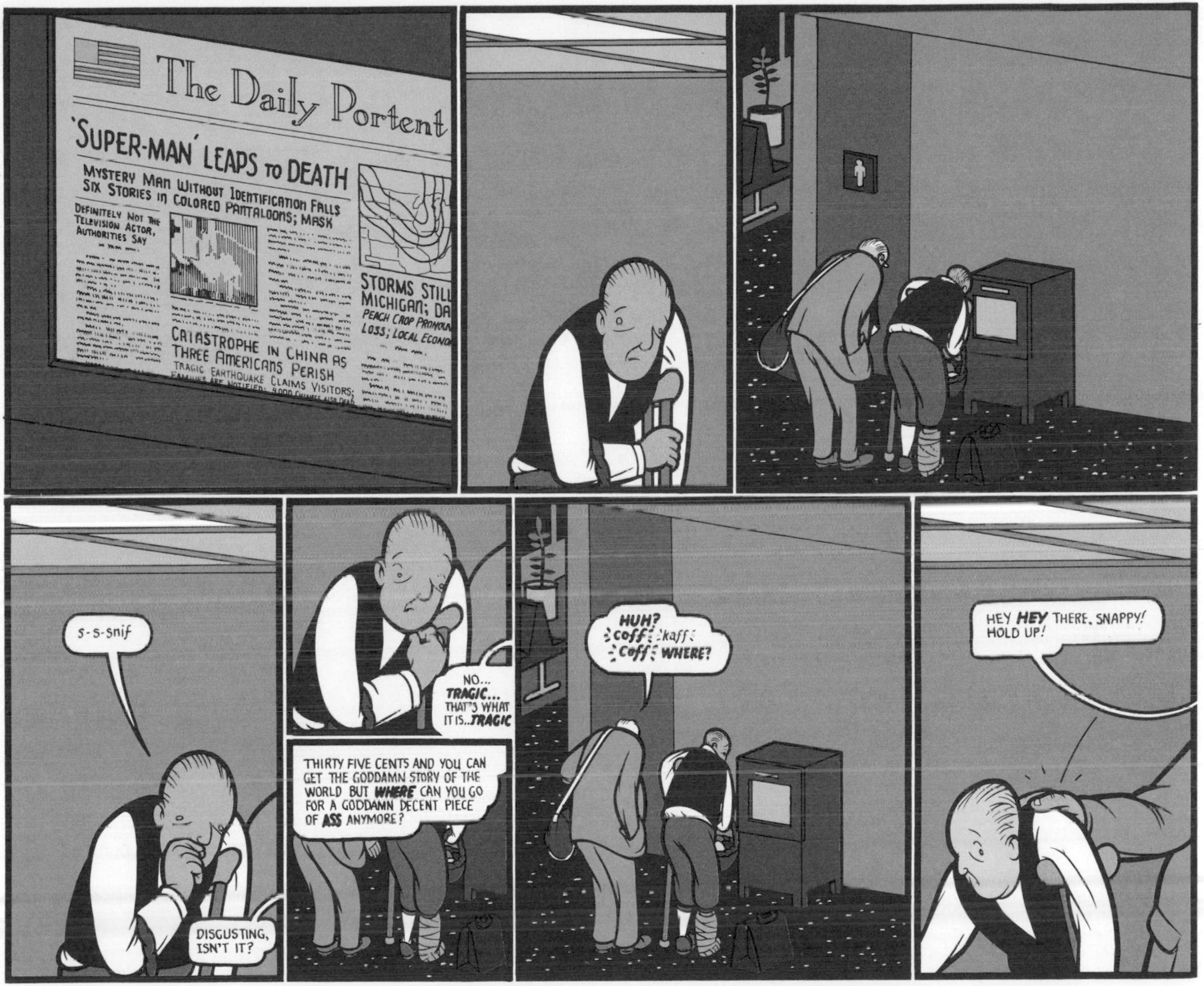
The Daily Portent
'SUPER-MAN' LEAPS TO DEATH
MYSTERY MAN WITHOUT IDENTIFICATION FALLS SIX STORIES IN COLORED PANTALOONS; MASK
DEFINITELY NOT THE TELEVISION ACTOR, AUTHORITIES SAY
CATASTROPHE IN CHINA AS THREE AMERICANS PERISH
TRAGIC EARTHQUAKE CLAIMS VISITORS;
STORMS STILL
s-s-snif
DISGUSTING, ISN'T IT?
NO... TRAGIC... THAT'S WHAT IT IS...TRAGIC
THIRTY FIVE CENTS AND YOU CAN GET THE GODDAMN STORY OF THE WORLD BUT WHERE CAN YOU GO FOR A GODDAMN DECENT PIECE OF ASS ANYMORE?
HUH? coff kaff Coff WHERE?
HEY HEY THERE, SNAPPY! HOLD UP!

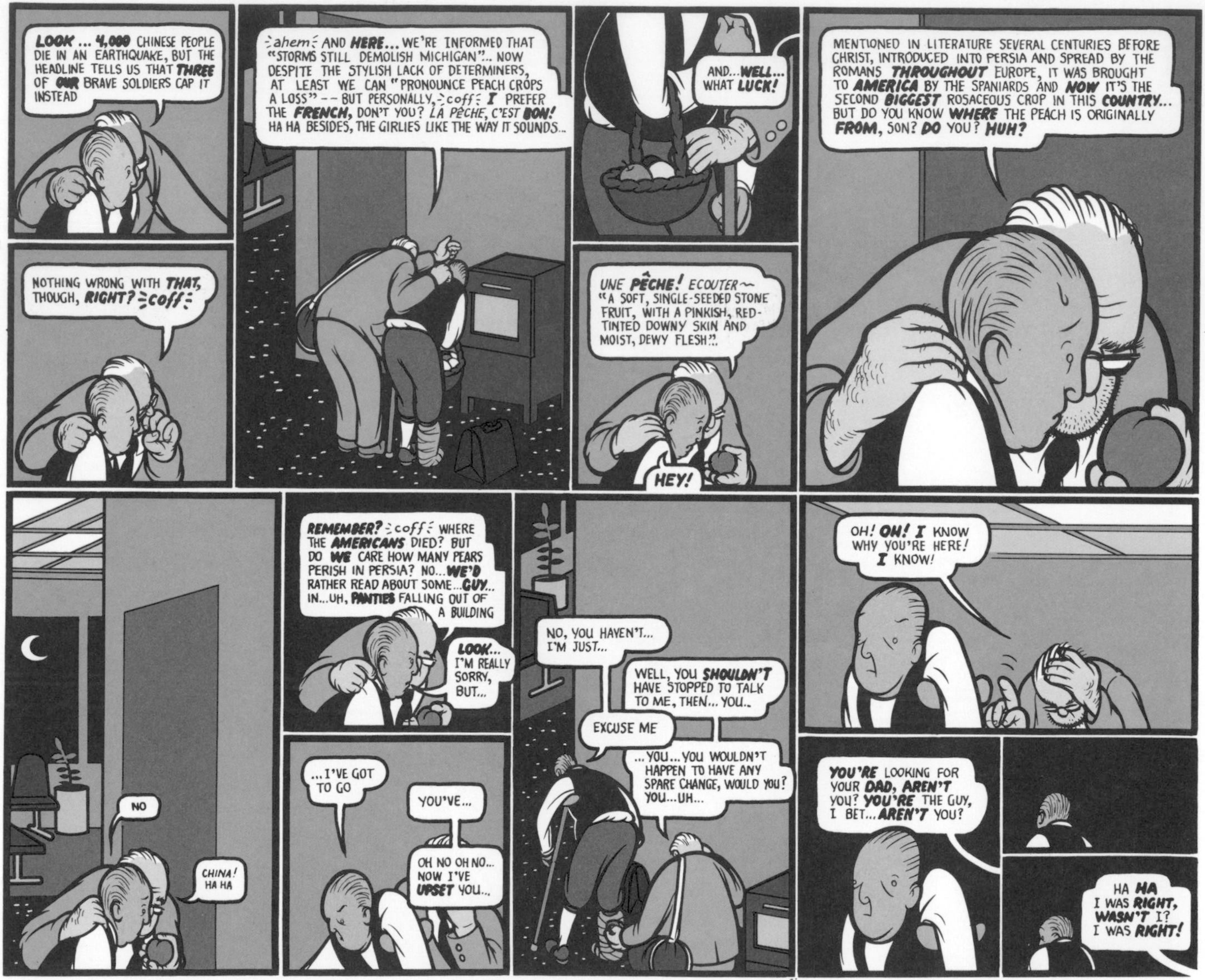
LOOK ... 4,000 CHINESE PEOPLE DIE IN AN EARTHQUAKE, BUT THE HEADLINE TELLS US THAT THREE OF OUR BRAVE SOLDIERS CAP IT INSTEAD
NOTHING WRONG WITH THAT, THOUGH, RIGHT? ≈coff≈
≈ahem≈ AND HERE... WE'RE INFORMED THAT "STORMS STILL DEMOLISH MICHIGAN"... NOW DESPITE THE STYLISH LACK OF DETERMINERS, AT LEAST WE CAN "PRONOUNCE PEACH CROPS A LOSS" -- BUT PERSONALLY, ≈coff≈ I PREFER THE FRENCH, DON'T YOU? LA PÊCHE, C'EST BON! HA HA BESIDES, THE GIRLIES LIKE THE WAY IT SOUNDS...
AND... WELL... WHAT LUCK!
UNE PÊCHE! ECOUTER~ "A SOFT, SINGLE-SEEDED STONE FRUIT, WITH A PINKISH, RED-TINTED DOWNY SKIN AND MOIST, DEWY FLESH".
HEY!
MENTIONED IN LITERATURE SEVERAL CENTURIES BEFORE CHRIST, INTRODUCED INTO PERSIA AND SPREAD BY THE ROMANS THROUGHOUT EUROPE, IT WAS BROUGHT TO AMERICA BY THE SPANIARDS AND NOW IT'S THE SECOND BIGGEST ROSACEOUS CROP IN THIS COUNTRY... BUT DO YOU KNOW WHERE THE PEACH IS ORIGINALLY FROM, SON? DO YOU? HUH?
NO
CHINA! HA HA
REMEMBER? ≈coff≈ WHERE THE AMERICANS DIED? BUT DO WE CARE HOW MANY PEARS PERISH IN PERSIA? NO... WE'D RATHER READ ABOUT SOME... GUY... IN... UH, PANTIES FALLING OUT OF A BUILDING
LOOK... I'M REALLY SORRY, BUT...
...I'VE GOT TO GO
YOU'VE...
OH NO OH NO... NOW I'VE UPSET YOU...
NO, YOU HAVEN'T... I'M JUST...
WELL, YOU SHOULDN'T HAVE STOPPED TO TALK TO ME, THEN... YOU..
EXCUSE ME
...YOU... YOU WOULDN'T HAPPEN TO HAVE ANY SPARE CHANGE, WOULD YOU? YOU... UH...
OH! OH! I KNOW WHY YOU'RE HERE! I KNOW!
YOU'RE LOOKING FOR YOUR DAD, AREN'T YOU? YOU'RE THE GUY, I BET... AREN'T YOU?
HA HA I WAS RIGHT, WASN'T I? I WAS RIGHT!

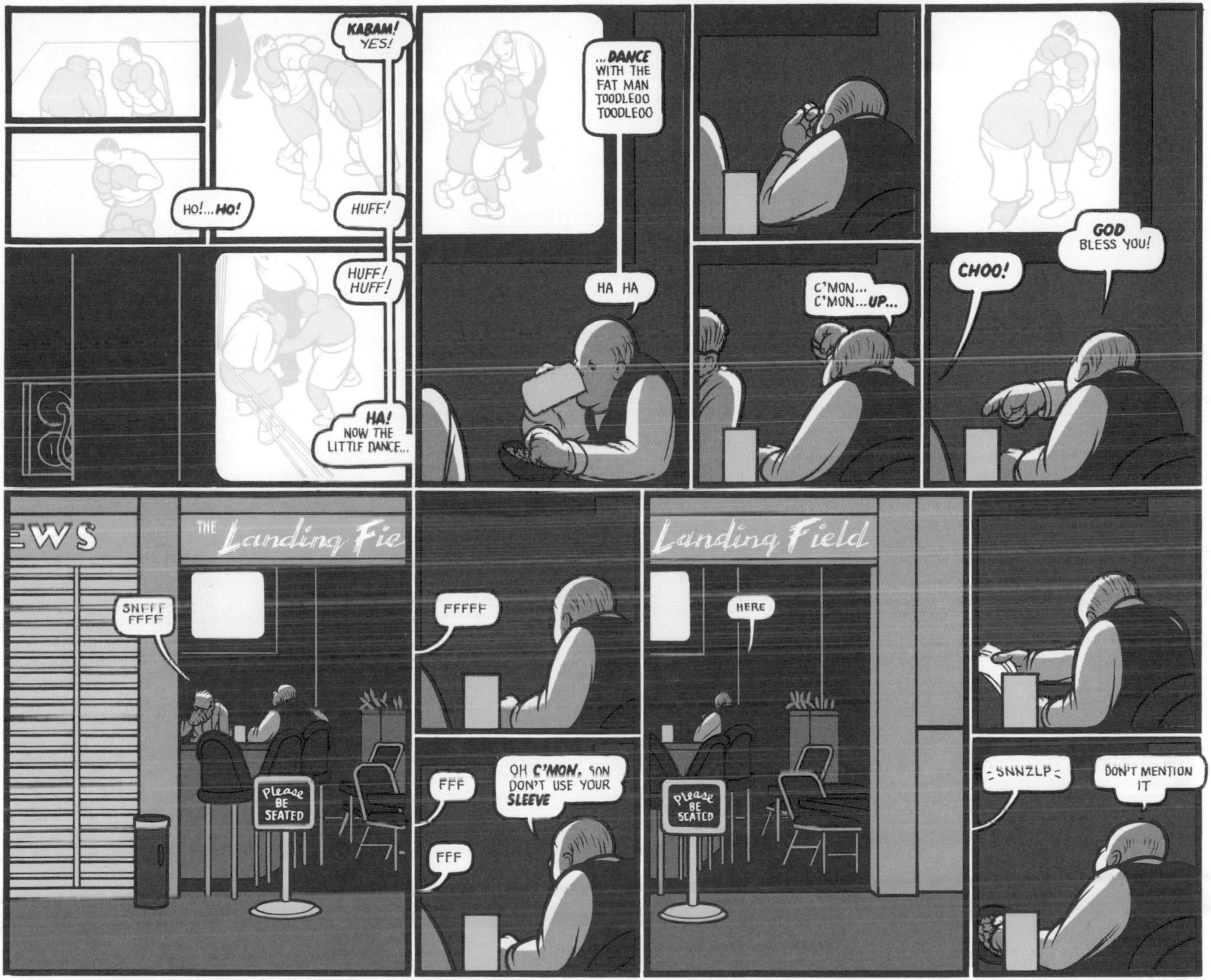
HO!...HO!
KABAM! YES!
HUFF!
HUFF! HUFF!
HA! NOW THE LITTLE DANCE...
...DANCE WITH THE FAT MAN TOODLEOO TOODLEOO
HA HA
C'MON... C'MON...UP...
CHOO!
GOD BLESS YOU!
EWS
THE Landing Fie
SNFFF FFFF
Please BE SEATED
FFFFF
FFF
OH C'MON, SON DON'T USE YOUR SLEEVE
FFF
Landing Field
HERE
Please BE SEATED
SNNZLP
DON'T MENTION IT

OOP--COMMERCIAL BREAK! TIME FOR *EDUCATION!*

THE *Landing Field*

PFF

"THREE AMERICANS MISSING IN CHINESE EARTHQUAKE"

PLEASE BE SEATED

YESTERDAY'S PAPER

I PROMISE I PROMISE

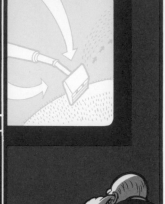

SO MUCH FOR EDUCATION

≥coff≥

MR. CORRIGAN MR. CORRIGAN!

≥grunt≥

I *FOUND* HIM! I *FOUND* HIM!

SEE? I *TOLD* YOU! I *FOUND* HIM! I *TOLD* YOU!

WELL *HOT DAMN* LOOK AT THAT! WHAT HAPPENED TO YOUR *FOOT?*

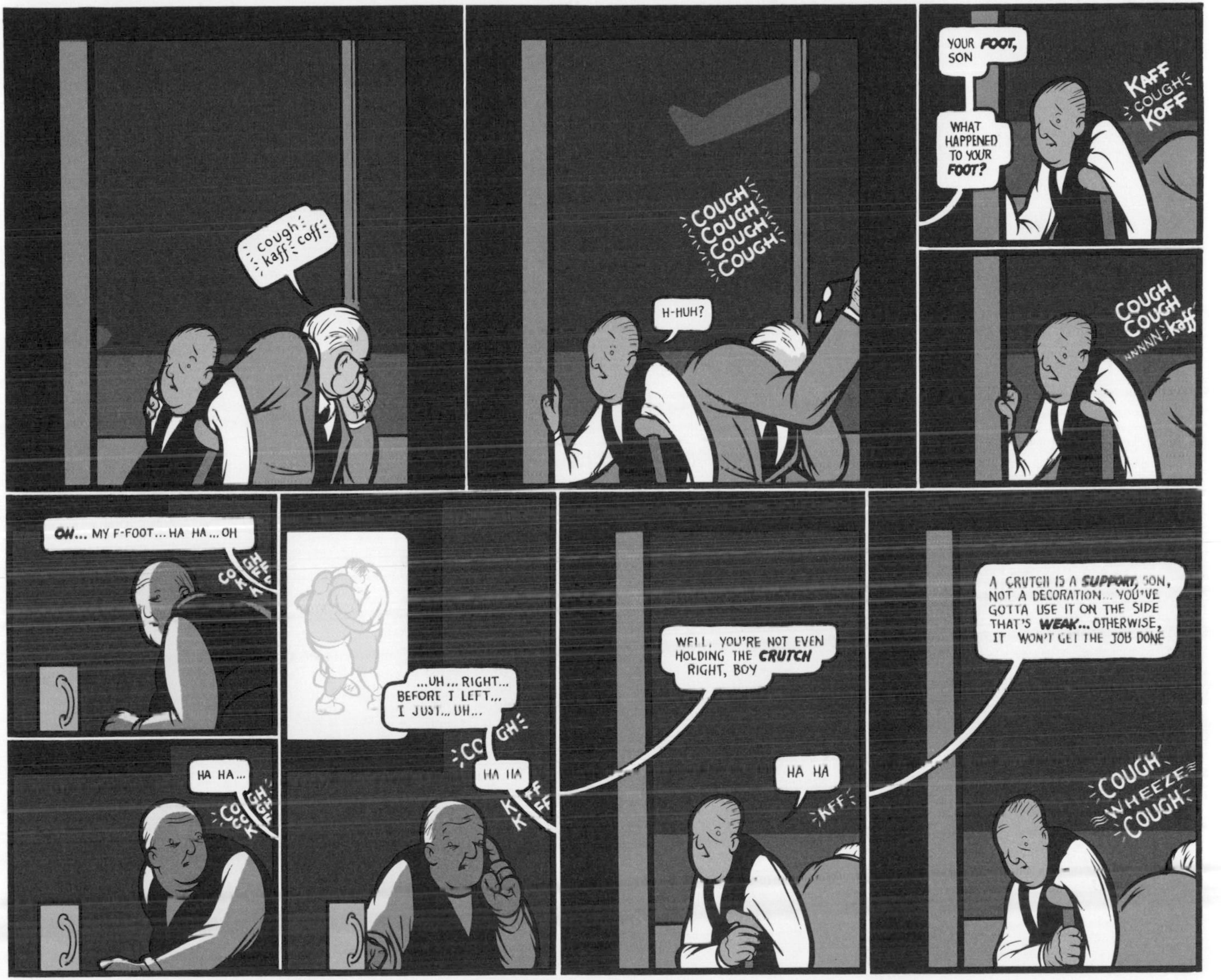
cough kaff coff
COUGH COUGH COUGH COUGH
H-HUH?
YOUR FOOT, SON
WHAT HAPPENED TO YOUR FOOT?
KAFF COUGH KOFF
COUGH COUGH NNNNN kaff
OH... MY F-FOOT... HA HA... OH
HA HA...
...UH... RIGHT... BEFORE I LEFT... I JUST... UH...
HA HA
WELL, YOU'RE NOT EVEN HOLDING THE CRUTCH RIGHT, BOY
HA HA
KFF
A CRUTCH IS A SUPPORT, SON, NOT A DECORATION... YOU'VE GOTTA USE IT ON THE SIDE THAT'S WEAK... OTHERWISE, IT WON'T GET THE JOB DONE
COUGH WHEEZE COUGH

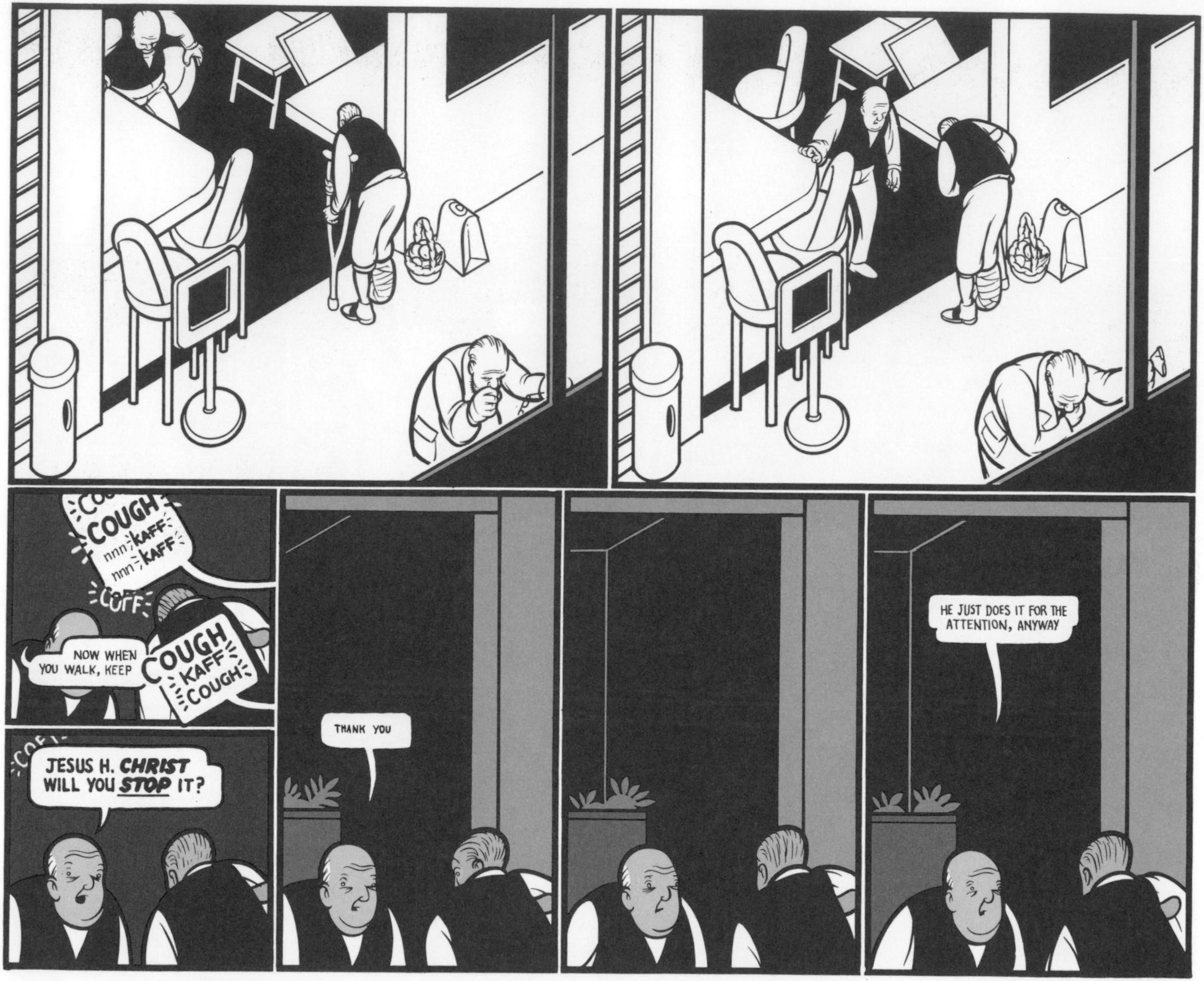

COUGH
nnn KAFF
nnn KAFF
COFF
NOW WHEN YOU WALK, KEEP
COUGH KAFF COUGH
JESUS H. CHRIST WILL YOU STOP IT?
THANK YOU
HE JUST DOES IT FOR THE ATTENTION, ANYWAY

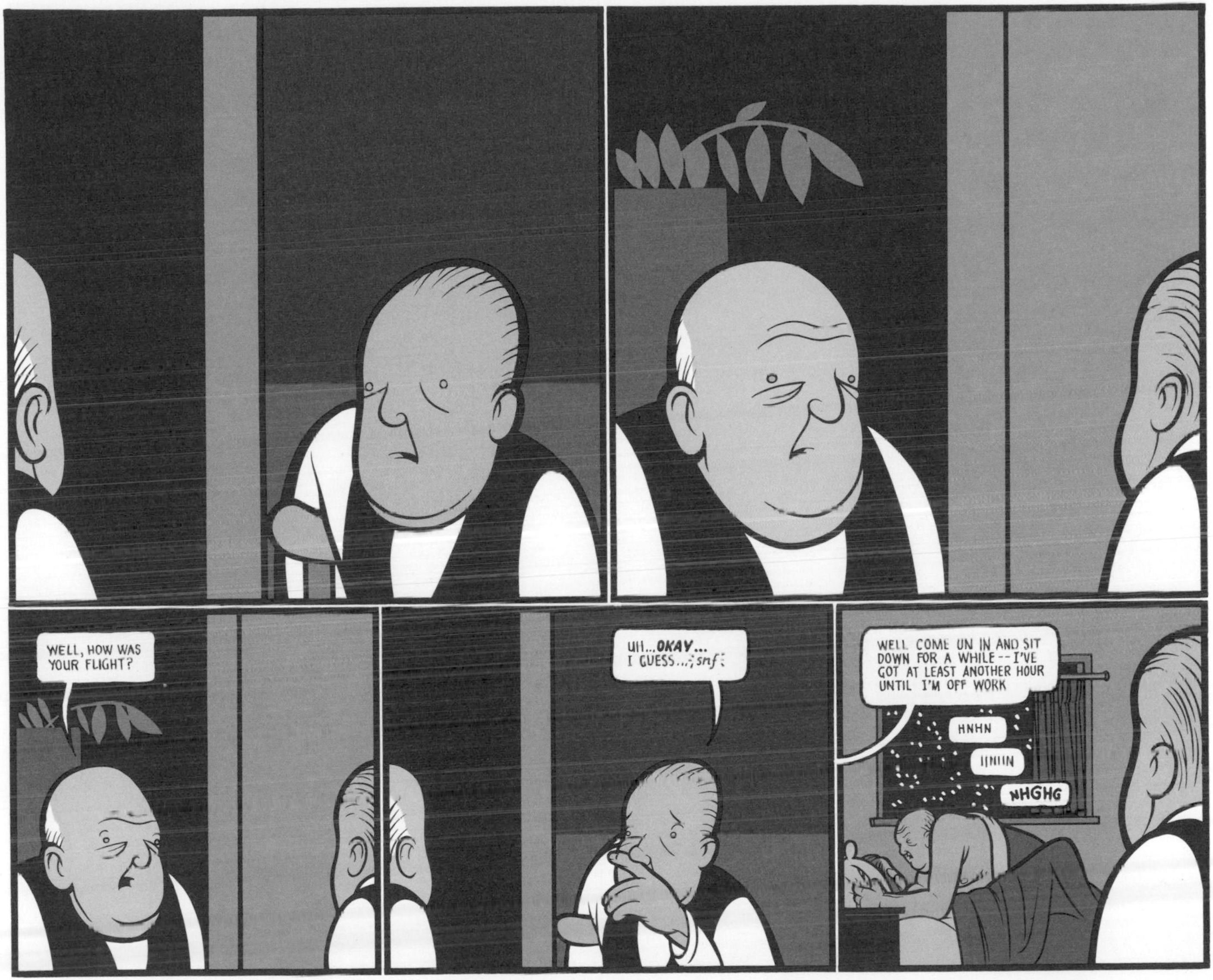
WELL, HOW WAS YOUR FLIGHT?
UH...*OKAY*... I GUESS...;snf;
WELL COME UN IN AND SIT DOWN FOR A WHILE--I'VE GOT AT LEAST ANOTHER HOUR UNTIL I'M OFF WORK
HNHN
HNHN
NHGHG

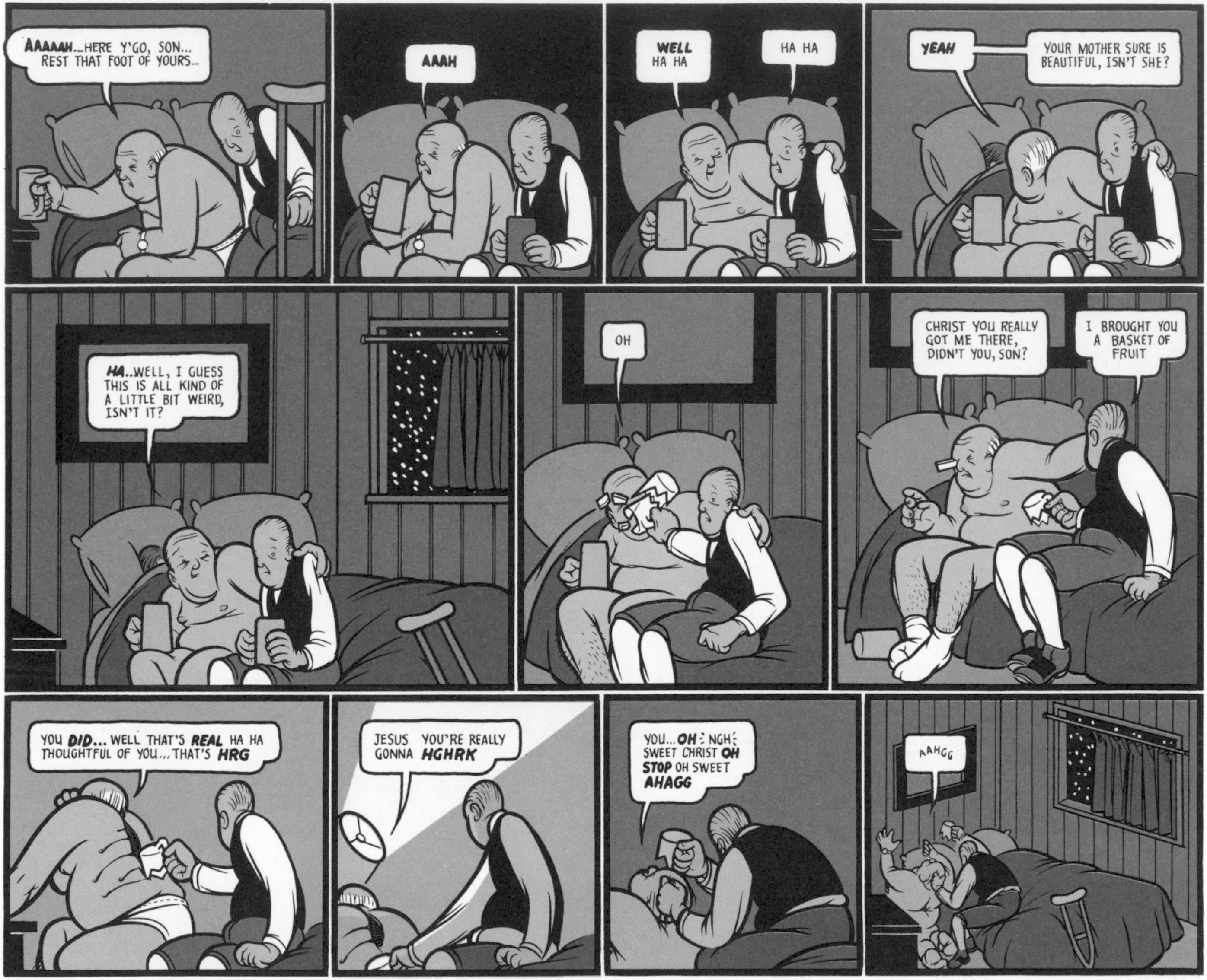
AAAAAH...HERE Y'GO, SON... REST THAT FOOT OF YOURS...
AAAH
WELL HA HA
HA HA
YEAH
YOUR MOTHER SURE IS BEAUTIFUL, ISN'T SHE?
HA..WELL, I GUESS THIS IS ALL KIND OF A LITTLE BIT WEIRD, ISN'T IT?
OH
CHRIST YOU REALLY GOT ME THERE, DIDN'T YOU, SON?
I BROUGHT YOU A BASKET OF FRUIT
YOU DID... WELL THAT'S REAL HA HA THOUGHTFUL OF YOU... THAT'S HRG
JESUS YOU'RE REALLY GONNA HGHRK
YOU...OH NGH SWEET CHRIST OH STOP OH SWEET AHAGG
AAHGG

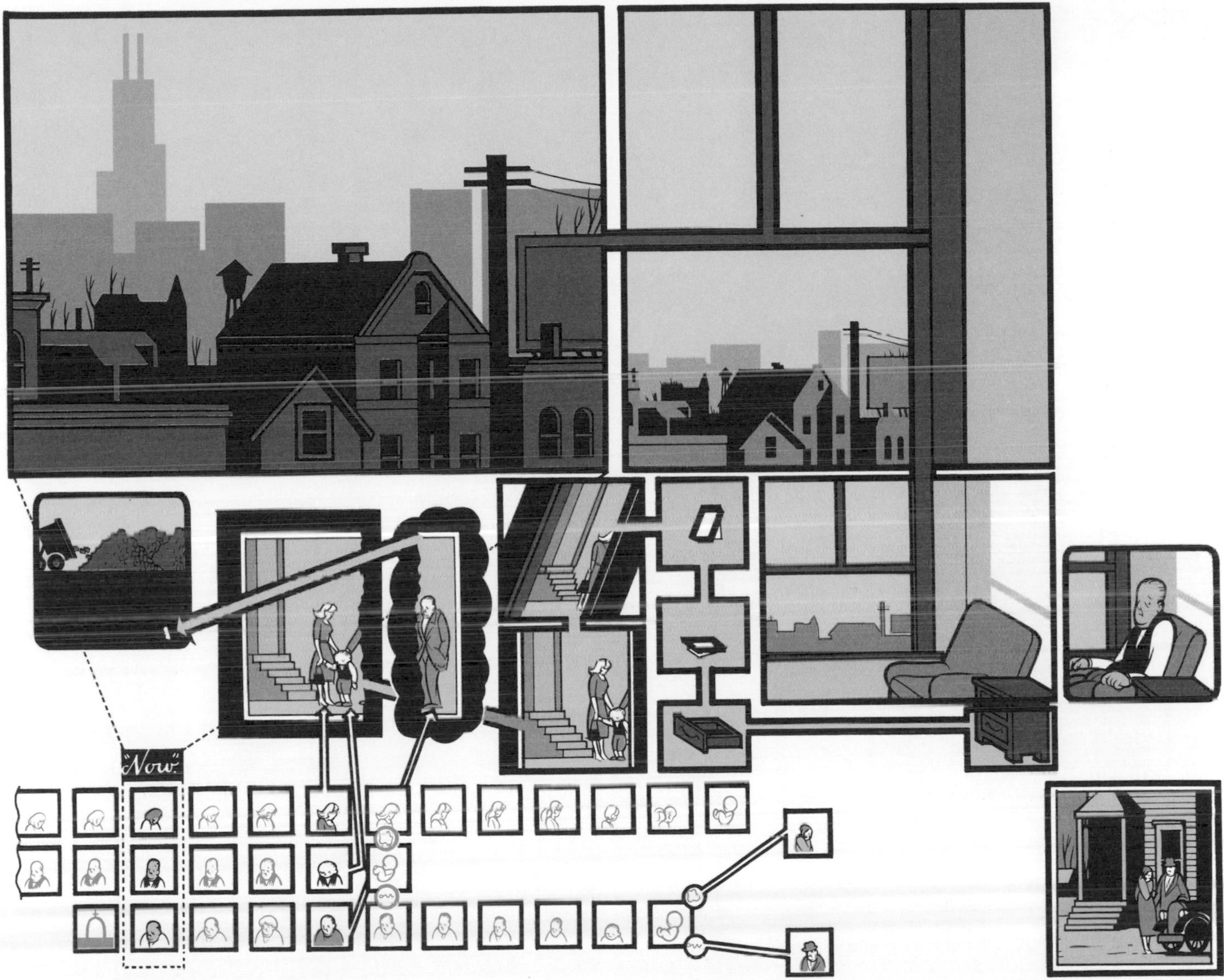
"Now"

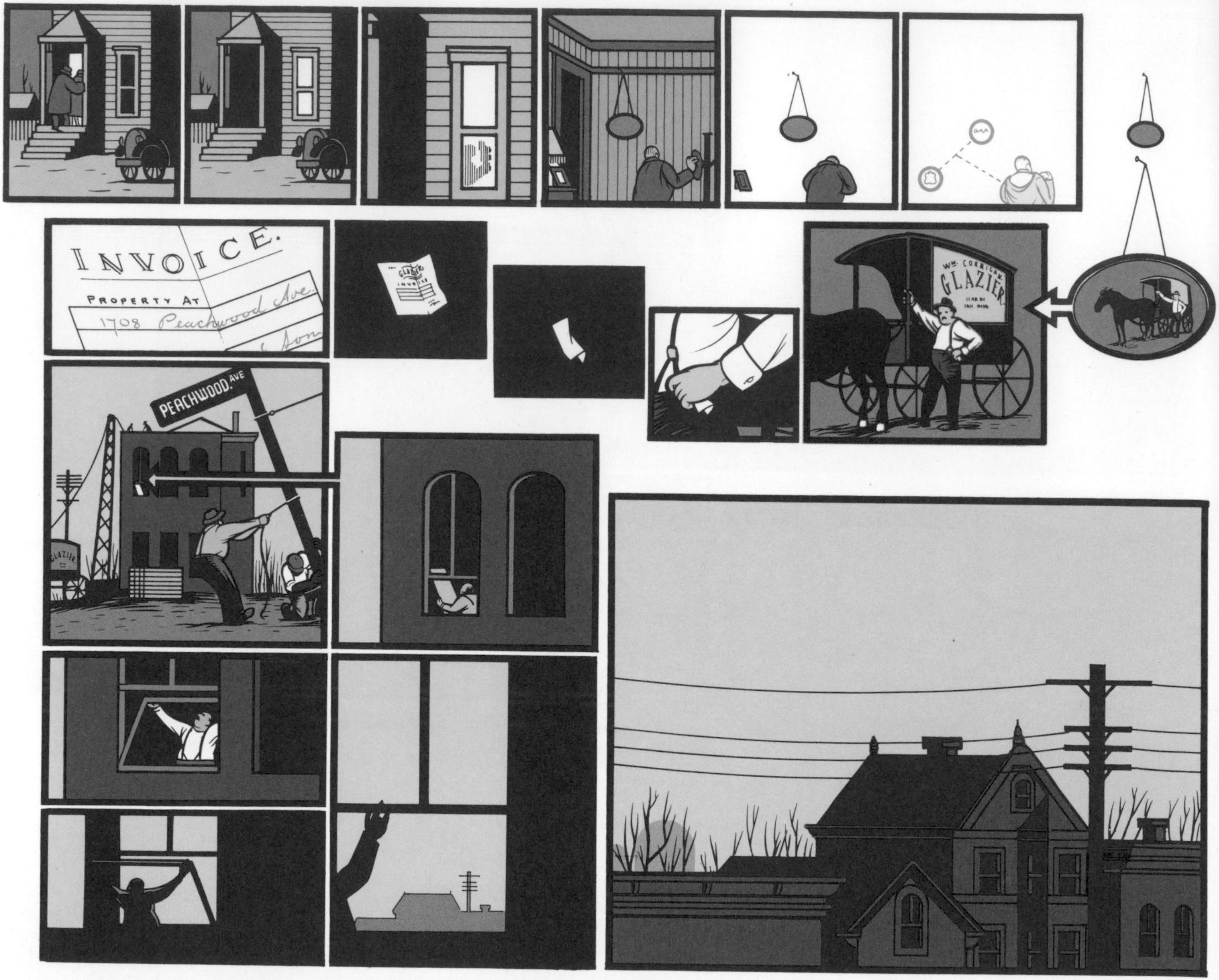
INVOICE.
PROPERTY AT
1708 Peachwood Ave.
& Son
WM. CORRIGAN.
GLAZIER.
PEACHWOOD AVE
GLAZIER

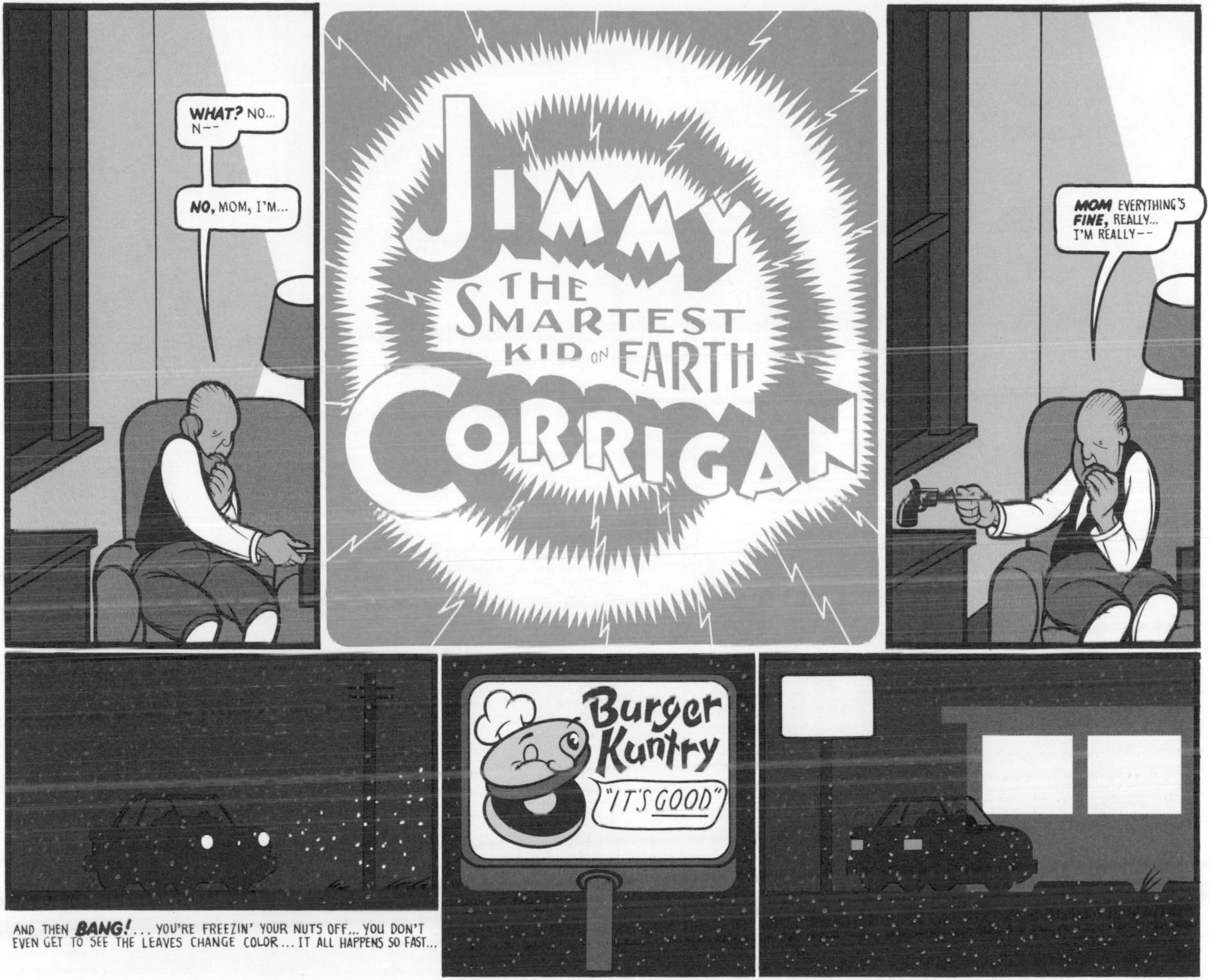
WHAT? NO... N--
NO, MOM, I'M...
JIMMY CORRIGAN
THE SMARTEST KID ON EARTH
MOM EVERYTHING'S FINE, REALLY... I'M REALLY--
Burger Kuntry
"IT'S GOOD"
AND THEN BANG!... YOU'RE FREEZIN' YOUR NUTS OFF... YOU DON'T EVEN GET TO SEE THE LEAVES CHANGE COLOR... IT ALL HAPPENS SO FAST...

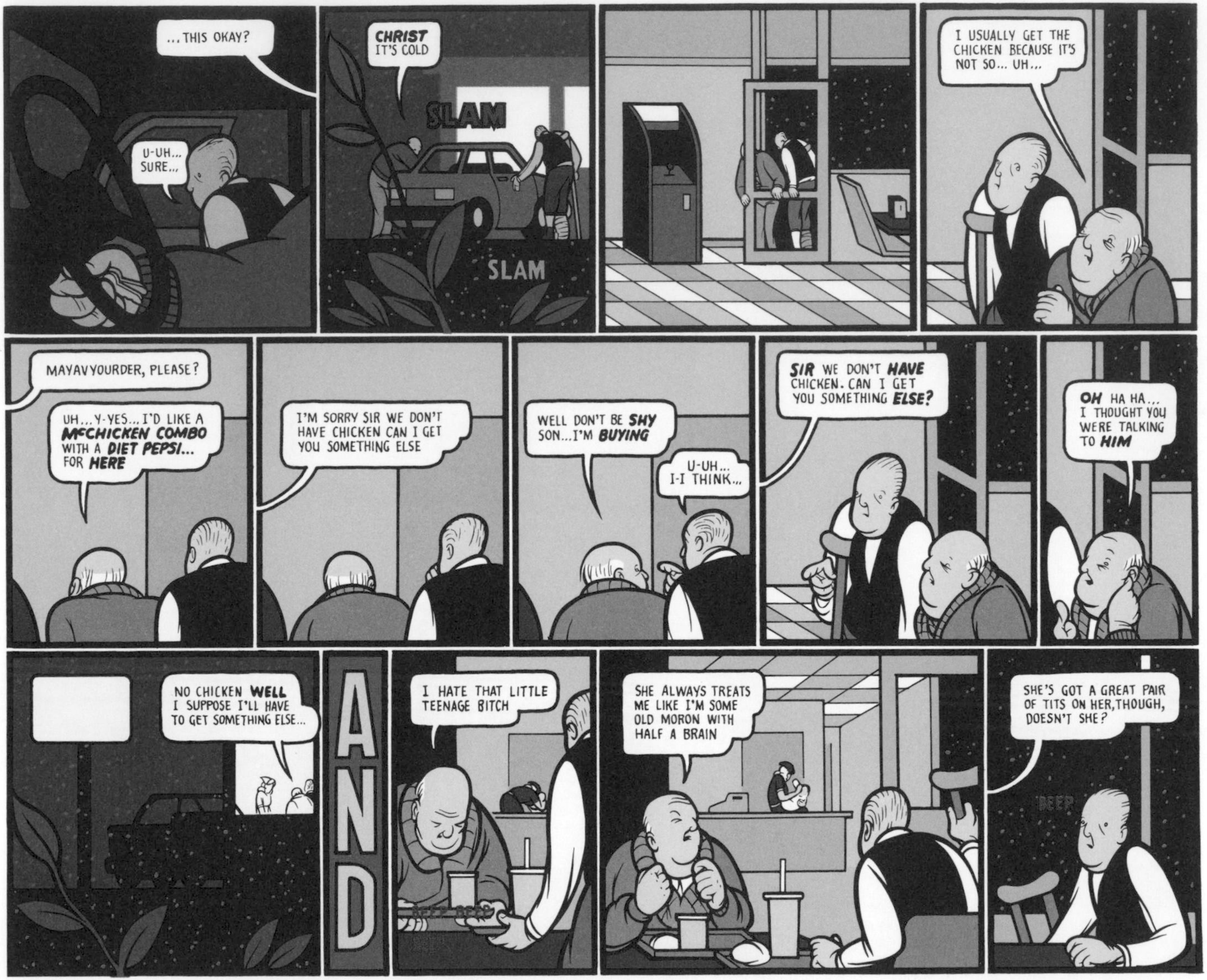

... THIS OKAY?
U-UH... SURE...
CHRIST IT'S COLD
SLAM
SLAM
I USUALLY GET THE CHICKEN BECAUSE IT'S NOT SO... UH...
MAYAVYOURDER, PLEASE?
UH... Y-YES... I'D LIKE A McCHICKEN COMBO WITH A DIET PEPSI... FOR HERE
I'M SORRY SIR WE DON'T HAVE CHICKEN CAN I GET YOU SOMETHING ELSE
WELL DON'T BE SHY SON... I'M BUYING
U-UH... I-I THINK...
SIR WE DON'T HAVE CHICKEN. CAN I GET YOU SOMETHING ELSE?
OH HA HA... I THOUGHT YOU WERE TALKING TO HIM
NO CHICKEN WELL I SUPPOSE I'LL HAVE TO GET SOMETHING ELSE...
AND
I HATE THAT LITTLE TEENAGE BITCH
SHE ALWAYS TREATS ME LIKE I'M SOME OLD MORON WITH HALF A BRAIN
SHE'S GOT A GREAT PAIR OF TITS ON HER, THOUGH, DOESN'T SHE?
BEEP

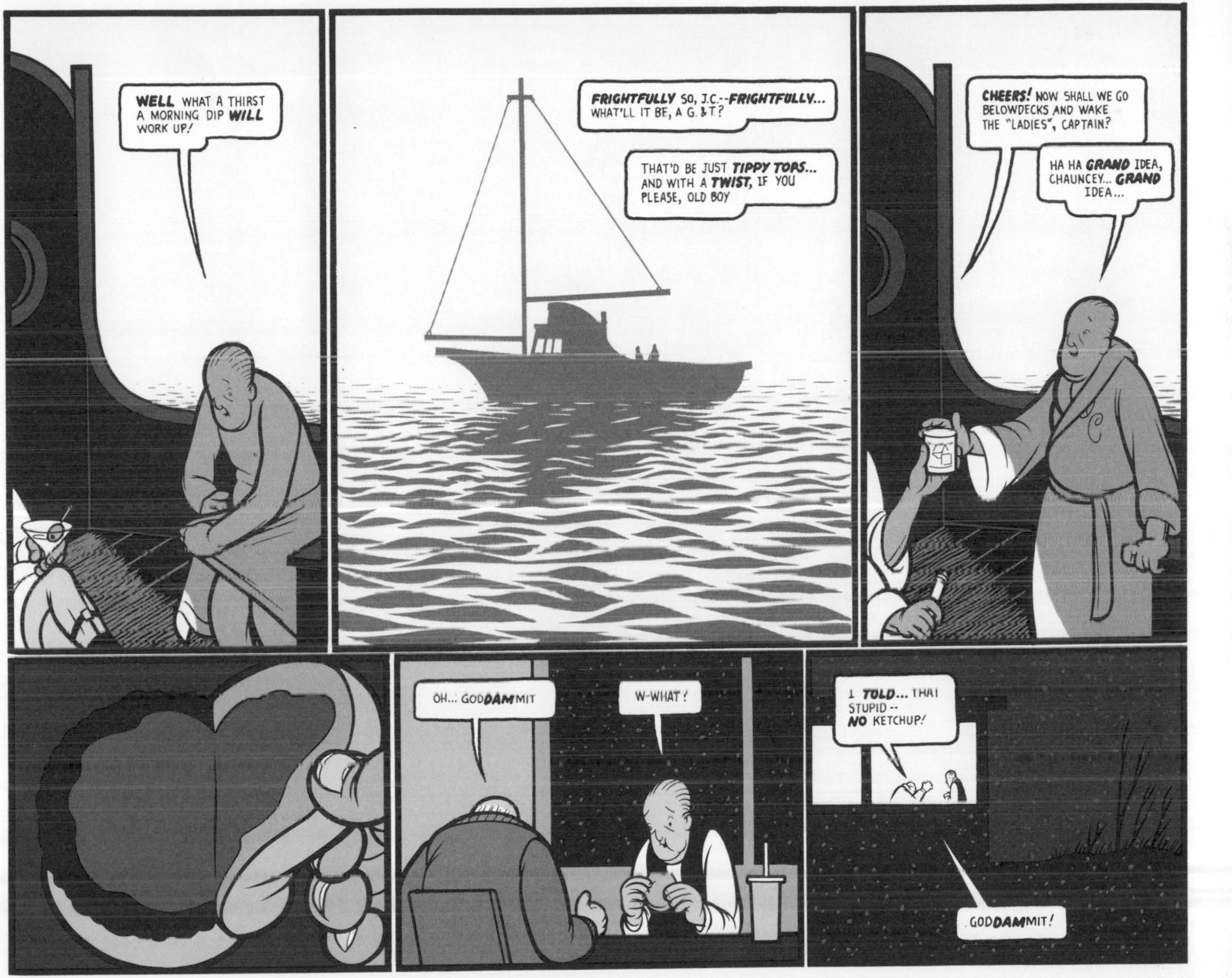

WELL WHAT A THIRST A MORNING DIP WILL WORK UP!
FRIGHTFULLY SO, J.C.--FRIGHTFULLY... WHAT'LL IT BE, A G.&T.?
THAT'D BE JUST TIPPY TOPS... AND WITH A TWIST, IF YOU PLEASE, OLD BOY
CHEERS! NOW SHALL WE GO BELOWDECKS AND WAKE THE "LADIES", CAPTAIN?
HA HA GRAND IDEA, CHAUNCEY... GRAND IDEA...
OH... GODDAMMIT
W-WHAT?
I TOLD... THAT STUPID -- NO KETCHUP!
GODDAMMIT!

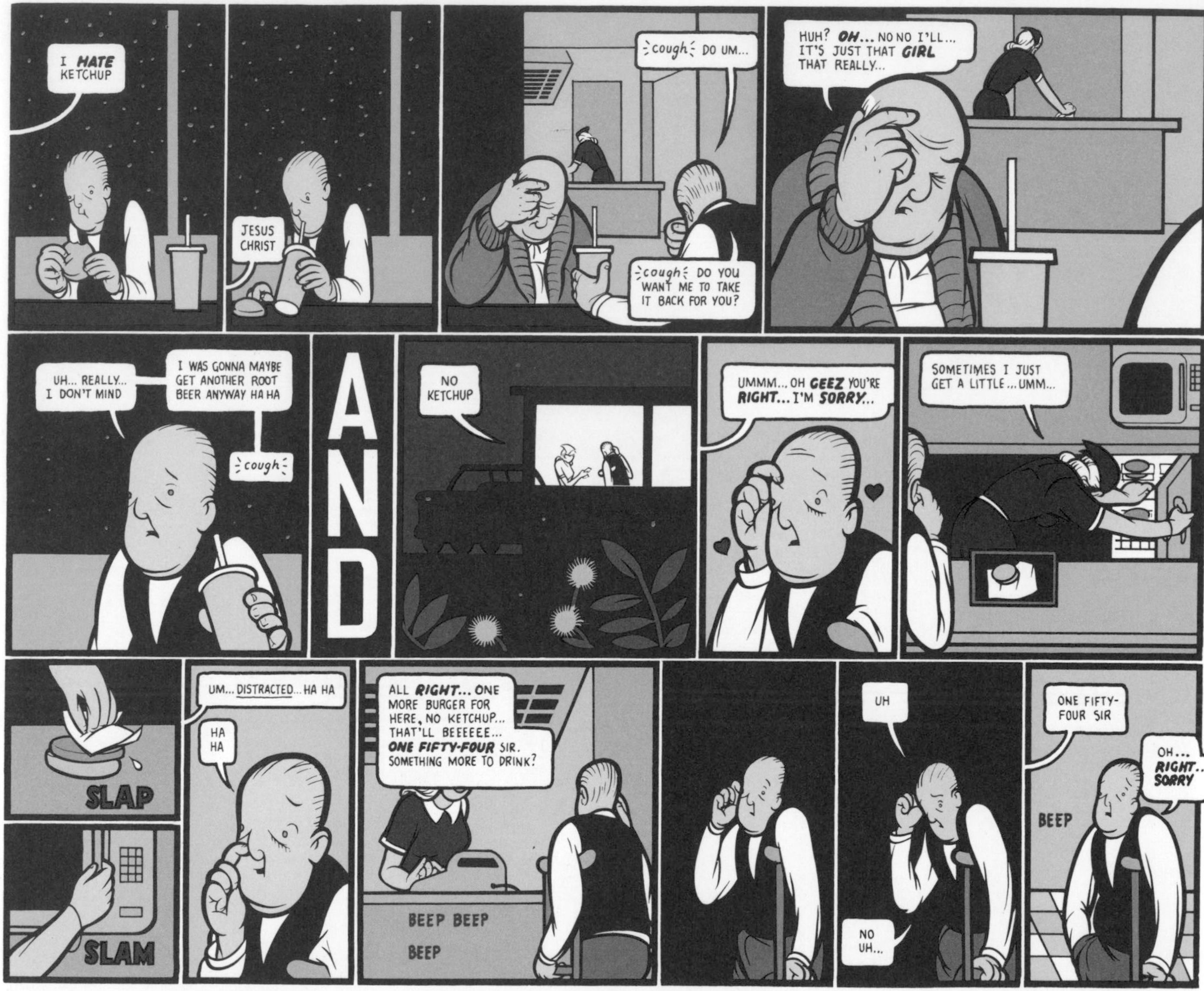

I **HATE** KETCHUP
JESUS CHRIST
cough DO UM...
cough DO YOU WANT ME TO TAKE IT BACK FOR YOU?
HUH? **OH...** NO NO I'LL... IT'S JUST THAT **GIRL** THAT REALLY...
UH... REALLY... I DON'T MIND
I WAS GONNA MAYBE GET ANOTHER ROOT BEER ANYWAY HA HA
cough
AND
NO KETCHUP
UMMM... OH **GEEZ** YOU'RE **RIGHT...** I'M **SORRY...**
SOMETIMES I JUST GET A LITTLE... UMM...
SLAP
SLAM
UM... DISTRACTED... HA HA
HA HA
ALL **RIGHT...** ONE MORE BURGER FOR HERE, NO KETCHUP... THAT'LL BEEEEEE... **ONE FIFTY-FOUR** SIR. SOMETHING MORE TO DRINK?
BEEP BEEP
BEEP
UH
NO UH...
ONE FIFTY-FOUR SIR
OH... **RIGHT... SORRY**
BEEP

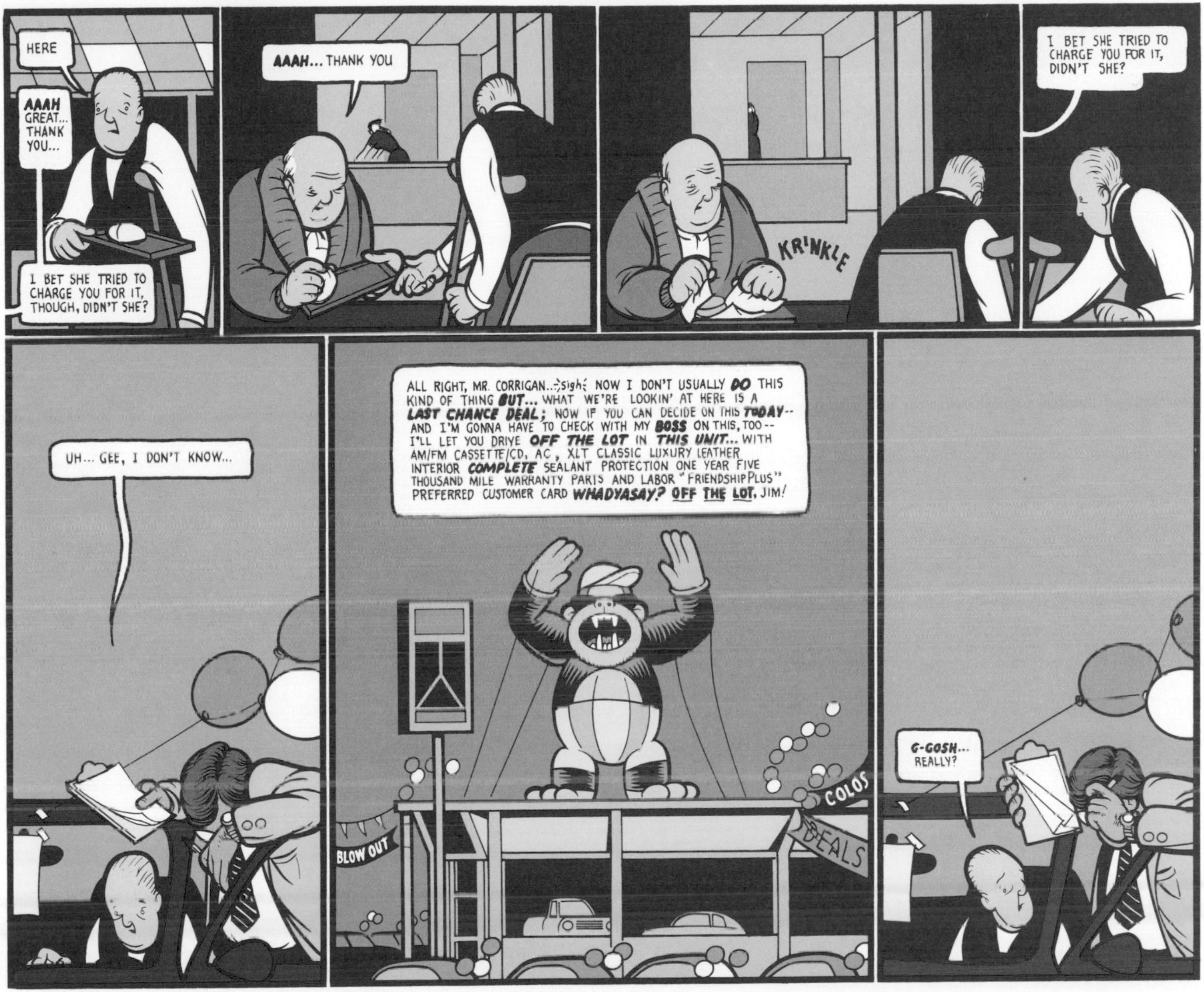
HERE
AAAH GREAT... THANK YOU...
I BET SHE TRIED TO CHARGE YOU FOR IT, THOUGH, DIDN'T SHE?
AAAH... THANK YOU
KRINKLE
I BET SHE TRIED TO CHARGE YOU FOR IT, DIDN'T SHE?
UH... GEE, I DON'T KNOW...
ALL RIGHT, MR. CORRIGAN... sigh NOW I DON'T USUALLY DO THIS KIND OF THING BUT... WHAT WE'RE LOOKIN' AT HERE IS A LAST CHANCE DEAL; NOW IF YOU CAN DECIDE ON THIS TODAY-- AND I'M GONNA HAVE TO CHECK WITH MY BOSS ON THIS, TOO-- I'LL LET YOU DRIVE OFF THE LOT IN THIS UNIT... WITH AM/FM CASSETTE/CD, AC, XLT CLASSIC LUXURY LEATHER INTERIOR COMPLETE SEALANT PROTECTION ONE YEAR FIVE THOUSAND MILE WARRANTY PARTS AND LABOR "FRIENDSHIPPLUS" PREFERRED CUSTOMER CARD WHADYASAY? OFF THE LOT, JIM!
BLOW OUT
COLOS
DEALS
G-GOSH... REALLY?

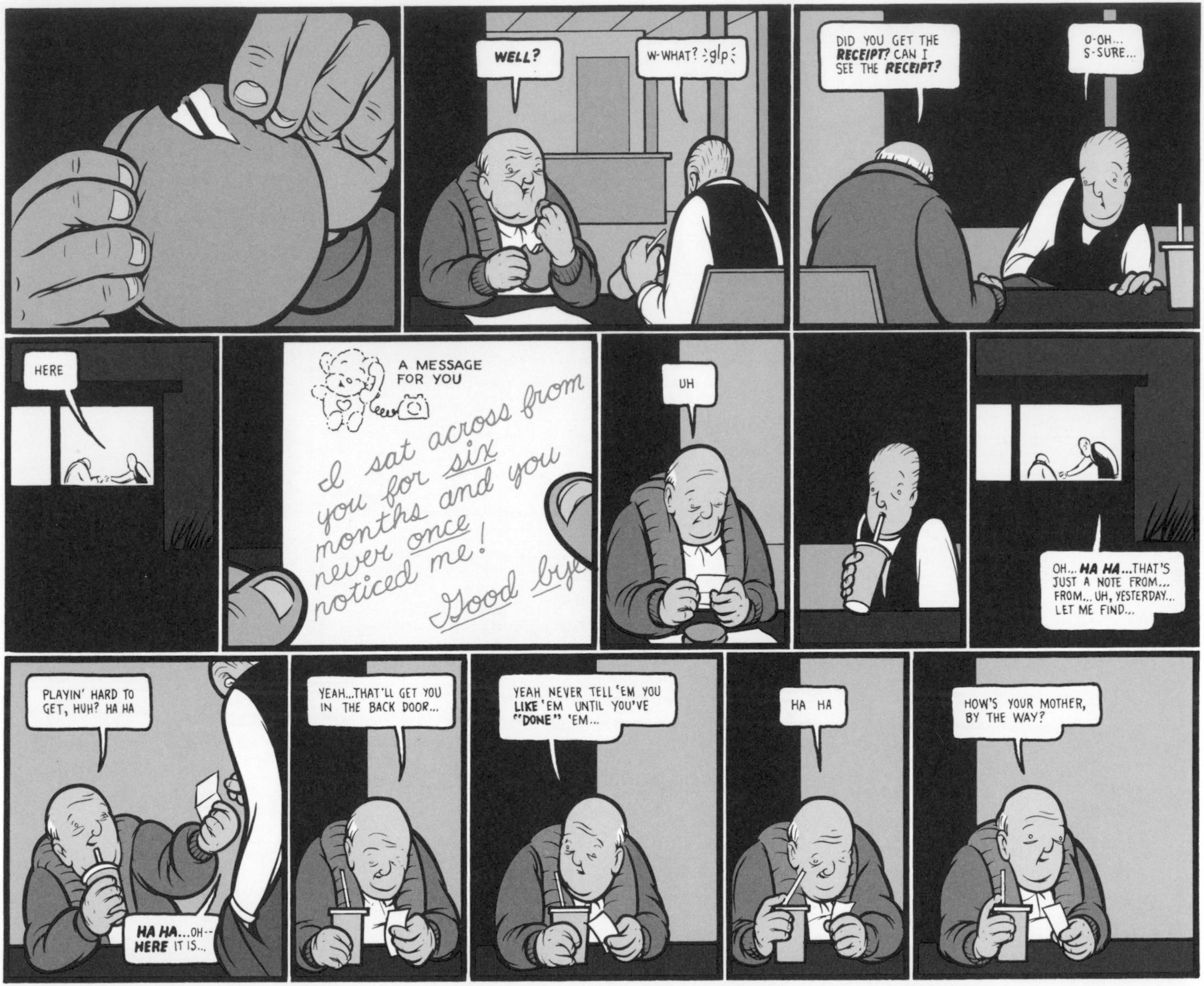
WELL?
W-WHAT? glp
DID YOU GET THE RECEIPT? CAN I SEE THE RECEIPT?
O-OH... S-SURE...
HERE
A MESSAGE FOR YOU
I sat across from you for six months and you never once noticed me! Good bye
UH
OH... HA HA...THAT'S JUST A NOTE FROM... FROM... UH, YESTERDAY... LET ME FIND...
PLAYIN' HARD TO GET, HUH? HA HA
HA HA...OH-- HERE IT IS...
YEAH...THAT'LL GET YOU IN THE BACK DOOR...
YEAH NEVER TELL 'EM YOU LIKE 'EM UNTIL YOU'VE "DONE" 'EM...
HA HA
HOW'S YOUR MOTHER, BY THE WAY?

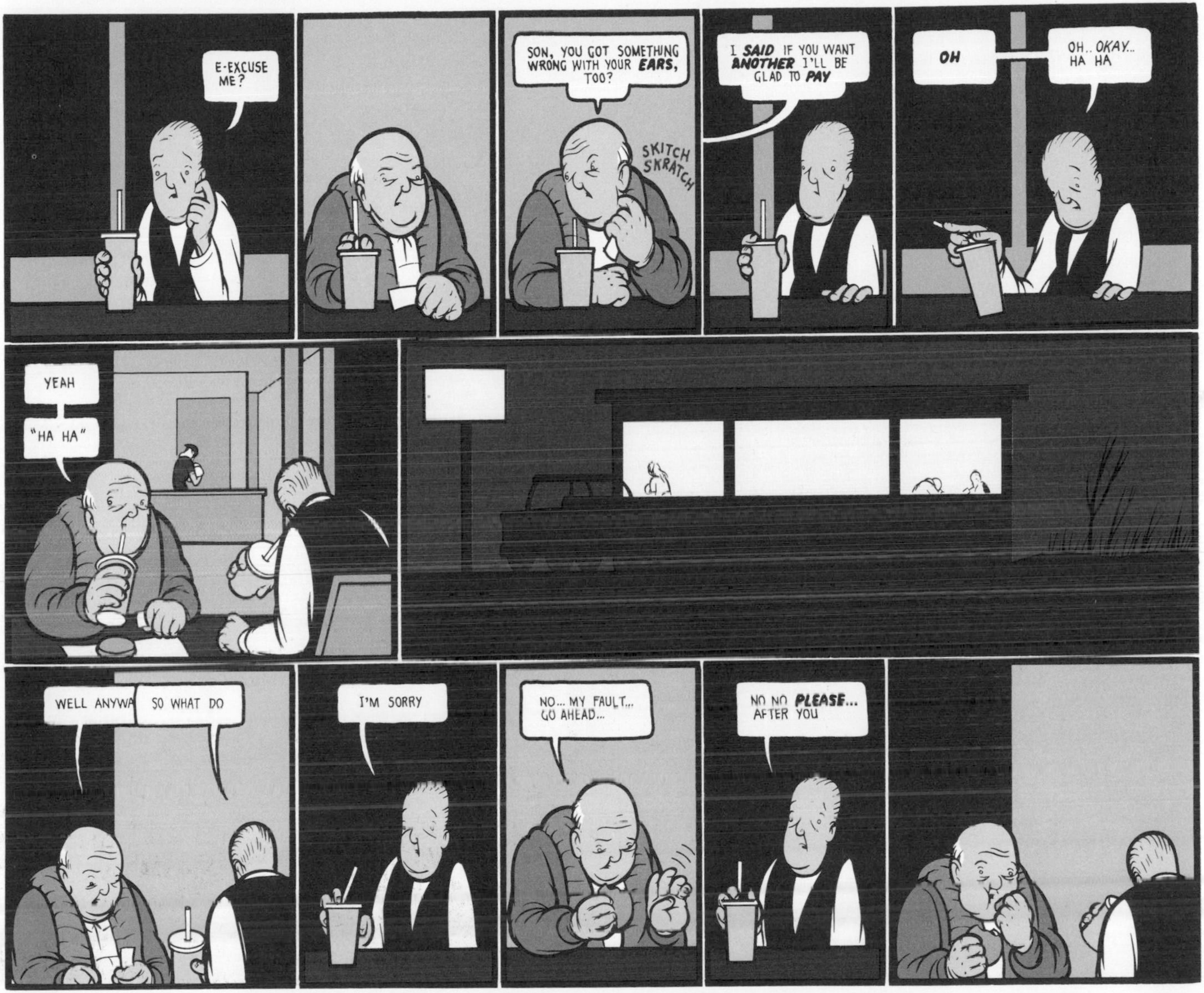
E-EXCUSE ME?
SON, YOU GOT SOMETHING WRONG WITH YOUR **EARS,** TOO?
SKITCH SKRATCH
I **SAID** IF YOU WANT **ANOTHER** I'LL BE GLAD TO **PAY**
OH
OH.. *OKAY*... HA HA
YEAH
"HA HA"
WELL ANYWA
SO WHAT DO
I'M SORRY
NO... MY FAULT... GO AHEAD...
NO NO **PLEASE...** AFTER YOU

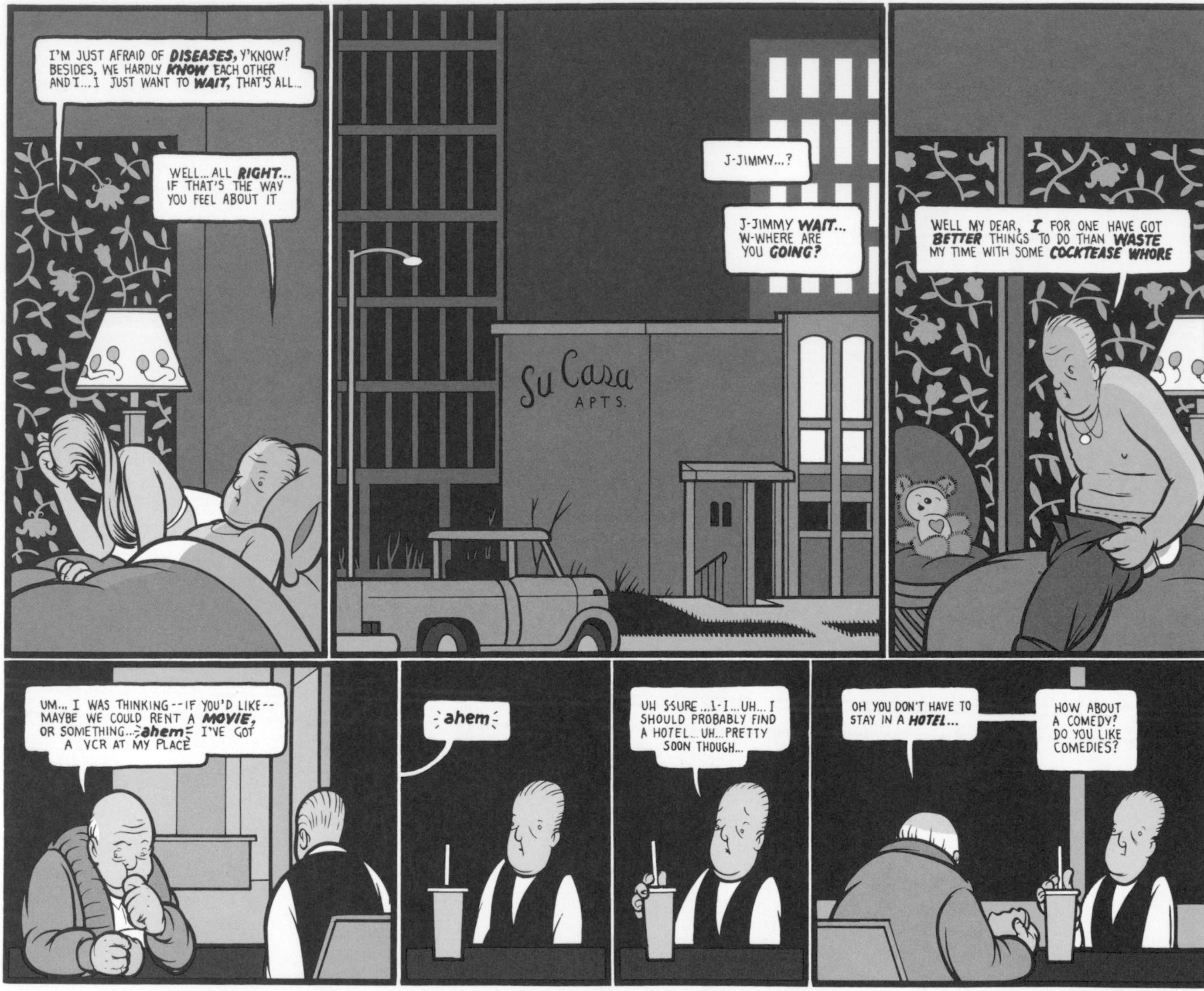

I'M JUST AFRAID OF DISEASES, Y'KNOW? BESIDES, WE HARDLY KNOW EACH OTHER AND I... I JUST WANT TO WAIT, THAT'S ALL...
WELL... ALL RIGHT... IF THAT'S THE WAY YOU FEEL ABOUT IT
Su Casa APTS.
J-JIMMY...?
J-JIMMY WAIT... W-WHERE ARE YOU GOING?
WELL MY DEAR, I FOR ONE HAVE GOT BETTER THINGS TO DO THAN WASTE MY TIME WITH SOME COCKTEASE WHORE
UM... I WAS THINKING -- IF YOU'D LIKE -- MAYBE WE COULD RENT A MOVIE, OR SOMETHING... ahem I'VE GOT A VCR AT MY PLACE
ahem
UH S-SURE... I-I... UH... I SHOULD PROBABLY FIND A HOTEL... UH... PRETTY SOON THOUGH...
OH YOU DON'T HAVE TO STAY IN A HOTEL...
HOW ABOUT A COMEDY? DO YOU LIKE COMEDIES?

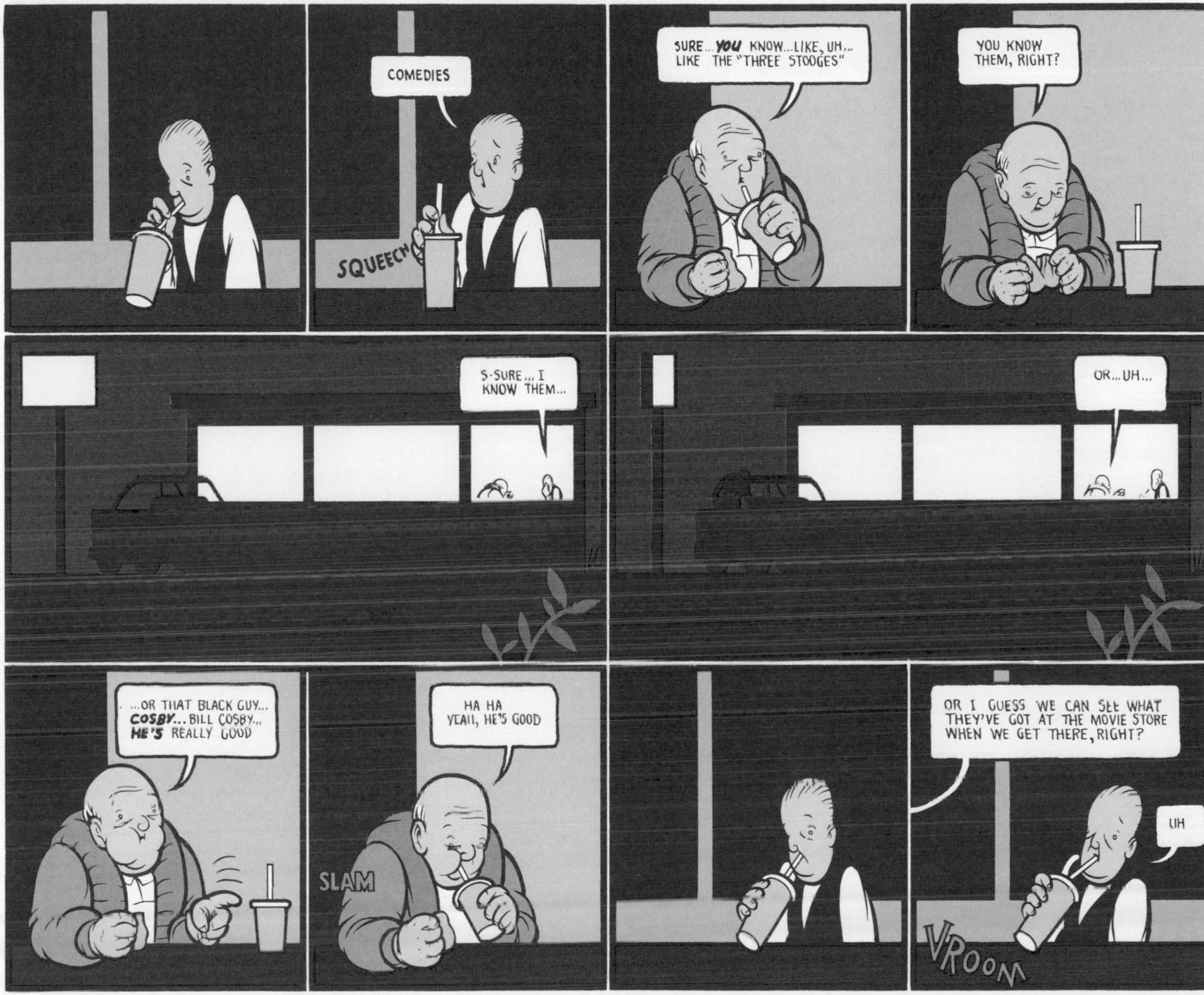

COMEDIES
SQUEECH
SURE... YOU KNOW...LIKE, UH... LIKE THE "THREE STOOGES"
YOU KNOW THEM, RIGHT?
S-SURE... I KNOW THEM...
OR... UH...
...OR THAT BLACK GUY... COSBY... BILL COSBY... HE'S REALLY GOOD
HA HA YEAH, HE'S GOOD
SLAM
OR I GUESS WE CAN SEE WHAT THEY'VE GOT AT THE MOVIE STORE WHEN WE GET THERE, RIGHT?
UH
VROOM

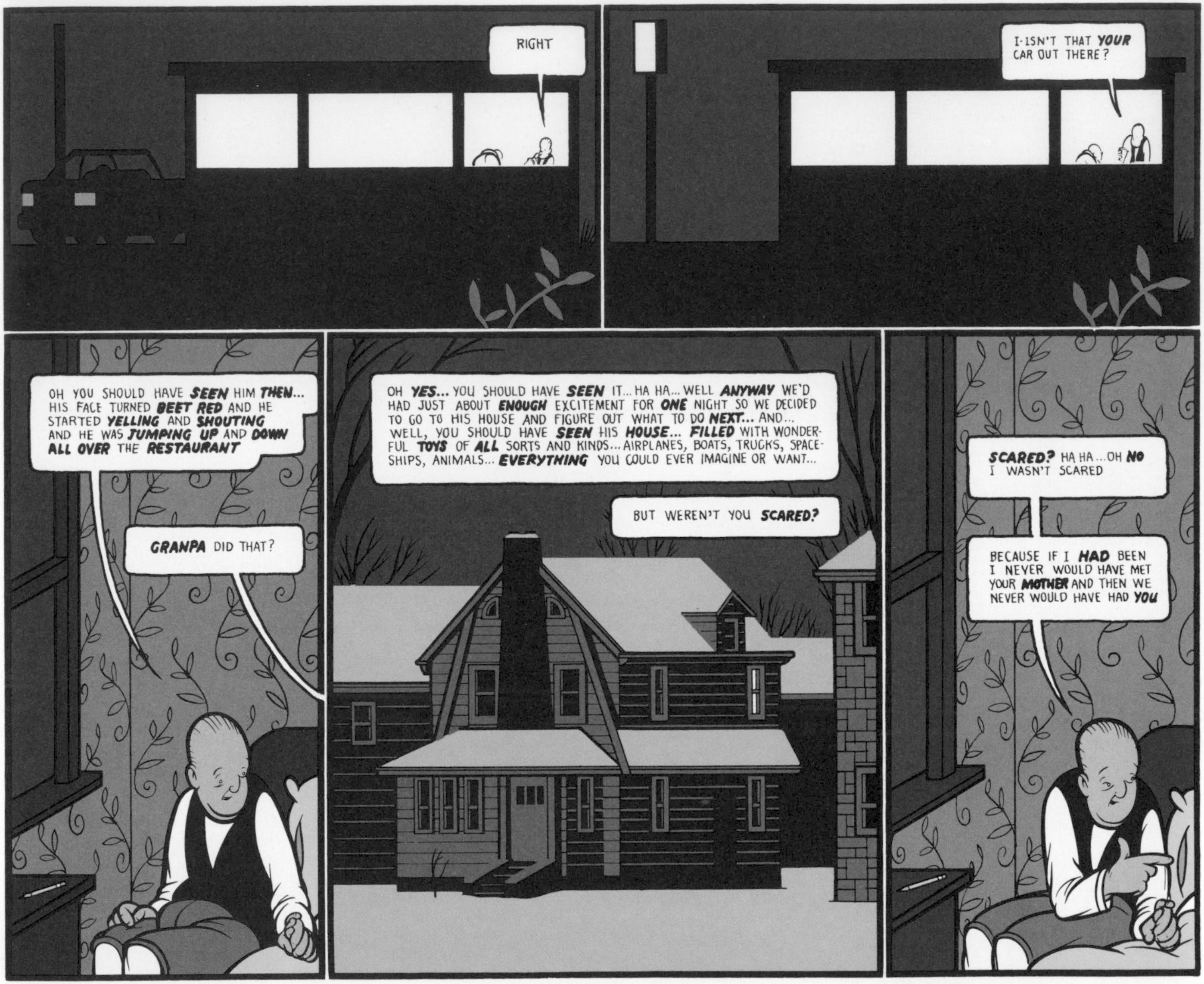
RIGHT
I-ISN'T THAT YOUR CAR OUT THERE?
OH YOU SHOULD HAVE SEEN HIM THEN... HIS FACE TURNED BEET RED AND HE STARTED YELLING AND SHOUTING AND HE WAS JUMPING UP AND DOWN ALL OVER THE RESTAURANT
GRANPA DID THAT?
OH YES... YOU SHOULD HAVE SEEN IT... HA HA... WELL ANYWAY WE'D HAD JUST ABOUT ENOUGH EXCITEMENT FOR ONE NIGHT SO WE DECIDED TO GO TO HIS HOUSE AND FIGURE OUT WHAT TO DO NEXT... AND... WELL, YOU SHOULD HAVE SEEN HIS HOUSE... FILLED WITH WONDERFUL TOYS OF ALL SORTS AND KINDS... AIRPLANES, BOATS, TRUCKS, SPACESHIPS, ANIMALS... EVERYTHING YOU COULD EVER IMAGINE OR WANT...
BUT WEREN'T YOU SCARED?
SCARED? HA HA... OH NO I WASN'T SCARED
BECAUSE IF I HAD BEEN I NEVER WOULD HAVE MET YOUR MOTHER AND THEN WE NEVER WOULD HAVE HAD YOU

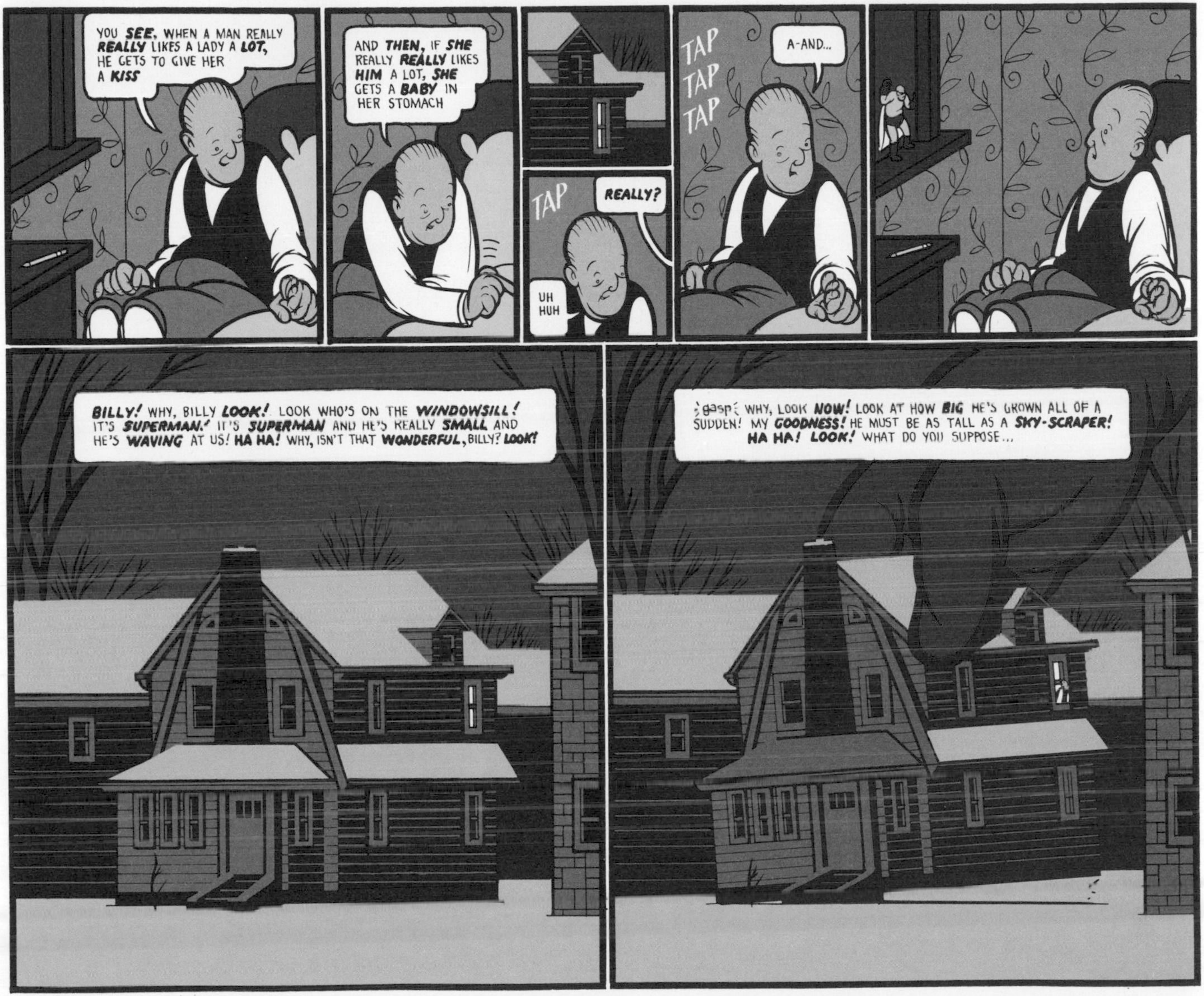

YOU SEE, WHEN A MAN REALLY REALLY LIKES A LADY A LOT, HE GETS TO GIVE HER A KISS
AND THEN, IF SHE REALLY REALLY LIKES HIM A LOT, SHE GETS A BABY IN HER STOMACH
TAP
REALLY?
UH HUH
TAP TAP TAP
A-AND...
BILLY! WHY, BILLY LOOK! LOOK WHO'S ON THE WINDOWSILL! IT'S SUPERMAN! IT'S SUPERMAN AND HE'S REALLY SMALL AND HE'S WAVING AT US! HA HA! WHY, ISN'T THAT WONDERFUL, BILLY? LOOK!
gasp WHY, LOOK NOW! LOOK AT HOW BIG HE'S GROWN ALL OF A SUDDEN! MY GOODNESS! HE MUST BE AS TALL AS A SKY-SCRAPER! HA HA! LOOK! WHAT DO YOU SUPPOSE...

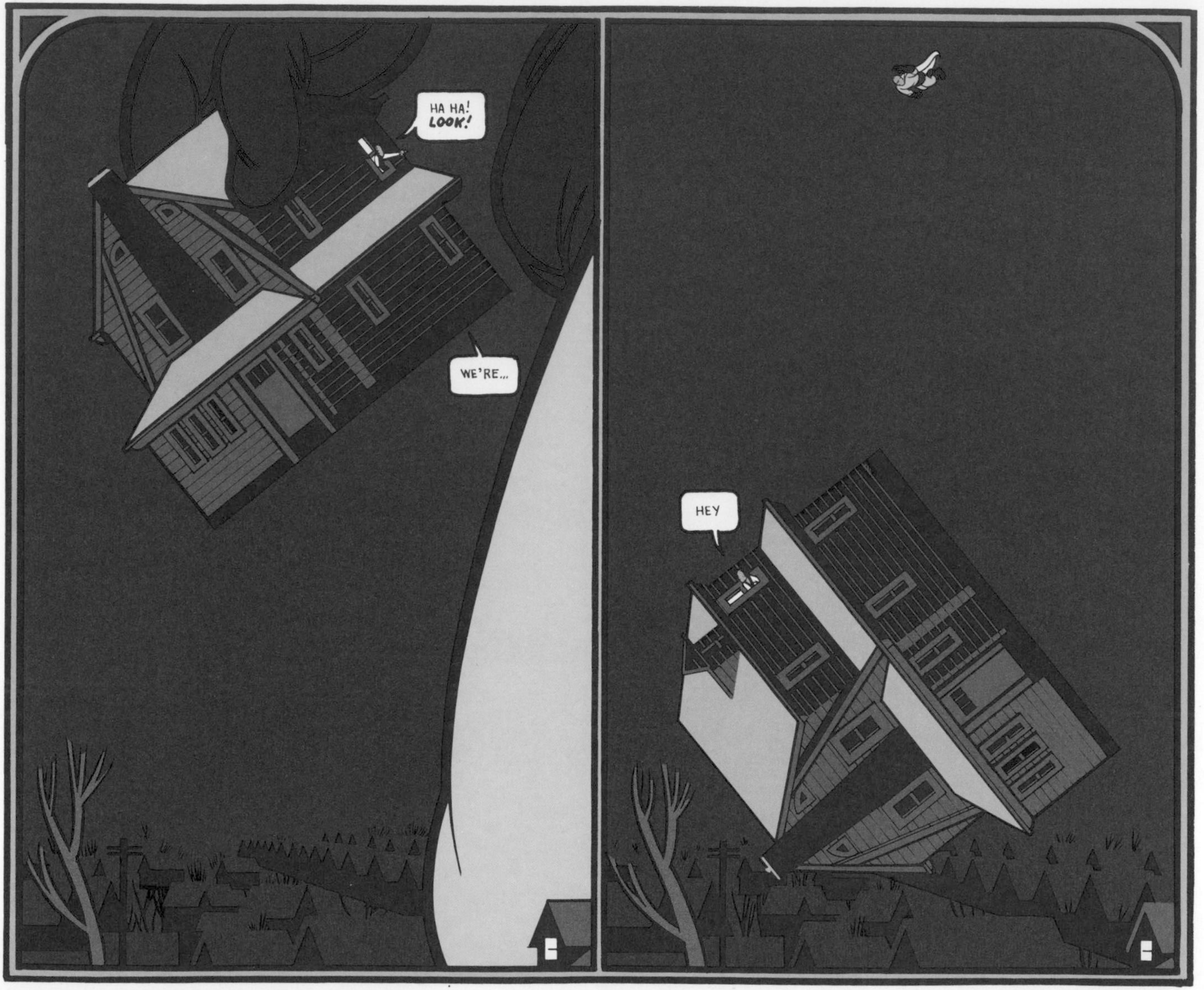
HA HA! **LOOK!**
WE'RE...
HEY

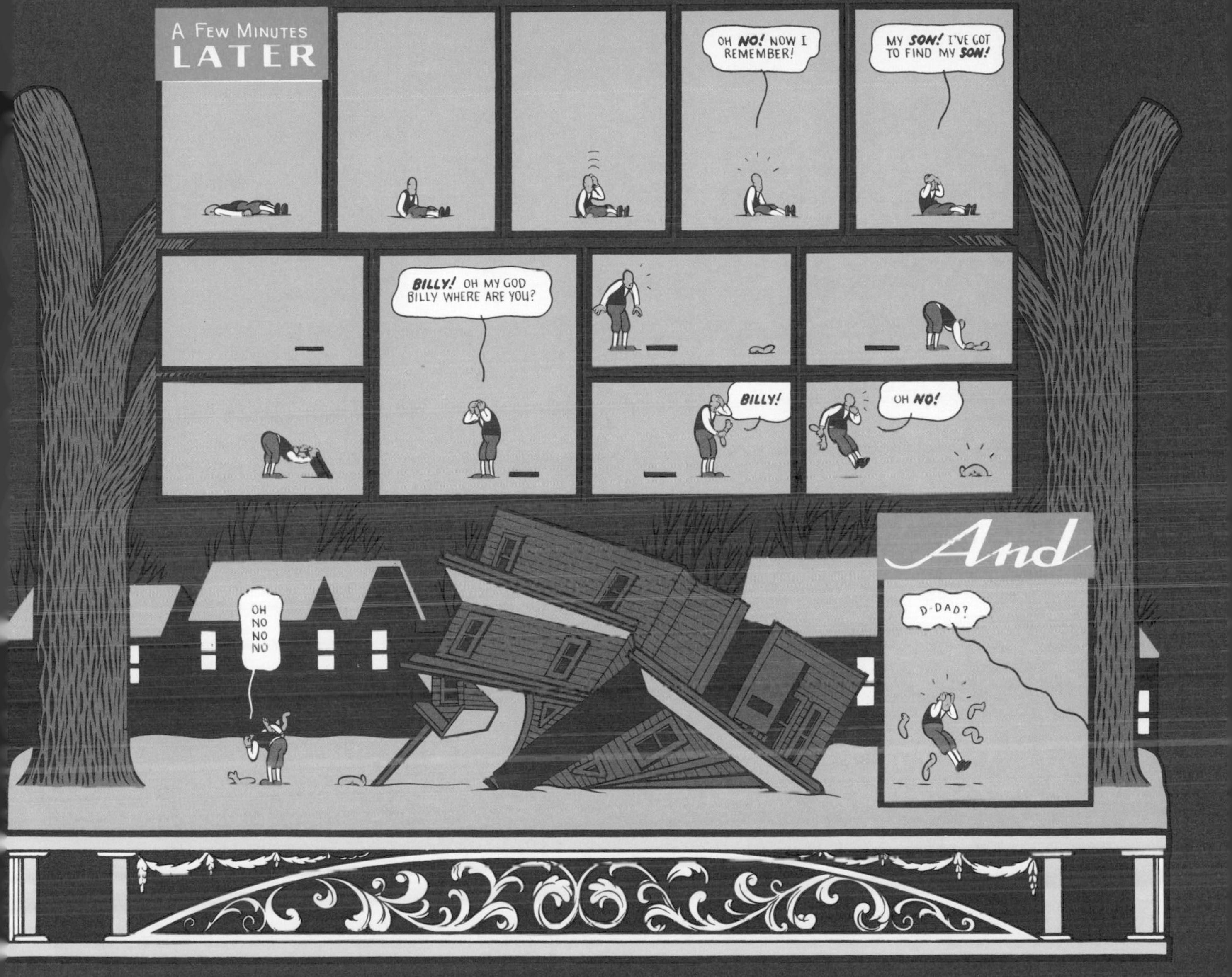
A FEW MINUTES LATER
OH NO! NOW I REMEMBER!
MY SON! I'VE GOT TO FIND MY SON!
BILLY! OH MY GOD BILLY WHERE ARE YOU?
BILLY!
OH NO!
OH NO NO NO
And
D-DAD?

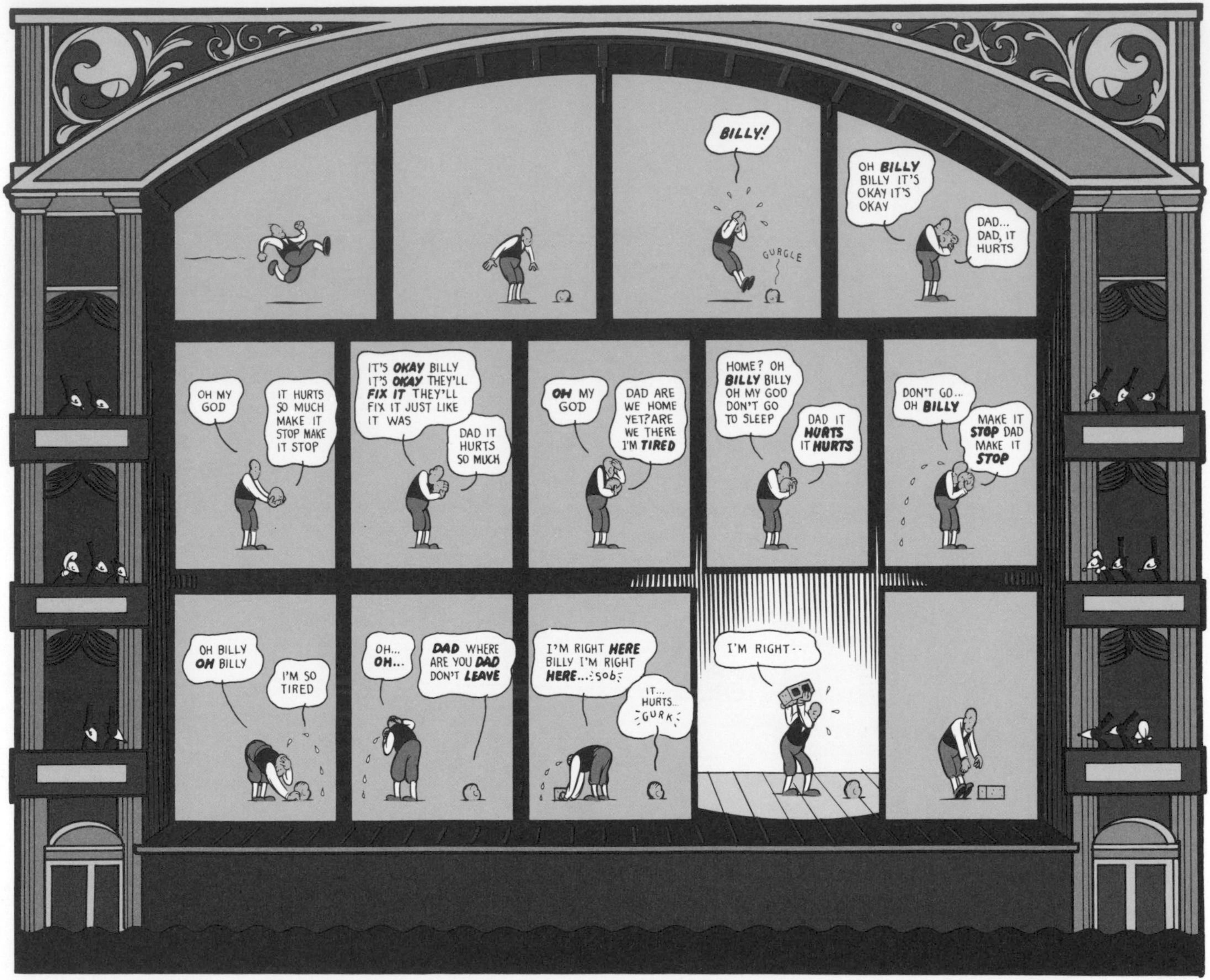
BILLY!
GURGLE
OH BILLY BILLY IT'S OKAY IT'S OKAY
DAD... DAD, IT HURTS
OH MY GOD
IT HURTS SO MUCH MAKE IT STOP MAKE IT STOP
IT'S OKAY BILLY IT'S OKAY THEY'LL FIX IT THEY'LL FIX IT JUST LIKE IT WAS
DAD IT HURTS SO MUCH
OH MY GOD
DAD ARE WE HOME YET? ARE WE THERE I'M TIRED
HOME? OH BILLY BILLY OH MY GOD DON'T GO TO SLEEP
DAD IT HURTS IT HURTS
DON'T GO... OH BILLY
MAKE IT STOP DAD MAKE IT STOP
OH BILLY OH BILLY
I'M SO TIRED
OH... OH...
DAD WHERE ARE YOU DAD DON'T LEAVE
I'M RIGHT HERE BILLY I'M RIGHT HERE... sob
IT... HURTS... GURK
I'M RIGHT--

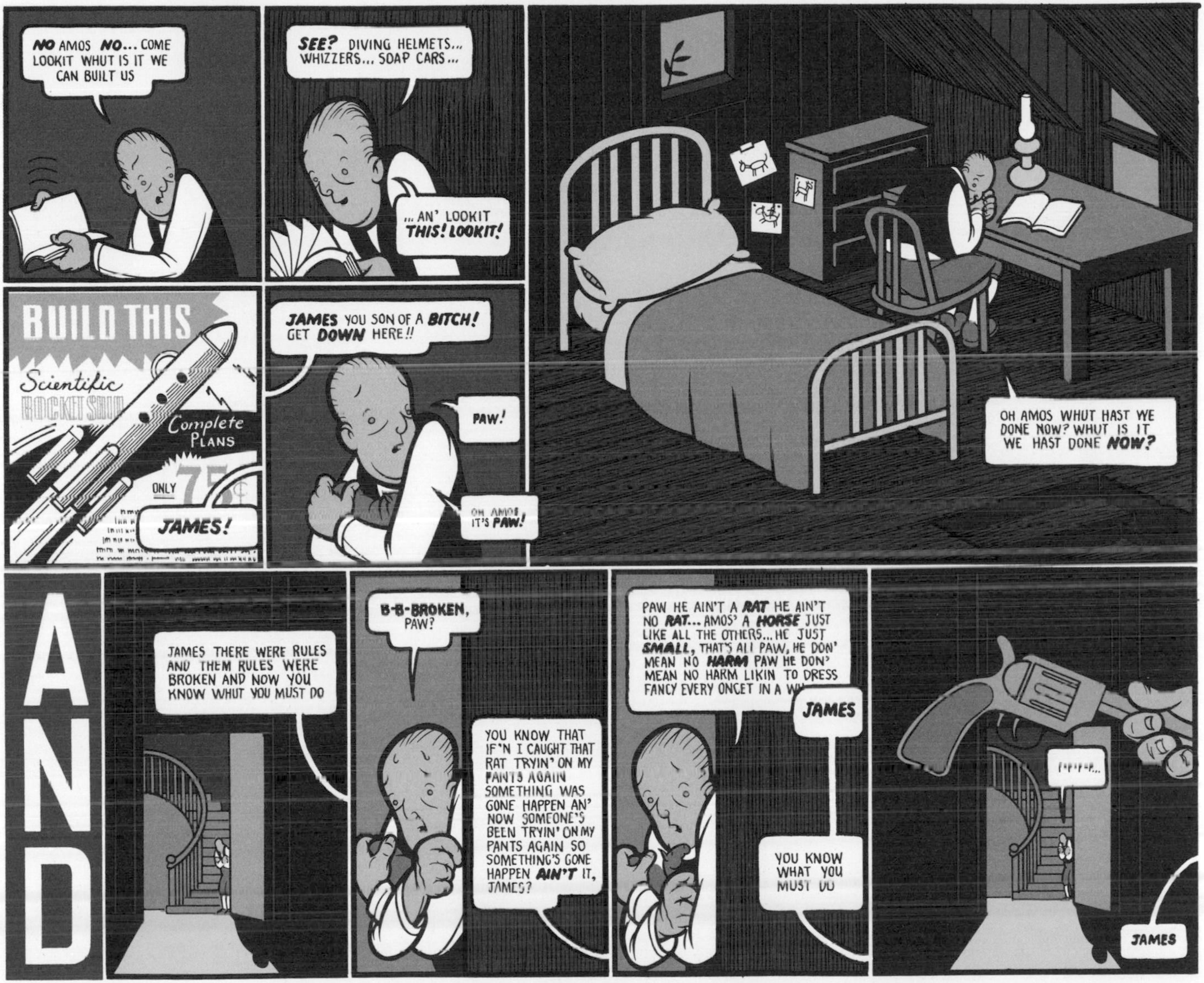

NO AMOS NO... COME LOOKIT WHUT IS IT WE CAN BUILT US
SEE? DIVING HELMETS... WHIZZERS... SOAP CARS...
... AN' LOOKIT THIS! LOOKIT!
BUILD THIS
Scientific
ROCKET SHIP
Complete PLANS
ONLY 75¢
JAMES!
JAMES YOU SON OF A BITCH! GET DOWN HERE!!
PAW!
OH AMOS IT'S PAW!
OH AMOS WHUT HAST WE DONE NOW? WHUT IS IT WE HAST DONE NOW?
AND
JAMES THERE WERE RULES AND THEM RULES WERE BROKEN AND NOW YOU KNOW WHUT YOU MUST DO
B-B-BROKEN, PAW?
YOU KNOW THAT IF'N I CAUGHT THAT RAT TRYIN' ON MY PANTS AGAIN SOMETHING WAS GONE HAPPEN AN' NOW SOMEONE'S BEEN TRYIN' ON MY PANTS AGAIN SO SOMETHING'S GONE HAPPEN AIN'T IT, JAMES?
PAW HE AIN'T A RAT HE AIN'T NO RAT... AMOS' A HORSE JUST LIKE ALL THE OTHERS... HE JUST SMALL, THAT'S ALL PAW, HE DON' MEAN NO HARM PAW HE DON' MEAN NO HARM LIKIN TO DRESS FANCY EVERY ONCET IN A WH
JAMES
YOU KNOW WHAT YOU MUST DO
JAMES

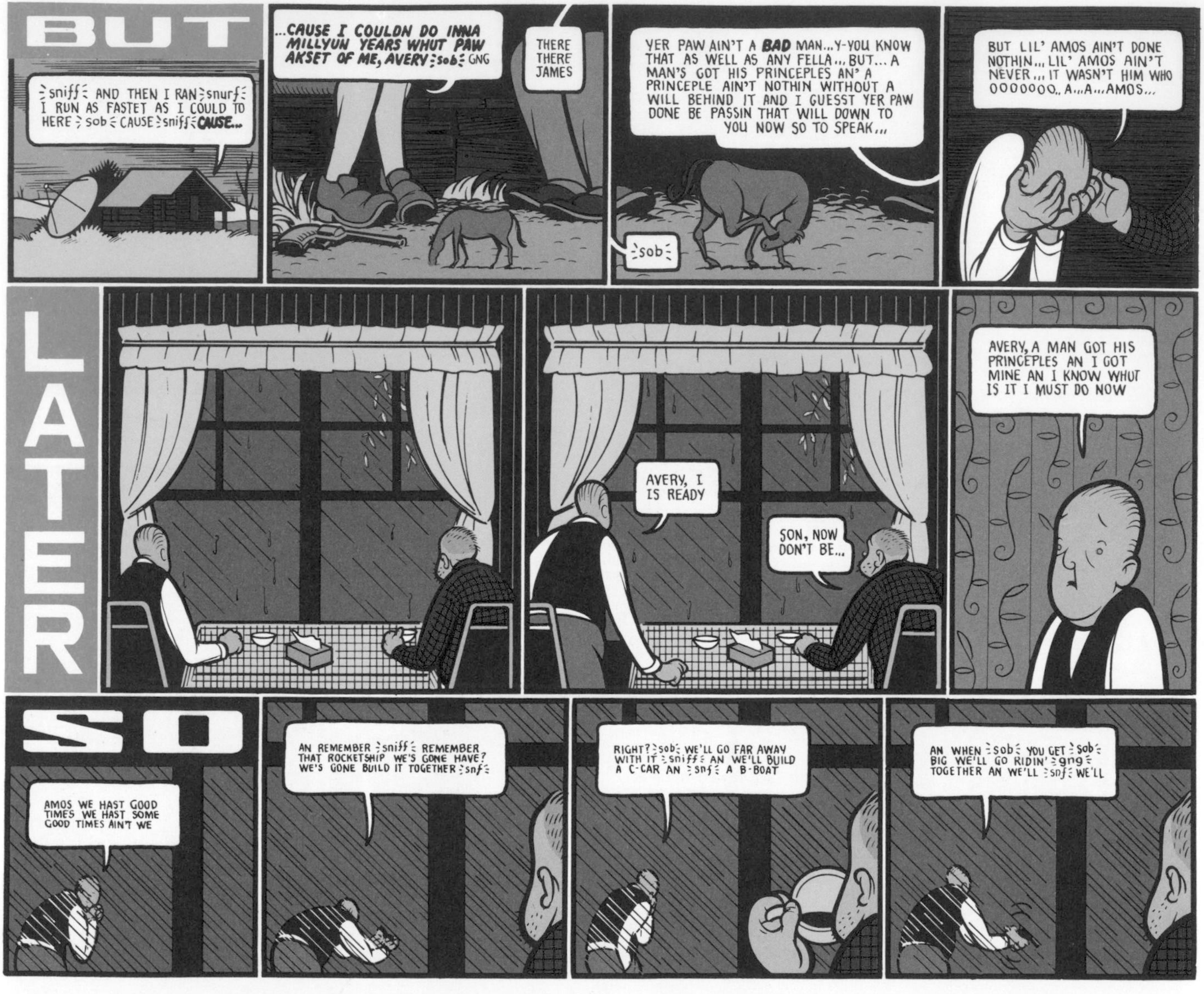
BUT
⁝sniff⁝ AND THEN I RAN ⁝snurf⁝ I RUN AS FASTET AS I COULD TO HERE ⁝sob⁝ CAUSE ⁝sniff⁝ CAUSE...
...CAUSE I COULDN DO INNA MILLYUN YEARS WHUT PAW AKSET OF ME, AVERY ⁝sob⁝ GNG
THERE THERE JAMES
YER PAW AIN'T A BAD MAN... Y-YOU KNOW THAT AS WELL AS ANY FELLA... BUT... A MAN'S GOT HIS PRINCEPLES AN' A PRINCEPLE AIN'T NOTHIN WITHOUT A WILL BEHIND IT AND I GUESST YER PAW DONE BE PASSIN THAT WILL DOWN TO YOU NOW SO TO SPEAK...
⁝sob⁝
BUT LIL' AMOS AIN'T DONE NOTHIN... LIL' AMOS AIN'T NEVER... IT WASN'T HIM WHO OOOOOOO.. A...A...AMOS...
LATER
AVERY, I IS READY
SON, NOW DON'T BE...
AVERY, A MAN GOT HIS PRINCEPLES AN I GOT MINE AN I KNOW WHUT IS IT I MUST DO NOW
SO
AMOS WE HAST GOOD TIMES WE HAST SOME GOOD TIMES AIN'T WE
AN REMEMBER ⁝sniff⁝ REMEMBER THAT ROCKETSHIP WE'S GONE HAVE? WE'S GONE BUILD IT TOGETHER ⁝snf⁝
RIGHT? ⁝sob⁝ WE'LL GO FAR AWAY WITH IT ⁝sniff⁝ AN WE'LL BUILD A C-CAR AN ⁝snf⁝ A B-BOAT
AN WHEN ⁝sob⁝ YOU GET ⁝sob⁝ BIG WE'LL GO RIDIN' ⁝gng⁝ TOGETHER AN WE'LL ⁝snf⁝ WE'LL

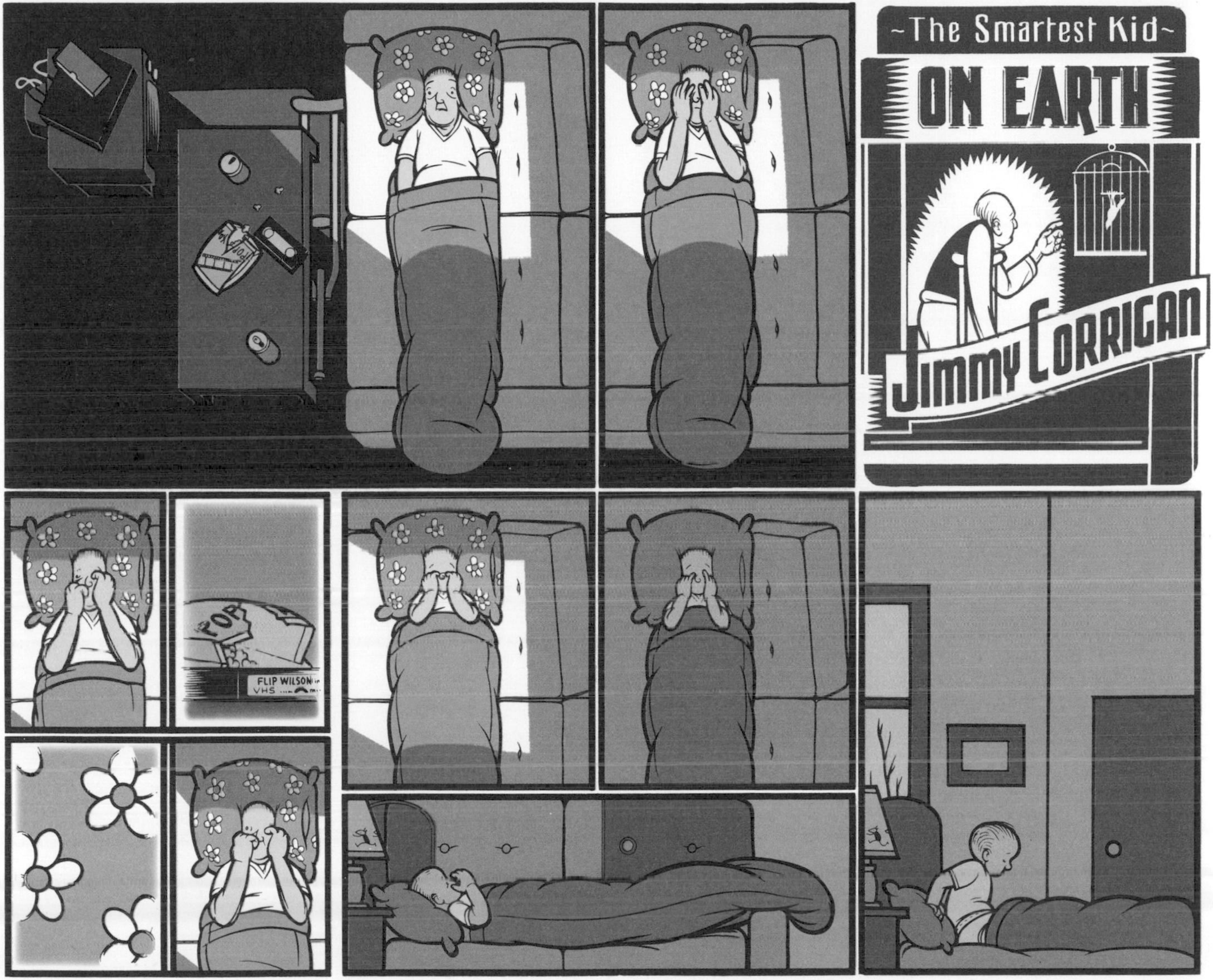
~The Smartest Kid~
ON EARTH
JIMMY CORRIGAN
POP
FLIP WILSON
VHS

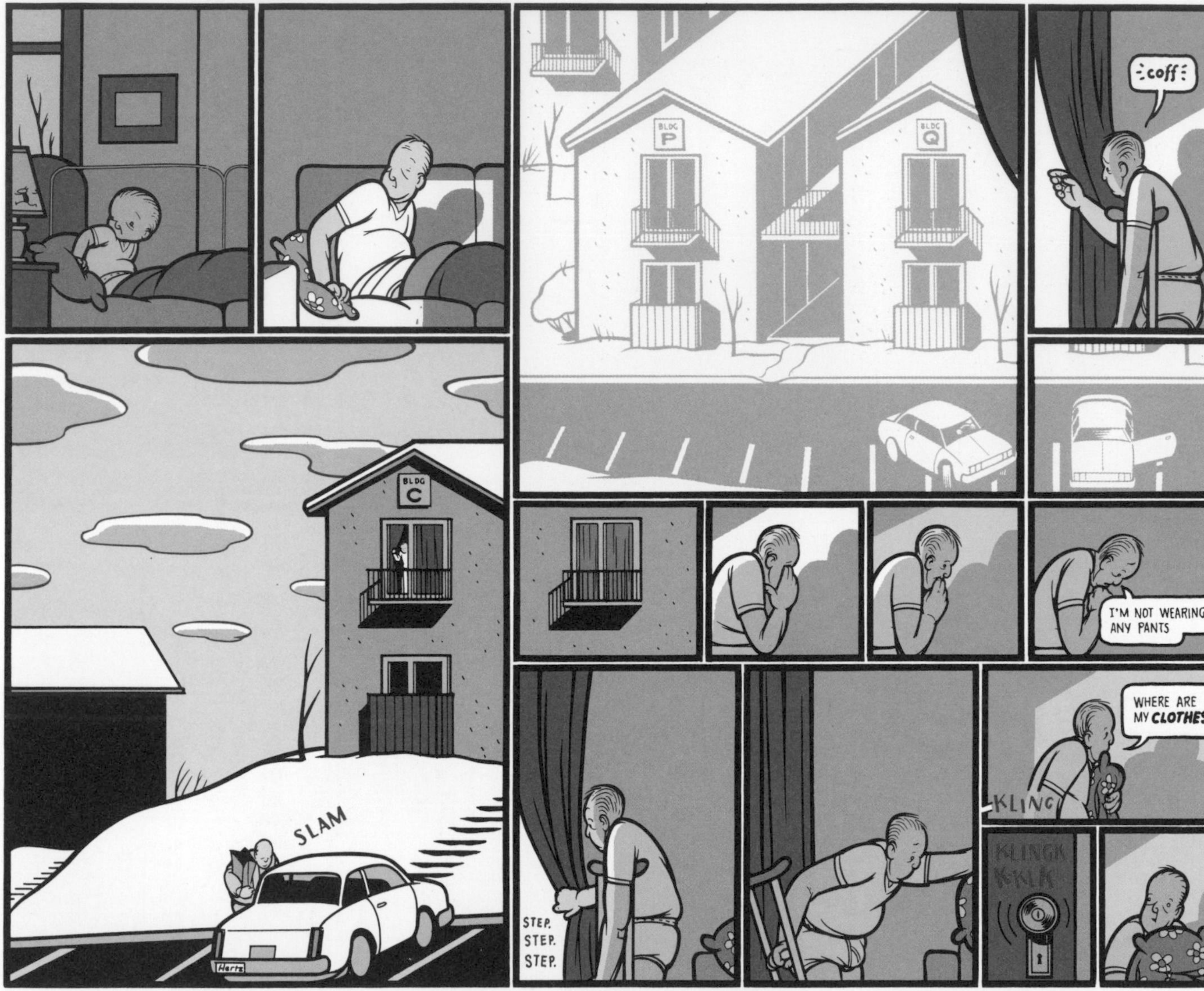

coff
SLAM
Hertz
I'M NOT WEARING ANY PANTS
STEP.
STEP.
STEP.
WHERE ARE MY CLOTHES?
KLING
KLINGK
KKLK

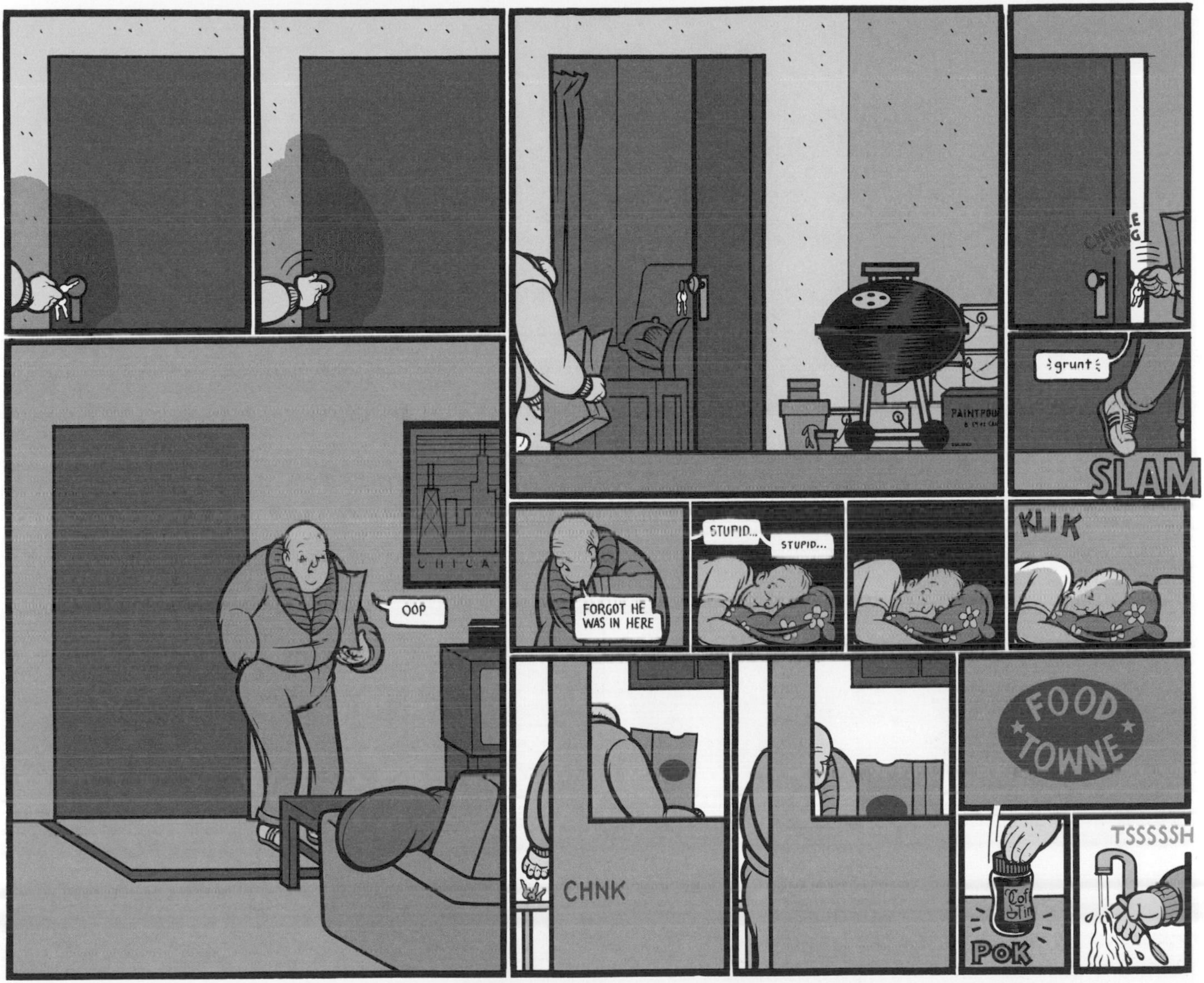
grunt
SLAM
OOP
FORGOT HE WAS IN HERE
STUPID...
STUPID...
KLIK
CHNK
FOOD TOWNE
POK
TSSSSSH

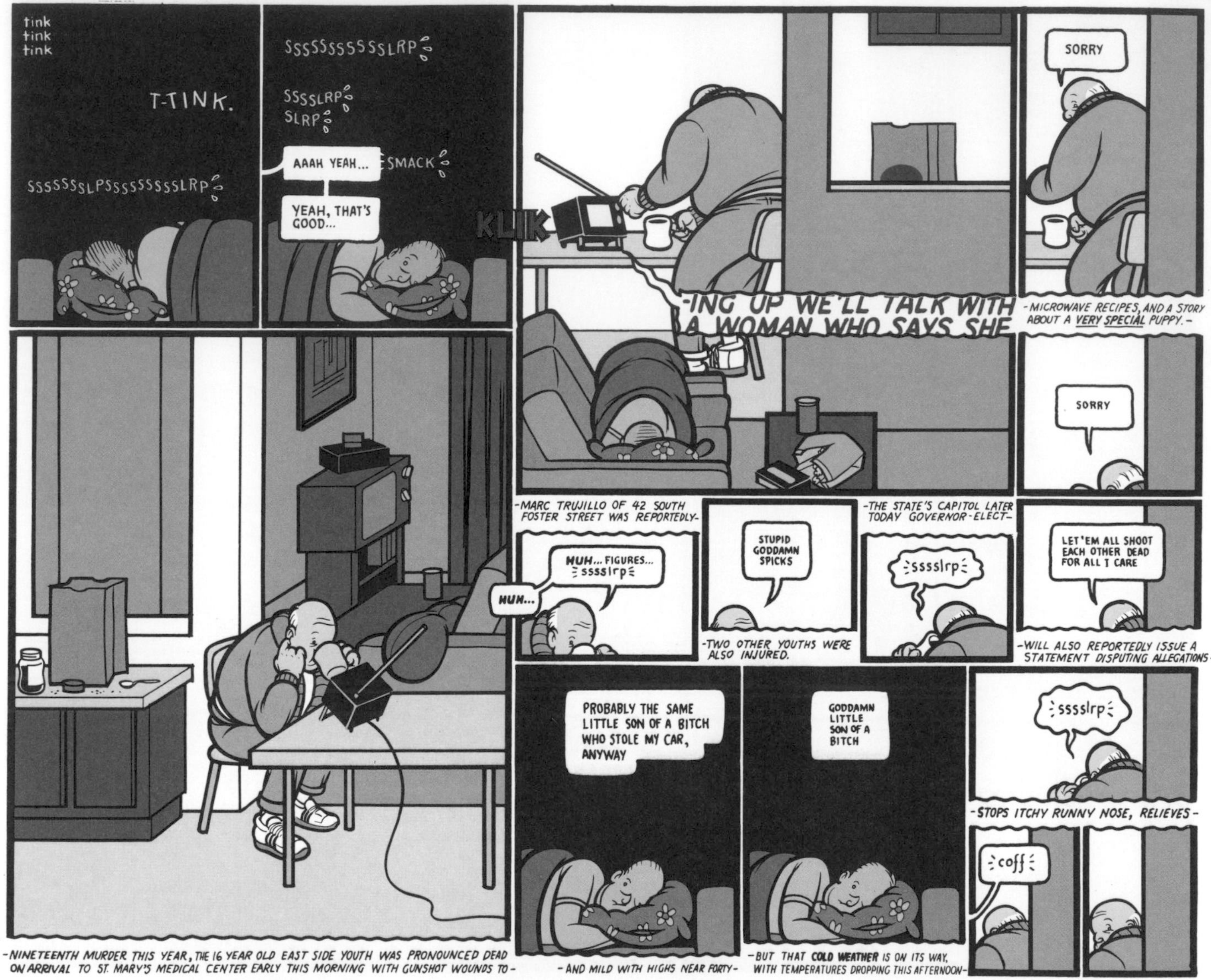
tink
tink
tink
T-TINK.
SSSSSSSLPSSSSSSSSSLRP
SSSSSSSSSSSLRP
SSSSLRP
SLRP
AAAH YEAH...
SMACK
YEAH, THAT'S GOOD...
KLIK
-ING UP WE'LL TALK WITH
A WOMAN WHO SAYS SHE
SORRY
-MICROWAVE RECIPES, AND A STORY ABOUT A VERY SPECIAL PUPPY.-
SORRY
-NINETEENTH MURDER THIS YEAR, THE 16 YEAR OLD EAST SIDE YOUTH WAS PRONOUNCED DEAD ON ARRIVAL TO ST. MARY'S MEDICAL CENTER EARLY THIS MORNING WITH GUNSHOT WOUNDS TO-
-MARC TRUJILLO OF 42 SOUTH FOSTER STREET WAS REPORTEDLY-
HUH...
HUH... FIGURES... ssssIrp
STUPID GODDAMN SPICKS
-TWO OTHER YOUTHS WERE ALSO INJURED.
-THE STATE'S CAPITOL LATER TODAY GOVERNOR-ELECT-
ssssIrp
LET'EM ALL SHOOT EACH OTHER DEAD FOR ALL I CARE
-WILL ALSO REPORTEDLY ISSUE A STATEMENT DISPUTING ALLEGATIONS-
PROBABLY THE SAME LITTLE SON OF A BITCH WHO STOLE MY CAR, ANYWAY
-AND MILD WITH HIGHS NEAR FORTY-
GODDAMN LITTLE SON OF A BITCH
-BUT THAT COLD WEATHER IS ON ITS WAY, WITH TEMPERATURES DROPPING THIS AFTERNOON-
ssssIrp
-STOPS ITCHY RUNNY NOSE, RELIEVES-
coff

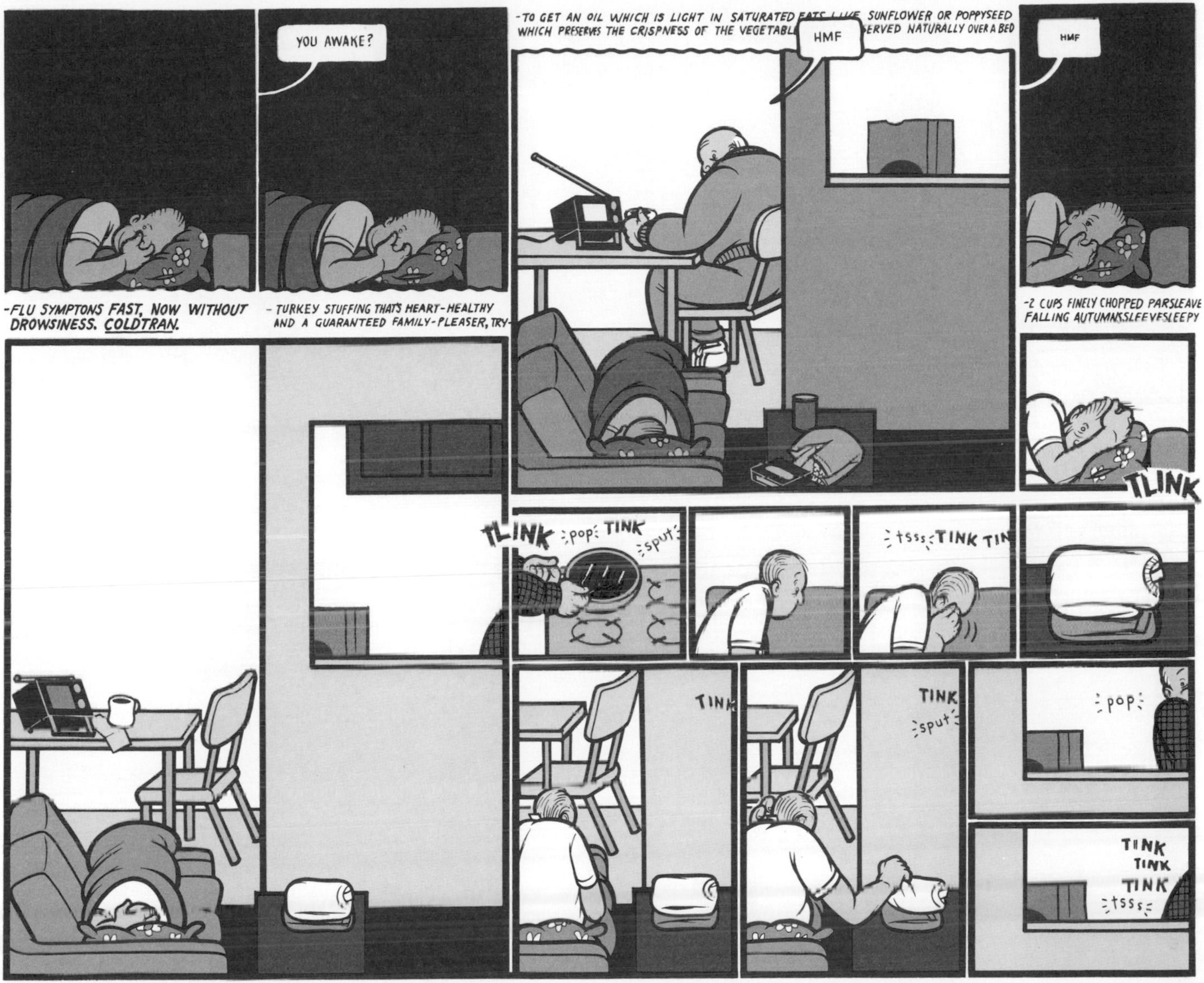
-FLU SYMPTONS FAST, NOW WITHOUT DROWSINESS. COLDTRAN.
YOU AWAKE?
- TURKEY STUFFING THAT'S HEART-HEALTHY AND A GUARANTEED FAMILY-PLEASER, TRY-
-TO GET AN OIL WHICH IS LIGHT IN SATURATED
SUNFLOWER OR POPPYSEED
WHICH PRESERVES THE CRISPNESS OF THE VEGETABL
ERVED NATURALLY OVER A BED
HMF
HMF
-2 CUPS FINELY CHOPPED PARSLEAVE FALLING AUTUMNSSLEEVESLEEPY
TLINK
TLINK pop TINK sput
tsss TINK TIN
TINK
TINK sput
pop
TINK TINK TINK tsss

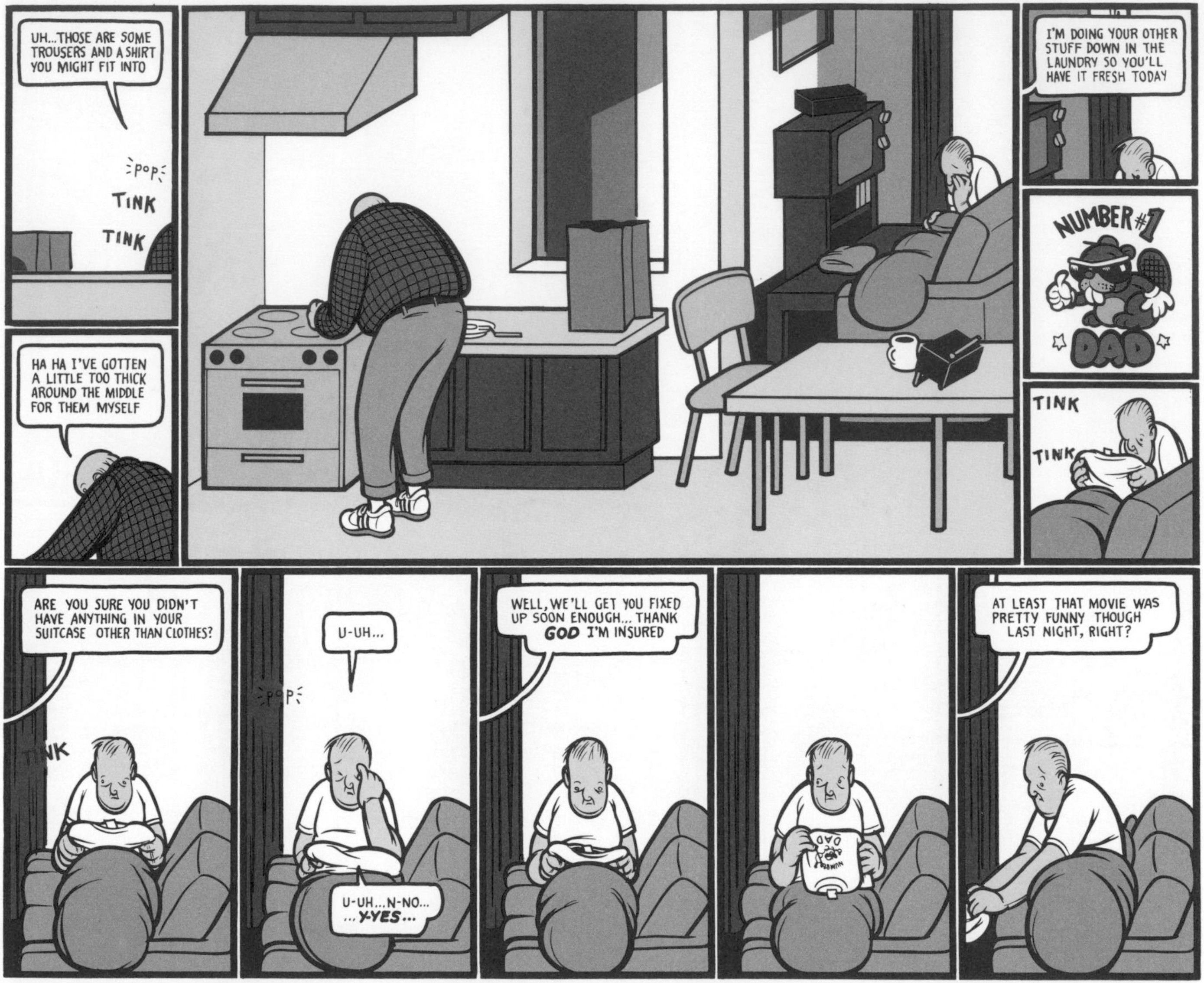
UH...THOSE ARE SOME TROUSERS AND A SHIRT YOU MIGHT FIT INTO
POP
TINK
TINK
HA HA I'VE GOTTEN A LITTLE TOO THICK AROUND THE MIDDLE FOR THEM MYSELF
I'M DOING YOUR OTHER STUFF DOWN IN THE LAUNDRY SO YOU'LL HAVE IT FRESH TODAY
NUMBER #1
DAD
TINK
TINK
ARE YOU SURE YOU DIDN'T HAVE ANYTHING IN YOUR SUITCASE OTHER THAN CLOTHES?
TINK
U-UH...
POP
U-UH...N-NO... ...Y-YES...
WELL, WE'LL GET YOU FIXED UP SOON ENOUGH... THANK GOD I'M INSURED
AT LEAST THAT MOVIE WAS PRETTY FUNNY THOUGH LAST NIGHT, RIGHT?

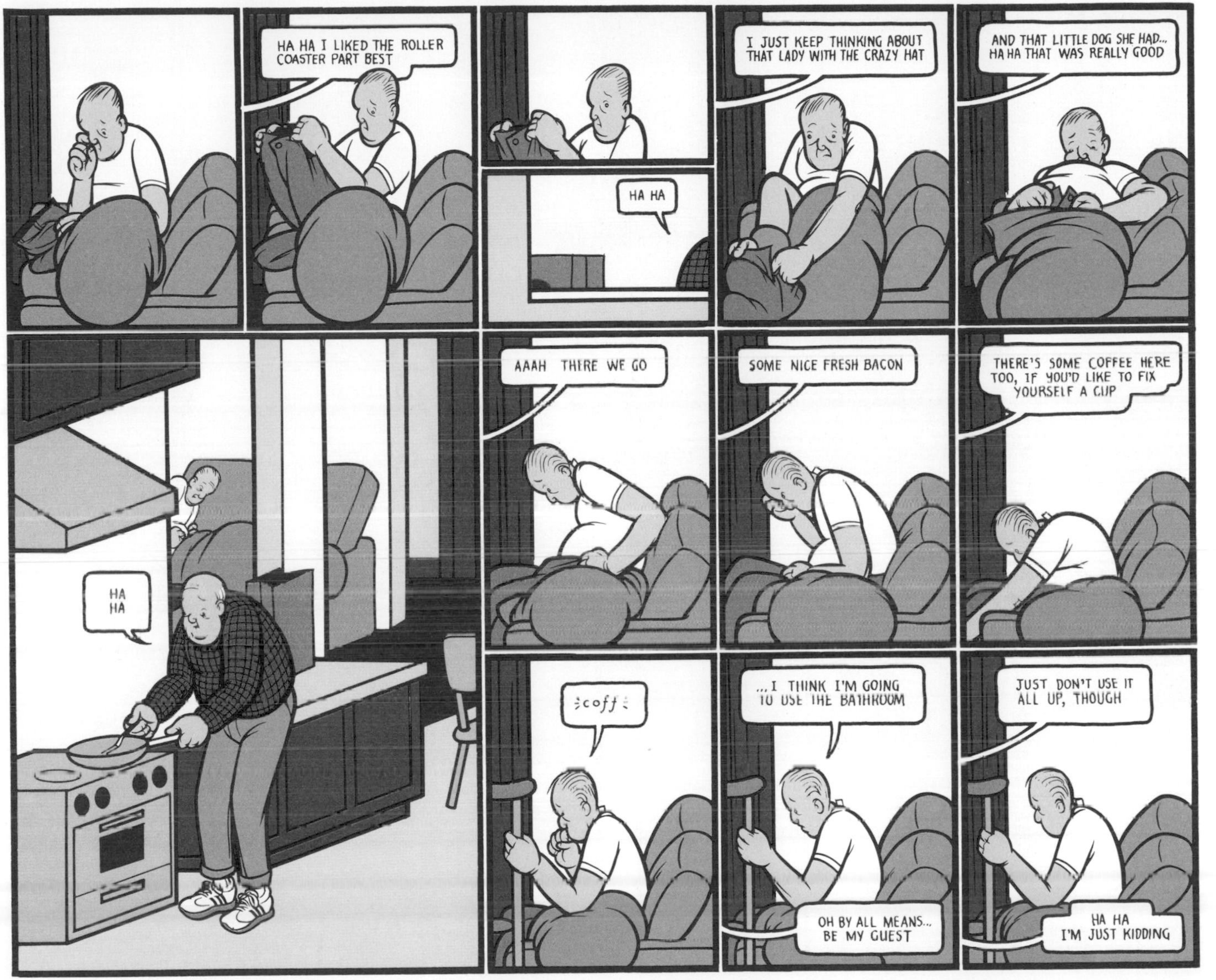
HA HA I LIKED THE ROLLER COASTER PART BEST
HA HA
I JUST KEEP THINKING ABOUT THAT LADY WITH THE CRAZY HAT
AND THAT LITTLE DOG SHE HAD... HA HA THAT WAS REALLY GOOD
HA HA
AAAH THERE WE GO
SOME NICE FRESH BACON
THERE'S SOME COFFEE HERE TOO, IF YOU'D LIKE TO FIX YOURSELF A CUP
coff
...I THINK I'M GOING TO USE THE BATHROOM
OH BY ALL MEANS... BE MY GUEST
JUST DON'T USE IT ALL UP, THOUGH
HA HA I'M JUST KIDDING

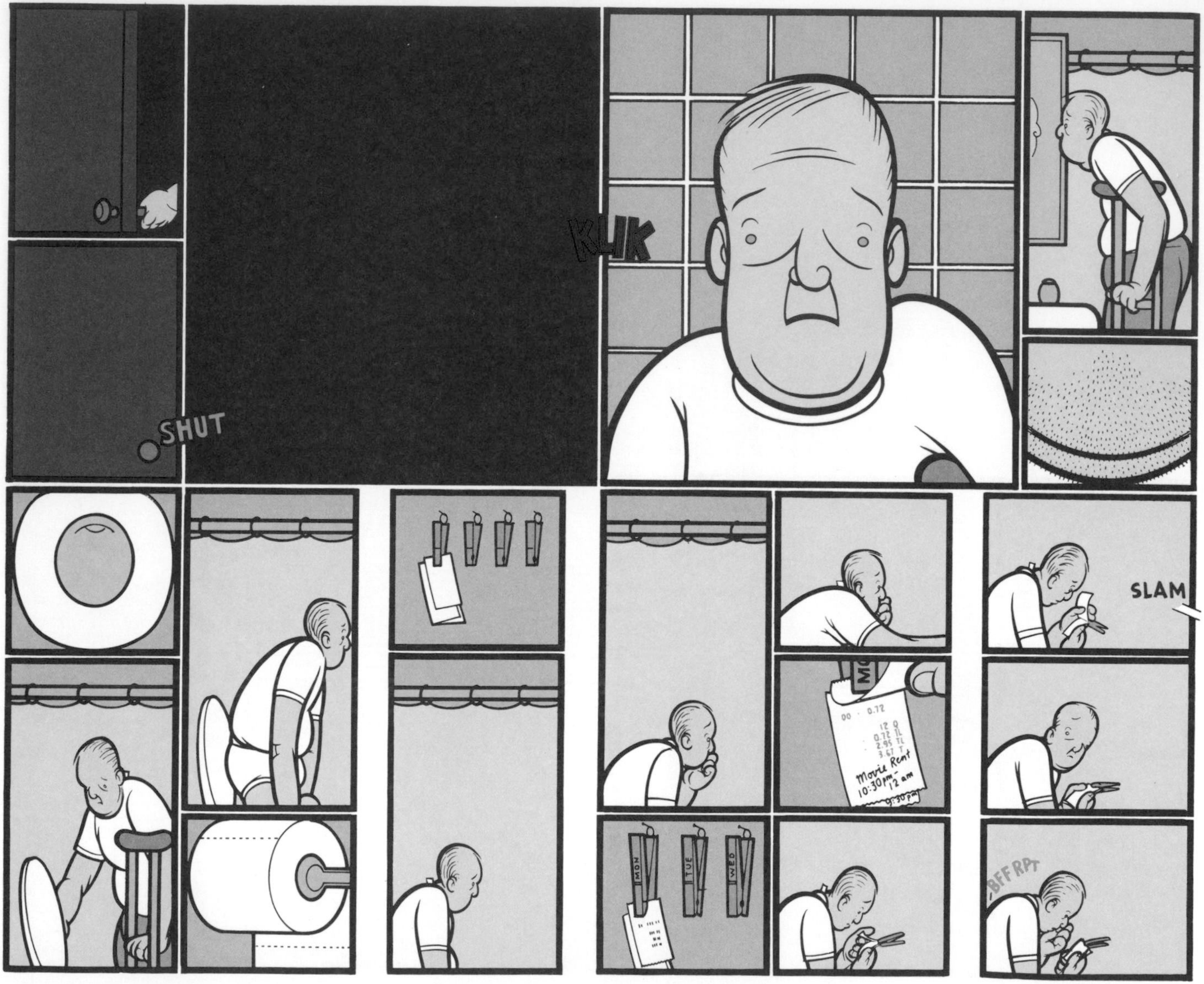
SHUT
KLIK
Movie Rent
10:30pm–12 am
9:30pm
MON
TUE
WED
SLAM
BFFRPT

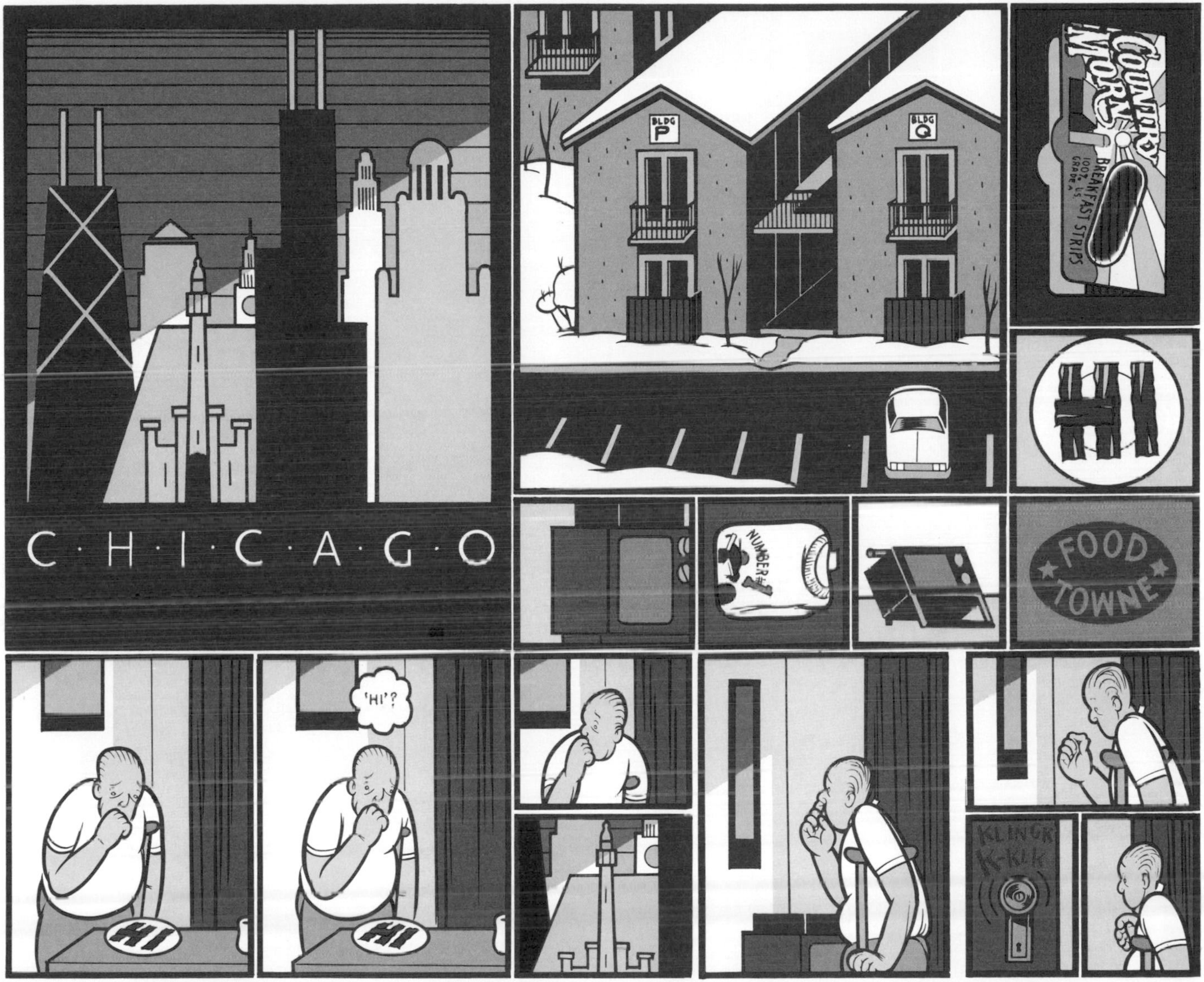
C·H·I·C·A·G·O
BLDG P
BLDG Q
COUNTRY MORN
BREAKFAST STRIPS
HI
NUMBER
FOOD TOWNE
HI
'HI'?
HI
KLINCK
K-KLK

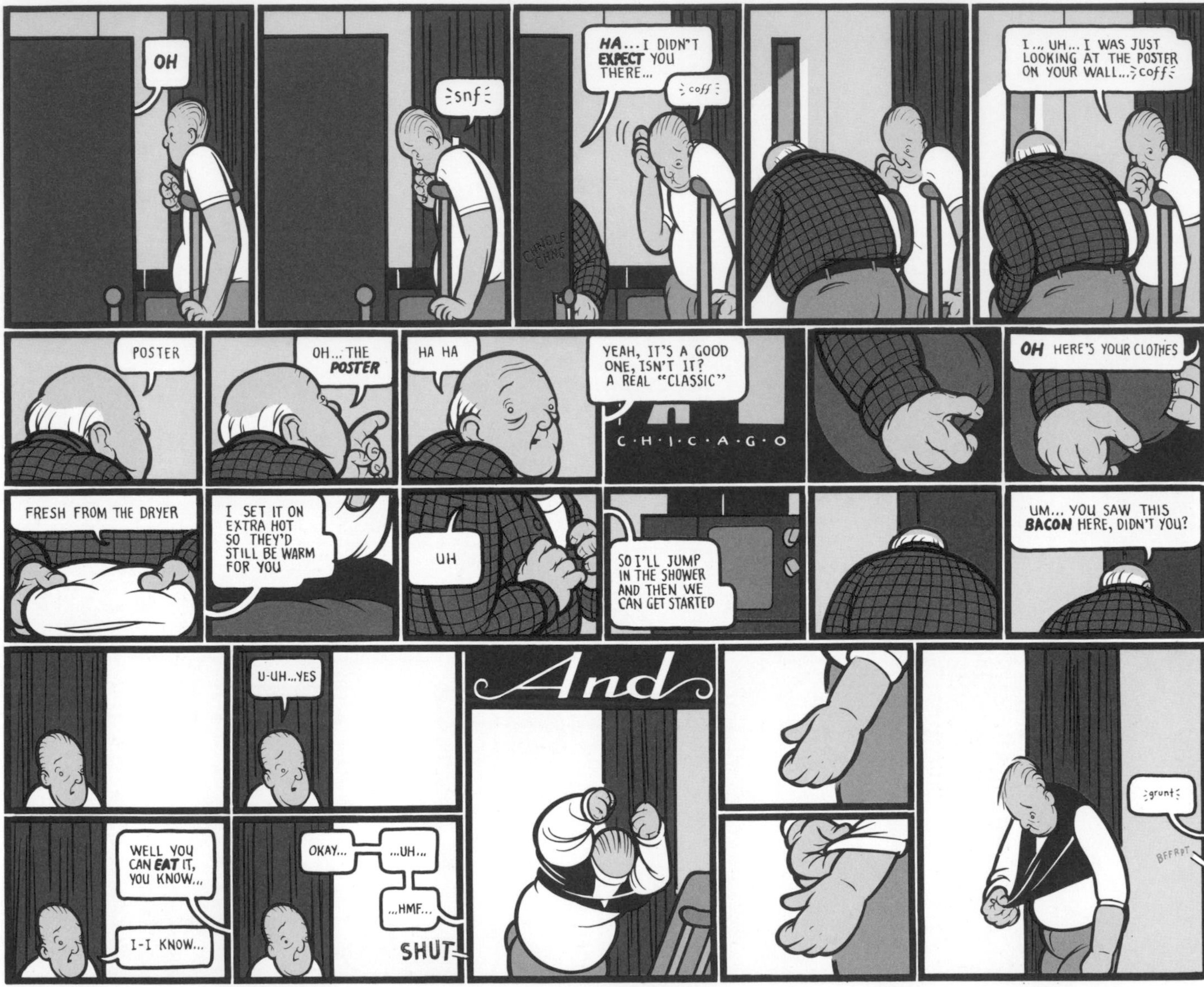
OH
snf
HA... I DIDN'T EXPECT YOU THERE...
coff
I... UH... I WAS JUST LOOKING AT THE POSTER ON YOUR WALL... coff
POSTER
OH... THE POSTER
HA HA
YEAH, IT'S A GOOD ONE, ISN'T IT? A REAL "CLASSIC"
C·H·I·C·A·G·O
OH HERE'S YOUR CLOTHES
FRESH FROM THE DRYER
I SET IT ON EXTRA HOT SO THEY'D STILL BE WARM FOR YOU
UH
SO I'LL JUMP IN THE SHOWER AND THEN WE CAN GET STARTED
UM... YOU SAW THIS BACON HERE, DIDN'T YOU?
U-UH...YES
WELL YOU CAN EAT IT, YOU KNOW...
I-I KNOW...
OKAY...
...UH...
...HMF...
SHUT
And
grunt

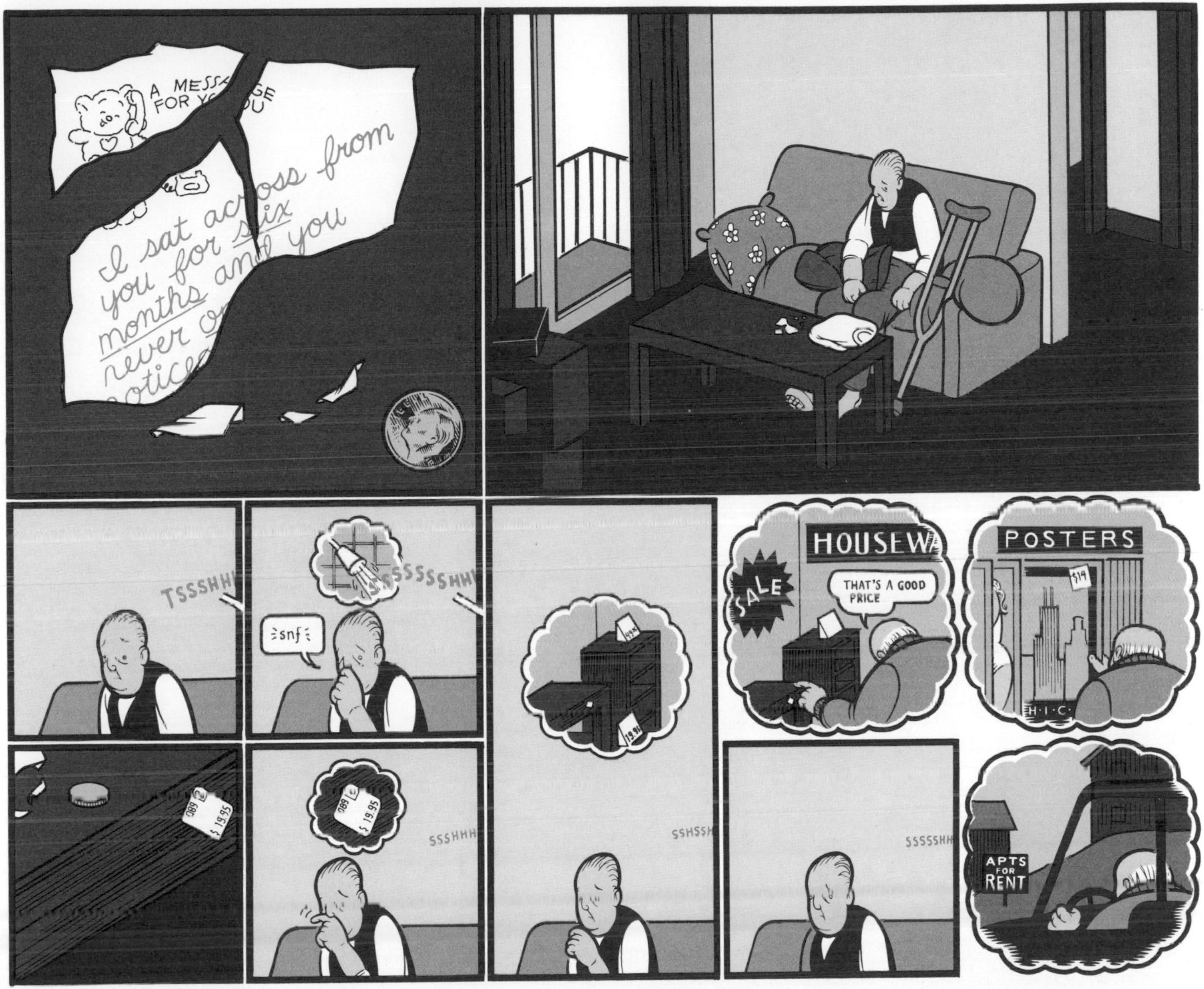

A MESS GE
FOR YO U
I sat across from
you for six
months and you
TSSSHH
snf
SSSSSSSHH
SSSHHH
$ 19.95
SSHSSH
HOUSEW
SALE
THAT'S A GOOD PRICE
POSTERS
$14
H·I·C·
SSSSSHH
APTS FOR RENT

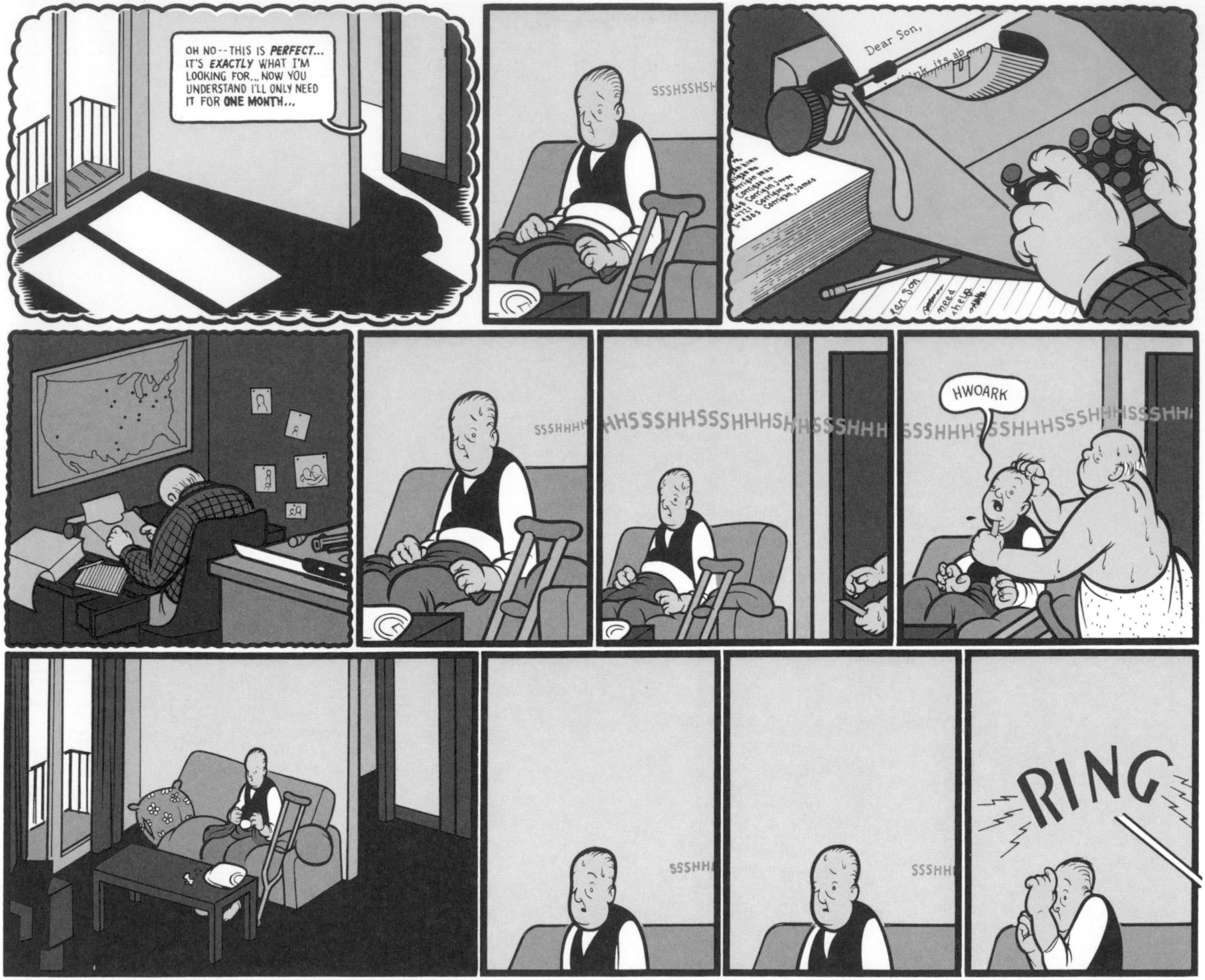

OH NO--THIS IS PERFECT... IT'S EXACTLY WHAT I'M LOOKING FOR... NOW YOU UNDERSTAND I'LL ONLY NEED IT FOR ONE MONTH...
SSSHSSHSH
Dear Son,
SSSHHHH
HHSSSHHSSSHHHSHHSSSHHH
HWOARK
SSSHHHSSSHHHSSSHHHSSSHH
SSSHH
SSSHH
RING

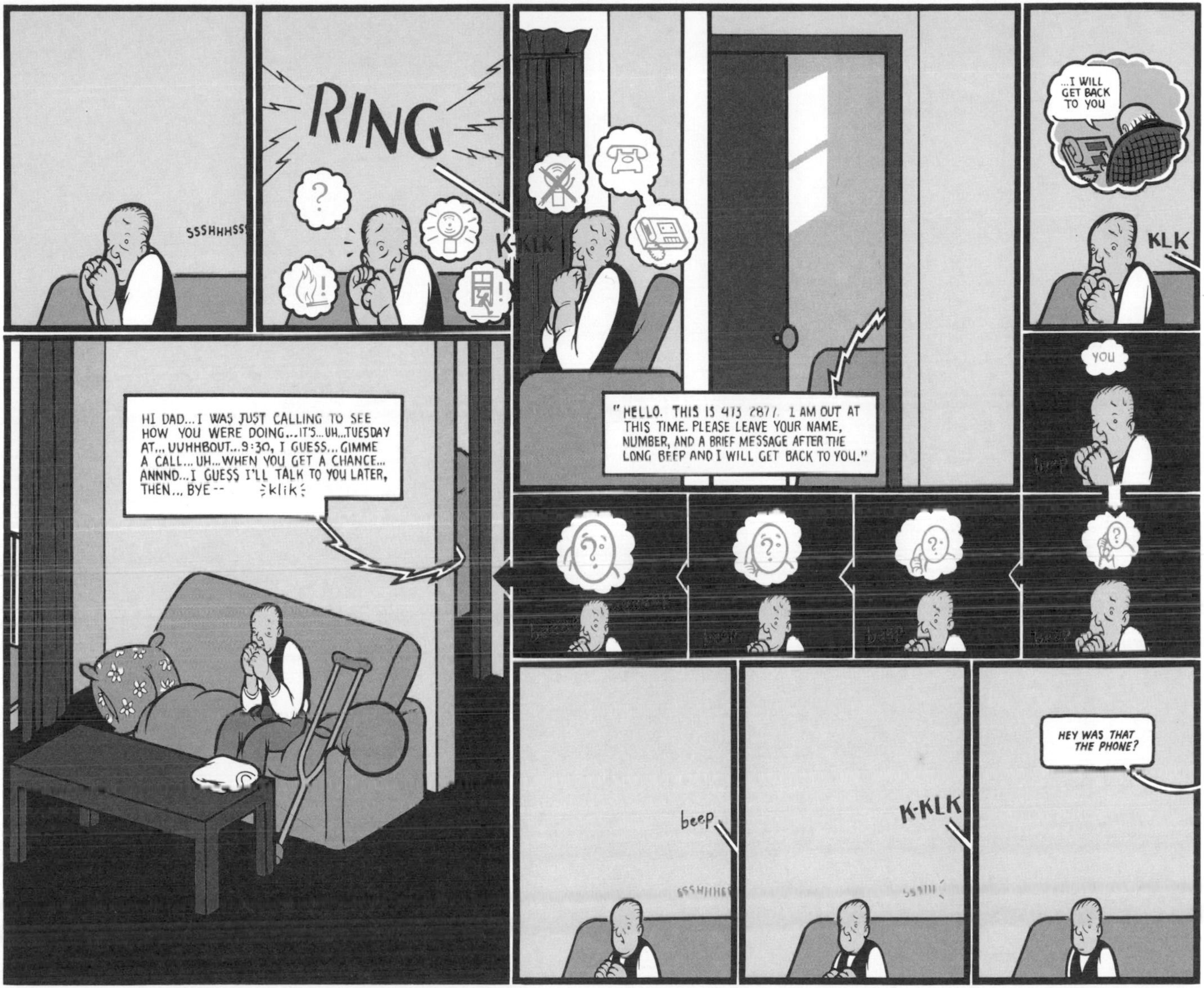
SSSHHHSSS
RING
K-KLK
...I WILL GET BACK TO YOU
KLK
"HELLO. THIS IS 473 2877. I AM OUT AT THIS TIME. PLEASE LEAVE YOUR NAME, NUMBER, AND A BRIEF MESSAGE AFTER THE LONG BEEP AND I WILL GET BACK TO YOU."
YOU
beep
HI DAD... I WAS JUST CALLING TO SEE HOW YOU WERE DOING... IT'S... UH... TUESDAY AT... UUHHBOUT... 9:30, I GUESS... GIMME A CALL... UH... WHEN YOU GET A CHANCE... ANNND... I GUESS I'LL TALK TO YOU LATER, THEN... BYE -- klik
beep
K-KLK
HEY WAS THAT THE PHONE?

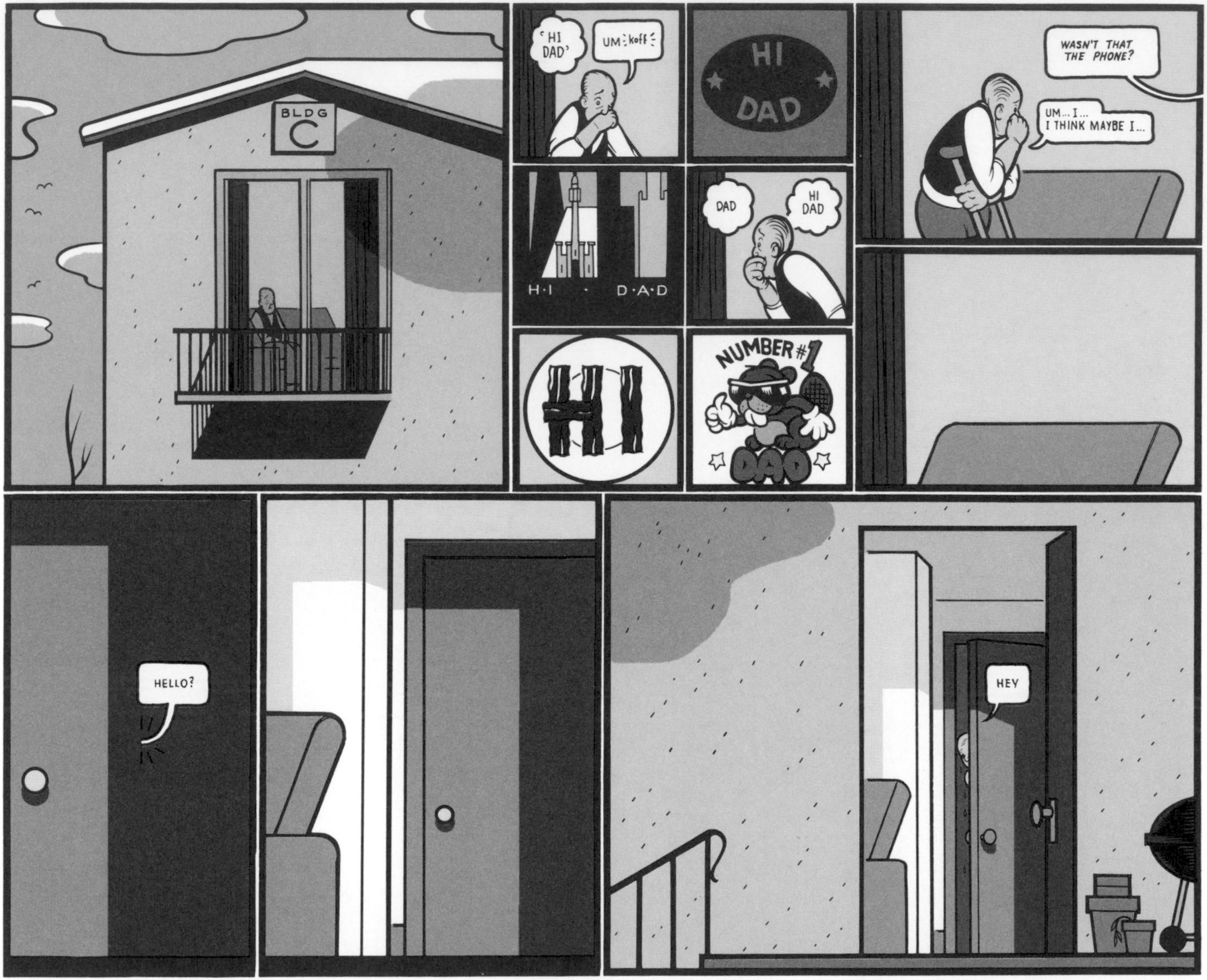
BLDG C
'HI DAD'
UM koff
HI DAD
H·I · D·A·D
DAD
HI DAD
HI
NUMBER #1 DAD
WASN'T THAT THE PHONE?
UM... I... I THINK MAYBE I...
HELLO?
HEY

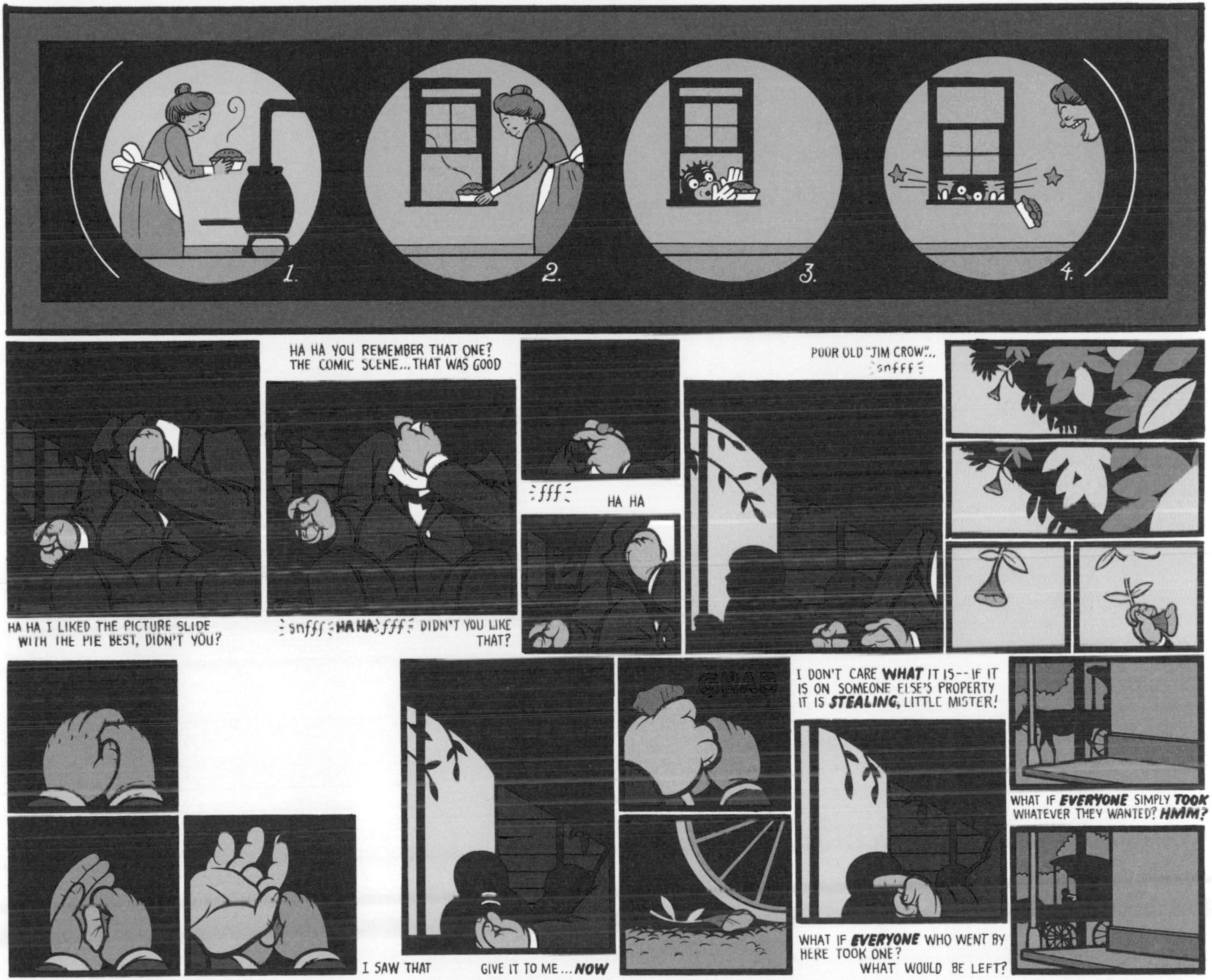
1.
2.
3.
4.
HA HA I LIKED THE PICTURE SLIDE WITH THE PIE BEST, DIDN'T YOU?
HA HA YOU REMEMBER THAT ONE? THE COMIC SCENE... THAT WAS GOOD
snfff HA HA fff DIDN'T YOU LIKE THAT?
fff
HA HA
POOR OLD "JIM CROW"...
snfff
I SAW THAT
GIVE IT TO ME... NOW
GRAB
I DON'T CARE WHAT IT IS-- IF IT IS ON SOMEONE ELSE'S PROPERTY IT IS STEALING, LITTLE MISTER!
WHAT IF EVERYONE WHO WENT BY HERE TOOK ONE?
WHAT WOULD BE LEFT?
WHAT IF EVERYONE SIMPLY TOOK WHATEVER THEY WANTED? HMM?

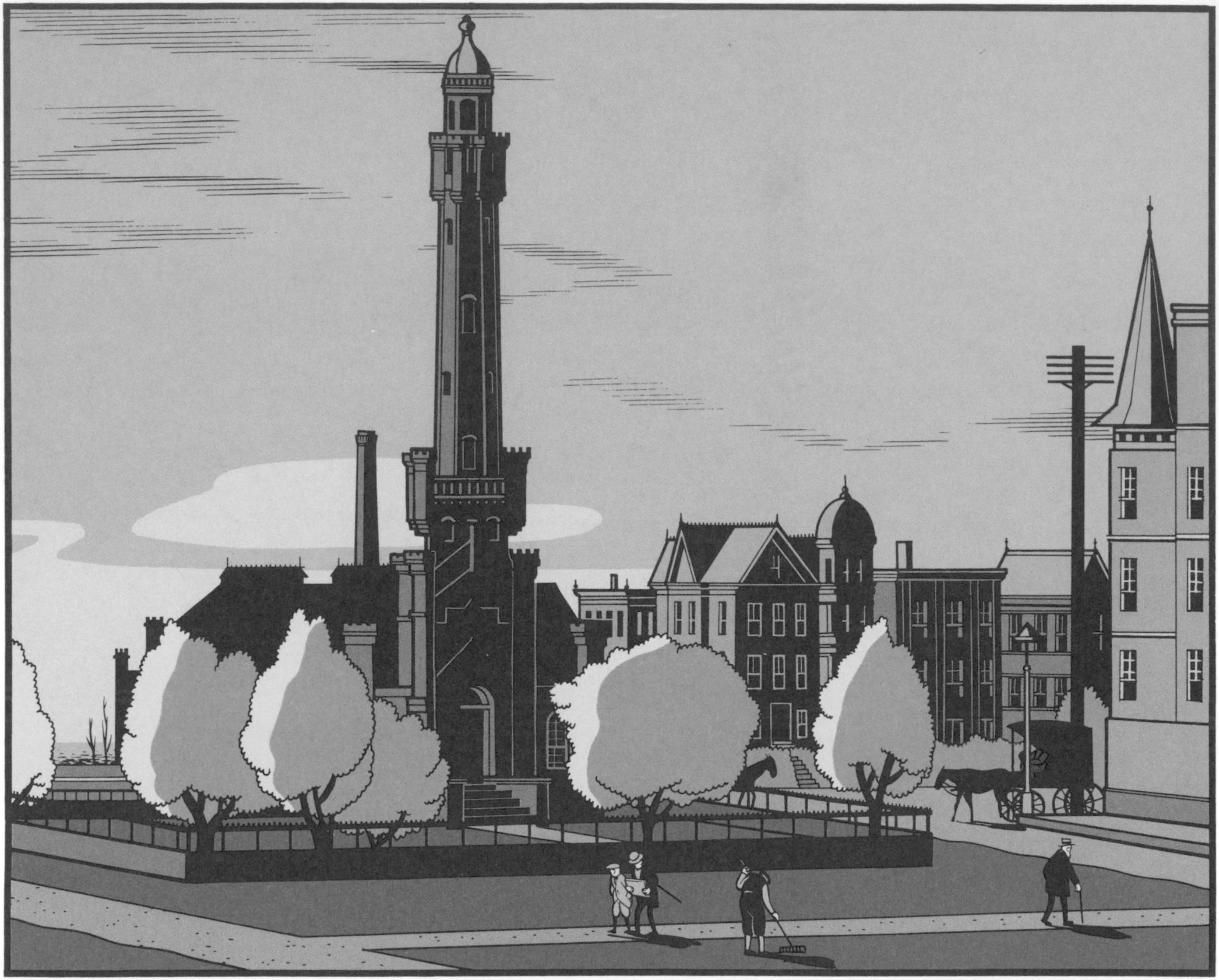

HMM? THEN WHERE WOULD WE BE?

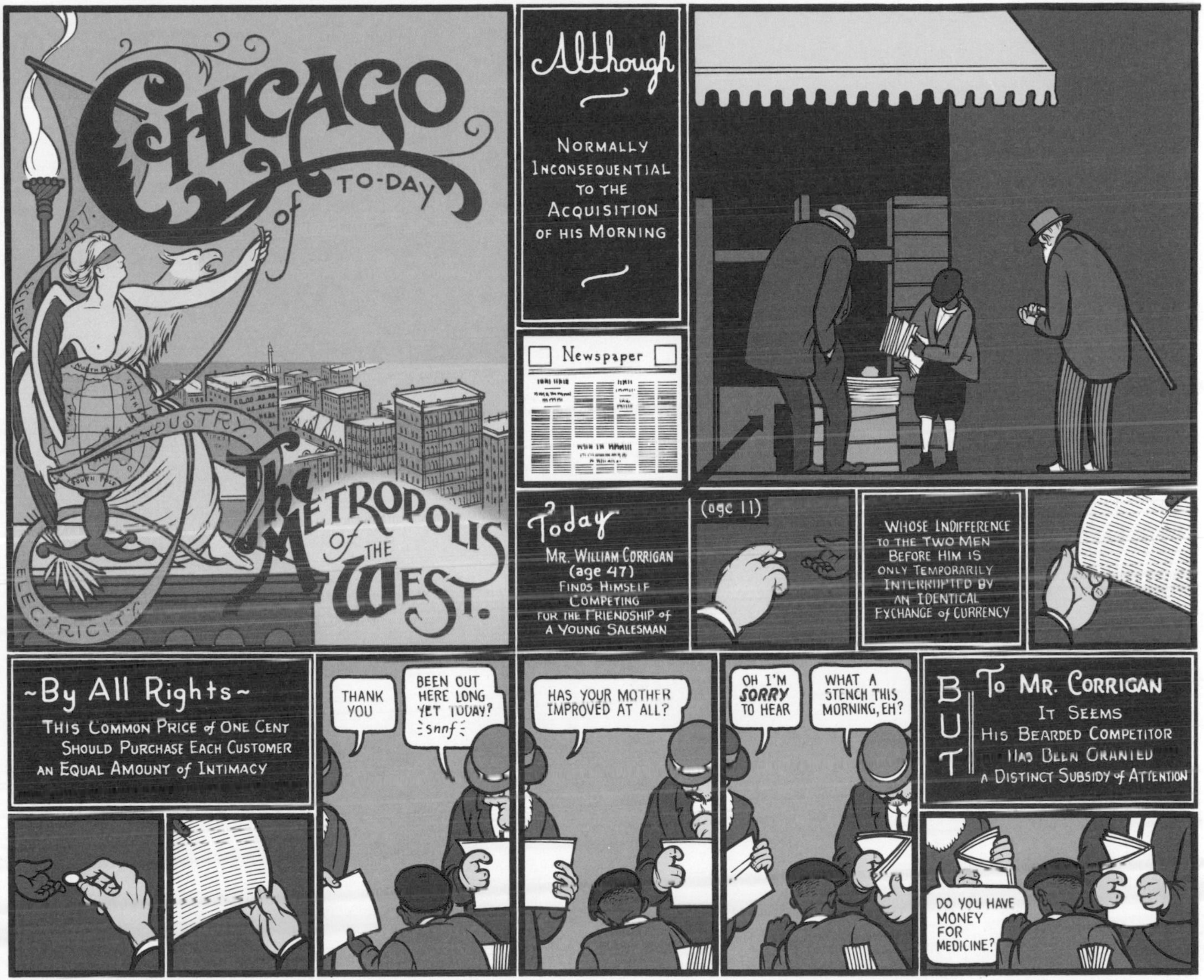

CHICAGO of TO-DAY
ART.
SCIENCE.
INDUSTRY
ELECTRICITY
The METROPOLIS of THE WEST.
Although
NORMALLY INCONSEQUENTIAL TO THE ACQUISITION OF HIS MORNING
Newspaper
Today
MR. WILLIAM CORRIGAN (age 47) FINDS HIMSELF COMPETING FOR THE FRIENDSHIP of A YOUNG SALESMAN
(age 11)
WHOSE INDIFFERENCE TO THE TWO MEN BEFORE HIM IS ONLY TEMPORARILY INTERRUPTED BY AN IDENTICAL EXCHANGE of CURRENCY
~By All Rights~
THIS COMMON PRICE of ONE CENT SHOULD PURCHASE EACH CUSTOMER AN EQUAL AMOUNT of INTIMACY
THANK YOU
BEEN OUT HERE LONG YET TODAY?
snnf
HAS YOUR MOTHER IMPROVED AT ALL?
OH I'M SORRY TO HEAR
WHAT A STENCH THIS MORNING, EH?
BUT To MR. CORRIGAN IT SEEMS HIS BEARDED COMPETITOR HAS BEEN GRANTED A DISTINCT SUBSIDY of ATTENTION
DO YOU HAVE MONEY FOR MEDICINE?

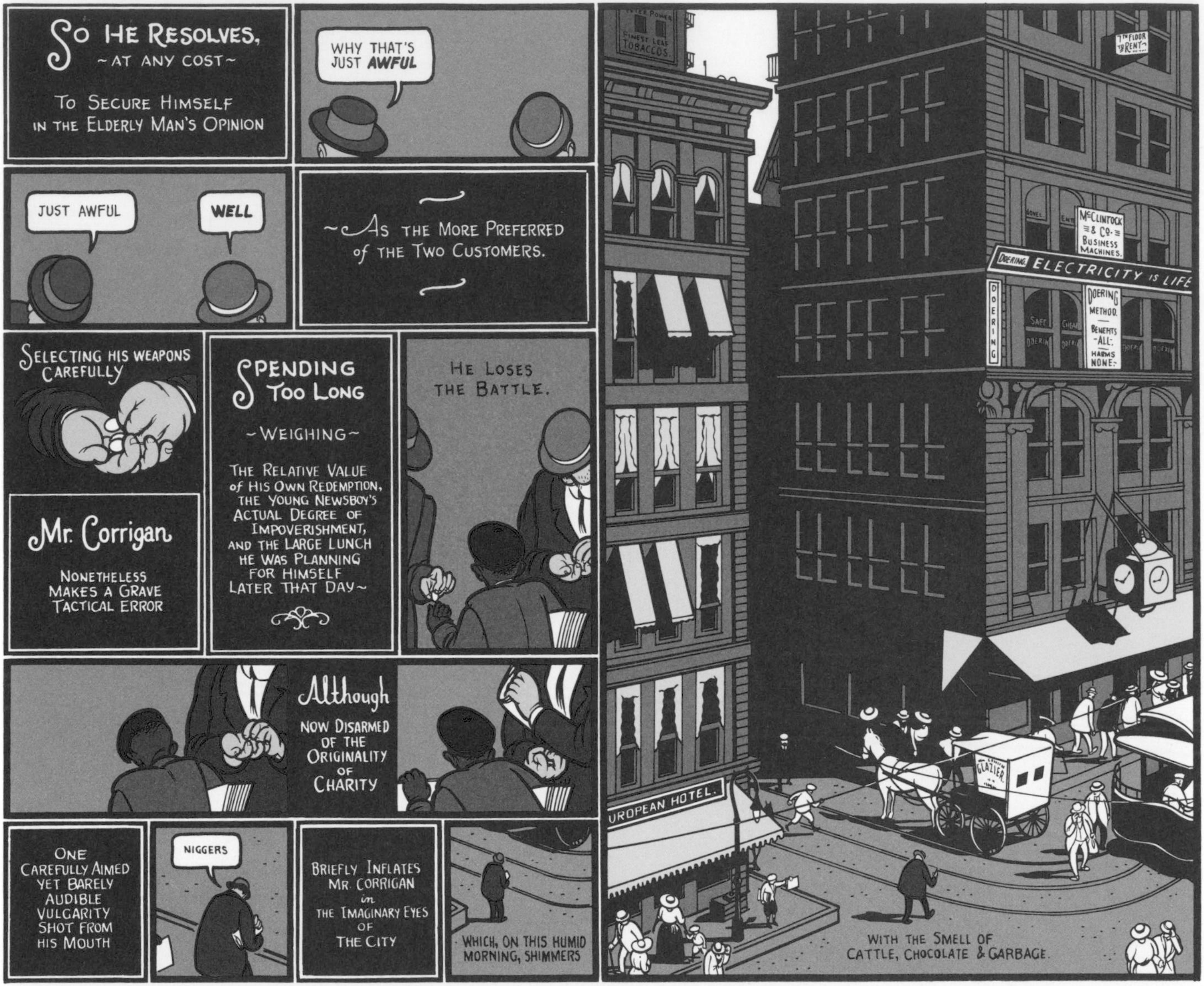
So He Resolves,
~at any cost~
To Secure Himself in the Elderly Man's Opinion
WHY THAT'S JUST AWFUL
JUST AWFUL
WELL
~As the More Preferred of the Two Customers.
Selecting his weapons carefully
Mr. Corrigan
Nonetheless makes a grave tactical error
Spending Too Long
~Weighing~
The Relative Value of His Own Redemption, the Young Newsboy's Actual Degree of Impoverishment, and the Large Lunch He Was Planning for Himself Later That Day~
He Loses the Battle.
Although
Now Disarmed of the Originality of Charity
One Carefully Aimed yet Barely Audible Vulgarity Shot from His Mouth
NIGGERS
Briefly Inflates Mr. Corrigan in the Imaginary Eyes of The City
Which, on this humid morning, shimmers
FINEST LEAF TOBACCOS
McCLINTOCK & Co. BUSINESS MACHINES.
DOERING ELECTRICITY IS LIFE
DOERING
DOERING METHOD. BENEFITS ALL: HARMS NONE.
UROPEAN HOTEL.
GLAZIER
With the Smell of Cattle, Chocolate & Garbage.

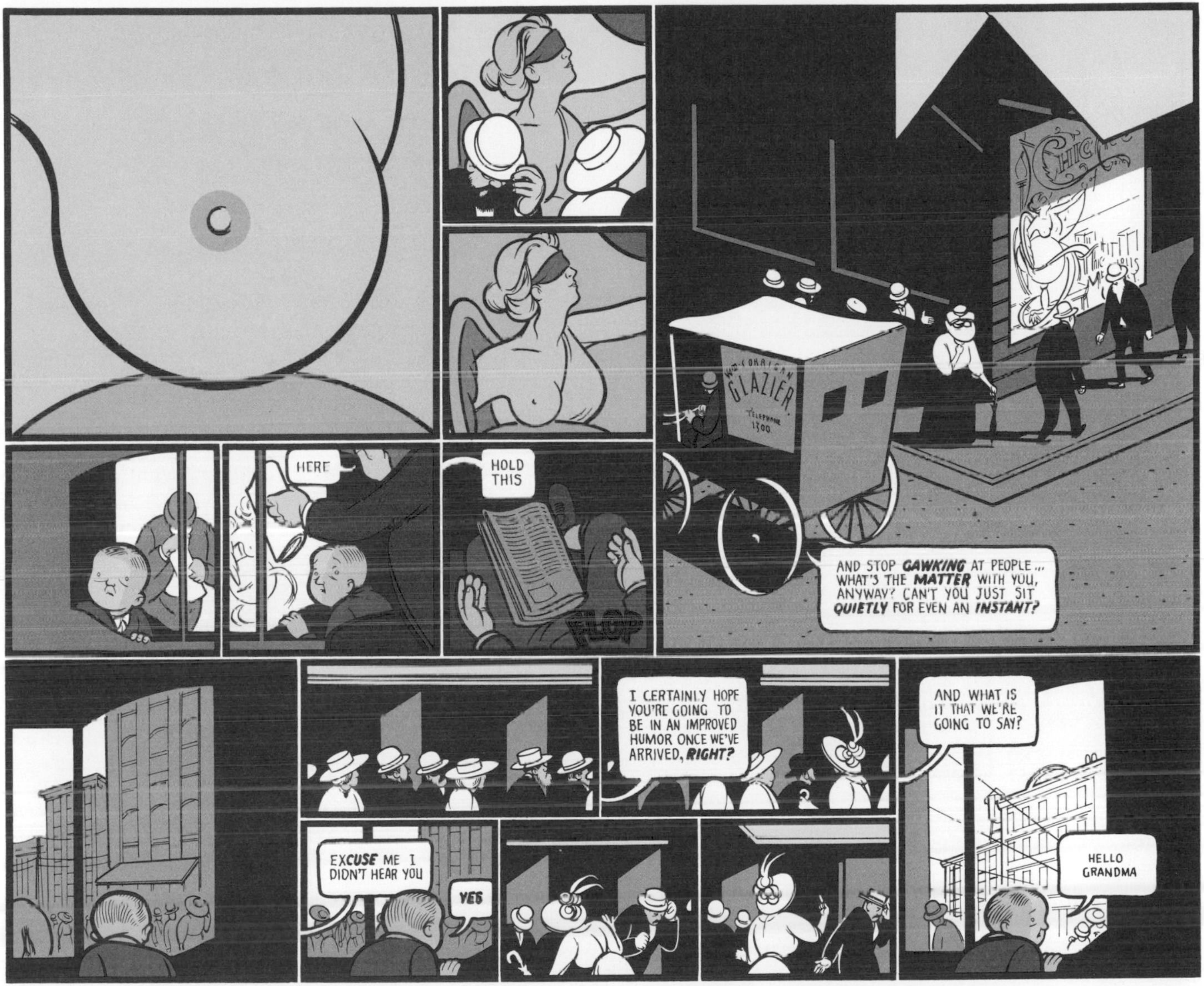
HERE
HOLD THIS
FLOP
GLAZIER
TELEPHONE
1300
AND STOP GAWKING AT PEOPLE ... WHAT'S THE MATTER WITH YOU, ANYWAY? CAN'T YOU JUST SIT QUIETLY FOR EVEN AN INSTANT?
I CERTAINLY HOPE YOU'RE GOING TO BE IN AN IMPROVED HUMOR ONCE WE'VE ARRIVED, RIGHT?
EXCUSE ME I DIDN'T HEAR YOU
YES
AND WHAT IS IT THAT WE'RE GOING TO SAY?
HELLO GRANDMA

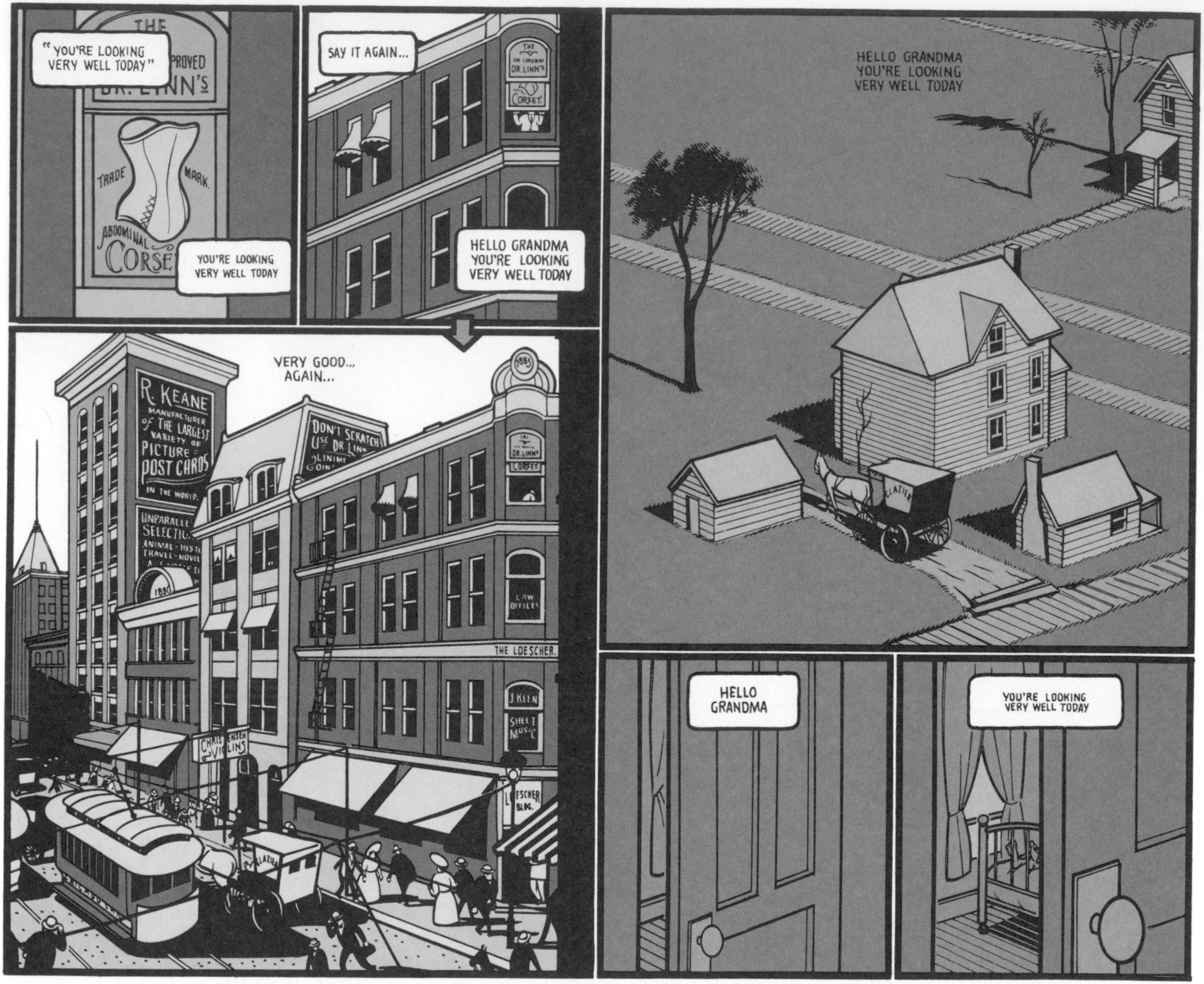
"YOU'RE LOOKING VERY WELL TODAY"
THE
PROVED
TRADE
MARK.
ABDOMINAL CORSET
YOU'RE LOOKING VERY WELL TODAY
SAY IT AGAIN...
THE
DR. LINN'S
CORSET.
HELLO GRANDMA YOU'RE LOOKING VERY WELL TODAY
VERY GOOD... AGAIN...
R. KEANE
MANUFACTURER OF THE LARGEST VARIETY OF PICTURE POST CARDS IN THE WORLD.
1894
1883
DON'T SCRATCH
DR. LINN'S
CORSET
LAW OFFICES
THE LOESCHER.
J. KEEN
SHEET MUSIC
VIOLINS
BLDG.
HELLO GRANDMA YOU'RE LOOKING VERY WELL TODAY
GLAZIER
HELLO GRANDMA
YOU'RE LOOKING VERY WELL TODAY

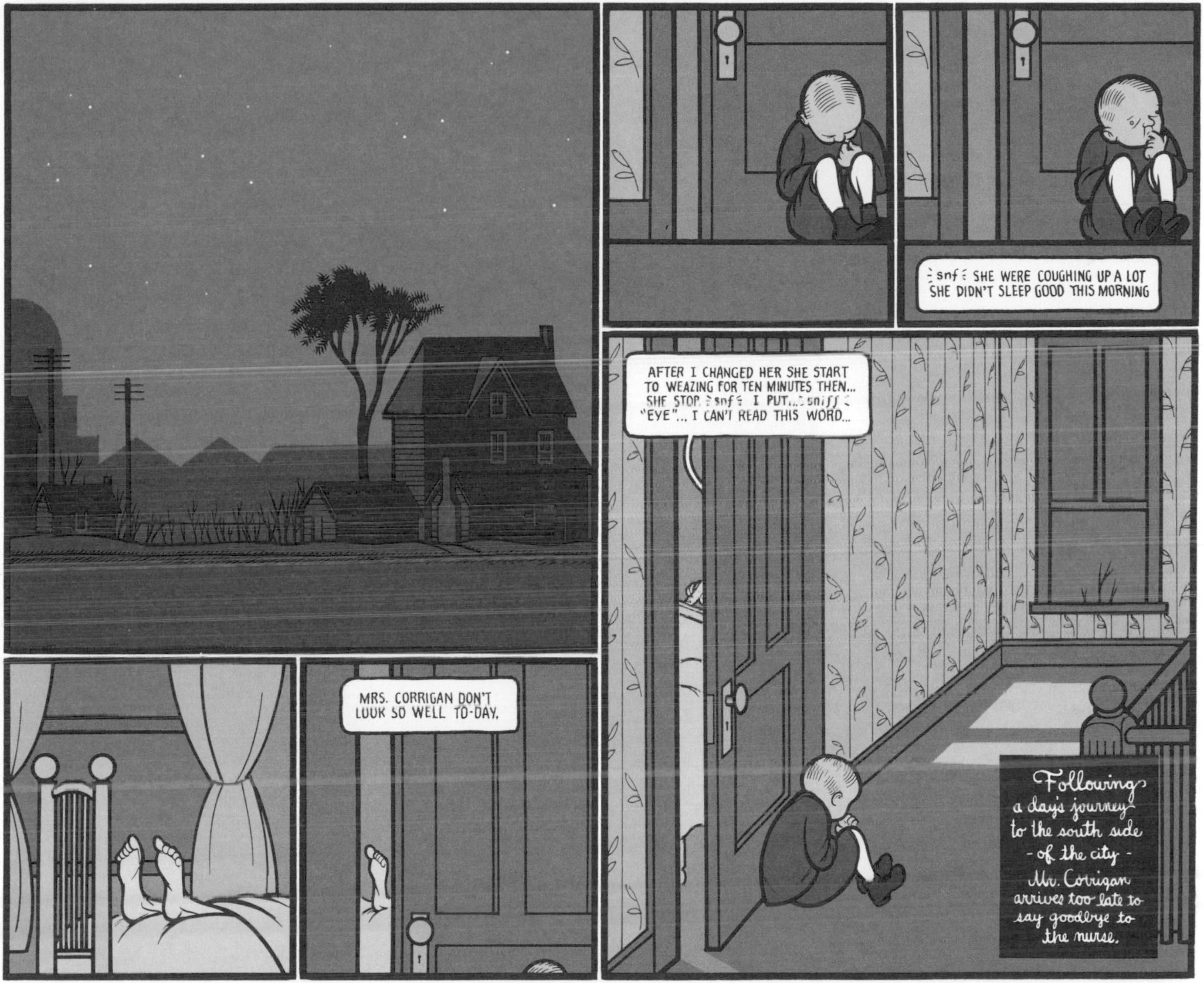
MRS. CORRIGAN DON'T LOOK SO WELL TO-DAY.
snf SHE WERE COUGHING UP A LOT SHE DIDN'T SLEEP GOOD THIS MORNING
AFTER I CHANGED HER SHE START TO WEAZING FOR TEN MINUTES THEN... SHE STOP. snf I PUT... sniff "EYE"... I CAN'T READ THIS WORD...
Following a day's journey to the south side - of the city - Mr. Corrigan arrives too late to say goodbye to the nurse.

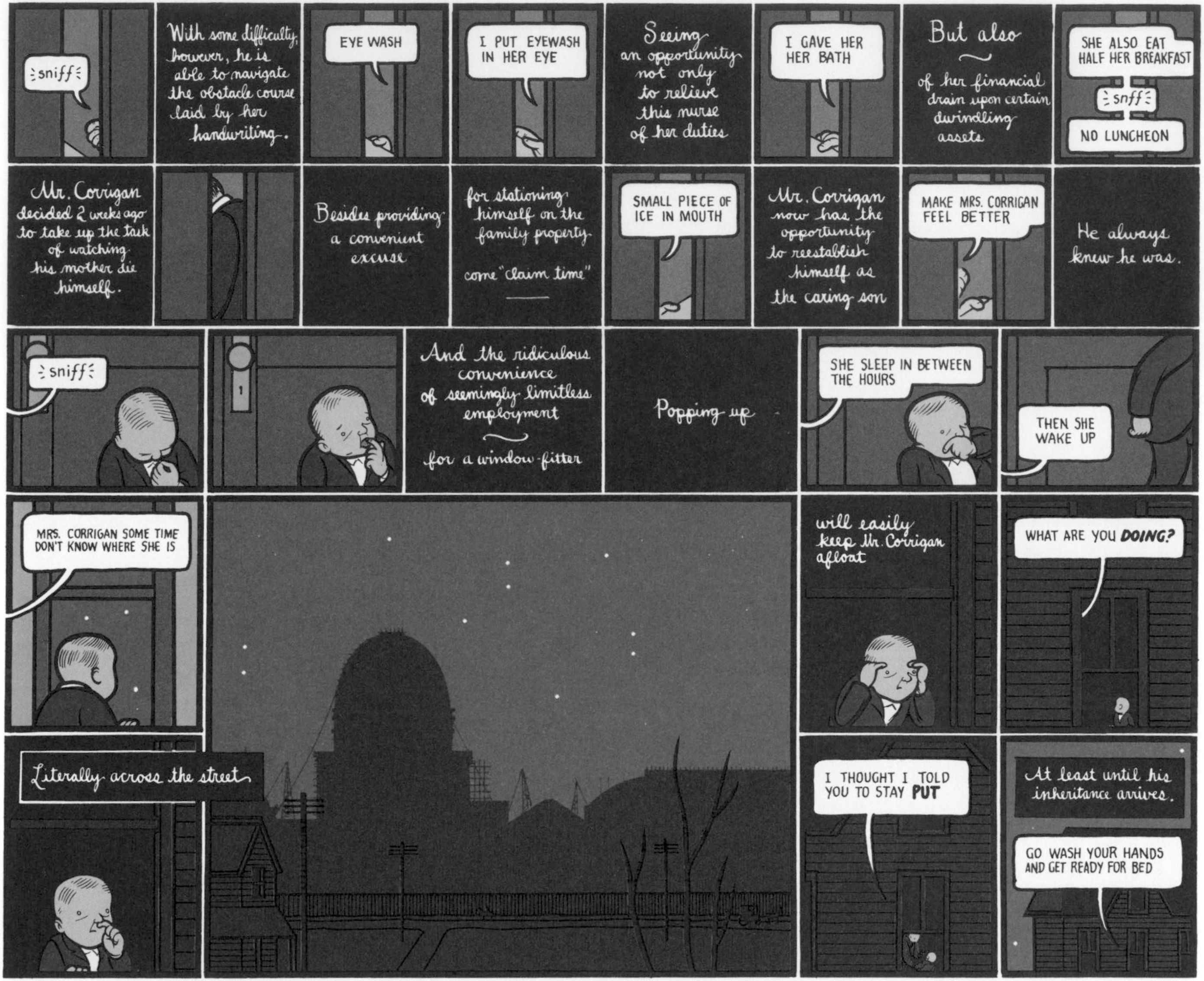
sniff
With some difficulty, however, he is able to navigate the obstacle course laid by her handwriting.
EYE WASH
I PUT EYEWASH IN HER EYE
Seeing an opportunity not only to relieve this nurse of her duties
I GAVE HER HER BATH
But also of her financial drain upon certain dwindling assets
SHE ALSO EAT HALF HER BREAKFAST
snff
NO LUNCHEON
Mr. Corrigan decided 2 weeks ago to take up the task of watching his mother die himself.
Besides providing a convenient excuse
for stationing himself on the family property come "claim time"
SMALL PIECE OF ICE IN MOUTH
Mr. Corrigan now has the opportunity to reestablish himself as the caring son
MAKE MRS. CORRIGAN FEEL BETTER
He always knew he was.
sniff
1
And the ridiculous convenience of seemingly limitless employment for a window-fitter
Popping up
SHE SLEEP IN BETWEEN THE HOURS
THEN SHE WAKE UP
MRS. CORRIGAN SOME TIME DON'T KNOW WHERE SHE IS
Literally across the street
will easily keep Mr. Corrigan afloat
WHAT ARE YOU DOING?
I THOUGHT I TOLD YOU TO STAY PUT
At least until his inheritance arrives.
GO WASH YOUR HANDS AND GET READY FOR BED

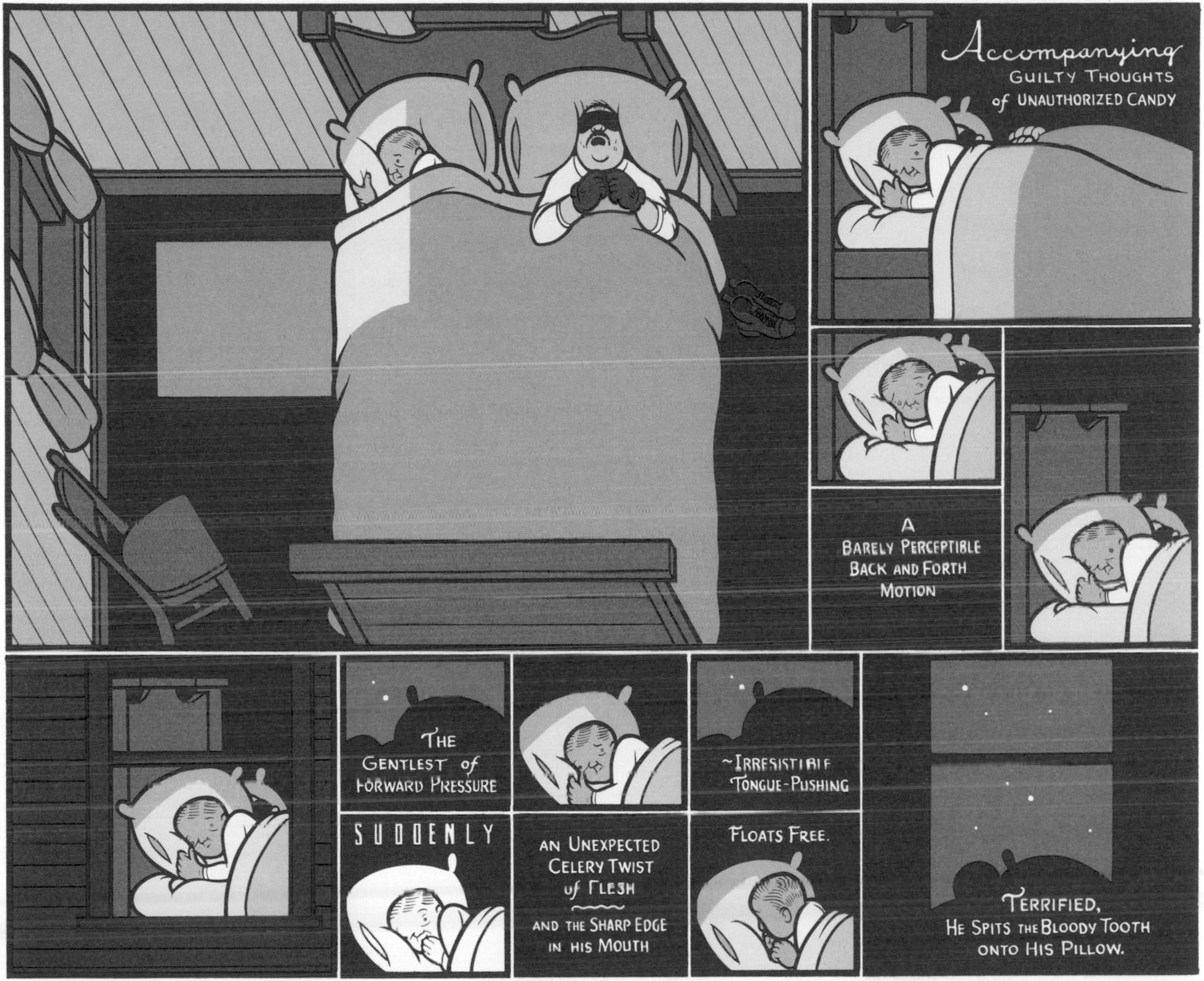
Accompanying
GUILTY THOUGHTS
of UNAUTHORIZED CANDY
A
BARELY PERCEPTIBLE
BACK AND FORTH
MOTION
THE
GENTLEST of
FORWARD PRESSURE
~IRRESISTIBLE
TONGUE-PUSHING
SUDDENLY
AN UNEXPECTED
CELERY TWIST
of FLESH
AND THE SHARP EDGE
IN HIS MOUTH
FLOATS FREE.
TERRIFIED,
HE SPITS THE BLOODY TOOTH
ONTO HIS PILLOW.

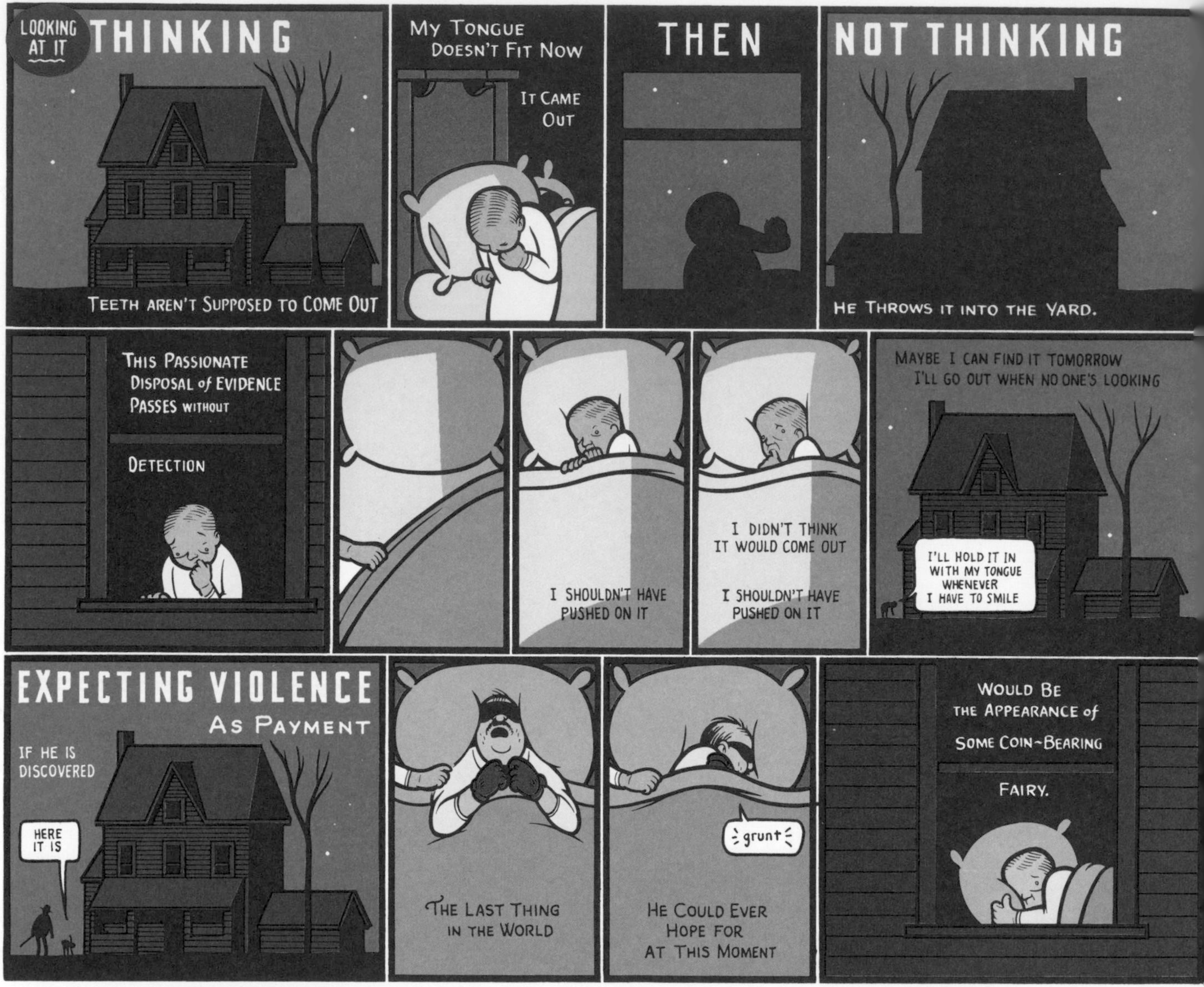
LOOKING AT IT
THINKING
TEETH AREN'T SUPPOSED TO COME OUT
MY TONGUE DOESN'T FIT NOW
IT CAME OUT
THEN
NOT THINKING
HE THROWS IT INTO THE YARD.
THIS PASSIONATE DISPOSAL of EVIDENCE PASSES WITHOUT
DETECTION
I SHOULDN'T HAVE PUSHED ON IT
I DIDN'T THINK IT WOULD COME OUT
I SHOULDN'T HAVE PUSHED ON IT
MAYBE I CAN FIND IT TOMORROW
I'LL GO OUT WHEN NO ONE'S LOOKING
I'LL HOLD IT IN WITH MY TONGUE WHENEVER I HAVE TO SMILE
EXPECTING VIOLENCE
AS PAYMENT
IF HE IS DISCOVERED
HERE IT IS
THE LAST THING IN THE WORLD
grunt
HE COULD EVER HOPE FOR AT THIS MOMENT
WOULD BE THE APPEARANCE of SOME COIN-BEARING
FAIRY.

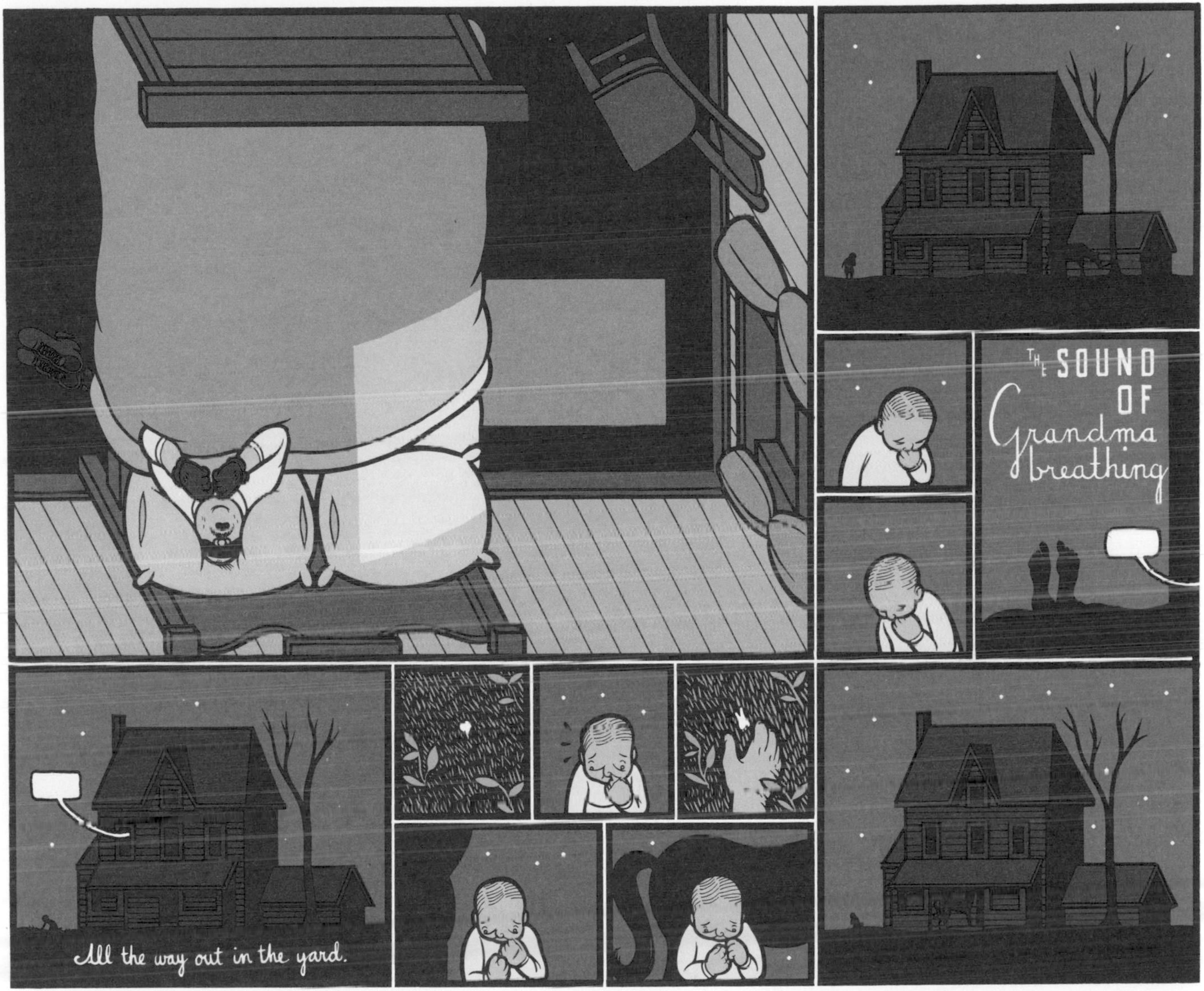
THE SOUND OF Grandma breathing
All the way out in the yard.

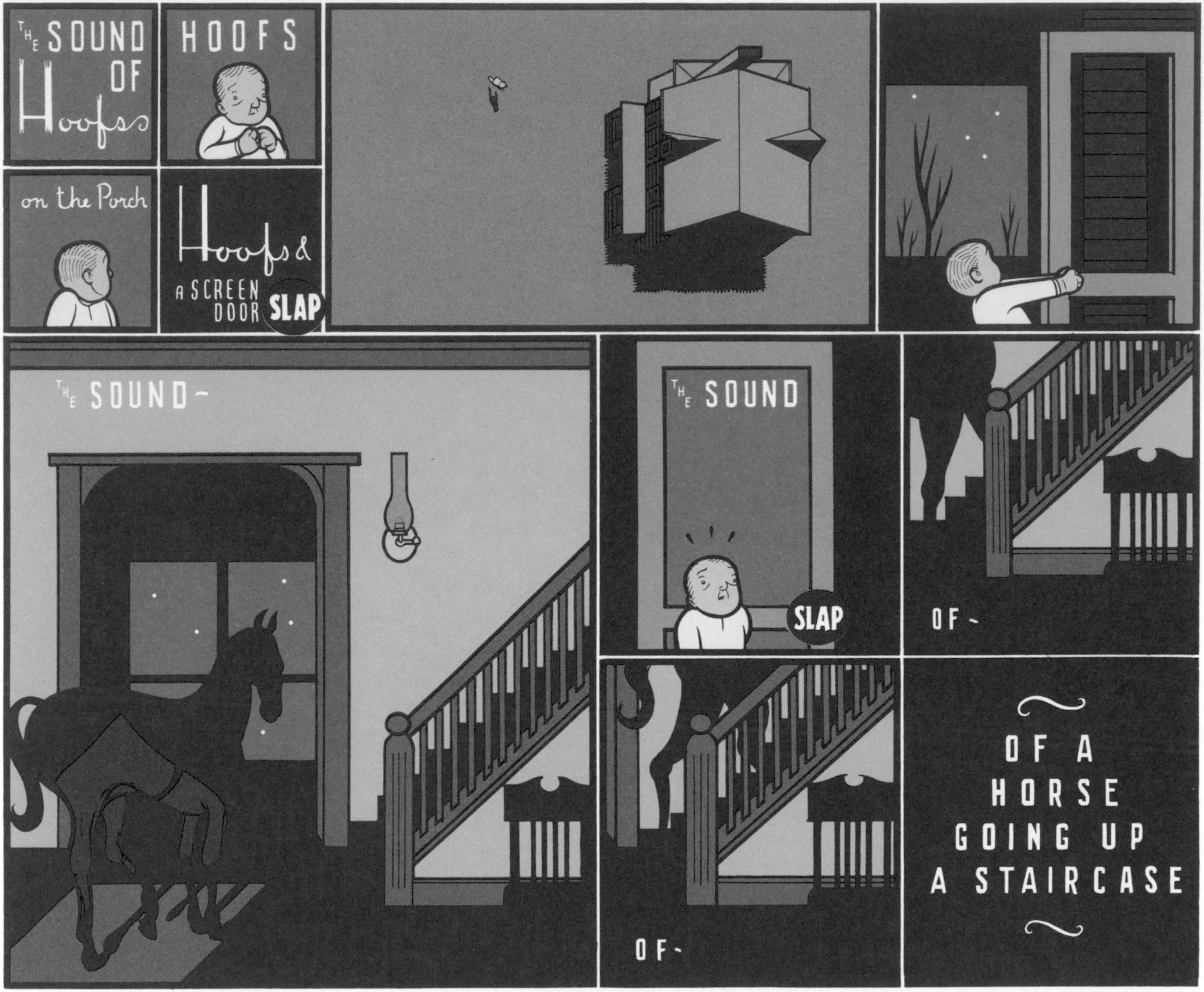
THE SOUND OF Hoofs
HOOFS
on the Porch
Hoofs & A SCREEN DOOR SLAP
THE SOUND~
THE SOUND
SLAP
OF~
OF~
OF A HORSE GOING UP A STAIRCASE

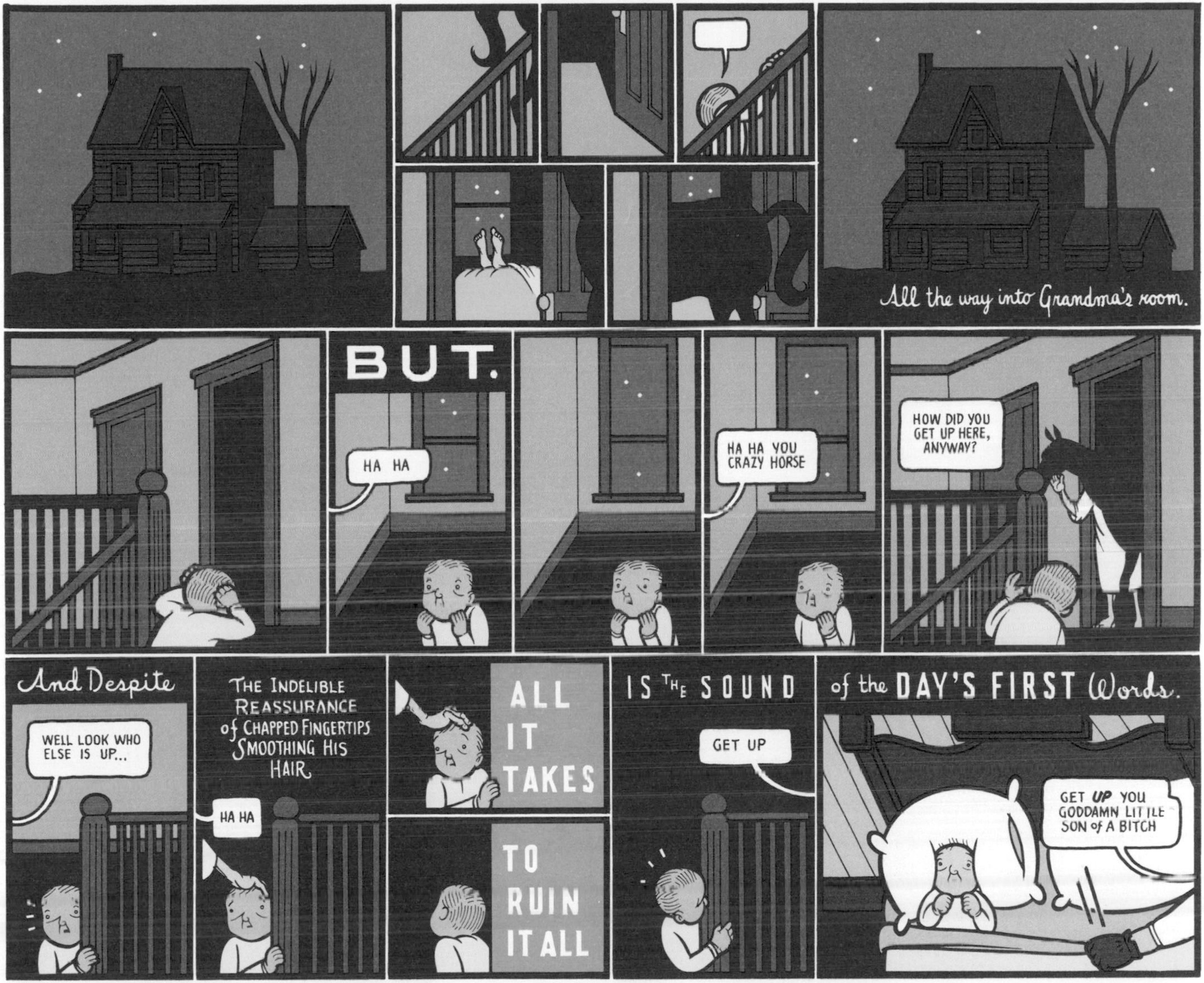
All the way into Grandma's room.
BUT.
HA HA
HA HA YOU CRAZY HORSE
HOW DID YOU GET UP HERE, ANYWAY?
And Despite
WELL LOOK WHO ELSE IS UP...
THE INDELIBLE REASSURANCE of CHAPPED FINGERTIPS SMOOTHING HIS HAIR
HA HA
ALL IT TAKES
TO RUIN IT ALL
IS THE SOUND
GET UP
of the DAY'S FIRST Words.
GET UP YOU GODDAMN LITTLE SON of A BITCH

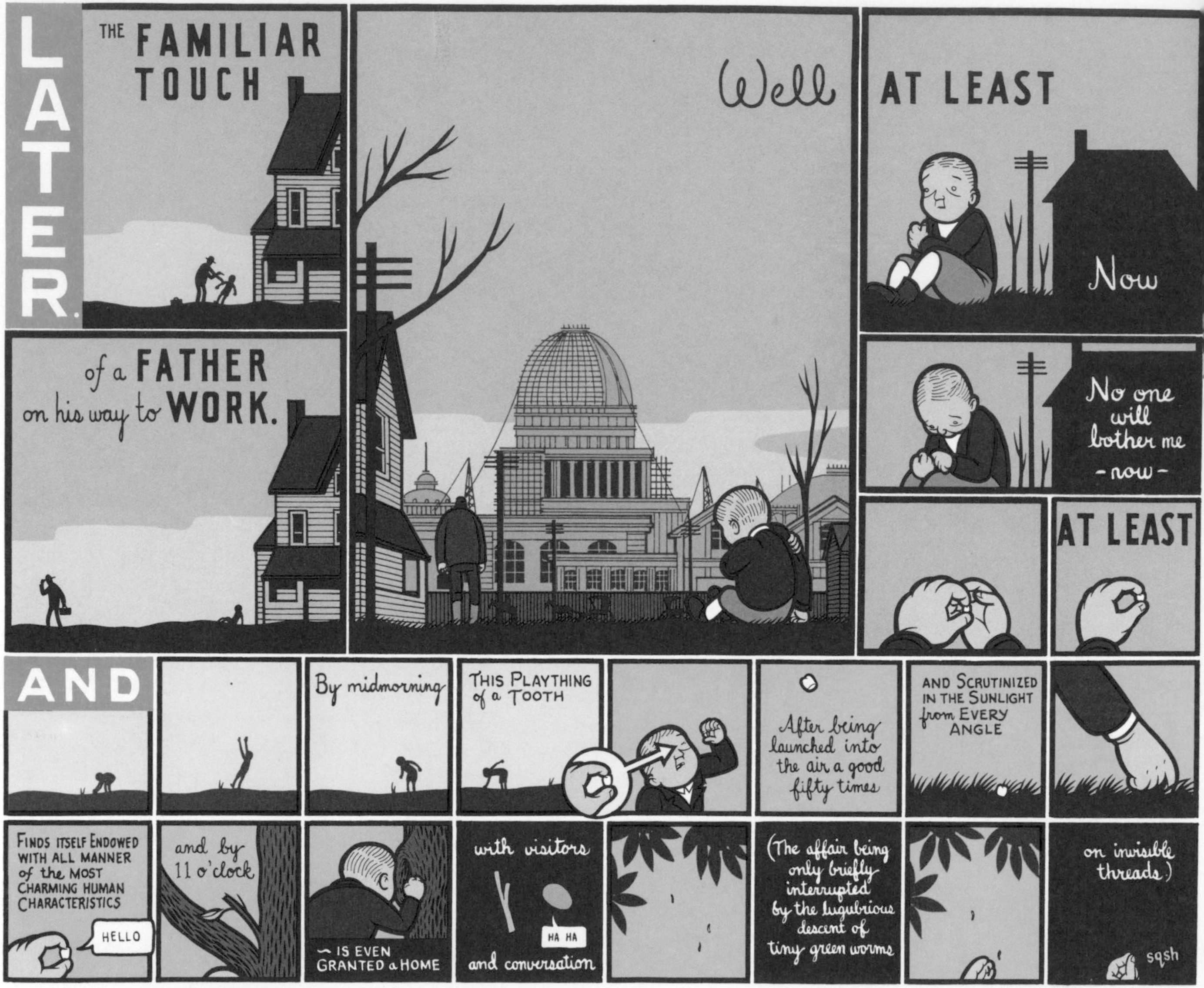
LATER.
THE FAMILIAR TOUCH
of a FATHER on his way to WORK.
Well
AT LEAST
Now
No one will bother me -now-
AT LEAST
AND
By midmorning
THIS PLAYTHING of a TOOTH
After being launched into the air a good fifty times
AND SCRUTINIZED IN THE SUNLIGHT from EVERY ANGLE
FINDS ITSELF ENDOWED WITH ALL MANNER of the MOST CHARMING HUMAN CHARACTERISTICS
HELLO
and by 11 o'clock
~IS EVEN GRANTED a HOME
with visitors
HA HA
and conversation
(The affair being only briefly interrupted by the lugubrious descent of tiny green worms
on invisible threads.)
sqsh

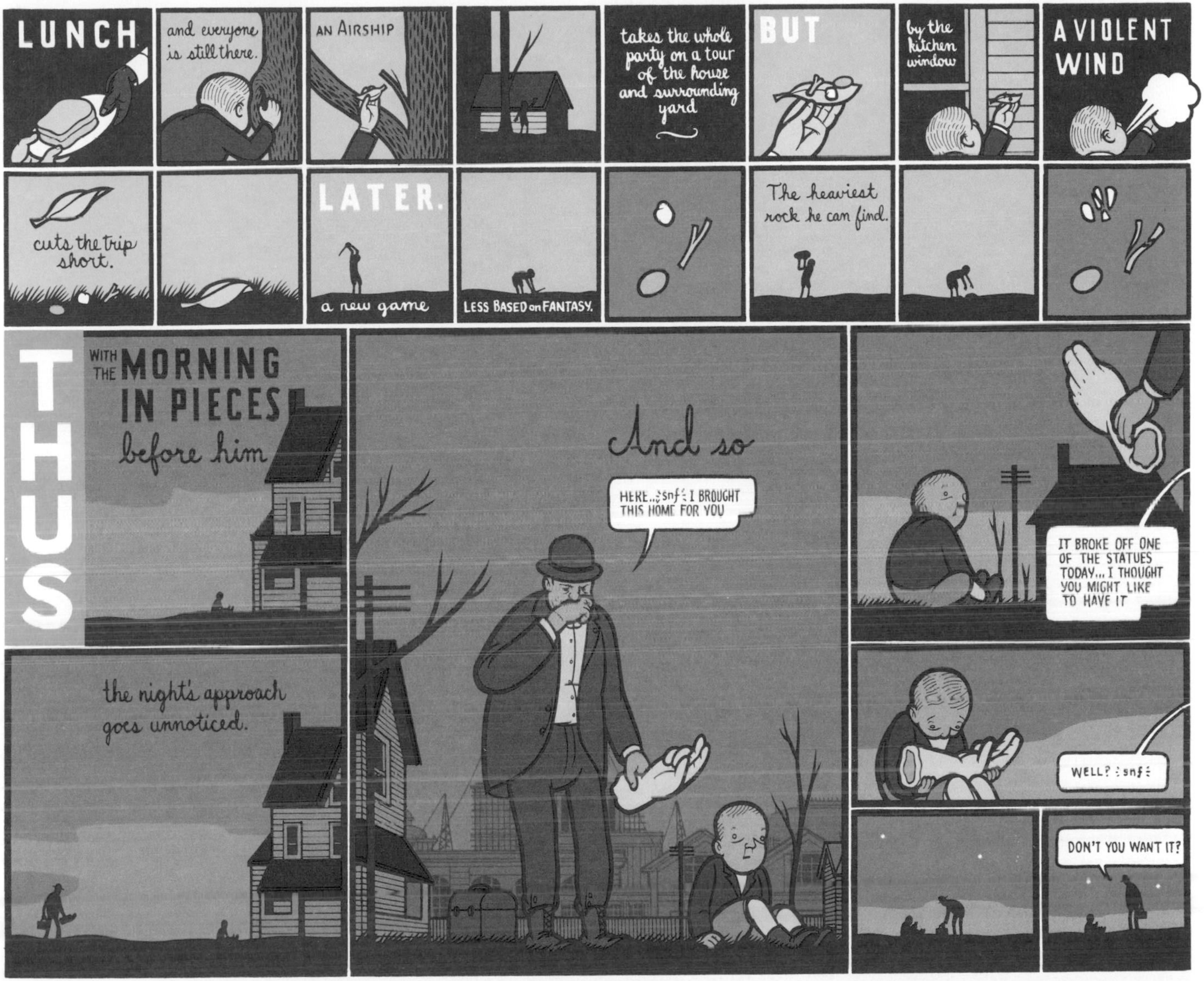

LUNCH
and everyone is still there.
AN AIRSHIP
takes the whole party on a tour of the house and surrounding yard
BUT
by the kitchen window
A VIOLENT WIND
cuts the trip short.
LATER.
a new game
LESS BASED on FANTASY.
The heaviest rock he can find.
THUS
WITH THE MORNING IN PIECES before him
the night's approach goes unnoticed.
And so
HERE...snf I BROUGHT THIS HOME FOR YOU
IT BROKE OFF ONE OF THE STATUES TODAY... I THOUGHT YOU MIGHT LIKE TO HAVE IT
WELL? snf
DON'T YOU WANT IT?

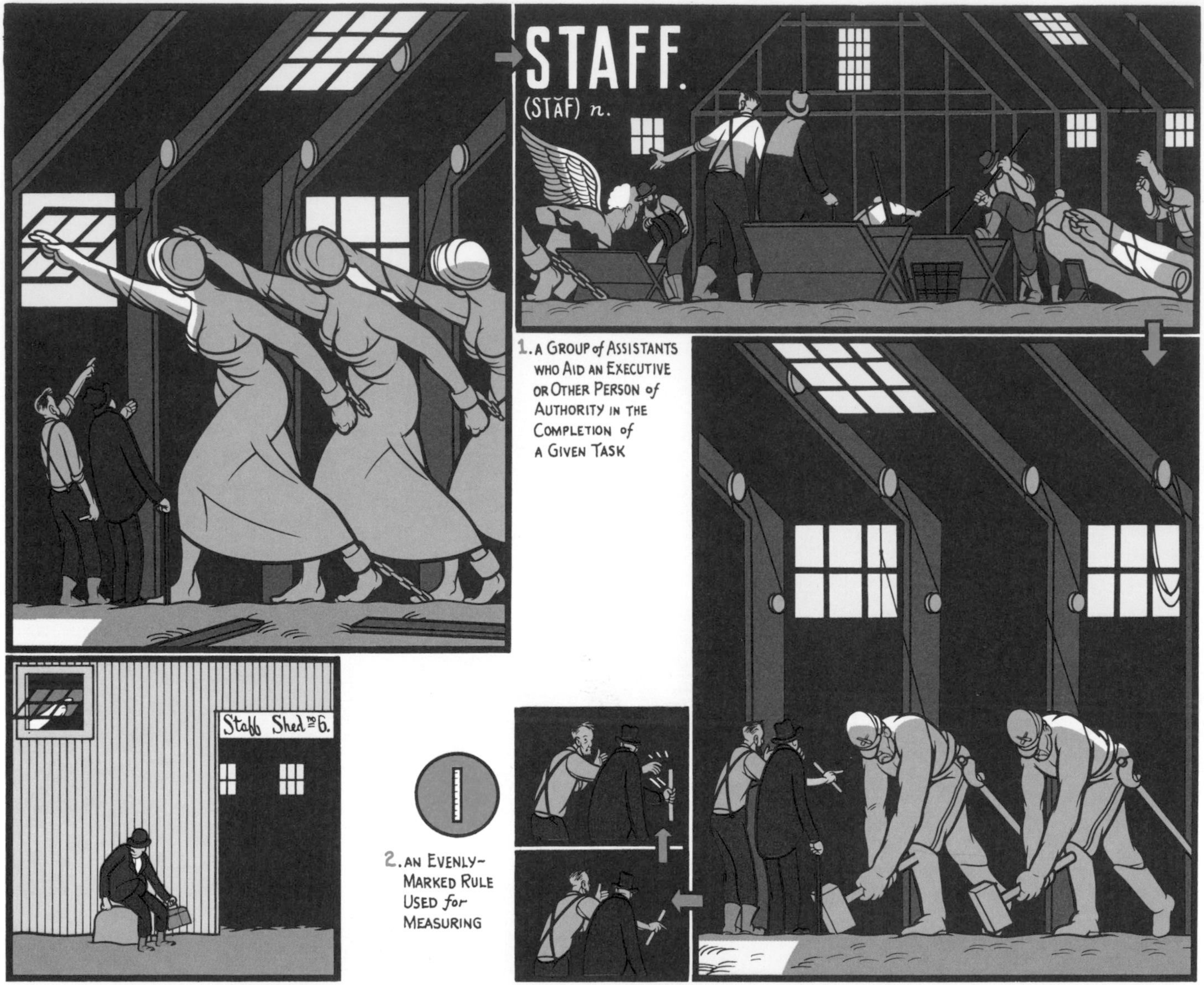
STAFF.
(STĂF) n.
1. A GROUP of ASSISTANTS WHO AID AN EXECUTIVE OR OTHER PERSON of AUTHORITY IN THE COMPLETION of A GIVEN TASK
2. AN EVENLY-MARKED RULE USED for MEASURING
Staff Shed No 6.

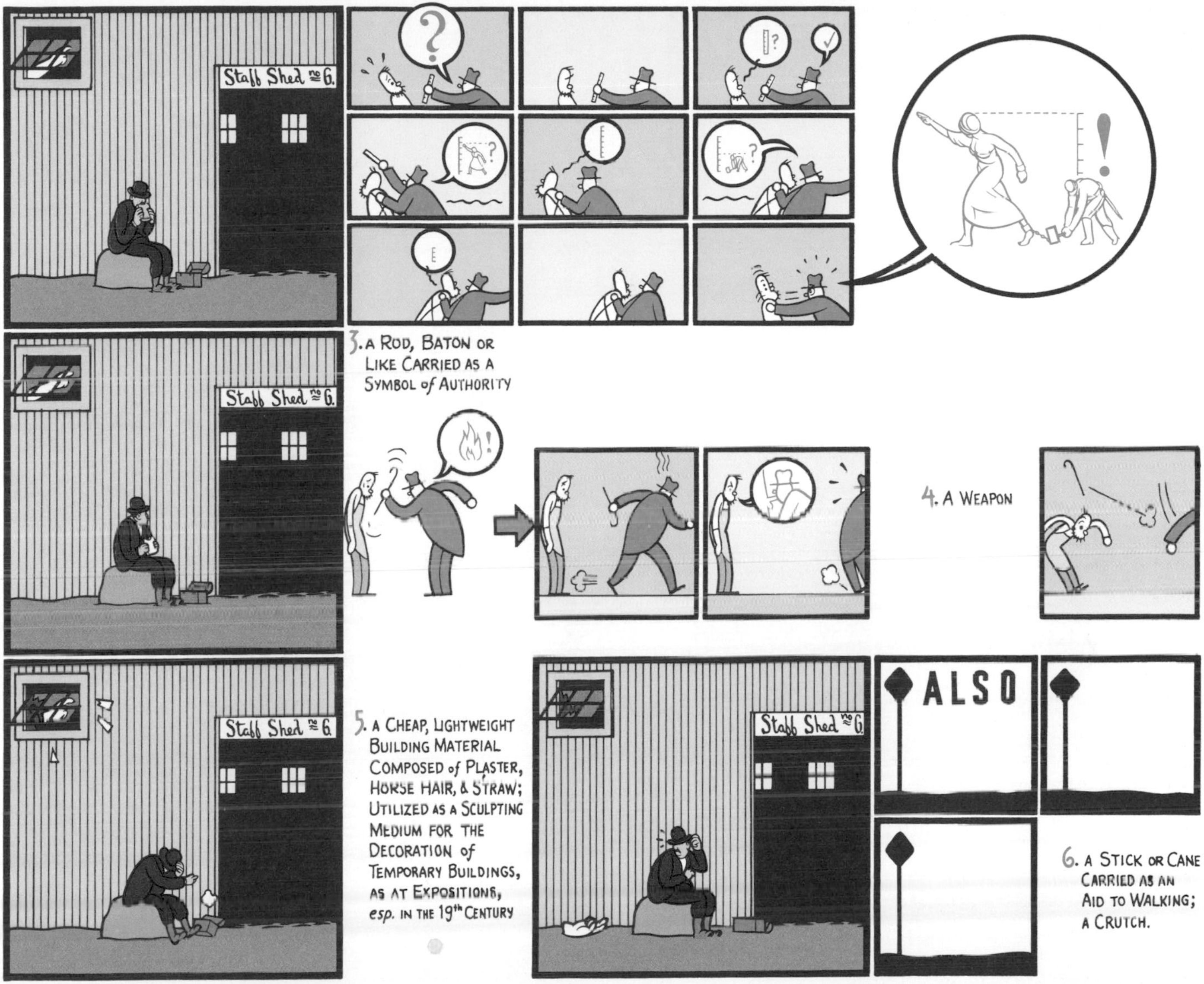

Staff Shed No 6.
?
?
!
Staff Shed No 6.
3. A Rod, Baton or Like Carried as a Symbol of Authority
!
4. A Weapon
Staff Shed No 6.
5. A Cheap, Lightweight Building Material Composed of Plaster, Horse Hair, & Straw; Utilized as a Sculpting Medium for the Decoration of Temporary Buildings, as at Expositions, esp. in the 19th Century
Staff Shed No 6.
ALSO
6. A Stick or Cane Carried as an Aid to Walking; a Crutch.

STAGECOACH STALLION STATUE

STICKS STONES STOP

STRANGLE STREAM *of* CONSCIOUSNESS

STRICT STUMBLE STUPID

SUMMARY □ **SUMMARY.** OF OUR STORY THUS FAR WITH NOTES AND EXPLANATIONS.

Prologue

IN WHICH WE LEARN THAT JIMMY CORRIGAN, THE SMARTEST KID ON EARTH IS A LONELY, EMOTIONALLY~IMPAIRED HUMAN CASTAWAY.

I AM A LONELY EMOTIONALLY-IMPAIRED HUMAN CASTAWAY

ONE DAY

JIMMY GETS AN AIRPLANE TICKET IN THE MAIL FROM HIS DAD.

OH BOY!

Dear Jimmy, Come visit me. Love, Dad

BUT

JIMMY HASN'T EVER MET HIS REAL DAD BEFORE

I'VE NEVER MET MY REAL DAD BEFORE

SO

HE BUYS HIMSELF A SNACK

AND THEN HE GOES TO THE BATHROOM.

LATER *That Night*

JIMMY DREAMS THAT HE IS A METAL MAN.

And Also THAT HE HAS A DATE WITH A GIRL OUT IN THE COUNTRY

HA HA

CLIP n' SAVE

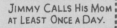 THINGS TO REMEMBER

JIMMY CAN'T MEET GIRLS.

JIMMY WEARS OLD-FASHIONED PANTS.

 JIMMY CALLS HIS MOM AT LEAST ONCE A DAY.

Anyway

THE AIRPLANE LANDS BUT JIMMY'S DAD ISN'T THERE TO MEET HIM.

I WASN'T!

AND A GIRL TELLS HIM TO QUIT STARING AT HER CHEST.

THEN HE WAKES UP ON AN AIRPLANE

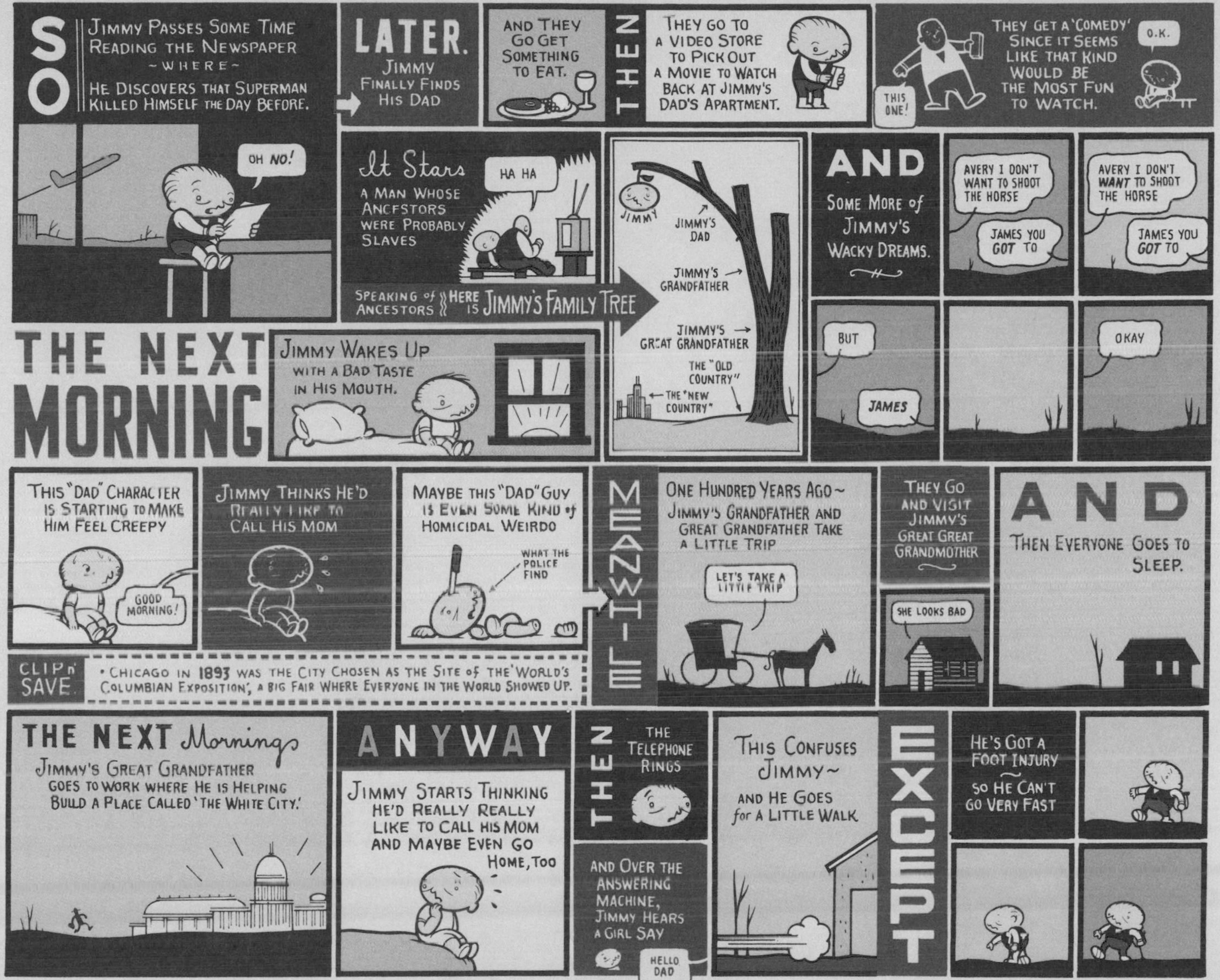

SO
JIMMY PASSES SOME TIME READING THE NEWSPAPER
~WHERE~
HE DISCOVERS THAT SUPERMAN KILLED HIMSELF THE DAY BEFORE.
OH NO!
LATER.
JIMMY FINALLY FINDS HIS DAD
AND THEY GO GET SOMETHING TO EAT.
THEN
THEY GO TO A VIDEO STORE TO PICK OUT A MOVIE TO WATCH BACK AT JIMMY'S DAD'S APARTMENT.
THEY GET A 'COMEDY' SINCE IT SEEMS LIKE THAT KIND WOULD BE THE MOST FUN TO WATCH.
THIS ONE!
O.K.
It Stars
A MAN WHOSE ANCESTORS WERE PROBABLY SLAVES
HA HA
SPEAKING of ANCESTORS
HERE IS JIMMY'S FAMILY TREE
JIMMY
JIMMY'S DAD
JIMMY'S GRANDFATHER
JIMMY'S GREAT GRANDFATHER
THE "OLD COUNTRY"
THE "NEW COUNTRY"
AND
SOME MORE of JIMMY'S WACKY DREAMS.
AVERY I DON'T WANT TO SHOOT THE HORSE
JAMES YOU GOT TO
AVERY I DON'T WANT TO SHOOT THE HORSE
JAMES YOU GOT TO
BUT
JAMES
OKAY
THE NEXT MORNING
JIMMY WAKES UP WITH A BAD TASTE IN HIS MOUTH.
THIS "DAD" CHARACTER IS STARTING TO MAKE HIM FEEL CREEPY
GOOD MORNING!
JIMMY THINKS HE'D REALLY LIKE TO CALL HIS MOM
MAYBE THIS "DAD" GUY IS EVEN SOME KIND of HOMICIDAL WEIRDO
WHAT THE POLICE FIND
MEANWHILE
ONE HUNDRED YEARS AGO~ JIMMY'S GRANDFATHER AND GREAT GRANDFATHER TAKE A LITTLE TRIP
LET'S TAKE A LITTLE TRIP
THEY GO AND VISIT JIMMY'S GREAT GREAT GRANDMOTHER
SHE LOOKS BAD
AND
THEN EVERYONE GOES TO SLEEP.
CLIP n' SAVE.
• CHICAGO IN 1893 WAS THE CITY CHOSEN AS THE SITE of THE 'WORLD'S COLUMBIAN EXPOSITION', A BIG FAIR WHERE EVERYONE IN THE WORLD SHOWED UP.
THE NEXT Mornings
JIMMY'S GREAT GRANDFATHER GOES TO WORK WHERE HE IS HELPING BUILD A PLACE CALLED 'THE WHITE CITY.'
ANYWAY
JIMMY STARTS THINKING HE'D REALLY REALLY LIKE TO CALL HIS MOM AND MAYBE EVEN GO HOME, TOO
THEN
THE TELEPHONE RINGS
AND OVER THE ANSWERING MACHINE, JIMMY HEARS A GIRL SAY
HELLO DAD
THIS CONFUSES JIMMY~
AND HE GOES for A LITTLE WALK
EXCEPT
HE'S GOT A FOOT INJURY
SO HE CAN'T GO VERY FAST

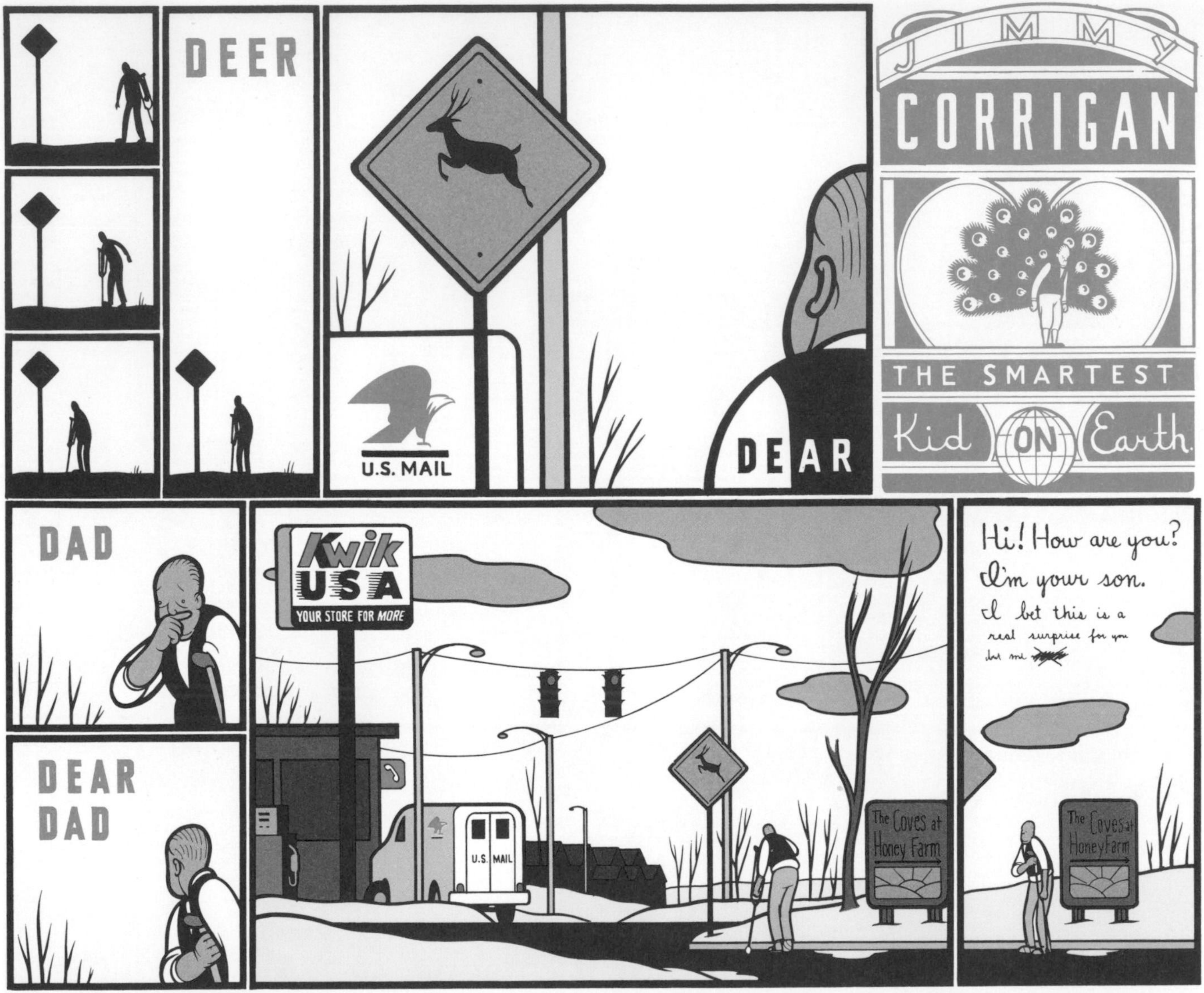
DEER
U.S. MAIL
DEAR
JIMMY
CORRIGAN
THE SMARTEST
Kid ON Earth.
DAD
DEAR
DAD
Kwik
USA
YOUR STORE FOR MORE
U.S. MAIL
The Coves at Honey Farm
Hi! How are you?
I'm your son.
I bet this is a
real surprise for you
The Coves at Honey Farm

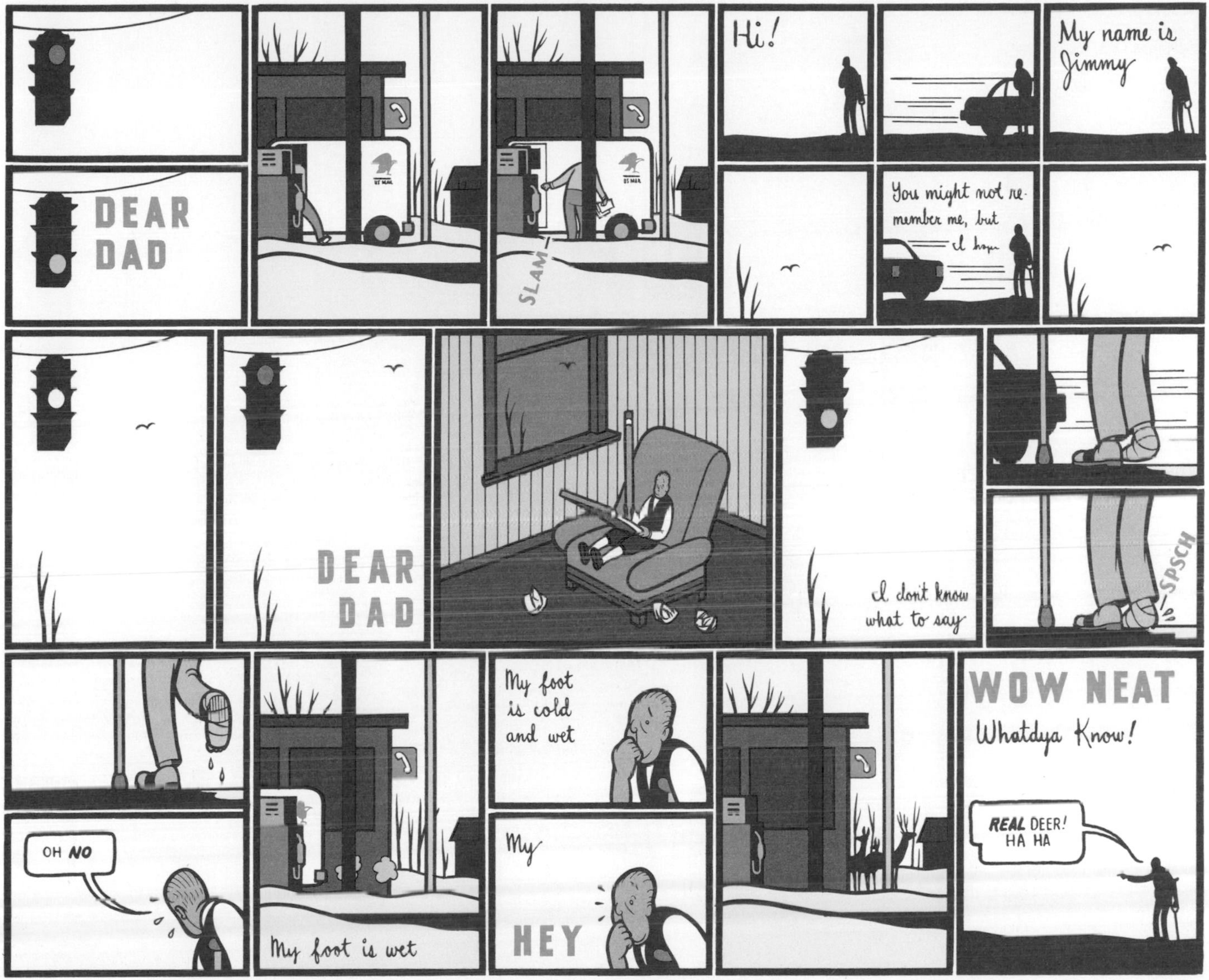

DEAR DAD
SLAM
Hi!
My name is Jimmy
You might not re-member me, but I hope
DEAR DAD
I don't know what to say
SPSCH
OH NO
My foot is wet
My foot is cold and wet
My
HEY
WOW NEAT
Whatdya Know!
REAL DEER! HA HA

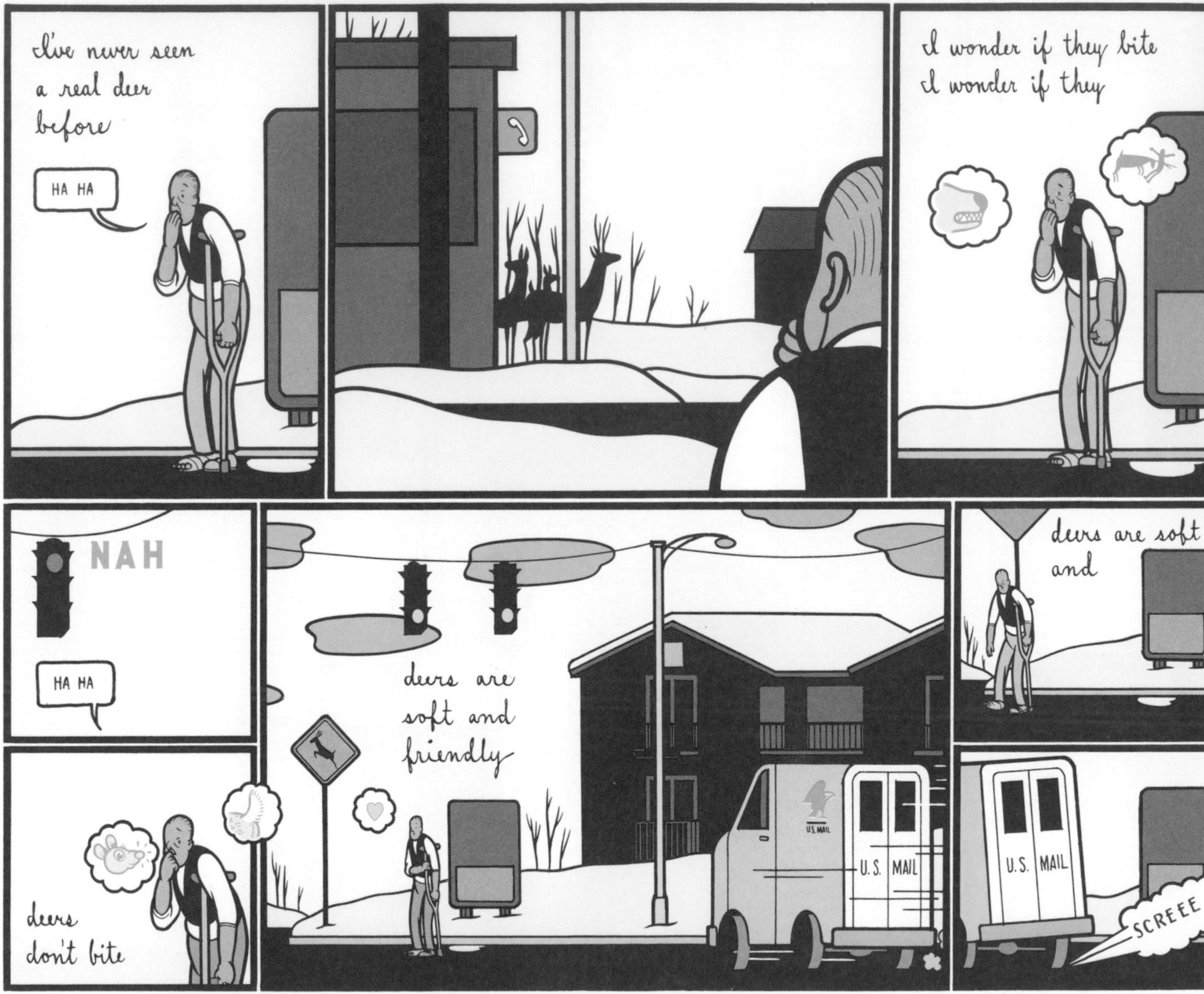

I've never seen
a real deer
before
HA HA
I wonder if they bite
I wonder if they
NAH
HA HA
deers
don't bite
deers are
soft and
friendly
U.S. MAIL
U. S. MAIL
deers are soft
and
U. S. MAIL
SCREEE

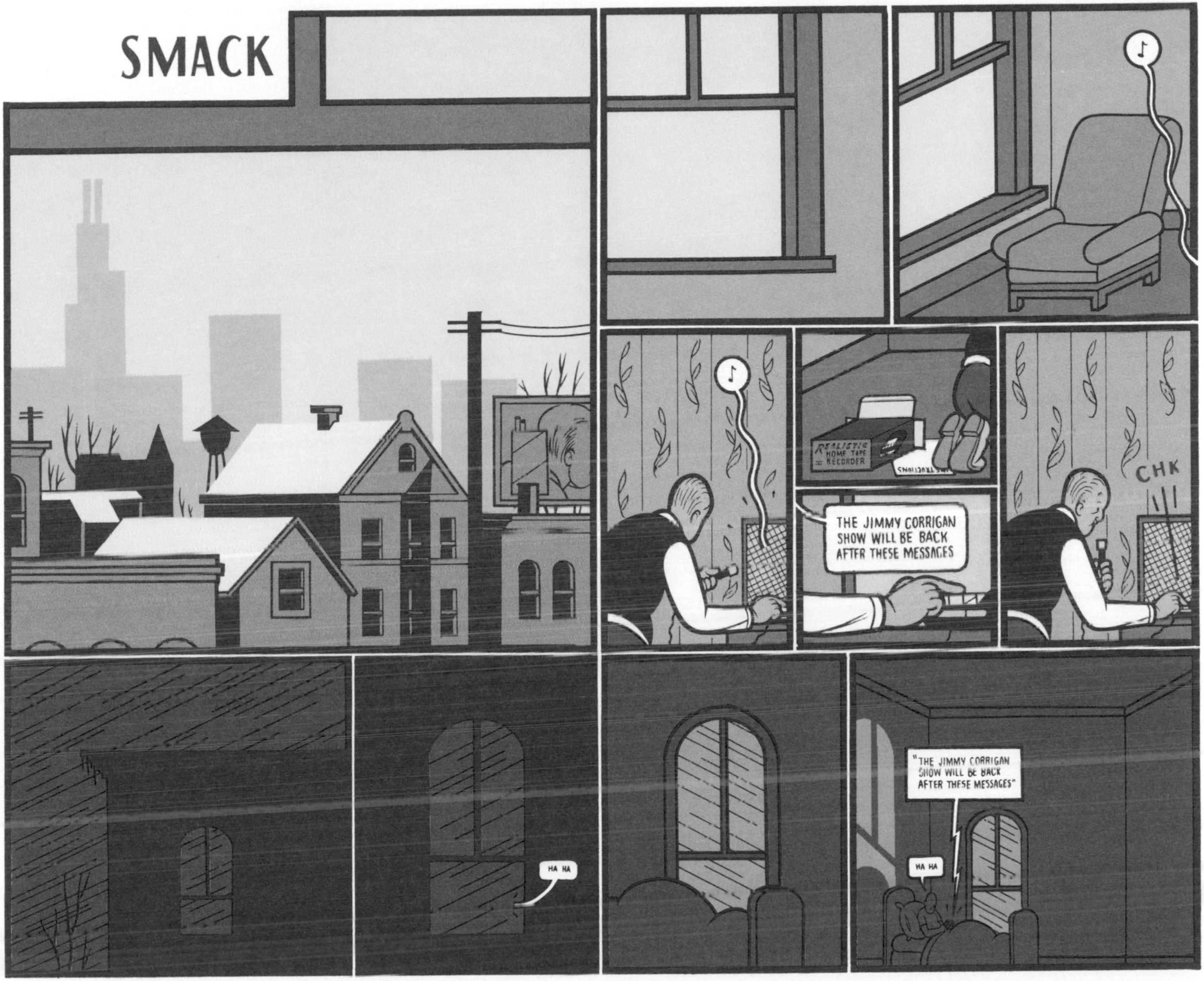
SMACK
HOME TAPE RECORDER
THE JIMMY CORRIGAN SHOW WILL BE BACK AFTER THESE MESSAGES
CHK
HA HA
"THE JIMMY CORRIGAN SHOW WILL BE BACK AFTER THESE MESSAGES"
HA HA

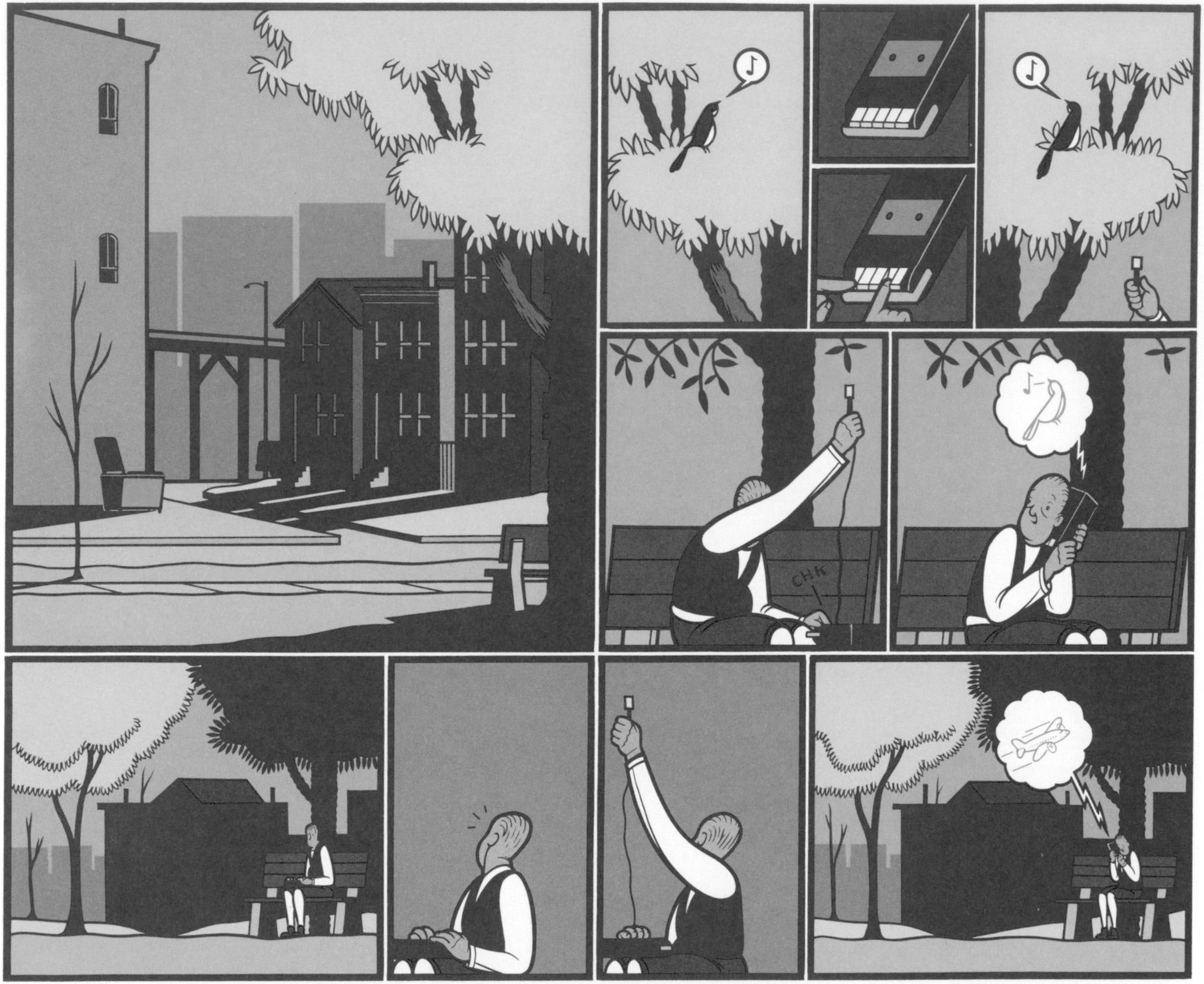
CHK

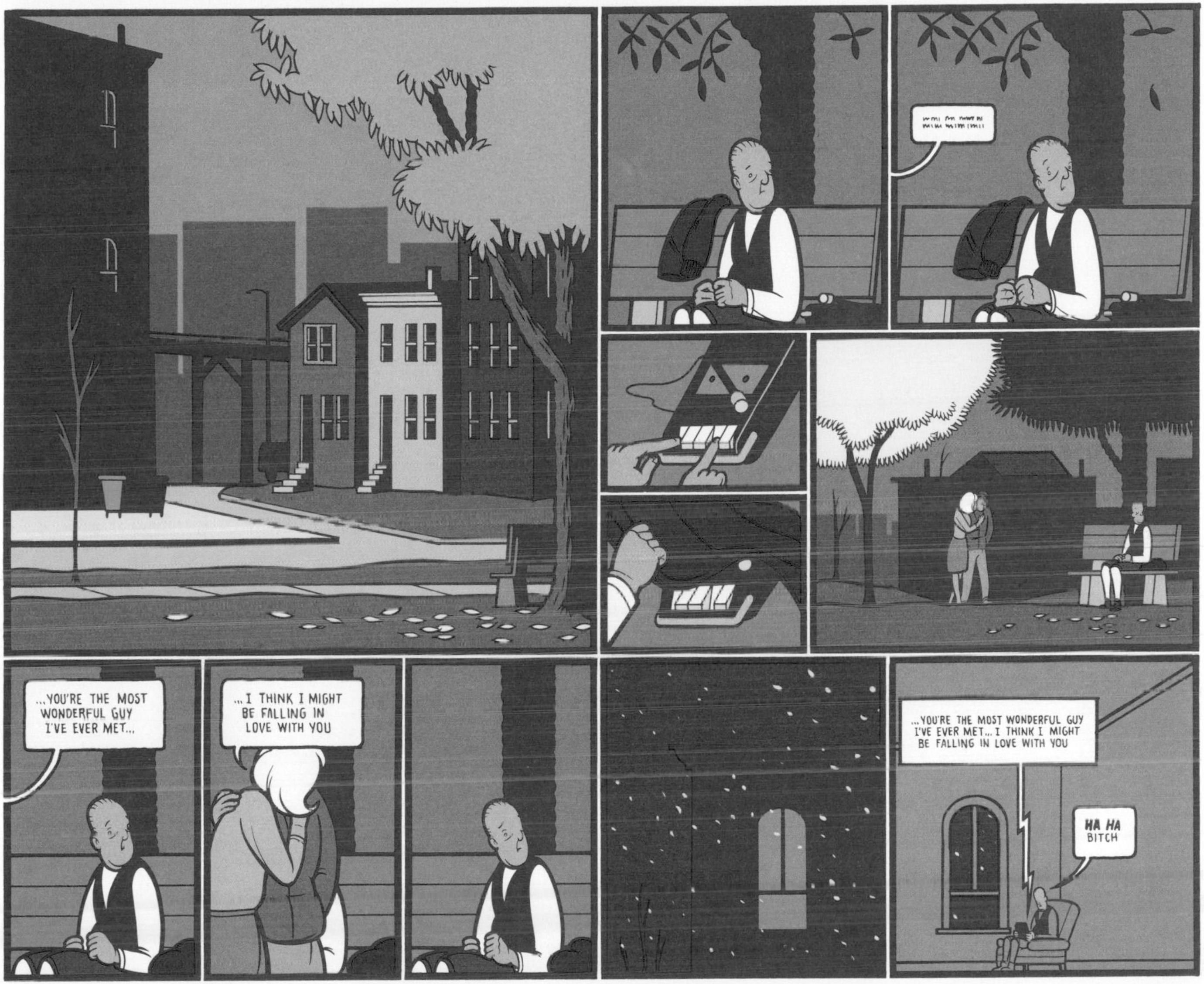
...YOU'RE THE MOST WONDERFUL GUY I'VE EVER MET...
...I THINK I MIGHT BE FALLING IN LOVE WITH YOU
...YOU'RE THE MOST WONDERFUL GUY I'VE EVER MET... I THINK I MIGHT BE FALLING IN LOVE WITH YOU
HA HA BITCH

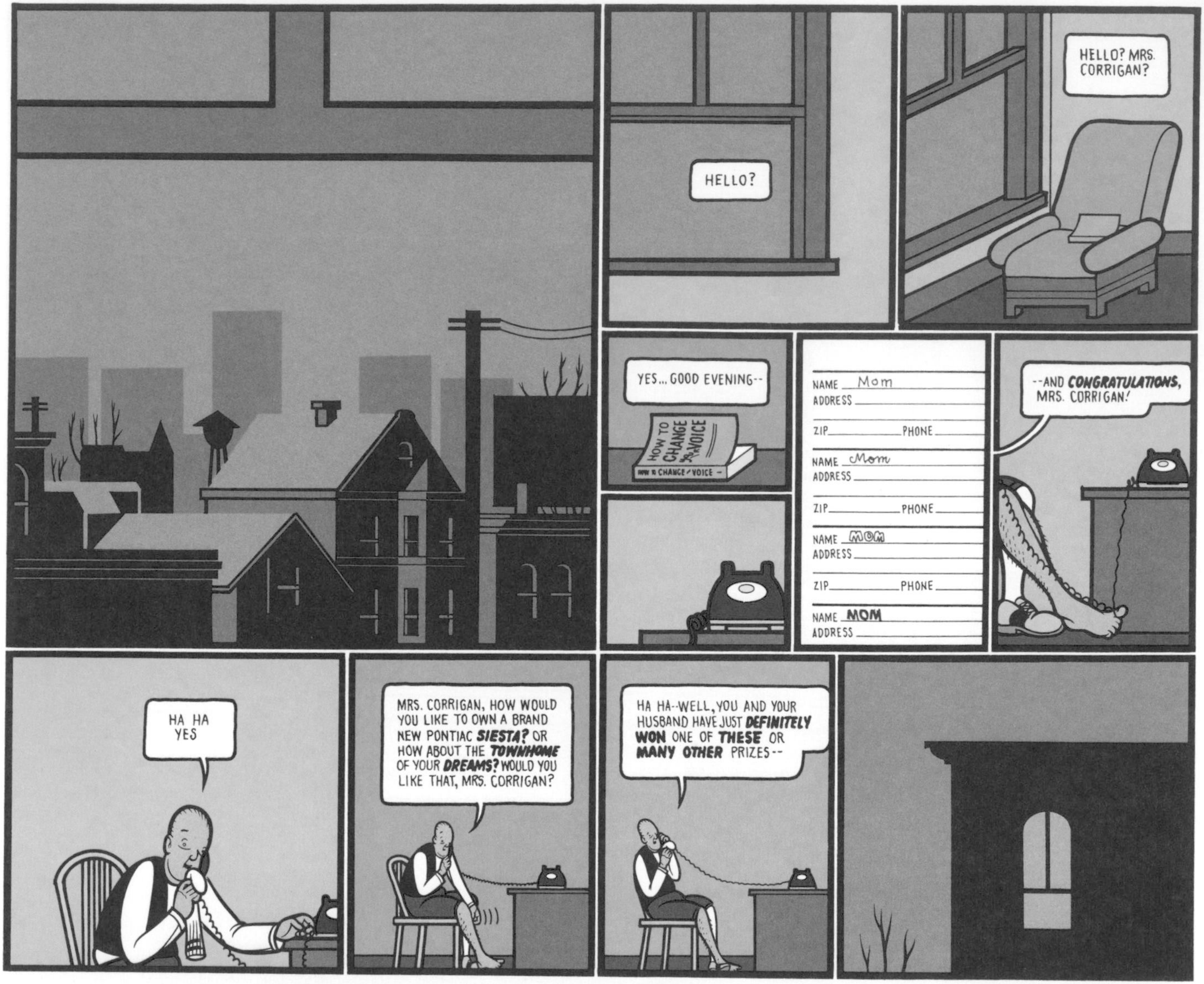
HELLO?
HELLO? MRS. CORRIGAN?
YES... GOOD EVENING--
HOW TO CHANGE YOUR VOICE
NAME Mom
ADDRESS
ZIP PHONE
NAME Mom
ADDRESS
ZIP PHONE
NAME MOM
ADDRESS
ZIP PHONE
NAME MOM
ADDRESS
--AND CONGRATULATIONS, MRS. CORRIGAN!
HA HA YES
MRS. CORRIGAN, HOW WOULD YOU LIKE TO OWN A BRAND NEW PONTIAC SIESTA? OR HOW ABOUT THE TOWNHOME OF YOUR DREAMS? WOULD YOU LIKE THAT, MRS. CORRIGAN?
HA HA--WELL, YOU AND YOUR HUSBAND HAVE JUST DEFINITELY WON ONE OF THESE OR MANY OTHER PRIZES--

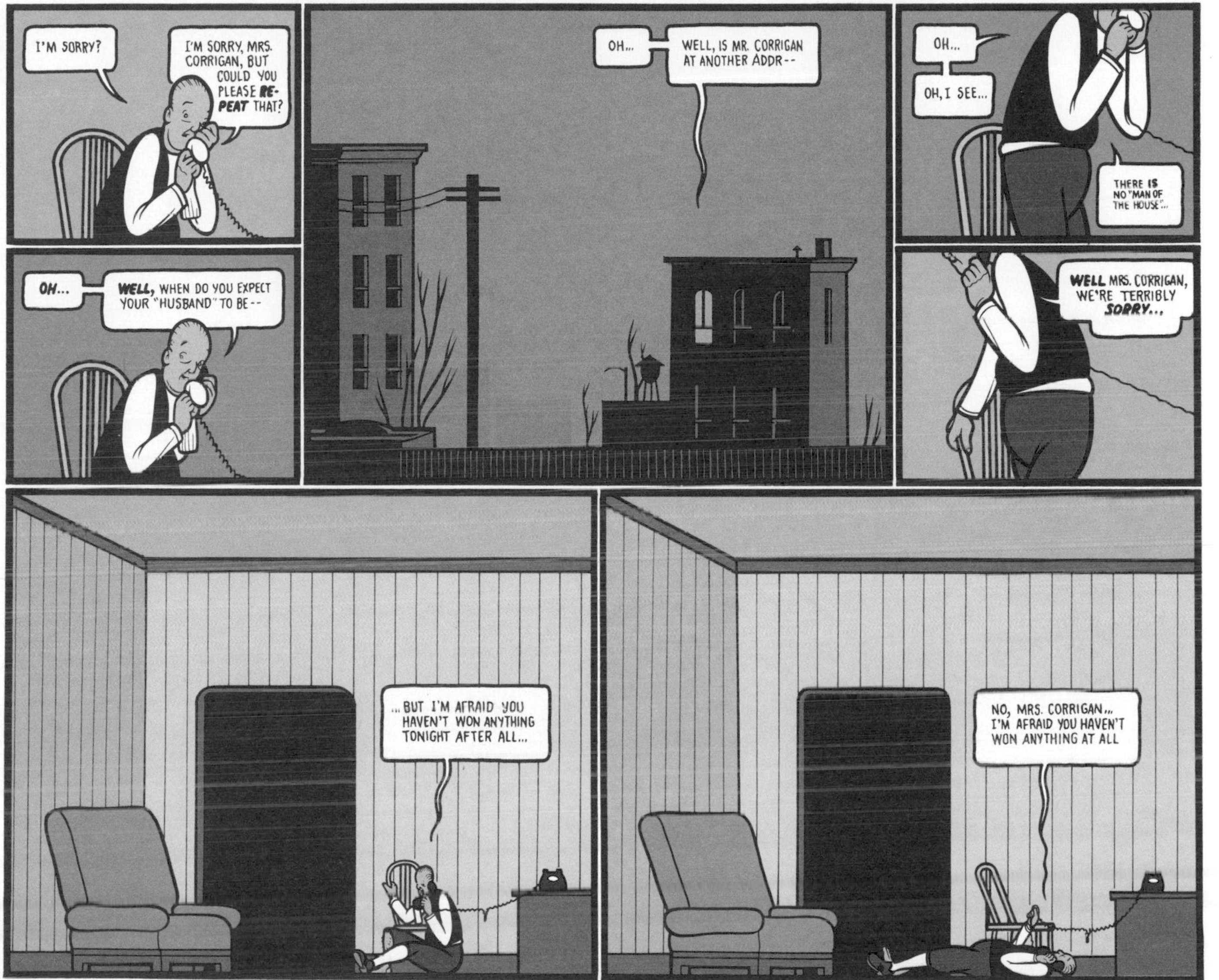
I'M SORRY?
I'M SORRY, MRS. CORRIGAN, BUT COULD YOU PLEASE RE-PEAT THAT?
OH...
WELL, WHEN DO YOU EXPECT YOUR "HUSBAND" TO BE--
OH...
WELL, IS MR. CORRIGAN AT ANOTHER ADDR--
OH...
OH, I SEE...
THERE IS NO "MAN OF THE HOUSE"...
WELL MRS. CORRIGAN, WE'RE TERRIBLY SORRY...
...BUT I'M AFRAID YOU HAVEN'T WON ANYTHING TONIGHT AFTER ALL...
NO, MRS. CORRIGAN... I'M AFRAID YOU HAVEN'T WON ANYTHING AT ALL

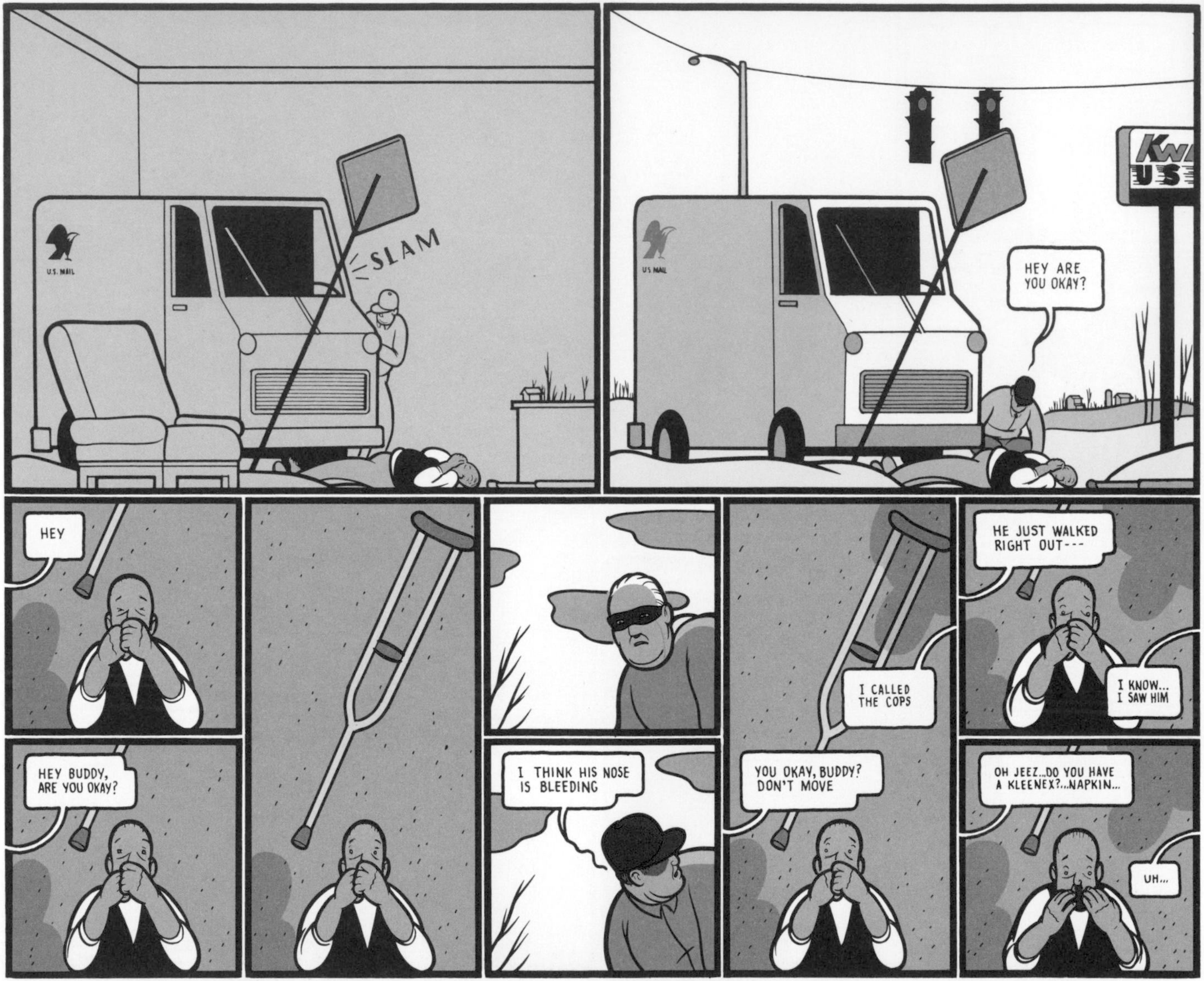
U.S. MAIL
SLAM
U.S. MAIL
HEY ARE YOU OKAY?
HEY
HEY BUDDY, ARE YOU OKAY?
I THINK HIS NOSE IS BLEEDING
I CALLED THE COPS
YOU OKAY, BUDDY? DON'T MOVE
HE JUST WALKED RIGHT OUT---
I KNOW... I SAW HIM
OH JEEZ...DO YOU HAVE A KLEENEX?...NAPKIN...
UH...

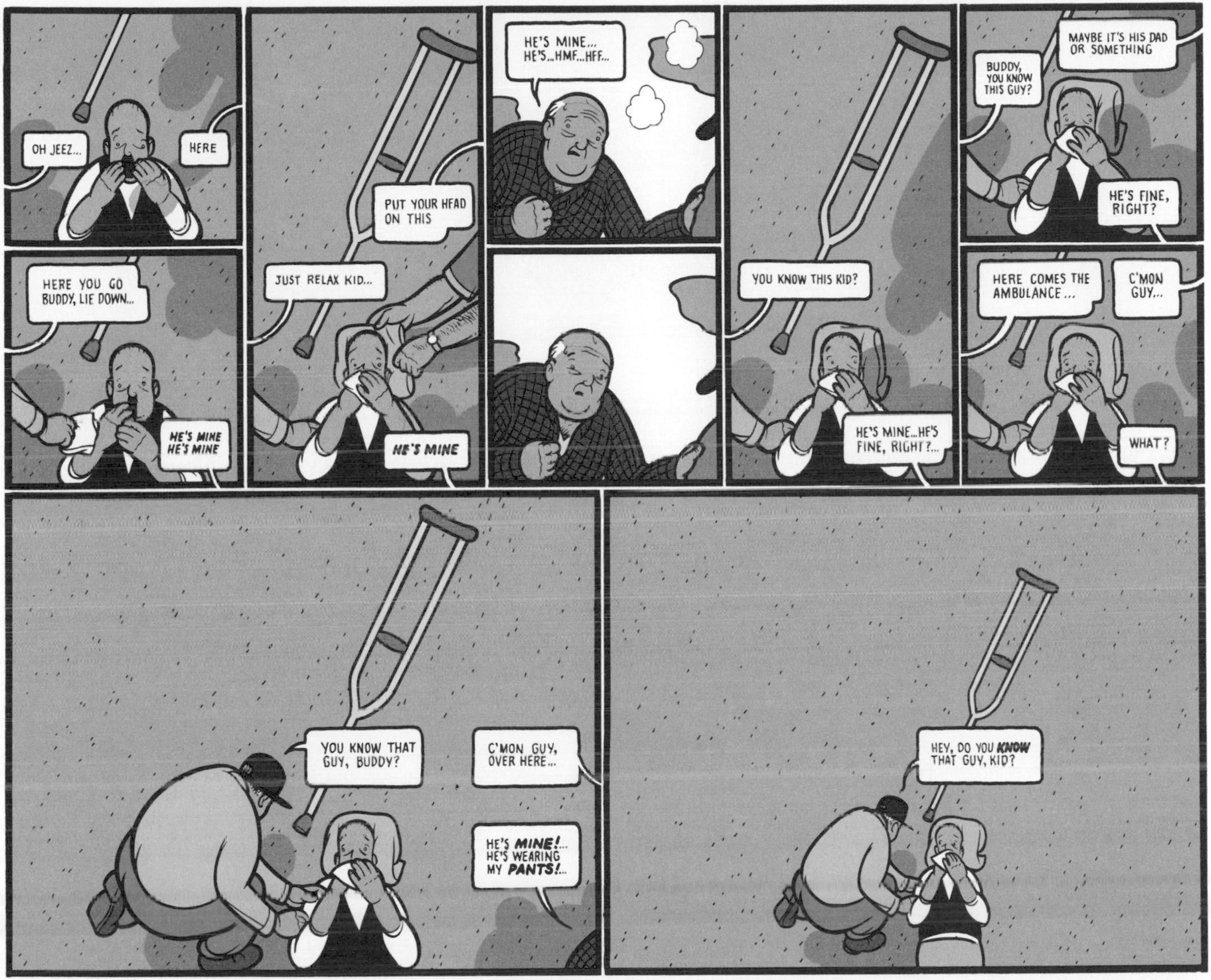
OH JEEZ...
HERE
HERE YOU GO BUDDY, LIE DOWN...
HE'S MINE HE'S MINE
PUT YOUR HEAD ON THIS
JUST RELAX KID...
HE'S MINE
HE'S MINE... HE'S...HMF...HFF...
YOU KNOW THIS KID?
HE'S MINE...HE'S FINE, RIGHT?...
MAYBE IT'S HIS DAD OR SOMETHING
BUDDY, YOU KNOW THIS GUY?
HE'S FINE, RIGHT?
HERE COMES THE AMBULANCE...
C'MON GUY...
WHAT?
YOU KNOW THAT GUY, BUDDY?
C'MON GUY, OVER HERE...
HE'S MINE!... HE'S WEARING MY PANTS!...
HEY, DO YOU KNOW THAT GUY, KID?

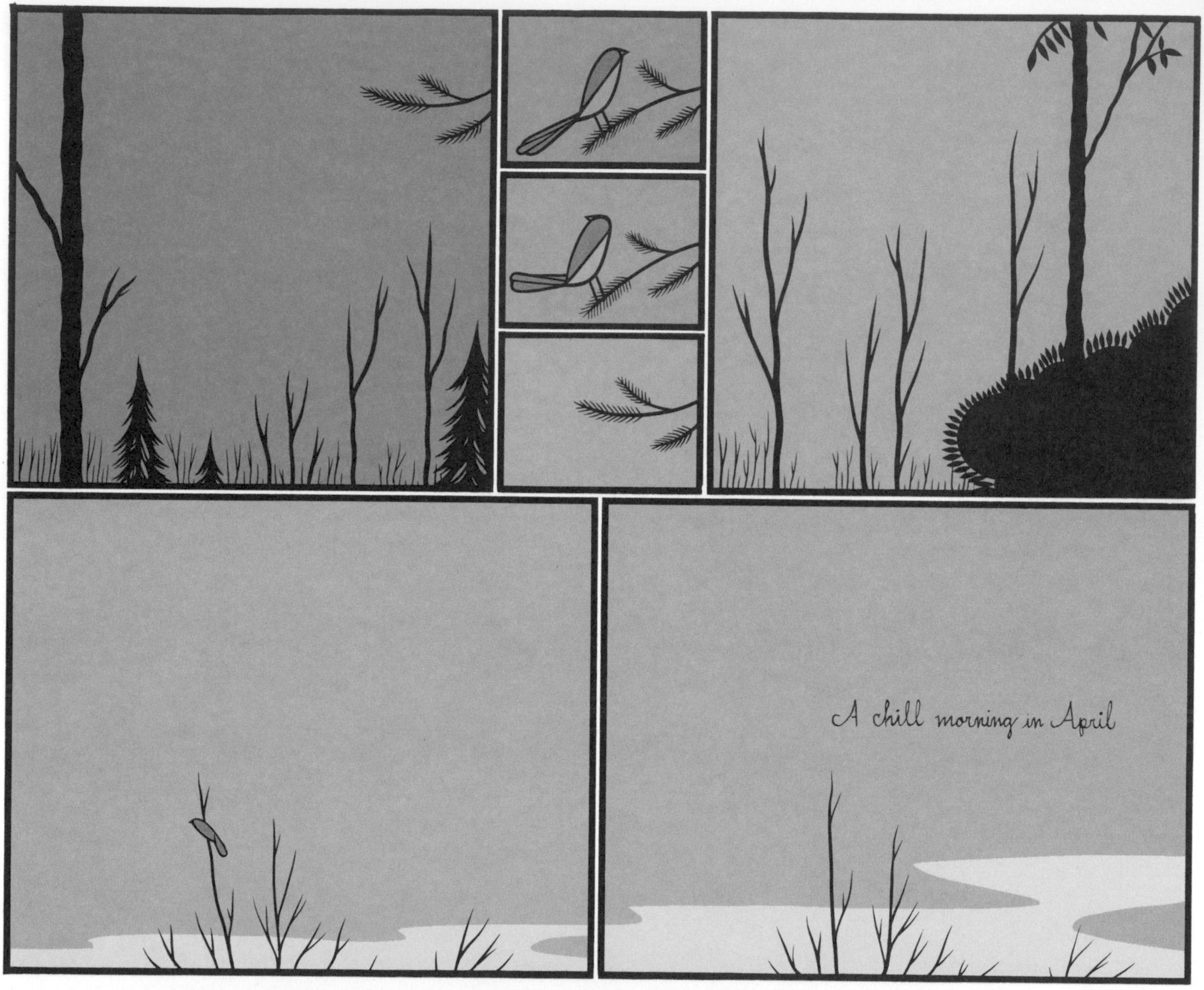
A chill morning in April

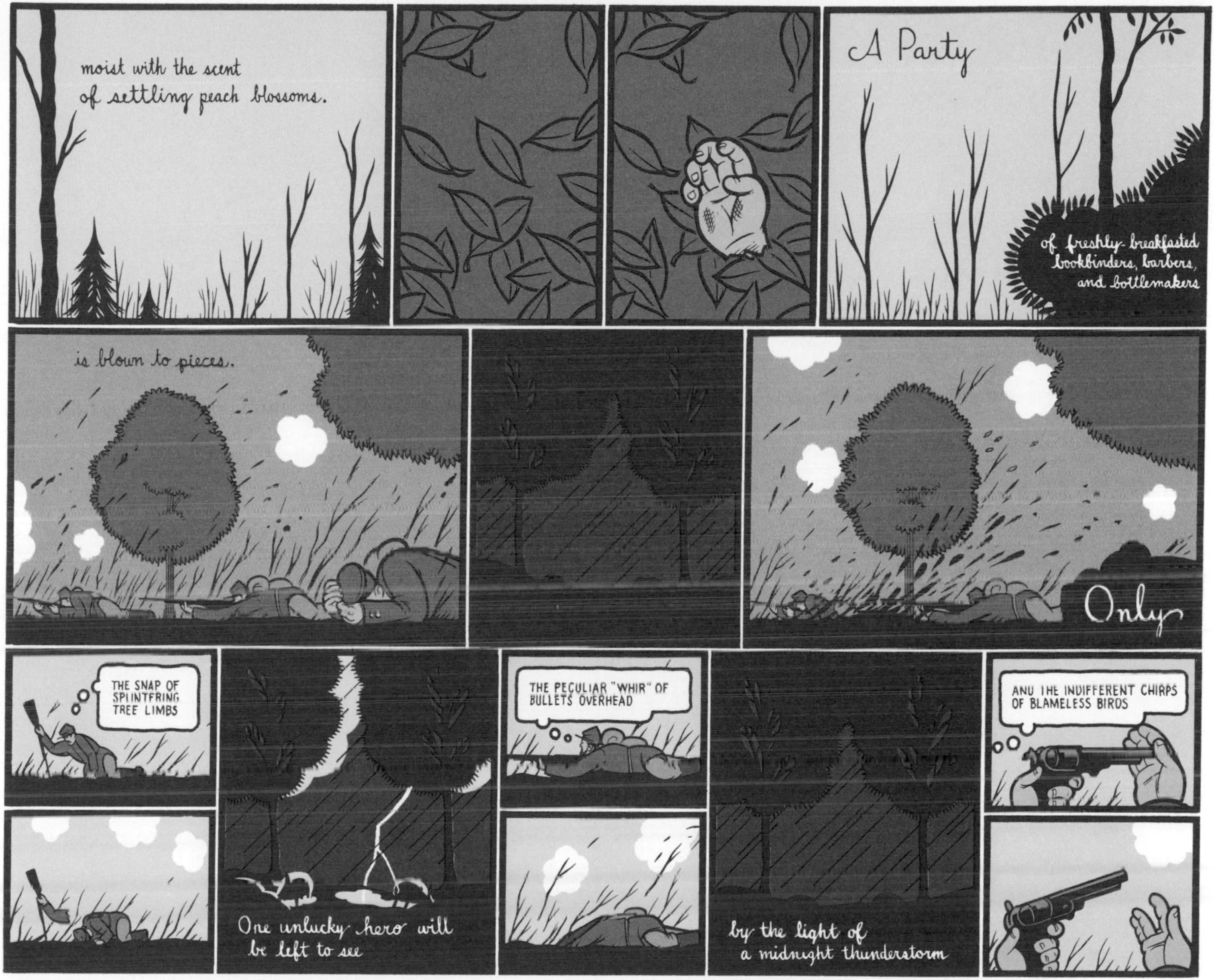
moist with the scent
of settling peach blossoms.
A Party
of freshly-breakfasted
bookbinders, barbers,
and bottlemakers
is blown to pieces.
Only
THE SNAP OF SPLINTERING TREE LIMBS
One unlucky hero will
be left to see
THE PECULIAR "WHIR" OF BULLETS OVERHEAD
by the light of
a midnight thunderstorm
AND THE INDIFFERENT CHIRPS OF BLAMELESS BIRDS

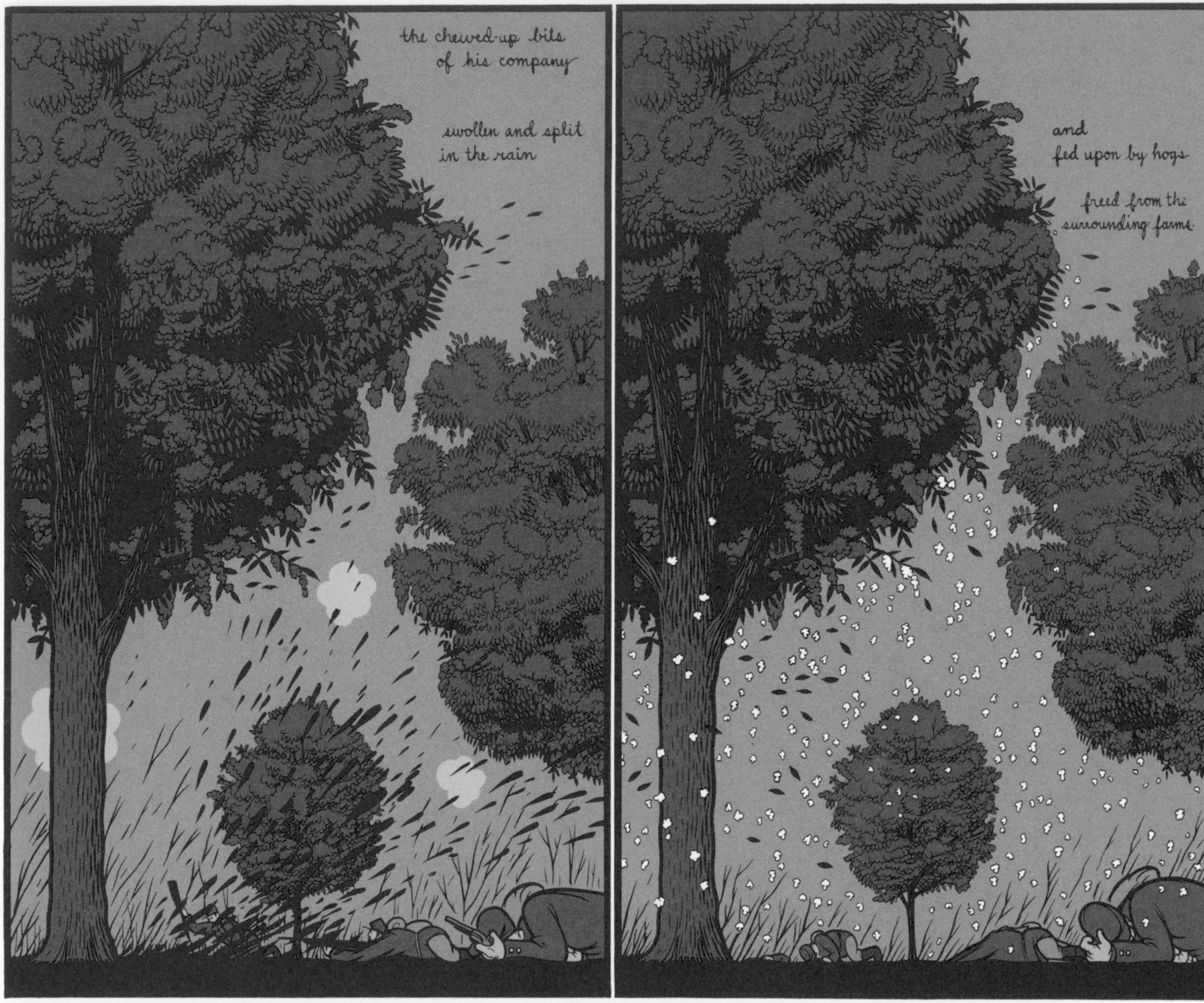
the chewed-up bits
of his company
swollen and split
in the rain
and
fed upon by hogs
freed from the
surrounding farms

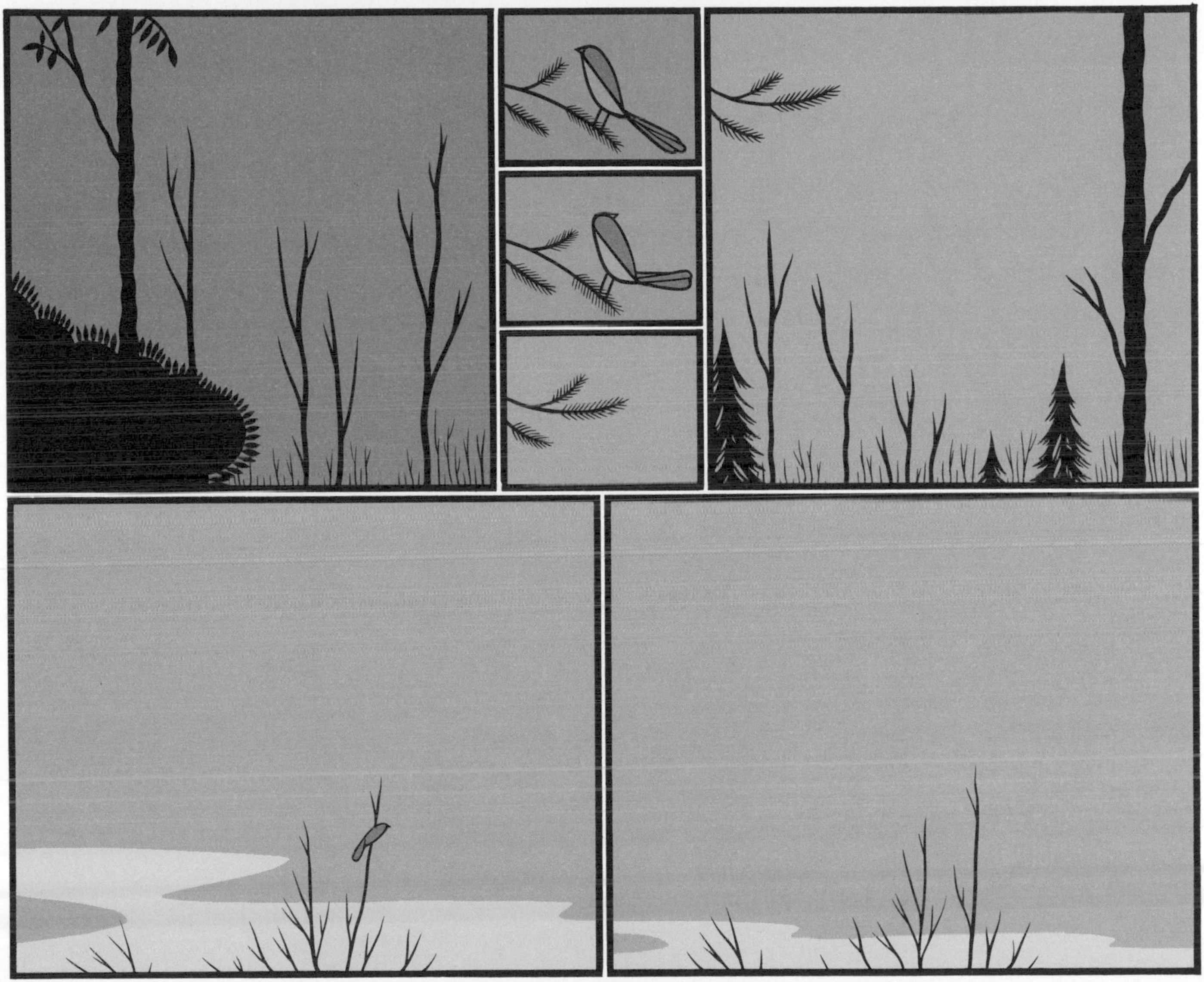

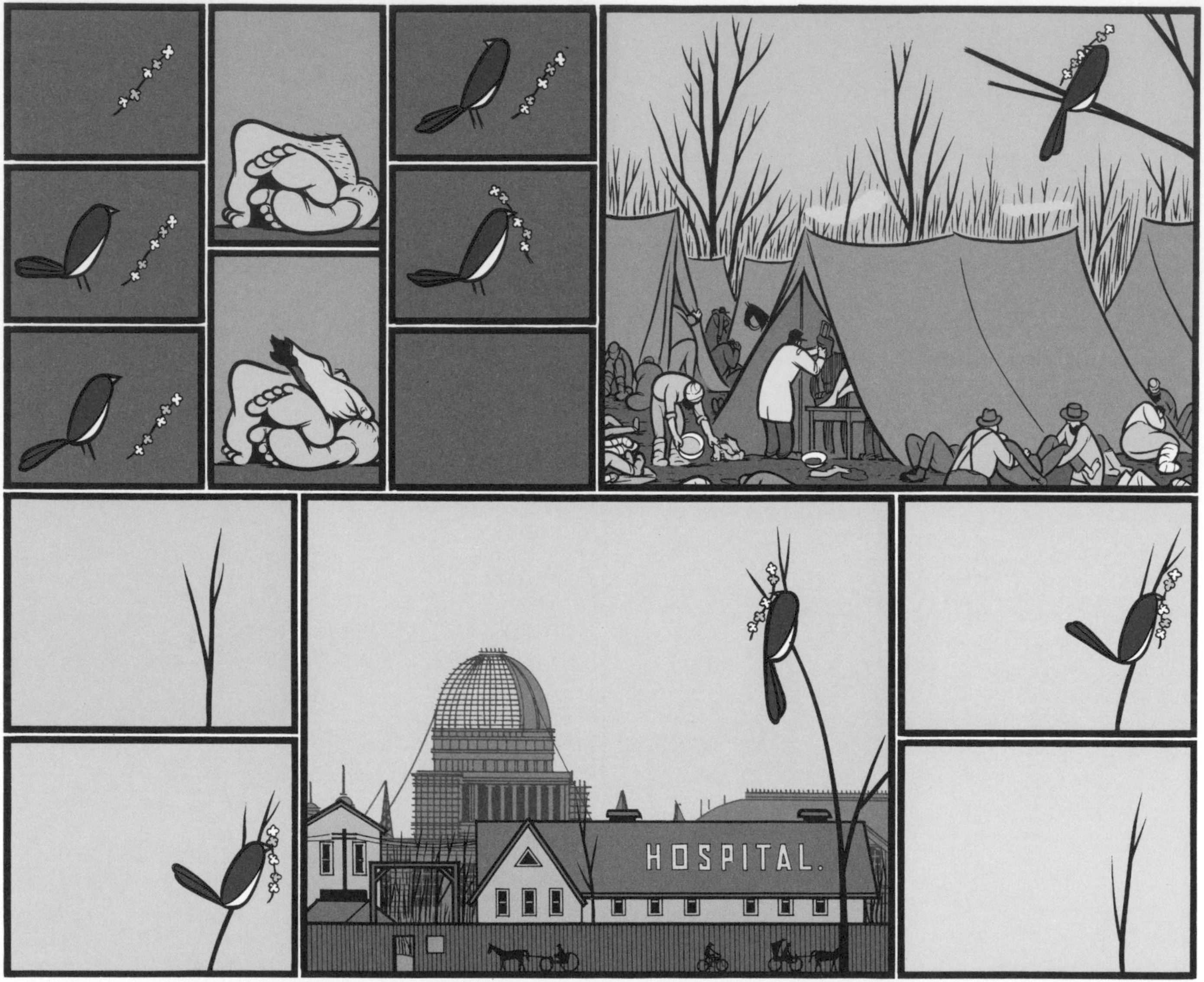
HOSPITAL.

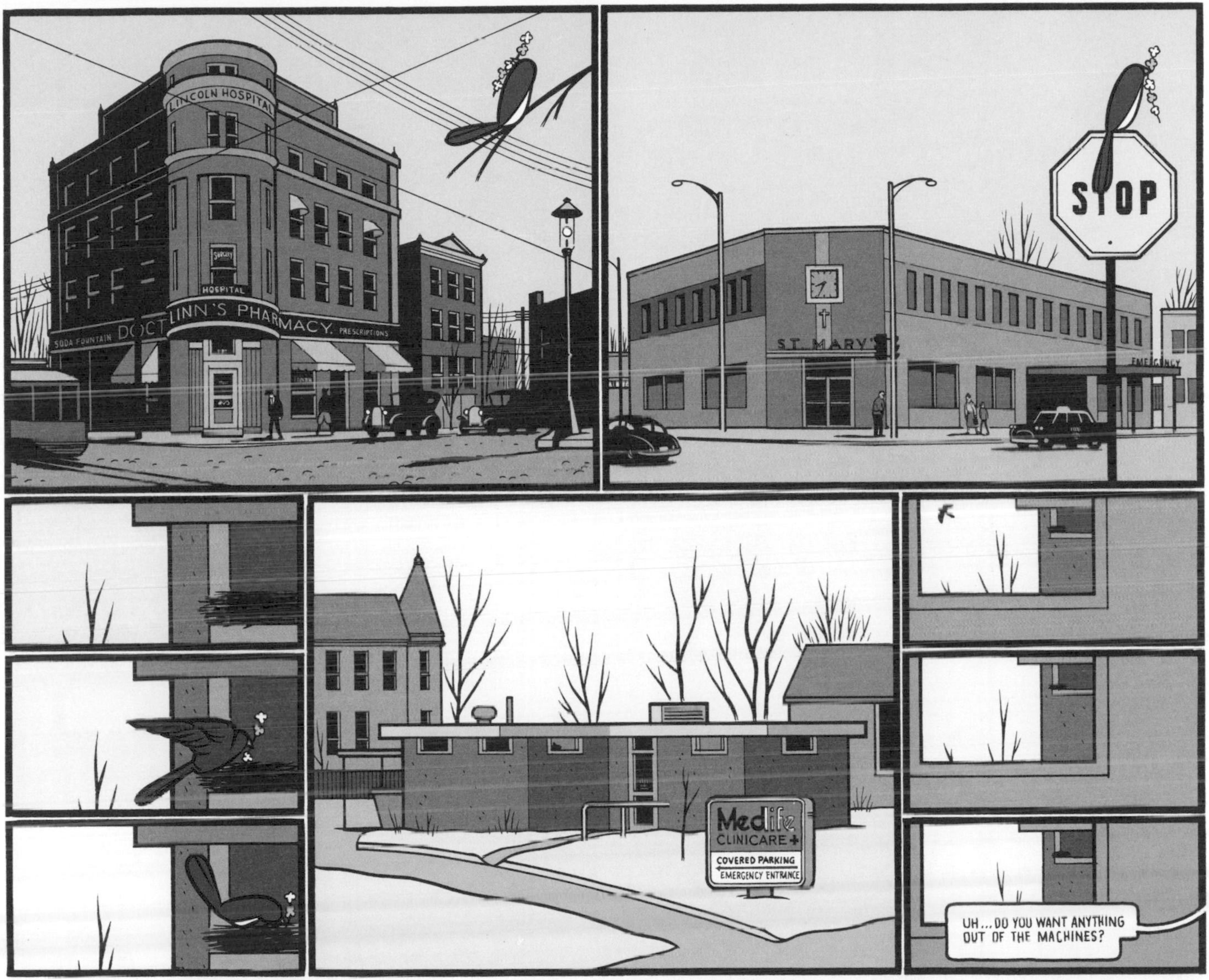
LINCOLN HOSPITAL
SURGERY
HOSPITAL
DOCT LINN'S PHARMACY.
SODA FOUNTAIN
PRESCRIPTIONS
STOP
ST. MARY'S
EMERGENCY
Medlife CLINICARE+
COVERED PARKING
EMERGENCY ENTRANCE
UH... DO YOU WANT ANYTHING OUT OF THE MACHINES?

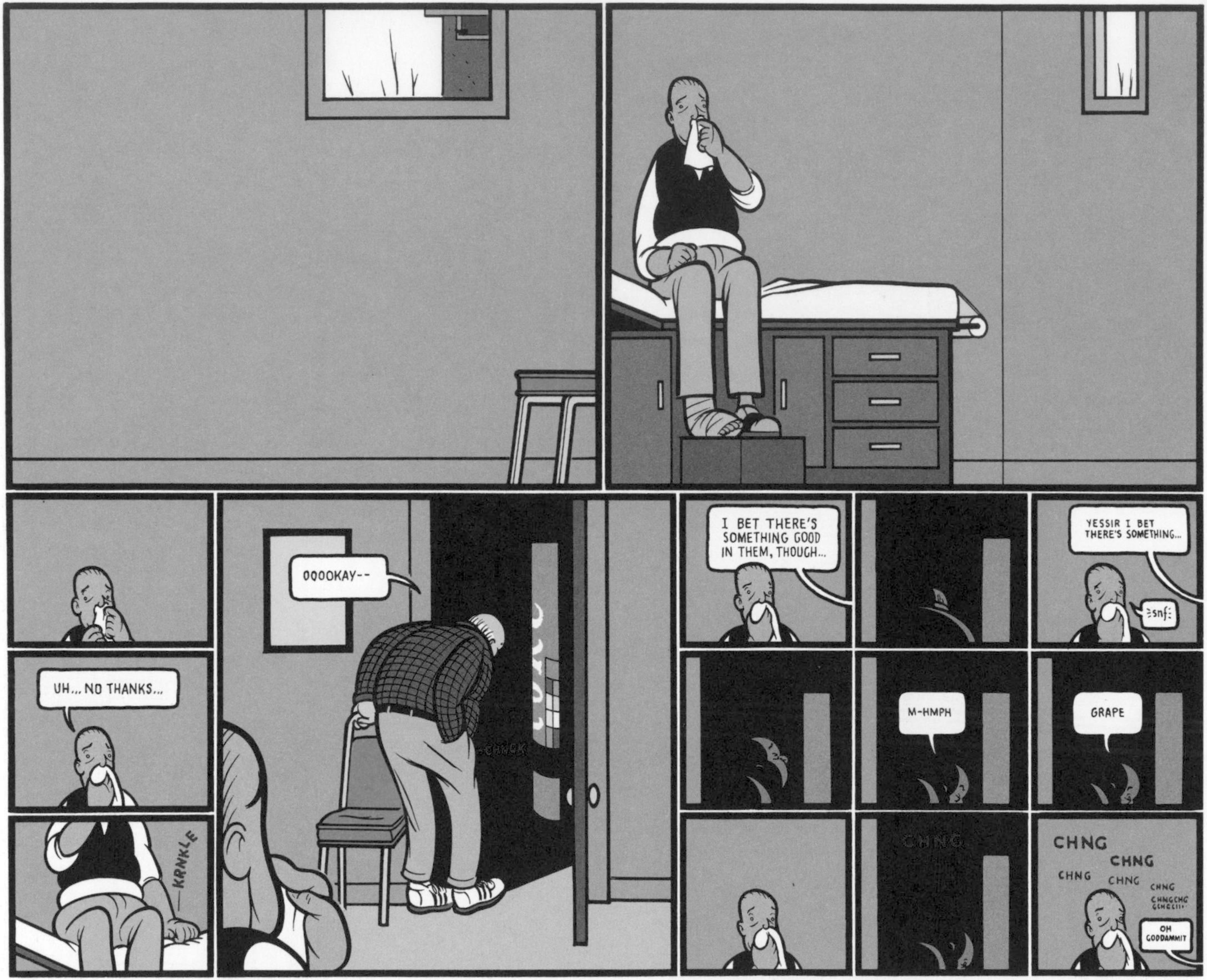
UH... NO THANKS...
KRNKLE
OOOOKAY--
I BET THERE'S SOMETHING GOOD IN THEM, THOUGH...
YESSIR I BET THERE'S SOMETHING...
snf
M-HMPH
GRAPE
CHNG
CHNG
CHNG
CHNG
CHNG
CHNG
CHNGCHG
OH GODDAMMIT

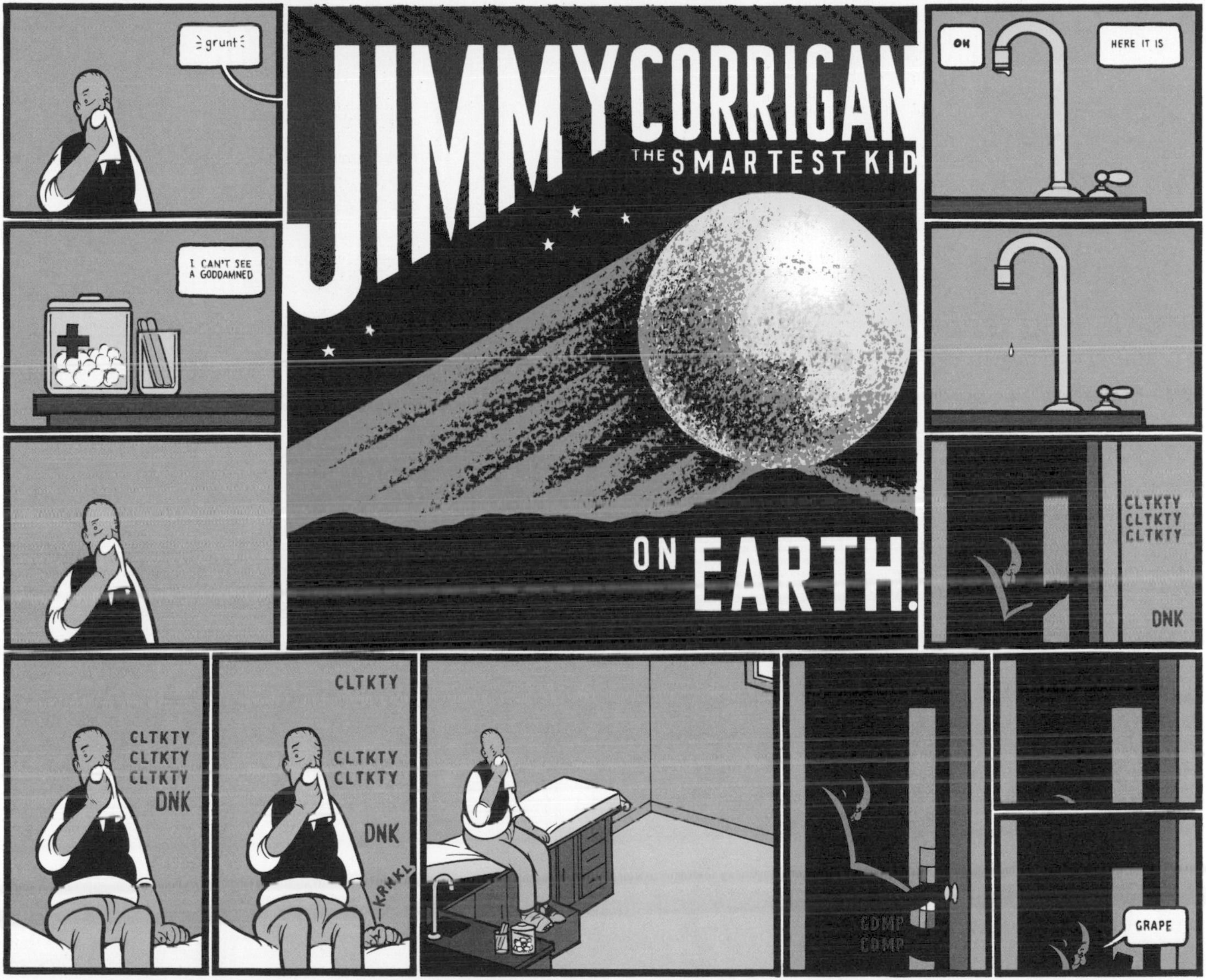
grunt
I CAN'T SEE A GODDAMNED
JIMMY CORRIGAN
THE SMARTEST KID
ON EARTH.
OH
HERE IT IS
CLTKTY CLTKTY CLTKTY
DNK
CLTKTY CLTKTY CLTKTY
DNK
CLTKTY
CLTKTY CLTKTY
DNK
KRNKL
COMP COMP
GRAPE

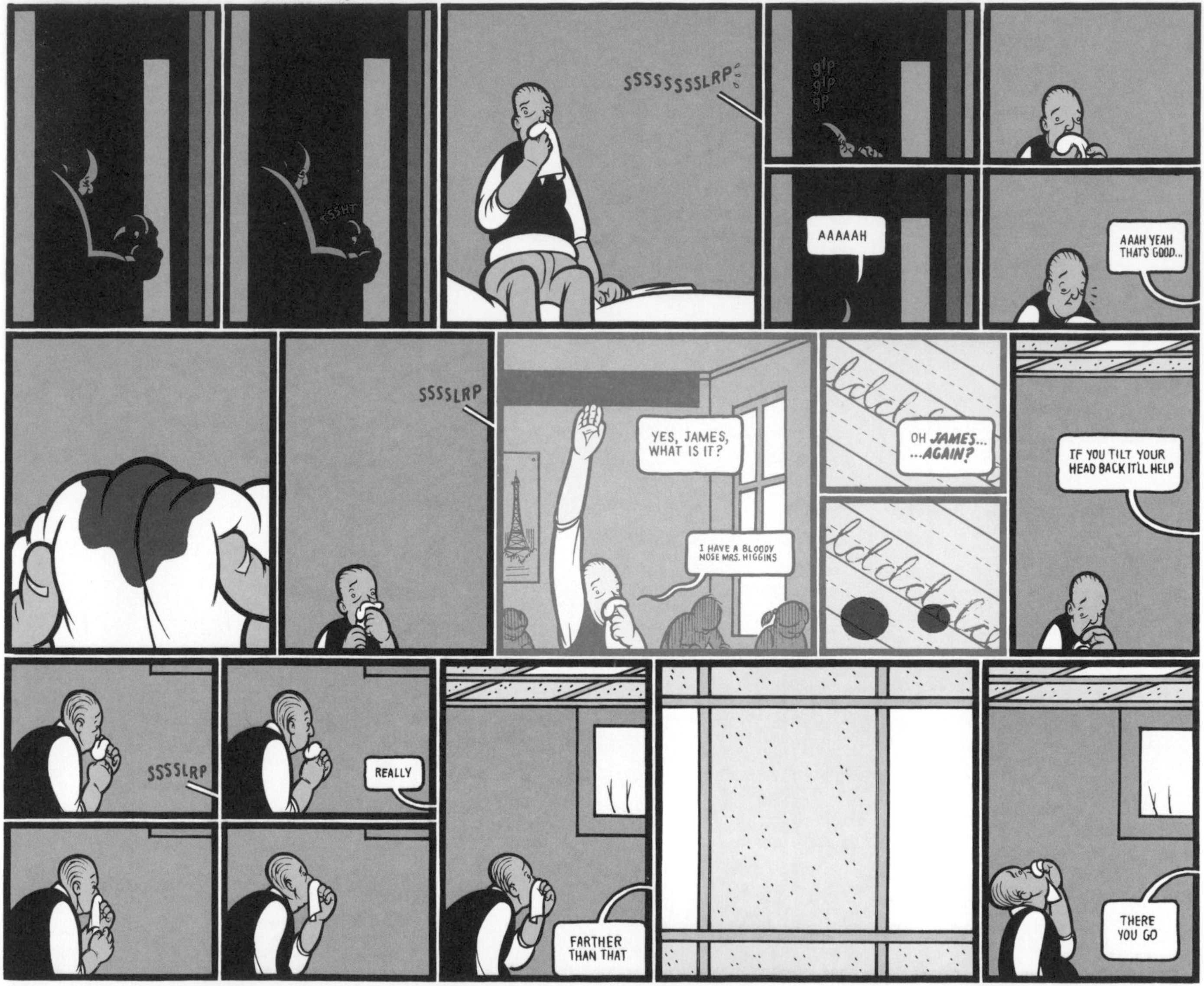
SSSSSSSSLRP
glp
glp
gp
AAAAAH
AAAH YEAH THAT'S GOOD...
SSSSLRP
YES, JAMES, WHAT IS IT?
I HAVE A BLOODY NOSE MRS. HIGGINS
OH JAMES... ...AGAIN?
IF YOU TILT YOUR HEAD BACK IT'LL HELP
SSSSLRP
REALLY
FARTHER THAN THAT
THERE YOU GO

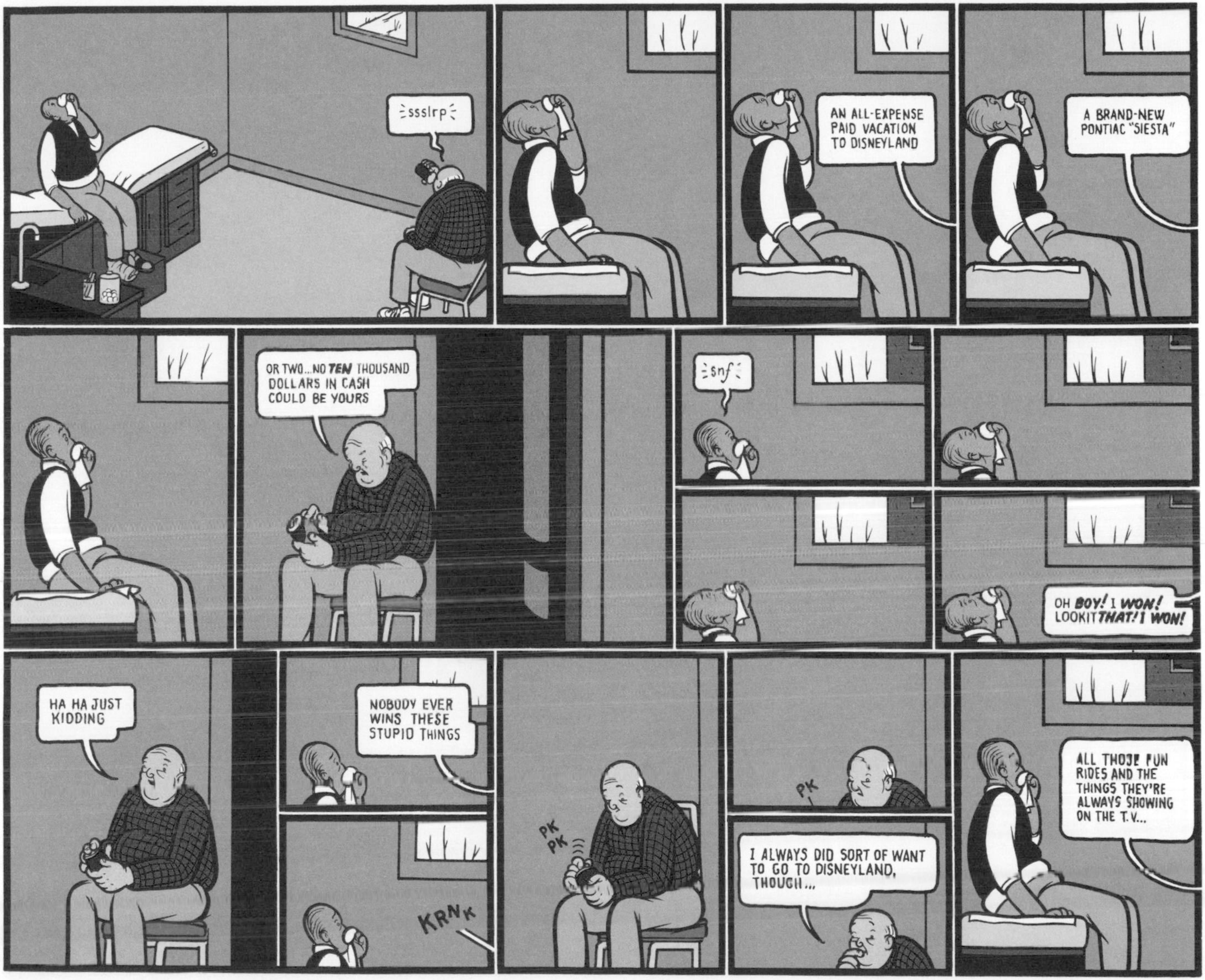
sssIrp
AN ALL-EXPENSE PAID VACATION TO DISNEYLAND
A BRAND-NEW PONTIAC "SIESTA"
OR TWO...NO TEN THOUSAND DOLLARS IN CASH COULD BE YOURS
snf
OH BOY! I WON! LOOKIT THAT! I WON!
HA HA JUST KIDDING
NOBODY EVER WINS THESE STUPID THINGS
KRNK
PK PK
PK
I ALWAYS DID SORT OF WANT TO GO TO DISNEYLAND, THOUGH...
ALL THOSE FUN RIDES AND THE THINGS THEY'RE ALWAYS SHOWING ON THE T.V...

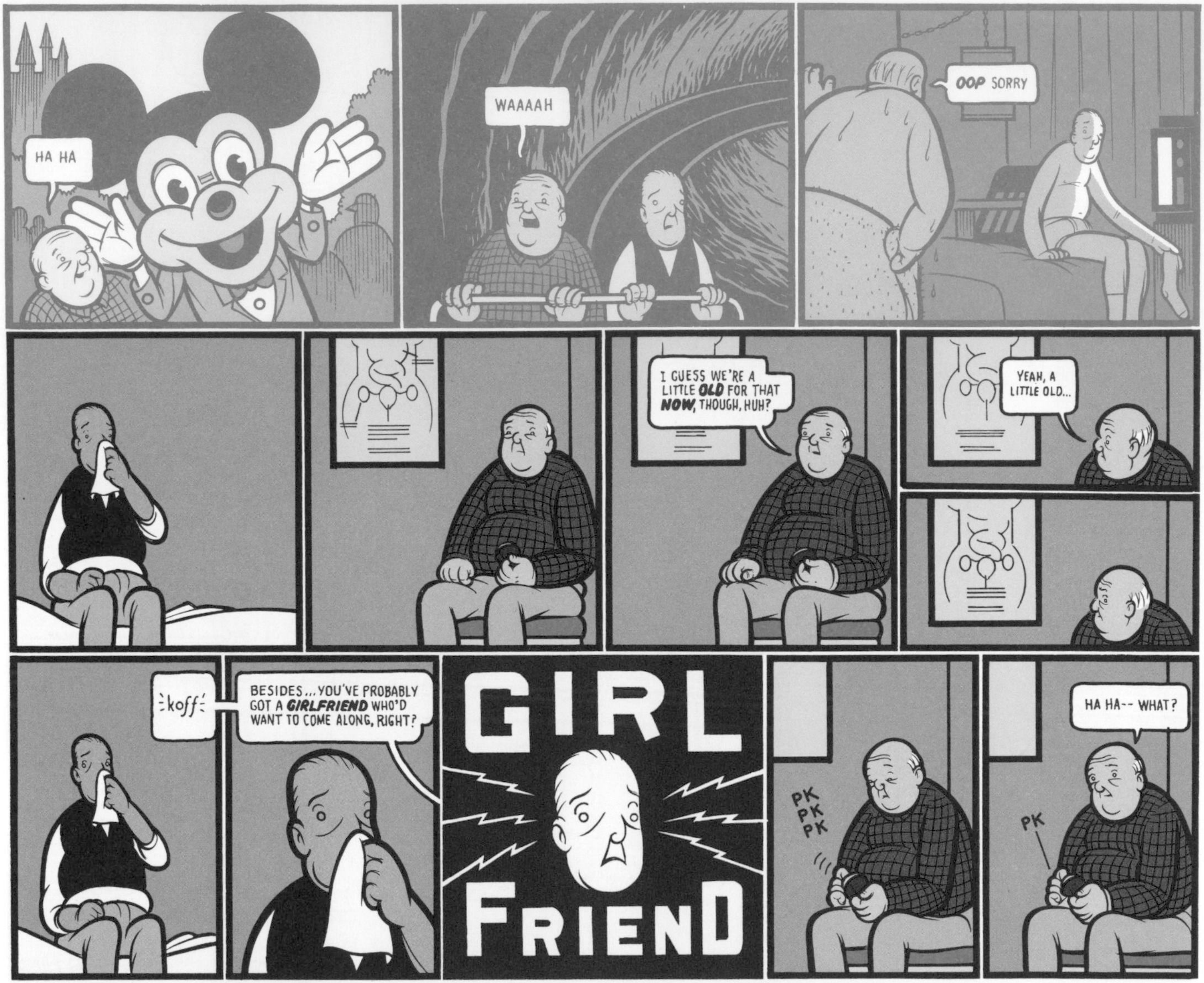
HA HA
WAAAAH
OOP SORRY
I GUESS WE'RE A LITTLE **OLD** FOR THAT **NOW**, THOUGH, HUH?
YEAH, A LITTLE OLD...
koff
BESIDES... YOU'VE PROBABLY GOT A **GIRLFRIEND** WHO'D WANT TO COME ALONG, RIGHT?
GIRL FRIEND
PK PK PK
PK
HA HA-- WHAT?

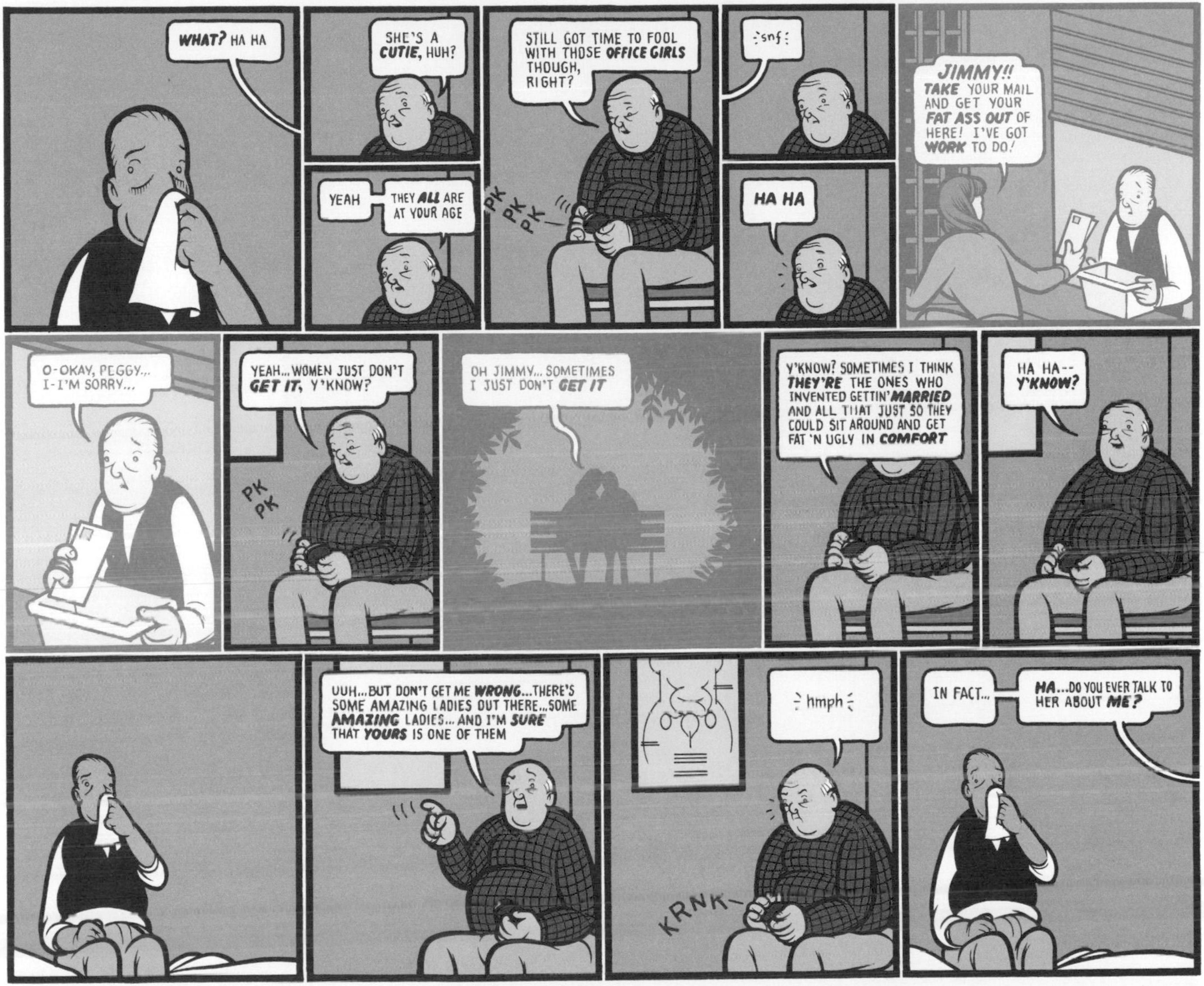
WHAT? HA HA
SHE'S A CUTIE, HUH?
YEAH
THEY ALL ARE AT YOUR AGE
STILL GOT TIME TO FOOL WITH THOSE OFFICE GIRLS THOUGH, RIGHT?
PK PK PK
snf
HA HA
JIMMY!! TAKE YOUR MAIL AND GET YOUR FAT ASS OUT OF HERE! I'VE GOT WORK TO DO!
O-OKAY, PEGGY... I-I'M SORRY...
YEAH... WOMEN JUST DON'T GET IT, Y'KNOW?
PK PK
OH JIMMY... SOMETIMES I JUST DON'T GET IT
Y'KNOW? SOMETIMES I THINK THEY'RE THE ONES WHO INVENTED GETTIN' MARRIED AND ALL THAT JUST SO THEY COULD SIT AROUND AND GET FAT 'N UGLY IN COMFORT
HA HA-- Y'KNOW?
UUH... BUT DON'T GET ME WRONG... THERE'S SOME AMAZING LADIES OUT THERE... SOME AMAZING LADIES... AND I'M SURE THAT YOURS IS ONE OF THEM
hmph
KRNK-
IN FACT...
HA... DO YOU EVER TALK TO HER ABOUT ME?

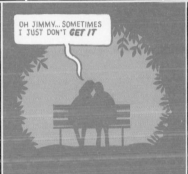

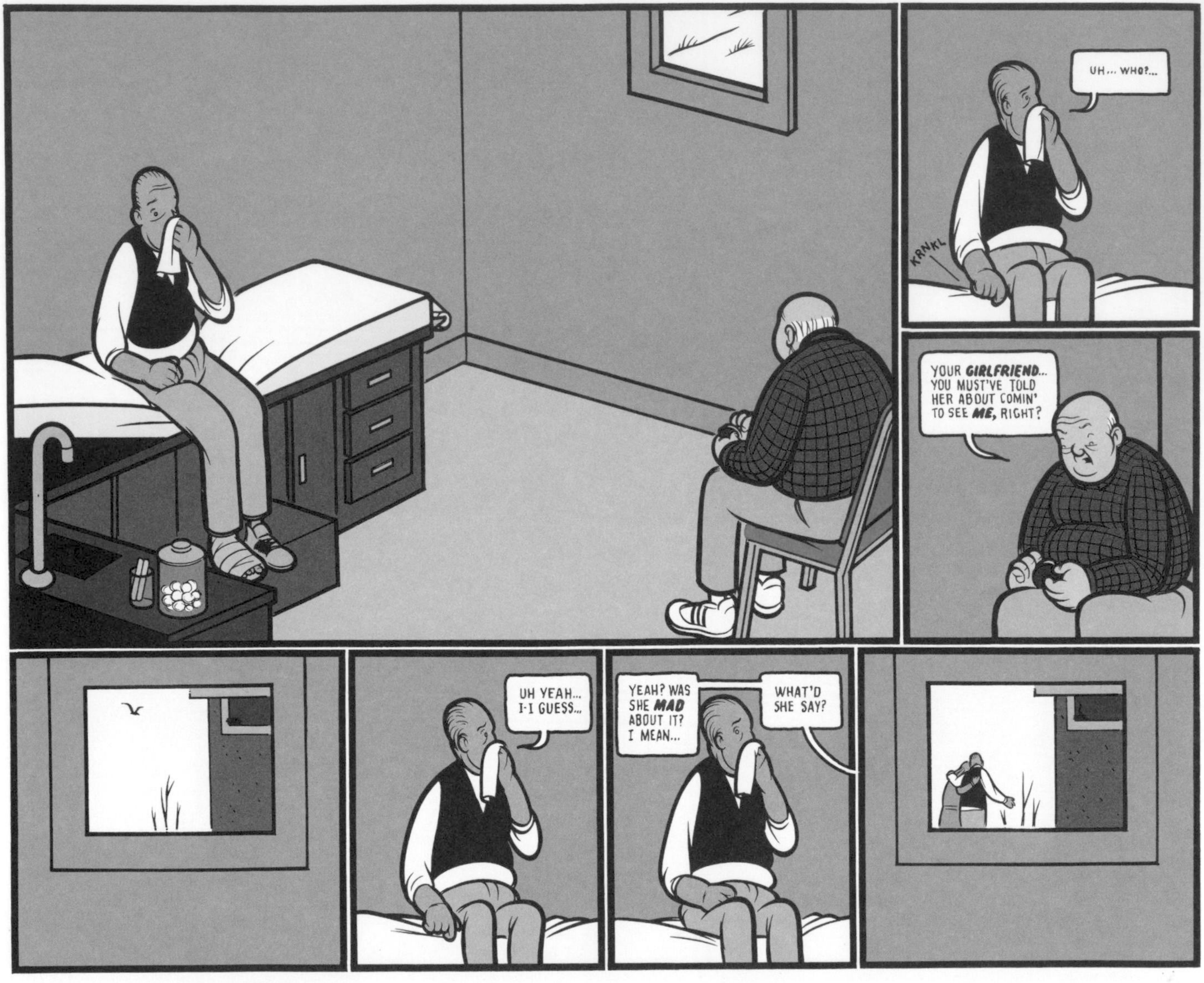
UH... WHO?...
KRNKL
YOUR GIRLFRIEND... YOU MUST'VE TOLD HER ABOUT COMIN' TO SEE ME, RIGHT?
UH YEAH... I-I GUESS...
YEAH? WAS SHE MAD ABOUT IT? I MEAN...
WHAT'D SHE SAY?

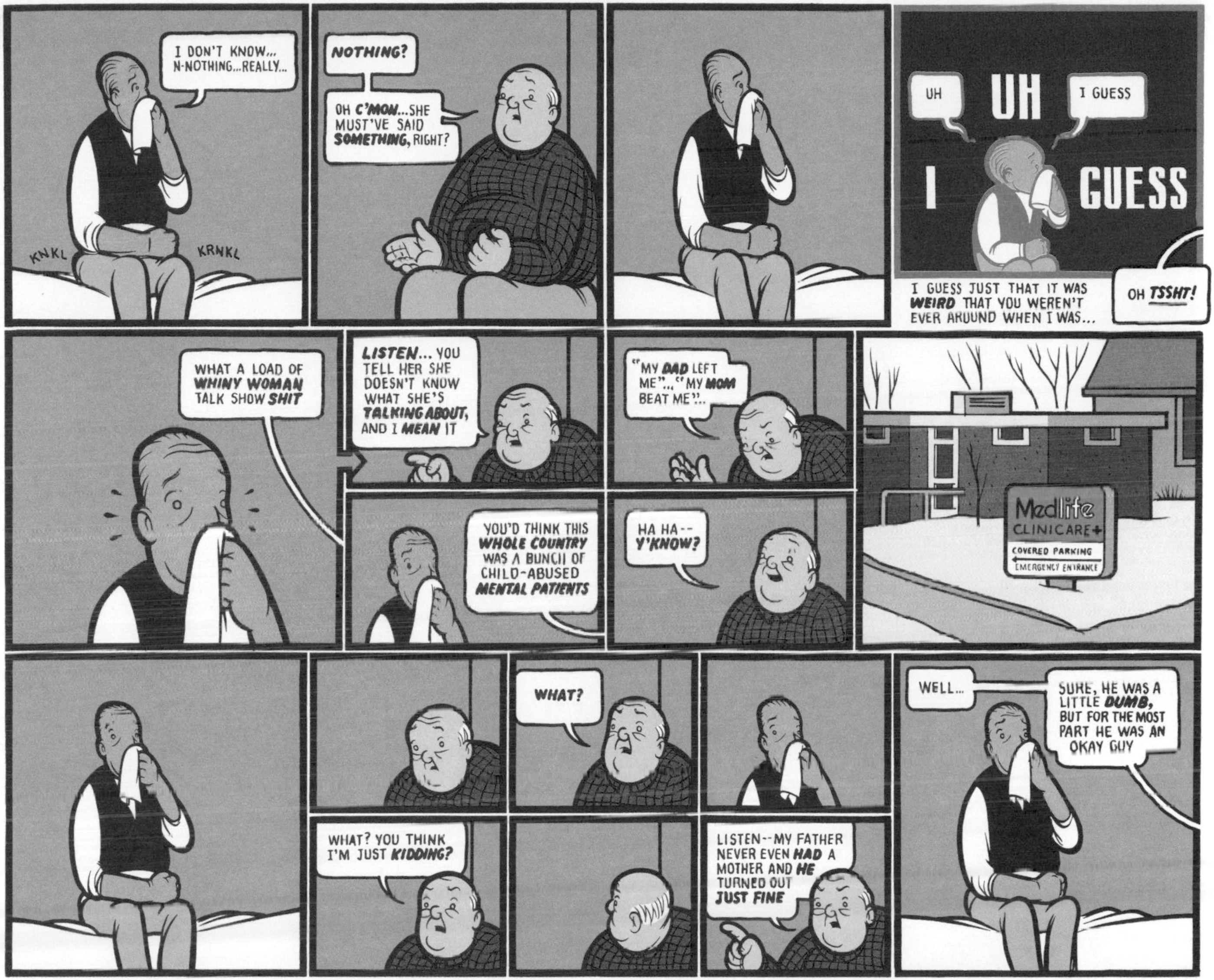
I DON'T KNOW... N-NOTHING...REALLY...
KNKL
KRNKL
NOTHING?
OH C'MON...SHE MUST'VE SAID SOMETHING, RIGHT?
UH
UH
I GUESS
I
GUESS
I GUESS JUST THAT IT WAS WEIRD THAT YOU WEREN'T EVER AROUND WHEN I WAS...
OH TSSHT!
WHAT A LOAD OF WHINY WOMAN TALK SHOW SHIT
LISTEN... YOU TELL HER SHE DOESN'T KNOW WHAT SHE'S TALKING ABOUT, AND I MEAN IT
"MY DAD LEFT ME"... "MY MOM BEAT ME"...
YOU'D THINK THIS WHOLE COUNTRY WAS A BUNCH OF CHILD-ABUSED MENTAL PATIENTS
HA HA-- Y'KNOW?
Medlife CLINICARE+
COVERED PARKING
EMERGENCY ENTRANCE
WHAT?
WHAT? YOU THINK I'M JUST KIDDING?
LISTEN--MY FATHER NEVER EVEN HAD A MOTHER AND HE TURNED OUT JUST FINE
WELL...
SURE, HE WAS A LITTLE DUMB, BUT FOR THE MOST PART HE WAS AN OKAY GUY

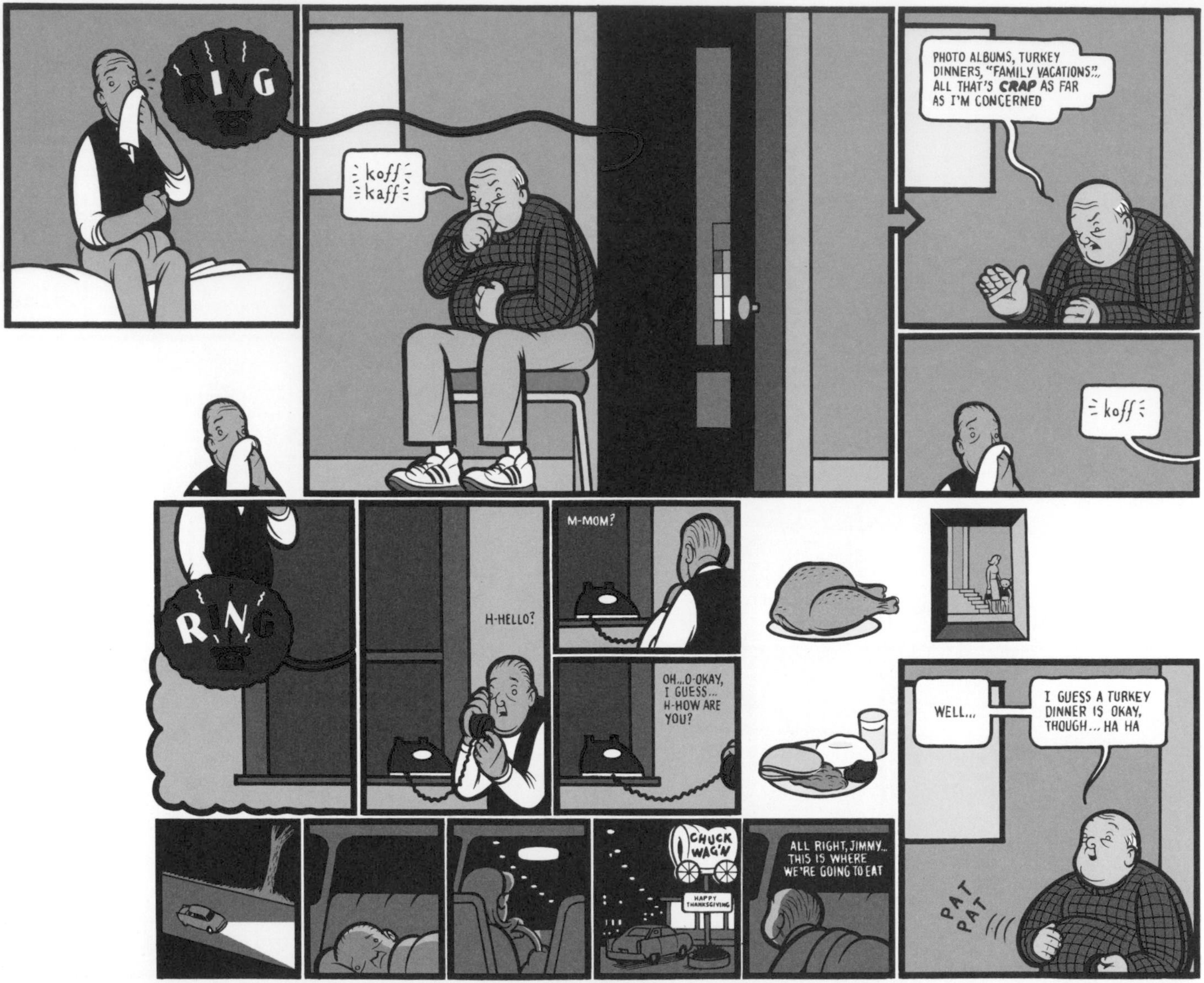
RING
koff
kaff
PHOTO ALBUMS, TURKEY DINNERS, "FAMILY VACATIONS"... ALL THAT'S CRAP AS FAR AS I'M CONCERNED
koff
RING
H-HELLO?
M-MOM?
OH...O-OKAY, I GUESS... H-HOW ARE YOU?
WELL...
I GUESS A TURKEY DINNER IS OKAY, THOUGH... HA HA
PAT PAT
CHUCK WAG'N
HAPPY THANKSGIVING
ALL RIGHT, JIMMY... THIS IS WHERE WE'RE GOING TO EAT

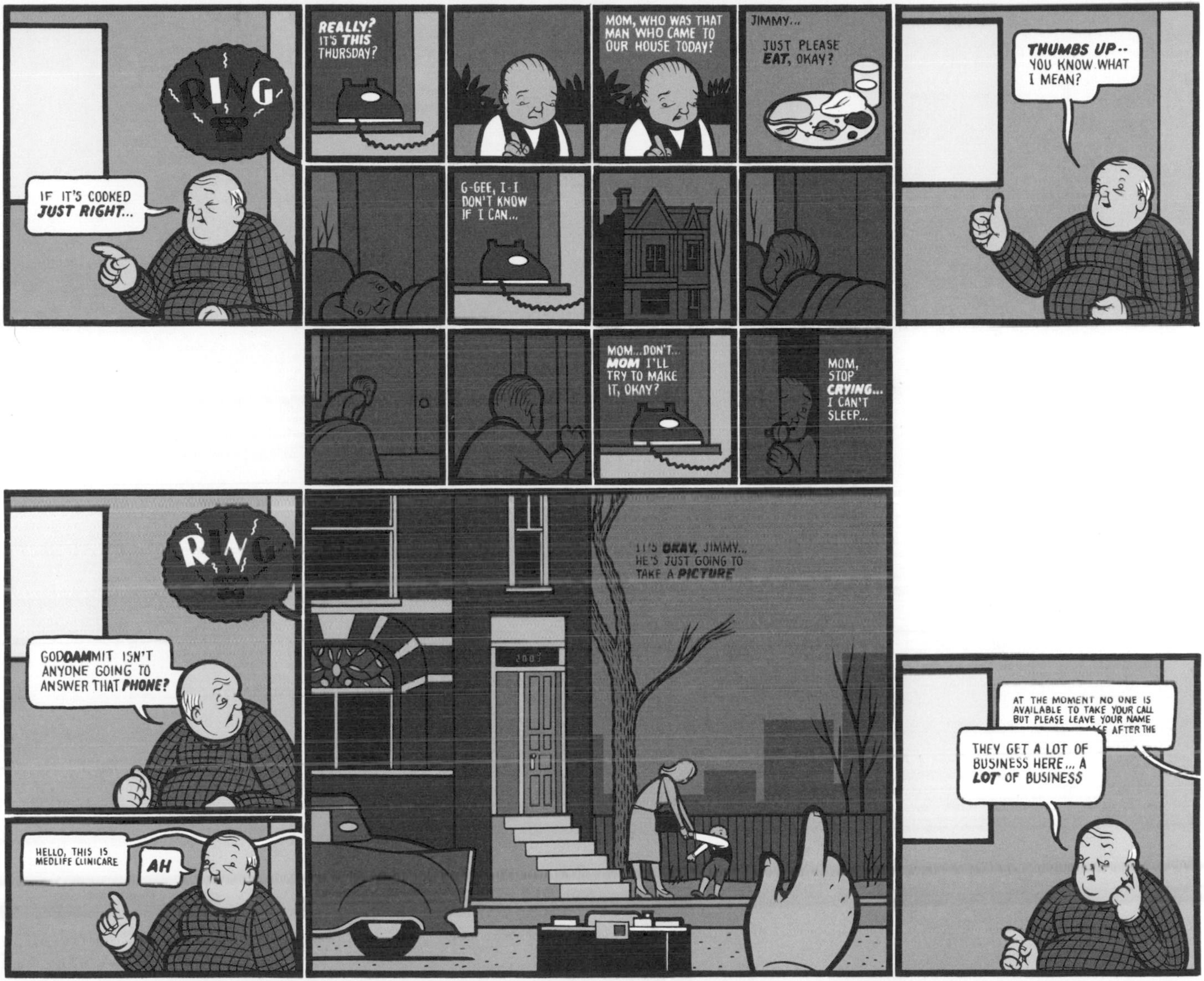

RING
IF IT'S COOKED **JUST RIGHT**...
REALLY? IT'S **THIS** THURSDAY?
MOM, WHO WAS THAT MAN WHO CAME TO OUR HOUSE TODAY?
JIMMY...
JUST PLEASE **EAT**, OKAY?
G-GEE, I-I DON'T KNOW IF I CAN...
THUMBS UP.. YOU KNOW WHAT I MEAN?
MOM...DON'T... **MOM** I'LL TRY TO MAKE IT, OKAY?
MOM, STOP **CRYING**... I CAN'T SLEEP...
RING
GOD**DAM**MIT ISN'T ANYONE GOING TO ANSWER THAT **PHONE**?
HELLO, THIS IS MEDLIFE CLINICARE
AH
IT'S **OKAY**, JIMMY... HE'S JUST GOING TO TAKE A **PICTURE**
AT THE MOMENT NO ONE IS AVAILABLE TO TAKE YOUR CALL BUT PLEASE LEAVE YOUR NAME
AFTER THE
THEY GET A LOT OF BUSINESS HERE... A **LOT** OF BUSINESS

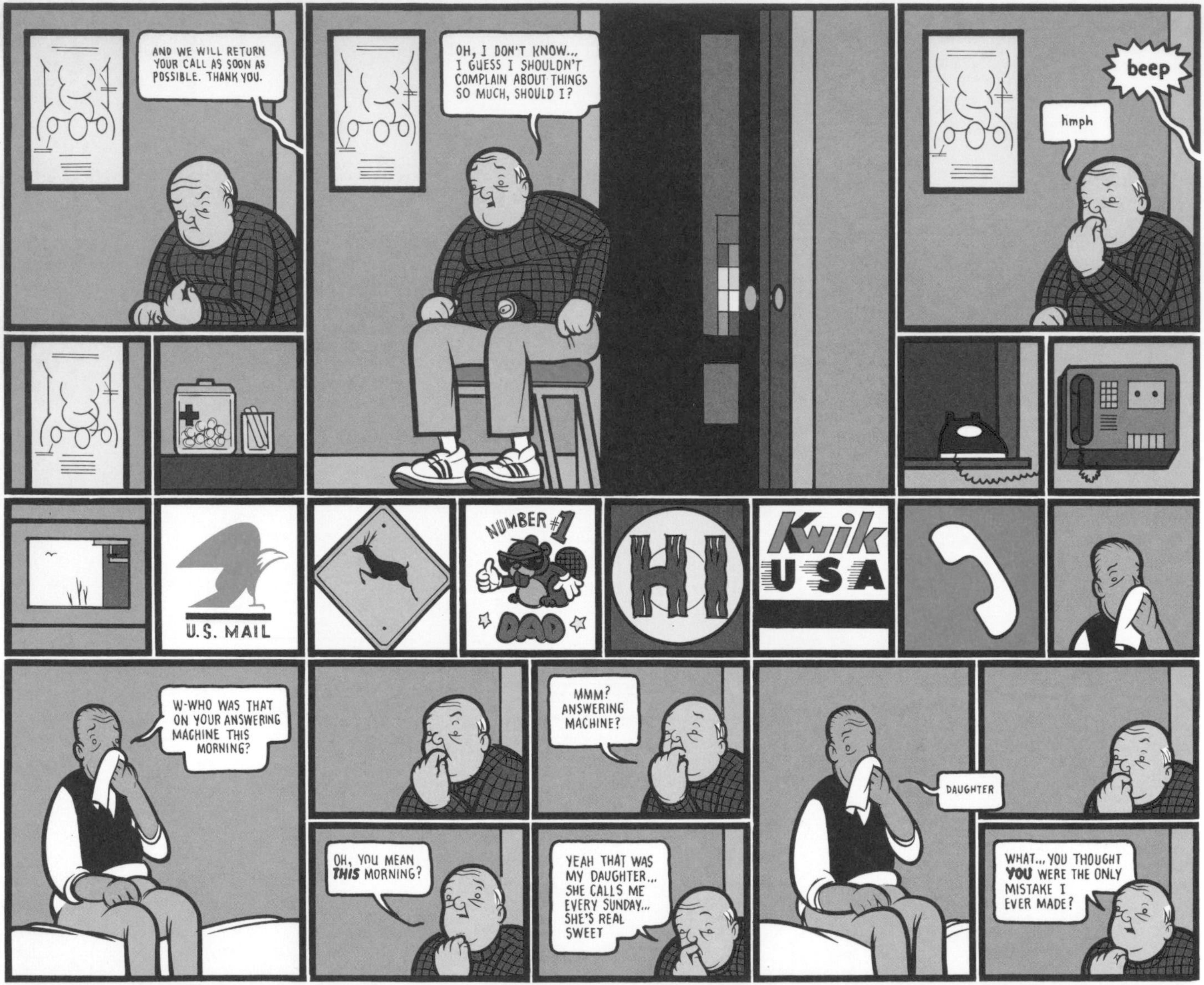

AND WE WILL RETURN YOUR CALL AS SOON AS POSSIBLE. THANK YOU.
OH, I DON'T KNOW... I GUESS I SHOULDN'T COMPLAIN ABOUT THINGS SO MUCH, SHOULD I?
hmph
beep
U.S. MAIL
NUMBER #1
DAD
HI
Kwik
USA
W-WHO WAS THAT ON YOUR ANSWERING MACHINE THIS MORNING?
MMM? ANSWERING MACHINE?
OH, YOU MEAN **THIS** MORNING?
YEAH THAT WAS MY DAUGHTER... SHE CALLS ME EVERY SUNDAY... SHE'S REAL SWEET
DAUGHTER
WHAT... YOU THOUGHT **YOU** WERE THE ONLY MISTAKE I EVER MADE?

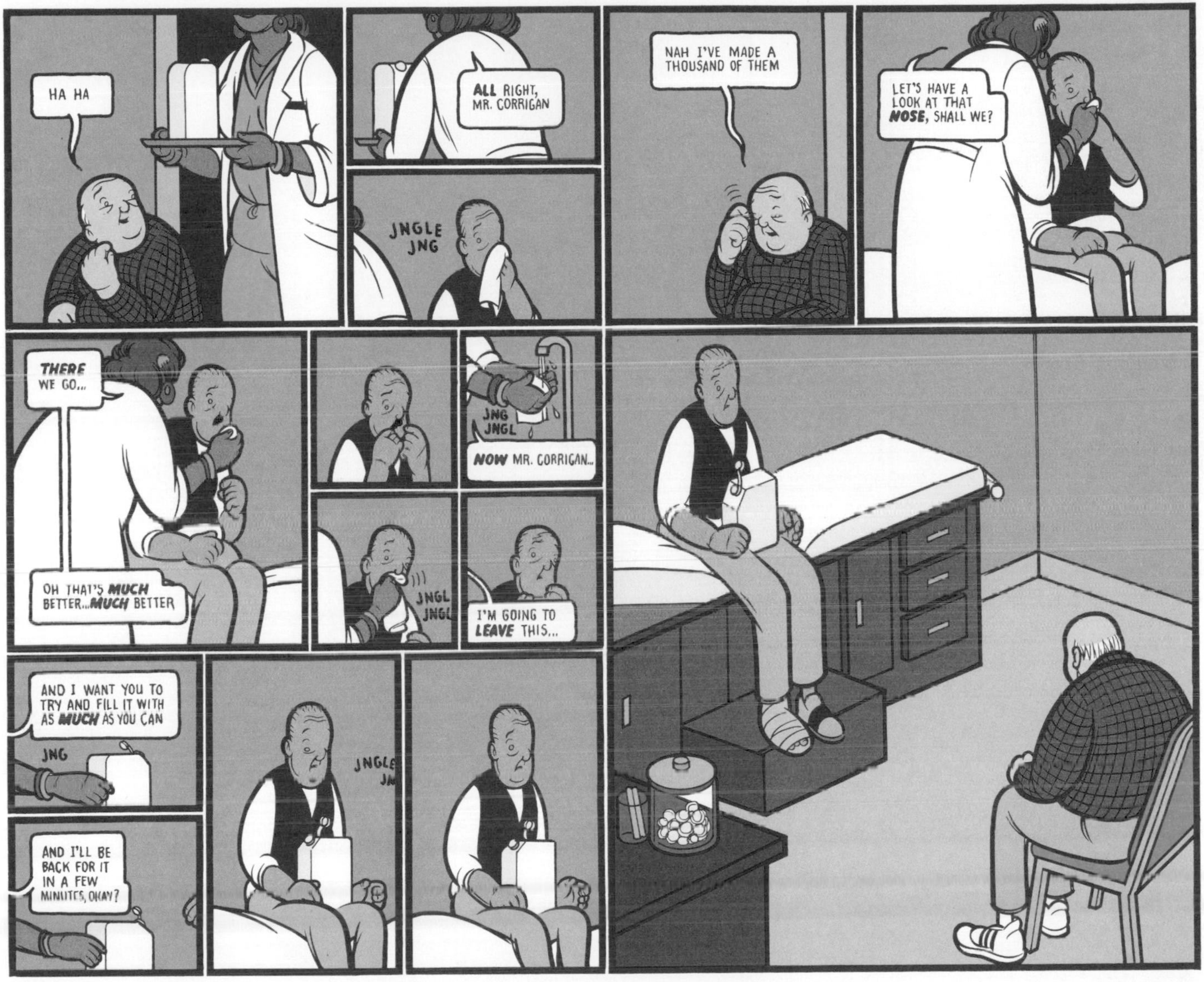

HA HA
ALL RIGHT, MR. CORRIGAN
JNGLE JNG
NAH I'VE MADE A THOUSAND OF THEM
LET'S HAVE A LOOK AT THAT NOSE, SHALL WE?
THERE WE GO...
OH THAT'S MUCH BETTER...MUCH BETTER
JNG JNGL
NOW MR. CORRIGAN...
JNGL JNGL
I'M GOING TO LEAVE THIS...
AND I WANT YOU TO TRY AND FILL IT WITH AS MUCH AS YOU CAN
JNG
AND I'LL BE BACK FOR IT IN A FEW MINUTES, OKAY?
JNGLE

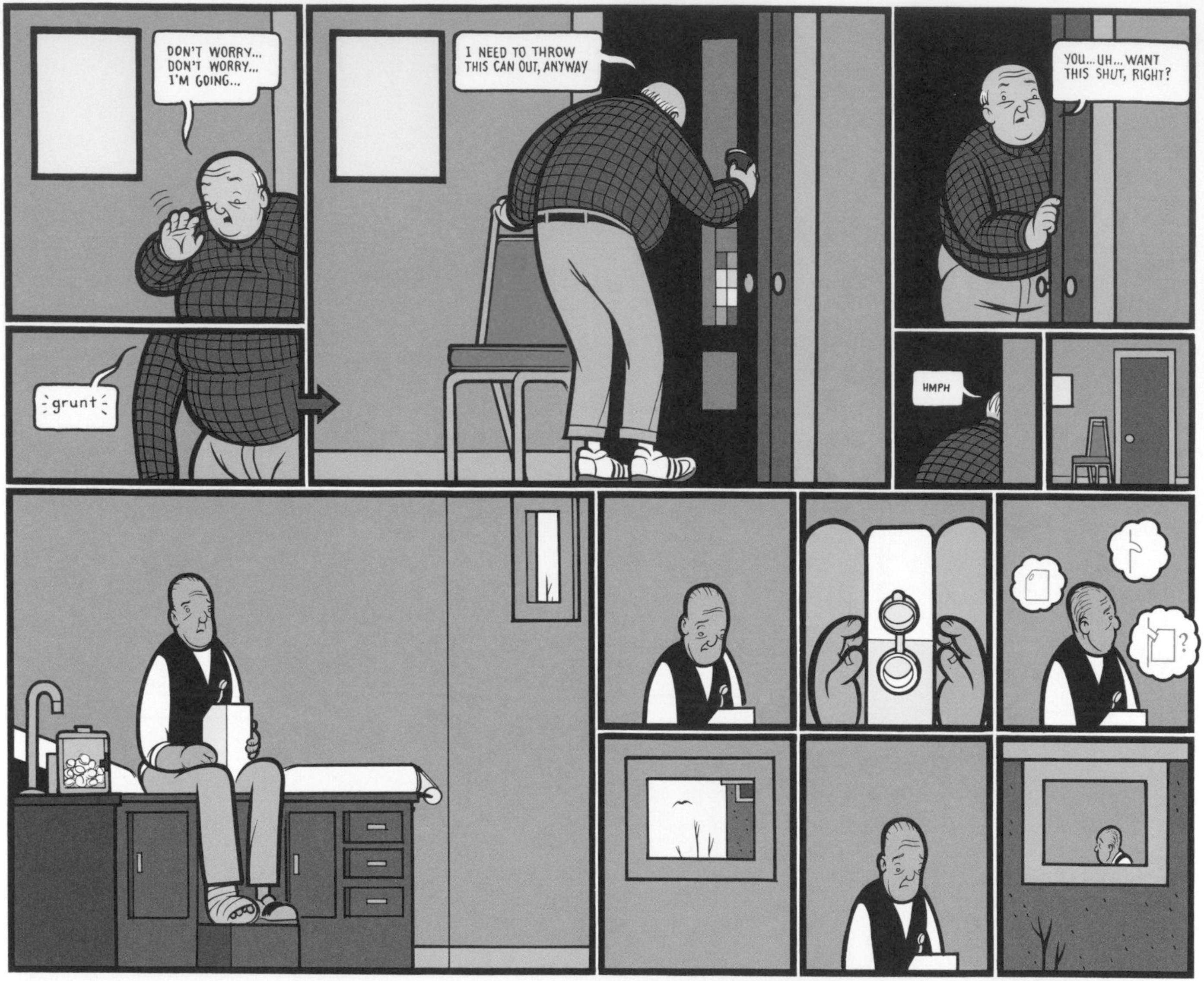
DON'T WORRY... DON'T WORRY... I'M GOING...
grunt
I NEED TO THROW THIS CAN OUT, ANYWAY
YOU... UH... WANT THIS SHUT, RIGHT?
HMPH
?

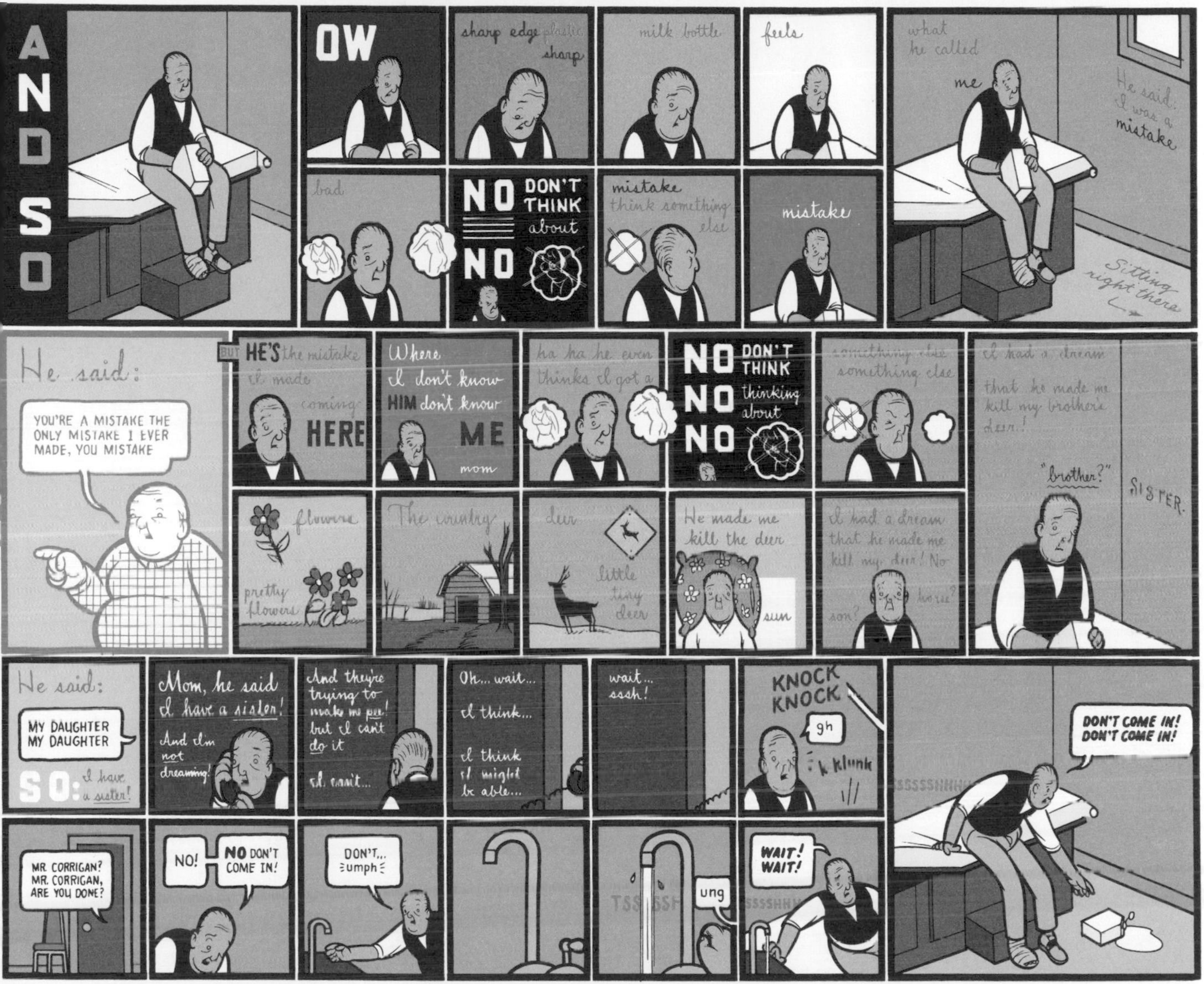

AND SO
OW
sharp edge plastic
sharp
milk bottle
feels
what he called
me
He said: I was a mistake
bad
NO DON'T THINK about
NO
mistake
think something else
mistake
Sitting right there
He said:
YOU'RE A MISTAKE THE ONLY MISTAKE I EVER MADE, YOU MISTAKE
BUT HE'S the mistake I made coming
HERE
Where
I don't know
HIM don't know
ME
mom
ha ha he even thinks I got a
NO DON'T THINK
NO thinking about
NO
something else
something else
I had a dream
that he made me kill my brother's deer!
"brother?"
SISTER.
flowers
pretty flowers
The country
deer
little tiny deer
He made me kill the deer
sun
I had a dream that he made me kill my deer! No
son?
worse?
He said:
MY DAUGHTER MY DAUGHTER
SO: I have a sister!
Mom, he said I have a sister!
And I'm not dreaming!
And they're trying to make me pee! but I can't do it
I can't...
Oh... wait...
I think...
I think I might be able...
wait... sssh!
KNOCK KNOCK
gh
k klunk
DON'T COME IN! DON'T COME IN!
SSSSSHHH
MR. CORRIGAN? MR. CORRIGAN, ARE YOU DONE?
NO!
NO DON'T COME IN!
DON'T... umph
TSSSSSH
ung
WAIT! WAIT!
SSSSSHHH

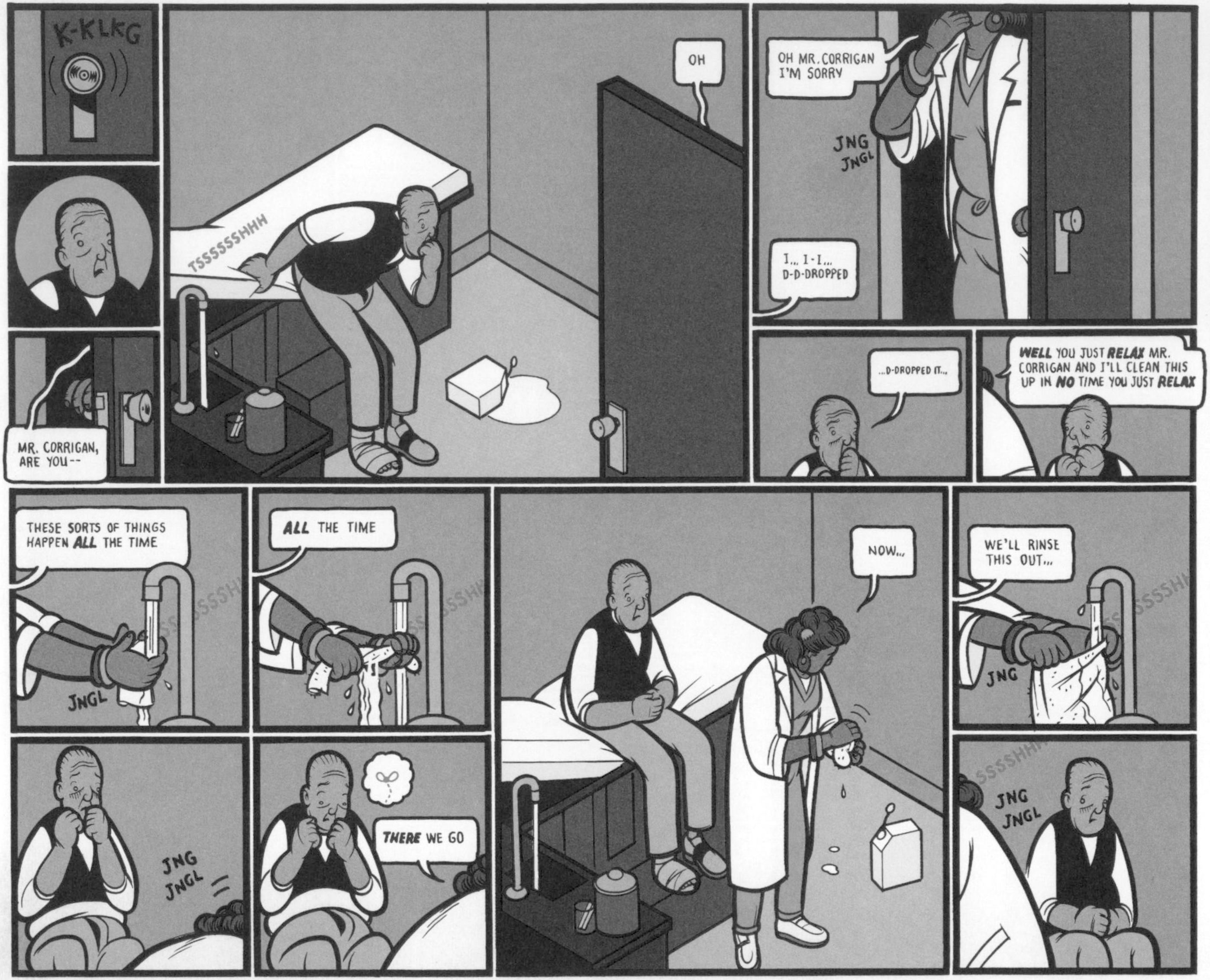
K-KLKG
MR. CORRIGAN, ARE YOU--
TSSSSSSHHH
OH
OH MR. CORRIGAN I'M SORRY
JNG JNGL
I... I-I... D-D-DROPPED
...D-DROPPED IT...
WELL YOU JUST RELAX MR. CORRIGAN AND I'LL CLEAN THIS UP IN NO TIME YOU JUST RELAX
THESE SORTS OF THINGS HAPPEN ALL THE TIME
JNGL
ALL THE TIME
NOW...
WE'LL RINSE THIS OUT...
JNG
JNG JNGL
THERE WE GO
JNG JNGL

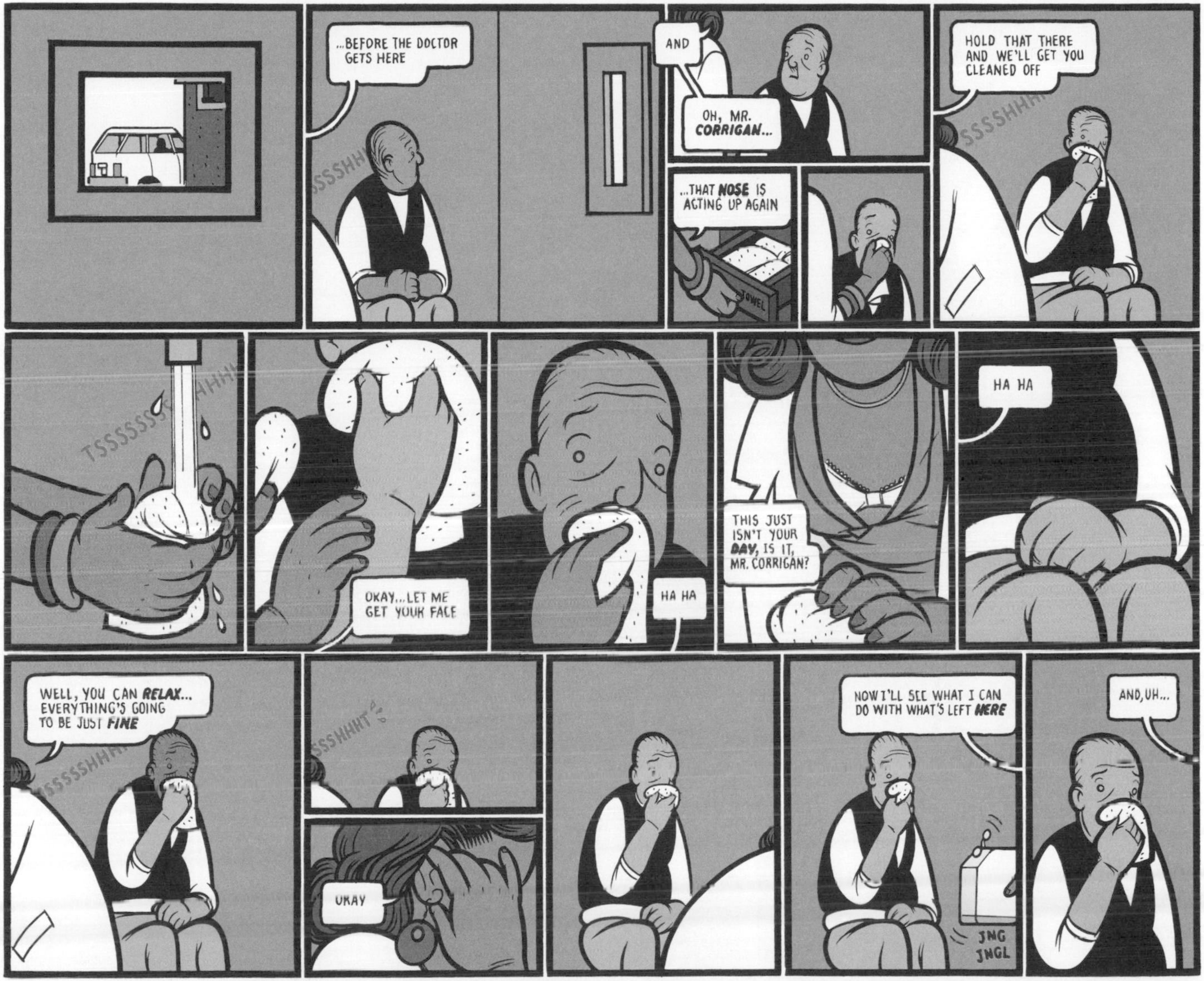
...BEFORE THE DOCTOR GETS HERE
SSSSHHH
AND
OH, MR. CORRIGAN...
...THAT NOSE IS ACTING UP AGAIN
TOWEL
HOLD THAT THERE AND WE'LL GET YOU CLEANED OFF
SSSSHHH
TSSSSSSSHHHH
OKAY...LET ME GET YOUR FACE
HA HA
THIS JUST ISN'T YOUR DAY, IS IT, MR. CORRIGAN?
HA HA
WELL, YOU CAN RELAX... EVERYTHING'S GOING TO BE JUST FINE
TSSSSSHHHH
SSSHHHT
OKAY
NOW I'LL SEE WHAT I CAN DO WITH WHAT'S LEFT HERE
JNG JNGL
AND, UH...

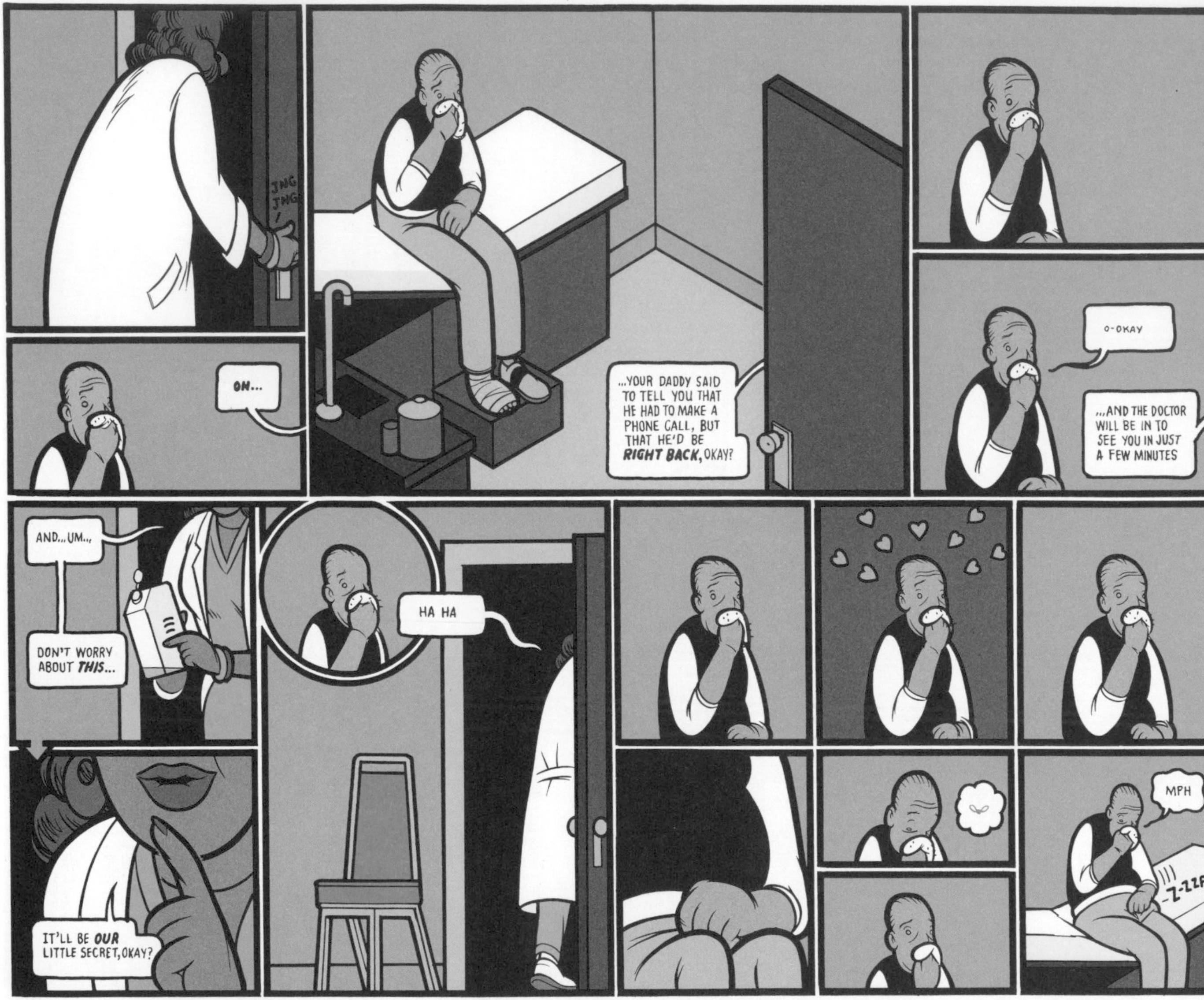
JNG JNG
OH...
...YOUR DADDY SAID TO TELL YOU THAT HE HAD TO MAKE A PHONE CALL, BUT THAT HE'D BE RIGHT BACK, OKAY?
...AND THE DOCTOR WILL BE IN TO SEE YOU IN JUST A FEW MINUTES
O-OKAY
AND... UM...,
DON'T WORRY ABOUT THIS...
IT'LL BE OUR LITTLE SECRET, OKAY?
HA HA
MPH
Z-ZZP

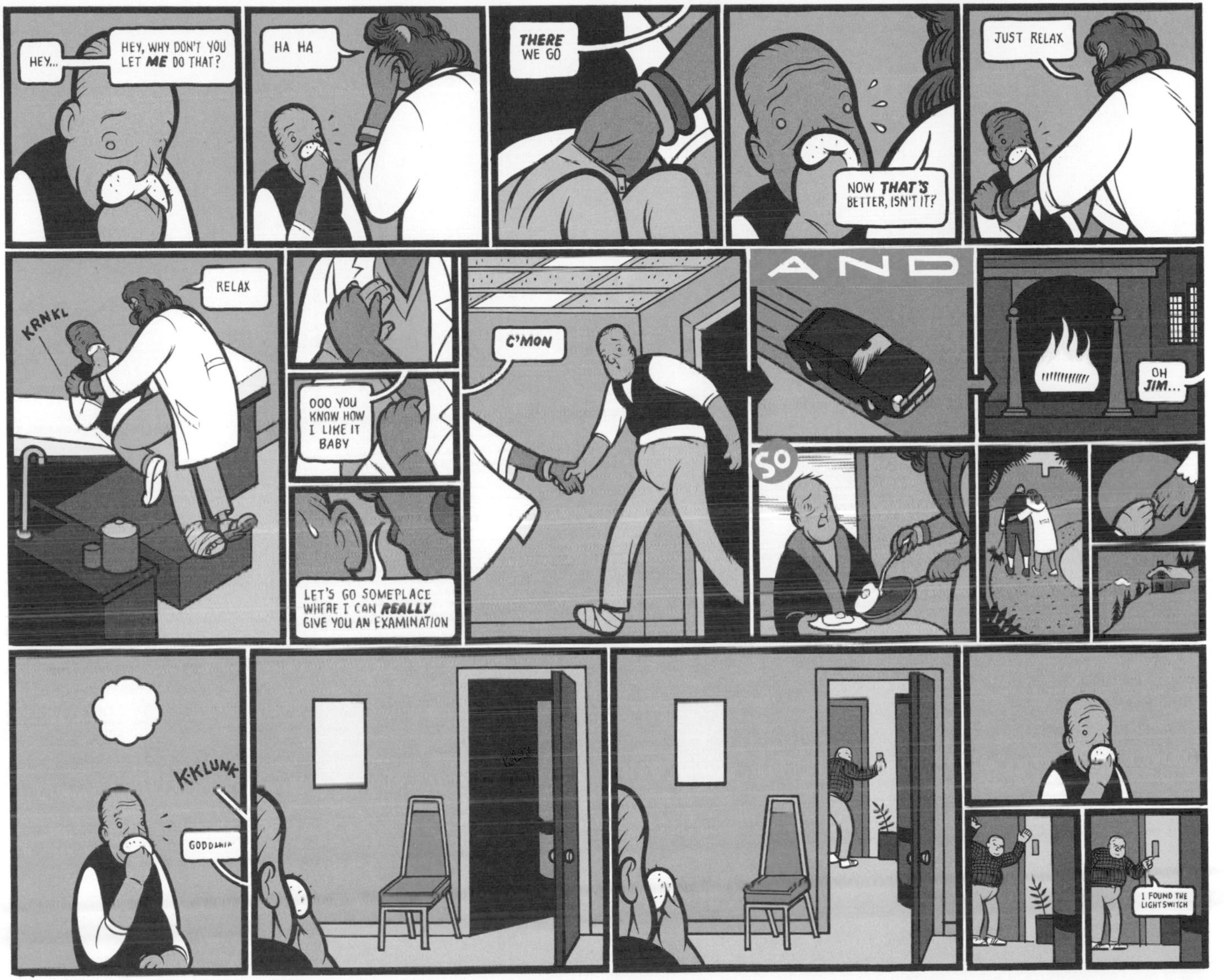
HEY...
HEY, WHY DON'T YOU LET **ME** DO THAT?
HA HA
THERE WE GO
NOW **THAT'S** BETTER, ISN'T IT?
JUST RELAX
RELAX
KRNKL
C'MON
OOO YOU KNOW HOW I LIKE IT BABY
LET'S GO SOMEPLACE WHERE I CAN **REALLY** GIVE YOU AN EXAMINATION
AND
OH **JIM**...
SO
K-KLUNK
GODDAMN
I FOUND THE LIGHTSWITCH

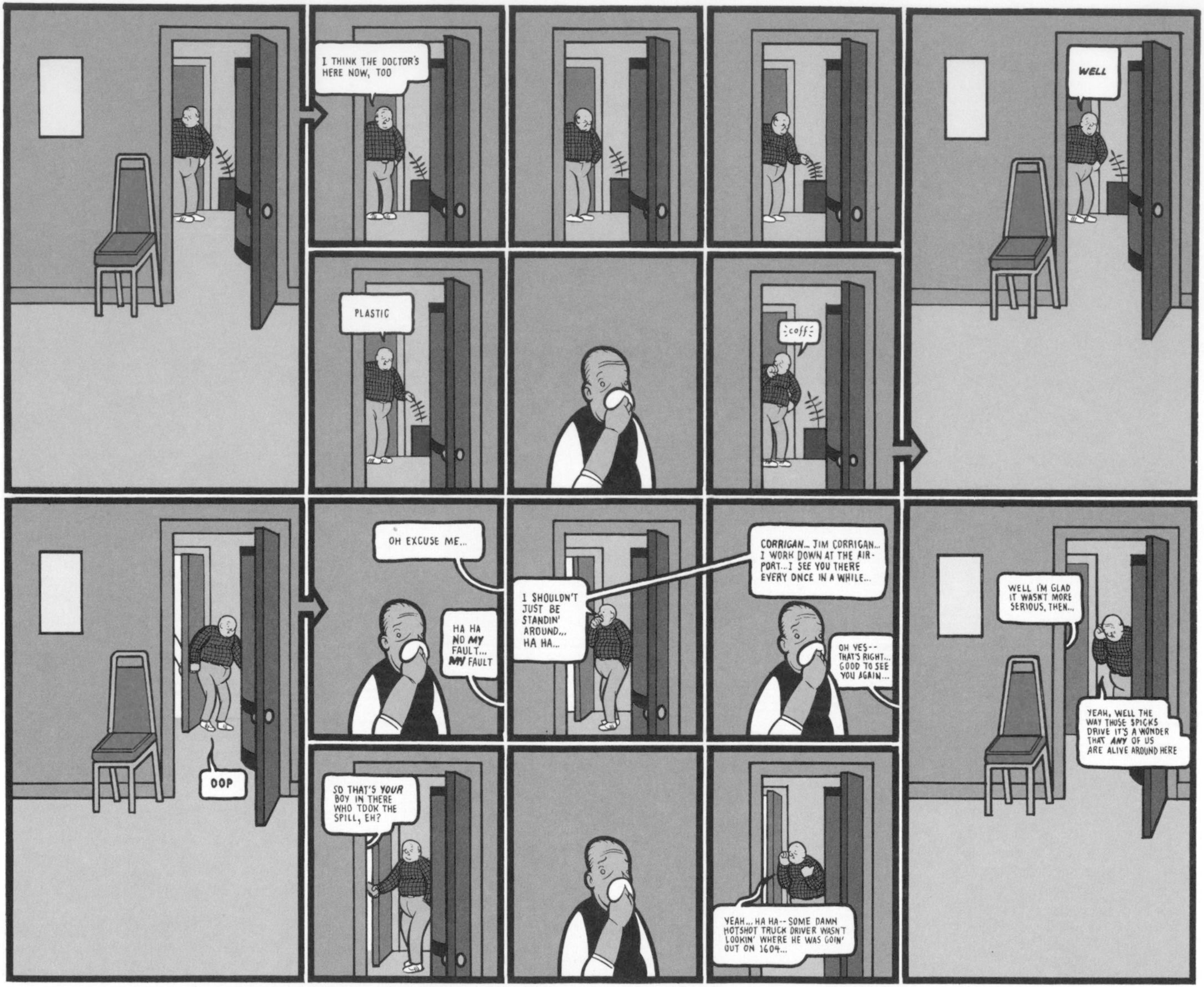
I THINK THE DOCTOR'S HERE NOW, TOO
PLASTIC
coff
WELL
OOP
OH EXCUSE ME...
HA HA NO MY FAULT... MY FAULT
I SHOULDN'T JUST BE STANDIN' AROUND... HA HA...
CORRIGAN... JIM CORRIGAN... I WORK DOWN AT THE AIR-PORT... I SEE YOU THERE EVERY ONCE IN A WHILE...
OH YES-- THAT'S RIGHT... GOOD TO SEE YOU AGAIN...
SO THAT'S YOUR BOY IN THERE WHO TOOK THE SPILL, EH?
YEAH... HA HA-- SOME DAMN HOTSHOT TRUCK DRIVER WASN'T LOOKIN' WHERE HE WAS GOIN' OUT ON 1604...
WELL I'M GLAD IT WASN'T MORE SERIOUS, THEN...
YEAH, WELL THE WAY THOSE SPICKS DRIVE IT'S A WONDER THAT ANY OF US ARE ALIVE AROUND HERE

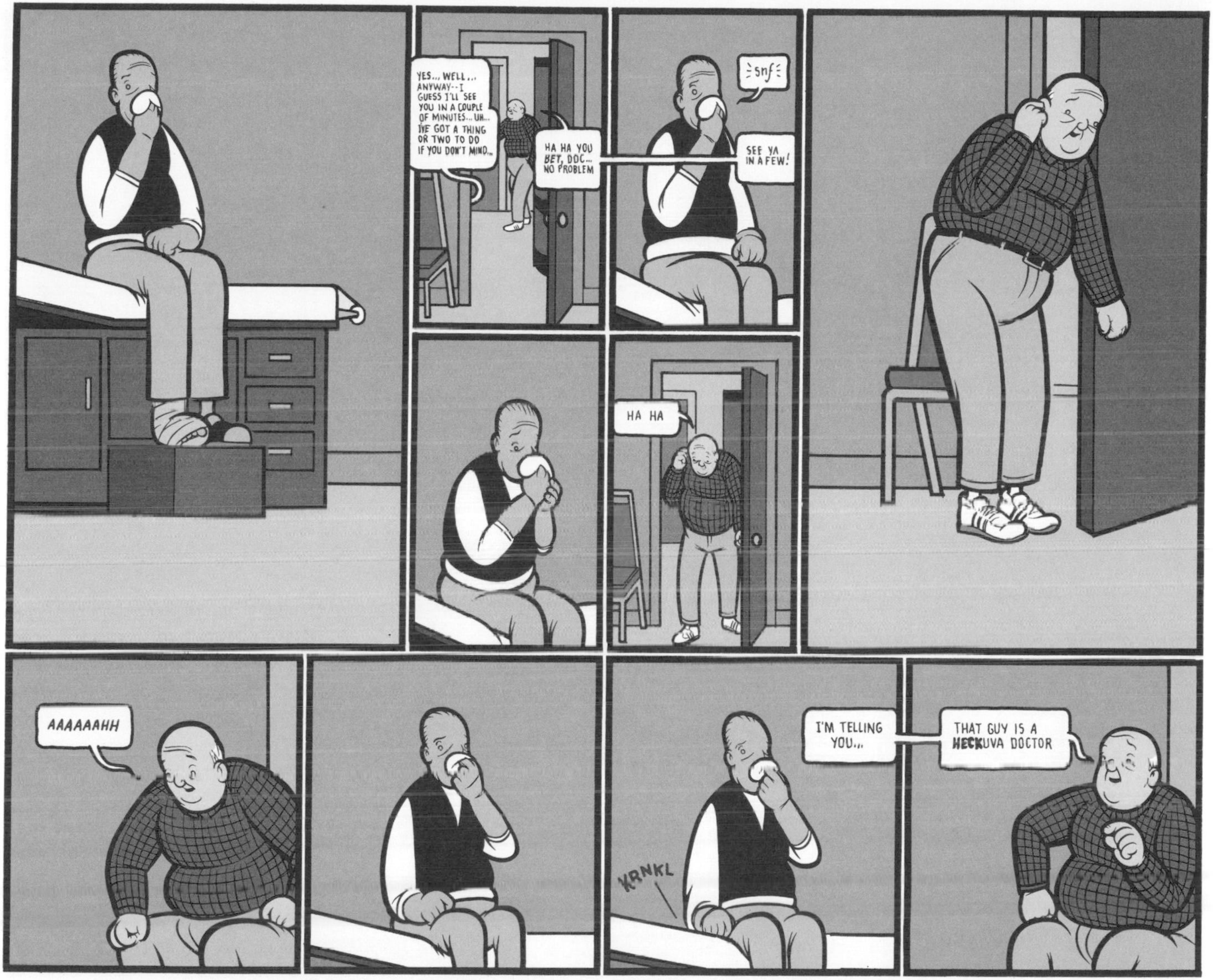

YES... WELL... ANYWAY--I GUESS I'LL SEE YOU IN A COUPLE OF MINUTES... UH... I'VE GOT A THING OR TWO TO DO IF YOU DON'T MIND...
HA HA YOU BET, DOC... NO PROBLEM
snf
SEE YA IN A FEW!
HA HA
AAAAAAHH
KRNKL
I'M TELLING YOU...
THAT GUY IS A HECKUVA DOCTOR

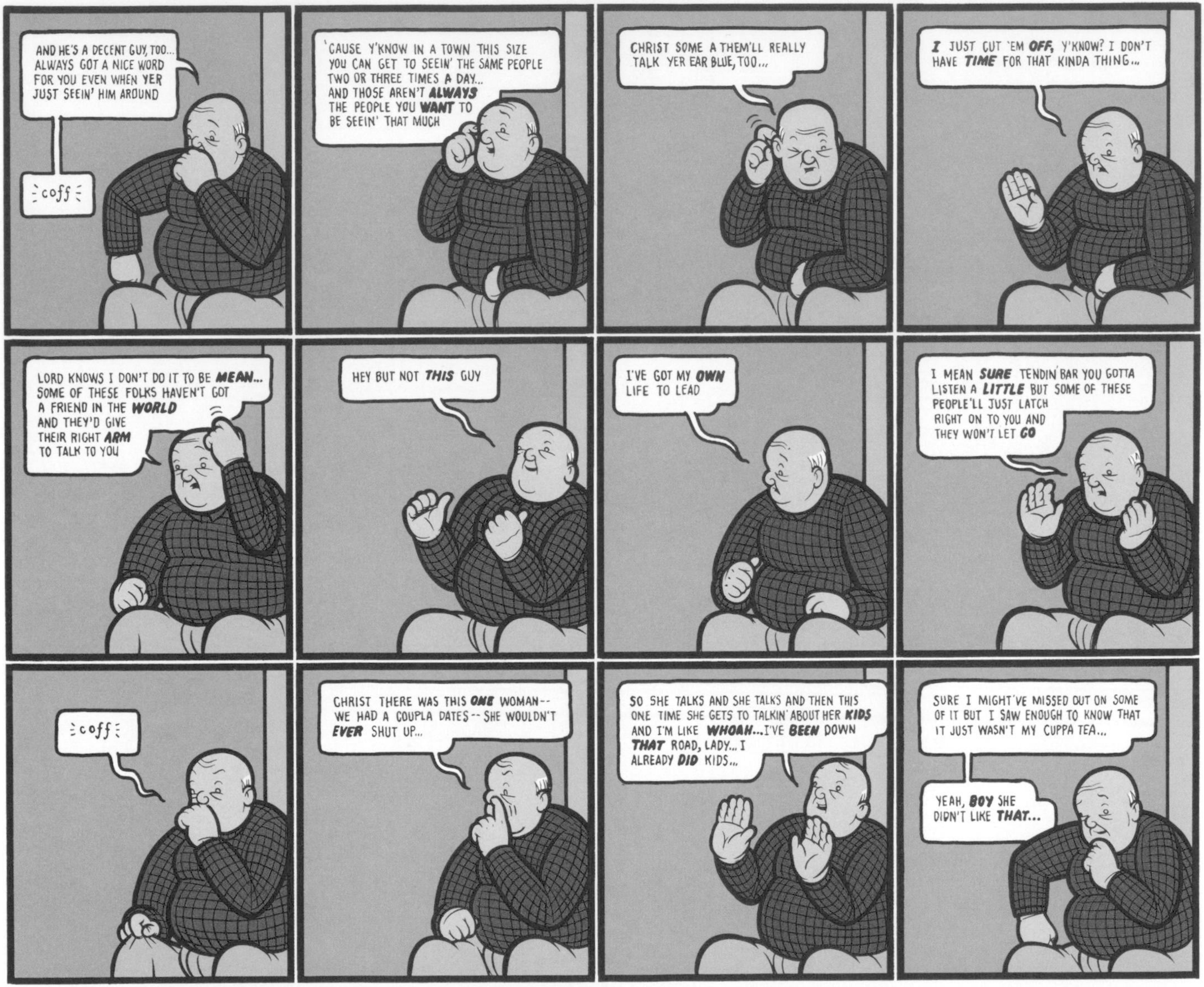
AND HE'S A DECENT GUY, TOO... ALWAYS GOT A NICE WORD FOR YOU EVEN WHEN YER JUST SEEIN' HIM AROUND
coff
'CAUSE Y'KNOW IN A TOWN THIS SIZE YOU CAN GET TO SEEIN' THE SAME PEOPLE TWO OR THREE TIMES A DAY... AND THOSE AREN'T ALWAYS THE PEOPLE YOU WANT TO BE SEEIN' THAT MUCH
CHRIST SOME A THEM'LL REALLY TALK YER EAR BLUE, TOO...
I JUST CUT 'EM OFF, Y'KNOW? I DON'T HAVE TIME FOR THAT KINDA THING...
LORD KNOWS I DON'T DO IT TO BE MEAN... SOME OF THESE FOLKS HAVEN'T GOT A FRIEND IN THE WORLD AND THEY'D GIVE THEIR RIGHT ARM TO TALK TO YOU
HEY BUT NOT THIS GUY
I'VE GOT MY OWN LIFE TO LEAD
I MEAN SURE TENDIN' BAR YOU GOTTA LISTEN A LITTLE BUT SOME OF THESE PEOPLE'LL JUST LATCH RIGHT ON TO YOU AND THEY WON'T LET GO
coff
CHRIST THERE WAS THIS ONE WOMAN-- WE HAD A COUPLA DATES-- SHE WOULDN'T EVER SHUT UP...
SO SHE TALKS AND SHE TALKS AND THEN THIS ONE TIME SHE GETS TO TALKIN' ABOUT HER KIDS AND I'M LIKE WHOAH... I'VE BEEN DOWN THAT ROAD, LADY... I ALREADY DID KIDS...
SURE I MIGHT'VE MISSED OUT ON SOME OF IT BUT I SAW ENOUGH TO KNOW THAT IT JUST WASN'T MY CUPPA TEA...
YEAH, BOY SHE DIDN'T LIKE THAT...

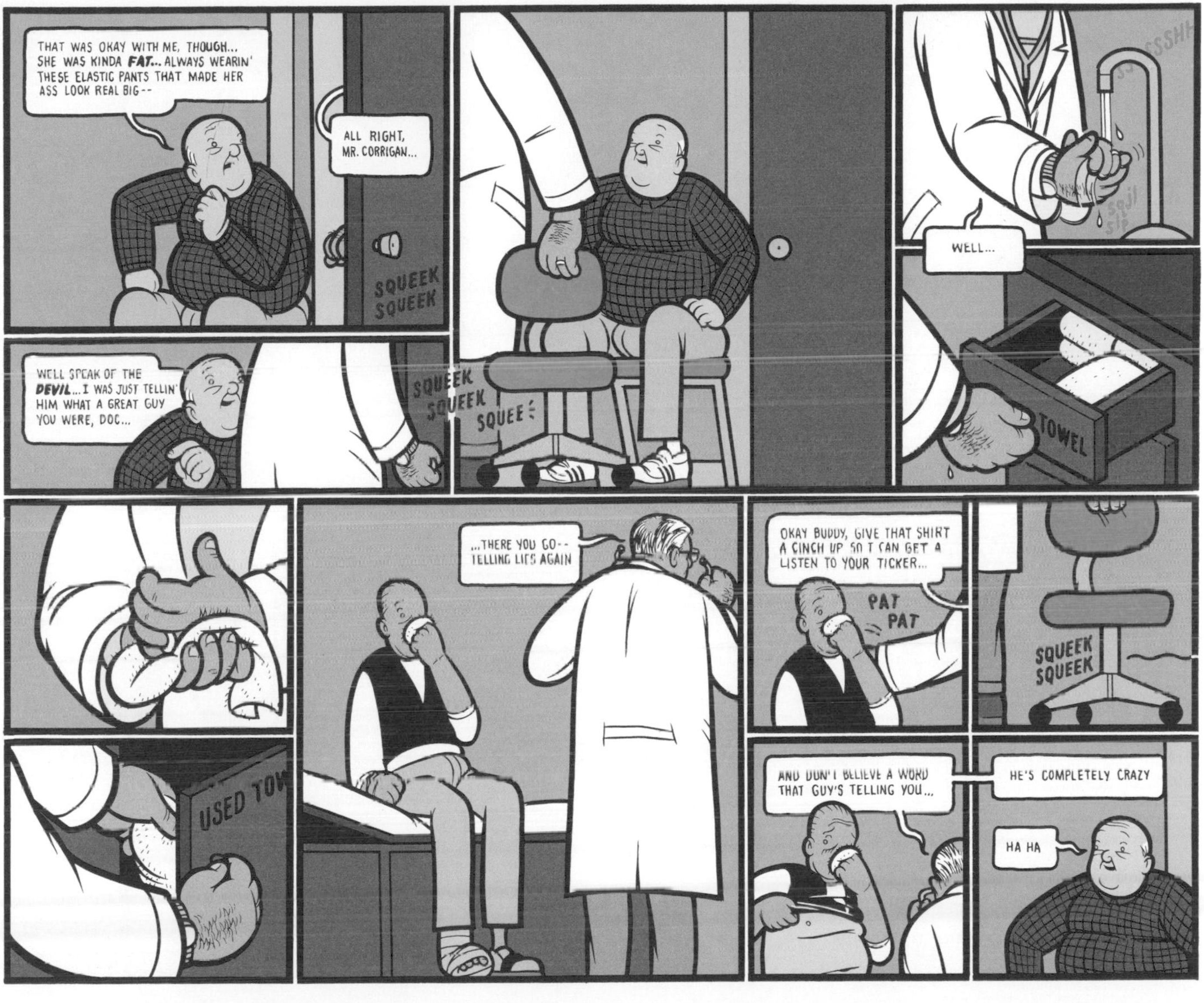
THAT WAS OKAY WITH ME, THOUGH... SHE WAS KINDA **FAT**... ALWAYS WEARIN' THESE ELASTIC PANTS THAT MADE HER ASS LOOK REAL BIG--
ALL RIGHT, MR. CORRIGAN...
SQUEEK SQUEEK
WELL SPEAK OF THE **DEVIL**... I WAS JUST TELLIN' HIM WHAT A GREAT GUY YOU WERE, DOC...
SQUEEK SQUEEK SQUEE
WELL...
TOWEL
USED TOW
...THERE YOU GO-- TELLING LIES AGAIN
OKAY BUDDY, GIVE THAT SHIRT A CINCH UP SO I CAN GET A LISTEN TO YOUR TICKER...
PAT PAT
SQUEEK SQUEEK
AND DON'T BELIEVE A WORD THAT GUY'S TELLING YOU...
HE'S COMPLETELY CRAZY
HA HA

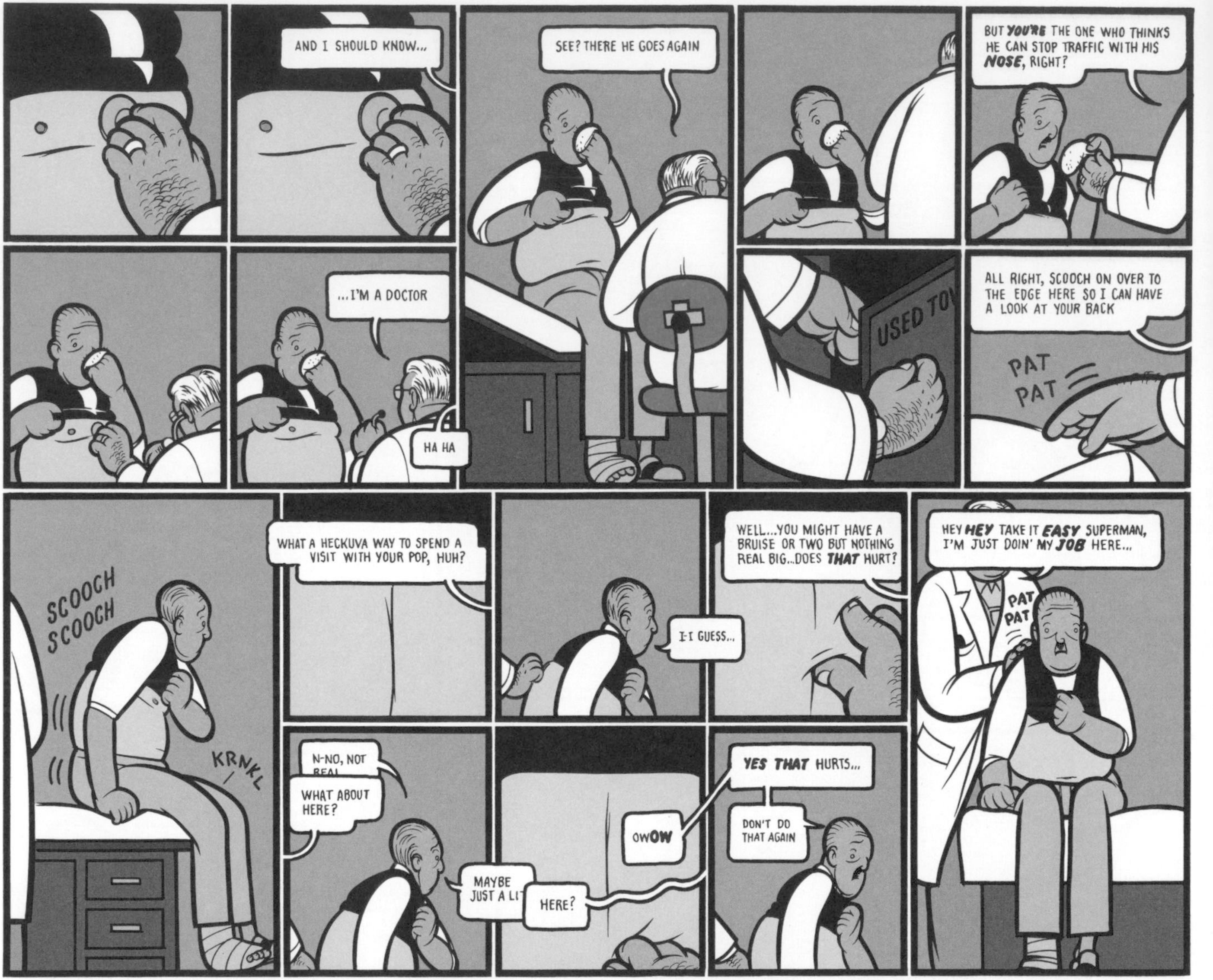
AND I SHOULD KNOW...
SEE? THERE HE GOES AGAIN
BUT YOU'RE THE ONE WHO THINKS HE CAN STOP TRAFFIC WITH HIS NOSE, RIGHT?
...I'M A DOCTOR
HA HA
USED TO
ALL RIGHT, SCOOCH ON OVER TO THE EDGE HERE SO I CAN HAVE A LOOK AT YOUR BACK
PAT PAT
SCOOCH SCOOCH
KRNKL
WHAT A HECKUVA WAY TO SPEND A VISIT WITH YOUR POP, HUH?
I-I GUESS...
WELL...YOU MIGHT HAVE A BRUISE OR TWO BUT NOTHING REAL BIG...DOES THAT HURT?
N-NO, NOT
WHAT ABOUT HERE?
MAYBE JUST A LI
HERE?
OWOW
YES THAT HURTS...
DON'T DO THAT AGAIN
HEY HEY TAKE IT EASY SUPERMAN, I'M JUST DOIN' MY JOB HERE...
PAT PAT

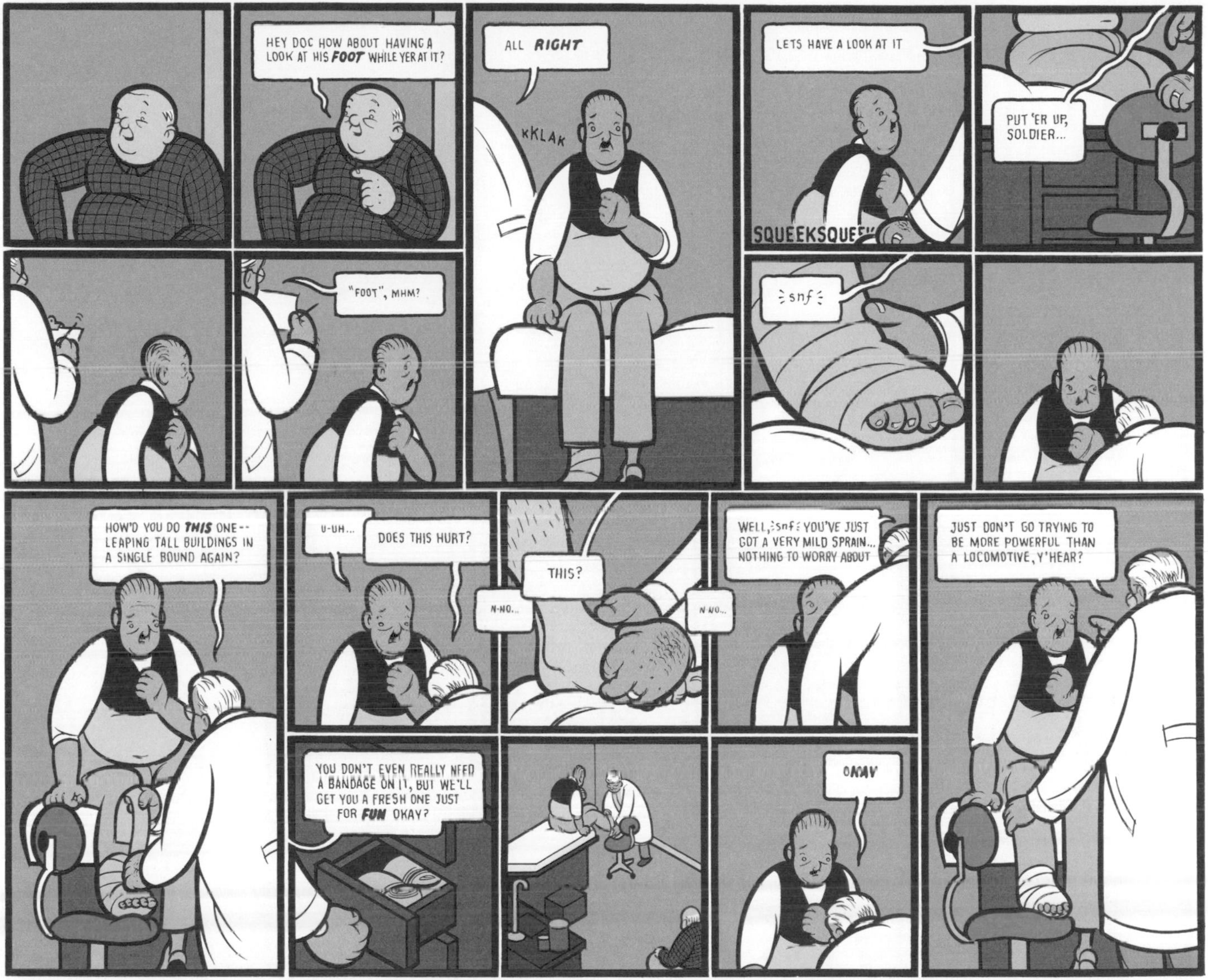

HEY DOC HOW ABOUT HAVING A LOOK AT HIS FOOT WHILE YER AT IT?
"FOOT", MHM?
ALL RIGHT
KKLAK
LETS HAVE A LOOK AT IT
SQUEEKSQUEE
PUT 'ER UP, SOLDIER...
snf
HOW'D YOU DO THIS ONE-- LEAPING TALL BUILDINGS IN A SINGLE BOUND AGAIN?
U-UH...
DOES THIS HURT?
THIS?
N-NO...
N-NO...
WELL, snf YOU'VE JUST GOT A VERY MILD SPRAIN... NOTHING TO WORRY ABOUT
YOU DON'T EVEN REALLY NEED A BANDAGE ON IT, BUT WE'LL GET YOU A FRESH ONE JUST FOR FUN OKAY?
OKAY
JUST DON'T GO TRYING TO BE MORE POWERFUL THAN A LOCOMOTIVE, Y'HEAR?

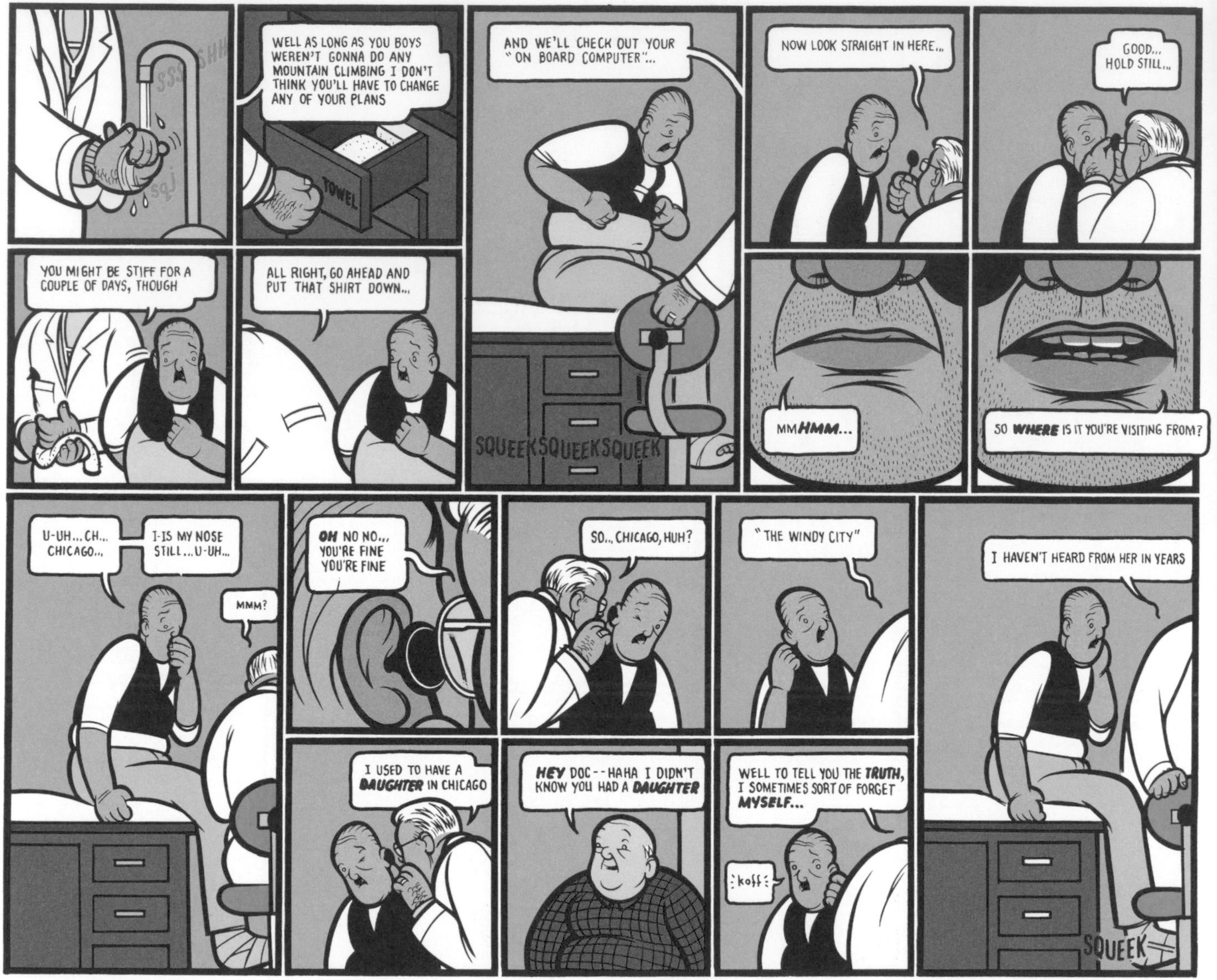
sqj
WELL AS LONG AS YOU BOYS WEREN'T GONNA DO ANY MOUNTAIN CLIMBING I DON'T THINK YOU'LL HAVE TO CHANGE ANY OF YOUR PLANS
TOWEL
AND WE'LL CHECK OUT YOUR "ON BOARD COMPUTER"...
SQUEEKSQUEEKSQUEEK
NOW LOOK STRAIGHT IN HERE...
GOOD... HOLD STILL...
YOU MIGHT BE STIFF FOR A COUPLE OF DAYS, THOUGH
ALL RIGHT, GO AHEAD AND PUT THAT SHIRT DOWN...
MM**HMM**...
SO **WHERE** IS IT YOU'RE VISITING FROM?
U-UH... CH... CHICAGO...
I-IS MY NOSE STILL... U-UH...
MMM?
OH NO NO... YOU'RE FINE YOU'RE FINE
SO... CHICAGO, HUH?
"THE WINDY CITY"
I USED TO HAVE A **DAUGHTER** IN CHICAGO
HEY DOC--HAHA I DIDN'T KNOW YOU HAD A **DAUGHTER**
WELL TO TELL YOU THE **TRUTH**, I SOMETIMES SORT OF FORGET **MYSELF**...
koff
I HAVEN'T HEARD FROM HER IN YEARS
SQUEEK

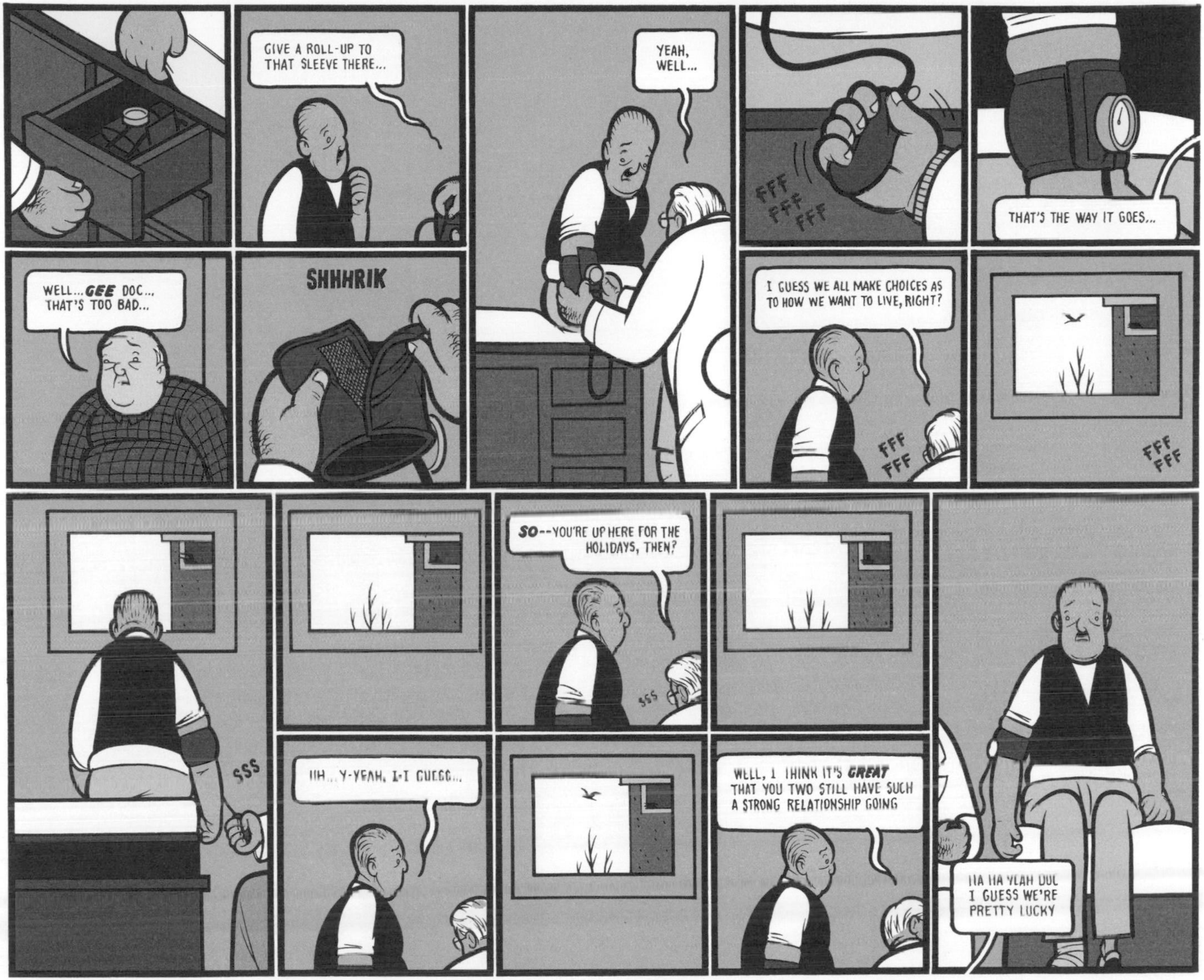
GIVE A ROLL-UP TO THAT SLEEVE THERE...
YEAH, WELL...
FFF FFF FFF
THAT'S THE WAY IT GOES...
WELL... **GEE** DOC... THAT'S TOO BAD...
SHHHRIK
I GUESS WE ALL MAKE CHOICES AS TO HOW WE WANT TO LIVE, RIGHT?
FFF FFF
FFF FFF
SSS
SO--YOU'RE UP HERE FOR THE HOLIDAYS, THEN?
SSS
UH... Y-YEAH, I-I GUESS...
WELL, I THINK IT'S **GREAT** THAT YOU TWO STILL HAVE SUCH A STRONG RELATIONSHIP GOING
HA HA YEAH DOC I GUESS WE'RE PRETTY LUCKY

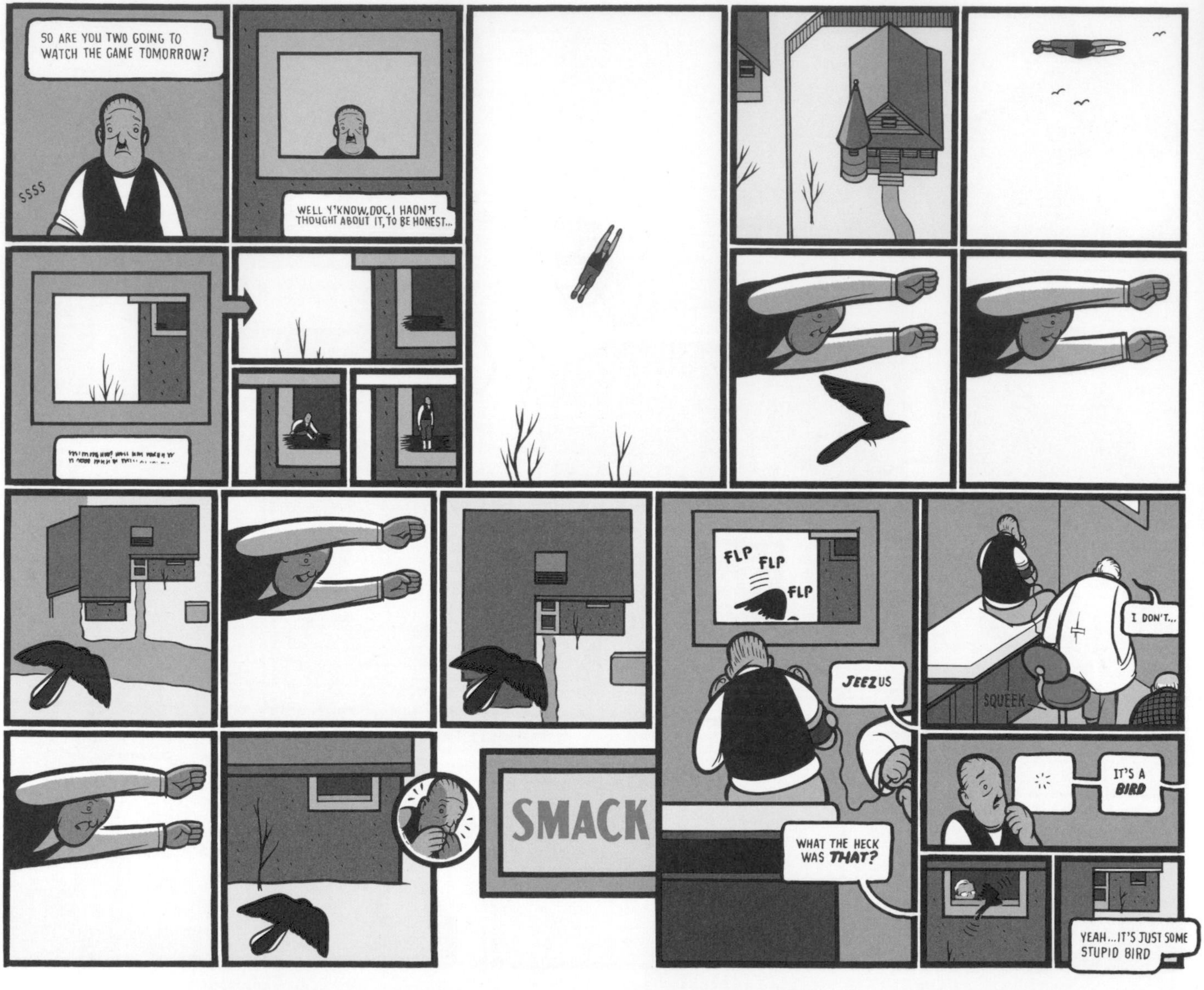

SO ARE YOU TWO GOING TO WATCH THE GAME TOMORROW?
SSSS
WELL Y'KNOW, DOC, I HADN'T THOUGHT ABOUT IT, TO BE HONEST...
FLP
FLP
FLP
JEEZUS
WHAT THE HECK WAS THAT?
I DON'T...
SQUEEK
IT'S A BIRD
SMACK
YEAH...IT'S JUST SOME STUPID BIRD

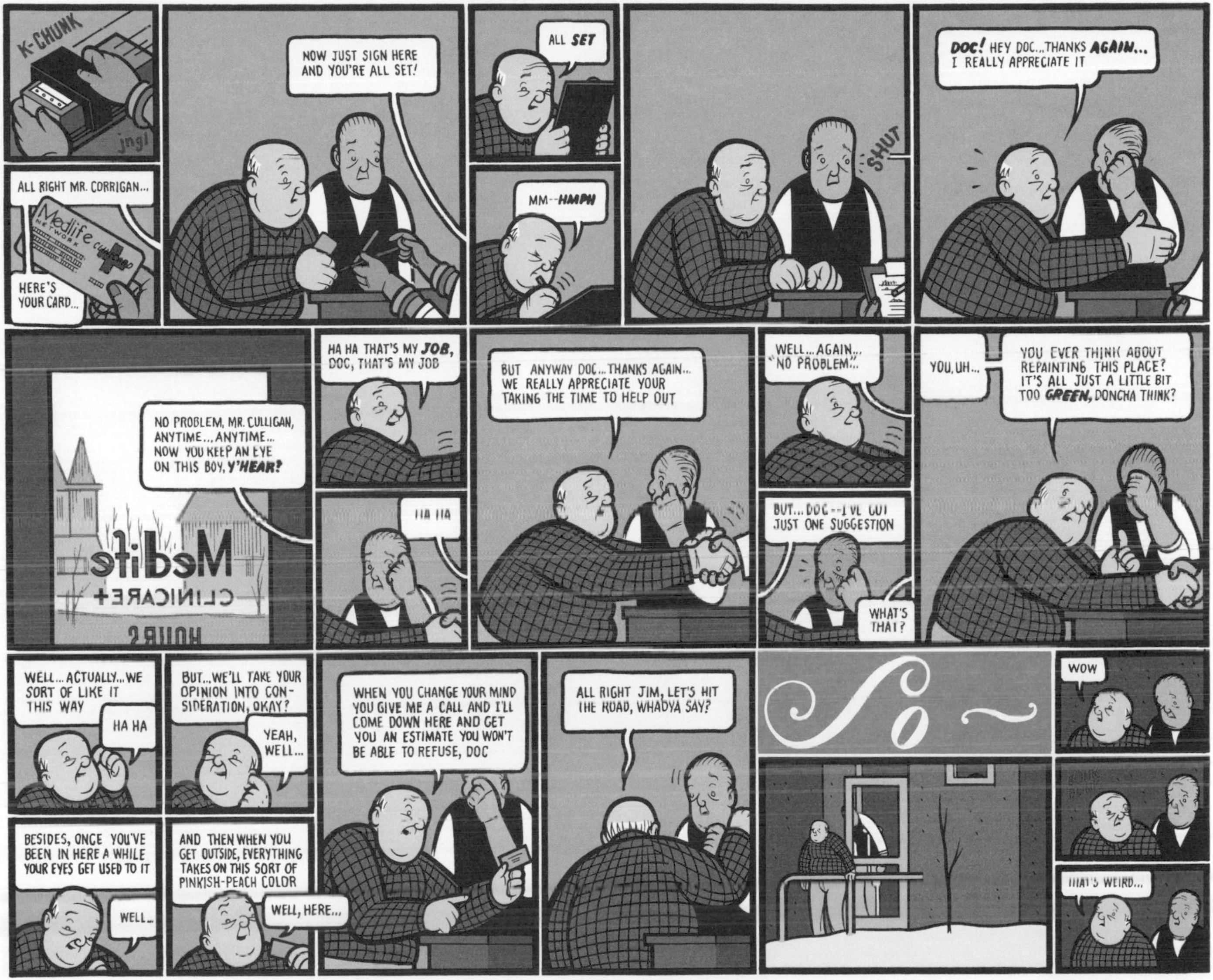

K-CHUNK
jngl
ALL RIGHT MR. CORRIGAN...
Medlife
NETWORK
HERE'S YOUR CARD...
NOW JUST SIGN HERE AND YOU'RE ALL SET!
ALL **SET**
MM--**HMPH**
SHUT
DOC! HEY DOC...THANKS **AGAIN...** I REALLY APPRECIATE IT
NO PROBLEM, MR. CULLIGAN, ANYTIME..., ANYTIME... NOW YOU KEEP AN EYE ON THIS BOY, **Y'HEAR?**
Medlife
CLINICARE+
HOURS
HA HA THAT'S MY **JOB,** DOC, THAT'S MY JOB
HA HA
BUT ANYWAY DOC...THANKS AGAIN... WE REALLY APPRECIATE YOUR TAKING THE TIME TO HELP OUT
WELL...AGAIN... "NO PROBLEM"...
BUT...DOC--I'VE GOT JUST ONE SUGGESTION
WHAT'S THAT?
YOU, UH...
YOU EVER THINK ABOUT REPAINTING THIS PLACE? IT'S ALL JUST A LITTLE BIT TOO **GREEN,** DONCHA THINK?
WELL...ACTUALLY...WE SORT OF LIKE IT THIS WAY
HA HA
BESIDES, ONCE YOU'VE BEEN IN HERE A WHILE YOUR EYES GET USED TO IT
WELL...
BUT...WE'LL TAKE YOUR OPINION INTO CON-SIDERATION, OKAY?
YEAH, WELL...
AND THEN WHEN YOU GET OUTSIDE, EVERYTHING TAKES ON THIS SORT OF PINKISH-PEACH COLOR
WELL, HERE...
WHEN YOU CHANGE YOUR MIND YOU GIVE ME A CALL AND I'LL COME DOWN HERE AND GET YOU AN ESTIMATE YOU WON'T BE ABLE TO REFUSE, DOC
ALL RIGHT JIM, LET'S HIT THE ROAD, WHADYA SAY?
WOW
THAT'S WEIRD...

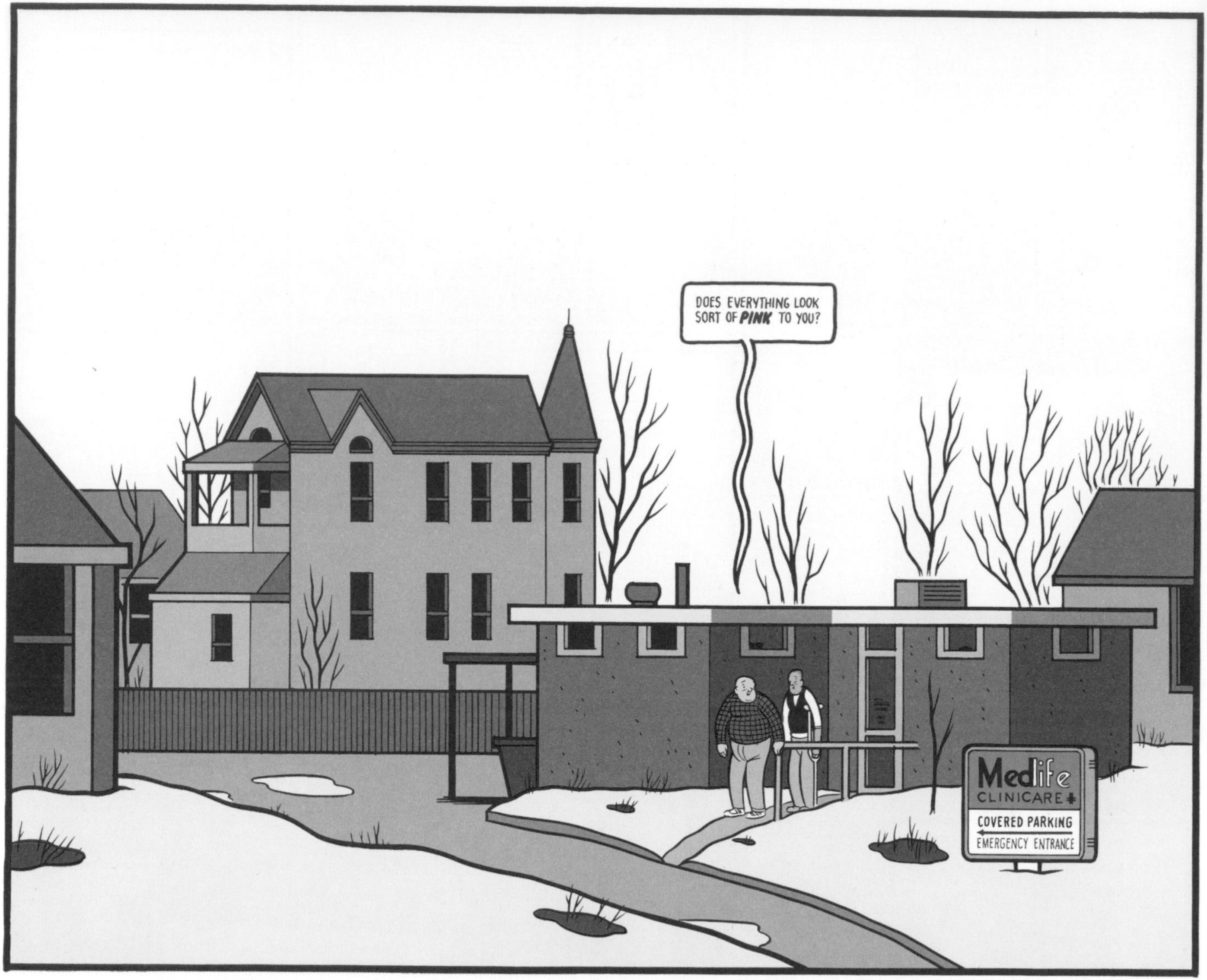
DOES EVERYTHING LOOK SORT OF PINK TO YOU?
Medlife CLINICARE
COVERED PARKING
EMERGENCY ENTRANCE

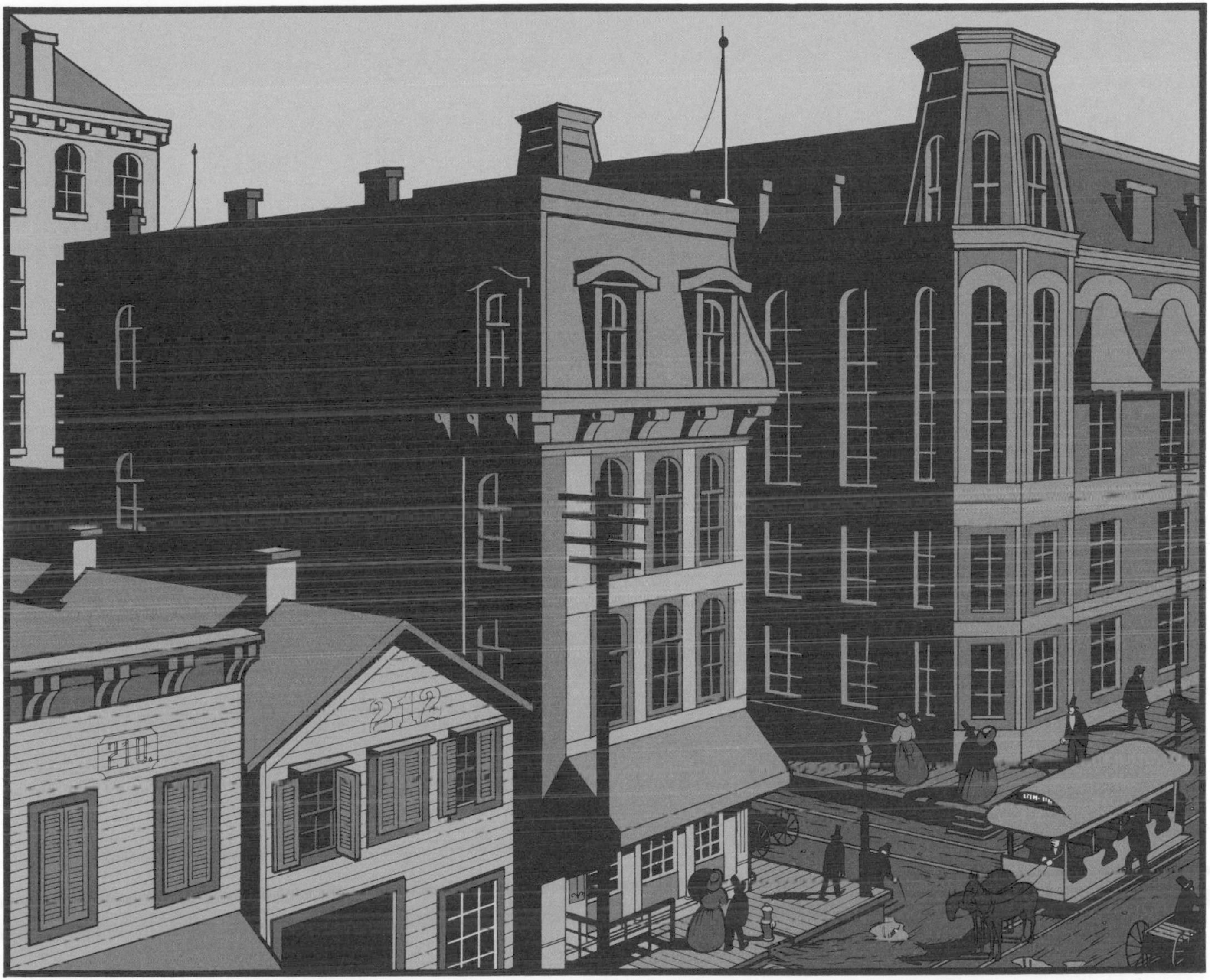
210.
212

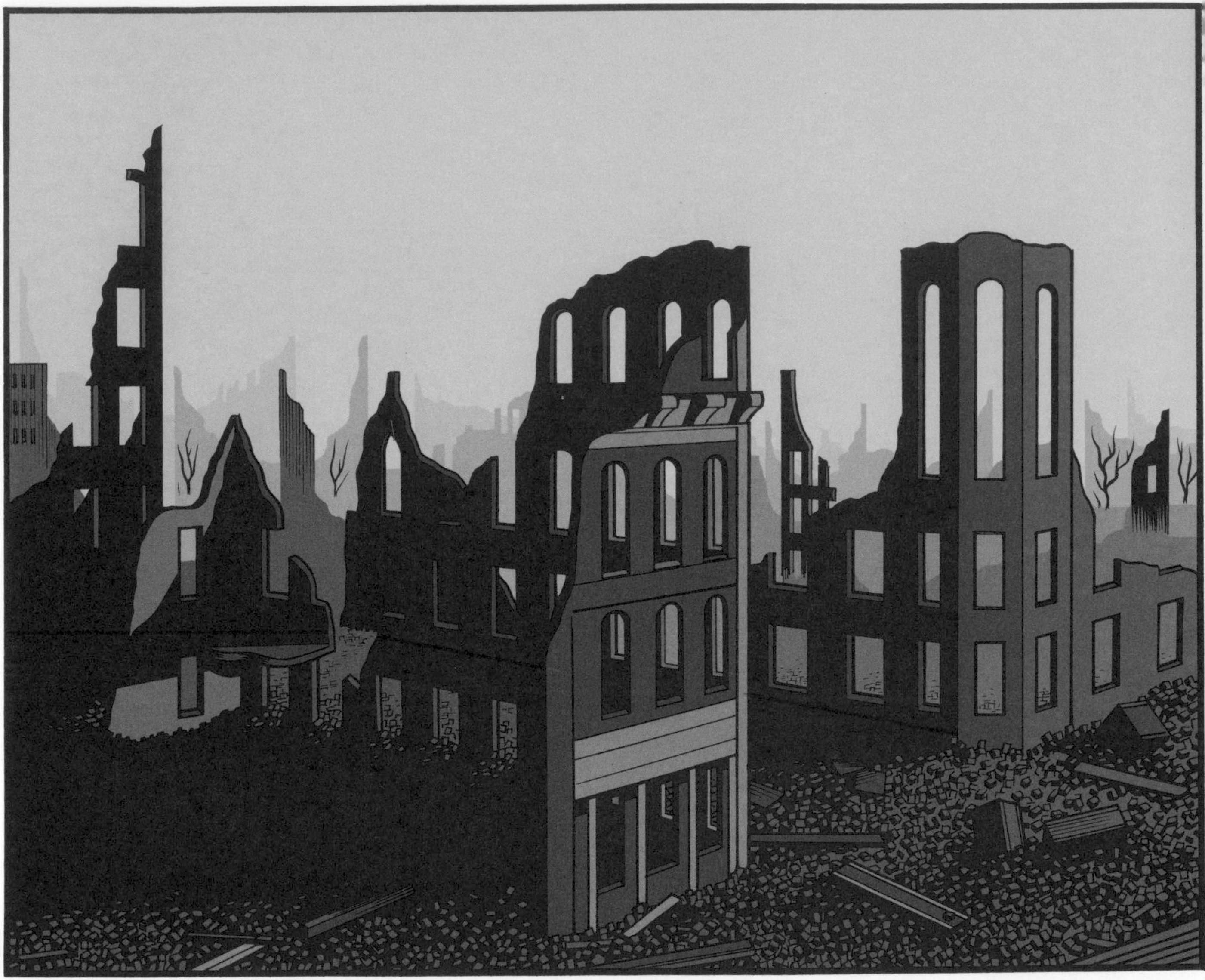

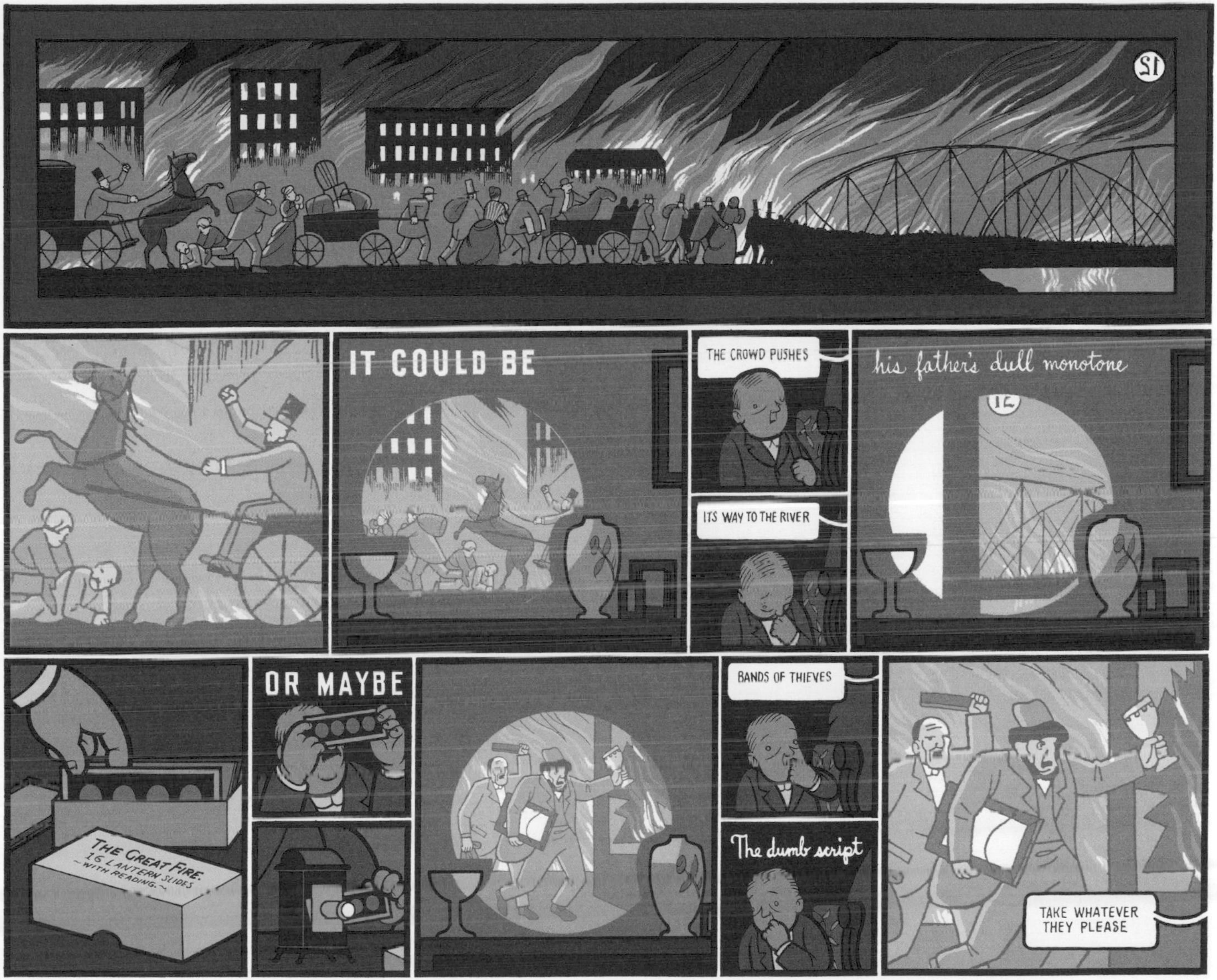
12
IT COULD BE
THE CROWD PUSHES
ITS WAY TO THE RIVER
his father's dull monotone
THE GREAT FIRE.
16 LANTERN SLIDES
~WITH READING.~
OR MAYBE
BANDS OF THIEVES
The dumb script
TAKE WHATEVER
THEY PLEASE

BUT THE *Brightly-colored shadows*

ORPHANED CHILDREN LEFT TO PERISH

FAIL *to capture the boy's interest.*

A MAN OUT OF HIS MIND WITH DRINK

DOUSES HIS DAUGHTER'S FIERY LOCKS WITH WHISKEY

instead being divided between

OH HOW AWFUL

His attention

ISN'T THERE SOMETHING A LITTLE LESS UPSETTING?

 A loose tooth

 an unpleasant powdery smell

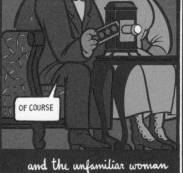 OF COURSE *and the unfamiliar woman*

 *his father's filthy hand*

 *occasionally fingers.*

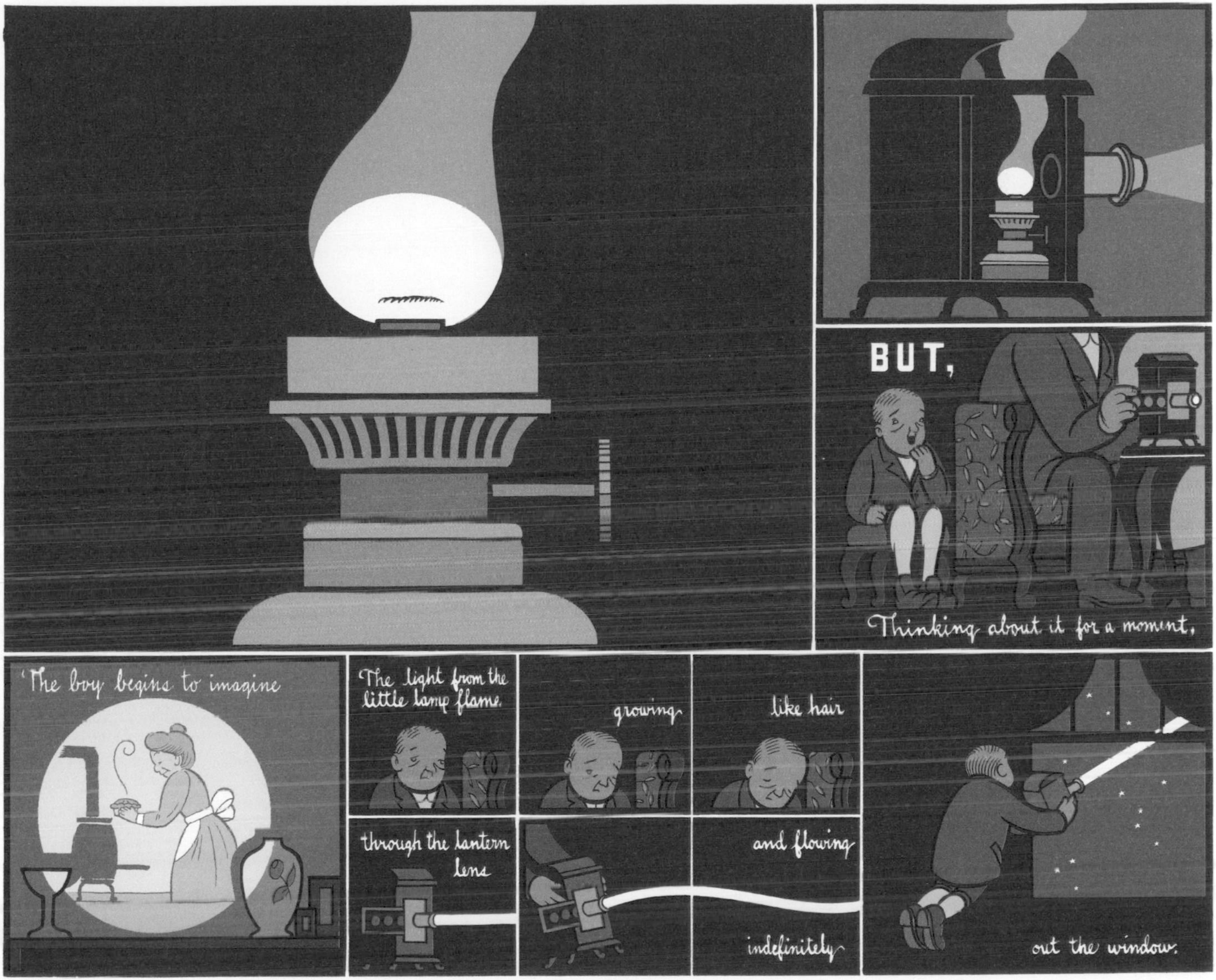
BUT,
Thinking about it for a moment,
'The boy begins to imagine
The light from the little lamp flame,
growing
like hair
through the lantern lens
and flowing
indefinitely
out the window.

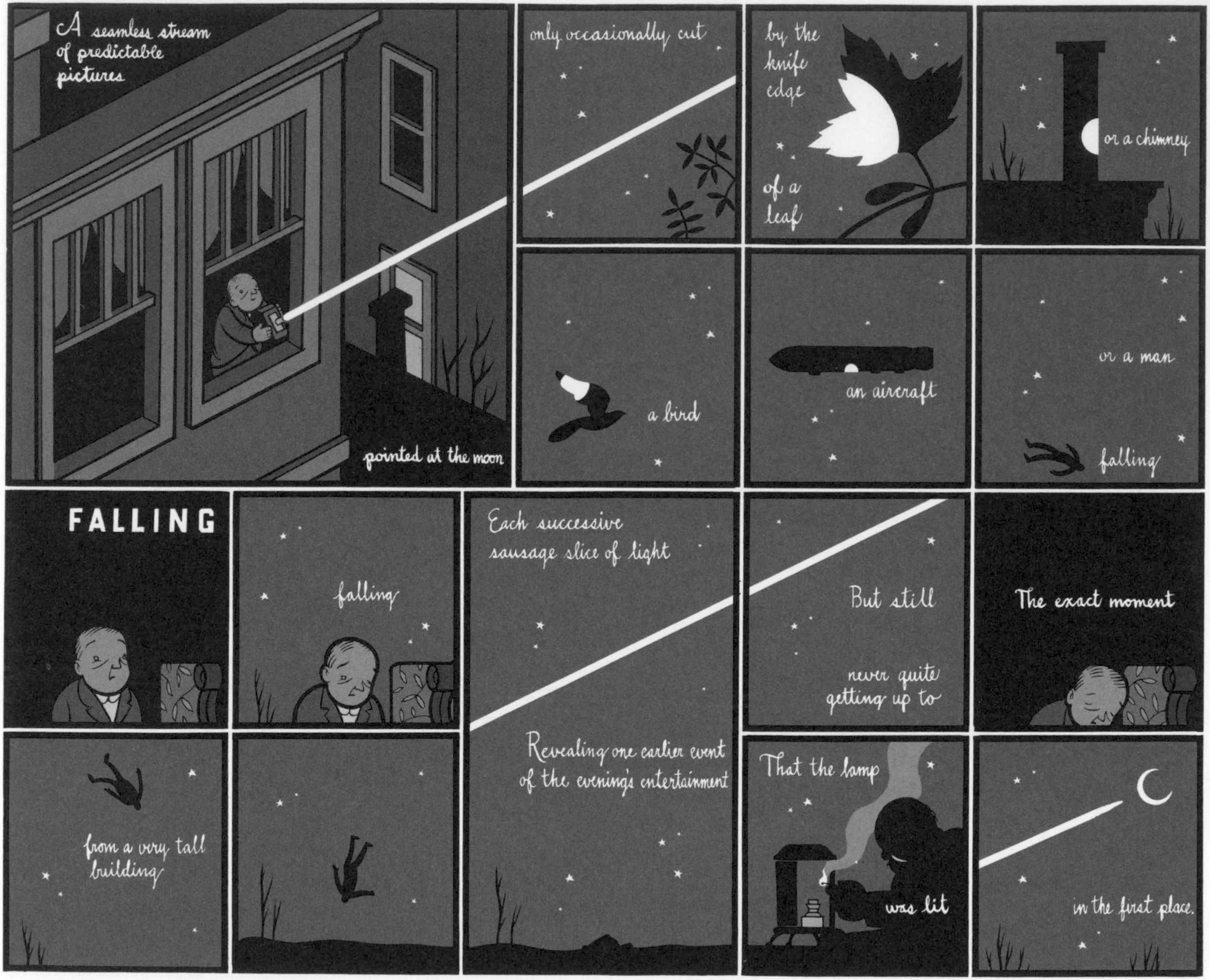
A seamless stream of predictable pictures
pointed at the moon
only occasionally cut
by the knife edge
of a leaf
or a chimney
a bird
an aircraft
or a man
falling
FALLING
falling
Each successive sausage slice of light
Revealing one earlier event of the evening's entertainment
But still
never quite getting up to
The exact moment
from a very tall building
That the lamp
was lit
in the first place.

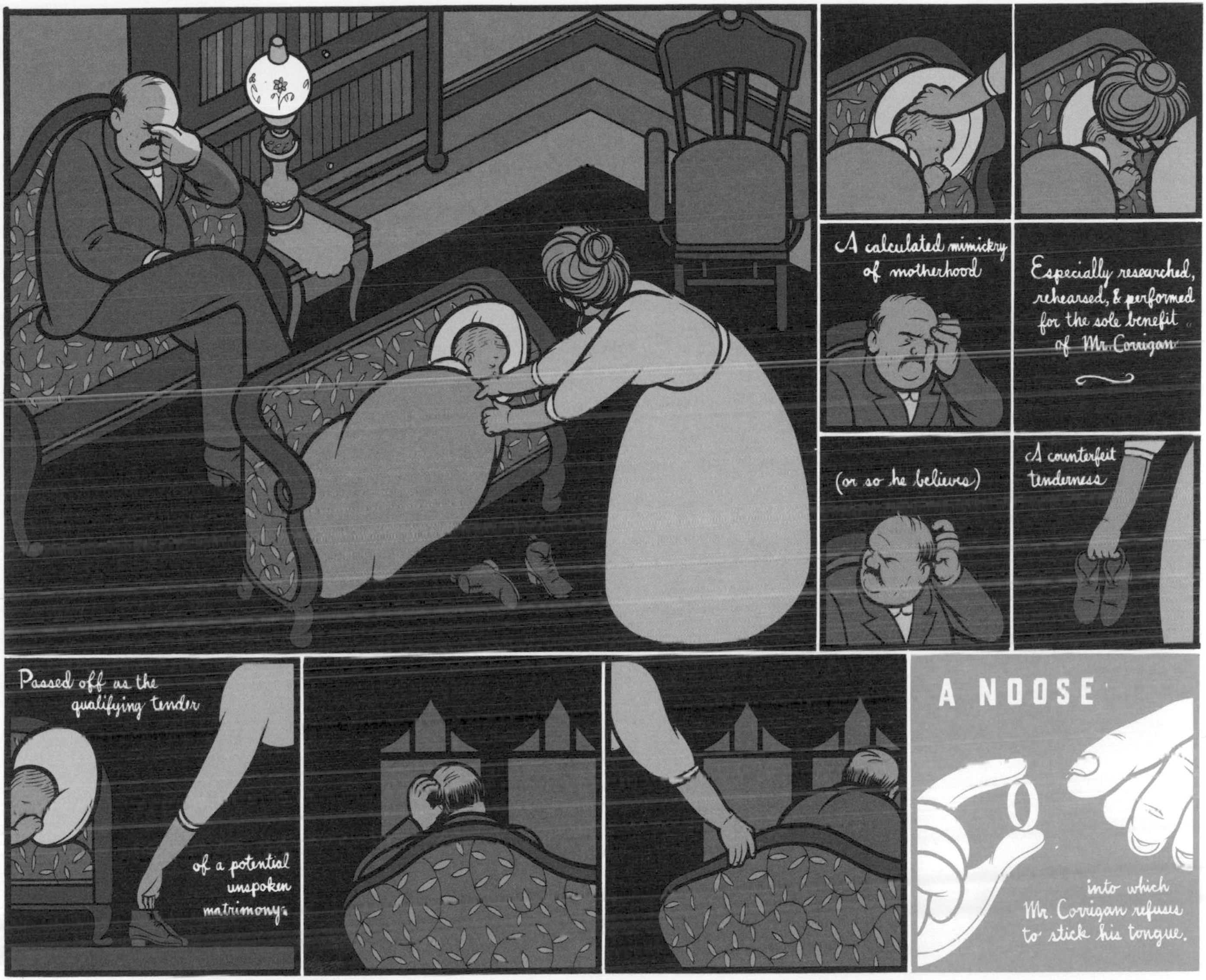
A calculated mimickry of motherhood
Especially researched, rehearsed, & performed for the sole benefit of Mr. Corrigan
(or so he believes)
A counterfeit tenderness
Passed off as the qualifying tender
of a potential unspoken matrimony.
A NOOSE
into which Mr. Corrigan refuses to stick his tongue.

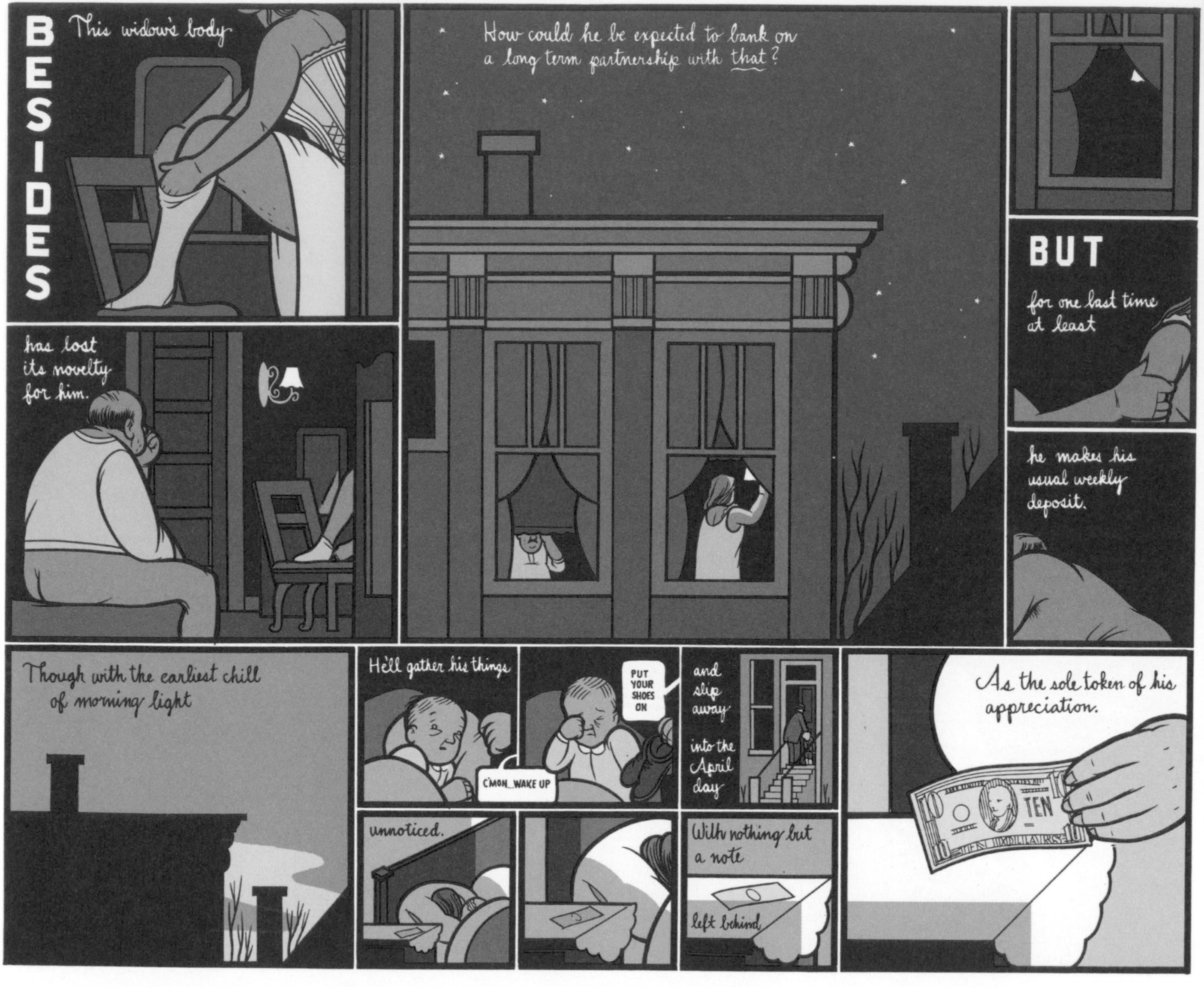
BESIDES
This widow's body
has lost its novelty for him.
How could he be expected to bank on a long term partnership with that?
BUT
for one last time at least
he makes his usual weekly deposit.
Though with the earliest chill of morning light
He'll gather his things
C'MON...WAKE UP
PUT YOUR SHOES ON
and slip away
into the April day
unnoticed.
With nothing but a note
left behind
As the sole token of his appreciation.
TEN
TEN DOLLARS

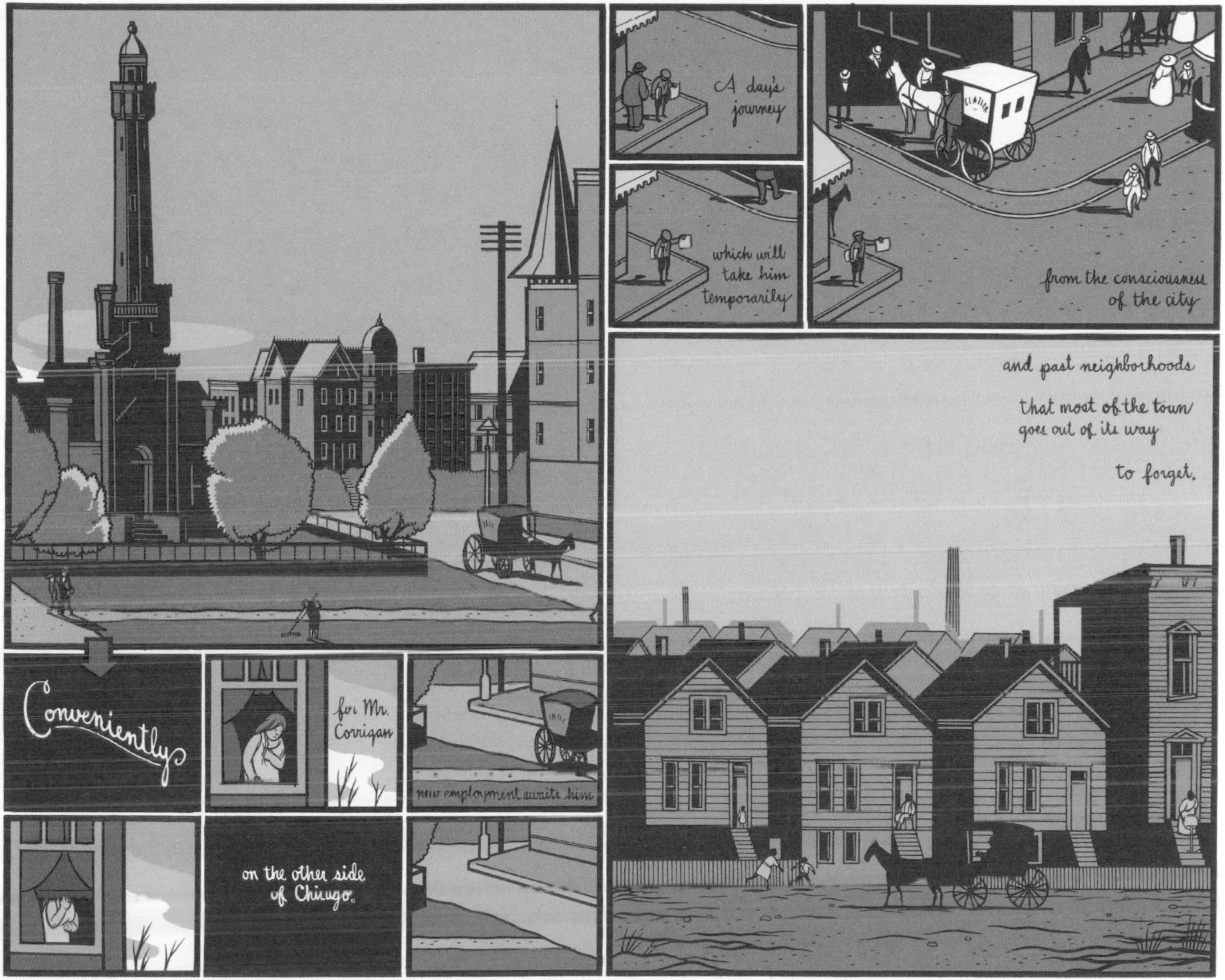
Conveniently
for Mr. Corrigan
new employment awaits him
on the other side of Chicago.
A day's journey
which will take him temporarily
from the consciousness of the city
and past neighborhoods
that most of the town goes out of its way
to forget.

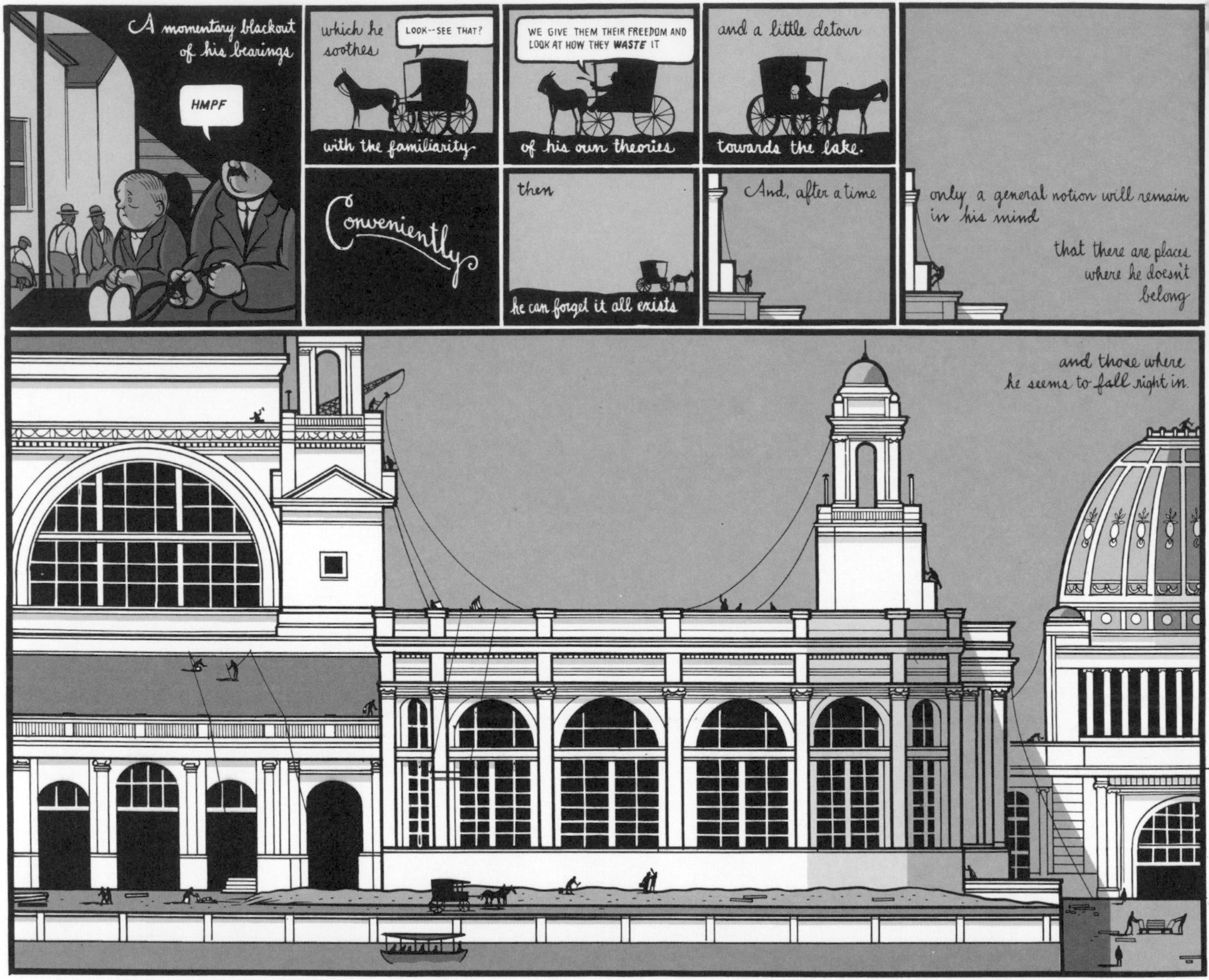
A momentary blackout of his bearings
HMPF
which he soothes
LOOK--SEE THAT?
with the familiarity
WE GIVE THEM THEIR FREEDOM AND LOOK AT HOW THEY WASTE IT
of his own theories
and a little detour
towards the lake.
Conveniently
then
he can forget it all exists
And, after a time
only a general notion will remain in his mind
that there are places where he doesn't belong
and those where he seems to fall right in.

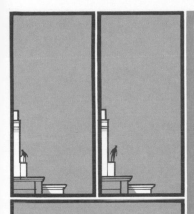

MEANWHILE.

THE **SOUND**

of One Lung

filling with water

DROWNED OUT by wave after wave

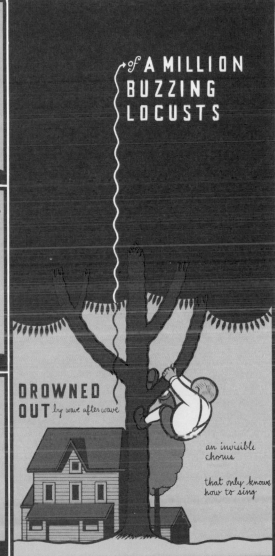

of **A MILLION BUZZING LOCUSTS**

an invisible chorus

that only knows how to sing

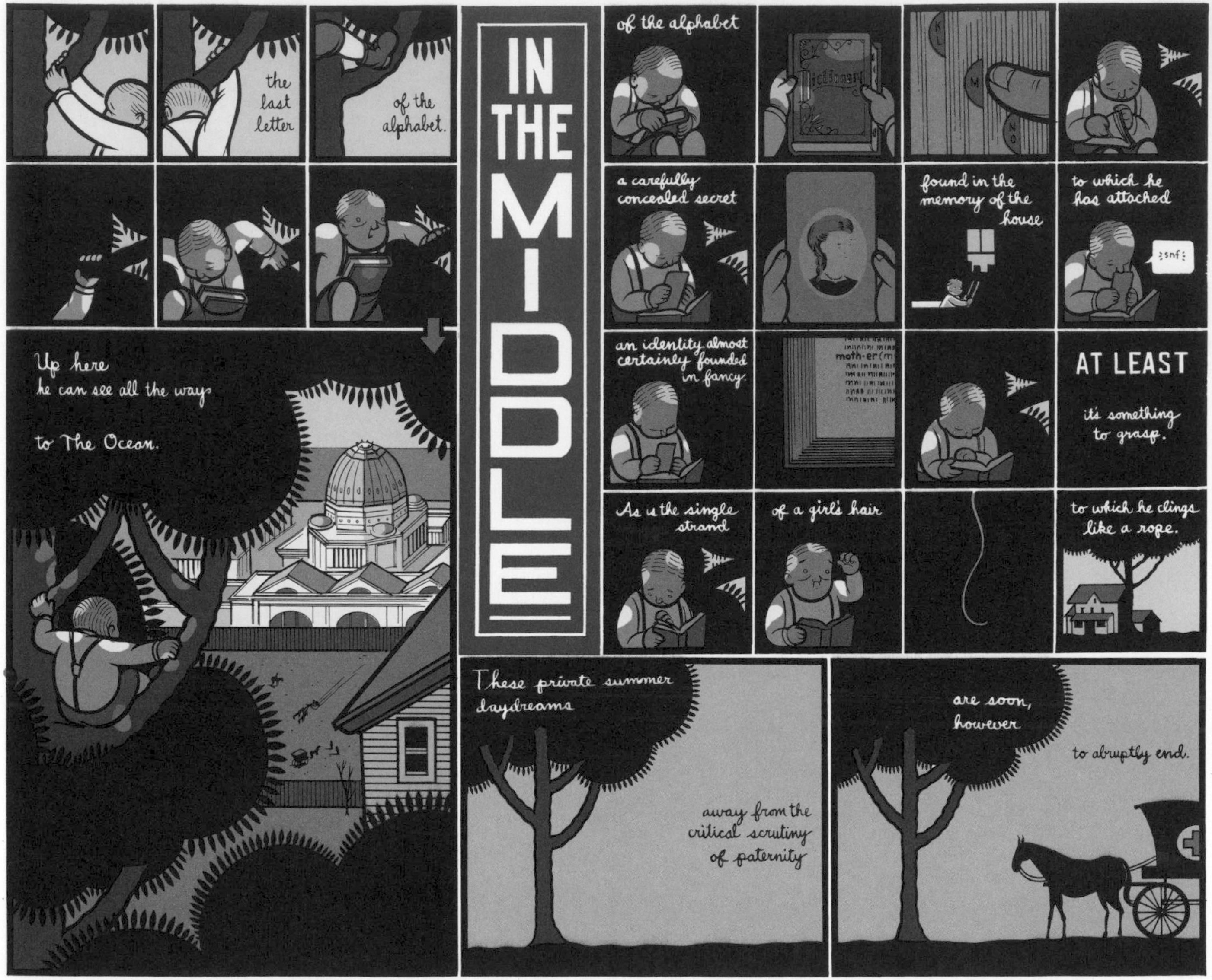
the last letter
of the alphabet.
Up here he can see all the ways
to The Ocean.
IN THE MIDDLE
of the alphabet
Dictionary
K L
M
N O
a carefully concealed secret
found in the memory of the house
to which he has attached
snf
an identity almost certainly founded in fancy.
moth-er (m
AT LEAST
it's something to grasp.
As is the single strand
of a girl's hair
to which he clings like a rope.
These private summer daydreams
away from the critical scrutiny of paternity
are soon, however
to abruptly end.

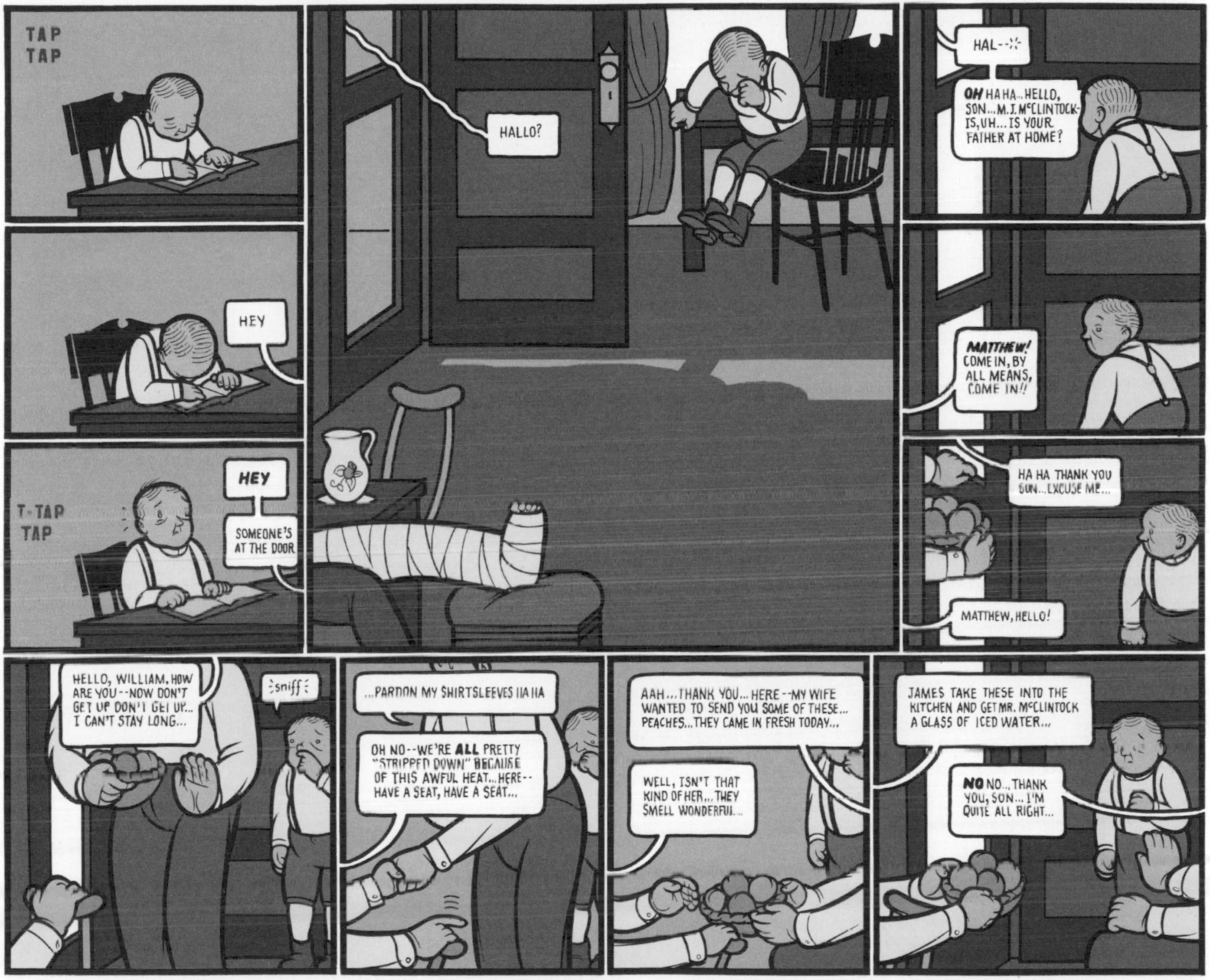
TAP
TAP
HEY
T-TAP
TAP
HEY
SOMEONE'S AT THE DOOR
HALLO?
HAL--
OH HA HA... HELLO, SON... M.J. McCLINTOCK- IS, UH... IS YOUR FATHER AT HOME?
MATTHEW! COME IN, BY ALL MEANS, COME IN!!
HA HA THANK YOU SON... EXCUSE ME...
MATTHEW, HELLO!
HELLO, WILLIAM, HOW ARE YOU--NOW DON'T GET UP DON'T GET UP... I CAN'T STAY LONG...
sniff
...PARDON MY SHIRTSLEEVES HA HA
OH NO--WE'RE ALL PRETTY "STRIPPED DOWN" BECAUSE OF THIS AWFUL HEAT... HERE-- HAVE A SEAT, HAVE A SEAT...
AAH... THANK YOU... HERE--MY WIFE WANTED TO SEND YOU SOME OF THESE... PEACHES... THEY CAME IN FRESH TODAY...
WELL, ISN'T THAT KIND OF HER... THEY SMELL WONDERFUL...
JAMES TAKE THESE INTO THE KITCHEN AND GET MR. McCLINTOCK A GLASS OF ICED WATER...
NO NO... THANK YOU, SON... I'M QUITE ALL RIGHT...

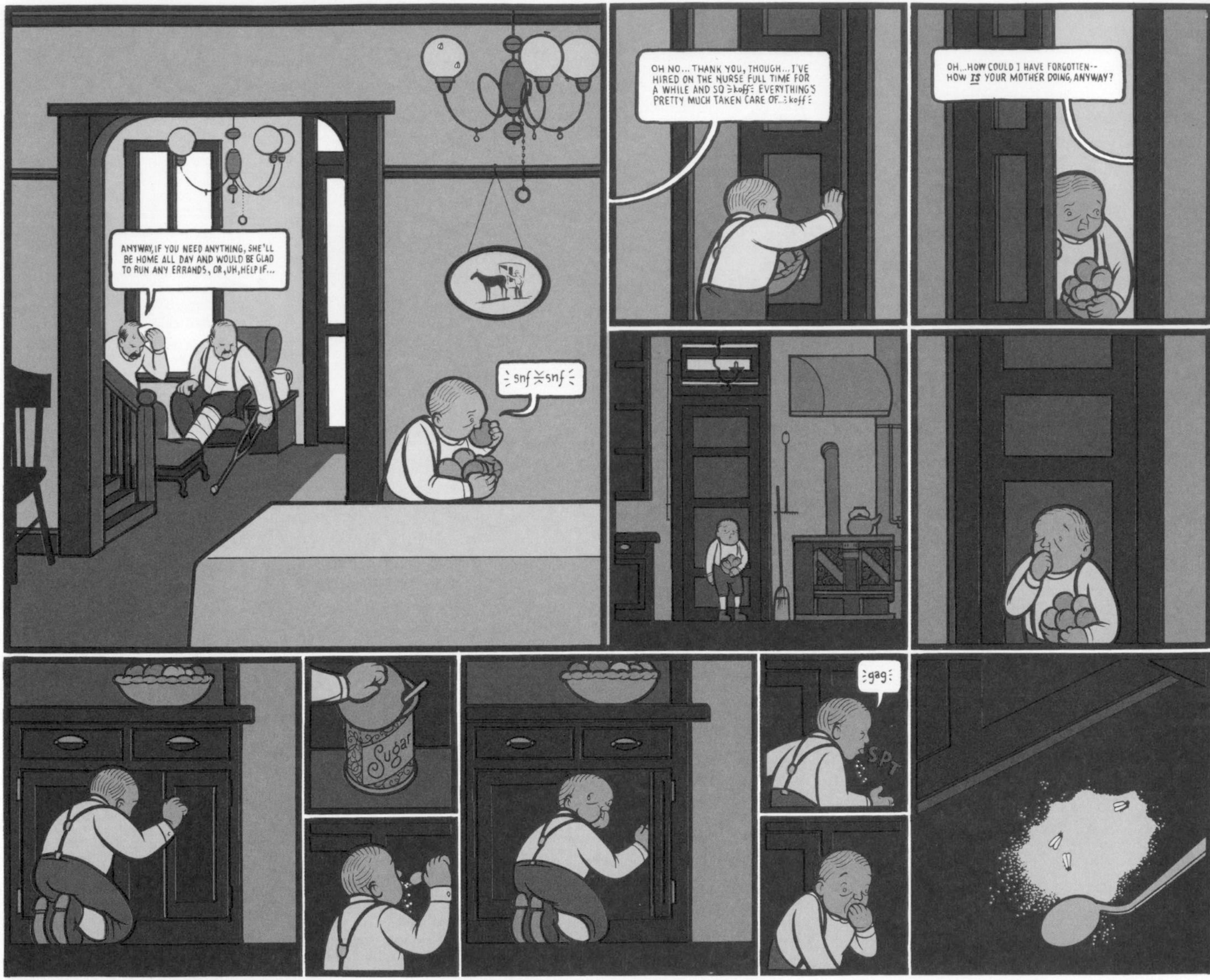
ANYWAY, IF YOU NEED ANYTHING, SHE'LL BE HOME ALL DAY AND WOULD BE GLAD TO RUN ANY ERRANDS, OR, UH, HELP IF...
snf snf
OH NO... THANK YOU, THOUGH... I'VE HIRED ON THE NURSE FULL TIME FOR A WHILE AND SO koff EVERYTHING'S PRETTY MUCH TAKEN CARE OF... koff
OH... HOW COULD I HAVE FORGOTTEN-- HOW *IS* YOUR MOTHER DOING, ANYWAY?
Sugar
gag
SPT

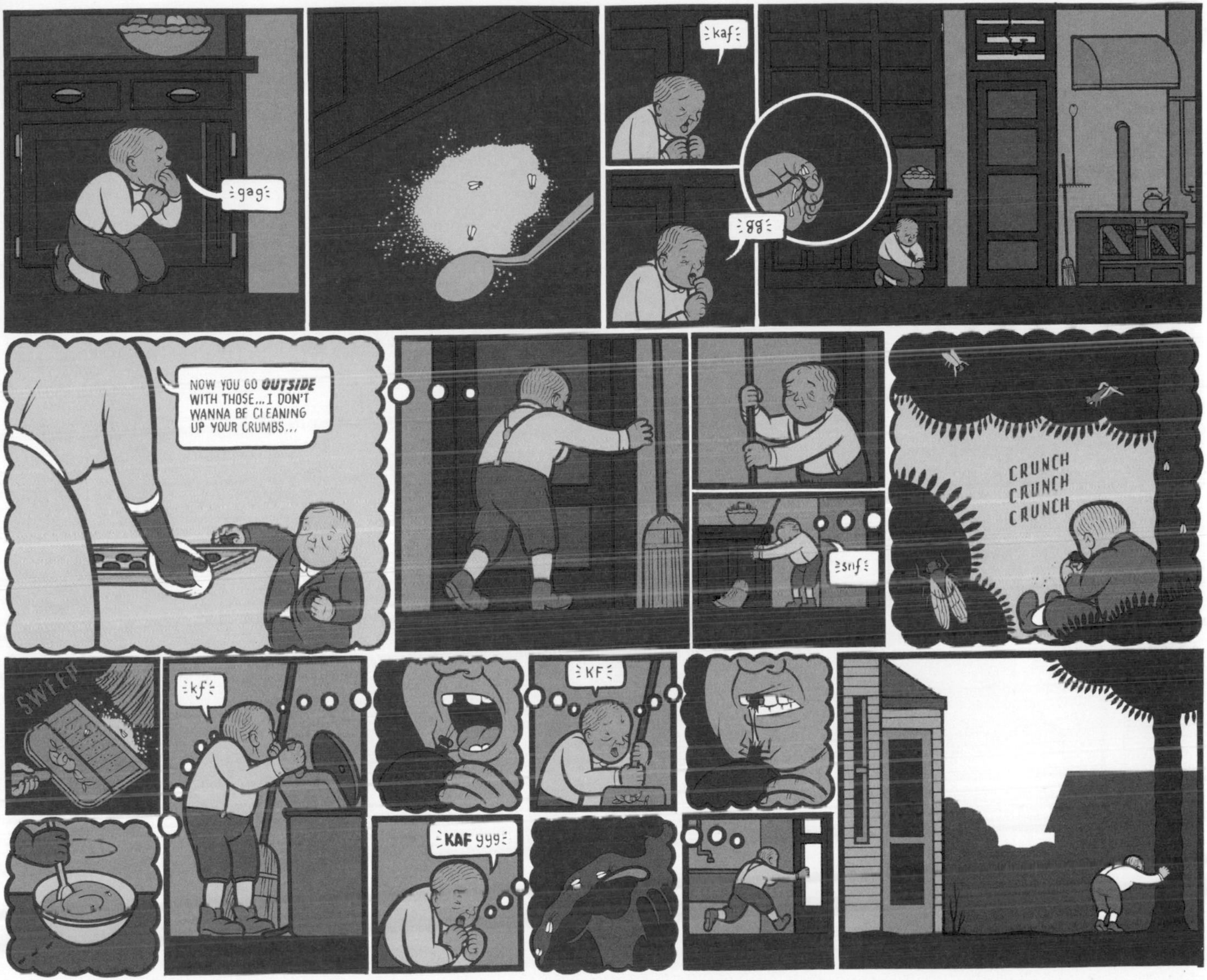
gag
kaf
gg
NOW YOU GO OUTSIDE WITH THOSE... I DON'T WANNA BE CLEANING UP YOUR CRUMBS...
snif
CRUNCH
CRUNCH
CRUNCH
SWEEP
kf
KF
KAF ggg

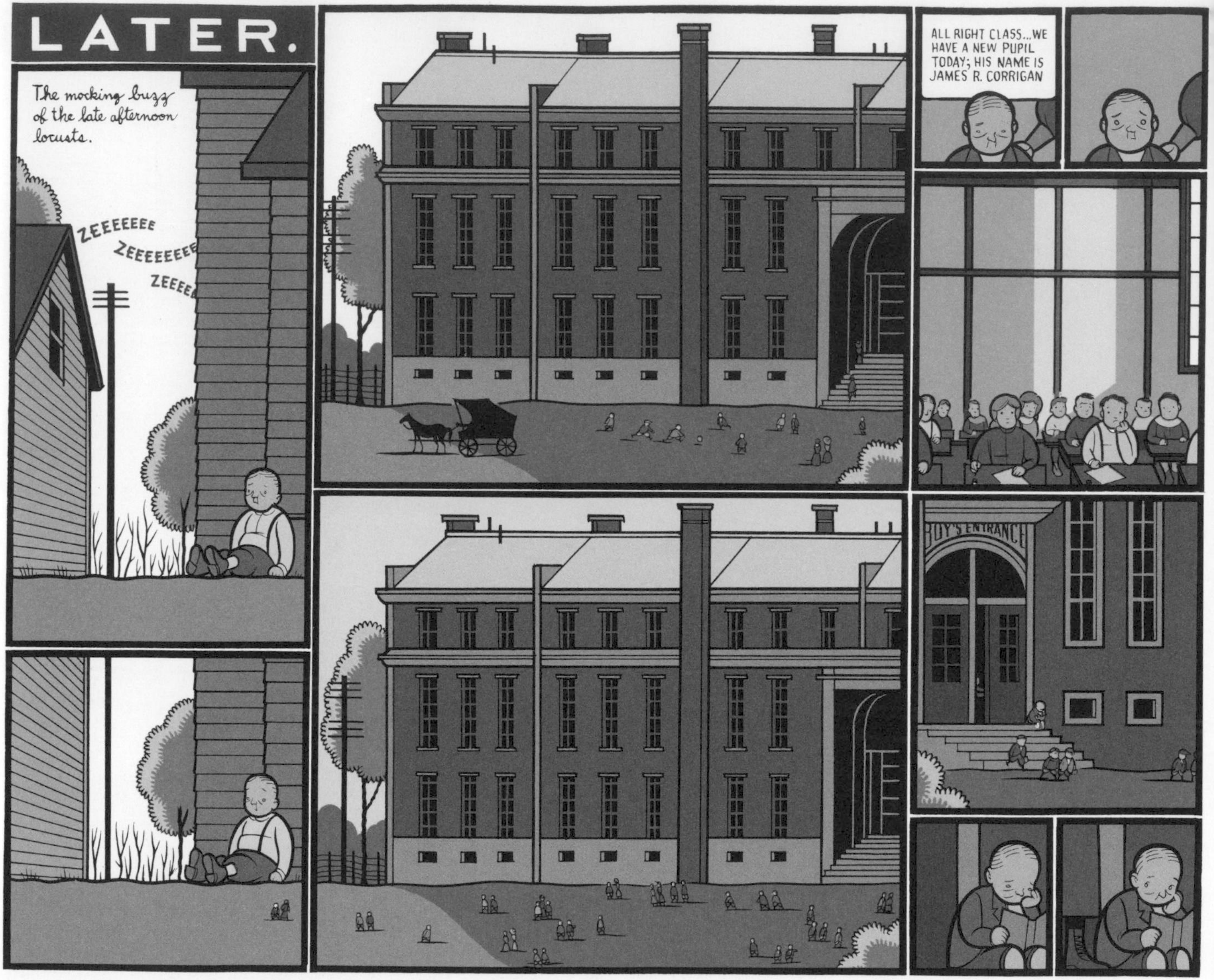
LATER.
The mocking buzz of the late afternoon locusts.
ZEEEEEEE
ZEEEEEEEE
ZEEEEE
ALL RIGHT CLASS...WE HAVE A NEW PUPIL TODAY; HIS NAME IS JAMES R. CORRIGAN
BOY'S ENTRANCE

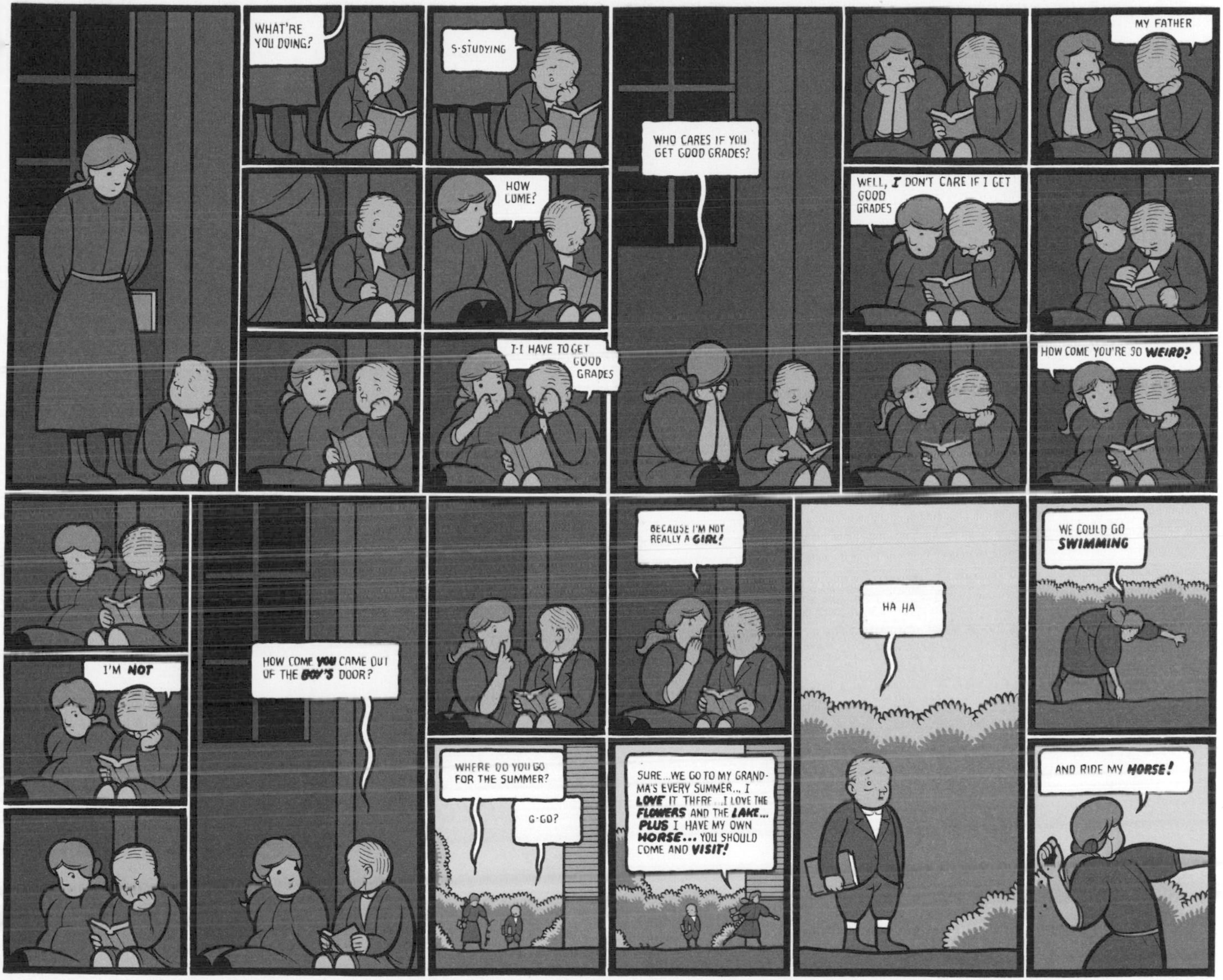
WHAT'RE YOU DOING?
S-STUDYING
HOW COME?
T-I HAVE TO GET GOOD GRADES
WHO CARES IF YOU GET GOOD GRADES?
MY FATHER
WELL, I DON'T CARE IF I GET GOOD GRADES
HOW COME YOU'RE SO WEIRD?
I'M NOT
HOW COME YOU CAME OUT OF THE BOY'S DOOR?
BECAUSE I'M NOT REALLY A GIRL!
WHERE DO YOU GO FOR THE SUMMER?
G-GO?
SURE...WE GO TO MY GRAND-MA'S EVERY SUMMER... I LOVE IT THERE...I LOVE THE FLOWERS AND THE LAKE... PLUS I HAVE MY OWN HORSE... YOU SHOULD COME AND VISIT!
HA HA
WE COULD GO SWIMMING
AND RIDE MY HORSE!

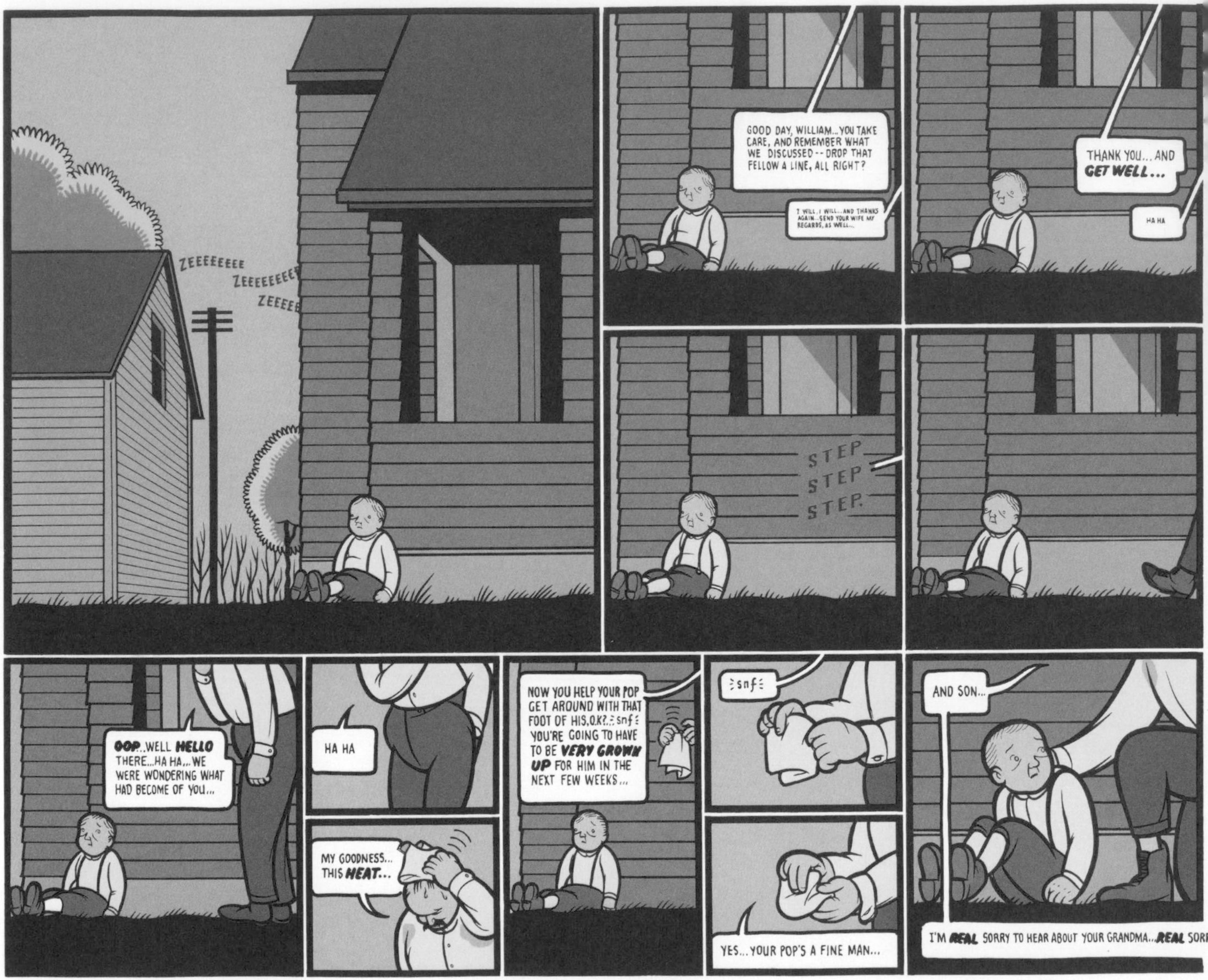
ZEEEEEEEE
ZEEEEEEEEE
ZEEEEE
GOOD DAY, WILLIAM... YOU TAKE CARE, AND REMEMBER WHAT WE DISCUSSED -- DROP THAT FELLOW A LINE, ALL RIGHT?
I WILL, I WILL... AND THANKS AGAIN... SEND YOUR WIFE MY REGARDS, AS WELL...
THANK YOU... AND GET WELL...
HA HA
STEP STEP STEP
OOP.. WELL HELLO THERE... HA HA... WE WERE WONDERING WHAT HAD BECOME OF YOU...
HA HA
MY GOODNESS... THIS HEAT...
NOW YOU HELP YOUR POP GET AROUND WITH THAT FOOT OF HIS, O.K.? snf YOU'RE GOING TO HAVE TO BE VERY GROWN UP FOR HIM IN THE NEXT FEW WEEKS...
snf
YES... YOUR POP'S A FINE MAN...
AND SON...
I'M REAL SORRY TO HEAR ABOUT YOUR GRANDMA... REAL SORRY.

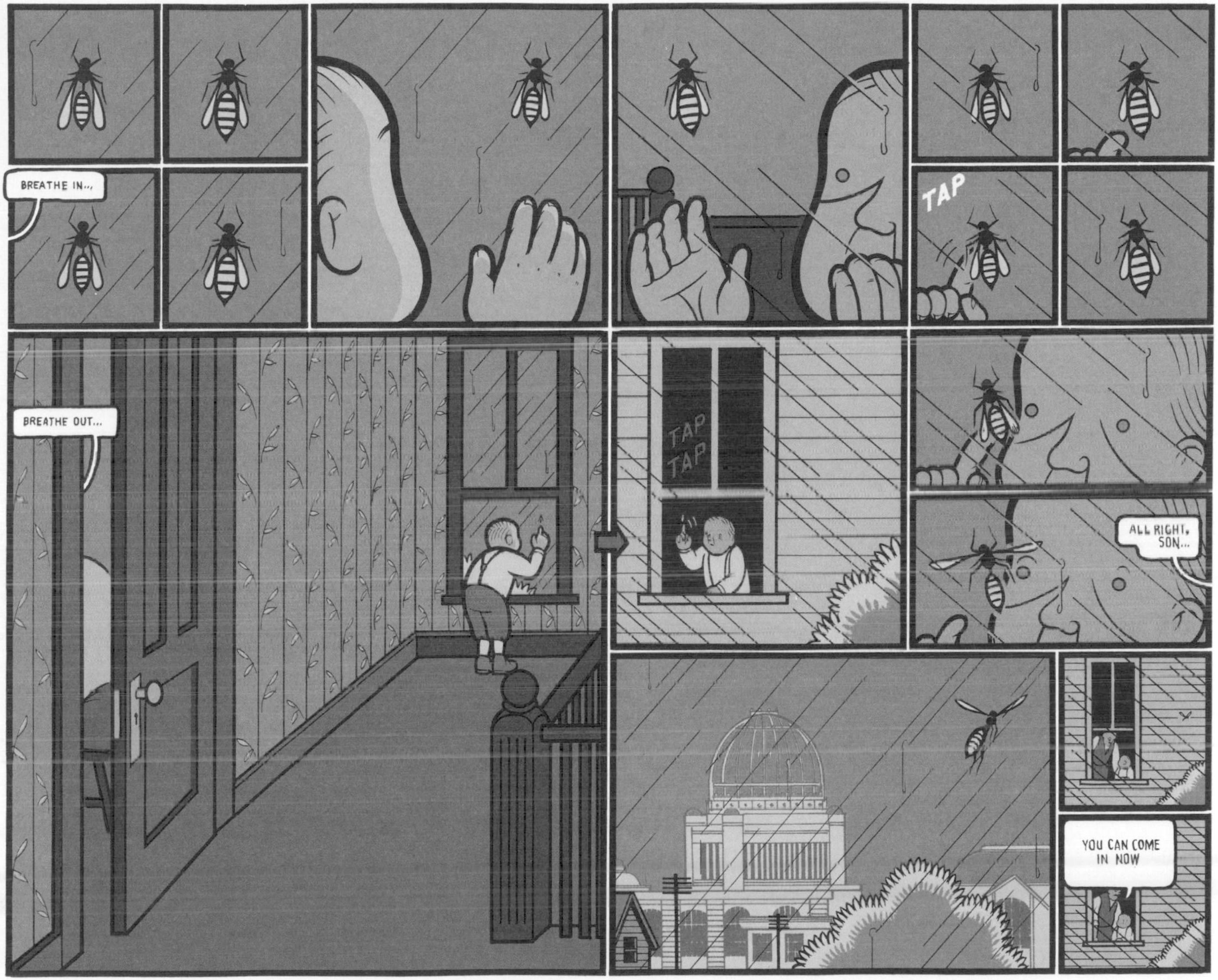
BREATHE IN...
TAP
BREATHE OUT...
TAP
TAP
ALL RIGHT, SON...
YOU CAN COME IN NOW

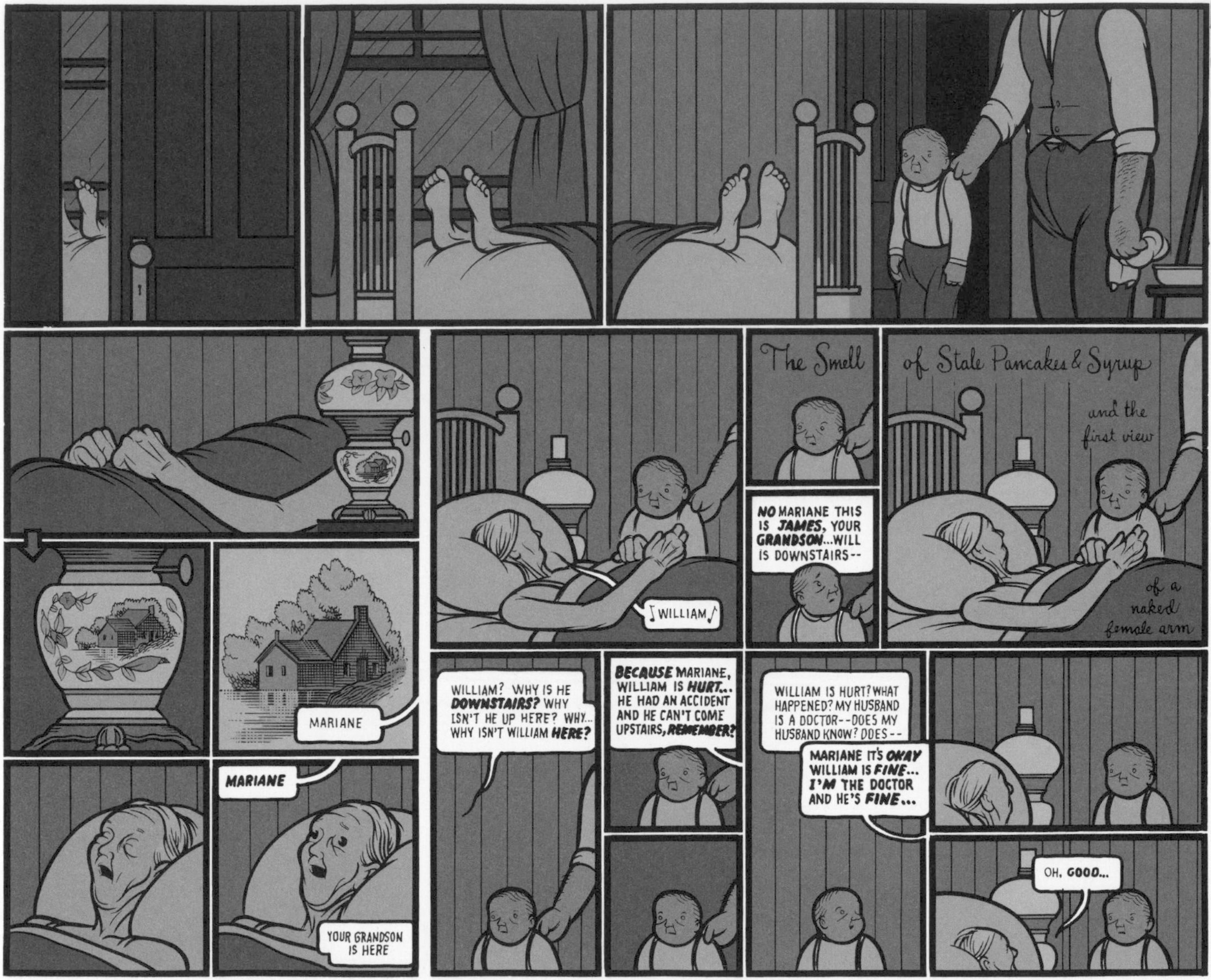

The Smell of Stale Pancakes & Syrup
and the first view
of a naked female arm
♪WILLIAM♪
NO MARIANE THIS IS JAMES, YOUR GRANDSON...WILL IS DOWNSTAIRS--
MARIANE
MARIANE
YOUR GRANDSON IS HERE
WILLIAM? WHY IS HE DOWNSTAIRS? WHY ISN'T HE UP HERE? WHY... WHY ISN'T WILLIAM HERE?
BECAUSE MARIANE, WILLIAM IS HURT... HE HAD AN ACCIDENT AND HE CAN'T COME UPSTAIRS, REMEMBER?
WILLIAM IS HURT? WHAT HAPPENED? MY HUSBAND IS A DOCTOR--DOES MY HUSBAND KNOW? DOES--
MARIANE IT'S OKAY WILLIAM IS FINE... I'M THE DOCTOR AND HE'S FINE...
OH, GOOD...

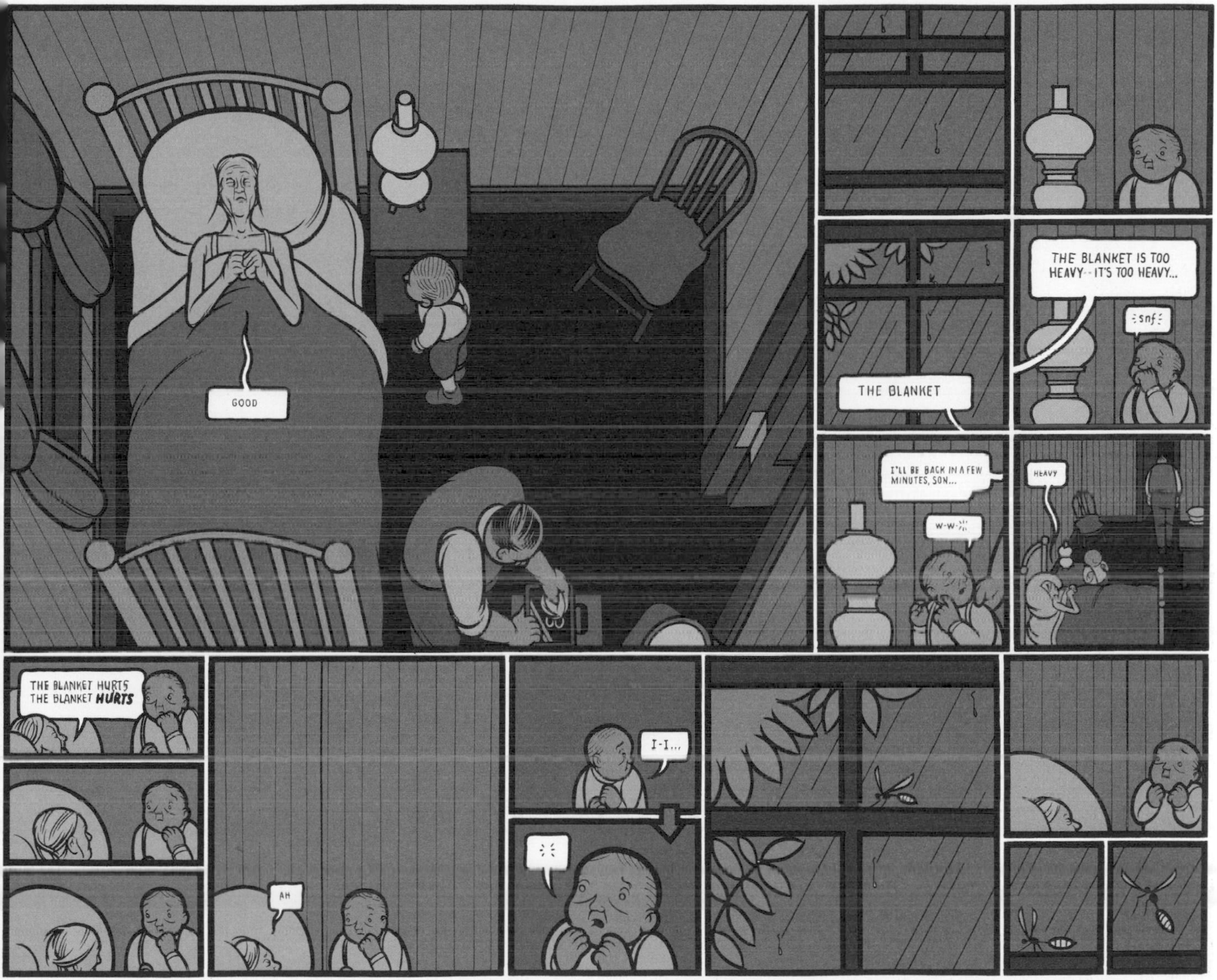
GOOD
THE BLANKET
THE BLANKET IS TOO HEAVY-- IT'S TOO HEAVY...
snf
I'LL BE BACK IN A FEW MINUTES, SON...
W-W-
HEAVY
THE BLANKET HURTS THE BLANKET **HURTS**
AH
I-I...

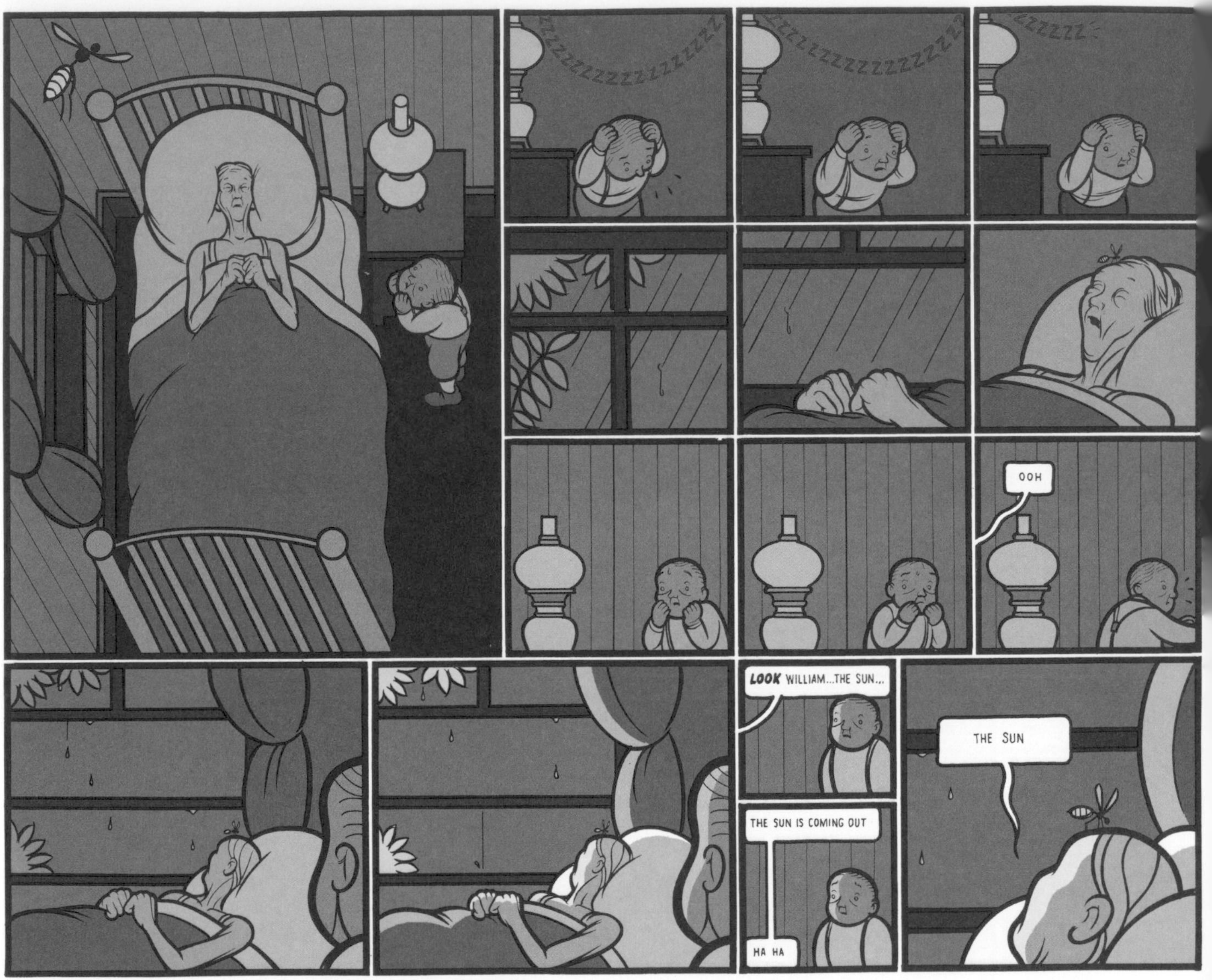
ZZZZZZZZZZZZZZZZZ
ZZZZZZZZZZZZZZZZZ
ZZZZZZ
OOH
LOOK WILLIAM...THE SUN...
THE SUN IS COMING OUT
HA HA
THE SUN

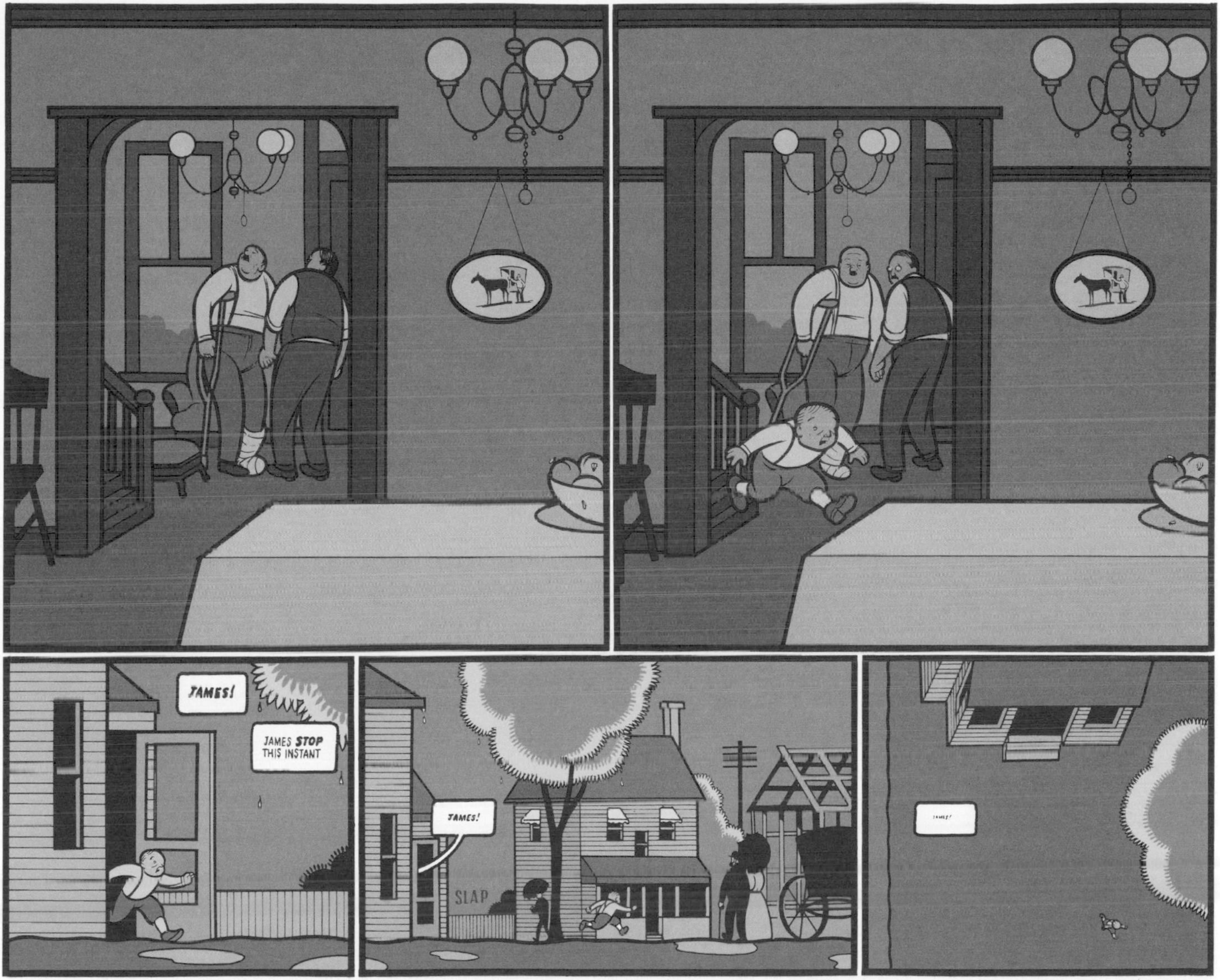
JAMES!
JAMES STOP THIS INSTANT
JAMES!
SLAP

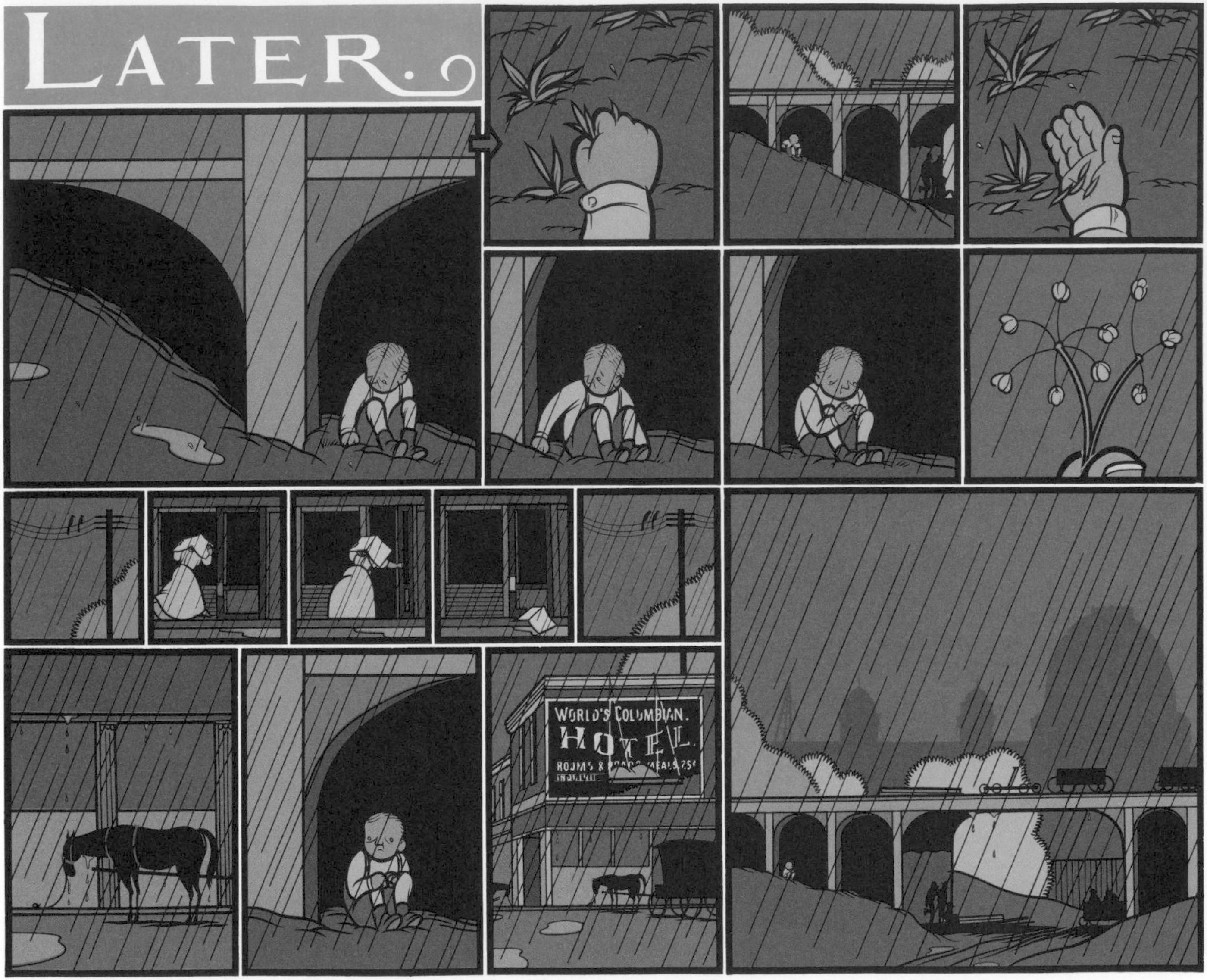
LATER.
WORLD'S COLUMBIAN.
HOTEL.
ROOMS &

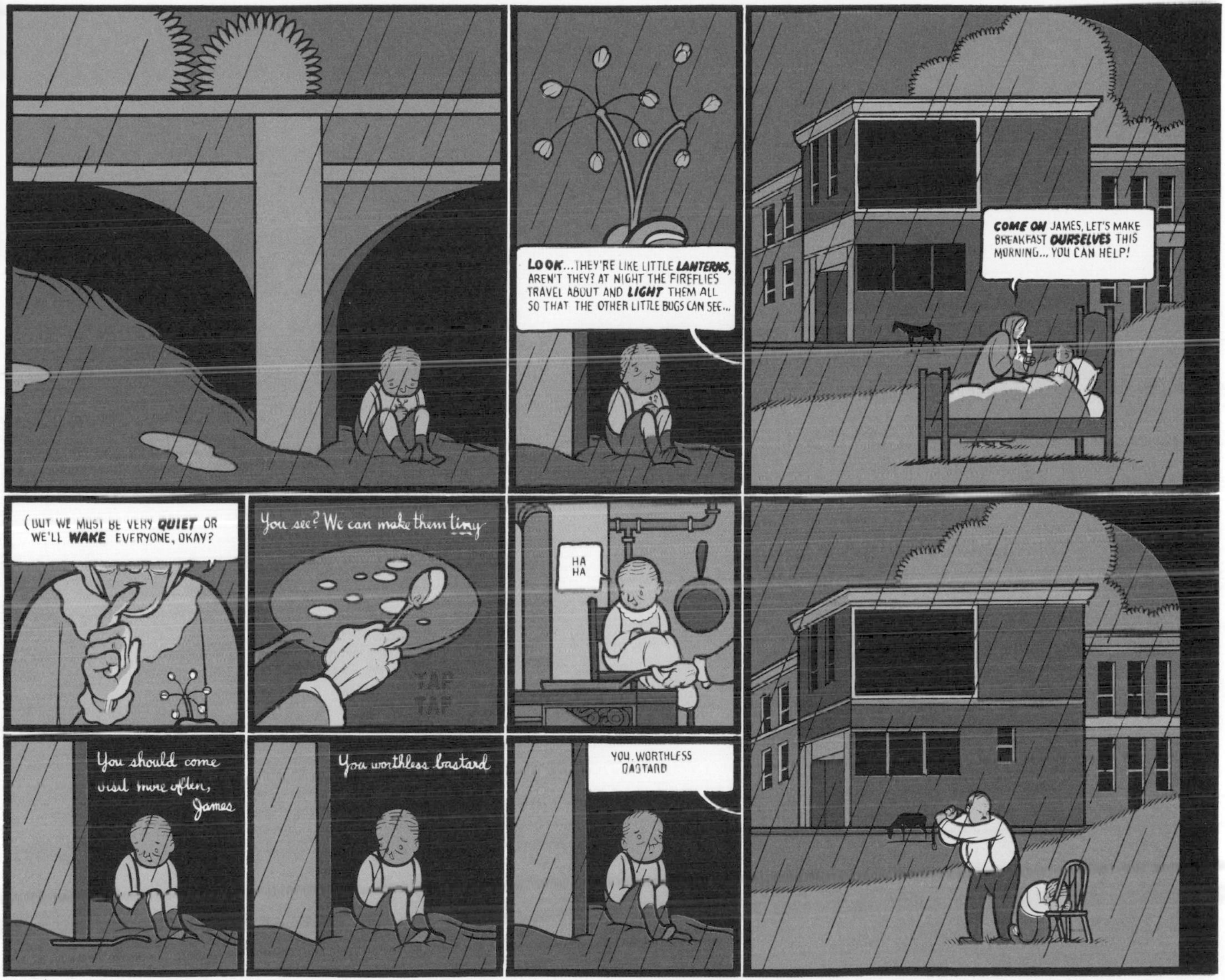
LOOK... THEY'RE LIKE LITTLE LANTERNS, AREN'T THEY? AT NIGHT THE FIREFLIES TRAVEL ABOUT AND LIGHT THEM ALL SO THAT THE OTHER LITTLE BUGS CAN SEE...
COME ON JAMES, LET'S MAKE BREAKFAST OURSELVES THIS MORNING... YOU CAN HELP!
(BUT WE MUST BE VERY QUIET OR WE'LL WAKE EVERYONE, OKAY?
You see? We can make them tiny
TAP TAP
HA HA
You should come visit more often, James
You worthless bastard
YOU. WORTHLESS BASTARD

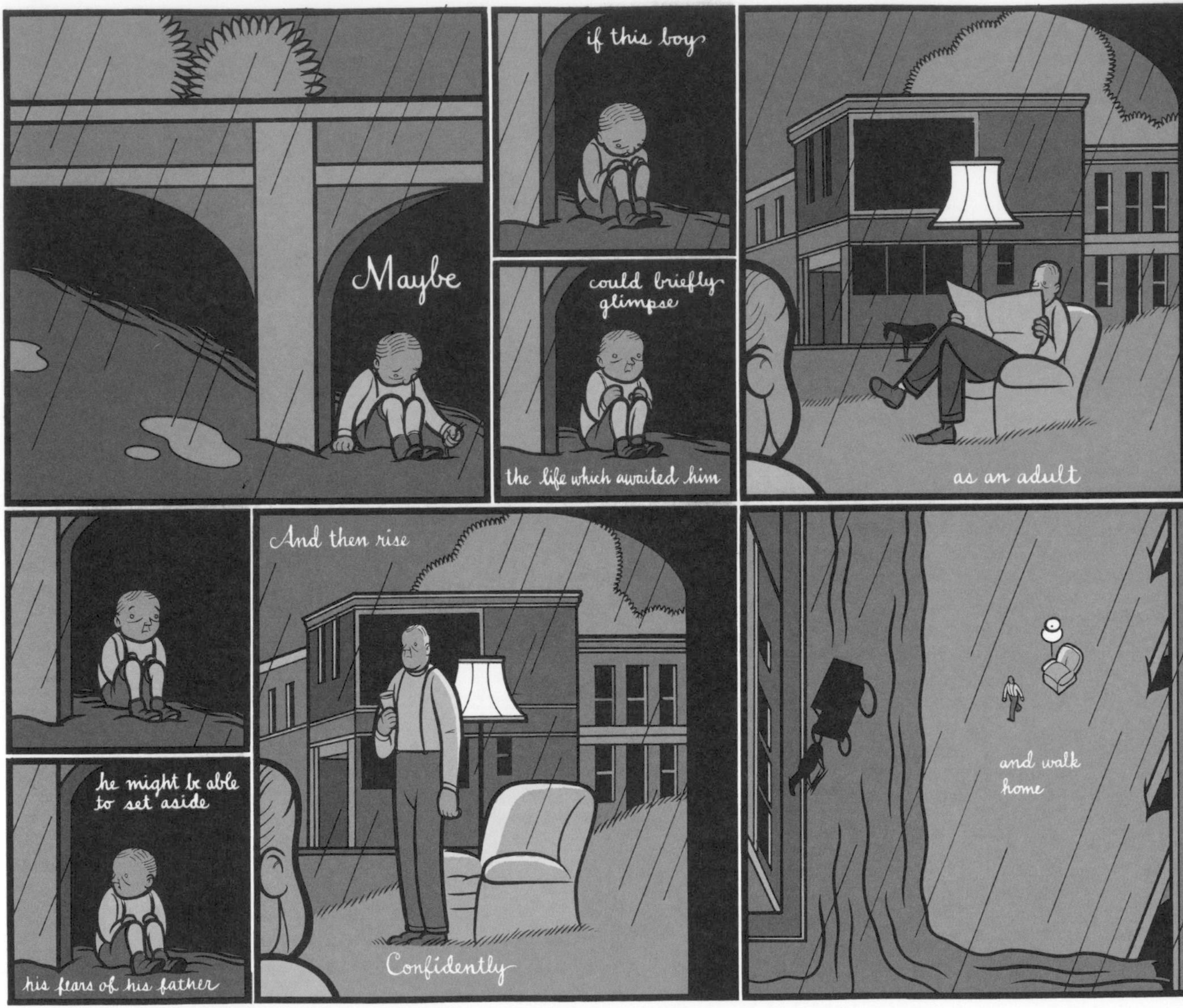
Maybe
if this boy
could briefly glimpse
the life which awaited him
as an adult
he might be able to set aside
his fears of his father
And then rise
Confidently
and walk home

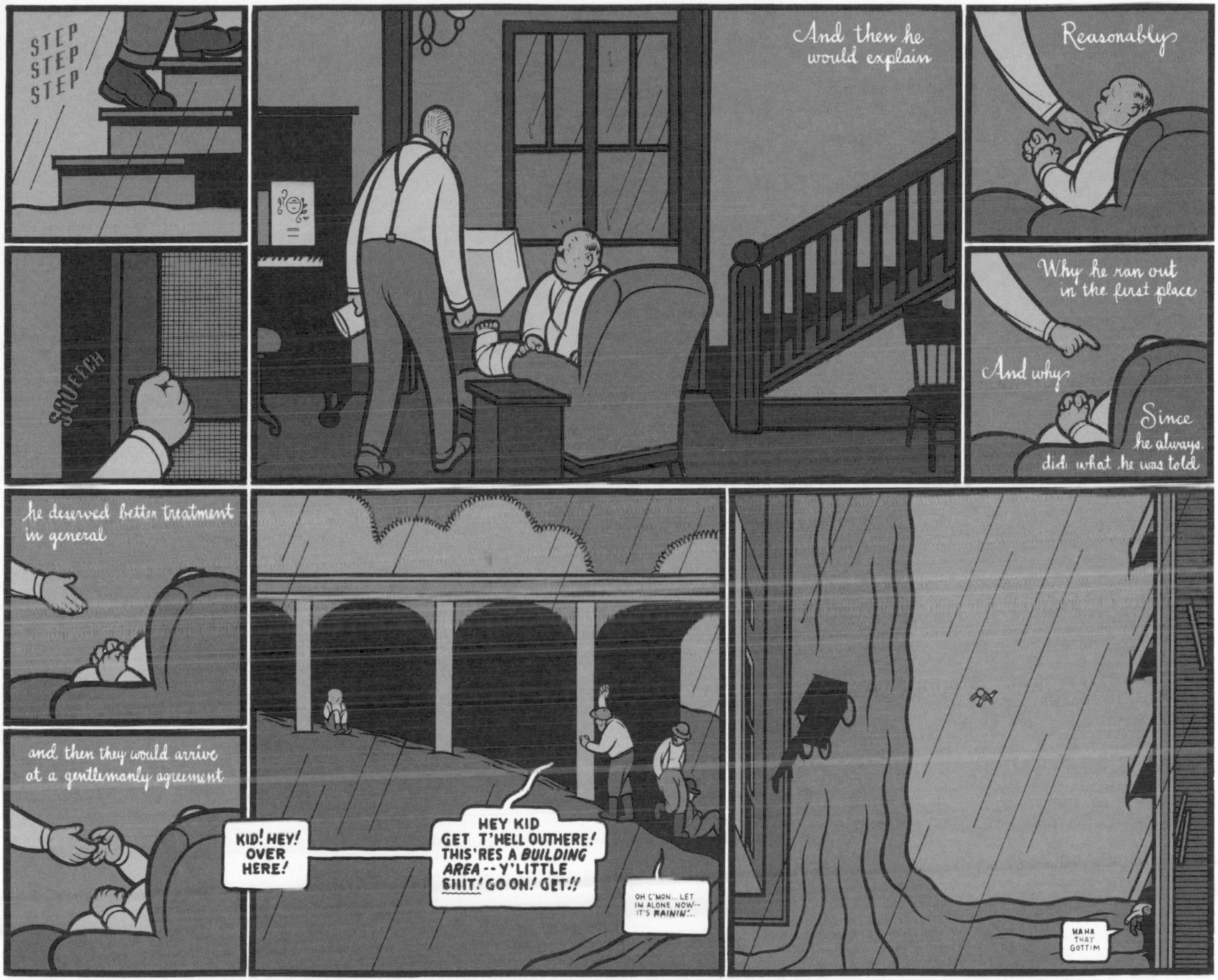
STEP
STEP
STEP
SQUEECH
And then he would explain
Reasonably
Why he ran out in the first place
And why
Since he always did what he was told
he deserved better treatment in general
and then they would arrive at a gentlemanly agreement
KID! HEY! OVER HERE!
HEY KID GET T'HELL OUTHERE! THIS'RES A BUILDING AREA -- Y'LITTLE SHIT! GO ON! GET!!
OH C'MON... LET IM ALONE NOW-- IT'S RAININ'...
HAHA THAT GOTTIM

A distant roll of thunder

and

A cooling breeze

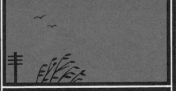

bearing the slur

of neighborhood voices emerging from the stale house heat

Crickets, fireflies...

All ruined

by a stomach-turning sense of dread.

It makes his toes hurt.

(and the familiar sniff of his own kneecaps

which always precedes any punishment.)

SOMETIMES
if he pushes on his eyeballs hard enough

he sees pictures

Red splotches and patterns of purple green sparkles, silvery smears

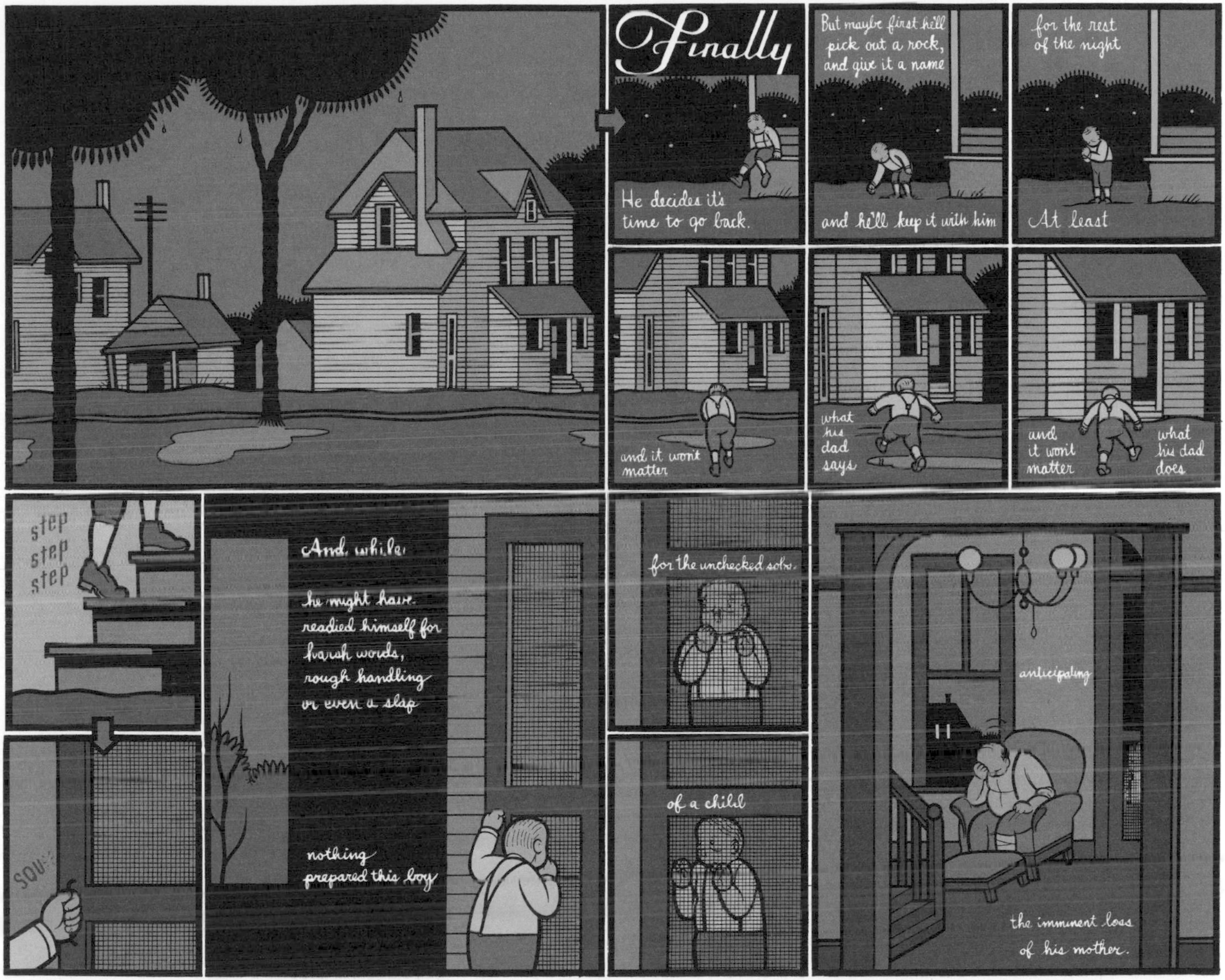
Finally
He decides it's time to go back.
But maybe first he'll pick out a rock, and give it a name
and he'll keep it with him
for the rest of the night
At least
and it won't matter
what his dad says
and it won't matter
what his dad does
step
step
step
SQU
And while
he might have readied himself for harsh words, rough handling or even a slap
nothing prepared this boy
for the unchecked sobs
of a child
anticipating
the imminent loss of his mother.

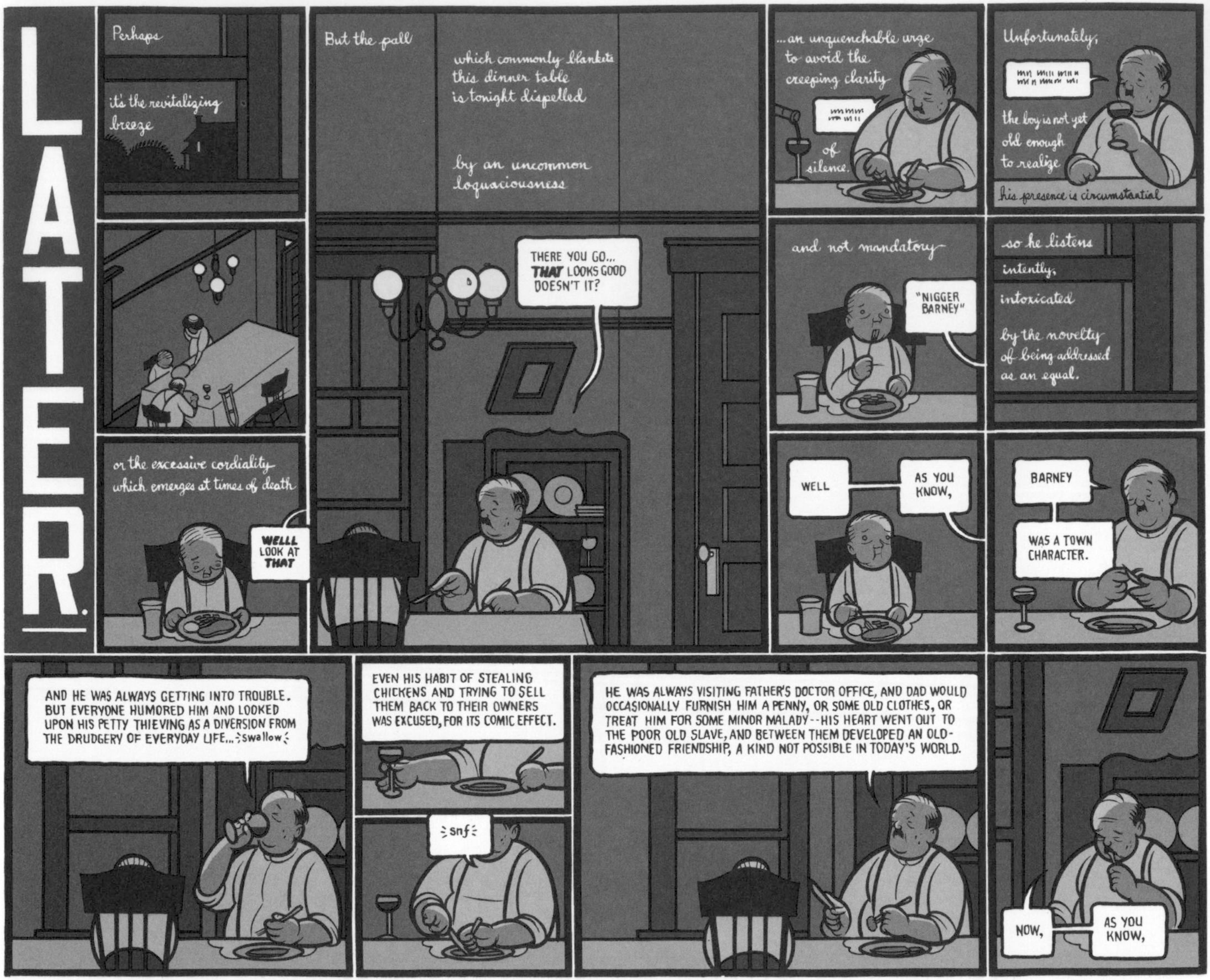

LATER.
Perhaps
it's the revitalizing breeze
or the excessive cordiality which emerges at times of death
WELLL LOOK AT THAT
But the pall
which commonly blankets this dinner table is tonight dispelled
by an uncommon loquaciousness
THERE YOU GO... THAT LOOKS GOOD DOESN'T IT?
...an unquenchable urge to avoid the creeping clarity
of silence.
Unfortunately,
the boy is not yet old enough to realize
his presence is circumstantial
and not mandatory—
"NIGGER BARNEY"
so he listens intently,
intoxicated
by the novelty of being addressed as an equal.
WELL
AS YOU KNOW,
BARNEY
WAS A TOWN CHARACTER.
AND HE WAS ALWAYS GETTING INTO TROUBLE. BUT EVERYONE HUMORED HIM AND LOOKED UPON HIS PETTY THIEVING AS A DIVERSION FROM THE DRUDGERY OF EVERYDAY LIFE... swallow
EVEN HIS HABIT OF STEALING CHICKENS AND TRYING TO SELL THEM BACK TO THEIR OWNERS WAS EXCUSED, FOR ITS COMIC EFFECT.
snf
HE WAS ALWAYS VISITING FATHER'S DOCTOR OFFICE, AND DAD WOULD OCCASIONALLY FURNISH HIM A PENNY, OR SOME OLD CLOTHES, OR TREAT HIM FOR SOME MINOR MALADY--HIS HEART WENT OUT TO THE POOR OLD SLAVE, AND BETWEEN THEM DEVELOPED AN OLD-FASHIONED FRIENDSHIP, A KIND NOT POSSIBLE IN TODAY'S WORLD.
NOW,
AS YOU KNOW,

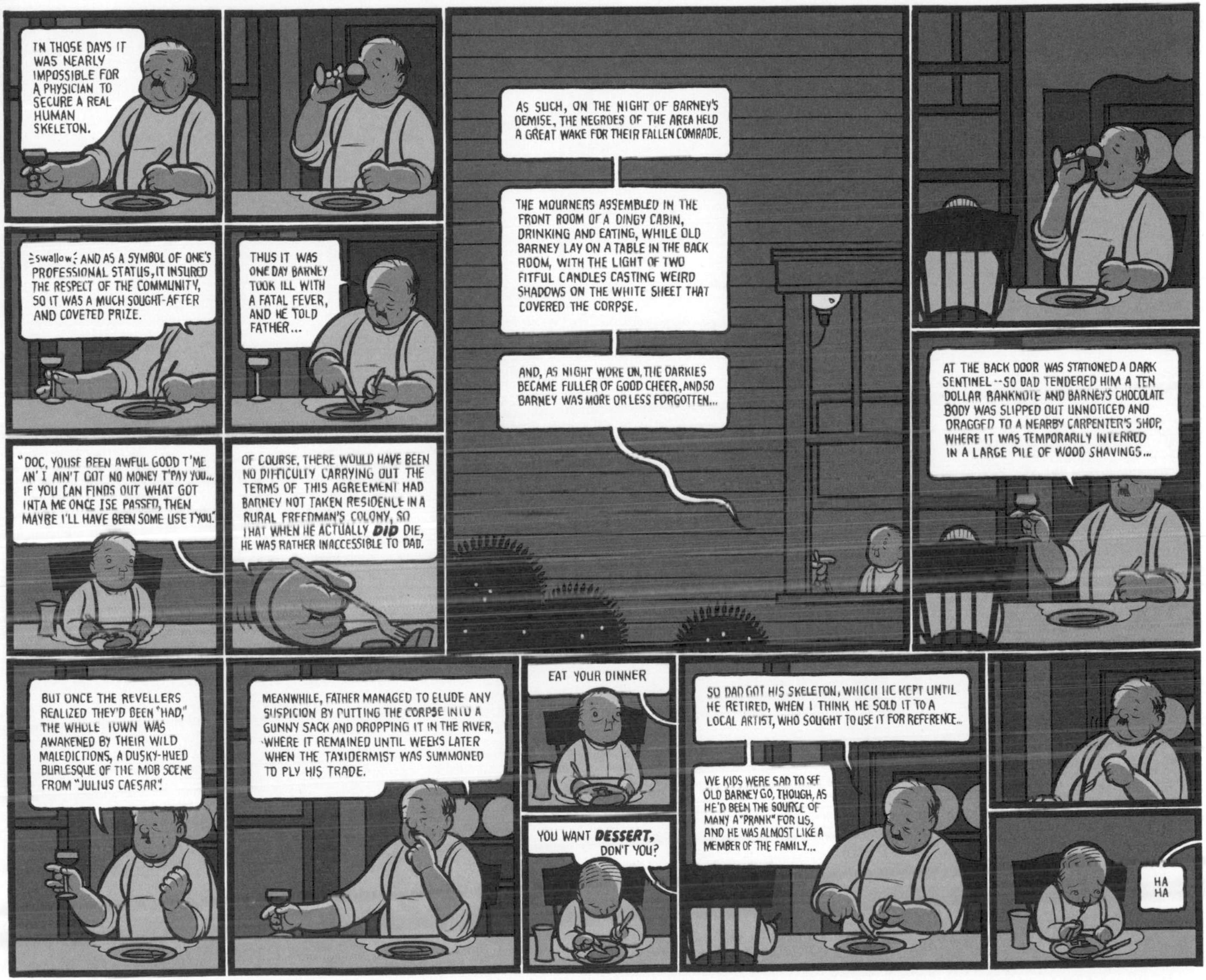
IN THOSE DAYS IT WAS NEARLY IMPOSSIBLE FOR A PHYSICIAN TO SECURE A REAL HUMAN SKELETON.
=swallow= AND AS A SYMBOL OF ONE'S PROFESSIONAL STATUS, IT INSURED THE RESPECT OF THE COMMUNITY, SO IT WAS A MUCH SOUGHT-AFTER AND COVETED PRIZE.
THUS IT WAS ONE DAY BARNEY TOOK ILL WITH A FATAL FEVER, AND HE TOLD FATHER...
"DOC, YOUSE BEEN AWFUL GOOD T'ME AN' I AIN'T GOT NO MONEY T'PAY YOU... IF YOU CAN FINDS OUT WHAT GOT INTA ME ONCE ISE PASSED, THEN MAYBE I'LL HAVE BEEN SOME USE T'YOU."
OF COURSE, THERE WOULD HAVE BEEN NO DIFFICULTY CARRYING OUT THE TERMS OF THIS AGREEMENT HAD BARNEY NOT TAKEN RESIDENCE IN A RURAL FREEDMAN'S COLONY, SO THAT WHEN HE ACTUALLY DID DIE, HE WAS RATHER INACCESSIBLE TO DAD.
AS SUCH, ON THE NIGHT OF BARNEY'S DEMISE, THE NEGROES OF THE AREA HELD A GREAT WAKE FOR THEIR FALLEN COMRADE.
THE MOURNERS ASSEMBLED IN THE FRONT ROOM OF A DINGY CABIN, DRINKING AND EATING, WHILE OLD BARNEY LAY ON A TABLE IN THE BACK ROOM, WITH THE LIGHT OF TWO FITFUL CANDLES CASTING WEIRD SHADOWS ON THE WHITE SHEET THAT COVERED THE CORPSE.
AND, AS NIGHT WORE ON, THE DARKIES BECAME FULLER OF GOOD CHEER, AND SO BARNEY WAS MORE OR LESS FORGOTTEN...
AT THE BACK DOOR WAS STATIONED A DARK SENTINEL--SO DAD TENDERED HIM A TEN DOLLAR BANKNOTE AND BARNEY'S CHOCOLATE BODY WAS SLIPPED OUT UNNOTICED AND DRAGGED TO A NEARBY CARPENTER'S SHOP, WHERE IT WAS TEMPORARILY INTERRED IN A LARGE PILE OF WOOD SHAVINGS...
BUT ONCE THE REVELLERS REALIZED THEY'D BEEN "HAD," THE WHOLE TOWN WAS AWAKENED BY THEIR WILD MALEDICTIONS, A DUSKY-HUED BURLESQUE OF THE MOB SCENE FROM "JULIUS CAESAR."
MEANWHILE, FATHER MANAGED TO ELUDE ANY SUSPICION BY PUTTING THE CORPSE INTO A GUNNY SACK AND DROPPING IT IN THE RIVER, WHERE IT REMAINED UNTIL WEEKS LATER WHEN THE TAXIDERMIST WAS SUMMONED TO PLY HIS TRADE.
EAT YOUR DINNER
YOU WANT DESSERT, DON'T YOU?
SO DAD GOT HIS SKELETON, WHICH HE KEPT UNTIL HE RETIRED, WHEN I THINK HE SOLD IT TO A LOCAL ARTIST, WHO SOUGHT TO USE IT FOR REFERENCE...
WE KIDS WERE SAD TO SEE OLD BARNEY GO, THOUGH, AS HE'D BEEN THE SOURCE OF MANY A "PRANK" FOR US, AND HE WAS ALMOST LIKE A MEMBER OF THE FAMILY...
HA HA

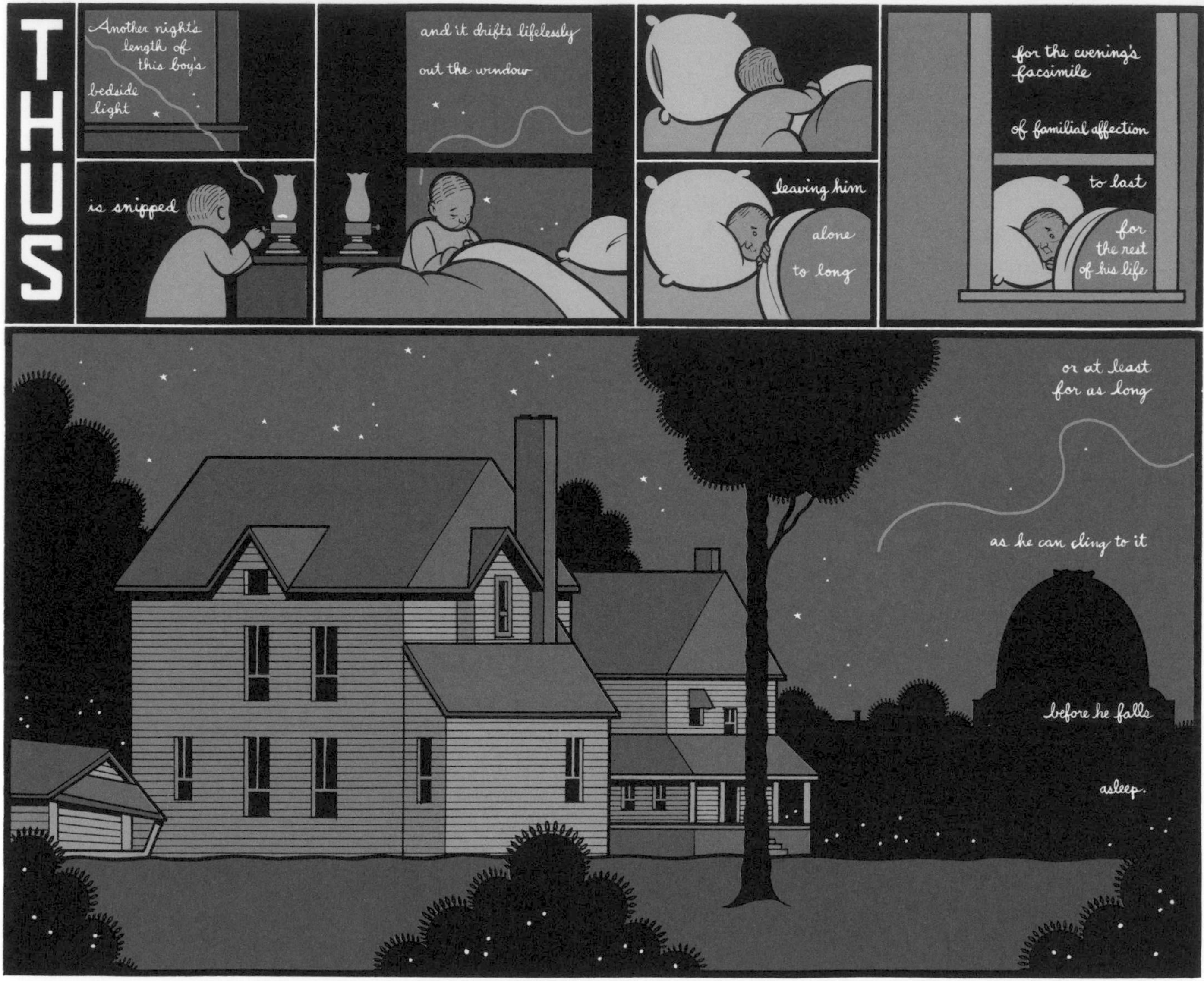
THUS
Another night's length of this boy's bedside light
is snipped
and it drifts lifelessly
out the window
leaving him
alone
to long
for the evening's facsimile
of familial affection
to last
for the rest of his life
or at least for as long
as he can cling to it
before he falls
asleep.

STOP
Dairy Queen
OPEN 24 HOURS
Buyalot
LIQUOR TOWN
CLUB MEGA
Pam's
Restaurant
wash
The Supper Club

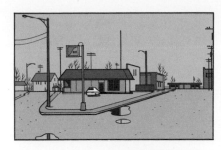

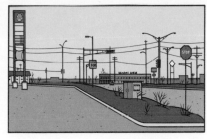

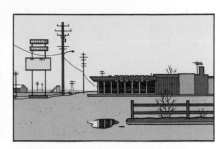

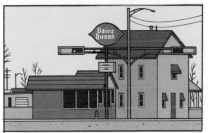

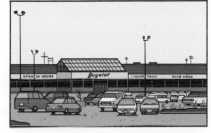

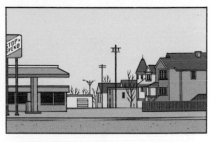

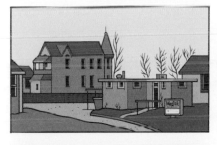

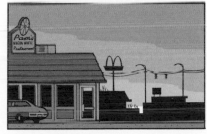

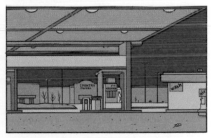

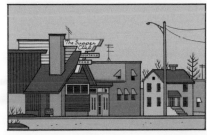

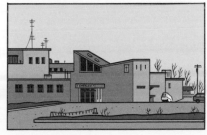

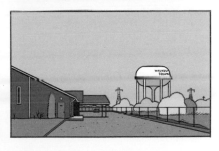

A DECLARATION OF GLORY.

Left to itself, this unpretentious scene of commercial beauty might garner ne'er a second glance from the casual passer-by, but in it may be found a striking model of modern elegance, form, and convenience. The "Bargain Showcase" (one of the most successful mercantiles in the history of the city of Waukosha) was established in 1964 as a means of providing quality goods at an affordable price to citizens of modest means, and it always went to great lengths and distant lands to procure such wares, often at risk of financial jeopardy and civic certification. Many of the younger residents of Waukosha also enjoyed gainful employment at this fine outlet, and, in some cases, founded a whole new generation of customers in the passenger seats of automobiles in the parking lot after closing time. While the lean honesty of the signage and the sleek, enthusiastic slope of the entryway invited thousands of local townspeople during its reign, it temporarily sits awaiting restoration; one hopes that the doors may once again swing open with the familiar strains of continuously playing popular ballads, and that the waft of polyester carpet binding may once again fill the nostrils with its promising allure and mystery.

VISTA.

No pine thicket, no birch grove, and no apple orchard could hope to compete with the the visual complexity of any scene selected from our contemporary interstate system, especially those cospes situated nearby the highway's many entries and exits, wherein the fagged voyager might seek sustenance and succor in the various eateries and refueling stations. The broad sweep of power lines, the delicate articulation of poles, signs, and warning lights, and the deep forest of advertisements all conspire to occasion countless views of complicated beauty, conceiving wonder in the curious onlooker at man's great achievement, however ductile. Great expanses of asphalt (here at the intersection of I-90 and highway 334) reflect the sun's blinding rays into the eyes of travellers, and provide an unconscious waste receptacle for items dropped overboard in haste to return to the comfort of the personal vehicle or land rover. Much history may be witnessed: the dinner wrappers, the emptied tins of flavored waters, and the frying pools of saliva all whispering a tale to those who might listen over the roar of the passing traffic. Such a fecund landscape! Such a rich heritage – oh! but it only could be frozen in time, for future generations to cherish.

GRAND PORT OF ENTRY.

Here's where it all begins for many sightseers and tourists, the Travel Bureau of the city of Waukosha, built in 1974 at the behest of the city's populace as a common meeting point for travellers seeking aid and advice. Note the rustic shingling, the modest porch, the way that the parking lot just seems to invite you -- all design concerns carefully incorporated by one of the city's leading contractors when designing the space. As well, the building is purposefully "open" on three sides, allowing sunlight to traverse its shallow carpeting in the course of an 8-hour workday, and to remind the visitor that this truly is a "port of all calls". Once a service for passengers of most major modes of transport, the Travel Bureau now focuses exclusively upon that of the public luxury coach, or bus system, as all railroad traffic was diverted from Waukosha in the early 1980s, and the airline which flies to Waukosha chose to handle such reservations itself. This more flexible, personal mode of transportation offers the citizens of Waukosha more than just a way to travel – it's a way to see the world. The new County Court House may be seen in the distance on the right, yet another testament to Waukosha's forward-looking spirit.

WINDSWEPT.

In 1878, when Siptus T. Bluntzer arrived at the arid plain which was to become the city of Concupiscence (renamed "Waukosha" in 1893 in honor of the Indians who once inhabited its dank promontory) little would he have guessed the variety of architecture, commerce, and culture which would one day populate the mild hills and rolling humps of his home. Sitting at the step of his grim little cabin, powder musket in hand, peering out from under the sticky edge of the muslin cheeseboard which he favored as a hat, how could he have known that little over eighty years hence he might simply rise from his perch and walk a few yards to the Stop n' Spend and purchase a sack of Corn Chips or a bottle of Orange spritzer, or perhaps a photo-magazine? Just imagine the lonely life that Mr. Bluntzer must have endured, the hardships he, his wife, and his thirteen children suffered. Their struggles simply to find food, to enjoy the gift of life on this Earth, the many times that he must have relieved himself of ardor against the wall of a barn, or behind a tree, or simply out in a field, and what grand edifice rises from his seed today. Such are the ways of history, and the grand scheme of the world, about which we shall always marvel.

MURMURING PINES.

Once an intraversable field of white pine and blue spruce forestland, this centrally-located plot of real estate was transformed by the City of Waukosha Planning Commission into an multi-purpose shopping facility for its suburban residents in 1987 – and well, the city has just never looked back. Created with ease of access and maximum parking potential (MPP) in mind, the striking simplicity of the majestic compound bespeaks a highly complex internetworking of æsthetic choices and intellectual theory, paired with a sharp sense of economy and surreptitious favors. Note the exciting pattern of windows, regularly spaced and only once interrupted by the main entryway, all harmonizing with the nettle of light-towers, evenly spaced as to provide the most efficient and convenient illumination under any conditions. Concomitantly, as an "open design" it tries to account for the fact that the visual field would be under constant flux, with the myriad automobiles and delivery trucks all coming and going; thus, the edifice remains stolid, stern – yet receptive – a beneficent reminder of the commercial bloodlines which bind us all together.

SILHOUETTE OF HISTORY.

Here's one of the most famous spots in all of Waukosha: "Treaty Rock", or "The Blood Stone" as old-timers like to call it. The site of one of the most potentially violent and fierce Indian uprisings in the city's history, it was the fearsomeness and pluck of one man which quelled a potential war upon the good people of "Concupiscence". Though many details of the event have been lost, the essential drama remains: our proud ancestors' families and livelihoods were threatened in 1881 by a small tribe of Indians who seemed to come from nowhere, with no regard at all for the society which was firmly established in God's name on the hallowed ground. The townspeople, of course, tried to reason with the unruly invaders, offering them sustenance and aid, but no words would seem to quell their fierce intent; none until Mr. Viscus Flatula, a local merchant, was able to speak with them. It is here that the details are sketchy, but the town was eventually renamed at the time of the Great Chicago Exposition in honor of these noble savages who saw the Christian reasoning of Mr. Flatula; votes to name the town after the great man himself were narrowly missed by two in the town council. *Note: rock is behind building, out of photo.*

CITY OF PERPETUAL MOONLIGHT.

One of the most novel and forward-looking features of the spritely city of Waukosha was its sophisticated illumination system established at the turn of the century, an ever-expanding array of tungsten, fluorescent, and halogen gas-burning glass globules which bathed the metropolis in a heavenly glow of dusty pinks, ambers, and icy blues – thus prompting the nickname "The City of Perpetual Moonlight". Almost entirely eliminating all ambient starlight, this *aurora artificialis* now allows for the continuance of commerce well into the wee hours, a whole new "segment" of the working-class population operating under an entrancing "færie sparkle". As well, this wonderful invention has engendered an exciting "night culture" of local meeting places and "after hours" supply depots all over Waukosha, some families even choosing to do their marketing at midnight, or to visit restaurants in their bedclothes when things get too emotionally stressful at home. Greatly expanding the possibilities for one's enjoyment of life, the "City of Perpetual Moonlight" was a bold step forward for the modest burgh of Waukosha, a path soon to be followed by cites all over this great land.

SUN'S FAREWELL KISS.

What could be better than a patty melt with curly fries, or a milkshake, or a good old-fashioned square of frozen mayonnaise? You bet. And Pam's "Wagon Wheel" has been serving up good, hearty fare like this for generations, ever since 1977. A favorite of young and old alike, the stories of its patrons are everywhere to be found: welded underneath table seventeen is a piece of gum stuck October 8th, 1981 at 8:24 AM by a heartbroken girl whose adoptive mother had just died of lung cancer in the city hospital the night before; crushed into the carpet by the southernmost window is a fragment of lettuce dislodged from the plate of an elderly man who for sixteen years was kept alive by a salad and a cup of coffee served in more or less that same spot; still adhering to the artificial leaves of the plant by the end of the center counter is the residue of a sneeze deposited by a widow whose most beloved feature of her college-aged body by her husband was the small dimple at the base of her skull into which his pinky would naturally rest when embracing her; and tucked away into the space between the ceiling tiles and the concrete above is a darkened space equal to the collective volume of a small church congregation, which no one ever thinks or cares about.

SIMPLICITY, SIMPLICITY.

What an easy blend of utility and domesticity may be glimpsed in this, a truly modern, yet nostalgic scene of midwestern modesty and efficiency. One of the many lovely "apothecary clinics" which conveniently dot the landscape of Waukosha – contrasted with the majesty and gentility of the ideal home world behind; see how these two sides of life complement and enrich each other; see how the bright blue sign and the trash removal receptacle counterpoint the quiet rhythms of the picket fence. Such "minor injury centers" cater to those citizens who have suffered only light complaints: common cuts and abrasions, sour stomach, and other "ow-ies" are well-served by the "on call" staff of specialists, while more major personal damage is attended to by physicians at the larger *hospital* down the street (from the Greek *hospes*, receiver of guests, and *tal*, meaning large, or tall) such as loss of limb, violent seizure, and unstoppable bleeding. No screams are to be heard sneaking through the walls of this happy little building, only the soft buzz of the central air conditioner, or the click and hum of the cozy heating unit switching on in the soft silence of a snowy November afternoon.

SERENE PANORAMA.

As one leaves or enters Waukosha, one cannot help but be struck by the majesty and dignity of the great aqueous tower which dominates the horizon, a common point of reference for all inhabitants of the happy hamlet, easily visible from most locales, especially from the periphery of the town. Painted with the name of the High School's 1992 State Champion Watersquad, the "Squaws", it is a solemn reminder of the great men and women who established themselves years ago on the lonely plain, and the noble savages they faced, befriended, and slaughtered. Many intoxicated teenagers have fallen to their deaths from the peripheral railing of this great monument, and many have attempted to inscribe their names in its marbly skin, not to mention the countless numbers who have chosen it as a "challenge destination" for trysting, the many discarded liquor bottles and crusted prophylactics clinging to its surface bespeaking the rich chronicle of loves won and lost. Tanking 85 thousand gallons of water to all inhabitants of Waukosha, each citizen should be grateful for the service it provides, bring the fresh elixir of life into every home, and providing a means for whisking away urine and feces at the pull of a lever.

SHARP TRUTH.

One of the finest medical facilities available to inhabitants of the Waukosha area, the Saint Mary Foundation was established in 1893 as the "Saint Mary Mother of God Sanitorium and Foundlings Infirmary or Beneficent Society", renamed "The College of Saint Mary Hospital" in 1928 (shortened to "Saint Mary's Hospital" in 1943 when the University lost accreditation), and finally renamed "Saint Mary: The Care Center" in 1989 when it was purchased by a service organization with "diversified interests in patient wellness". Note the striking angles and interesting spaces created by the unusual assemblage of buildings -- not the result of one architect's vision, but a by-product of necessity as the parent corporation grew. The original building – a neo-classical edifice interlaced with touches of "chinoiserie" and the motifs of ancient Egypt – was razed in 1943, and the newer structure, elements of which are still visible in the left of this image, was installed. Over the years, a modern entryway has been added, the parking lot expanded, and a helipad provided to allow for the removal of critical care patients to more specialized facilities in nearby Grand Loam or the Quad cities, insurance policy providing.

A SYMPHONY OF COLORS.

Probably one of the greatest creations of present times is the modern miracle known as *vinyl siding*. Available in a veritable nature's palette of bold and challenging hues, these brightly-toned sheathings are responsible for some of the most magical landscapes of contemporary life. Old, crumbling buildings are miraculously transformed in an autumn afternoon from cruel reminders of mortality into brightly-pigmented examples of hope and clarity, refreshed and renewed for a vernal generation of citizens to infest. A casement of chromatic complexion armoring rotting wood and weeping plaster, this delicate "second skin" can even conceal out-of-style doors, windows, and frivolous decoration; no need to rebuild or repaint when one can simply slather. Plus, with a texture of top-quality birchwood impressed into the plastic, who's the wiser? One watches as the lovely colors fade to a dusty tincture, and crack and pull away and sag as the structure underneath falls to its knees -- what greater metaphor could there be for our time on Earth than vinyl siding? Here, at the intersection of Dry and Futtock Streets in Waukosha such sublimity is readily apparent – and readily available – contact the realtors for particulars.

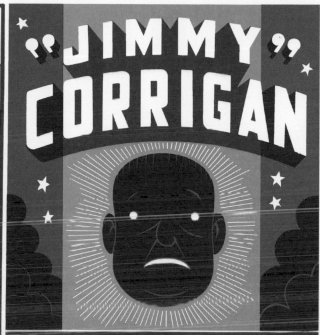

"JIMMY" CORRIGAN

THE SMARTEST KID on EARTH

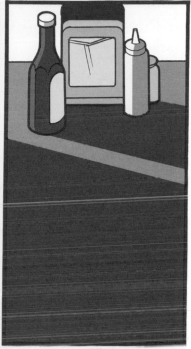

OKAY, I'LL GET YOU BUYS SOME MENUS IN A SECOND... YOU KNOW WHAT YOU WANNA HAVE TO DRINK?

COFFEE FOR ME, PLEASE...

UH... I'LL JUST HAVE A COKE, I GUESS...

COKE, OKAY... COFFEE AND A COKE

YEAH, THINGS WERE A LOT DIFFERENT THEN...

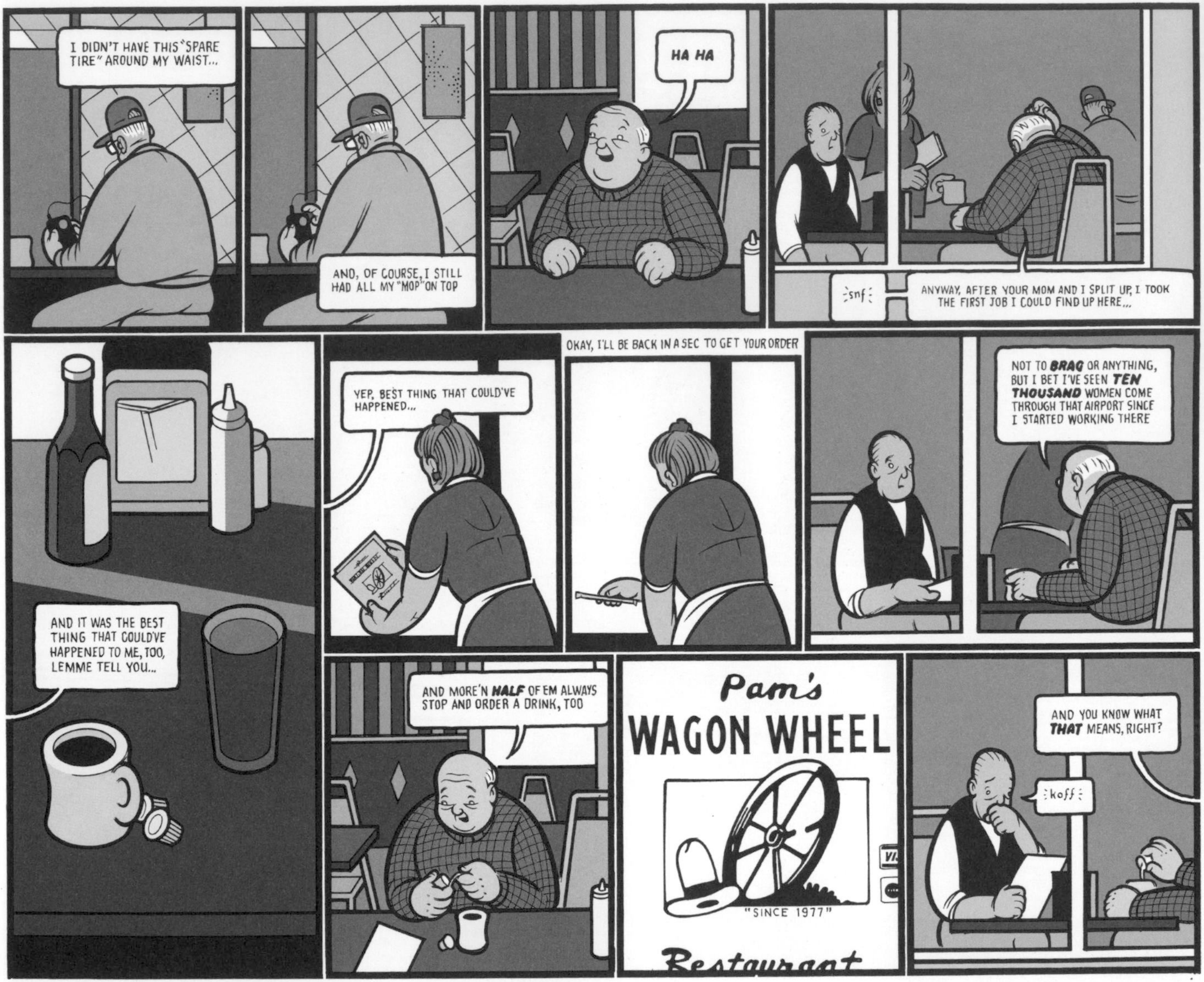
I DIDN'T HAVE THIS "SPARE TIRE" AROUND MY WAIST...
AND, OF COURSE, I STILL HAD ALL MY "MOP" ON TOP
HA HA
snf
ANYWAY, AFTER YOUR MOM AND I SPLIT UP, I TOOK THE FIRST JOB I COULD FIND UP HERE...
AND IT WAS THE BEST THING THAT COULD'VE HAPPENED TO ME, TOO, LEMME TELL YOU...
YEP, BEST THING THAT COULD'VE HAPPENED...
OKAY, I'LL BE BACK IN A SEC TO GET YOUR ORDER
NOT TO BRAG OR ANYTHING, BUT I BET I'VE SEEN TEN THOUSAND WOMEN COME THROUGH THAT AIRPORT SINCE I STARTED WORKING THERE
AND MORE'N HALF OF EM ALWAYS STOP AND ORDER A DRINK, TOO
Pam's
WAGON WHEEL
"SINCE 1977"
Restaurant
AND YOU KNOW WHAT THAT MEANS, RIGHT?
koff

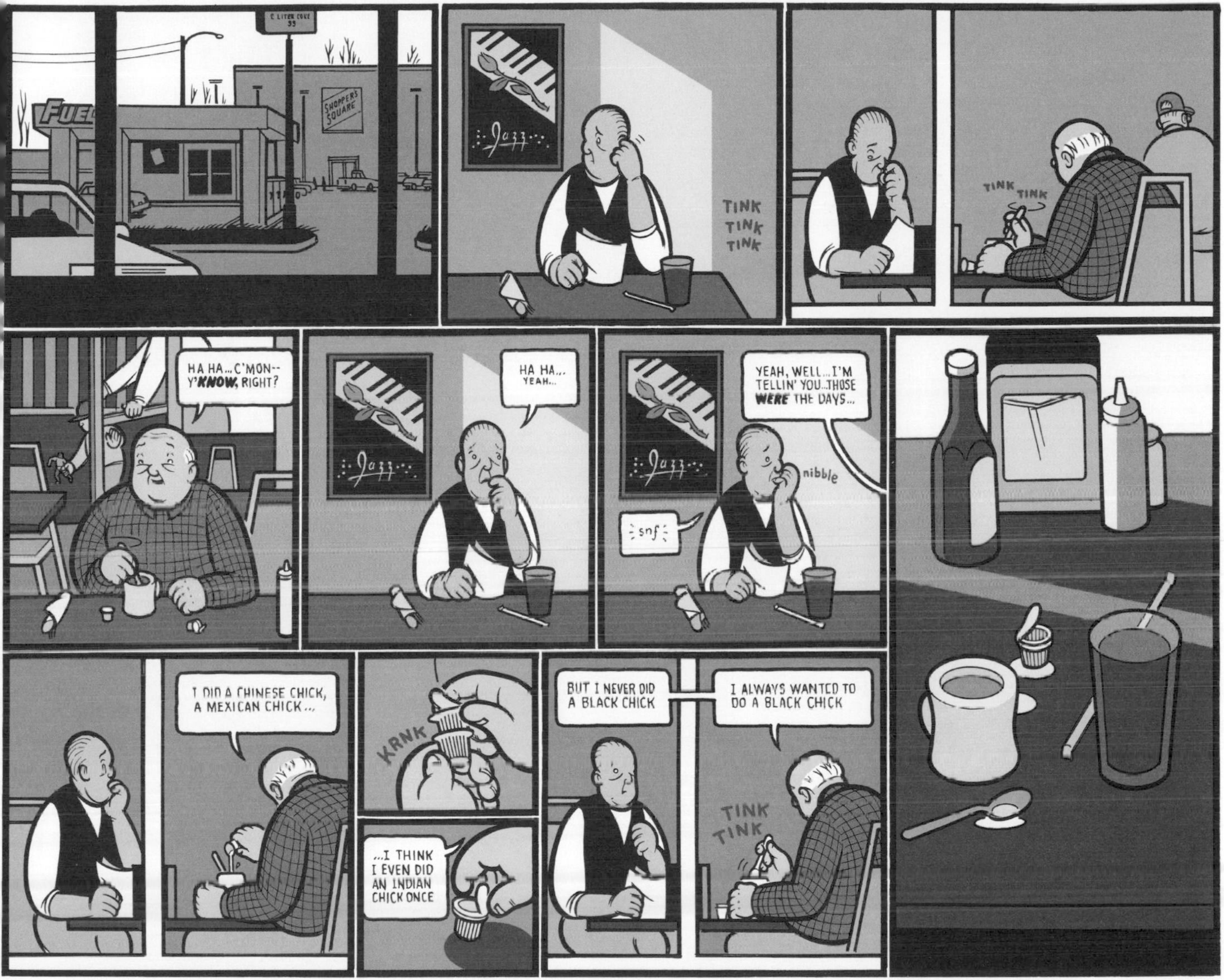
SHOPPER'S SQUARE
Jazz
TINK TINK TINK
TINK TINK
HA HA... C'MON-- Y'**KNOW**, RIGHT?
HA HA... YEAH...
Jazz
YEAH, WELL... I'M TELLIN' YOU... THOSE **WERE** THE DAYS...
nibble
snf
Jazz
I DID A CHINESE CHICK, A MEXICAN CHICK...
KRNK
...I THINK I EVEN DID AN INDIAN CHICK ONCE
BUT I NEVER DID A BLACK CHICK
I ALWAYS WANTED TO DO A BLACK CHICK
TINK TINK

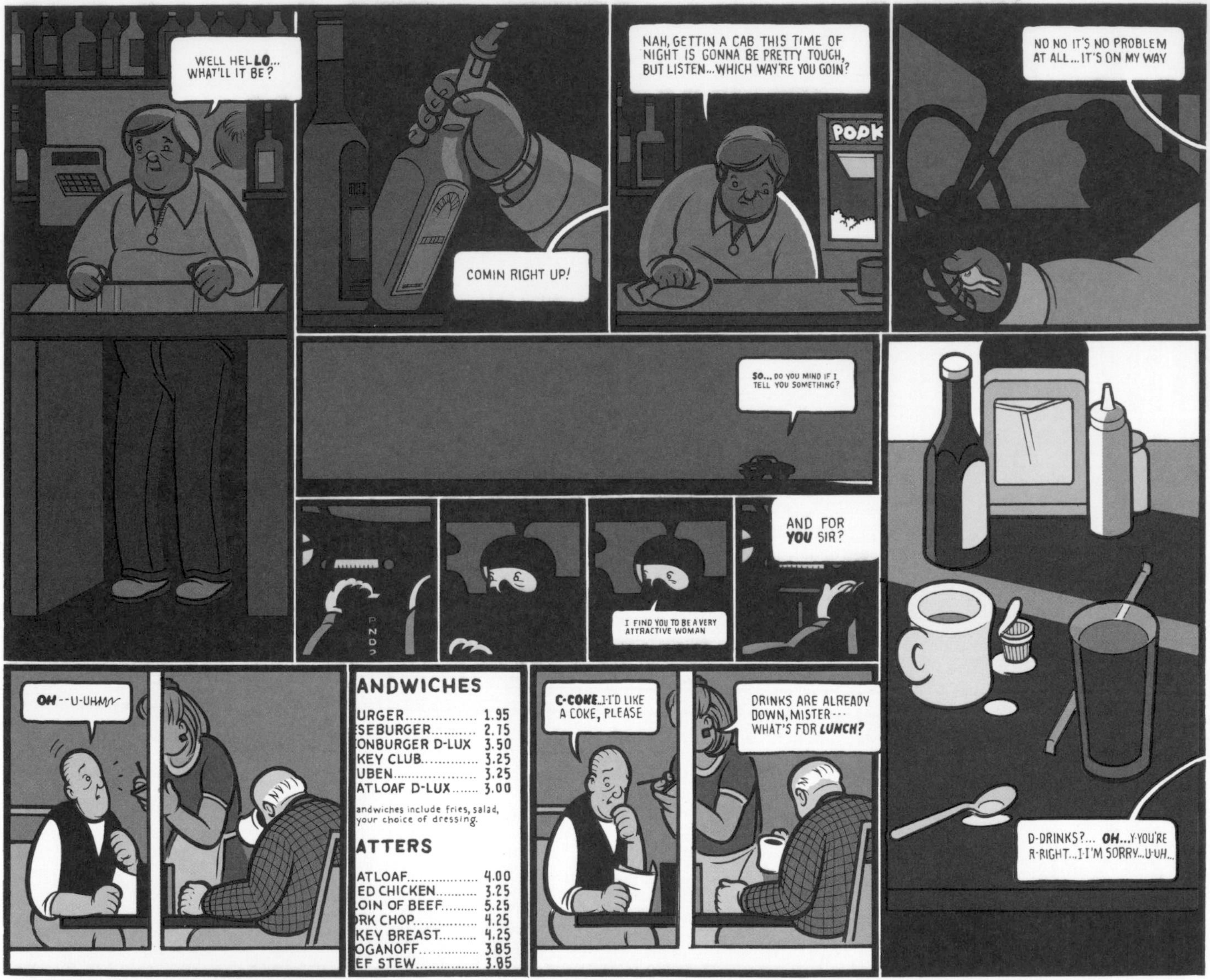
WELL HELLO... WHAT'LL IT BE?
COMIN RIGHT UP!
NAH, GETTIN A CAB THIS TIME OF NIGHT IS GONNA BE PRETTY TOUGH, BUT LISTEN... WHICH WAY'RE YOU GOIN?
POPK
NO NO IT'S NO PROBLEM AT ALL... IT'S ON MY WAY
SO... DO YOU MIND IF I TELL YOU SOMETHING?
I FIND YOU TO BE A VERY ATTRACTIVE WOMAN
AND FOR YOU SIR?
D-DRINKS?... OH... Y-YOU'RE R-RIGHT... I-I'M SORRY... U-UH...
OH --U-UHMM
ANDWICHES
URGER.................. 1.95
SEBURGER........... 2.75
ONBURGER D-LUX 3.50
KEY CLUB............. 3.25
UBEN..................... 3.25
ATLOAF D-LUX....... 3.00
andwiches include fries, salad, your choice of dressing.
ATTERS
ATLOAF.................. 4.00
ED CHICKEN........... 3.25
OIN OF BEEF......... 5.25
RK CHOP................ 4.25
KEY BREAST.......... 4.25
OGANOFF............... 3.85
EF STEW................ 3.85
C-COKE.. I-I'D LIKE A COKE, PLEASE
DRINKS ARE ALREADY DOWN, MISTER --- WHAT'S FOR LUNCH?

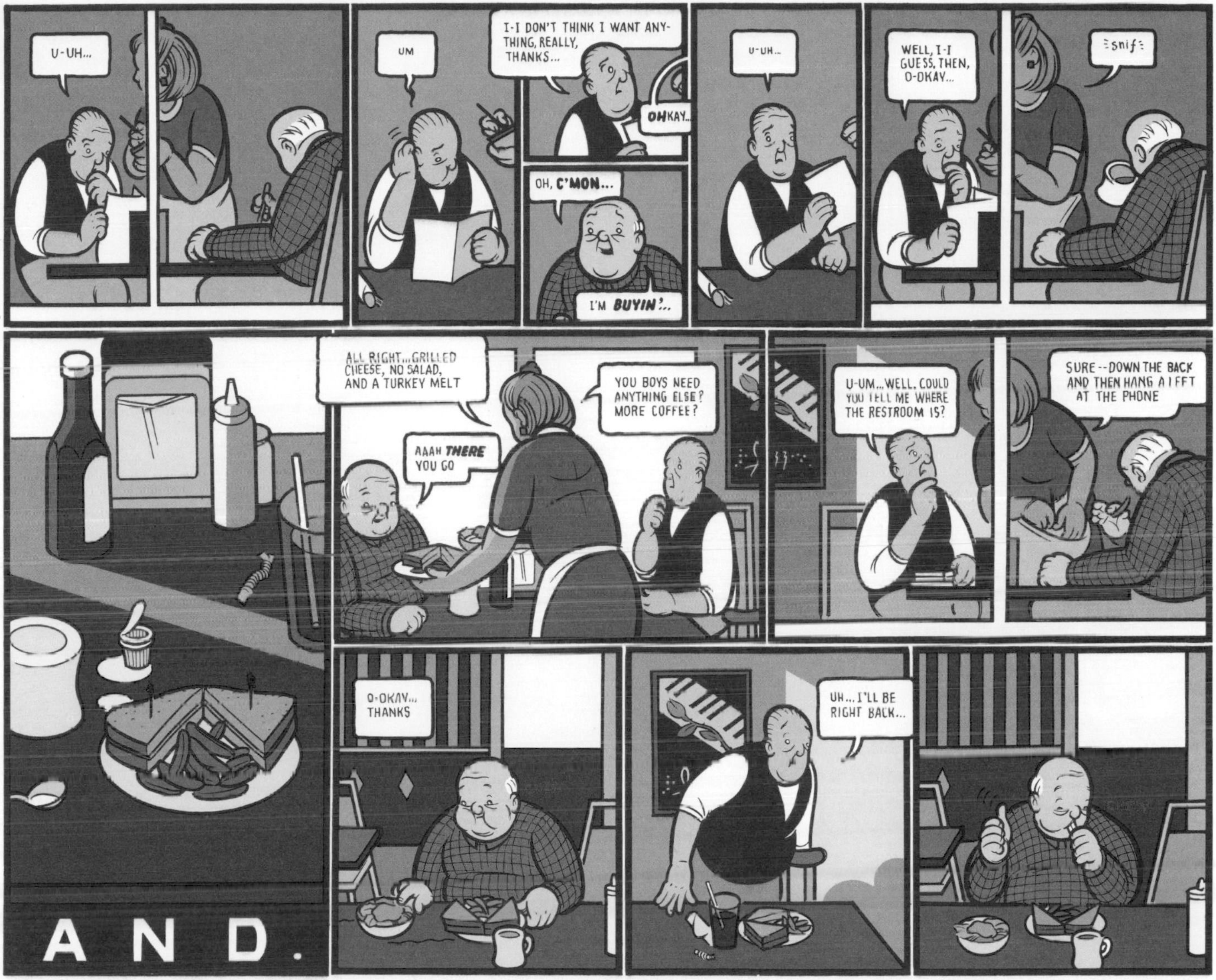

U-UH...
UM
I-I DON'T THINK I WANT ANYTHING, REALLY, THANKS...
OHKAY...
OH, C'MON...
I'M BUYIN'...
U-UH...
WELL, I-I GUESS, THEN, O-OKAY...
snif
ALL RIGHT... GRILLED CHEESE, NO SALAD, AND A TURKEY MELT
AAAH THERE YOU GO
YOU BOYS NEED ANYTHING ELSE? MORE COFFEE?
U-UM... WELL, COULD YOU TELL ME WHERE THE RESTROOM IS?
SURE -- DOWN THE BACK AND THEN HANG A LEFT AT THE PHONE
O-OKAY... THANKS
UH... I'LL BE RIGHT BACK...
AND.

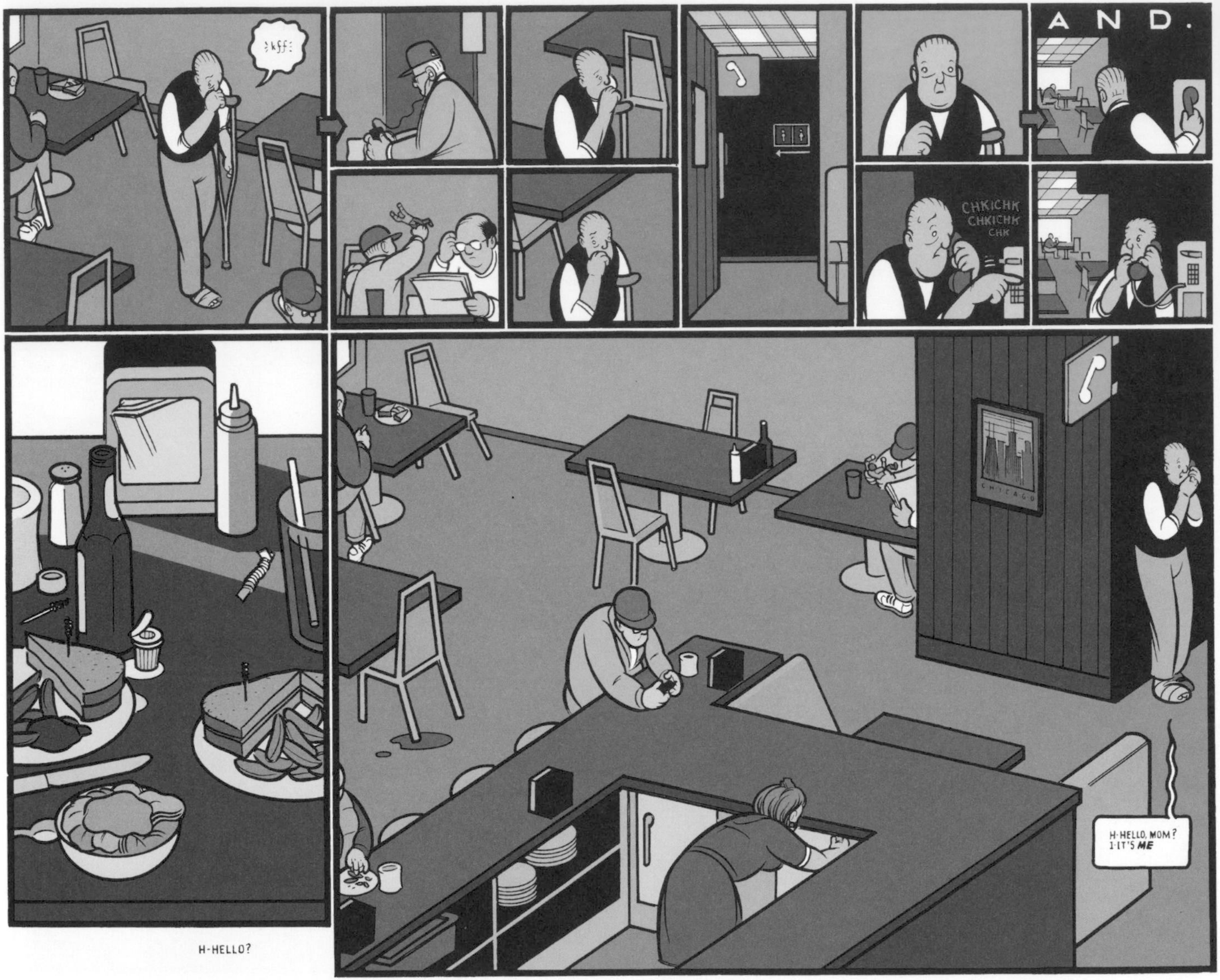
kff
AND.
CHKICHK
CHKICHK
CHK
CHICAGO
H-HELLO, MOM?
I-IT'S *ME*
H-HELLO?

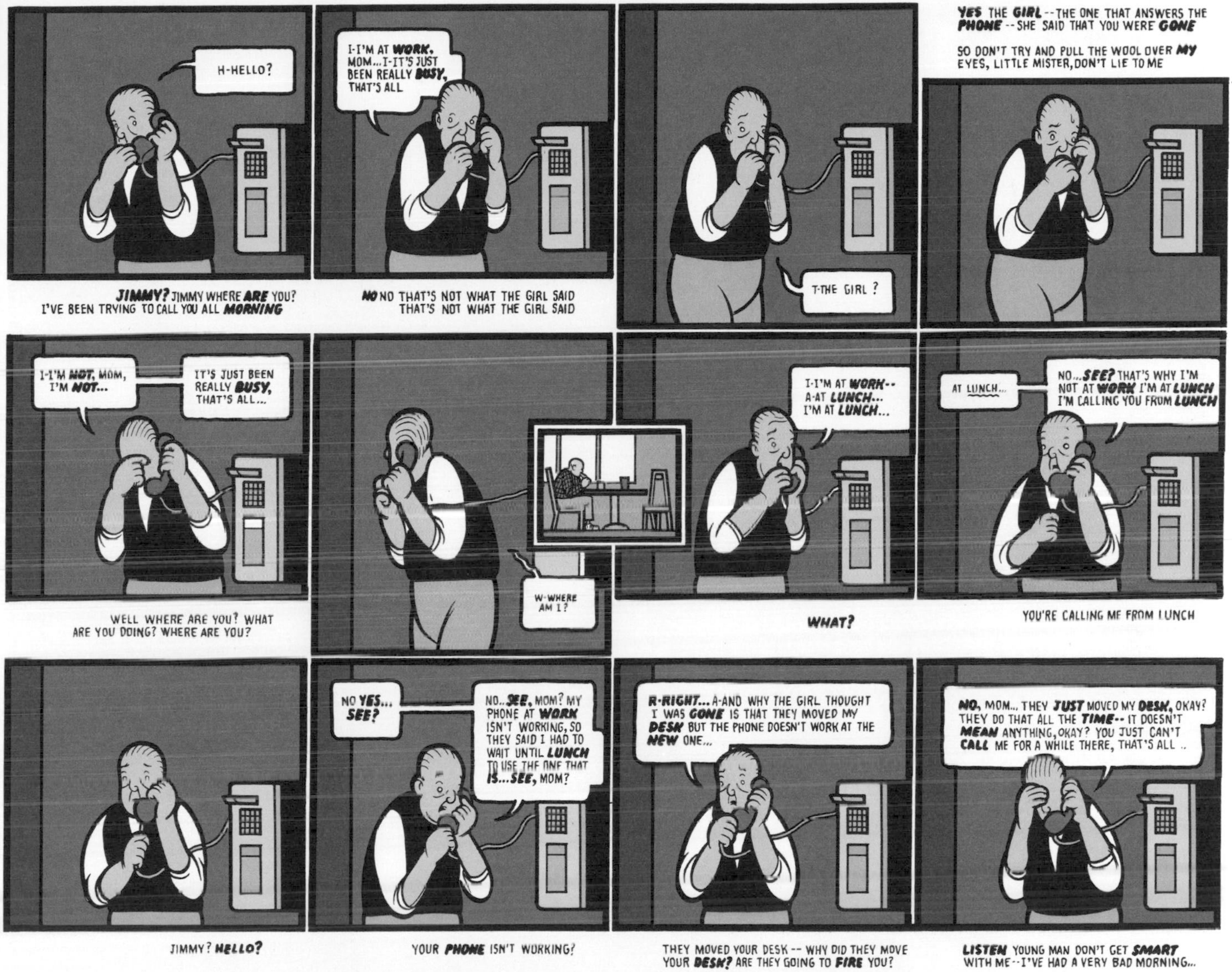

H-HELLO?
JIMMY? JIMMY WHERE ARE YOU? I'VE BEEN TRYING TO CALL YOU ALL MORNING
I-I'M AT WORK, MOM... I-IT'S JUST BEEN REALLY BUSY, THAT'S ALL
NO NO THAT'S NOT WHAT THE GIRL SAID THAT'S NOT WHAT THE GIRL SAID
T-THE GIRL ?
YES THE GIRL -- THE ONE THAT ANSWERS THE PHONE -- SHE SAID THAT YOU WERE GONE
SO DON'T TRY AND PULL THE WOOL OVER MY EYES, LITTLE MISTER, DON'T LIE TO ME
I-I'M NOT, MOM, I'M NOT...
IT'S JUST BEEN REALLY BUSY, THAT'S ALL...
WELL WHERE ARE YOU? WHAT ARE YOU DOING? WHERE ARE YOU?
W-WHERE AM I?
I-I'M AT WORK-- A-AT LUNCH... I'M AT LUNCH...
WHAT?
AT LUNCH...
NO... SEE? THAT'S WHY I'M NOT AT WORK I'M AT LUNCH I'M CALLING YOU FROM LUNCH
YOU'RE CALLING ME FROM LUNCH
JIMMY? HELLO?
NO YES... SEE?
NO.. SEE, MOM? MY PHONE AT WORK ISN'T WORKING, SO THEY SAID I HAD TO WAIT UNTIL LUNCH TO USE THE ONE THAT IS... SEE, MOM?
YOUR PHONE ISN'T WORKING?
R-RIGHT... A-AND WHY THE GIRL THOUGHT I WAS GONE IS THAT THEY MOVED MY DESK BUT THE PHONE DOESN'T WORK AT THE NEW ONE...
THEY MOVED YOUR DESK -- WHY DID THEY MOVE YOUR DESK? ARE THEY GOING TO FIRE YOU?
NO, MOM... THEY JUST MOVED MY DESK, OKAY? THEY DO THAT ALL THE TIME-- IT DOESN'T MEAN ANYTHING, OKAY? YOU JUST CAN'T CALL ME FOR A WHILE THERE, THAT'S ALL ..
LISTEN YOUNG MAN DON'T GET SMART WITH ME--I'VE HAD A VERY BAD MORNING...

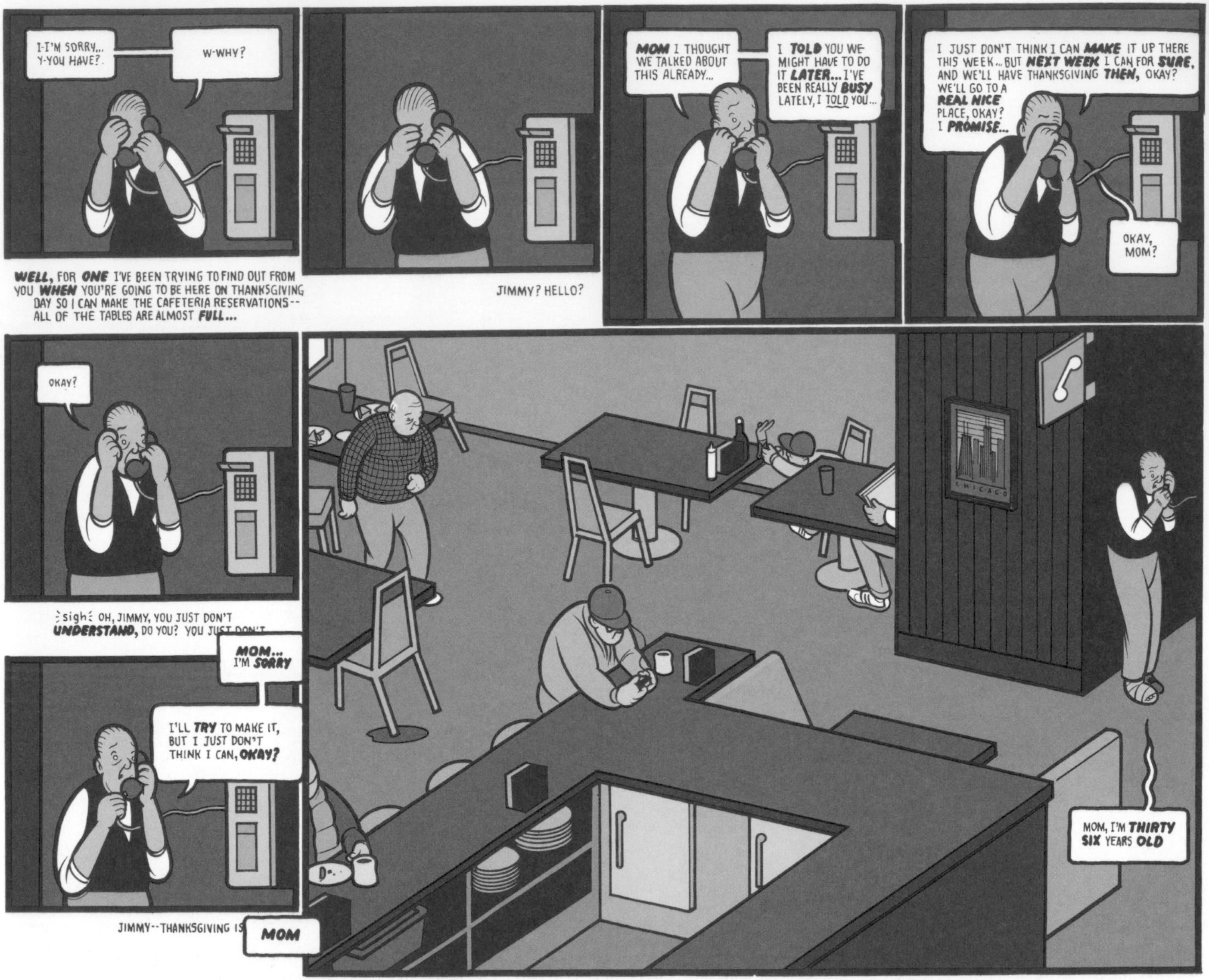

I-I'M SORRY... Y-YOU HAVE?
W-WHY?
WELL, FOR ONE I'VE BEEN TRYING TO FIND OUT FROM YOU WHEN YOU'RE GOING TO BE HERE ON THANKSGIVING DAY SO I CAN MAKE THE CAFETERIA RESERVATIONS-- ALL OF THE TABLES ARE ALMOST FULL...
JIMMY? HELLO?
MOM I THOUGHT WE TALKED ABOUT THIS ALREADY...
I TOLD YOU WE MIGHT HAVE TO DO IT LATER... I'VE BEEN REALLY BUSY LATELY, I TOLD YOU...
I JUST DON'T THINK I CAN MAKE IT UP THERE THIS WEEK... BUT NEXT WEEK I CAN FOR SURE, AND WE'LL HAVE THANKSGIVING THEN, OKAY? WE'LL GO TO A REAL NICE PLACE, OKAY? I PROMISE...
OKAY, MOM?
OKAY?
sigh OH, JIMMY, YOU JUST DON'T UNDERSTAND, DO YOU? YOU JUST DON'T
MOM... I'M SORRY
I'LL TRY TO MAKE IT, BUT I JUST DON'T THINK I CAN, OKAY?
JIMMY--THANKSGIVING IS
MOM
CHICAGO
MOM, I'M THIRTY SIX YEARS OLD

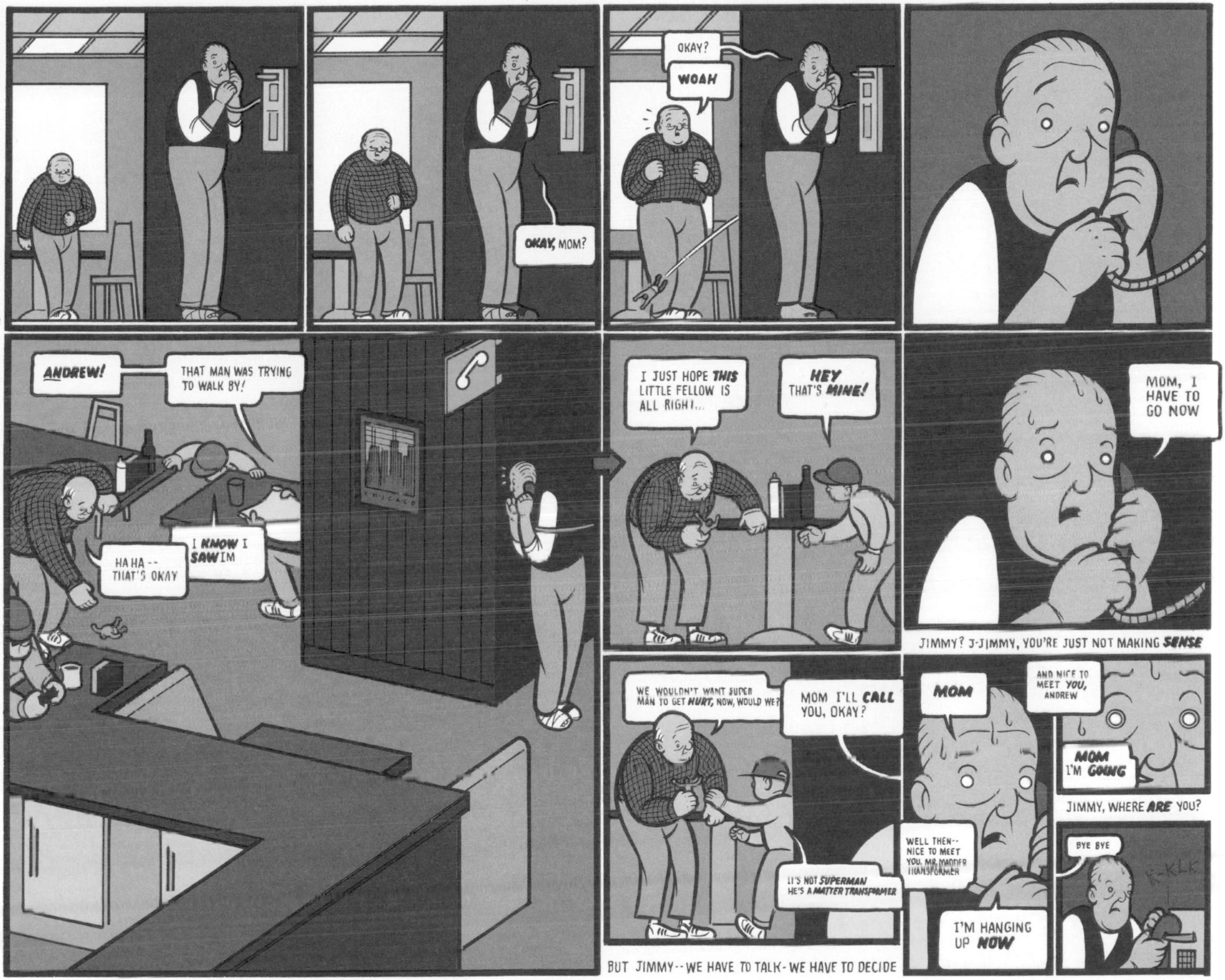
OKAY, MOM?
OKAY?
WOAH
ANDREW!
THAT MAN WAS TRYING TO WALK BY!
HA HA -- THAT'S OKAY
I KNOW I SAW IM
I JUST HOPE THIS LITTLE FELLOW IS ALL RIGHT...
HEY THAT'S MINE!
MOM, I HAVE TO GO NOW
JIMMY? J-JIMMY, YOU'RE JUST NOT MAKING SENSE
WE WOULDN'T WANT SUPER MAN TO GET HURT, NOW, WOULD WE?
MOM I'LL CALL YOU, OKAY?
IT'S NOT SUPERMAN HE'S A MATTER TRANSFORMER
BUT JIMMY -- WE HAVE TO TALK - WE HAVE TO DECIDE
MOM
WELL THEN-- NICE TO MEET YOU, MR. MATTER TRANSFORMER
I'M HANGING UP NOW
AND NICE TO MEET YOU, ANDREW
MOM I'M GOING
JIMMY, WHERE ARE YOU?
BYE BYE

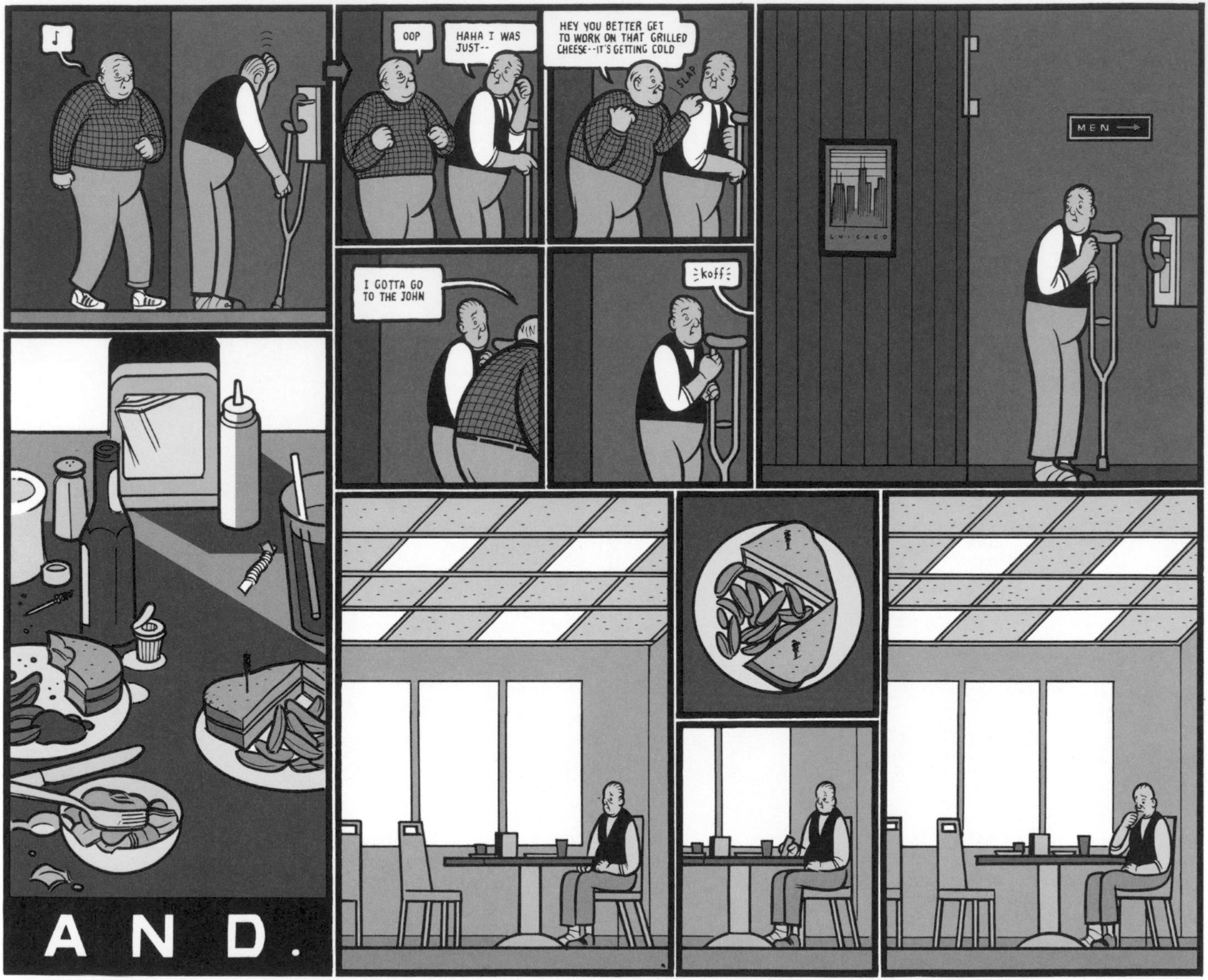
♩
OOP
HAHA I WAS JUST--
HEY YOU BETTER GET TO WORK ON THAT GRILLED CHEESE--IT'S GETTING COLD
SLAP
MEN →
CHICAGO
I GOTTA GO TO THE JOHN
koff
AND.

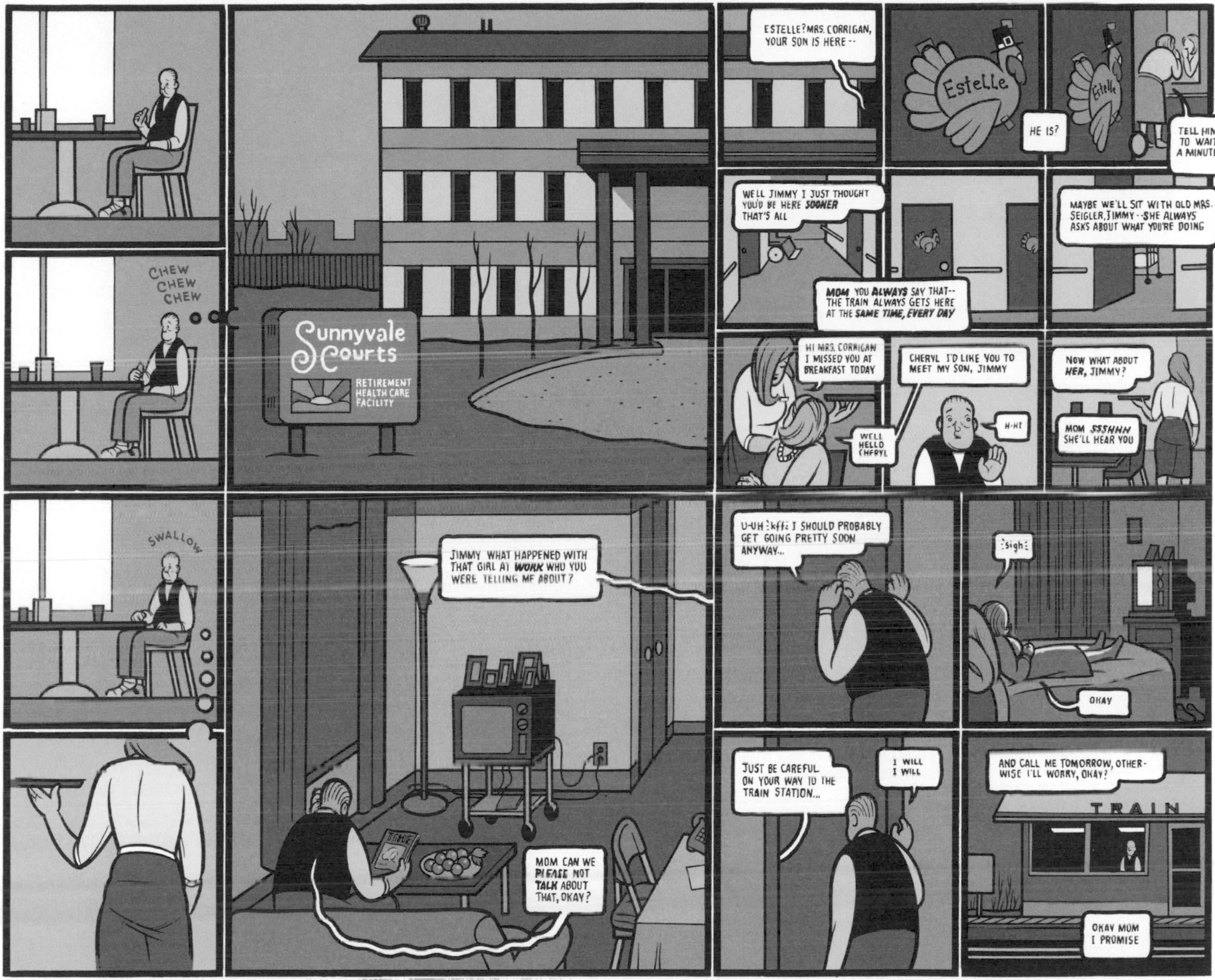

CHEW CHEW CHEW
SWALLOW
Sunnyvale Courts
RETIREMENT HEALTH CARE FACILITY
JIMMY WHAT HAPPENED WITH THAT GIRL AT WORK WHO YOU WERE TELLING ME ABOUT?
MOM CAN WE PLEASE NOT TALK ABOUT THAT, OKAY?
ESTELLE? MRS. CORRIGAN, YOUR SON IS HERE--
Estelle
HE IS?
TELL HIM TO WAIT A MINUTE
WELL JIMMY I JUST THOUGHT YOU'D BE HERE SOONER THAT'S ALL
MOM YOU ALWAYS SAY THAT-- THE TRAIN ALWAYS GETS HERE AT THE SAME TIME, EVERY DAY
MAYBE WE'LL SIT WITH OLD MRS. SEIGLER, JIMMY--SHE ALWAYS ASKS ABOUT WHAT YOU'RE DOING
HI MRS. CORRIGAN I MISSED YOU AT BREAKFAST TODAY
WELL HELLO CHERYL
CHERYL I'D LIKE YOU TO MEET MY SON, JIMMY
H-HI
NOW WHAT ABOUT HER, JIMMY?
MOM SSSHHH SHE'LL HEAR YOU
U-UH kff I SHOULD PROBABLY GET GOING PRETTY SOON ANYWAY...
sigh
OKAY
JUST BE CAREFUL ON YOUR WAY TO THE TRAIN STATION...
I WILL I WILL
AND CALL ME TOMORROW, OTHERWISE I'LL WORRY, OKAY?
TRAIN
OKAY MOM I PROMISE

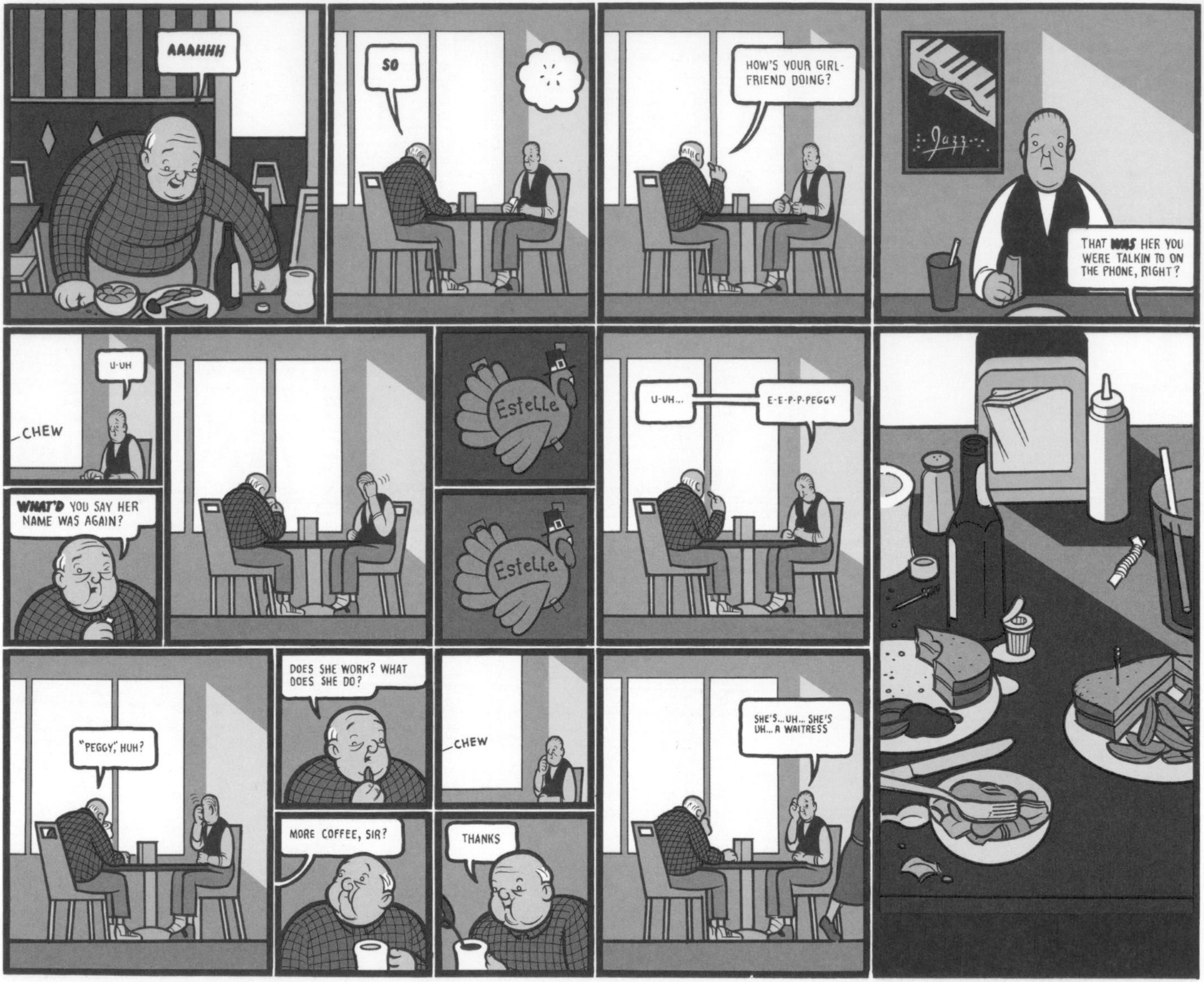
AAAHHH
SO
HOW'S YOUR GIRL-FRIEND DOING?
THAT WAS HER YOU WERE TALKIN TO ON THE PHONE, RIGHT?
Jazz
U-UH
CHEW
WHAT'D YOU SAY HER NAME WAS AGAIN?
Estelle
Estelle
U-UH...
E-E-P-P-PEGGY
"PEGGY," HUH?
DOES SHE WORK? WHAT DOES SHE DO?
CHEW
SHE'S... UH... SHE'S UH... A WAITRESS
MORE COFFEE, SIR?
THANKS

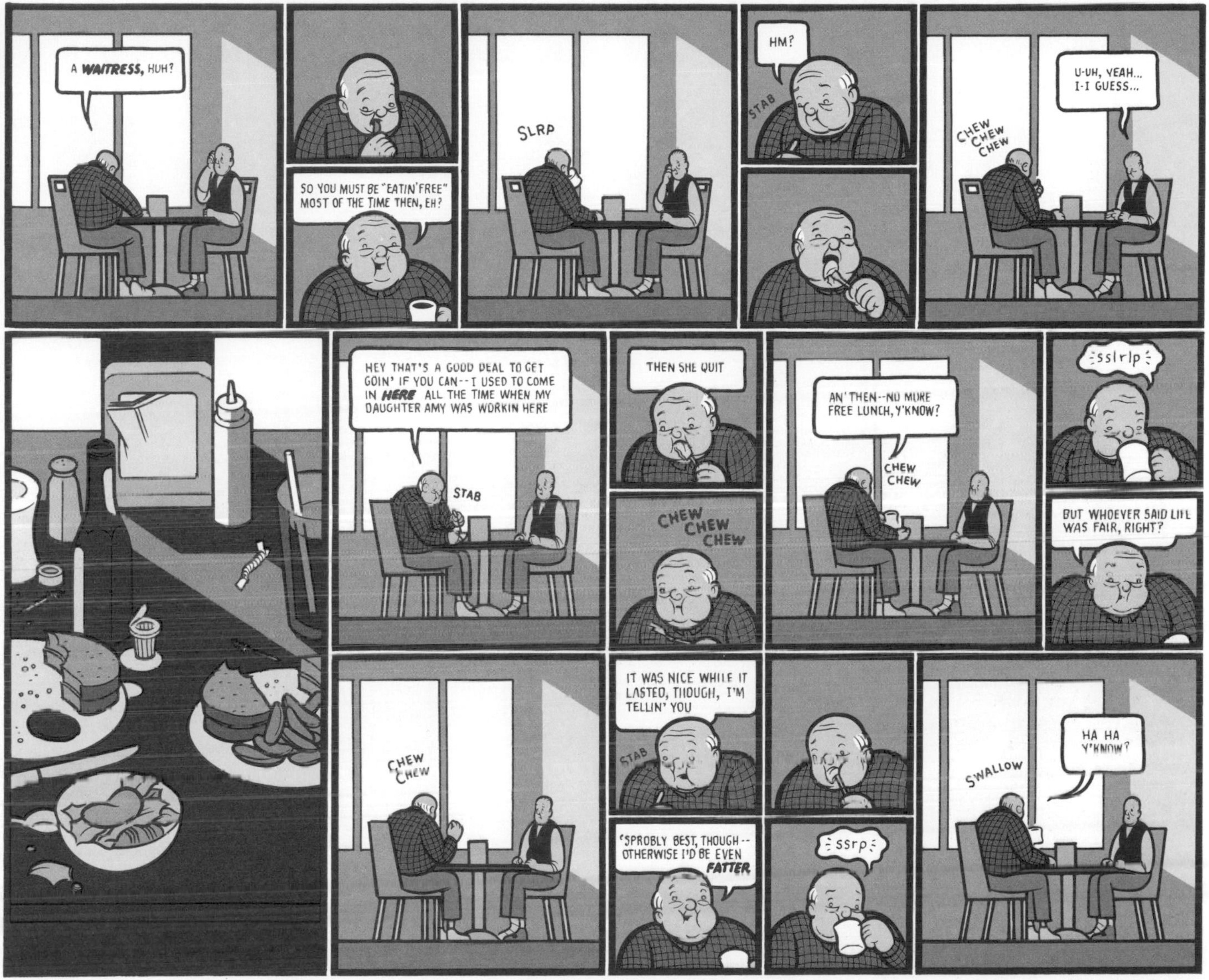

A WAITRESS, HUH?
SO YOU MUST BE "EATIN' FREE" MOST OF THE TIME THEN, EH?
SLRP
HM?
STAB
CHEW CHEW CHEW
U-UH, YEAH... I-I GUESS...
HEY THAT'S A GOOD DEAL TO GET GOIN' IF YOU CAN--I USED TO COME IN HERE ALL THE TIME WHEN MY DAUGHTER AMY WAS WORKIN HERE
STAB
THEN SHE QUIT
CHEW CHEW CHEW
AN' THEN--NO MORE FREE LUNCH, Y'KNOW?
CHEW CHEW
sslrlp
BUT WHOEVER SAID LIFE WAS FAIR, RIGHT?
CHEW CHEW
IT WAS NICE WHILE IT LASTED, THOUGH, I'M TELLIN' YOU
STAB
'SPROBLY BEST, THOUGH--OTHERWISE I'D BE EVEN FATTER
ssrp
SWALLOW
HA HA Y'KNOW?

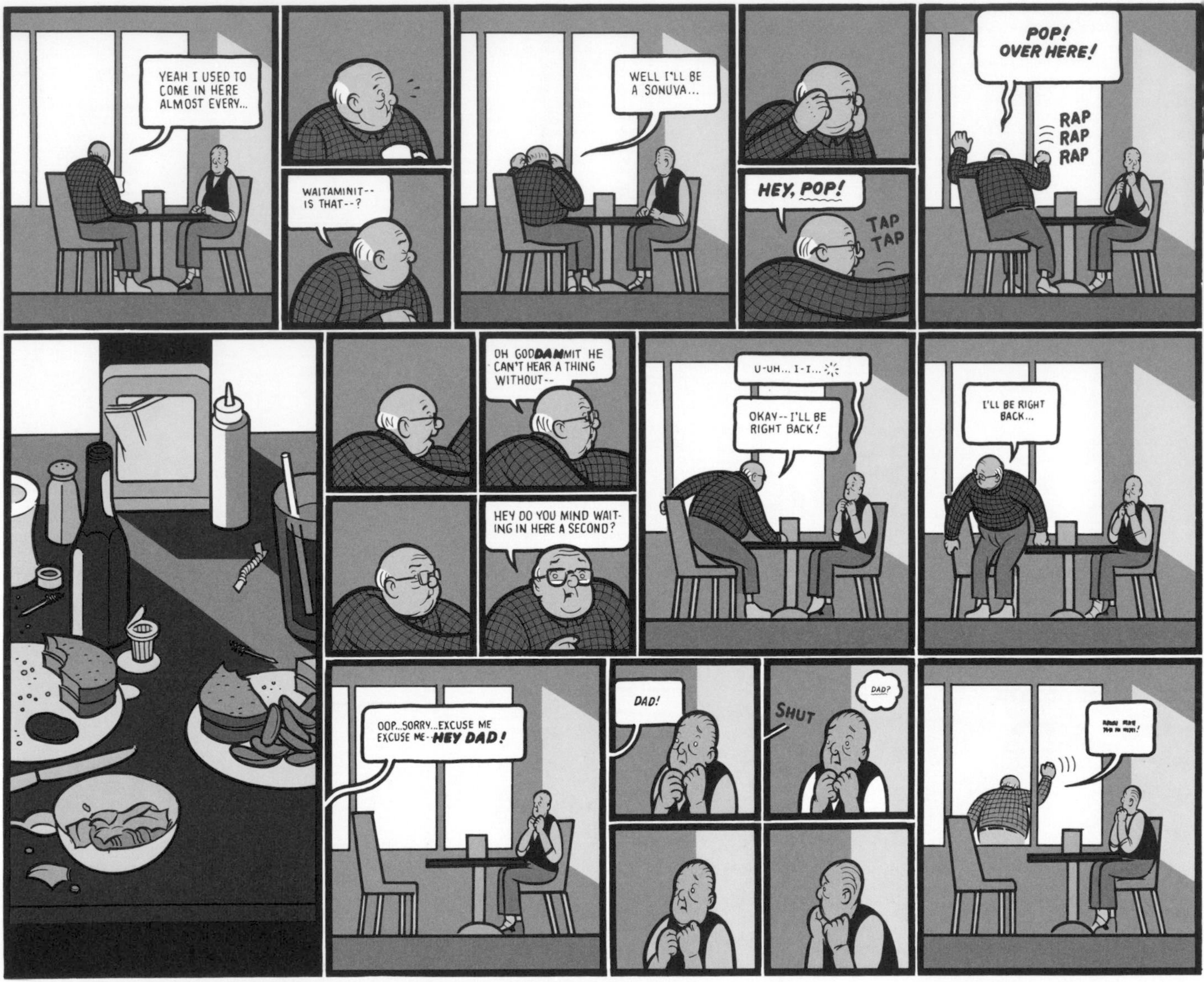
YEAH I USED TO COME IN HERE ALMOST EVERY...
WAITAMINIT-- IS THAT--?
WELL I'LL BE A SONUVA...
HEY, POP!
TAP TAP
POP! OVER HERE!
RAP RAP RAP
OH GODDAMMIT HE CAN'T HEAR A THING WITHOUT--
HEY DO YOU MIND WAITING IN HERE A SECOND?
U-UH... I-I...
OKAY-- I'LL BE RIGHT BACK!
I'LL BE RIGHT BACK...
OOP...SORRY...EXCUSE ME EXCUSE ME--HEY DAD!
DAD!
SHUT
DAD?

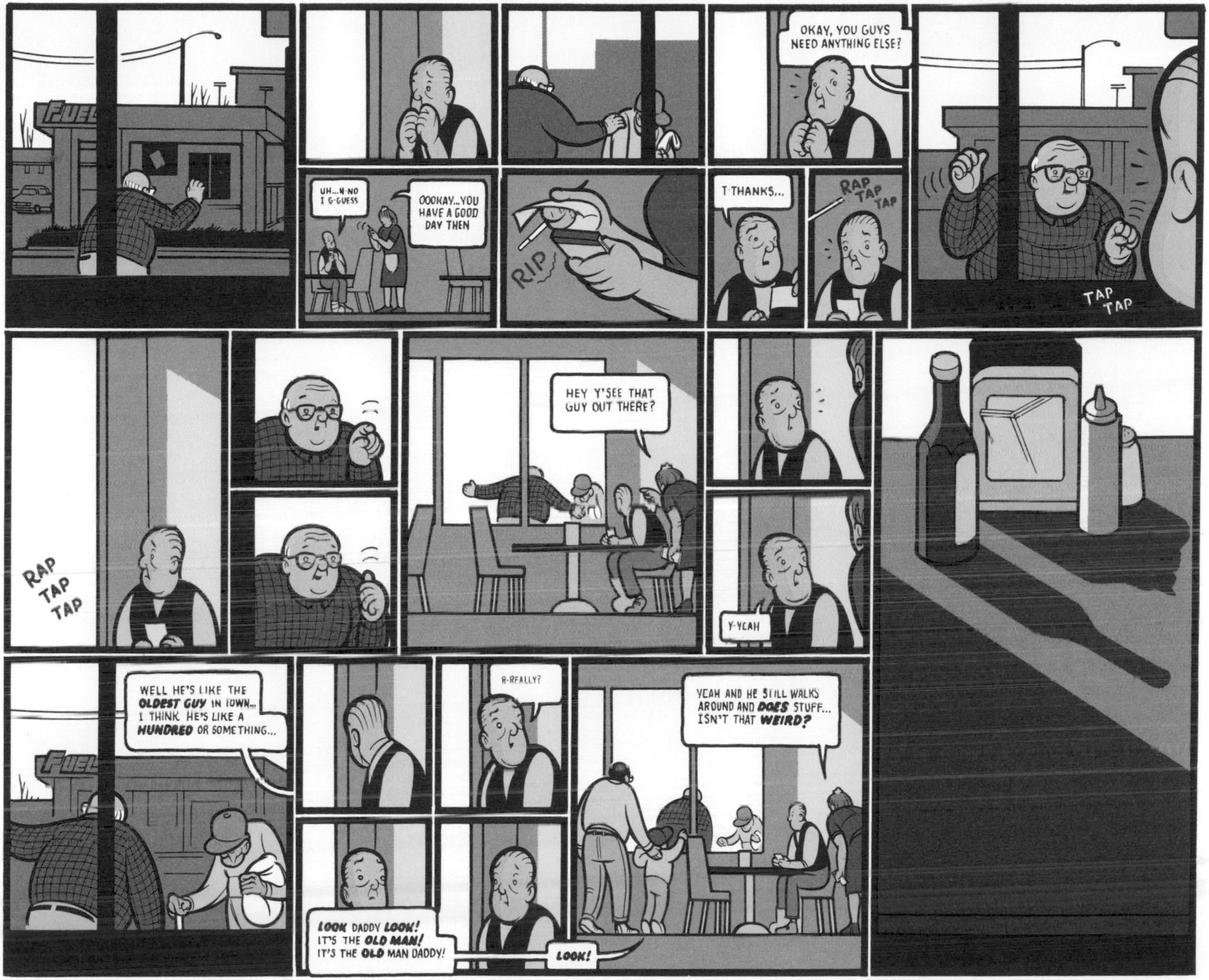

OKAY, YOU GUYS NEED ANYTHING ELSE?
UH...N-NO I G-GUESS
OOOKAY...YOU HAVE A GOOD DAY THEN
RIP
T-THANKS...
RAP TAP TAP
TAP TAP
RAP TAP TAP
HEY Y'SEE THAT GUY OUT THERE?
Y-YEAH
WELL HE'S LIKE THE OLDEST GUY IN TOWN... I THINK. HE'S LIKE A HUNDRED OR SOMETHING...
R-REALLY?
YEAH AND HE STILL WALKS AROUND AND DOES STUFF... ISN'T THAT WEIRD?
LOOK DADDY LOOK! IT'S THE OLD MAN! IT'S THE OLD MAN DADDY!
LOOK!

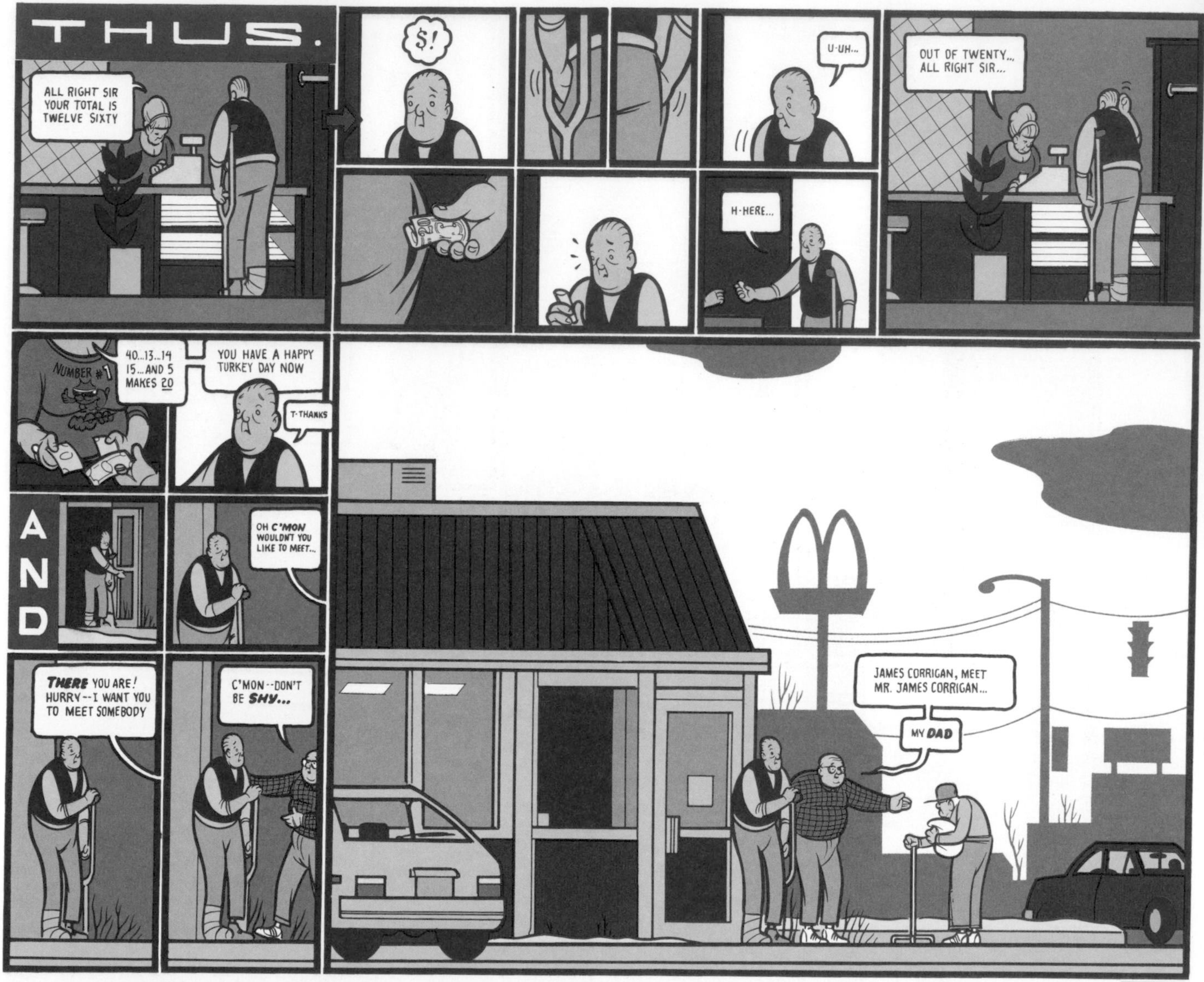
THUS.
ALL RIGHT SIR YOUR TOTAL IS TWELVE SIXTY
$!
U-UH...
OUT OF TWENTY... ALL RIGHT SIR...
H-HERE...
NUMBER #1
40...13...14 15...AND 5 MAKES 20
YOU HAVE A HAPPY TURKEY DAY NOW
T-THANKS
AND
OH C'MON WOULDN'T YOU LIKE TO MEET...
THERE YOU ARE! HURRY--I WANT YOU TO MEET SOMEBODY
C'MON--DON'T BE SHY...
JAMES CORRIGAN, MEET MR. JAMES CORRIGAN...
MY DAD

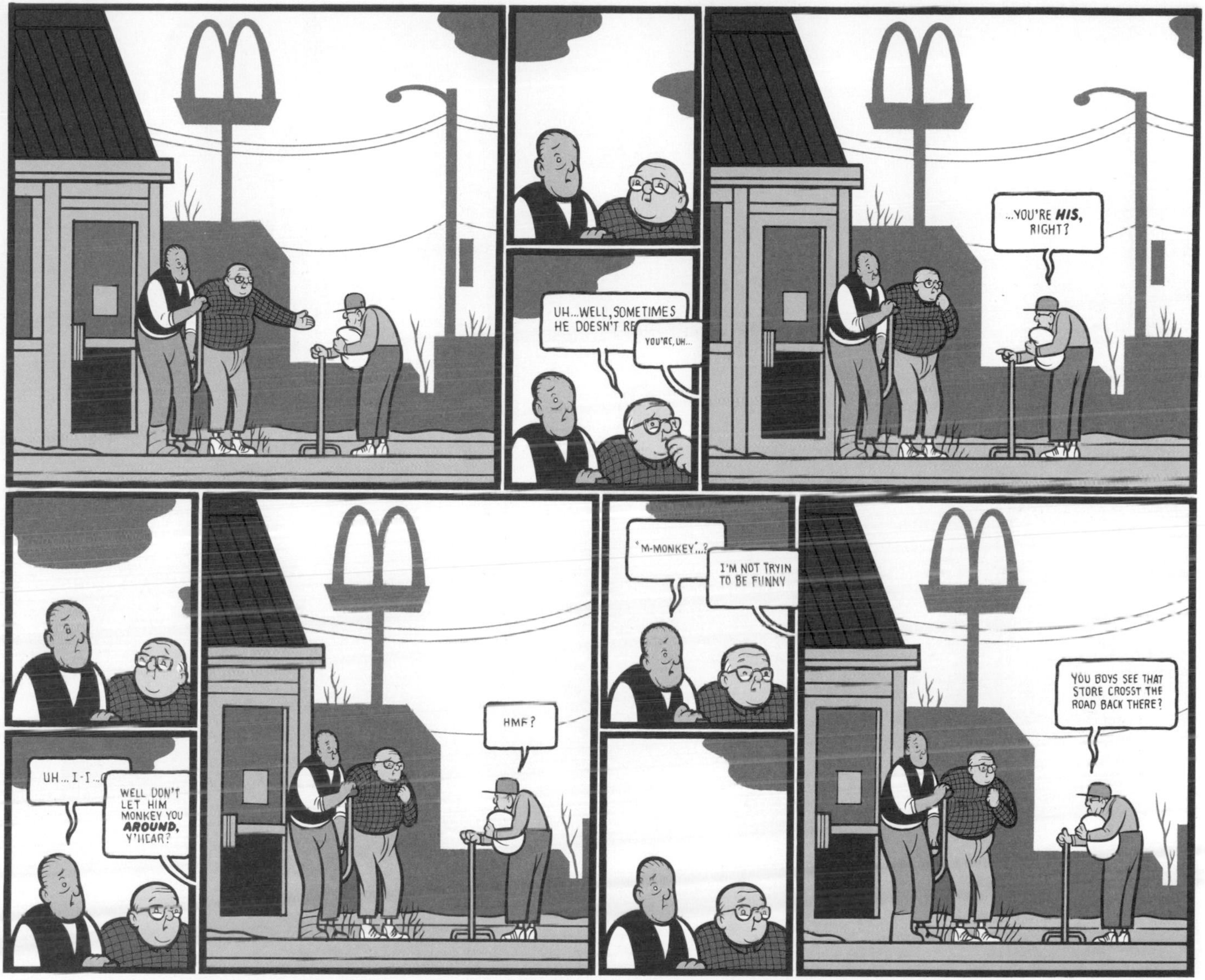
UH...WELL, SOMETIMES HE DOESN'T RE
YOU'RE, UH...
...YOU'RE HIS, RIGHT?
UH... I-I...
WELL DON'T LET HIM MONKEY YOU AROUND, Y'HEAR?
HMF?
"M-MONKEY"...?
I'M NOT TRYIN TO BE FUNNY
YOU BOYS SEE THAT STORE CROSST THE ROAD BACK THERE?

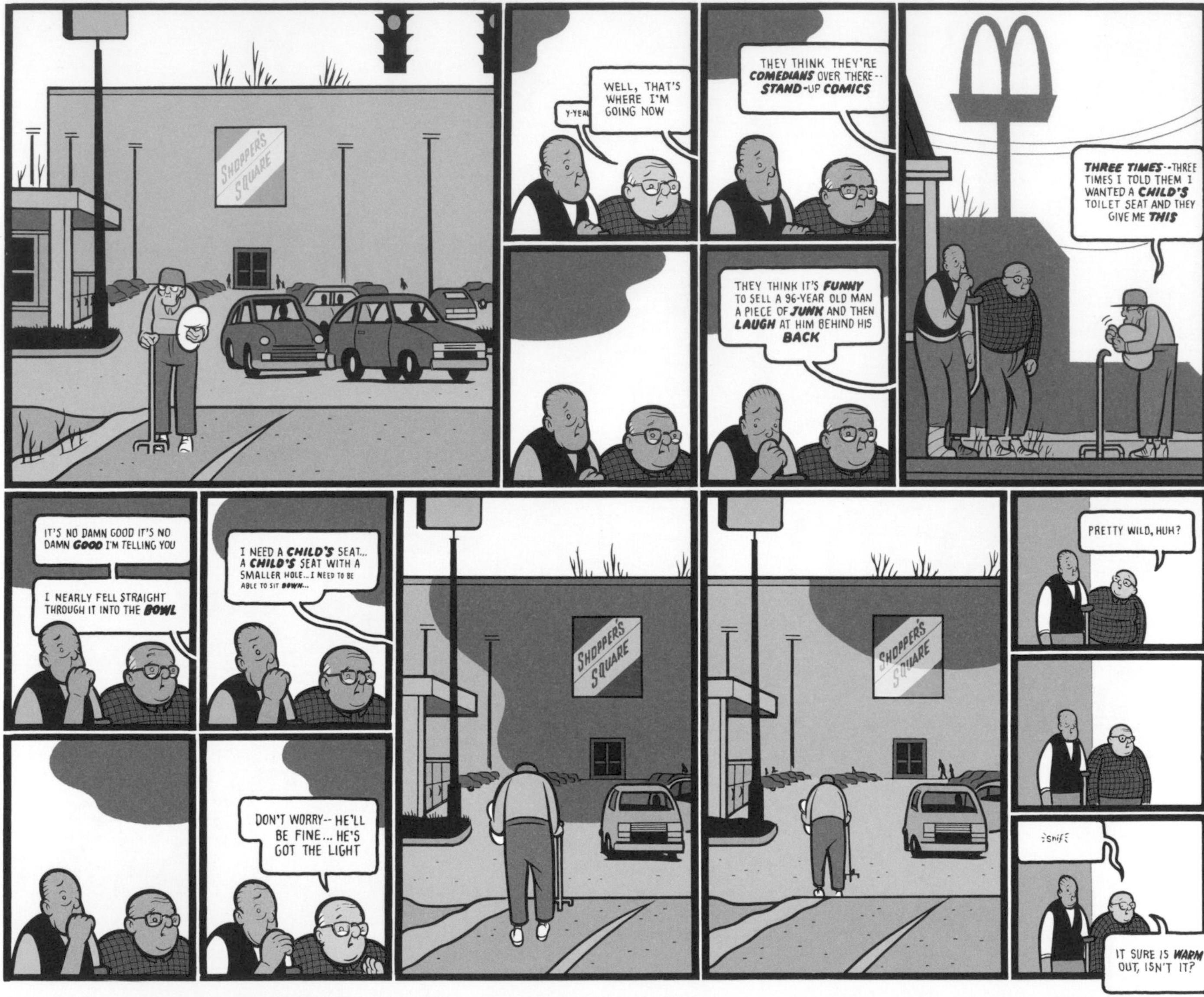
Y-YEAH
WELL, THAT'S WHERE I'M GOING NOW
THEY THINK THEY'RE COMEDIANS OVER THERE-- STAND-UP COMICS
THEY THINK IT'S FUNNY TO SELL A 96-YEAR OLD MAN A PIECE OF JUNK AND THEN LAUGH AT HIM BEHIND HIS BACK
THREE TIMES--THREE TIMES I TOLD THEM I WANTED A CHILD'S TOILET SEAT AND THEY GIVE ME THIS
IT'S NO DAMN GOOD IT'S NO DAMN GOOD I'M TELLING YOU
I NEARLY FELL STRAIGHT THROUGH IT INTO THE BOWL
I NEED A CHILD'S SEAT... A CHILD'S SEAT WITH A SMALLER HOLE... I NEED TO BE ABLE TO SIT DOWN...
DON'T WORRY-- HE'LL BE FINE... HE'S GOT THE LIGHT
PRETTY WILD, HUH?
snif
IT SURE IS WARM OUT, ISN'T IT?

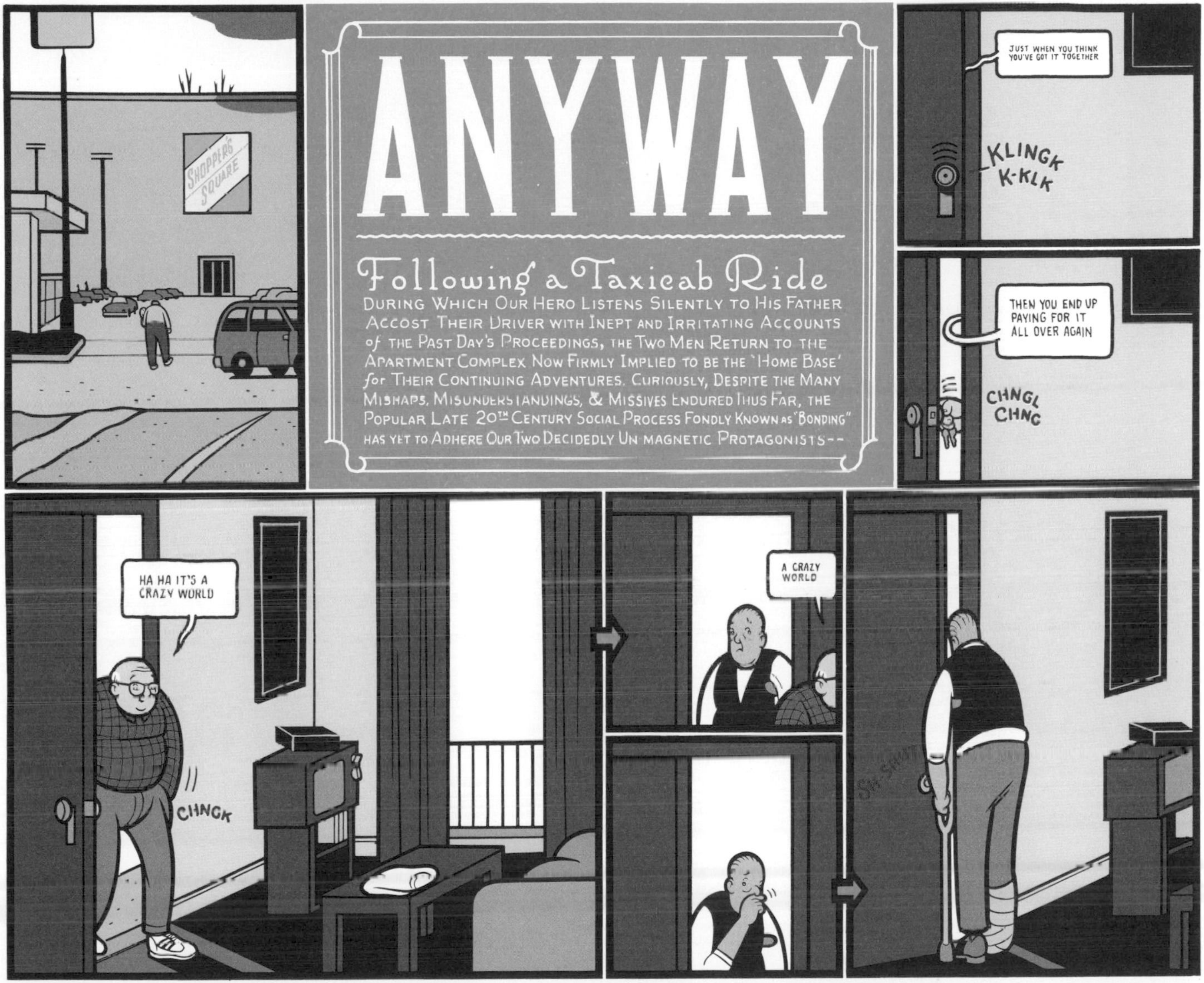
SHOPPER'S SQUARE
ANYWAY
Following a Taxicab Ride
During Which Our Hero Listens Silently to His Father Accost Their Driver with Inept and Irritating Accounts of the Past Day's Proceedings, the Two Men Return to the Apartment Complex Now Firmly Implied to be the 'Home Base' for Their Continuing Adventures. Curiously, Despite the Many Mishaps, Misunderstandings, & Missives Endured Thus Far, the Popular Late 20th Century Social Process Fondly Known as "Bonding" has yet to Adhere Our Two Decidedly Un magnetic Protagonists--
JUST WHEN YOU THINK YOU'VE GOT IT TOGETHER
KLINGK K-KLK
THEN YOU END UP PAYING FOR IT ALL OVER AGAIN
CHNGL CHNG
HA HA IT'S A CRAZY WORLD
CHNGK
A CRAZY WORLD
SH-SHUT

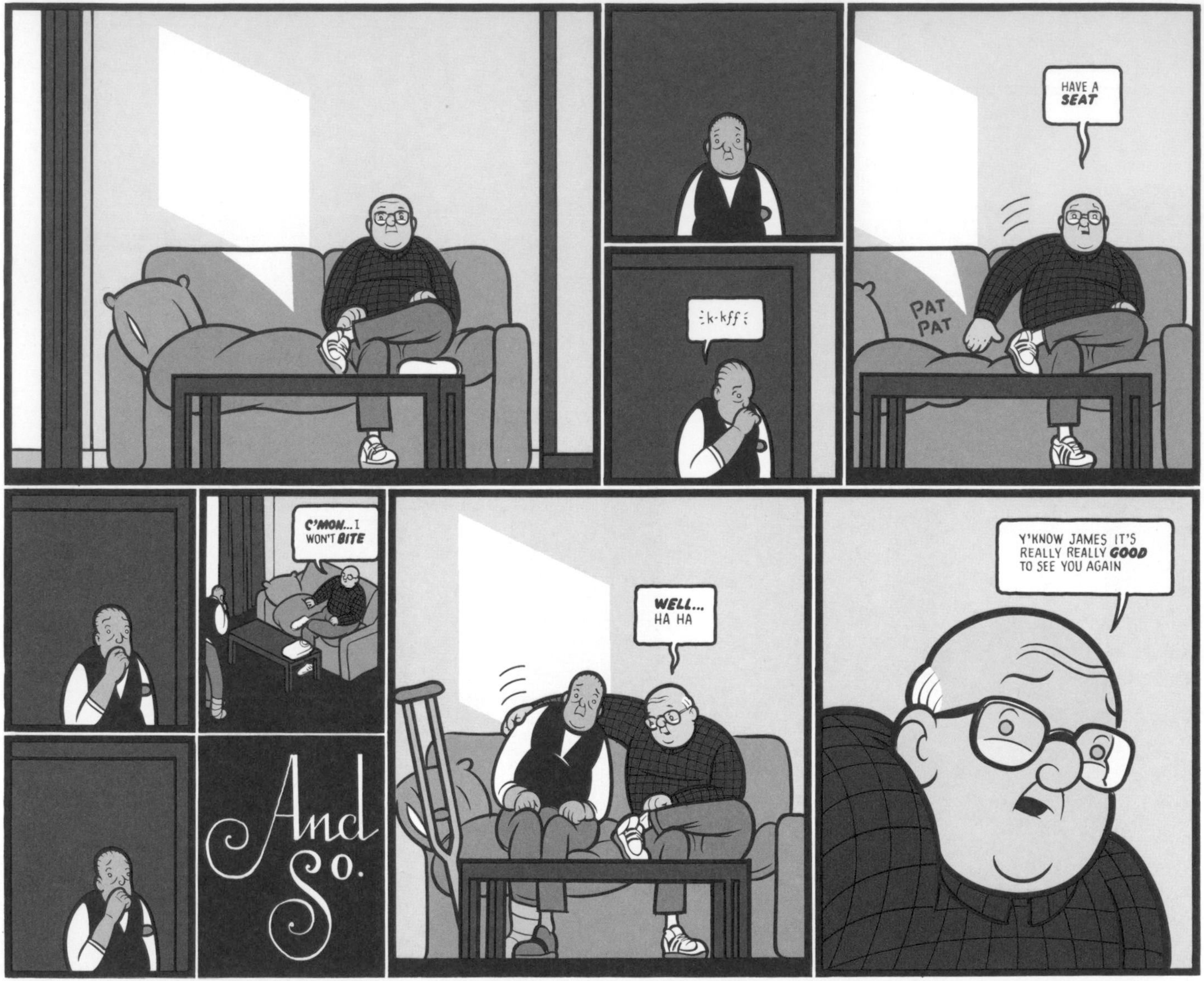

HAVE A SEAT
k-kff
PAT PAT
C'MON... I WON'T BITE
And So.
WELL... HA HA
Y'KNOW JAMES IT'S REALLY REALLY GOOD TO SEE YOU AGAIN

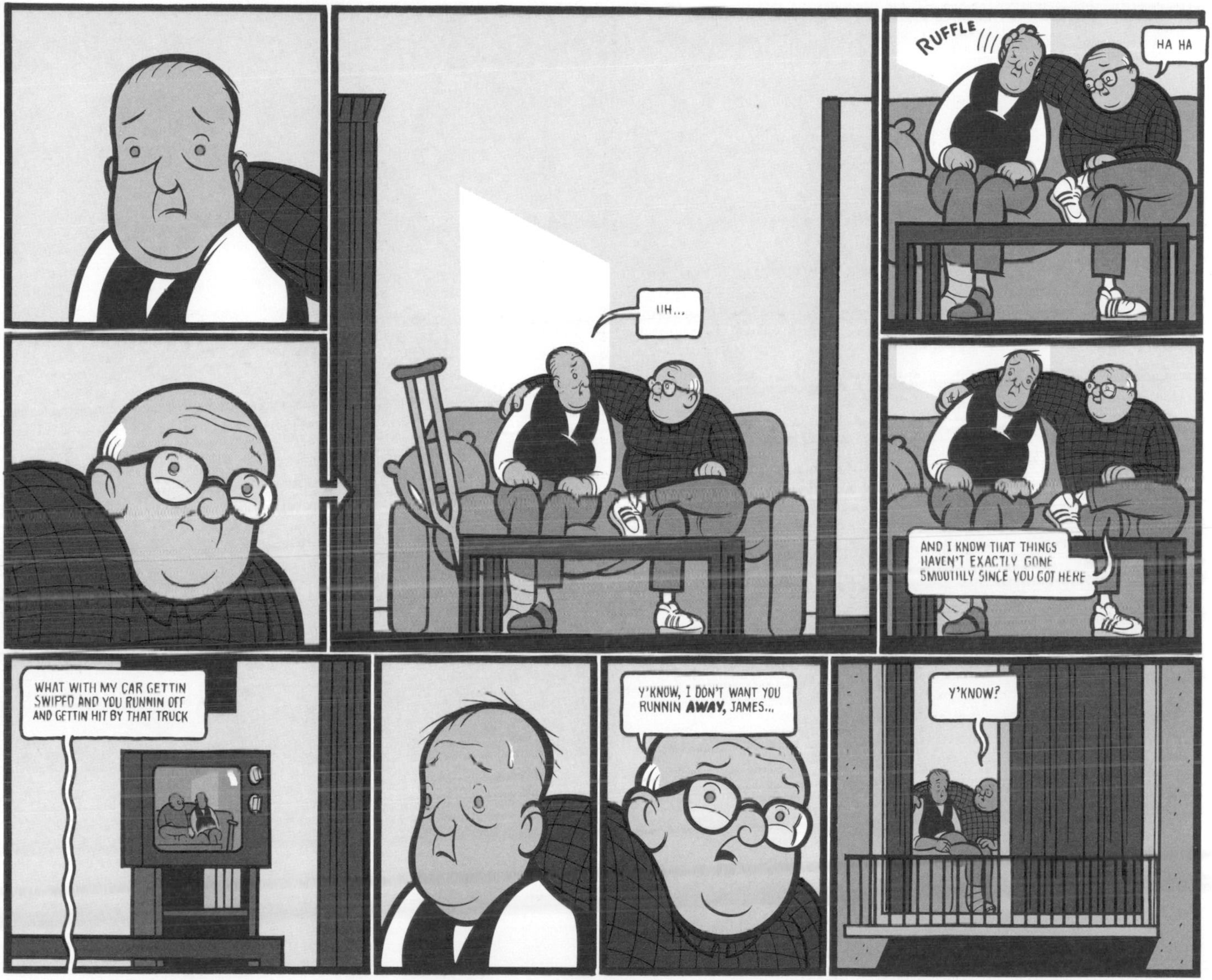

UH...
RUFFLE
HA HA
AND I KNOW THAT THINGS HAVEN'T EXACTLY GONE SMOOTHLY SINCE YOU GOT HERE
WHAT WITH MY CAR GETTIN SWIPED AND YOU RUNNIN OFF AND GETTIN HIT BY THAT TRUCK
Y'KNOW, I DON'T WANT YOU RUNNIN **AWAY,** JAMES...
Y'KNOW?

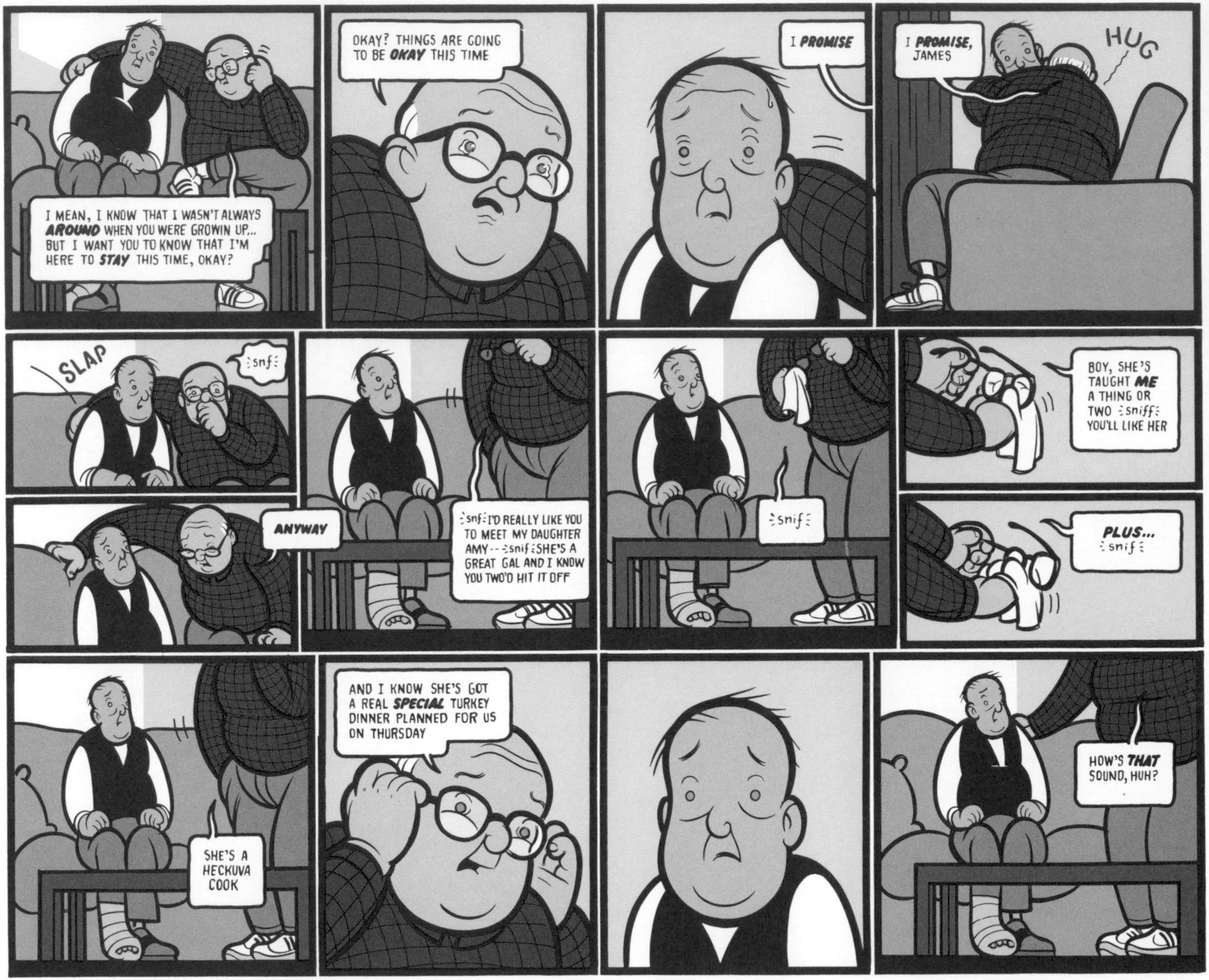
I MEAN, I KNOW THAT I WASN'T ALWAYS AROUND WHEN YOU WERE GROWIN UP... BUT I WANT YOU TO KNOW THAT I'M HERE TO STAY THIS TIME, OKAY?
OKAY? THINGS ARE GOING TO BE OKAY THIS TIME
I PROMISE
I PROMISE, JAMES
HUG
SLAP
snf
ANYWAY
snf I'D REALLY LIKE YOU TO MEET MY DAUGHTER AMY-- snif SHE'S A GREAT GAL AND I KNOW YOU TWO'D HIT IT OFF
snif
BOY, SHE'S TAUGHT ME A THING OR TWO sniff YOU'LL LIKE HER
PLUS... snif
SHE'S A HECKUVA COOK
AND I KNOW SHE'S GOT A REAL SPECIAL TURKEY DINNER PLANNED FOR US ON THURSDAY
HOW'S THAT SOUND, HUH?

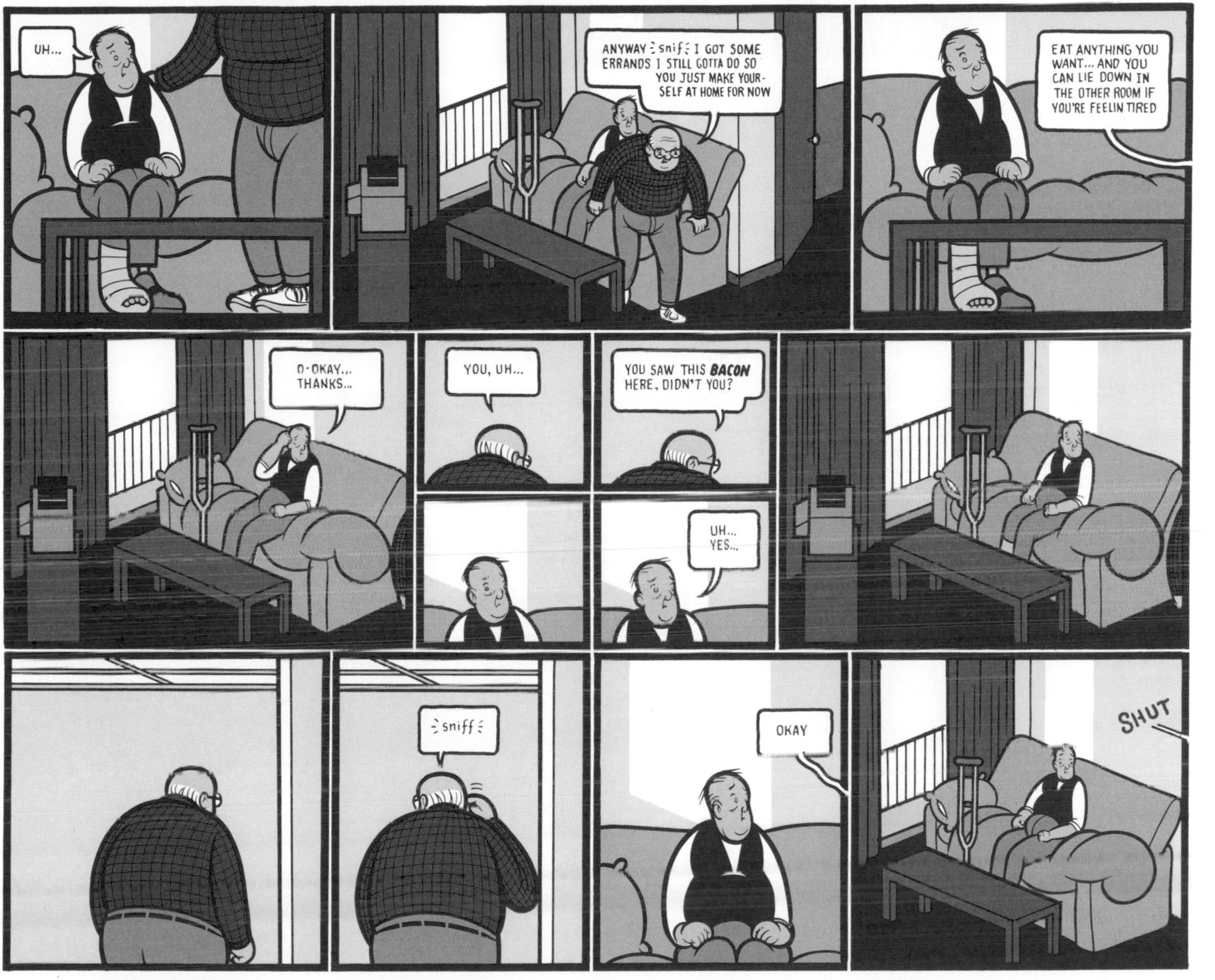
UH...
ANYWAY sniff I GOT SOME ERRANDS I STILL GOTTA DO SO YOU JUST MAKE YOURSELF AT HOME FOR NOW
EAT ANYTHING YOU WANT... AND YOU CAN LIE DOWN IN THE OTHER ROOM IF YOU'RE FEELIN TIRED
O-OKAY... THANKS...
YOU, UH...
YOU SAW THIS BACON HERE, DIDN'T YOU?
UH... YES...
sniff
OKAY
SHUT

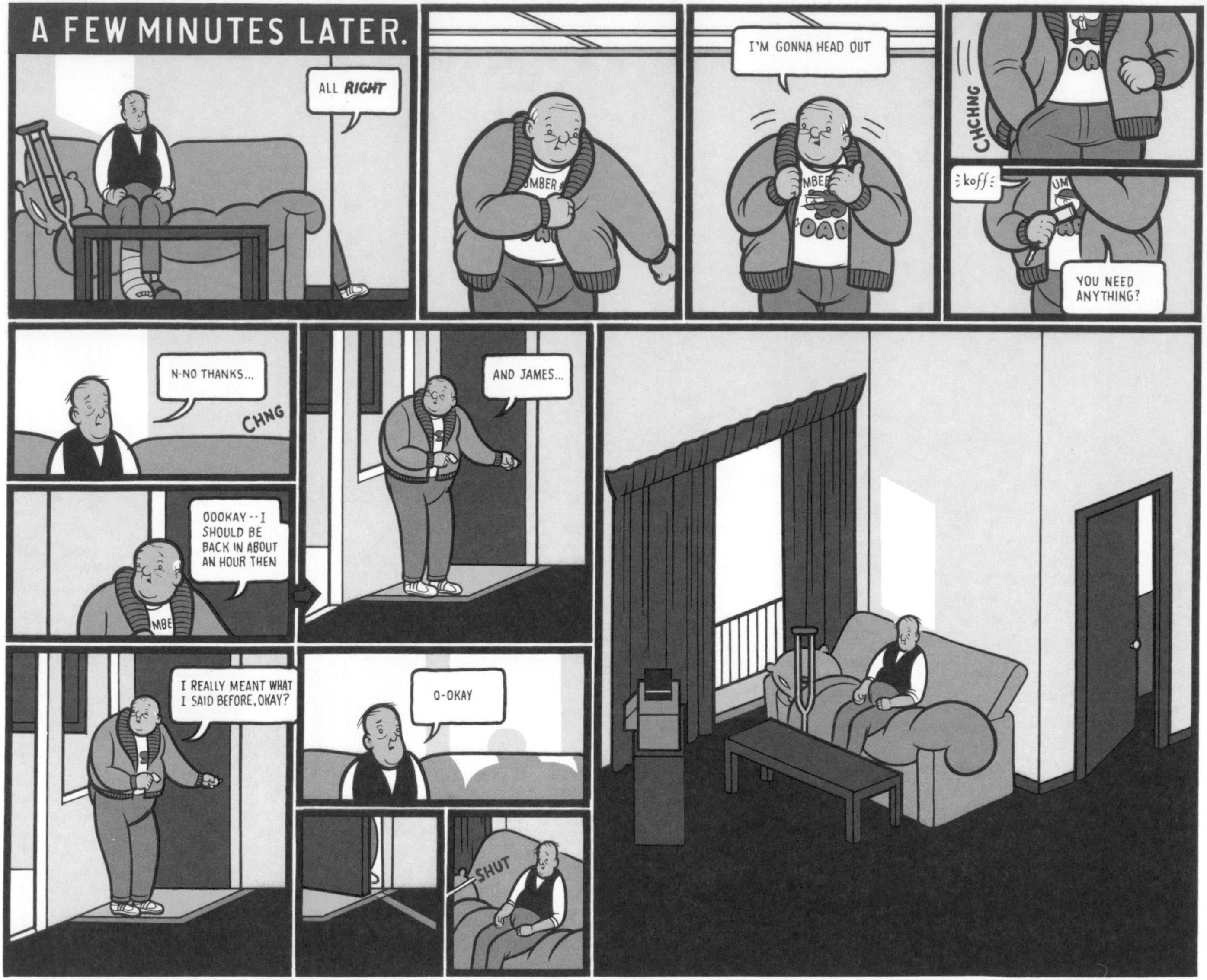
A FEW MINUTES LATER.
ALL RIGHT
I'M GONNA HEAD OUT
CHCHNG
DAD
koff
YOU NEED ANYTHING?
N-NO THANKS...
CHNG
AND JAMES...
OOOKAY--I SHOULD BE BACK IN ABOUT AN HOUR THEN
I REALLY MEANT WHAT I SAID BEFORE, OKAY?
O-OKAY
SHUT

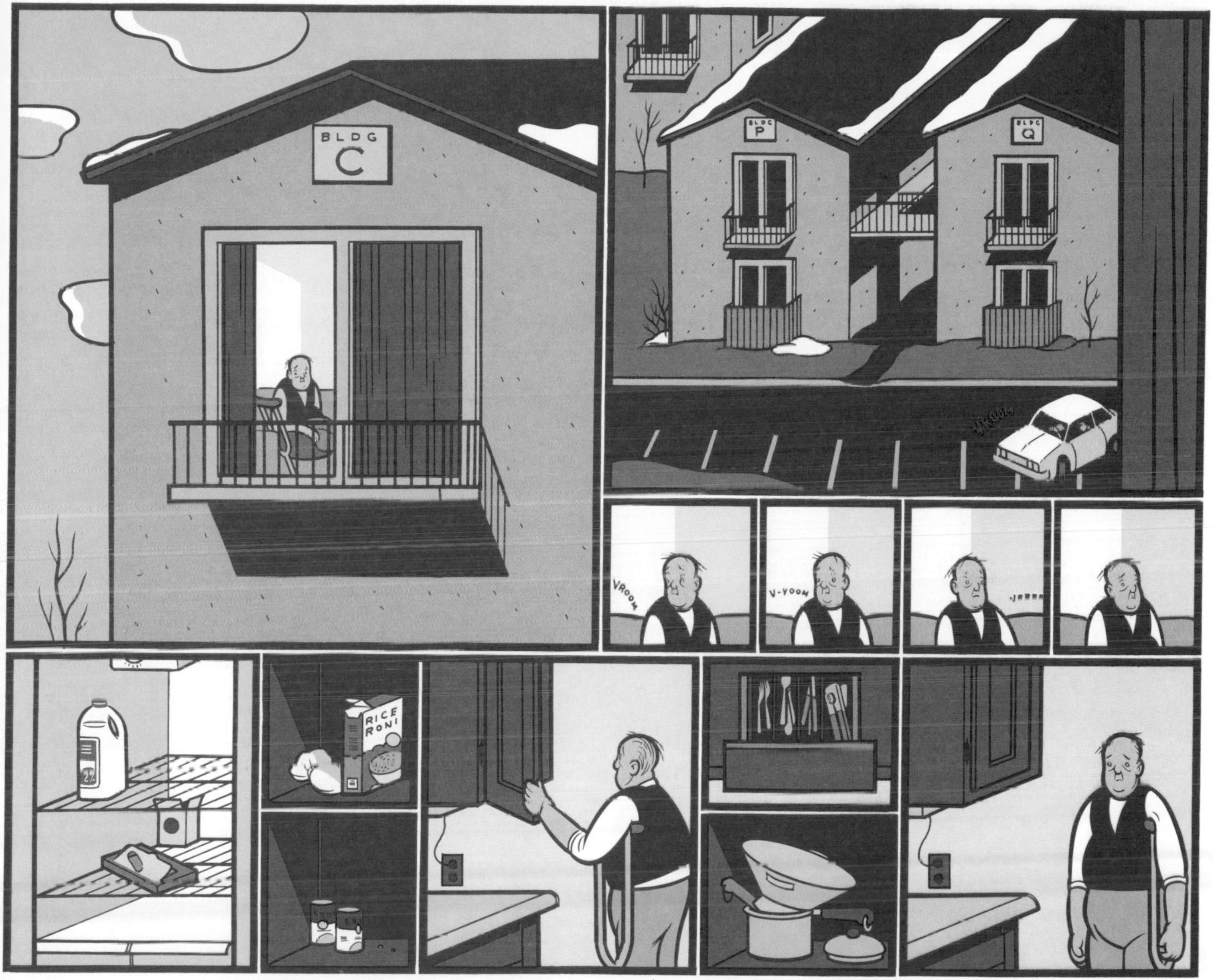
BLDG C
BLDG P
BLDG Q
VROOM
V-YOOM
RICE RONI

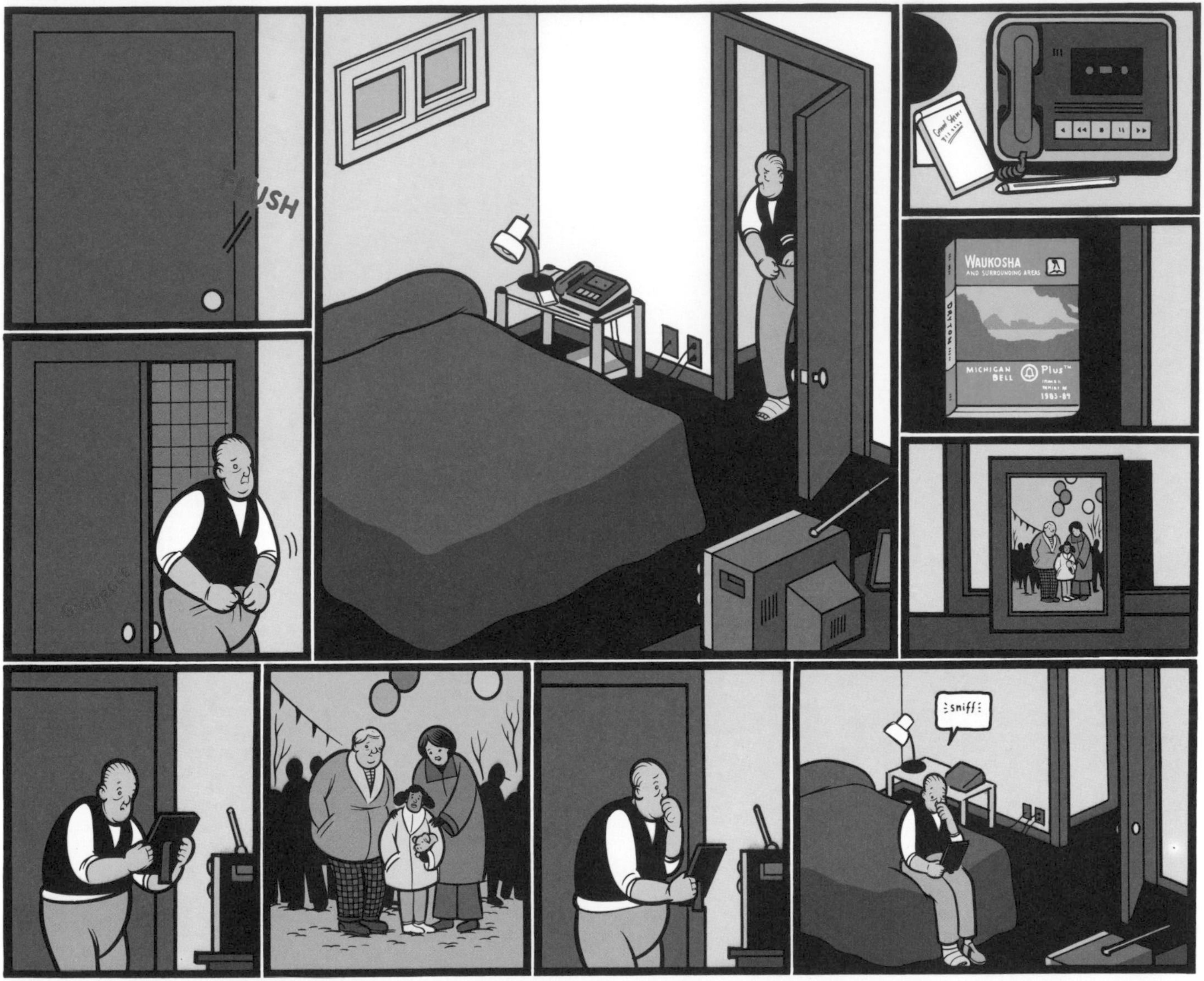
USH
WAUKOSHA
AND SURROUNDING AREAS
DAYTON
MICHIGAN BELL
Plus™
1983-84
sniff

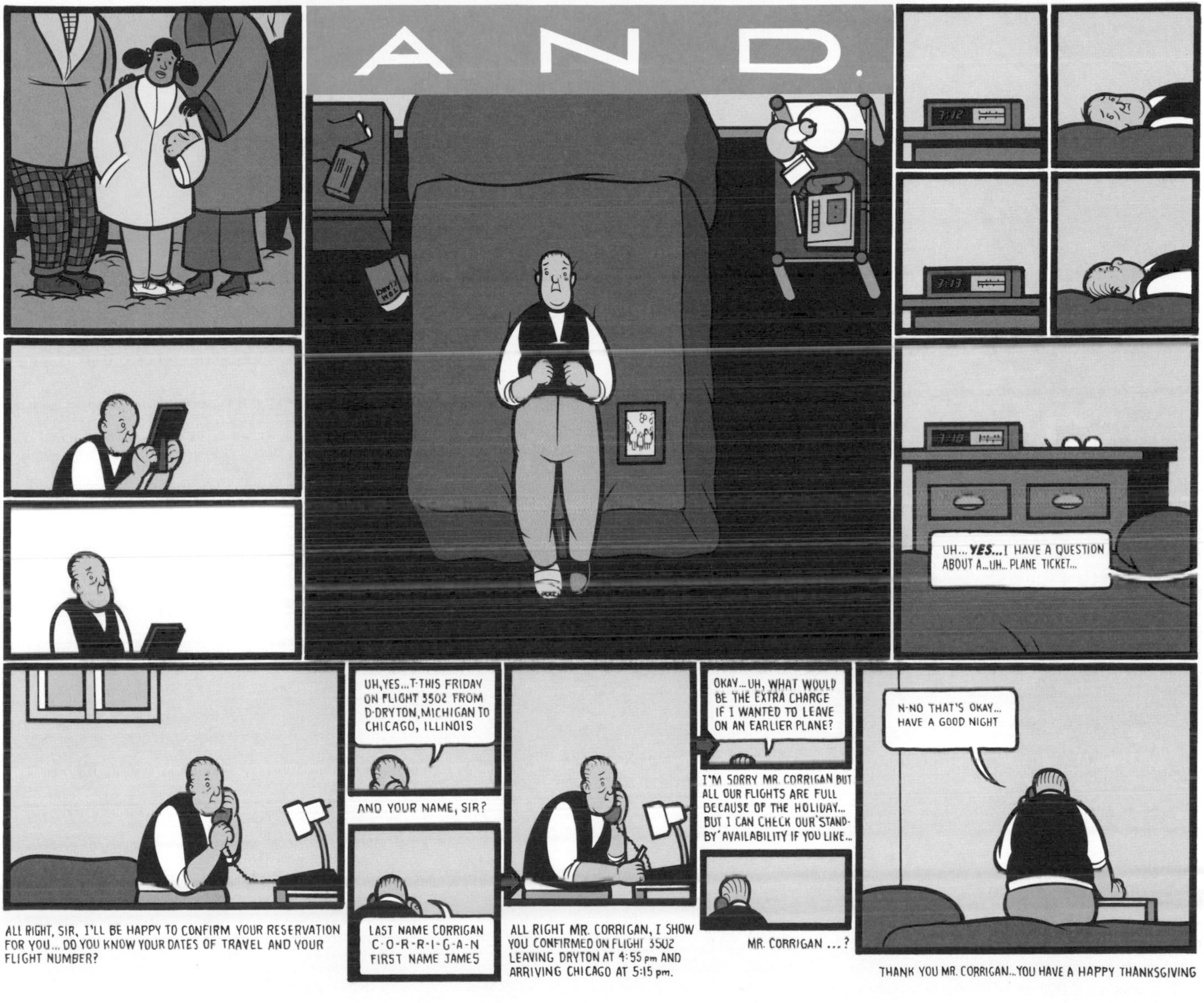
AND.
TOM CLANCY
UH... YES... I HAVE A QUESTION ABOUT A...UH... PLANE TICKET...
ALL RIGHT, SIR, I'LL BE HAPPY TO CONFIRM YOUR RESERVATION FOR YOU... DO YOU KNOW YOUR DATES OF TRAVEL AND YOUR FLIGHT NUMBER?
UH, YES... T-THIS FRIDAY ON FLIGHT 3502 FROM D-DRYTON, MICHIGAN TO CHICAGO, ILLINOIS
AND YOUR NAME, SIR?
LAST NAME CORRIGAN C-O-R-R-I-G-A-N FIRST NAME JAMES
ALL RIGHT MR. CORRIGAN, I SHOW YOU CONFIRMED ON FLIGHT 3502 LEAVING DRYTON AT 4:55 pm AND ARRIVING CHICAGO AT 5:15 pm.
OKAY... UH, WHAT WOULD BE THE EXTRA CHARGE IF I WANTED TO LEAVE ON AN EARLIER PLANE?
I'M SORRY MR. CORRIGAN BUT ALL OUR FLIGHTS ARE FULL BECAUSE OF THE HOLIDAY... BUT I CAN CHECK OUR 'STAND-BY' AVAILABILITY IF YOU LIKE...
MR. CORRIGAN ...?
N-NO THAT'S OKAY... HAVE A GOOD NIGHT
THANK YOU MR. CORRIGAN...YOU HAVE A HAPPY THANKSGIVING

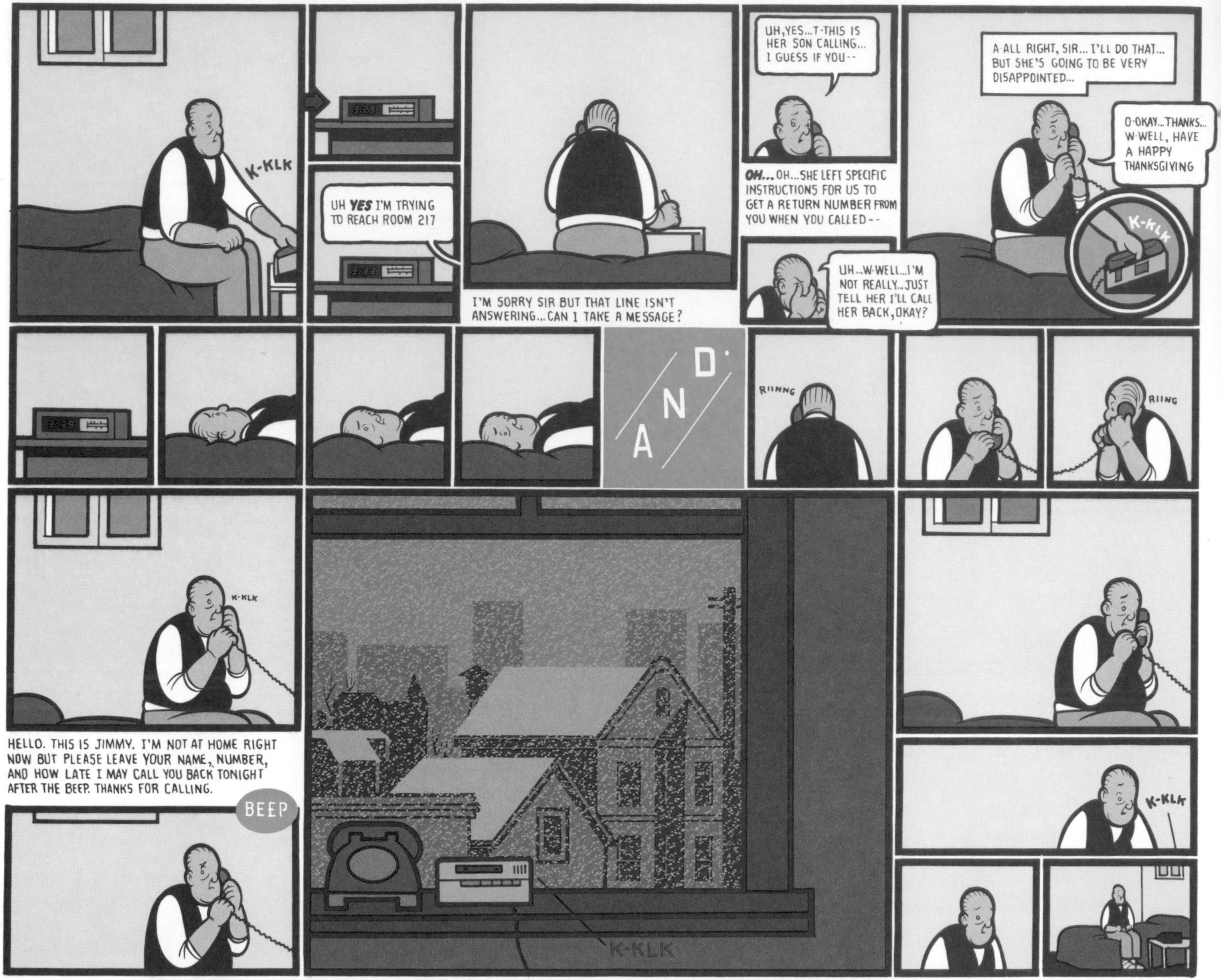

K-KLK
UH YES I'M TRYING TO REACH ROOM 217
I'M SORRY SIR BUT THAT LINE ISN'T ANSWERING... CAN I TAKE A MESSAGE?
UH, YES... T-THIS IS HER SON CALLING... I GUESS IF YOU--
OH... OH... SHE LEFT SPECIFIC INSTRUCTIONS FOR US TO GET A RETURN NUMBER FROM YOU WHEN YOU CALLED--
UH... W-WELL... I'M NOT REALLY... JUST TELL HER I'LL CALL HER BACK, OKAY?
A-ALL RIGHT, SIR... I'LL DO THAT... BUT SHE'S GOING TO BE VERY DISAPPOINTED...
O-OKAY... THANKS... W-WELL, HAVE A HAPPY THANKSGIVING
K-KLK
AND
RIINNG
RIING
K-KLK
HELLO. THIS IS JIMMY. I'M NOT AT HOME RIGHT NOW BUT PLEASE LEAVE YOUR NAME, NUMBER, AND HOW LATE I MAY CALL YOU BACK TONIGHT AFTER THE BEEP. THANKS FOR CALLING.
BEEP
K-KLK
K-KLK

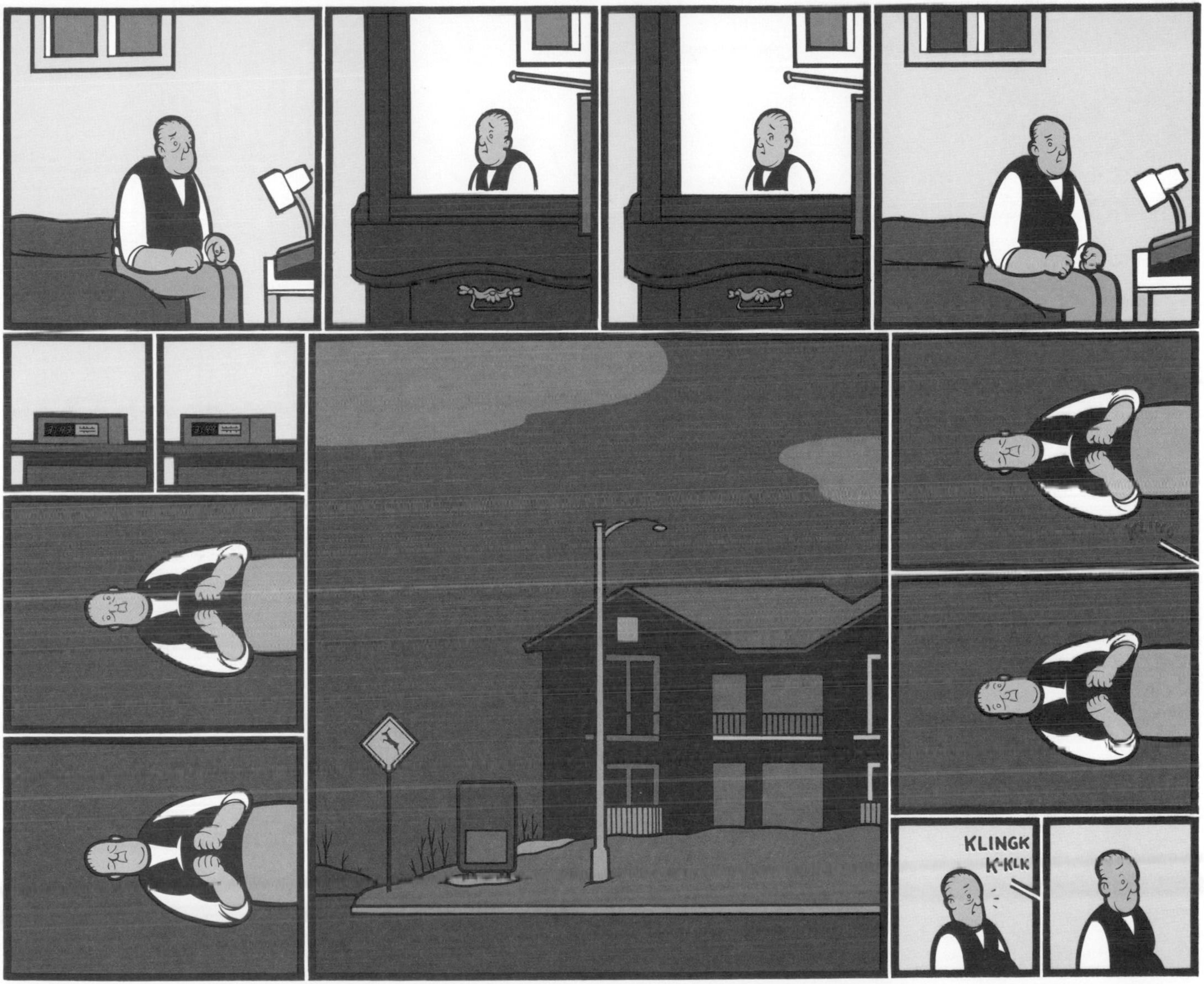
KLINGK
K-KLK

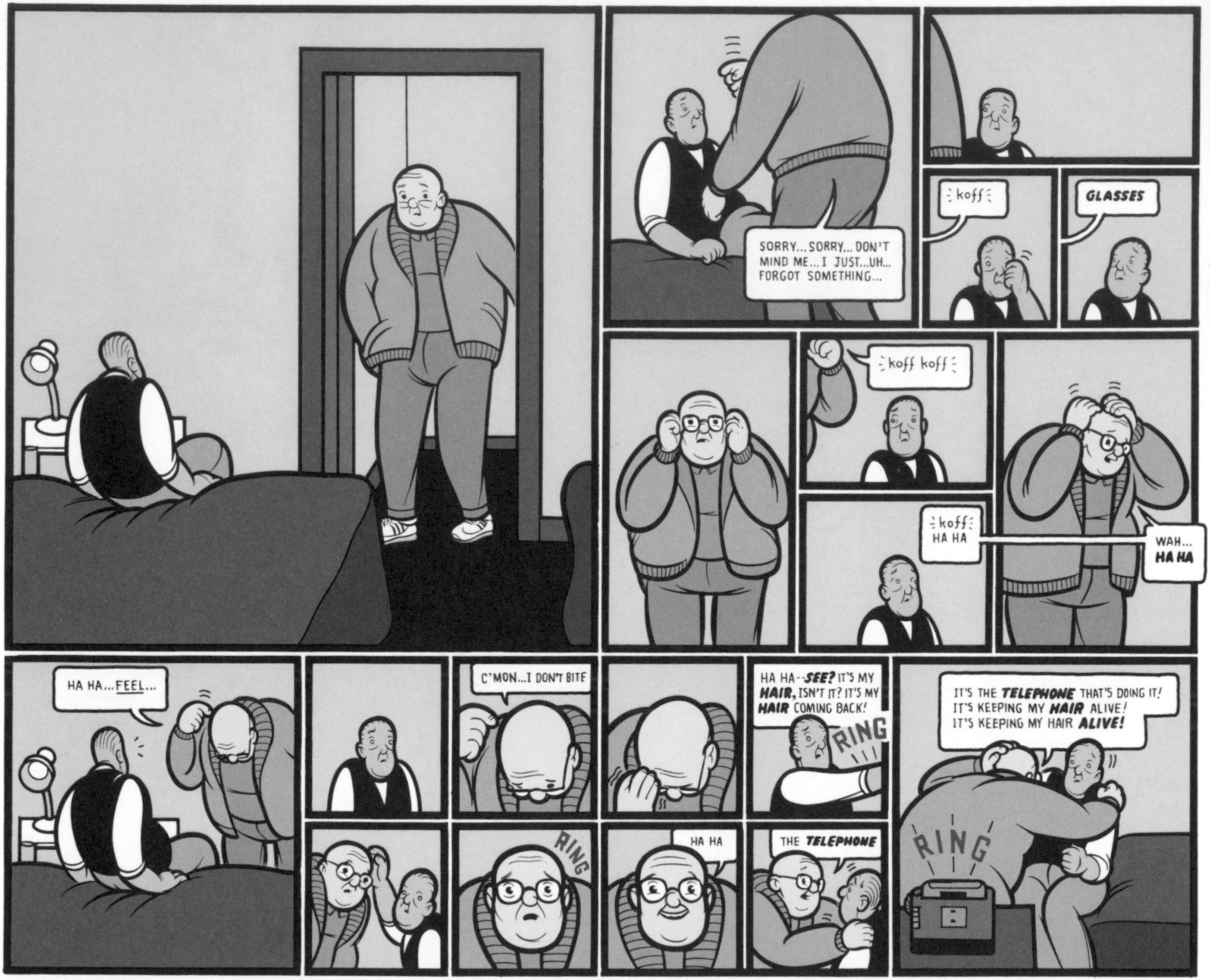
SORRY... SORRY... DON'T MIND ME... I JUST...UH... FORGOT SOMETHING...
koff
GLASSES
koff koff
koff
HA HA
WAH...
HA HA
HA HA...FEEL...
C'MON...I DON'T BITE
HA HA--SEE? IT'S MY HAIR, ISN'T IT? IT'S MY HAIR COMING BACK!
RING
RING
HA HA
THE TELEPHONE
IT'S THE TELEPHONE THAT'S DOING IT! IT'S KEEPING MY HAIR ALIVE! IT'S KEEPING MY HAIR ALIVE!
RING

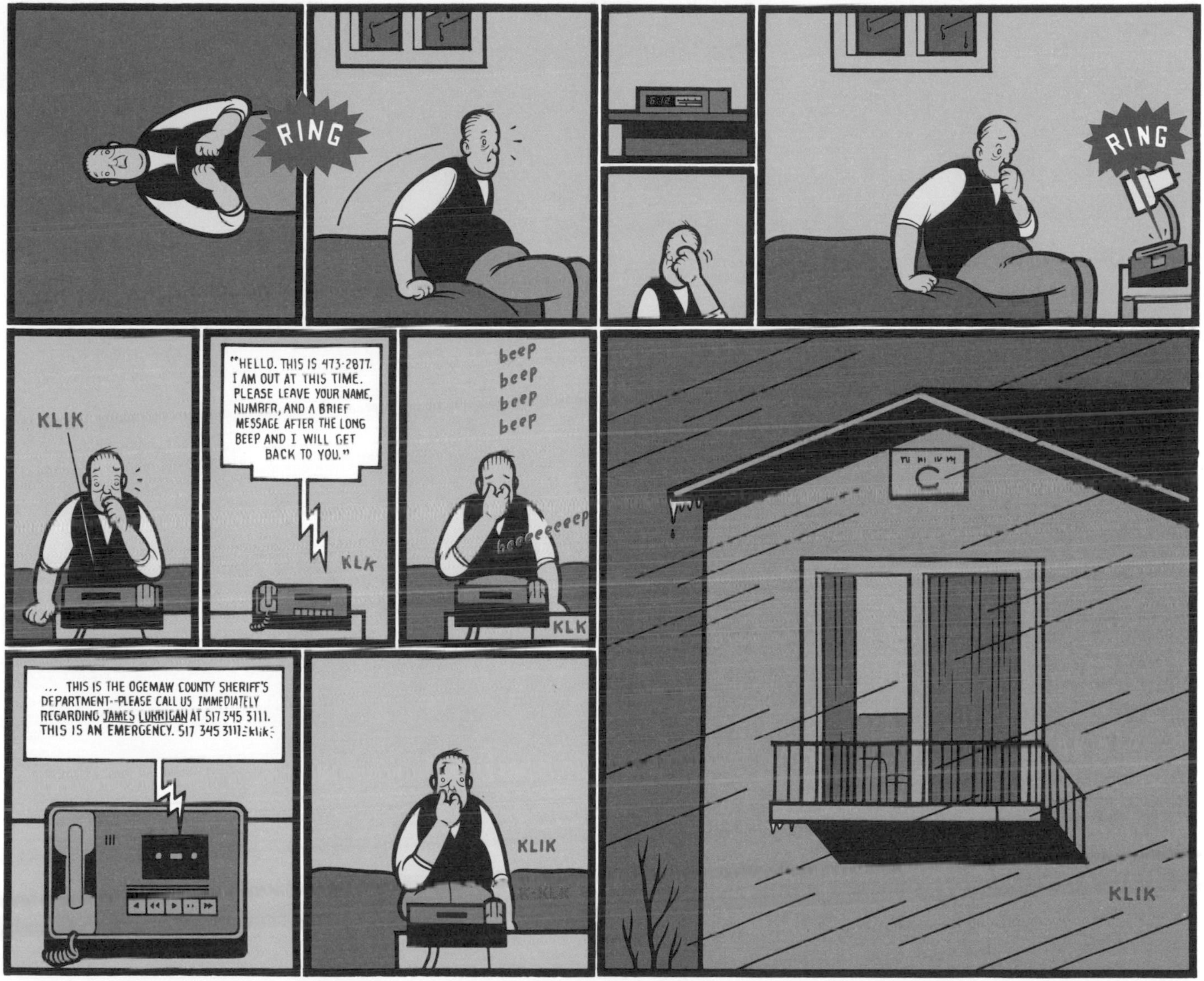
RING
RING
KLIK
"HELLO. THIS IS 473-2877. I AM OUT AT THIS TIME. PLEASE LEAVE YOUR NAME, NUMBER, AND A BRIEF MESSAGE AFTER THE LONG BEEP AND I WILL GET BACK TO YOU."
KLK
beep
beep
beep
beep
beeeeeeeep
KLK
... THIS IS THE OGEMAW COUNTY SHERIFF'S DEPARTMENT--PLEASE CALL US IMMEDIATELY REGARDING JAMES CORRIGAN AT 517 345 3111. THIS IS AN EMERGENCY. 517 345 3111 klik
KLIK
K-KLK
KLIK

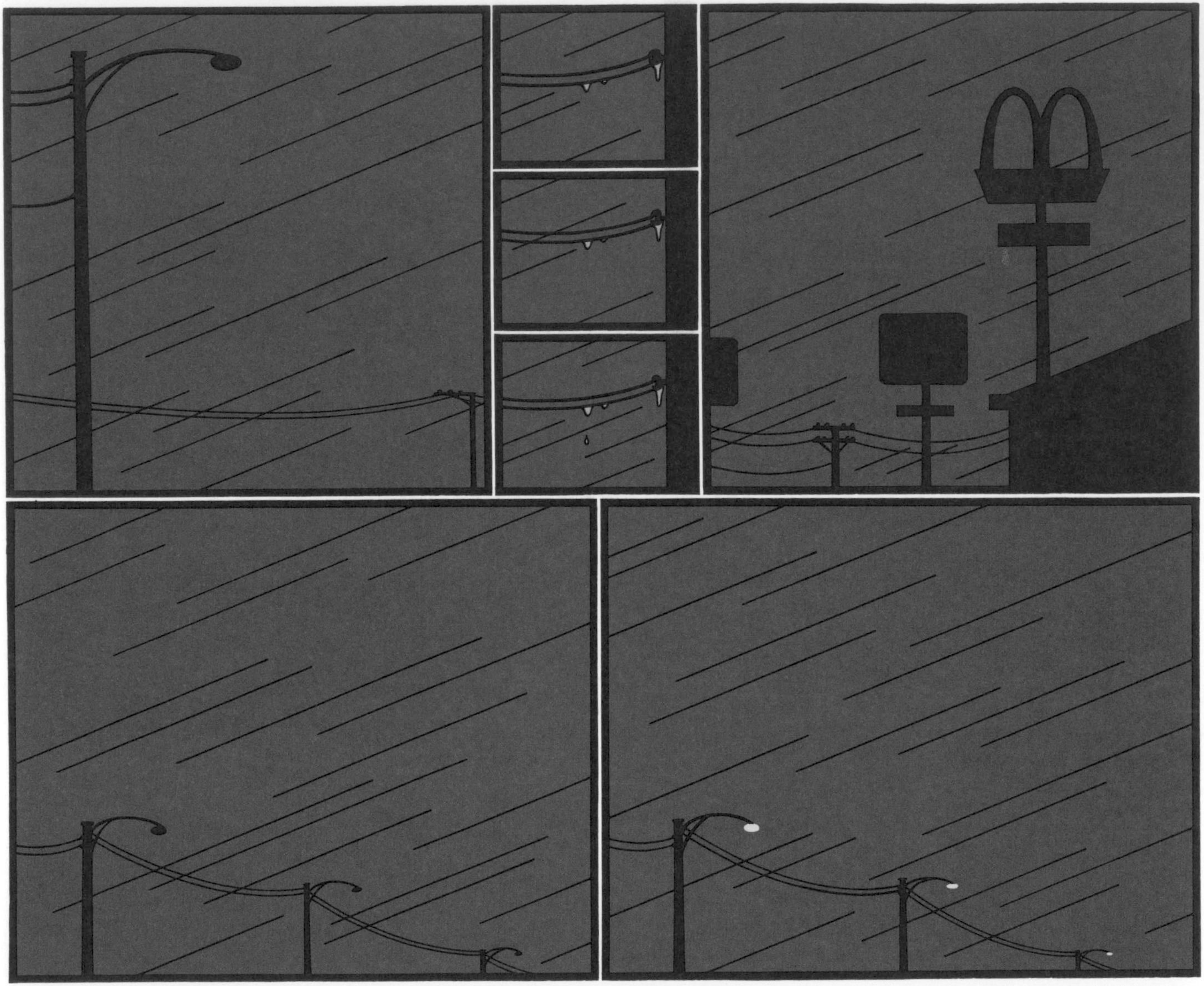

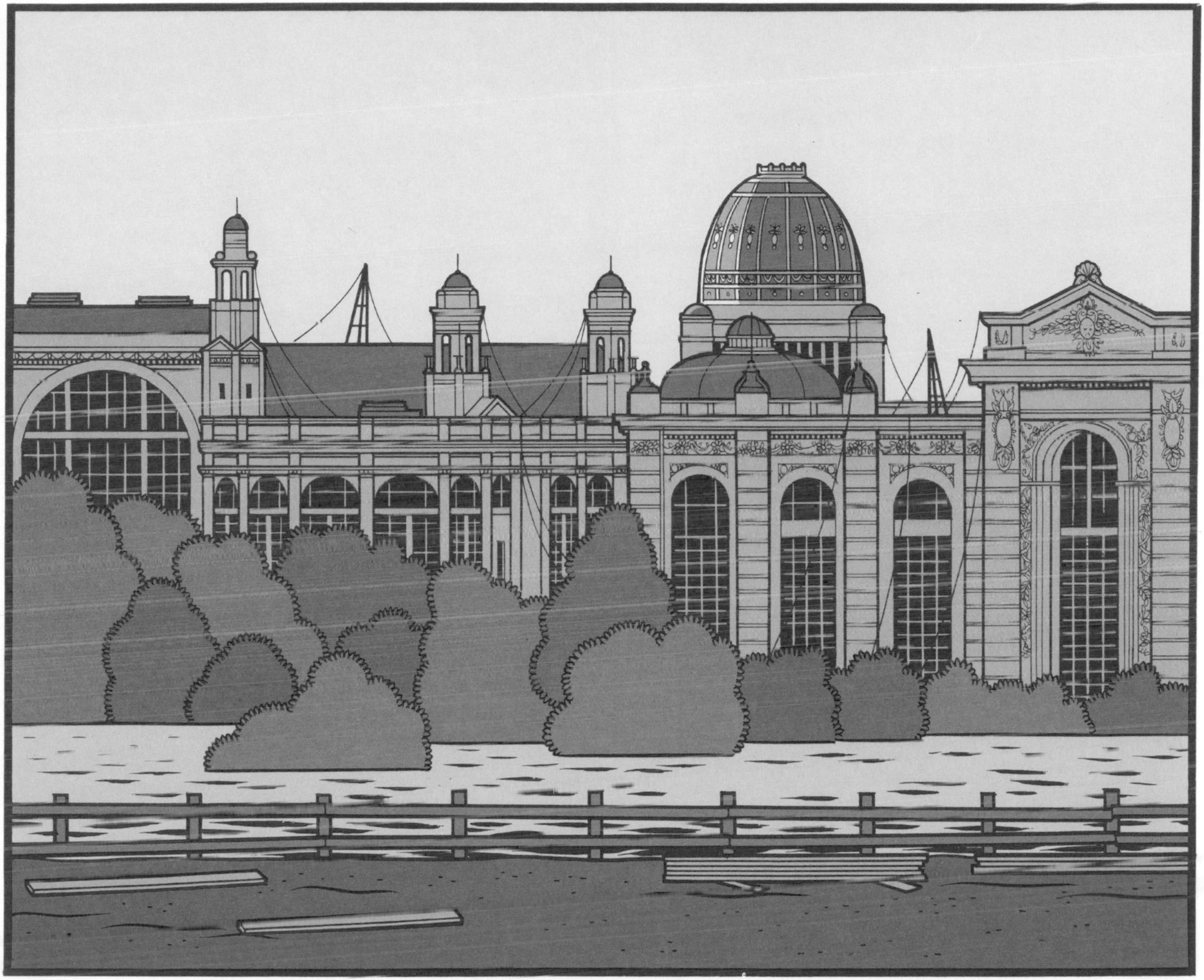

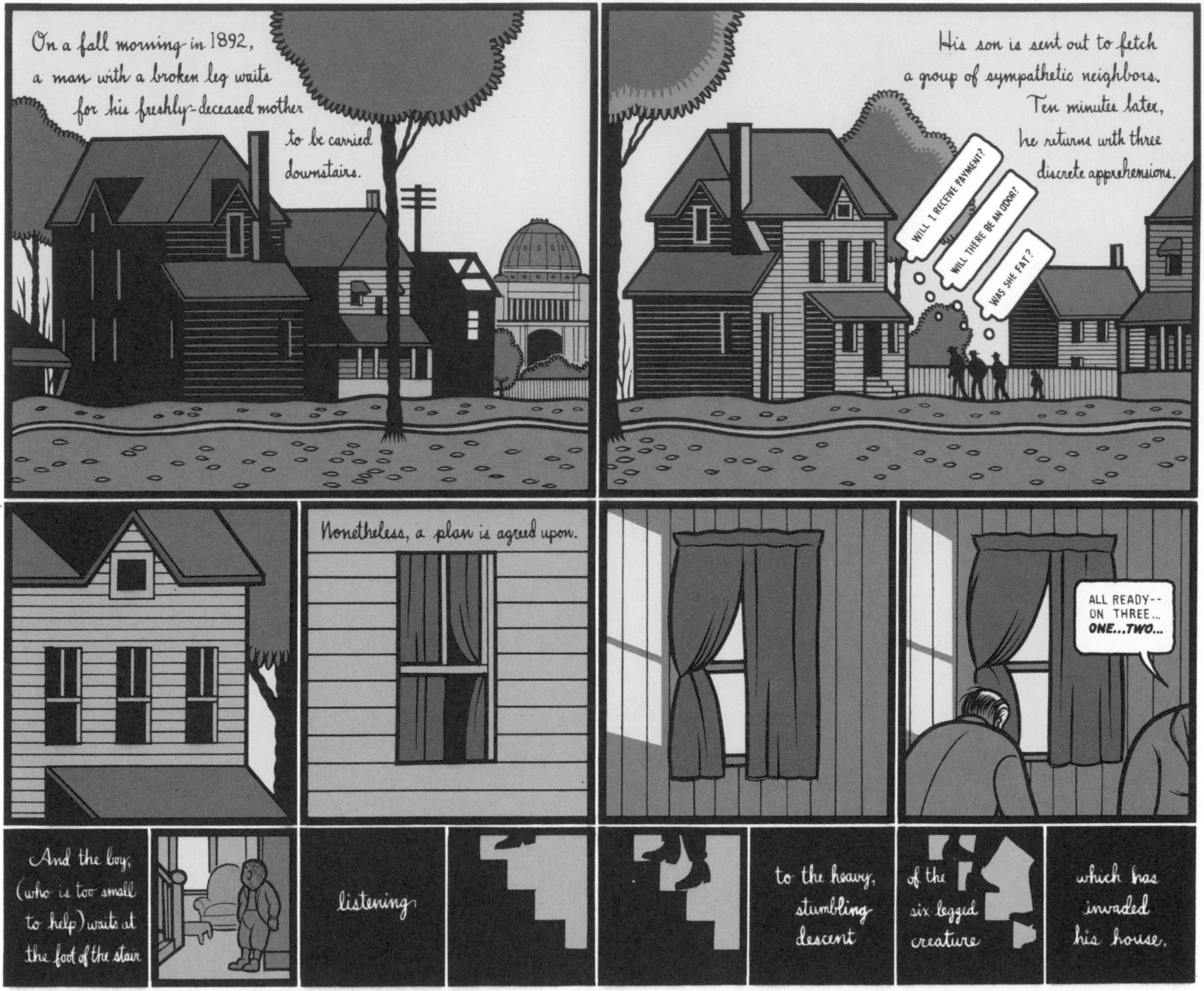
On a fall morning in 1892, a man with a broken leg waits for his freshly-deceased mother to be carried downstairs.
His son is sent out to fetch a group of sympathetic neighbors. Ten minutes later, he returns with three discrete apprehensions.
WILL I RECEIVE PAYMENT?
WILL THERE BE AN ODOR?
WAS SHE FAT?
Nonetheless, a plan is agreed upon.
ALL READY-- ON THREE... ONE...TWO...
And the boy, (who is too small to help) waits at the foot of the stair
listening,
to the heavy, stumbling descent
of the six-legged creature
which has invaded his house.

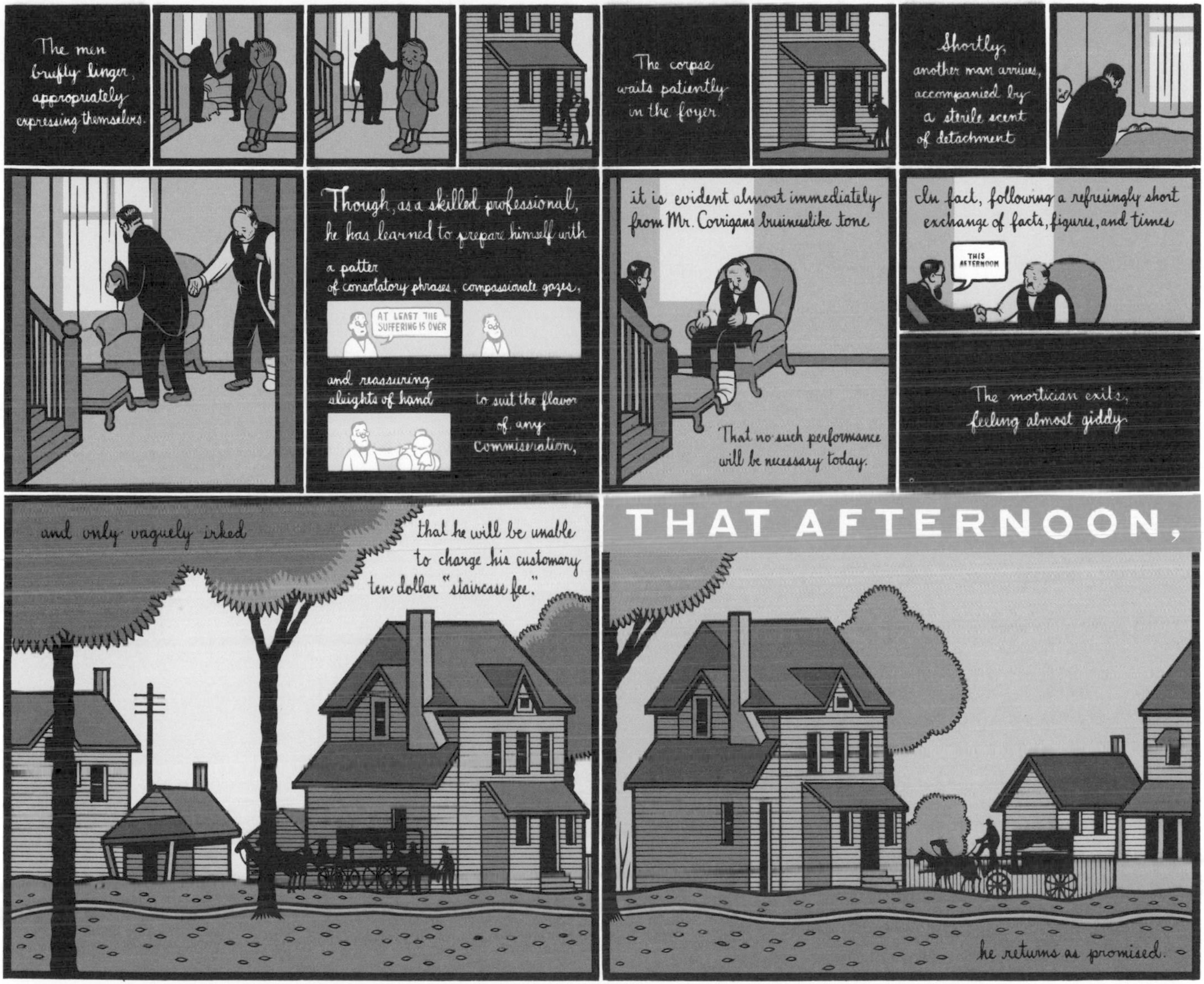

The men briefly linger, appropriately expressing themselves.
The corpse waits patiently in the foyer.
Shortly, another man arrives, accompanied by a sterile scent of detachment
Though, as a skilled professional, he has learned to prepare himself with
a patter of consolatory phrases,
AT LEAST THE SUFFERING IS OVER
compassionate gazes,
and reassuring sleights of hand
to suit the flavor of any commiseration,
it is evident almost immediately from Mr. Corrigan's businesslike tone
That no such performance will be necessary today.
In fact, following a refreshingly short exchange of facts, figures, and times
THIS AFTERNOON
The mortician exits, feeling almost giddy
and only vaguely irked
that he will be unable to charge his customary ten dollar "staircase fee."
THAT AFTERNOON,
he returns as promised.

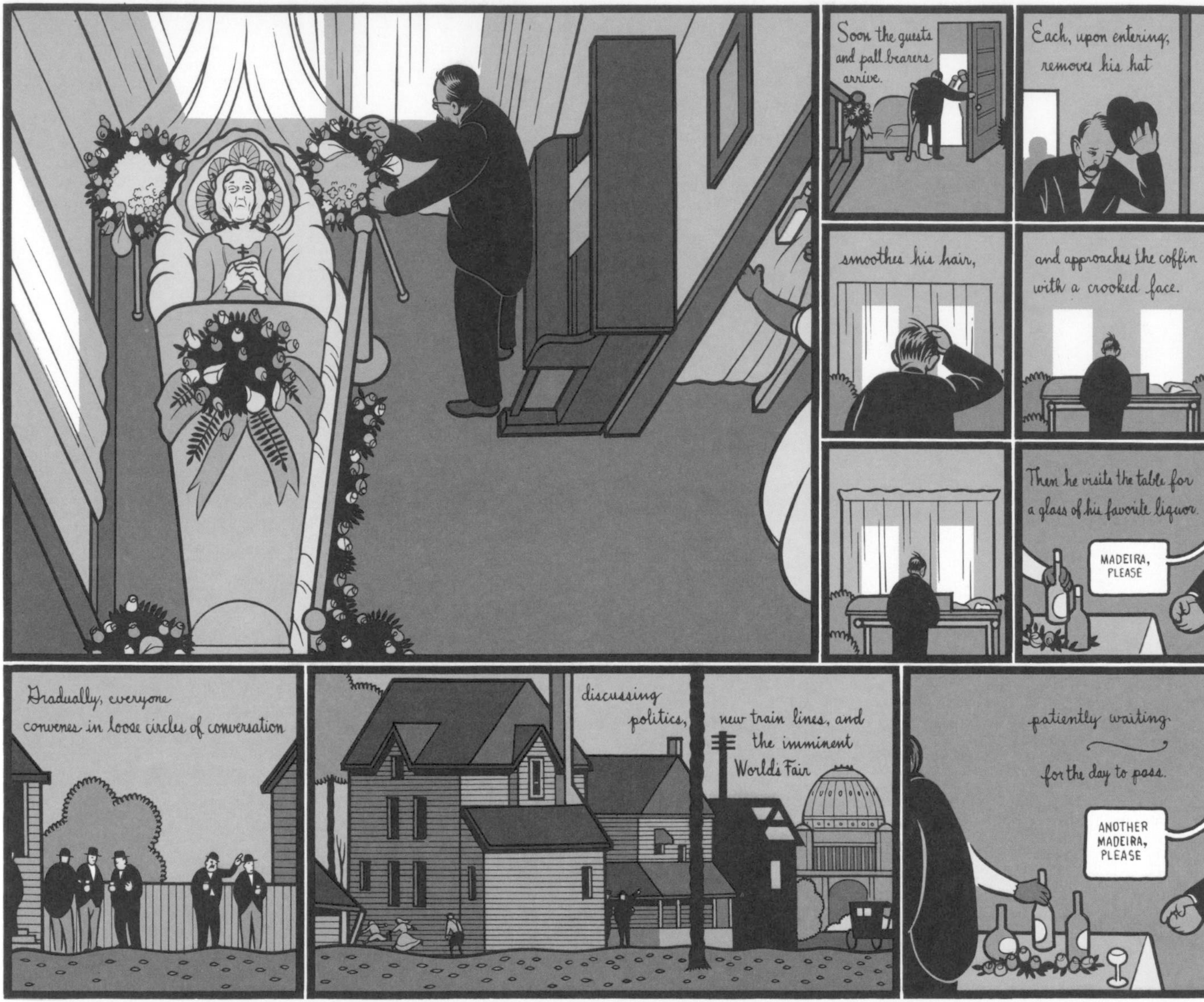
Soon the guests and pall bearers arrive.
Each, upon entering, removes his hat
smoothes his hair,
and approaches the coffin with a crooked face.
Then he visits the table for a glass of his favorite liquor.
MADEIRA, PLEASE
Gradually, everyone convenes in loose circles of conversation
discussing politics,
new train lines, and the imminent World's Fair
patiently waiting for the day to pass.
ANOTHER MADEIRA, PLEASE

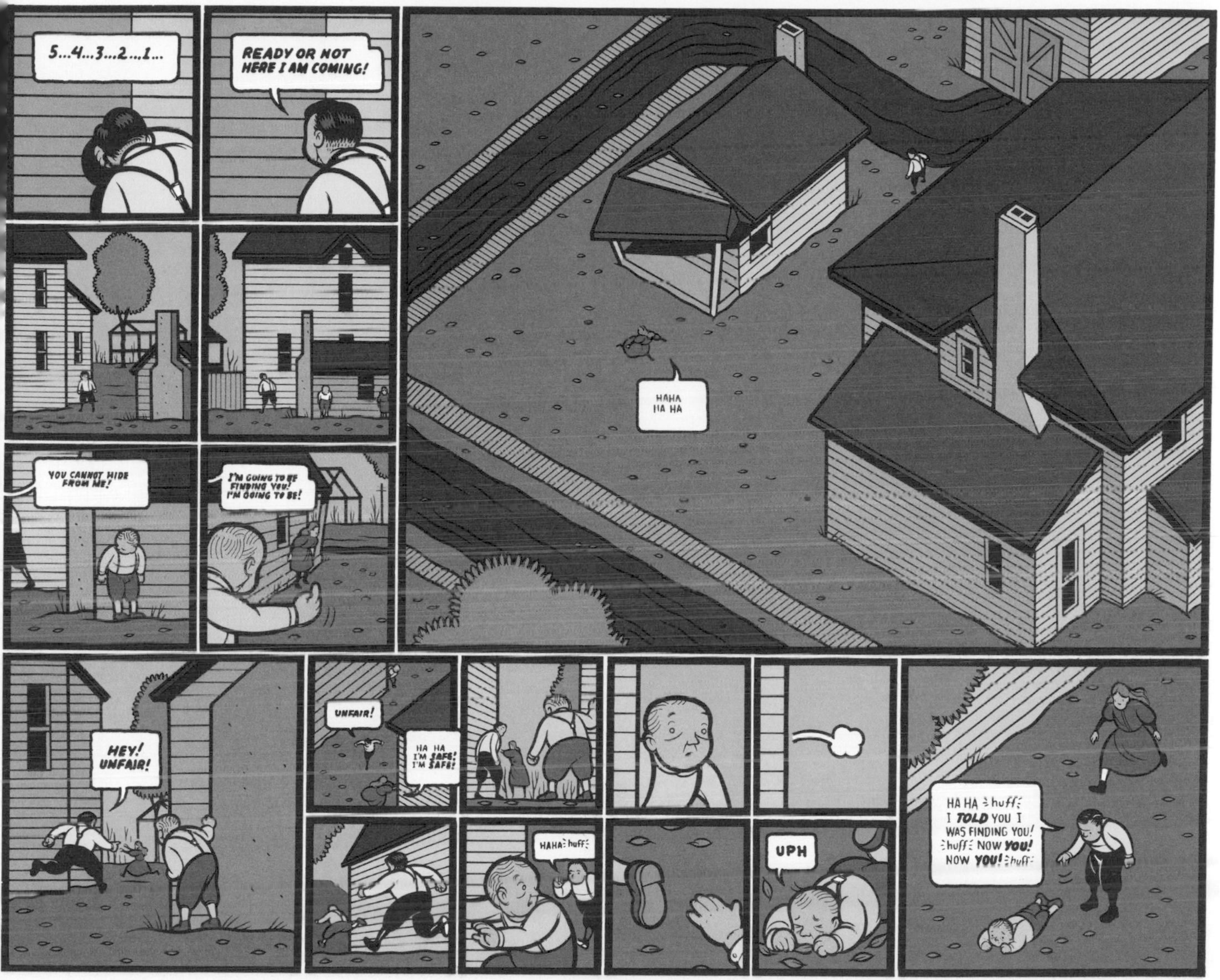
5...4...3...2...1...
READY OR NOT HERE I AM COMING!
HAHA HA HA
YOU CANNOT HIDE FROM ME!
I'M GOING TO BE FINDING YOU! I'M GOING TO BE!
HEY! UNFAIR!
UNFAIR!
HA HA I'M SAFE! I'M SAFE!
HAHA huff
UPH
HA HA huff I TOLD YOU I WAS FINDING YOU! huff NOW YOU! NOW YOU! huff

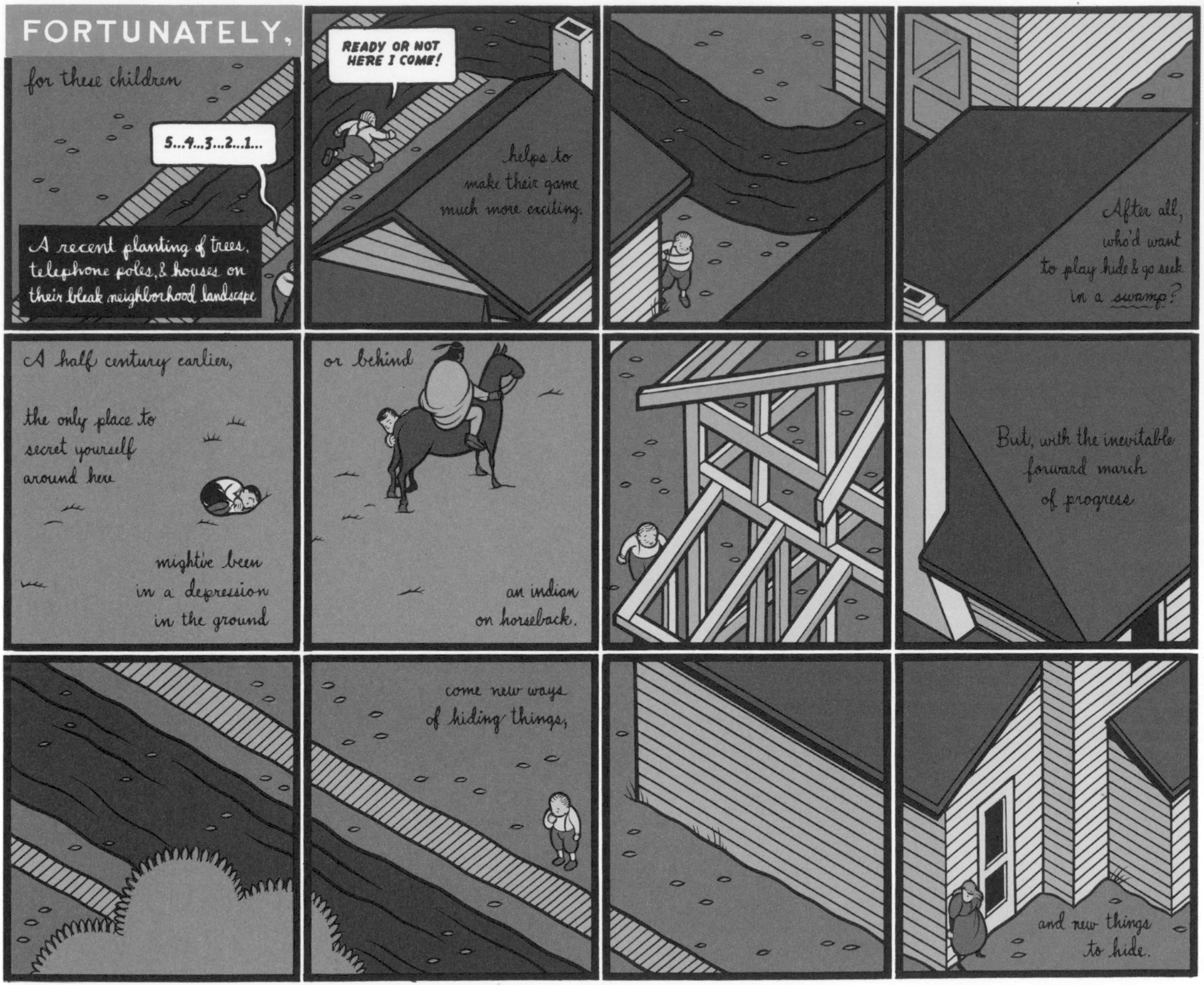
FORTUNATELY,
for these children
5...4...3...2...1...
A recent planting of trees, telephone poles, & houses on their bleak neighborhood landscape
READY OR NOT HERE I COME!
helps to make their game much more exciting.
After all, who'd want to play hide & go seek in a swamp?
A half century earlier,
the only place to secret yourself around here
might've been in a depression in the ground
or behind
an indian on horseback.
But, with the inevitable forward march of progress
come new ways of hiding things,
and new things to hide.

PAGES 206-207. – It should be readily apparent to even the most casual reader of this novella that supplied with it are a handful of piquant and diverting "cut out" reference guides; though such "paper activities" are sometimes dismissed as "child's play" or frivolous "hokum," of no value to the serious student of literature, it is hoped that these uncultured negative preconceptions – which really do serve no other purpose than to truncate one's experience of an evocative work – shall be disspelt by the dainties' masterful esthetic and artistic qualities. Besides, the increasing commonplace of such "paper toys" in respectable books, plays, and corporate presentations is enough to muzzle even the most vocal detractor towards the cause. Though admittedly printed too small to be constructed with any degree of satisfaction or pluck, pantographic or electrostatic enlargement of all primary shapes and careful study of the construction principia will potentially reward the concerted craftsman with models of relative usefulness. An outfit of water-color paints, a sharp knife, and limited background in human romantic contact are, of course, key.

It is, needless to say, not entirely necessary to complete these tasks to fully appreciate the story in question, though those who do attempt the feat will find themselves more acquainted with the rivulets and tributaries of its grander scope, and will besides have nice little miniatures to display to friends and family once the fantasy is nothing more than a swamp of misremembered trifles. However, given the relative intelligence and mathematical skills of this textbook's author, all culpability regarding measurement of parts, tabs, and joinery is hereby forfeit, and no submitted claims to the contrary shall be honored.

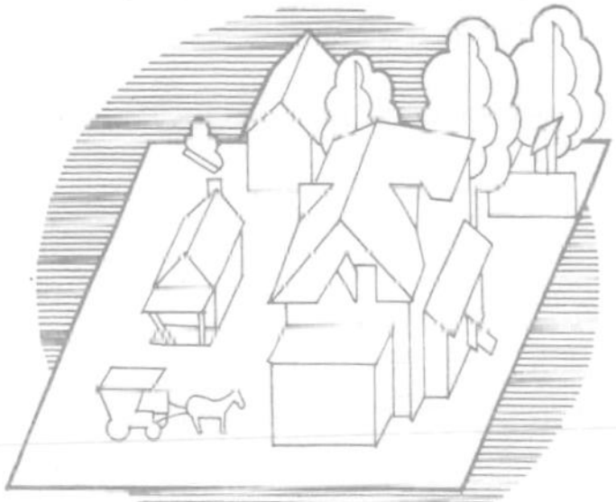

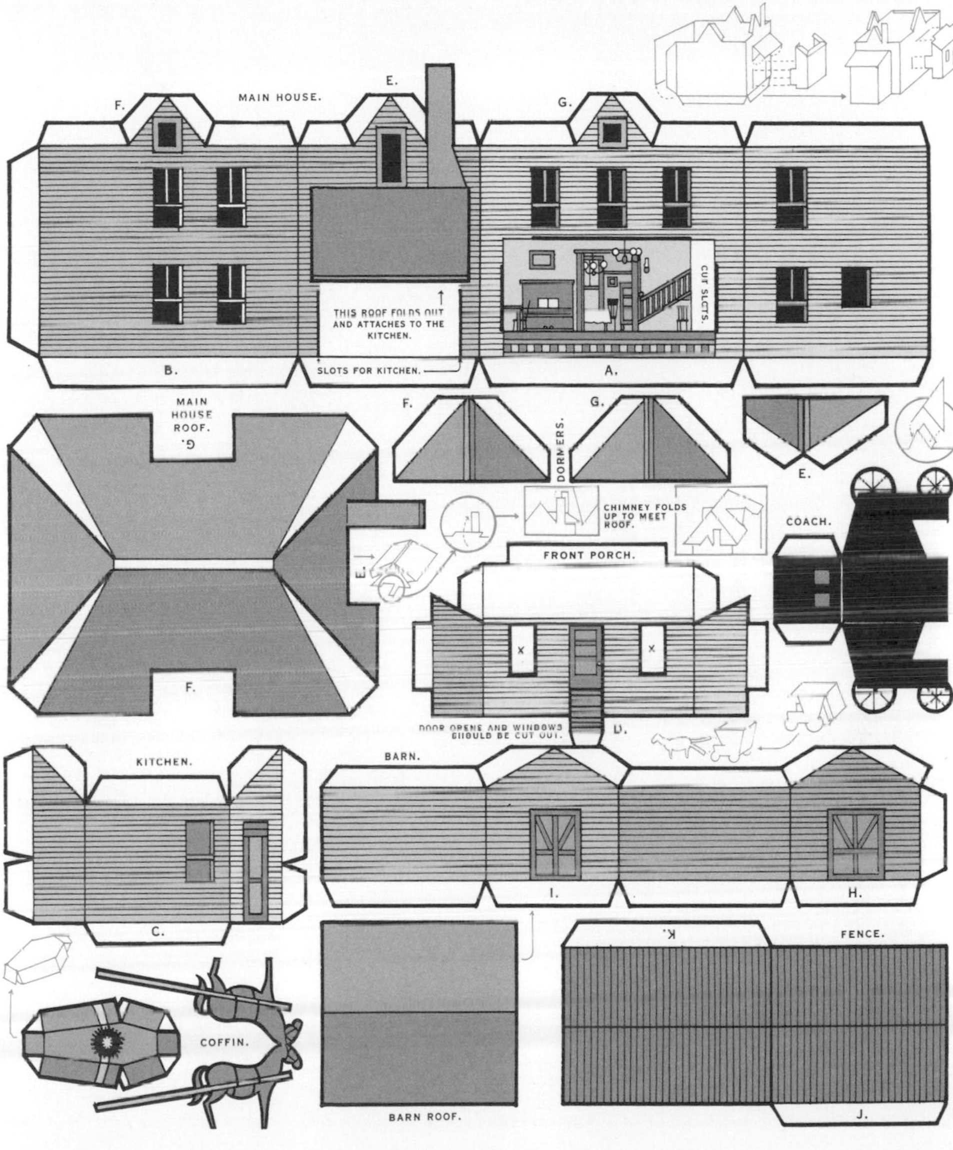

MAIN HOUSE.
E.
F.
G.
THIS ROOF FOLDS OUT AND ATTACHES TO THE KITCHEN.
CUT SLOTS.
B.
SLOTS FOR KITCHEN.
A.
MAIN HOUSE ROOF.
G.
F.
F.
G.
DORMERS.
E.
CHIMNEY FOLDS UP TO MEET ROOF.
E.
COACH.
FRONT PORCH.
DOOR OPENS AND WINDOWS SHOULD BE CUT OUT.
D.
KITCHEN.
C.
BARN.
I.
H.
COFFIN.
BARN ROOF.
K.
FENCE.
J.
CONTINUED ON INSIDE BACK COVER.

NOTE. – Any student of the history of the neighborhood in question will note that the reconstruction presented here is not without its inconsistencies; based, as it is, upon reminiscence and fragmentary recollection, some details reproduced may possibly contradict and/or overlap one another. Additionally, care should be taken when projecting any of this aid's details temporally forward or backward, as some street names have changed, vegetation has developed, and those personalities concerned with the area have either moved away, perished, or their relative sense of the scale of the world has changed. Regardless, and as elucidated above, those wishing a more fully-developed sense of the events related within these pages may find some diversion by crafting the attached, as it allows a simulated manoeuverability about the spaces described, and may, at the very least, prove a lightening influence upon a Sunday afternoon's weakened heart.

INSTRUCTIONS. – Given the generally intuitive level of the task, no detailed directions are provided; it is believed that the matching numerals, letters, and diagrams will be guidance enough to carry the intelligent reader through to completion of the chore. Follow all folds and outlines carefully, and avoid spreading of excess adhesive on exposed elements, as it will spoil the model and prevent attainment of the desired "finished" quality. As well, please take time to allow independent elements to thoroughly dry before committing final assembly; do not "test" parts, as this may compromise sensitive joinery. Those who suffer difficulty should abandon the enterprise immediately.

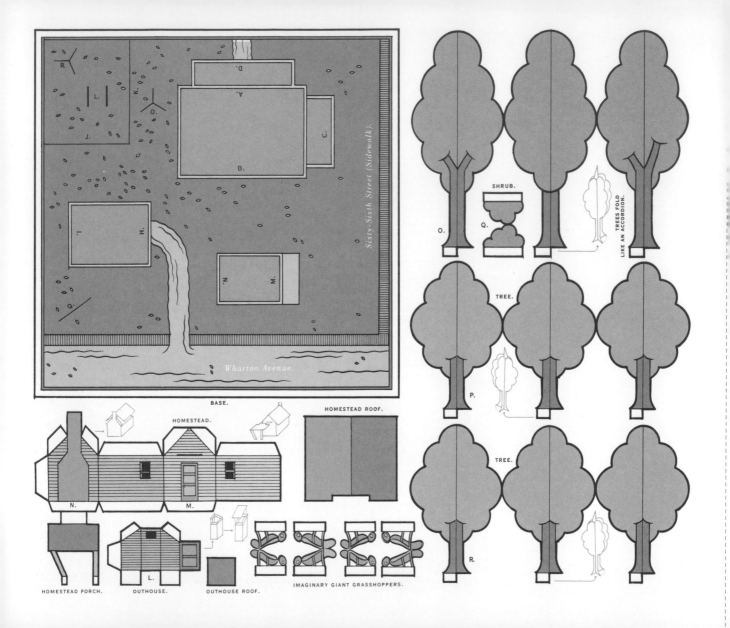

BASE.

Sixty-Sixth Street (Sidewalks).

Wharton Avenue.

SHRUB.

TREE.

TREE.

TREES FOLD LIKE AN ACCORDION.

HOMESTEAD.

HOMESTEAD ROOF.

HOMESTEAD PORCH.

OUTHOUSE.

OUTHOUSE ROOF.

IMAGINARY GIANT GRASSHOPPERS.

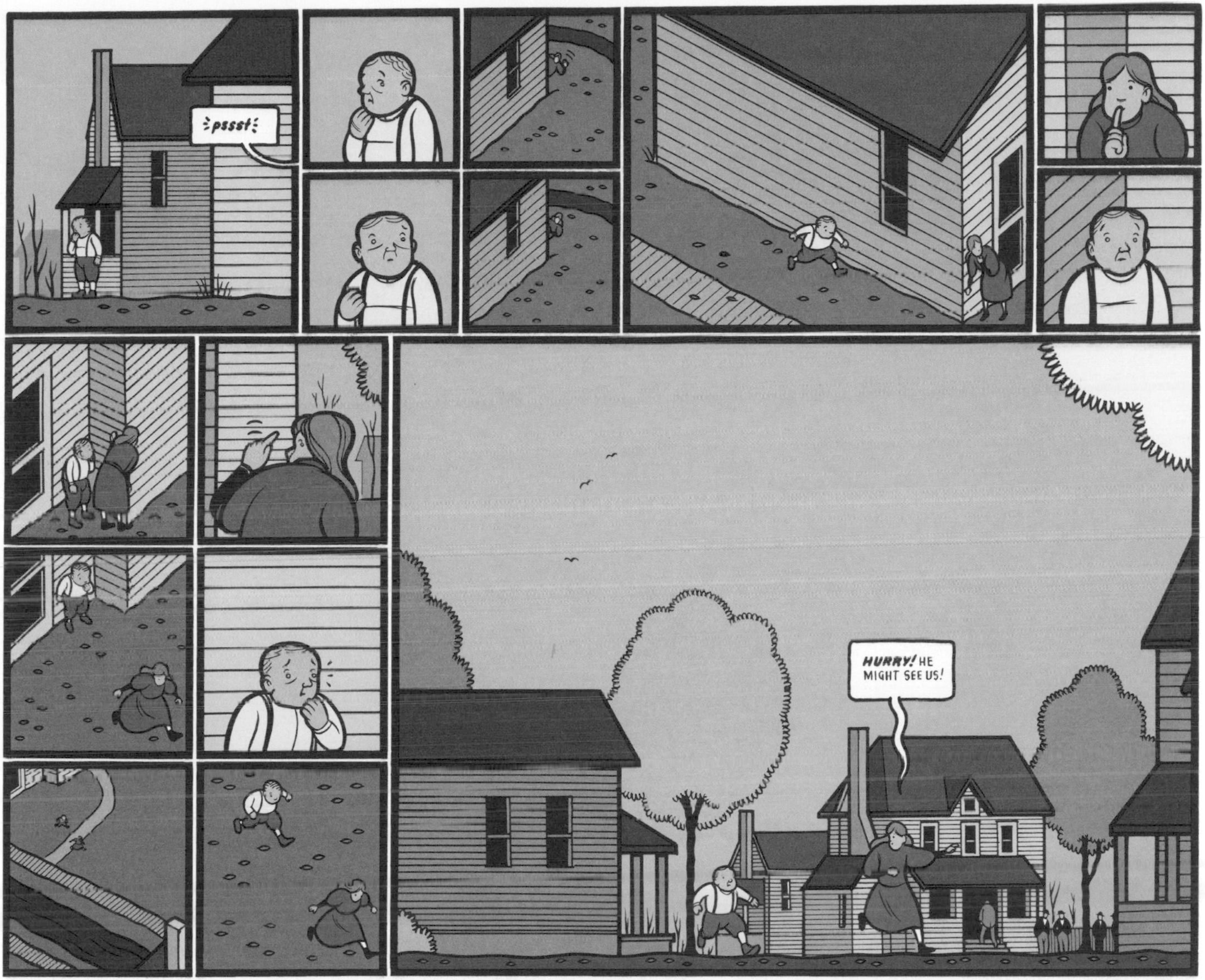
pssst
HURRY! HE MIGHT SEE US!

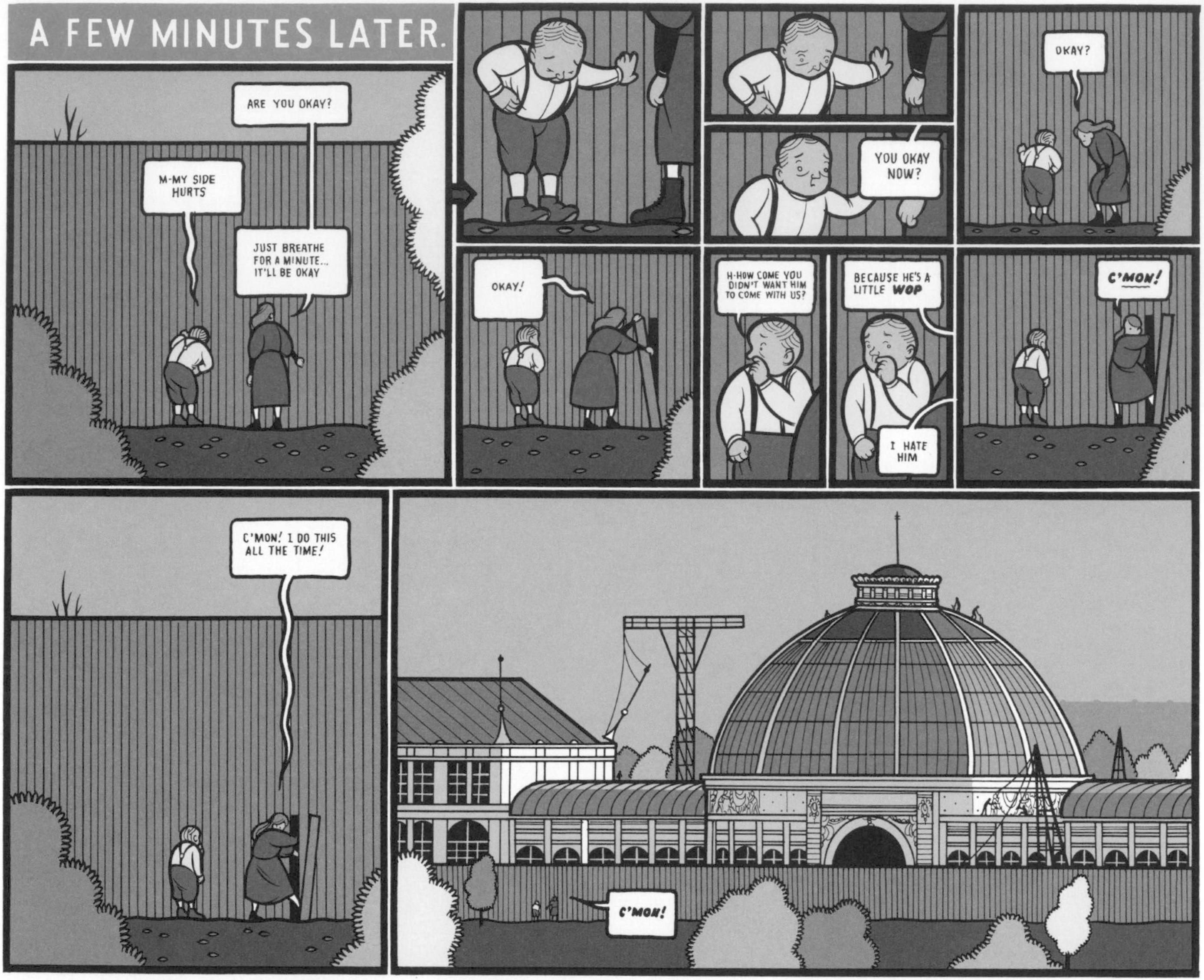
A FEW MINUTES LATER.
ARE YOU OKAY?
M-MY SIDE HURTS
JUST BREATHE FOR A MINUTE... IT'LL BE OKAY
YOU OKAY NOW?
OKAY?
OKAY!
H-HOW COME YOU DIDN'T WANT HIM TO COME WITH US?
BECAUSE HE'S A LITTLE WOP
I HATE HIM
C'MON!
C'MON! I DO THIS ALL THE TIME!
C'MON!

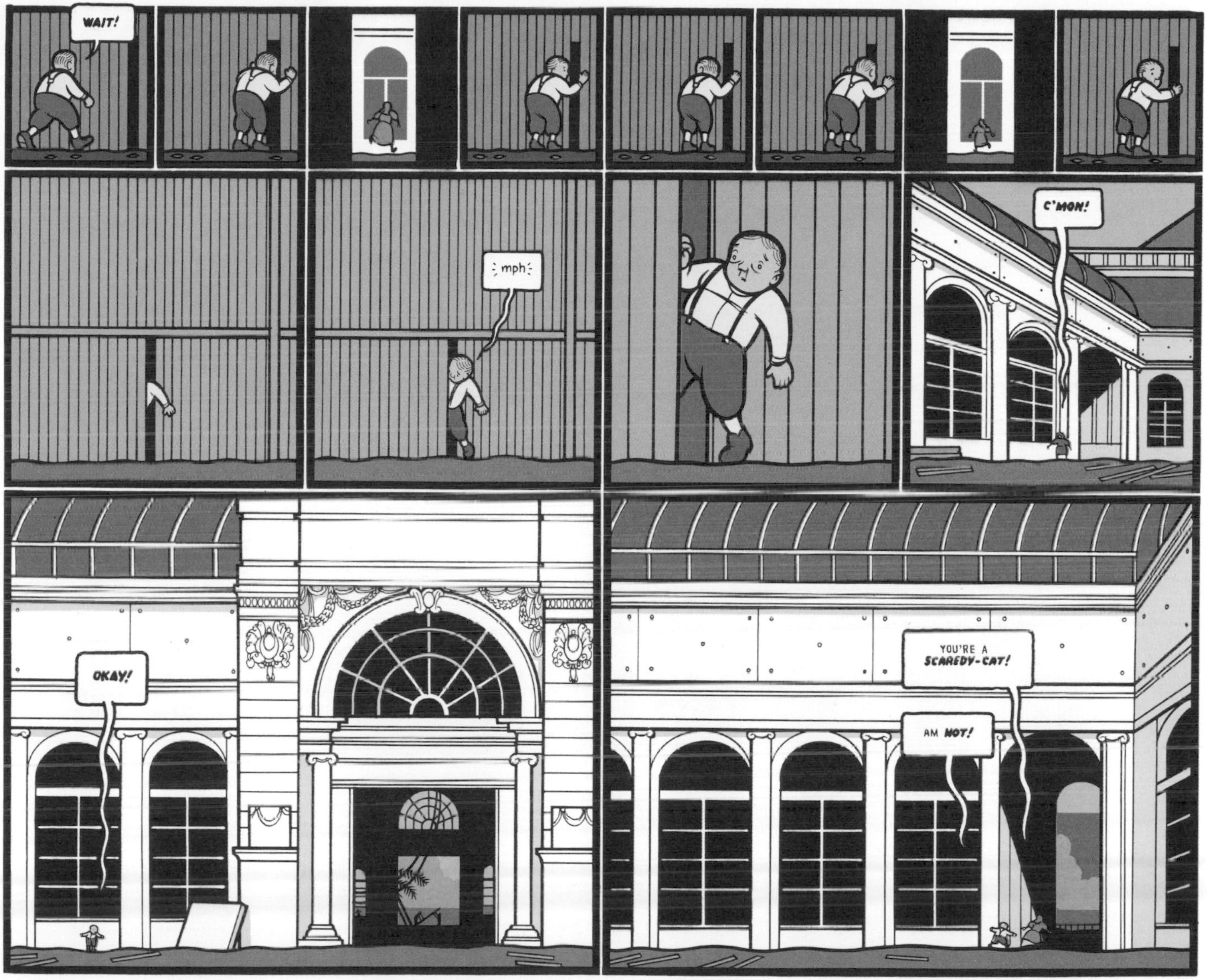
WAIT!
mph
C'MON!
OKAY!
YOU'RE A SCAREDY-CAT!
AM NOT!

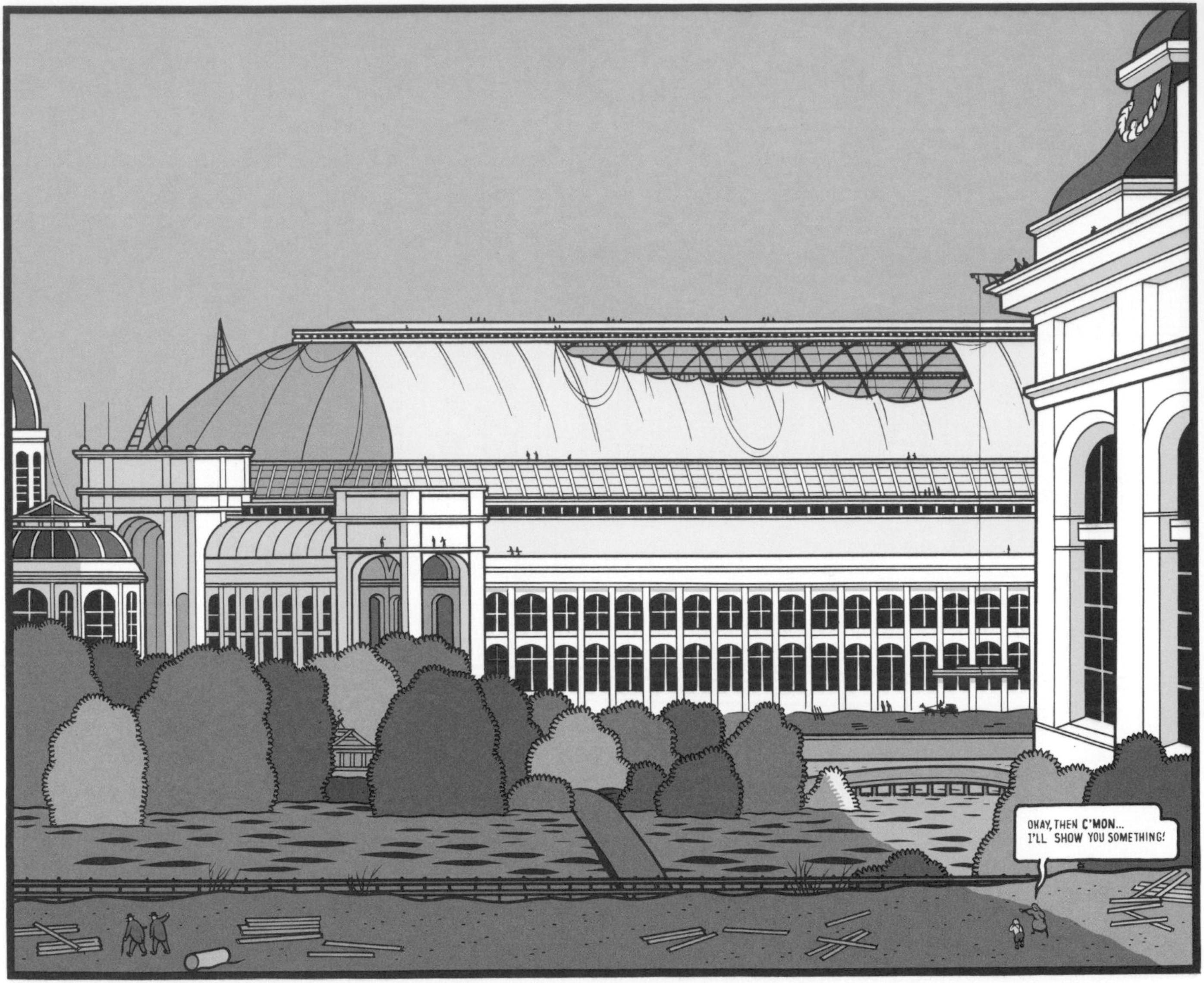
OKAY, THEN C'MON...
I'LL SHOW YOU SOMETHING!

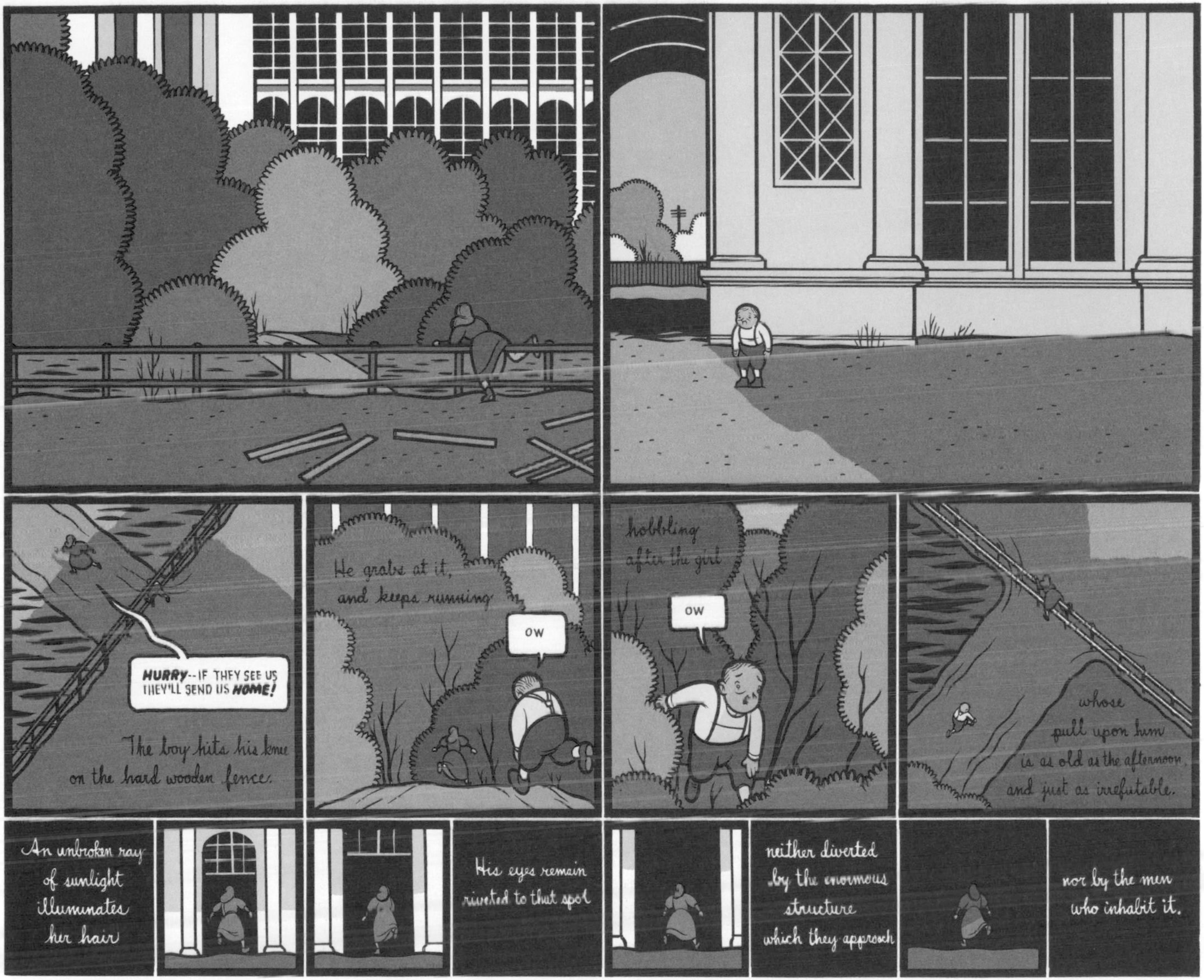
HURRY--IF THEY SEE US THEY'LL SEND US HOME!
The boy hits his knee on the hard wooden fence.
He grabs at it, and keeps running
OW
hobbling after the girl
OW
whose pull upon him is as old as the afternoon, and just as irrefutable.
An unbroken ray of sunlight illuminates her hair
His eyes remain riveted to that spot
neither diverted by the enormous structure which they approach
nor by the men who inhabit it.

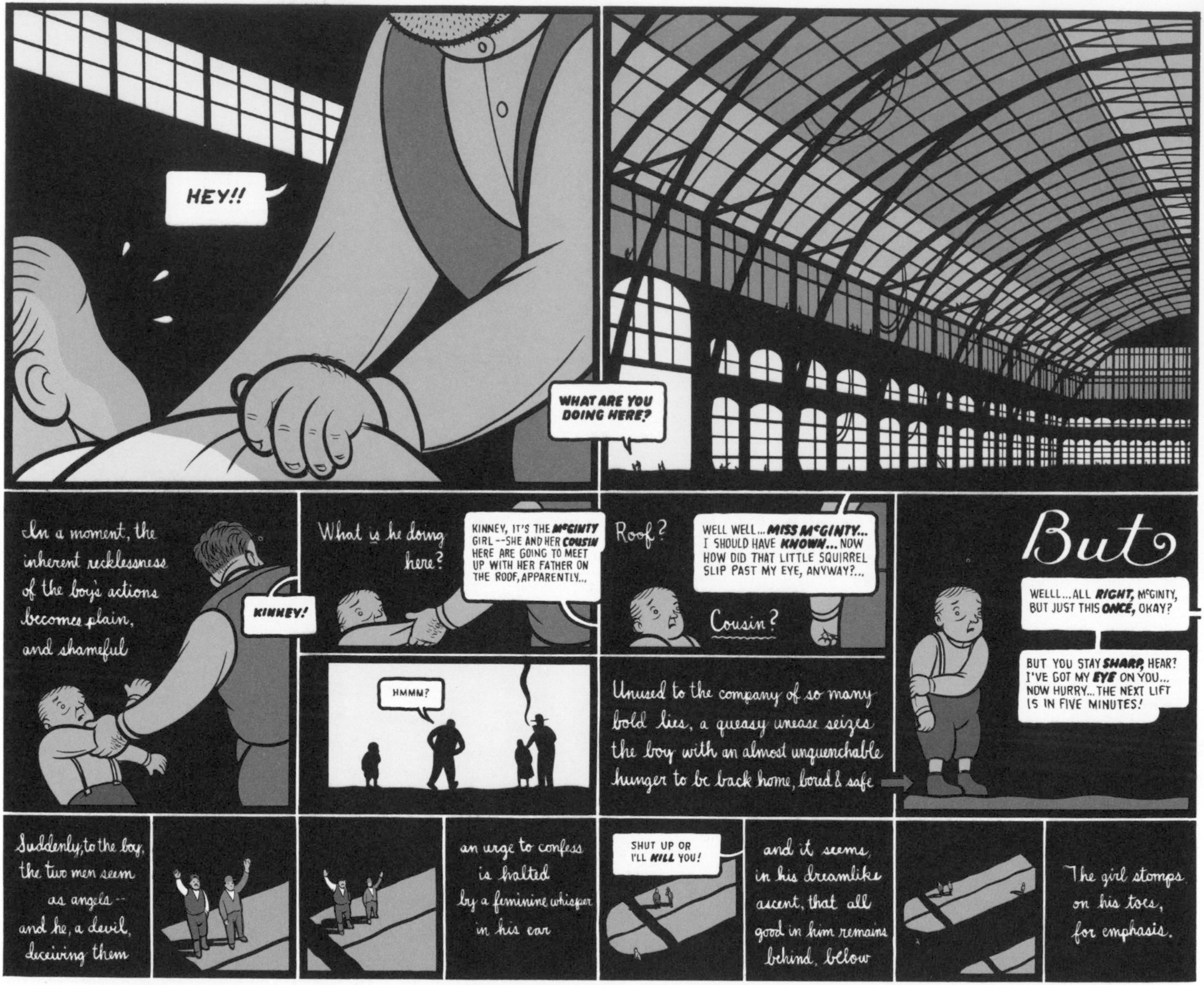
HEY!!
WHAT ARE YOU DOING HERE?
In a moment, the inherent recklessness of the boy's actions becomes plain, and shameful
KINNEY!
What is he doing here?
KINNEY, IT'S THE McGINTY GIRL --SHE AND HER COUSIN HERE ARE GOING TO MEET UP WITH HER FATHER ON THE ROOF, APPARENTLY...
Roof?
WELL WELL... MISS McGINTY... I SHOULD HAVE KNOWN... NOW HOW DID THAT LITTLE SQUIRREL SLIP PAST MY EYE, ANYWAY?...
Cousin?
But
WELLL... ALL RIGHT, McGINTY, BUT JUST THIS ONCE, OKAY?
BUT YOU STAY SHARP, HEAR? I'VE GOT MY EYE ON YOU... NOW HURRY... THE NEXT LIFT IS IN FIVE MINUTES!
HMMM?
Unused to the company of so many bold lies, a queasy unease seizes the boy with an almost unquenchable hunger to be back home, bored & safe
Suddenly, to the boy, the two men seem as angels -- and he, a devil, deceiving them
an urge to confess is halted by a feminine whisper in his ear
SHUT UP OR I'LL KILL YOU!
and it seems, in his dreamlike ascent, that all good in him remains behind, below
The girl stomps on his toes, for emphasis.

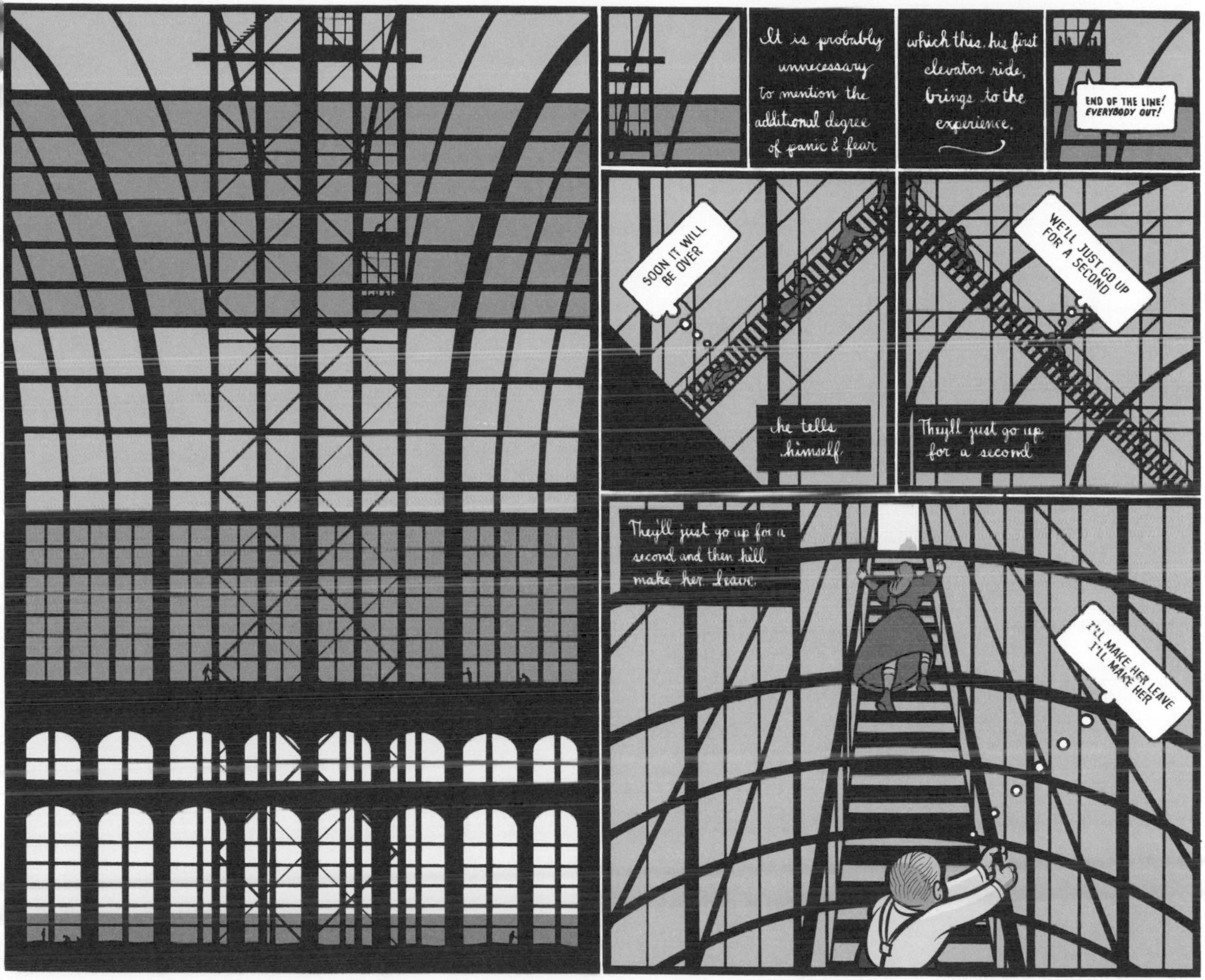
It is probably unnecessary to mention the additional degree of panic & fear
which this, his first elevator ride, brings to the experience.
END OF THE LINE! EVERYBODY OUT!
SOON IT WILL BE OVER
he tells himself.
WE'LL JUST GO UP FOR A SECOND
They'll just go up for a second
They'll just go up for a second and then he'll make her leave.
I'LL MAKE HER LEAVE I'LL MAKE HER

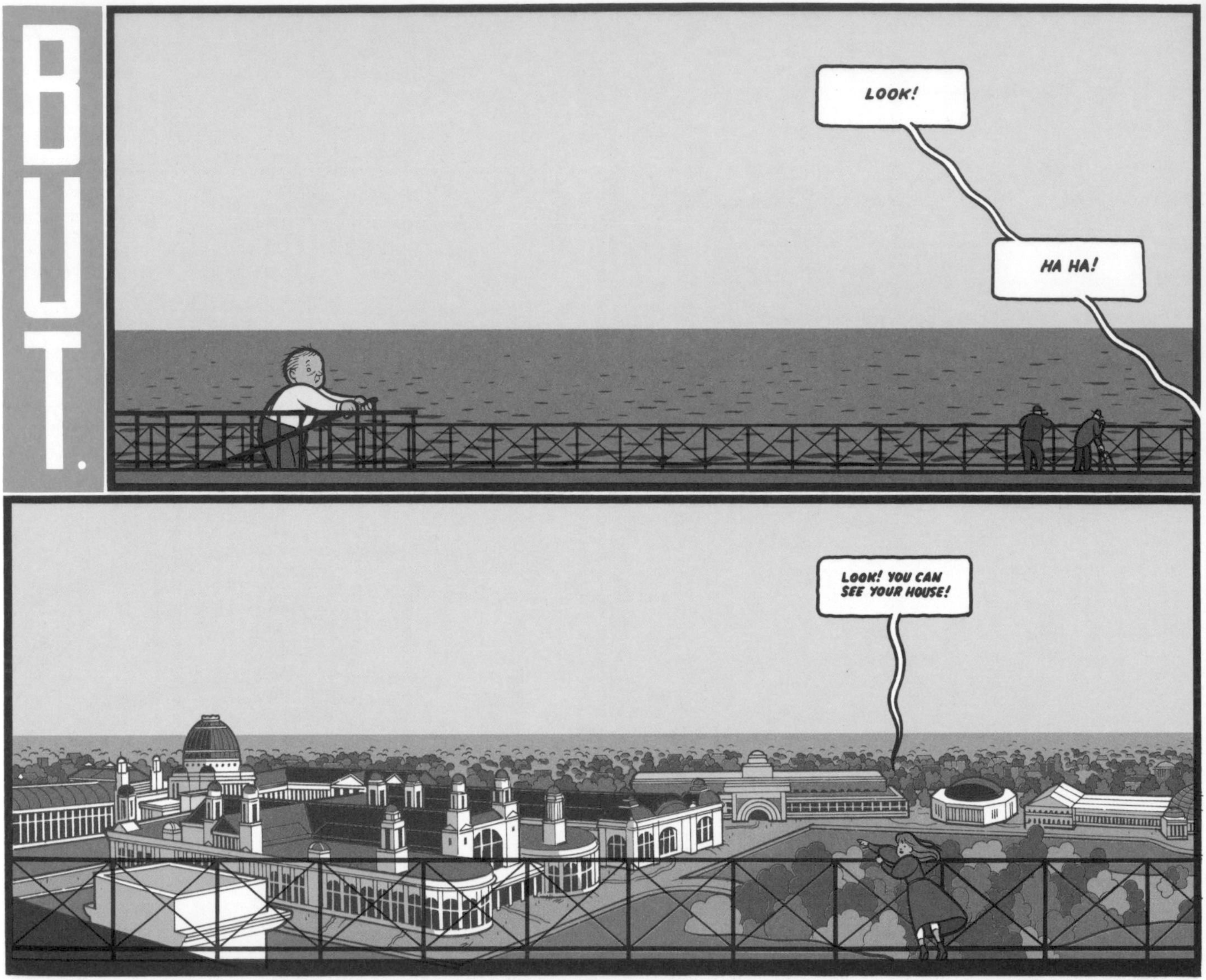
BUT.
LOOK!
HA HA!
LOOK! YOU CAN SEE YOUR HOUSE!

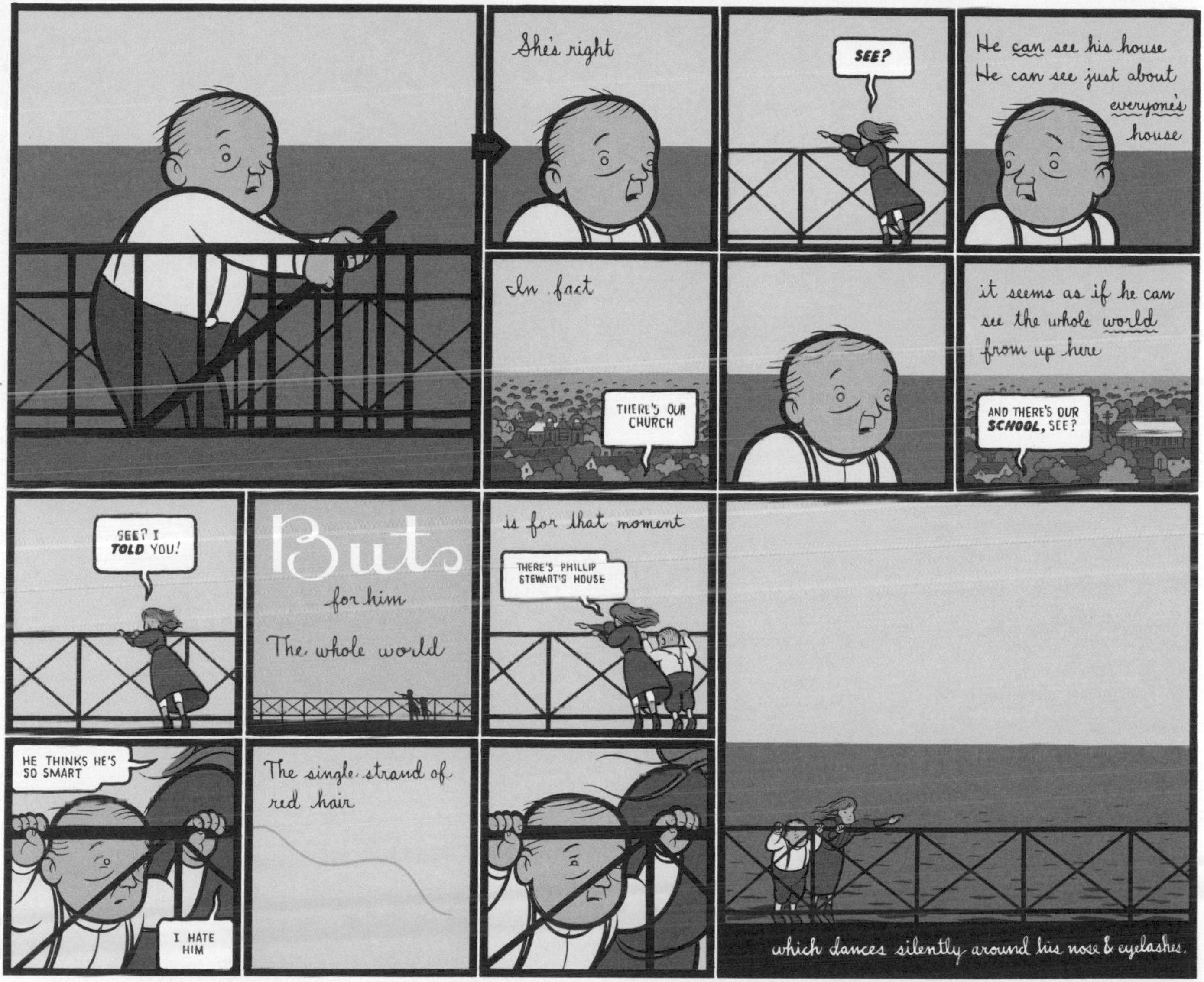

She's right
SEE?
He can see his house
He can see just about everyone's house
In fact
THERE'S OUR CHURCH
it seems as if he can see the whole world from up here
AND THERE'S OUR SCHOOL, SEE?
SEE? I TOLD YOU!
Buts
for him
The whole world
is for that moment
THERE'S PHILLIP STEWART'S HOUSE
HE THINKS HE'S SO SMART
I HATE HIM
The single strand of red hair
which dances silently around his nose & eyelashes.

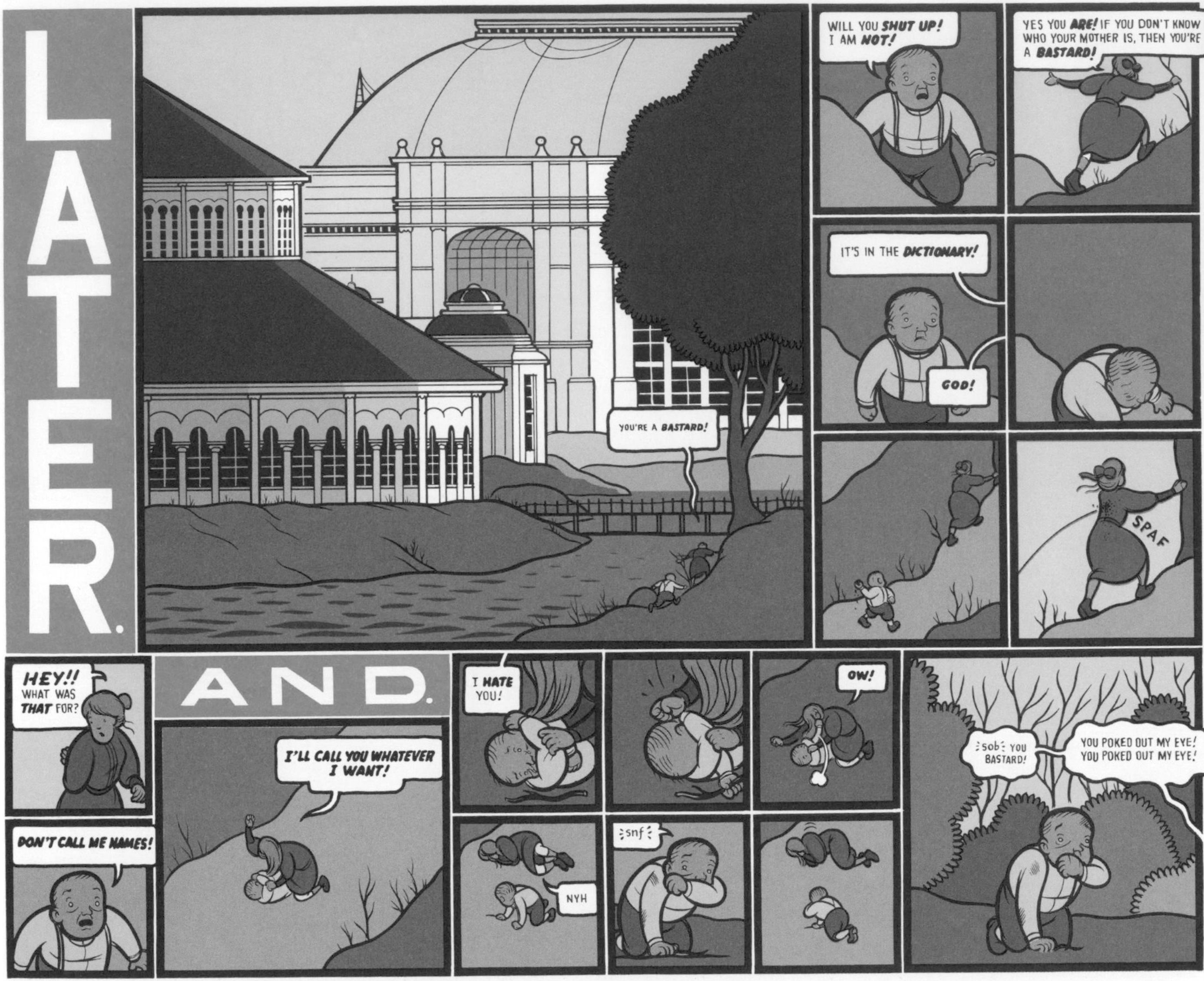
LATER.
YOU'RE A BASTARD!
WILL YOU SHUT UP! I AM NOT!
YES YOU ARE! IF YOU DON'T KNOW WHO YOUR MOTHER IS, THEN YOU'RE A BASTARD!
IT'S IN THE DICTIONARY!
GOD!
SPAF
HEY!! WHAT WAS THAT FOR?
DON'T CALL ME NAMES!
AND.
I'LL CALL YOU WHATEVER I WANT!
I HATE YOU!
OW!
NYH
snf
sob YOU BASTARD!
YOU POKED OUT MY EYE! YOU POKED OUT MY EYE!

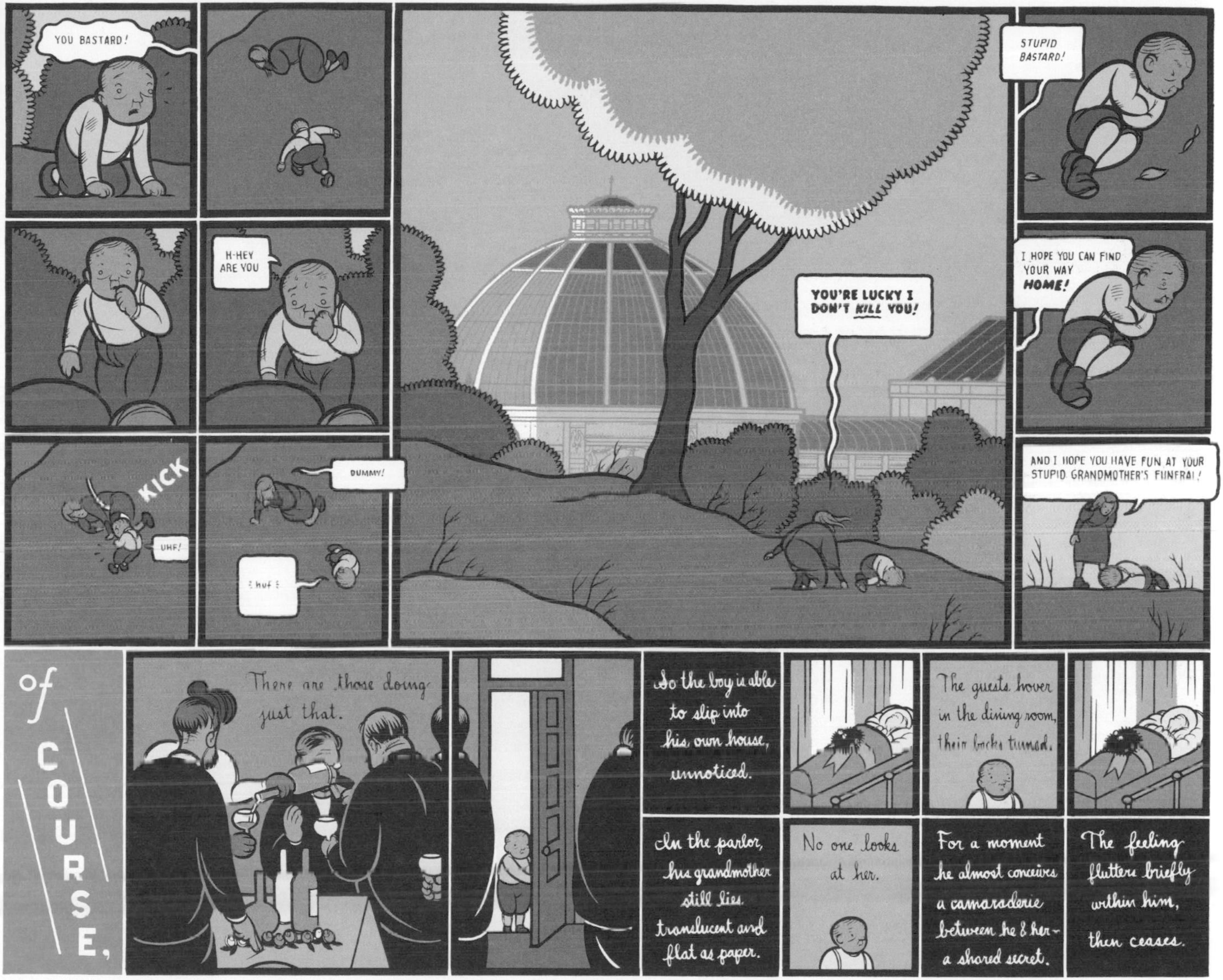

YOU BASTARD!
H-HEY ARE YOU
KICK
UHF!
DUMMY!
huf
YOU'RE LUCKY I DON'T KILL YOU!
STUPID BASTARD!
I HOPE YOU CAN FIND YOUR WAY HOME!
AND I HOPE YOU HAVE FUN AT YOUR STUPID GRANDMOTHER'S FUNERAL!
of COURSE,
There are those doing just that.
So the boy is able to slip into his own house, unnoticed.
The guests hover in the dining room, their backs turned.
In the parlor, his grandmother still lies translucent and flat as paper.
No one looks at her.
For a moment he almost conceives a camaraderie between he & her — a shared secret.
The feeling flutters briefly within him, then ceases.

UPSTAIRS,

The boy collapses in tears onto a strange woman's coat.

Screaming insensibly into a chiffon collar about the humiliations of the afternoon, he exhausts himself.

The drama of his emotion entices him, however, to induce its recurrence at least one or two more times.

He should be happy, anyway.

These semisincere sobs cannot keep his interest, though, so he soon stops.

After all, he somehow managed to get away with doing something for which the usual punishment would be severe, almost immeasurable

As long as that girl doesn't tell...

Why was she so mean to him, anyway?

His eyes closed, the image of his house seen from the rooftop returns to him, a puny pillbox, and he, a giant, plucking it from the earth

FLOP

The girl begs for his mercy.

CREAK

The guests wander through his house, like ghosts.

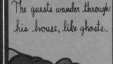

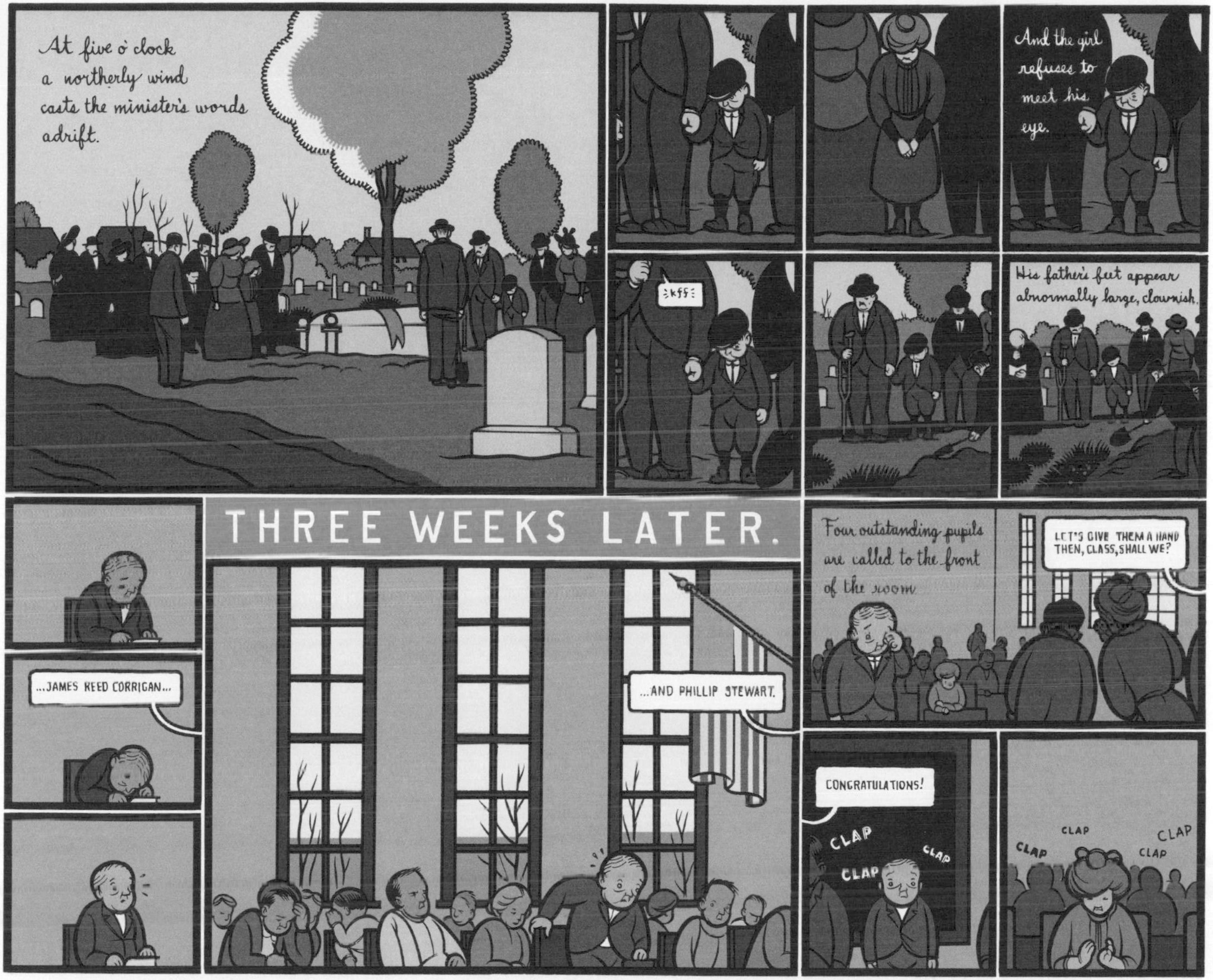
At five o' clock a northerly wind casts the minister's words adrift.
And the girl refuses to meet his eye.
kff
His father's feet appear abnormally large, clownish.
THREE WEEKS LATER.
...JAMES REED CORRIGAN...
...AND PHILLIP STEWART.
Four outstanding pupils are called to the front of the room
LET'S GIVE THEM A HAND THEN, CLASS, SHALL WE?
CONGRATULATIONS!
CLAP
CLAP
CLAP
CLAP
CLAP
CLAP
CLAP
CLAP

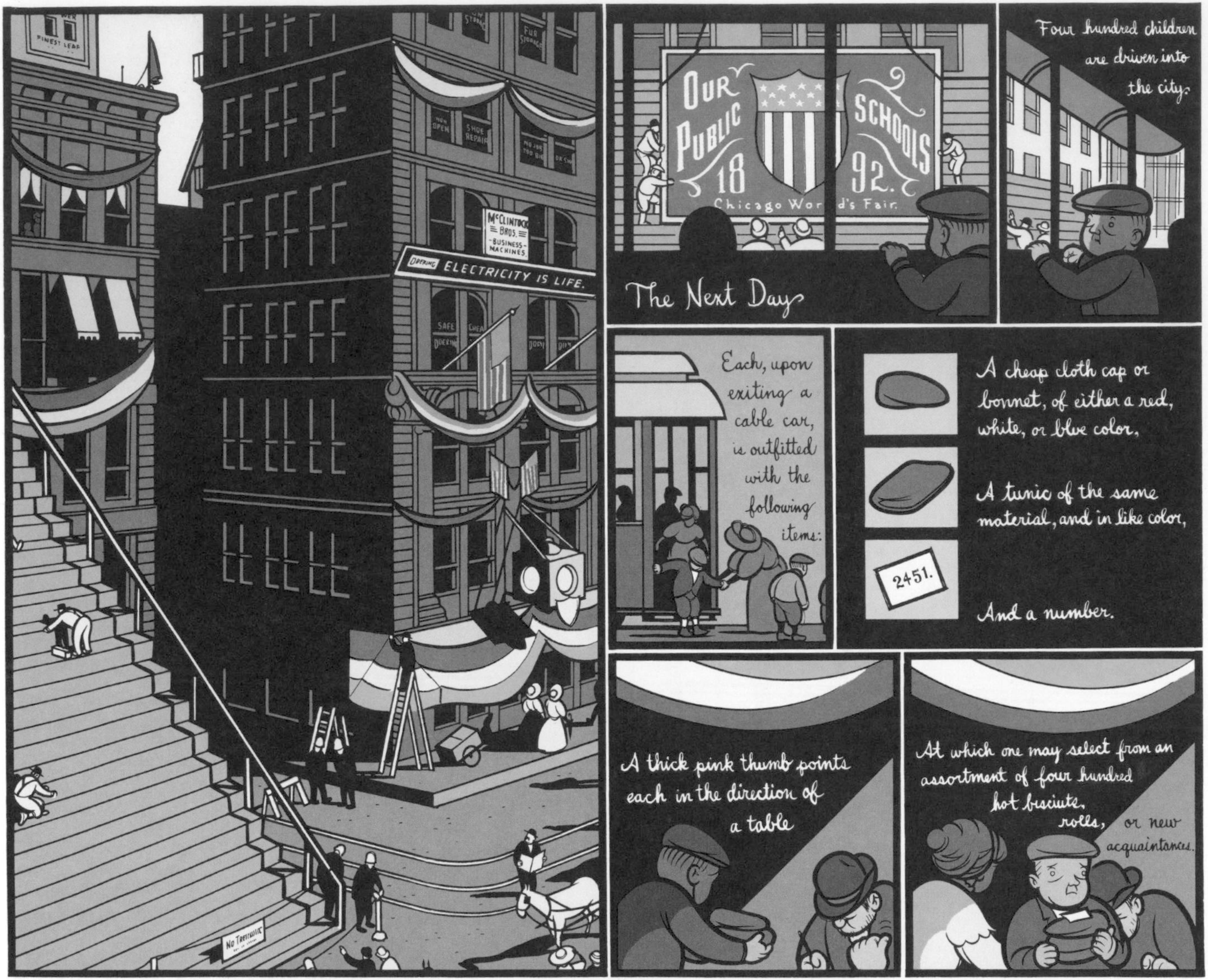
FINEST LEAF
FUR STORAGE
SHOE REPAIR
McCLINTOCK BROS. -BUSINESS- MACHINES.
ELECTRICITY IS LIFE.
OUR PUBLIC SCHOOLS
1892.
Chicago World's Fair.
The Next Day
Four hundred children are driven into the city.
Each, upon exiting a cable car, is outfitted with the following items:
A cheap cloth cap or bonnet, of either a red, white, or blue color,
A tunic of the same material, and in like color,
2451.
And a number.
A thick pink thumb points each in the direction of a table
At which one may select from an assortment of four hundred hot biscuits, rolls, or new acquaintances.

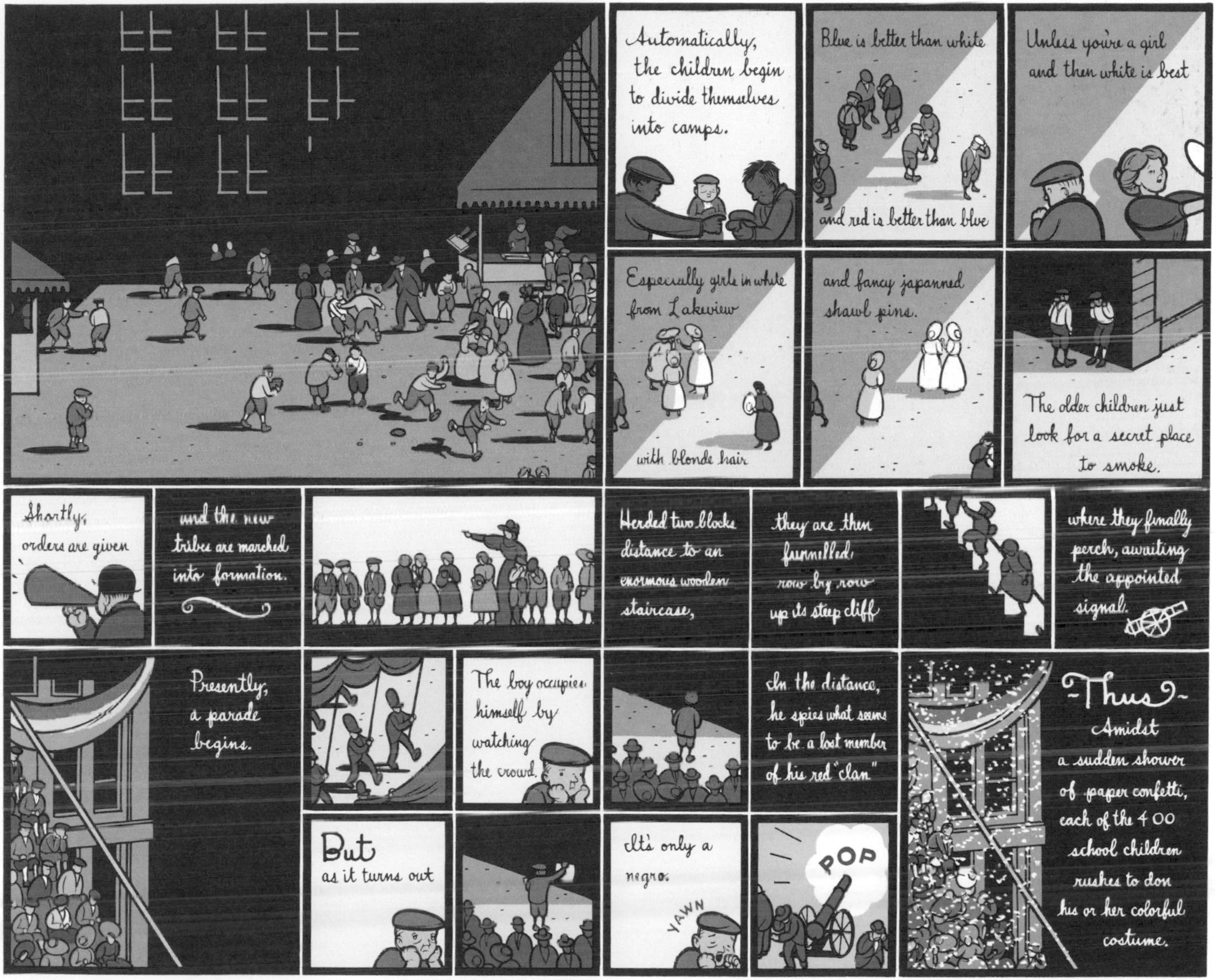
Automatically, the children begin to divide themselves into camps.
Blue is better than white
and red is better than blue
Unless you're a girl and then white is best
Especially girls in white from Lakeview
with blonde hair
and fancy japanned shawl pins.
The older children just look for a secret place to smoke.
Shortly, orders are given
and the new tribes are marched into formation.
Herded two blocks distance to an enormous wooden staircase,
they are then funnelled, row by row up its steep cliff
where they finally perch, awaiting the appointed signal.
Presently, a parade begins.
The boy occupies himself by watching the crowd.
In the distance, he spies what seems to be a lost member of his red "clan"
But as it turns out
It's only a negro.
YAWN
POP
Thus
Amidst a sudden shower of paper confetti, each of the 400 school children rushes to don his or her colorful costume.

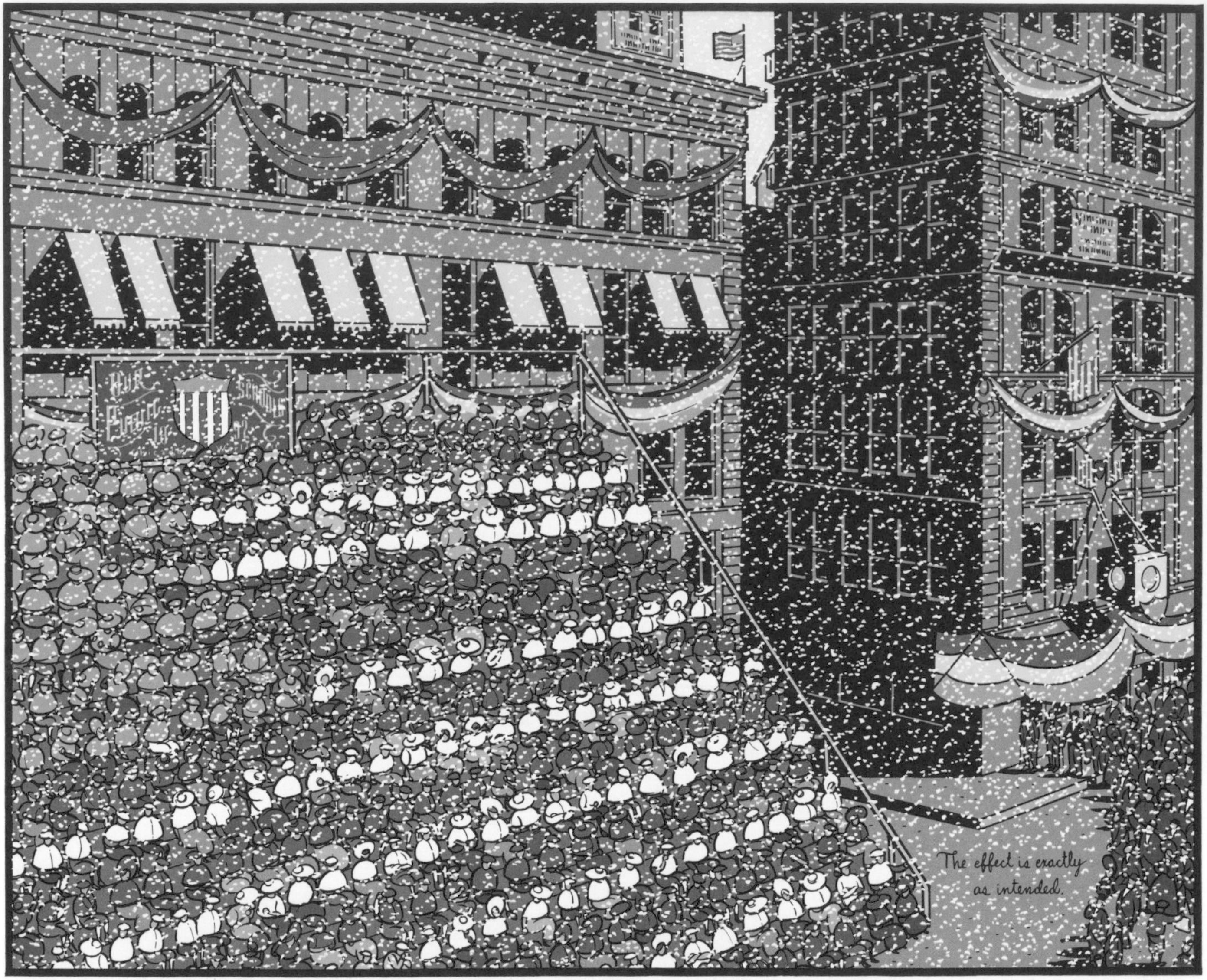
The effect is exactly as intended.

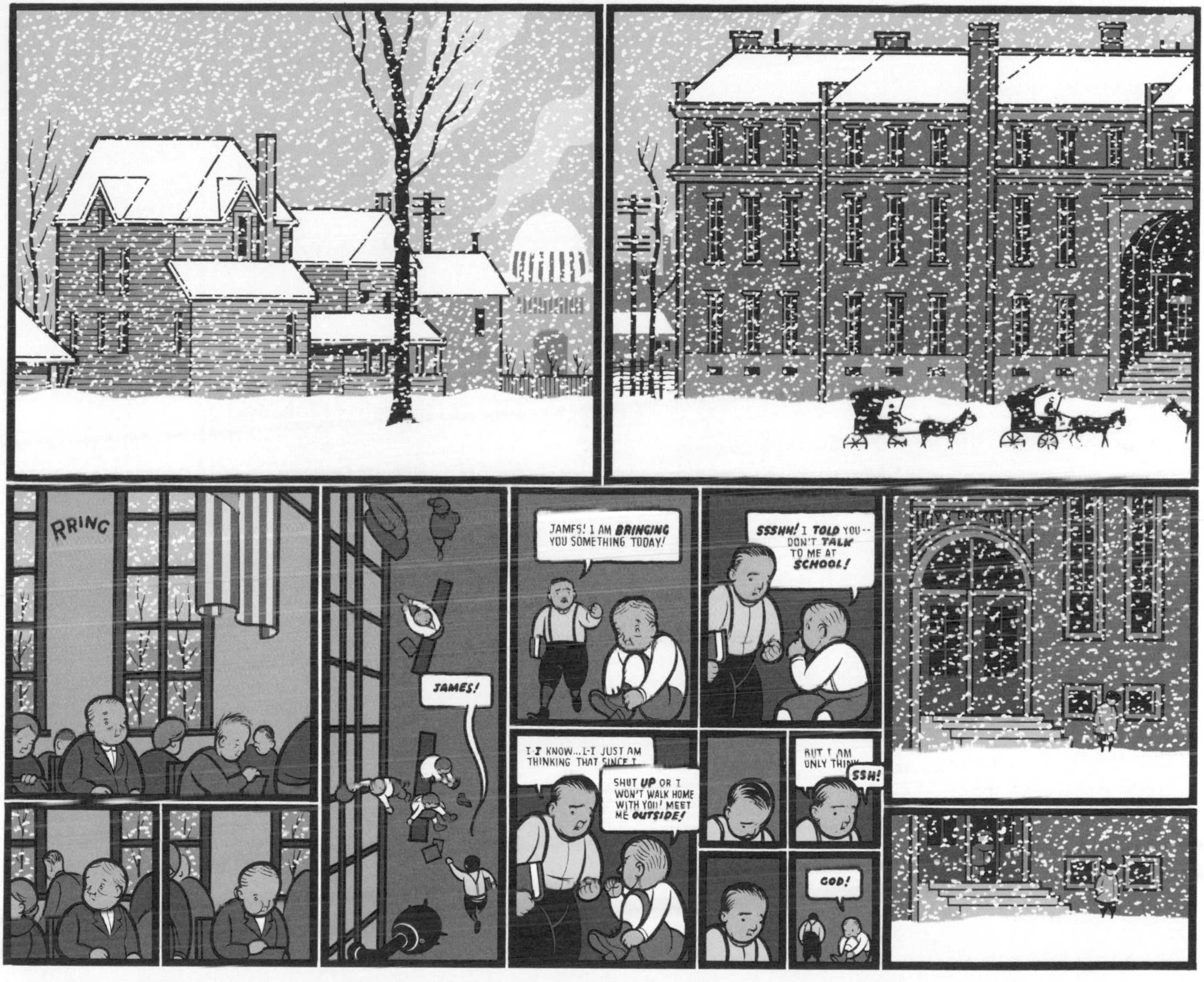
RRING
JAMES!
JAMES! I AM BRINGING YOU SOMETHING TODAY!
SSSHH! I TOLD YOU-- DON'T TALK TO ME AT SCHOOL!
I-I KNOW...I-I JUST AM THINKING THAT SINCE I
SHUT UP OR I WON'T WALK HOME WITH YOU! MEET ME OUTSIDE!
BUT I AM ONLY THI
SSH!
GOD!

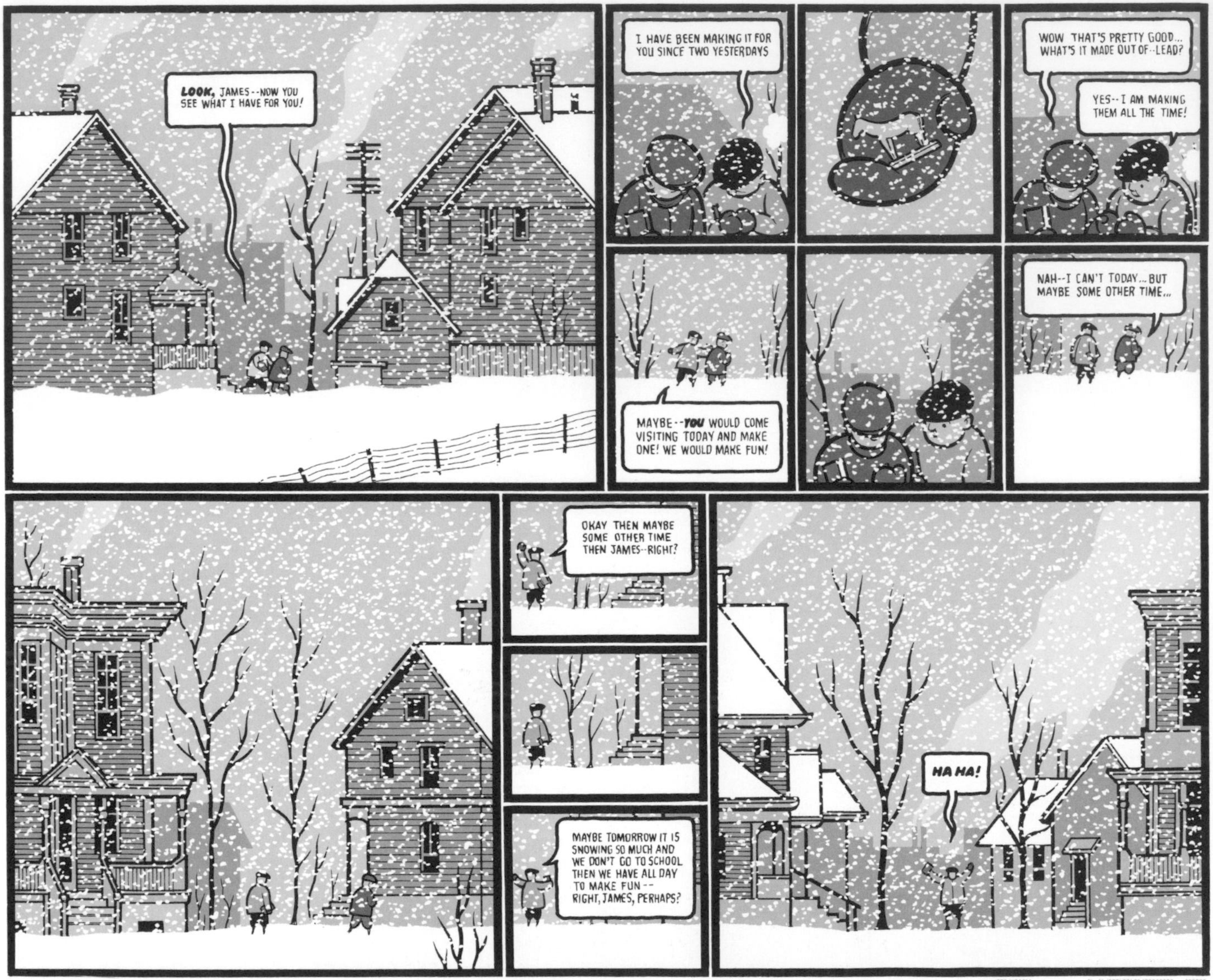
LOOK, JAMES--NOW YOU SEE WHAT I HAVE FOR YOU!
I HAVE BEEN MAKING IT FOR YOU SINCE TWO YESTERDAYS
WOW THAT'S PRETTY GOOD... WHAT'S IT MADE OUT OF--LEAD?
YES--I AM MAKING THEM ALL THE TIME!
MAYBE--YOU WOULD COME VISITING TODAY AND MAKE ONE! WE WOULD MAKE FUN!
NAH--I CAN'T TODAY... BUT MAYBE SOME OTHER TIME...
OKAY THEN MAYBE SOME OTHER TIME THEN JAMES--RIGHT?
MAYBE TOMORROW IT IS SNOWING SO MUCH AND WE DON'T GO TO SCHOOL THEN WE HAVE ALL DAY TO MAKE FUN--RIGHT, JAMES, PERHAPS?
HA HA!

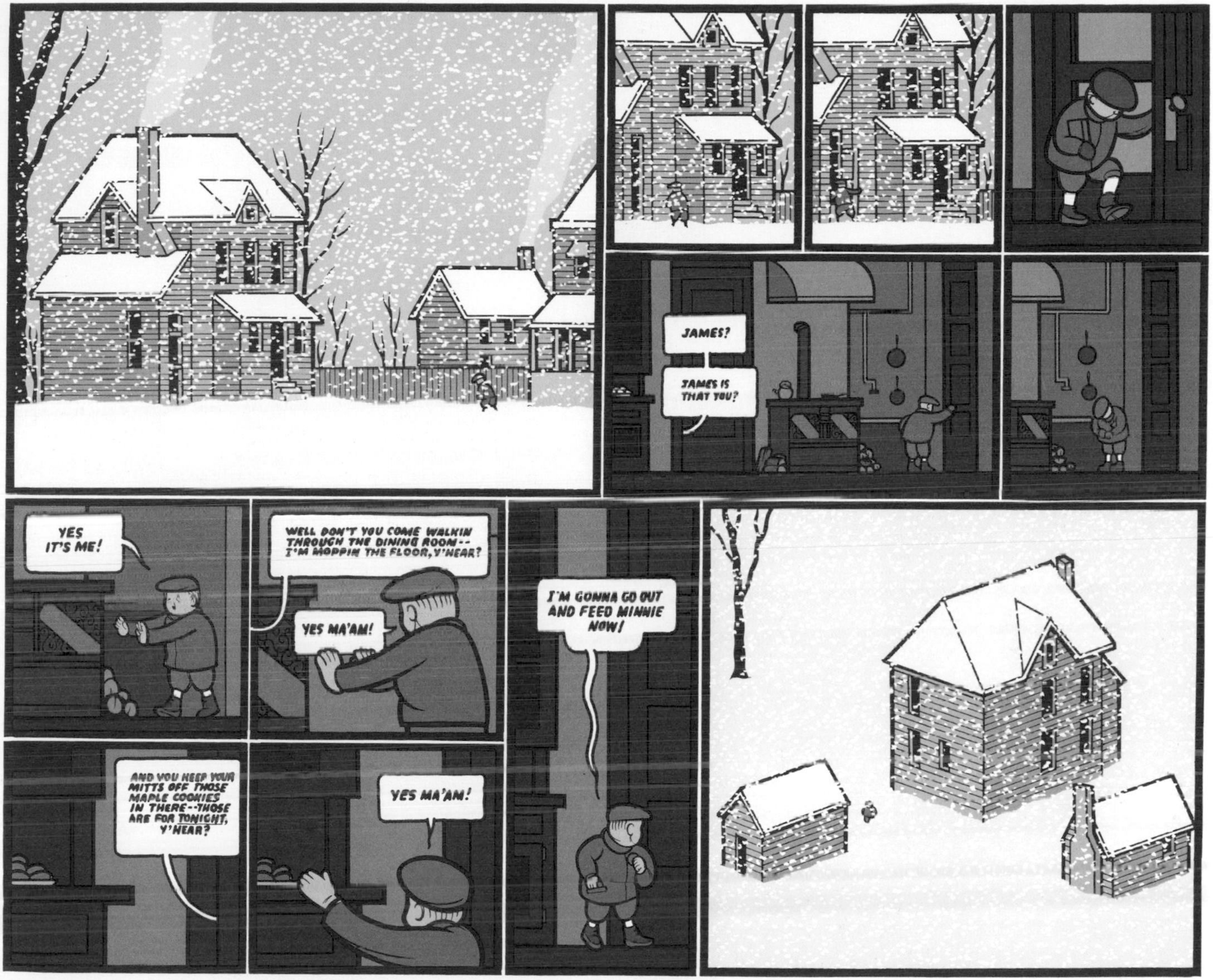
JAMES?
JAMES IS THAT YOU?
YES IT'S ME!
WELL DON'T YOU COME WALKIN THROUGH THE DINING ROOM-- I'M MOPPIN THE FLOOR, Y'HEAR?
YES MA'AM!
AND YOU KEEP YOUR MITTS OFF THOSE MAPLE COOKIES IN THERE--THOSE ARE FOR TONIGHT, Y'HEAR?
YES MA'AM!
I'M GONNA GO OUT AND FEED MINNIE NOW!

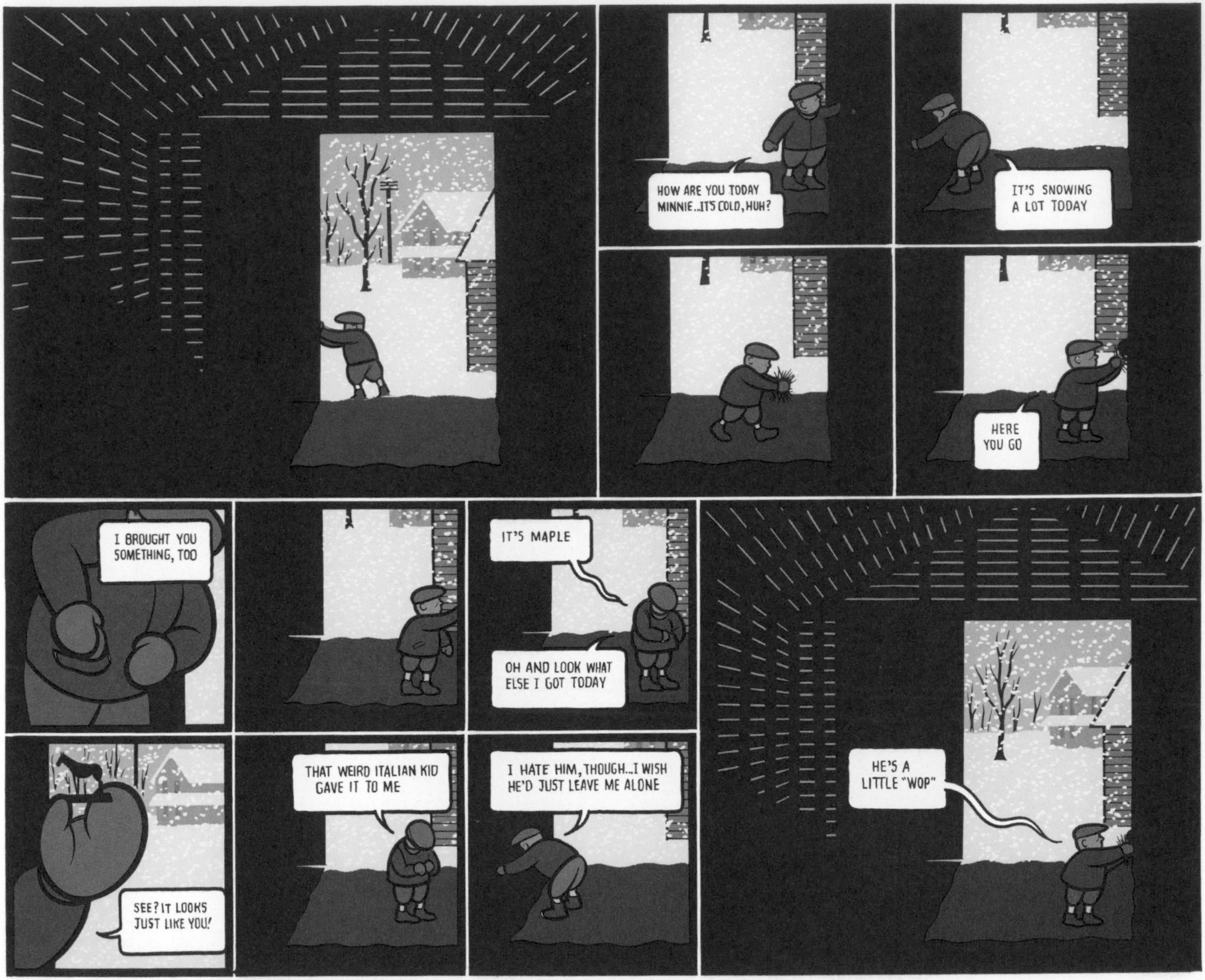
HOW ARE YOU TODAY MINNIE...IT'S COLD, HUH?
IT'S SNOWING A LOT TODAY
HERE YOU GO
I BROUGHT YOU SOMETHING, TOO
IT'S MAPLE
OH AND LOOK WHAT ELSE I GOT TODAY
SEE? IT LOOKS JUST LIKE YOU!
THAT WEIRD ITALIAN KID GAVE IT TO ME
I HATE HIM, THOUGH...I WISH HE'D JUST LEAVE ME ALONE
HE'S A LITTLE "WOP"

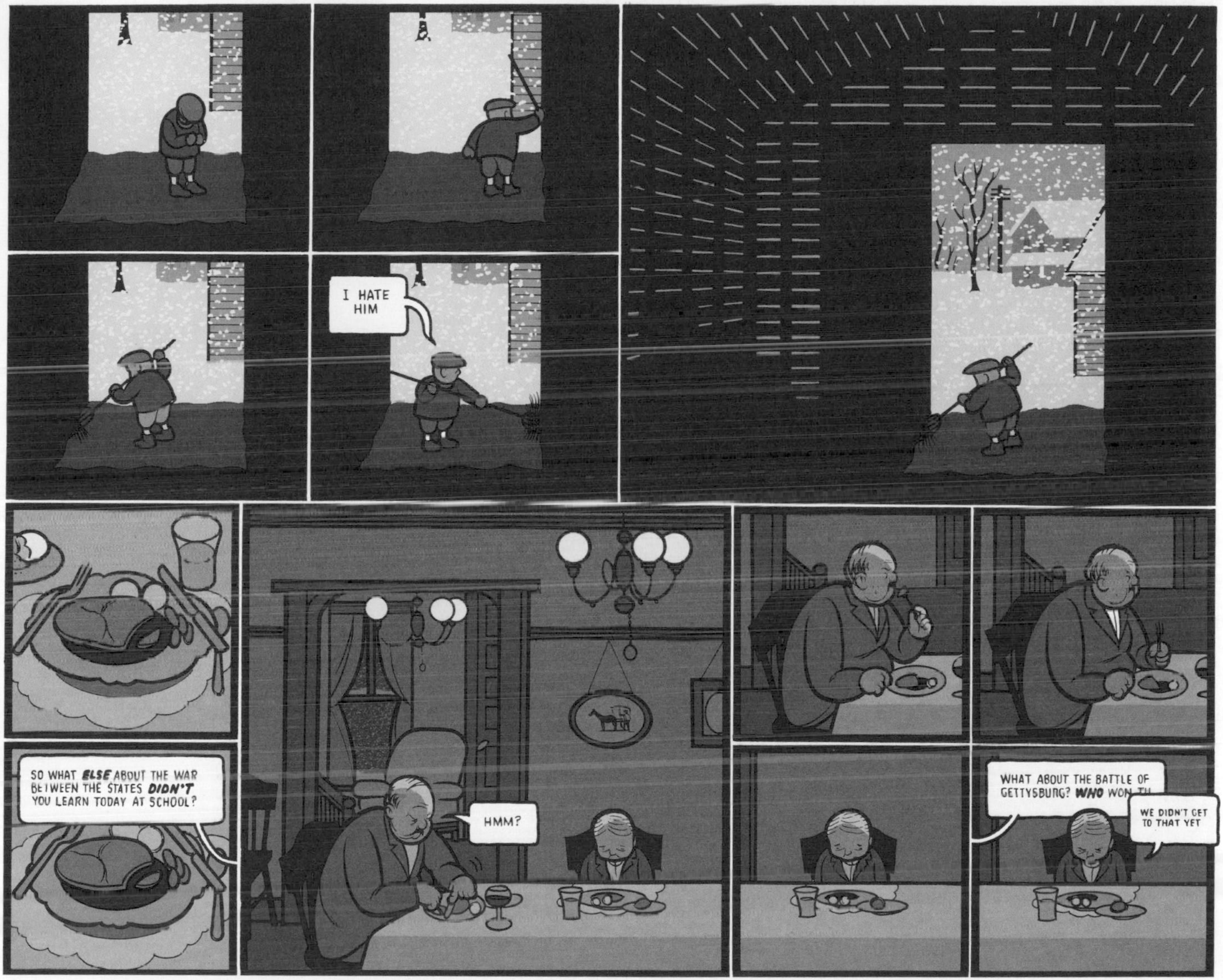

I HATE HIM
SO WHAT ELSE ABOUT THE WAR BETWEEN THE STATES DIDN'T YOU LEARN TODAY AT SCHOOL?
HMM?
WHAT ABOUT THE BATTLE OF GETTYSBURG? WHO WON TH
WE DIDN'T GET TO THAT YET

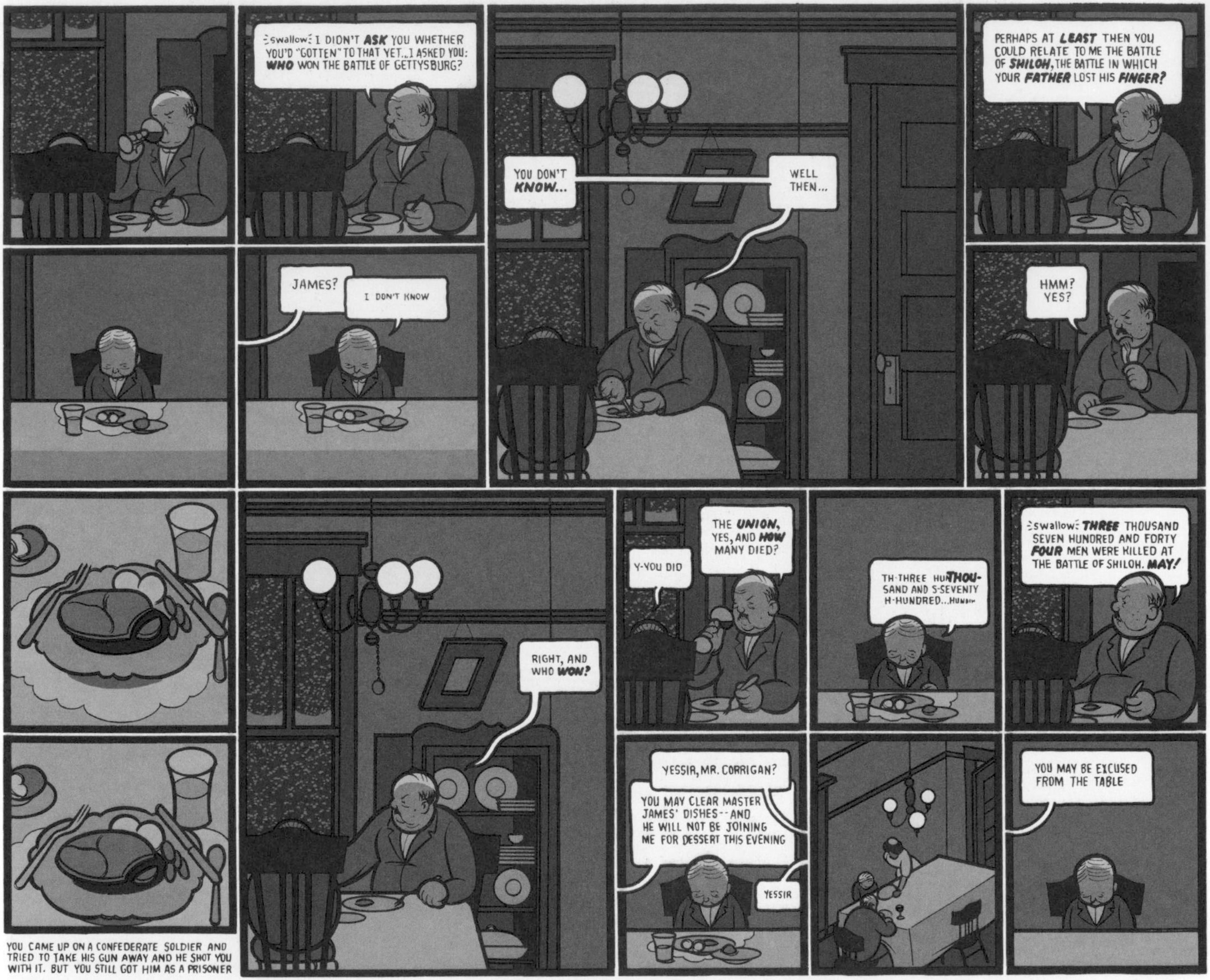

swallow I DIDN'T ASK YOU WHETHER YOU'D "GOTTEN" TO THAT YET... I ASKED YOU: WHO WON THE BATTLE OF GETTYSBURG?
JAMES?
I DON'T KNOW
YOU DON'T KNOW...
WELL THEN...
PERHAPS AT LEAST THEN YOU COULD RELATE TO ME THE BATTLE OF SHILOH, THE BATTLE IN WHICH YOUR FATHER LOST HIS FINGER?
HMM? YES?
YOU CAME UP ON A CONFEDERATE SOLDIER AND TRIED TO TAKE HIS GUN AWAY AND HE SHOT YOU WITH IT. BUT YOU STILL GOT HIM AS A PRISONER
RIGHT, AND WHO WON?
Y-YOU DID
THE UNION, YES, AND HOW MANY DIED?
TH-THREE HUTHOU-SAND AND S-SEVENTY H-HUNDRED...
swallow THREE THOUSAND SEVEN HUNDRED AND FORTY FOUR MEN WERE KILLED AT THE BATTLE OF SHILOH. MAY!
YESSIR, MR. CORRIGAN?
YOU MAY CLEAR MASTER JAMES' DISHES -- AND HE WILL NOT BE JOINING ME FOR DESSERT THIS EVENING
YESSIR
YOU MAY BE EXCUSED FROM THE TABLE

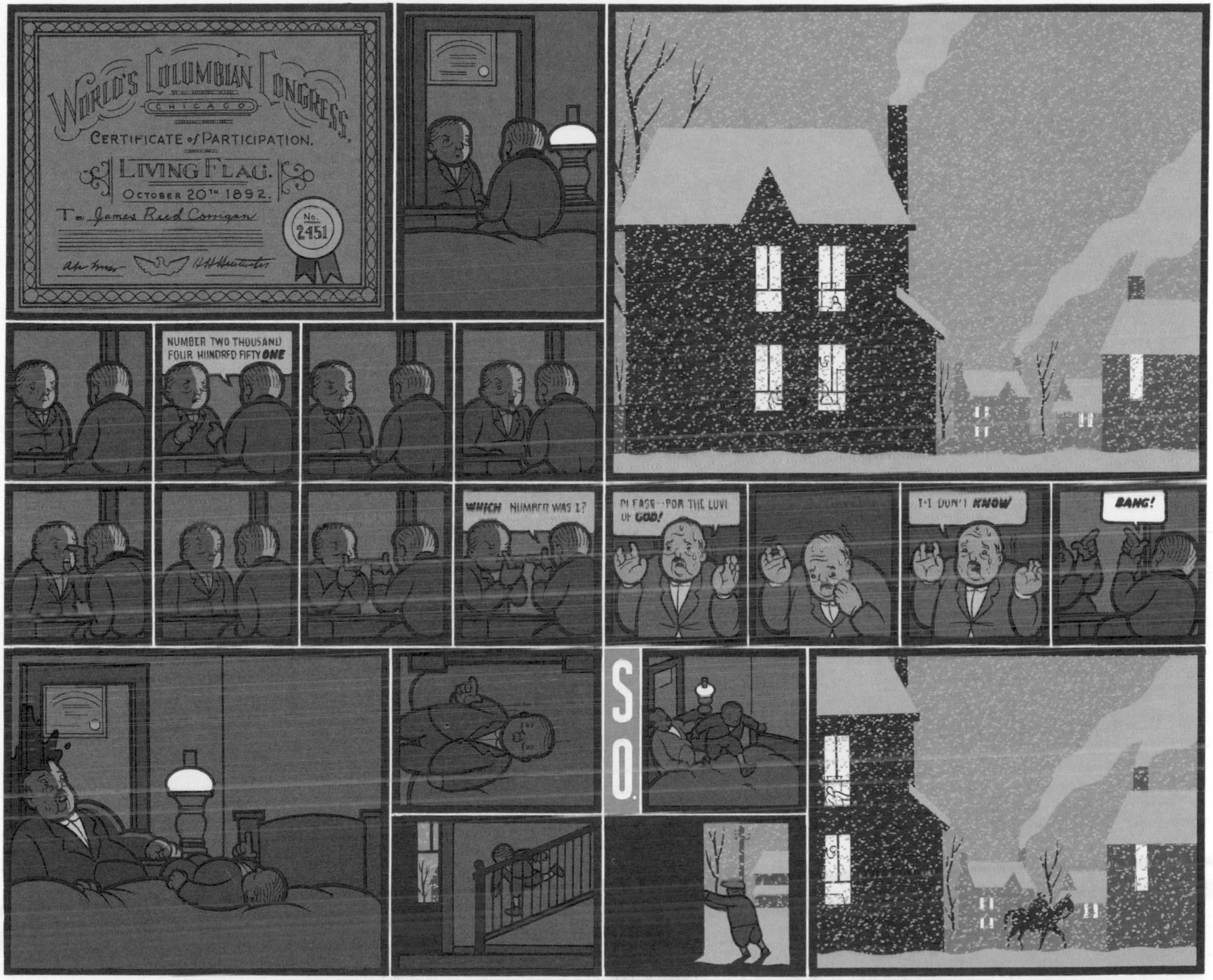

WORLD'S COLUMBIAN CONGRESS.
CHICAGO
CERTIFICATE of PARTICIPATION.
LIVING FLAG.
OCTOBER 20TH 1892.
To: James Reed Corrigan
No. 2451
NUMBER TWO THOUSAND FOUR HUNDRED FIFTY **ONE**
WHICH NUMBER WAS I?
PLEASE--FOR THE LOVE OF **GOD!**
I-I DON'T **KNOW**
BANG!
SO.

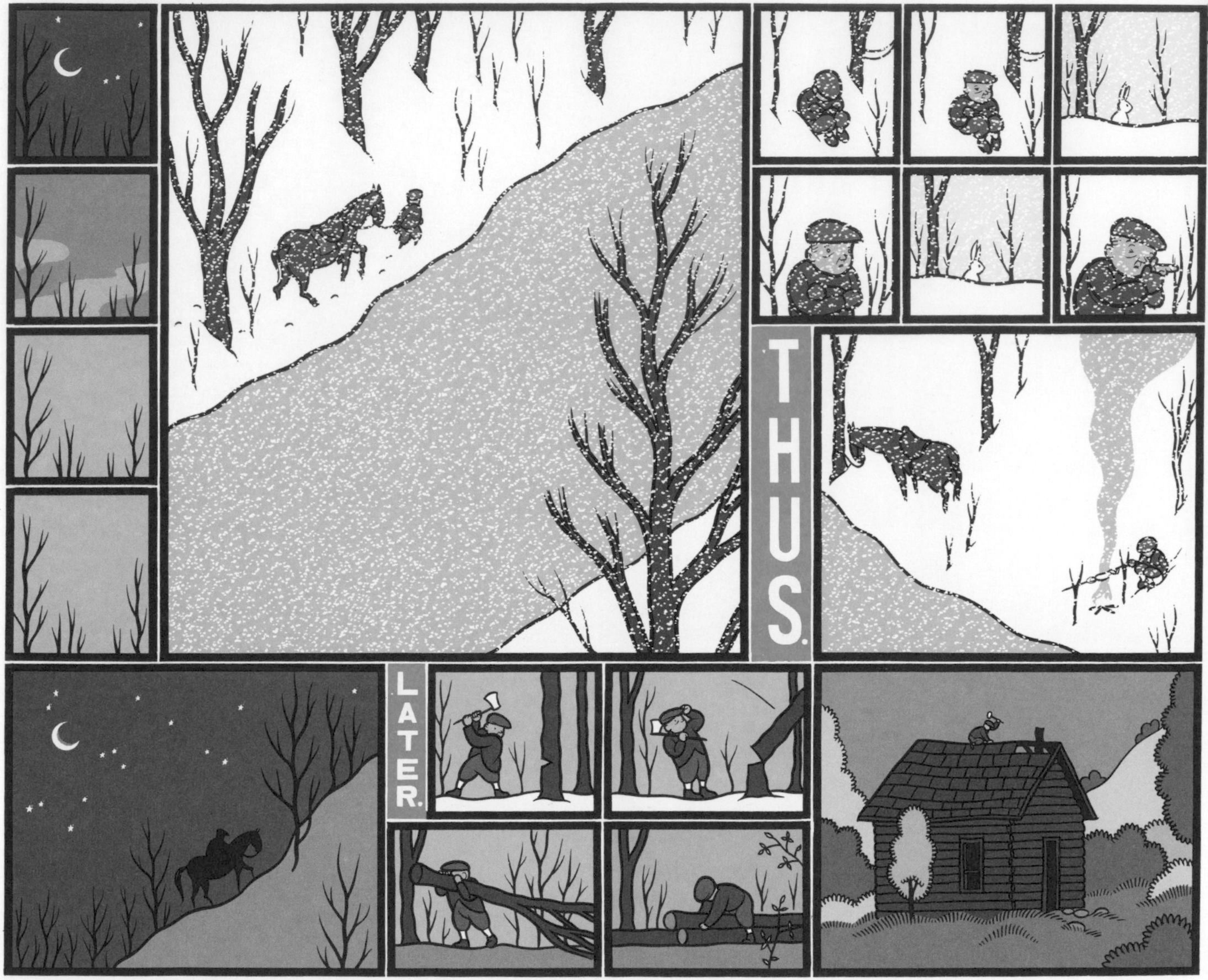
THUS.
LATER.

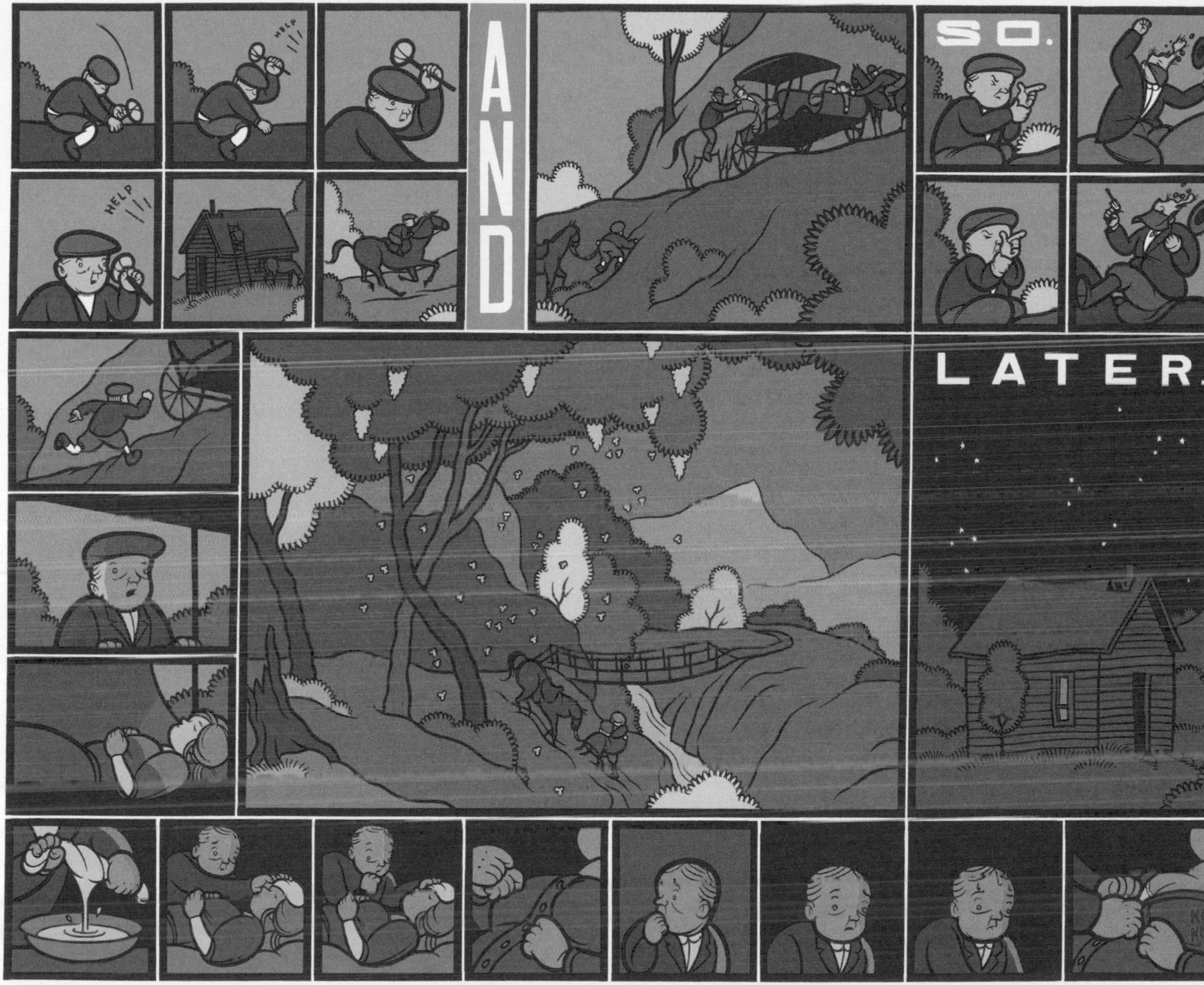

HELP
HELP
AND
SO.
LATER.
KNOCK
KNOCK

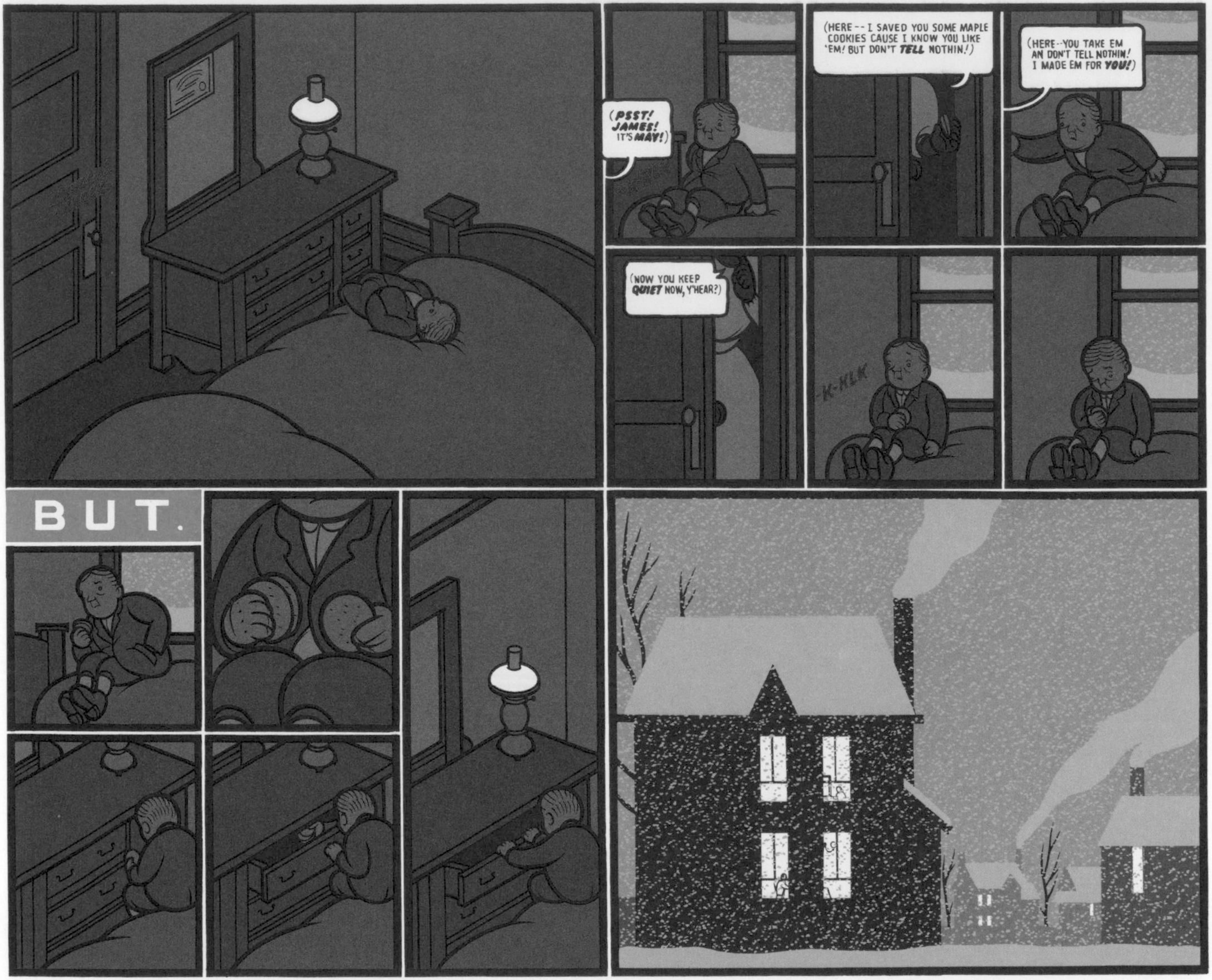
(PSST! JAMES! IT'S MAY!)
(HERE -- I SAVED YOU SOME MAPLE COOKIES CAUSE I KNOW YOU LIKE 'EM! BUT DON'T TELL NOTHIN!)
(HERE--YOU TAKE EM AN DON'T TELL NOTHIN! I MADE EM FOR YOU!)
(NOW YOU KEEP QUIET NOW, Y'HEAR?)
-K-HLK
BUT.

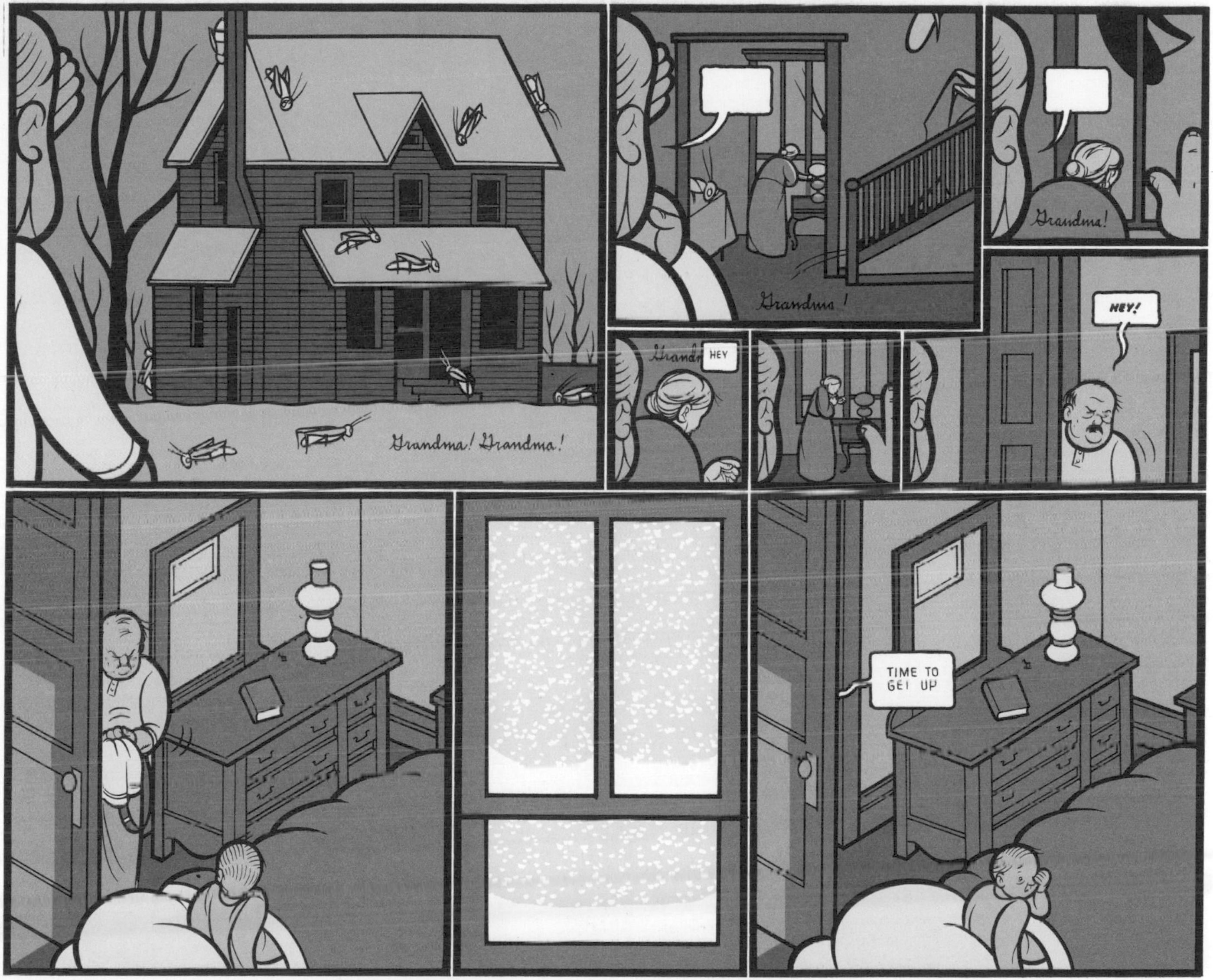

Grandma! Grandma!
Grandma!
Grandma!
Grandm
HEY
HEY!
TIME TO GET UP

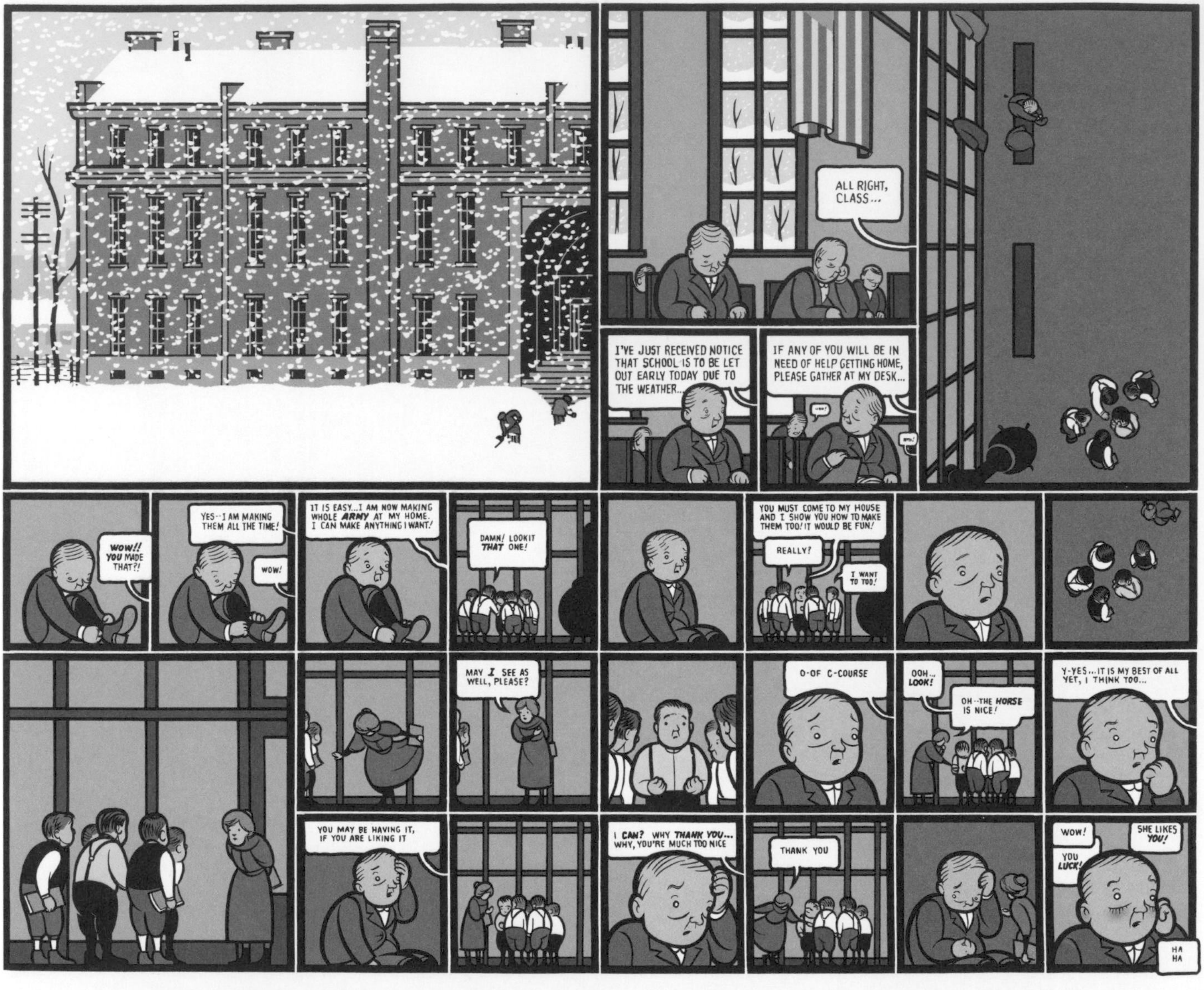
ALL RIGHT, CLASS...
I'VE JUST RECEIVED NOTICE THAT SCHOOL IS TO BE LET OUT EARLY TODAY DUE TO THE WEATHER...
IF ANY OF YOU WILL BE IN NEED OF HELP GETTING HOME, PLEASE GATHER AT MY DESK...
WOW!! YOU MADE THAT?!
YES--I AM MAKING THEM ALL THE TIME!
WOW!
IT IS EASY...I AM NOW MAKING WHOLE ARMY AT MY HOME. I CAN MAKE ANYTHING I WANT!
DAMN! LOOKIT THAT ONE!
YOU MUST COME TO MY HOUSE AND I SHOW YOU HOW TO MAKE THEM TOO! IT WOULD BE FUN!
REALLY?
I WANT TO TOO!
MAY I SEE AS WELL, PLEASE?
O-OF C-COURSE
OOH... LOOK!
OH--THE HORSE IS NICE!
Y-YES...IT IS MY BEST OF ALL YET, I THINK TOO...
YOU MAY BE HAVING IT, IF YOU ARE LIKING IT
I CAN? WHY THANK YOU... WHY, YOU'RE MUCH TOO NICE
THANK YOU
WOW!
YOU LUCK!
SHE LIKES YOU!
HA HA

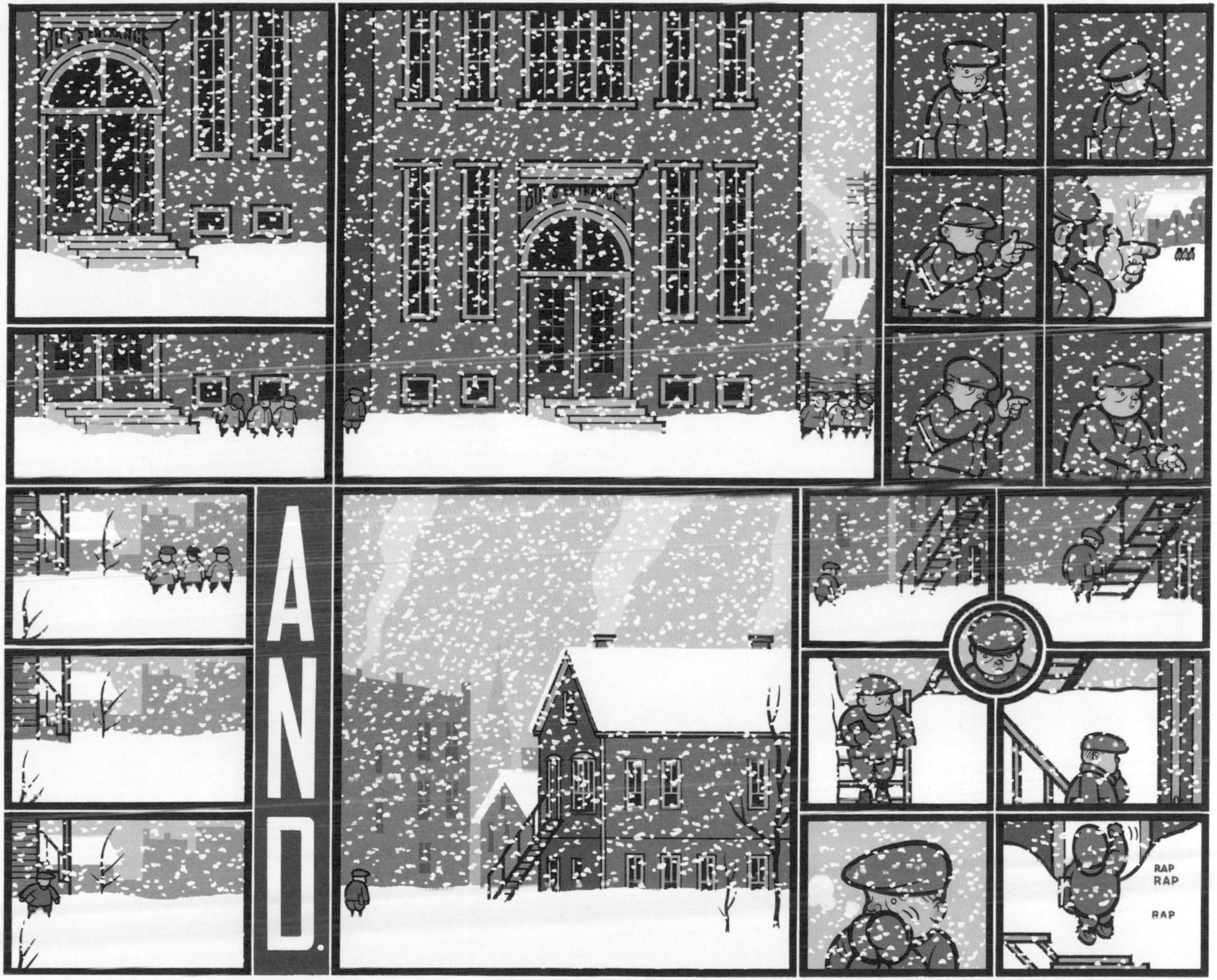
AND.
RAP
RAP
RAP

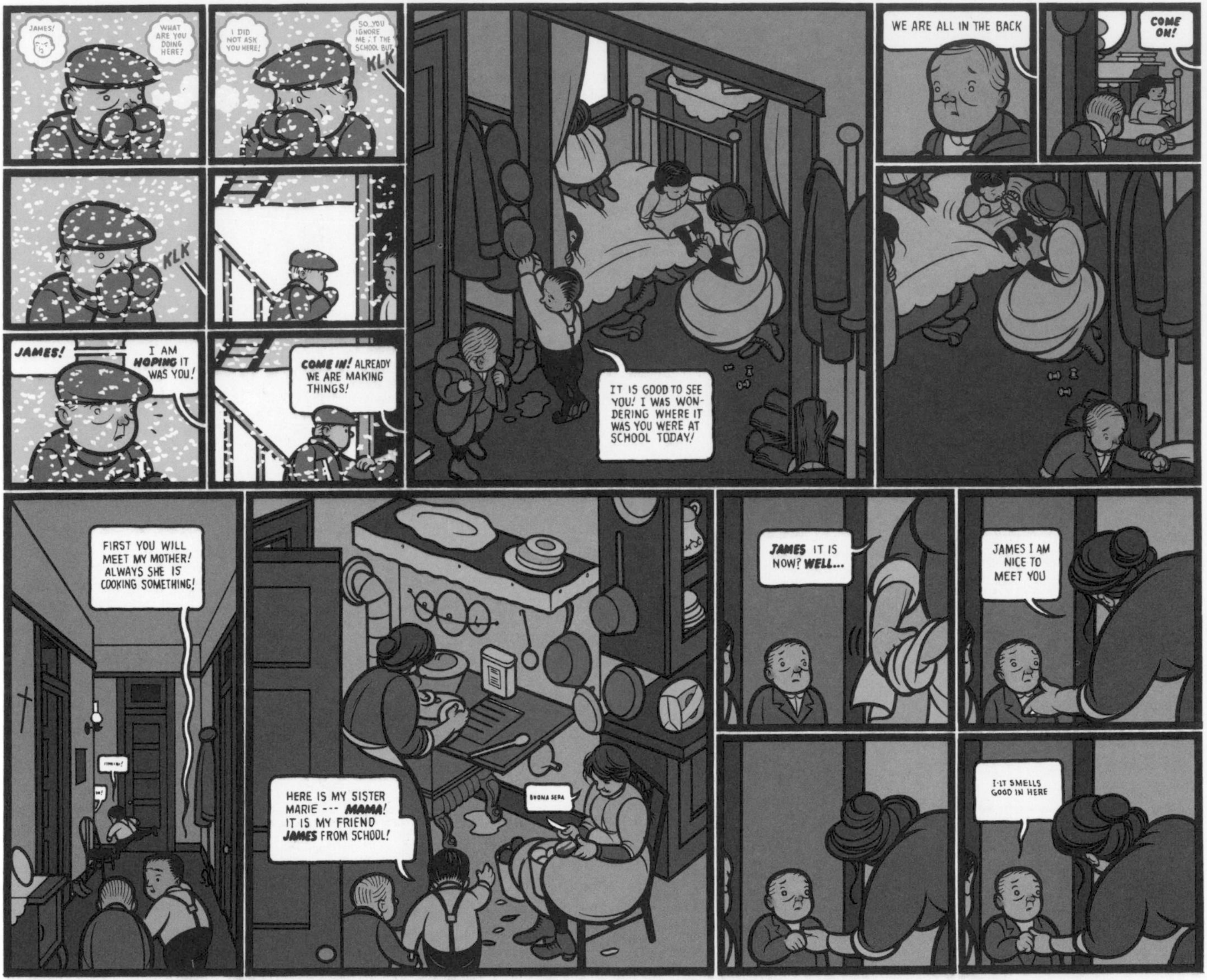
JAMES!
WHAT ARE YOU DOING HERE?
I DID NOT ASK YOU HERE!
SO..YOU IGNORE ME AT THE SCHOOL BUT
KLK
KLK
JAMES!
I AM HOPING IT WAS YOU!
COME IN! ALREADY WE ARE MAKING THINGS!
IT IS GOOD TO SEE YOU! I WAS WONDERING WHERE IT WAS YOU WERE AT SCHOOL TODAY!
WE ARE ALL IN THE BACK
COME ON!
FIRST YOU WILL MEET MY MOTHER! ALWAYS SHE IS COOKING SOMETHING!
HERE IS MY SISTER MARIE --- MAMA! IT IS MY FRIEND JAMES FROM SCHOOL!
BUONA SERA
JAMES IT IS NOW? WELL...
JAMES I AM NICE TO MEET YOU
I-IT SMELLS GOOD IN HERE

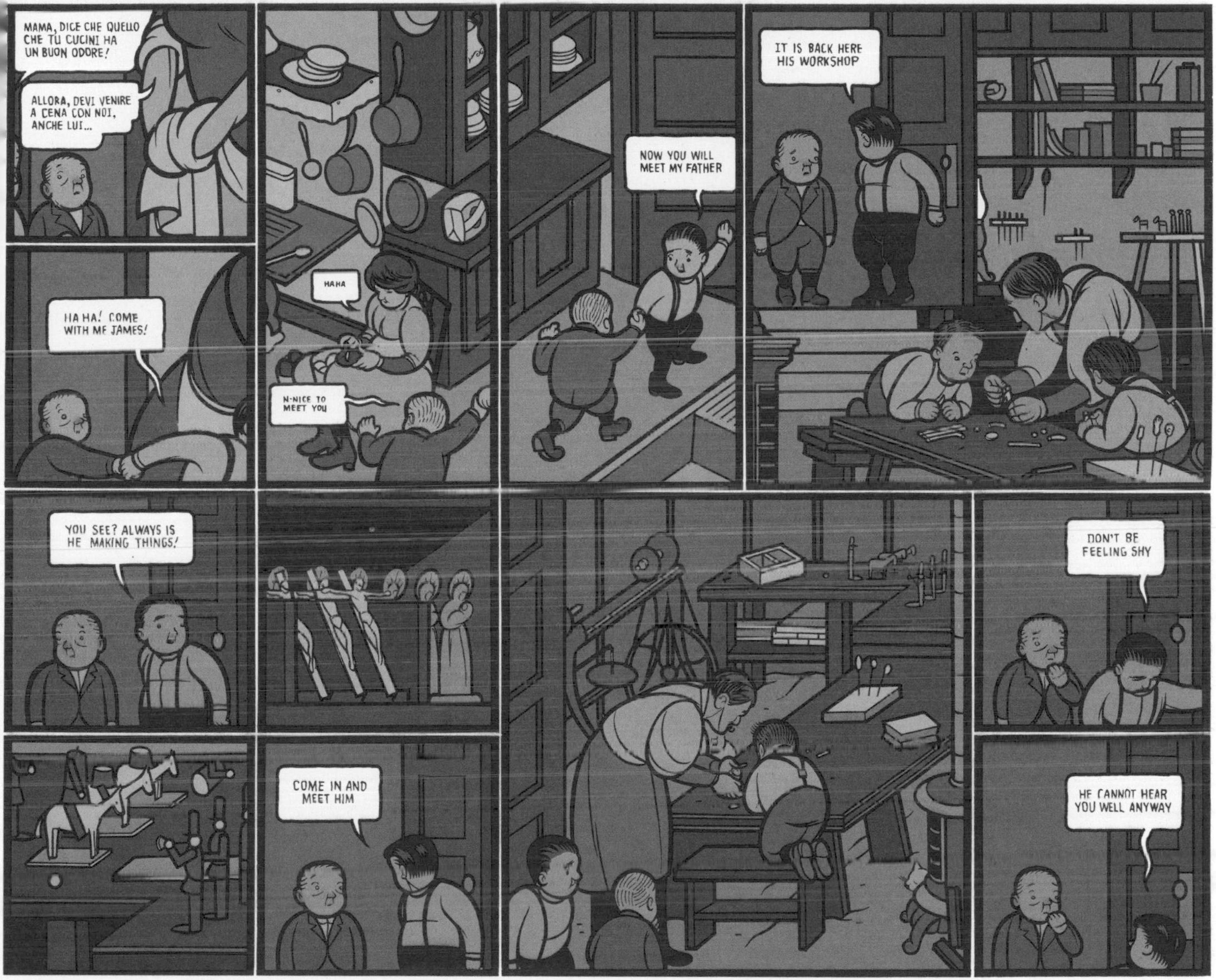
MAMA, DICE CHE QUELLO CHE TU CUCINI HA UN BUON ODORE!
ALLORA, DEVI VENIRE A CENA CON NOI, ANCHE LUI...
HA HA! COME WITH ME JAMES!
HAHA
N-NICE TO MEET YOU
NOW YOU WILL MEET MY FATHER
IT IS BACK HERE HIS WORKSHOP
YOU SEE? ALWAYS IS HE MAKING THINGS!
COME IN AND MEET HIM
DON'T BE FEELING SHY
HE CANNOT HEAR YOU WELL ANYWAY

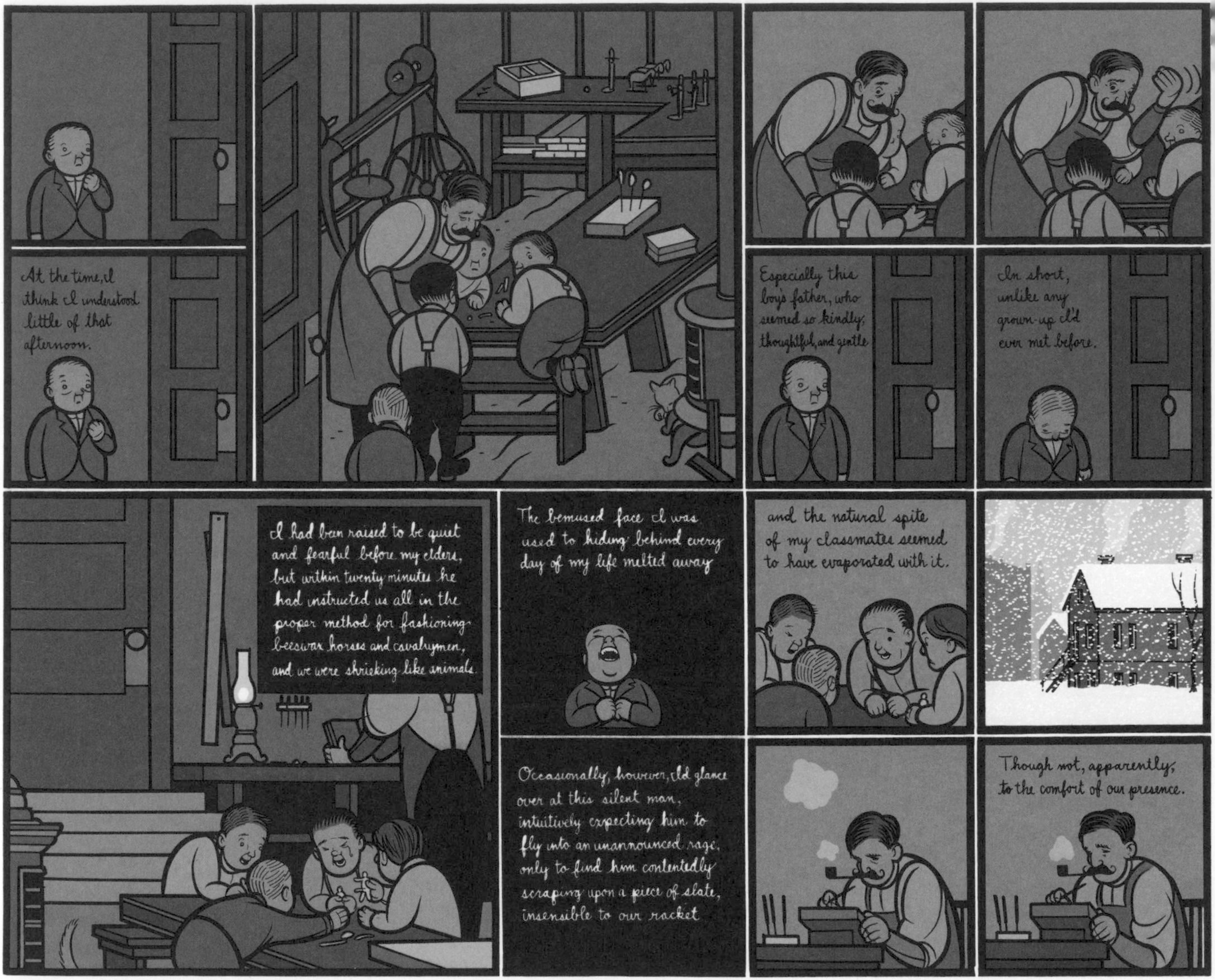
At the time, I think I understood little of that afternoon.
Especially this boy's father, who seemed so kindly, thoughtful, and gentle
In short, unlike any grown-up I'd ever met before.
I had been raised to be quiet and fearful before my elders, but within twenty minutes he had instructed us all in the proper method for fashioning beeswax horses and cavalrymen, and we were shrieking like animals.
The bemused face I was used to hiding behind every day of my life melted away
and the natural spite of my classmates seemed to have evaporated with it.
Occasionally, however, I'd glance over at this silent man, intuitively expecting him to fly into an unannounced rage, only to find him contentedly scraping upon a piece of slate, insensible to our racket
Though not, apparently, to the comfort of our presence.

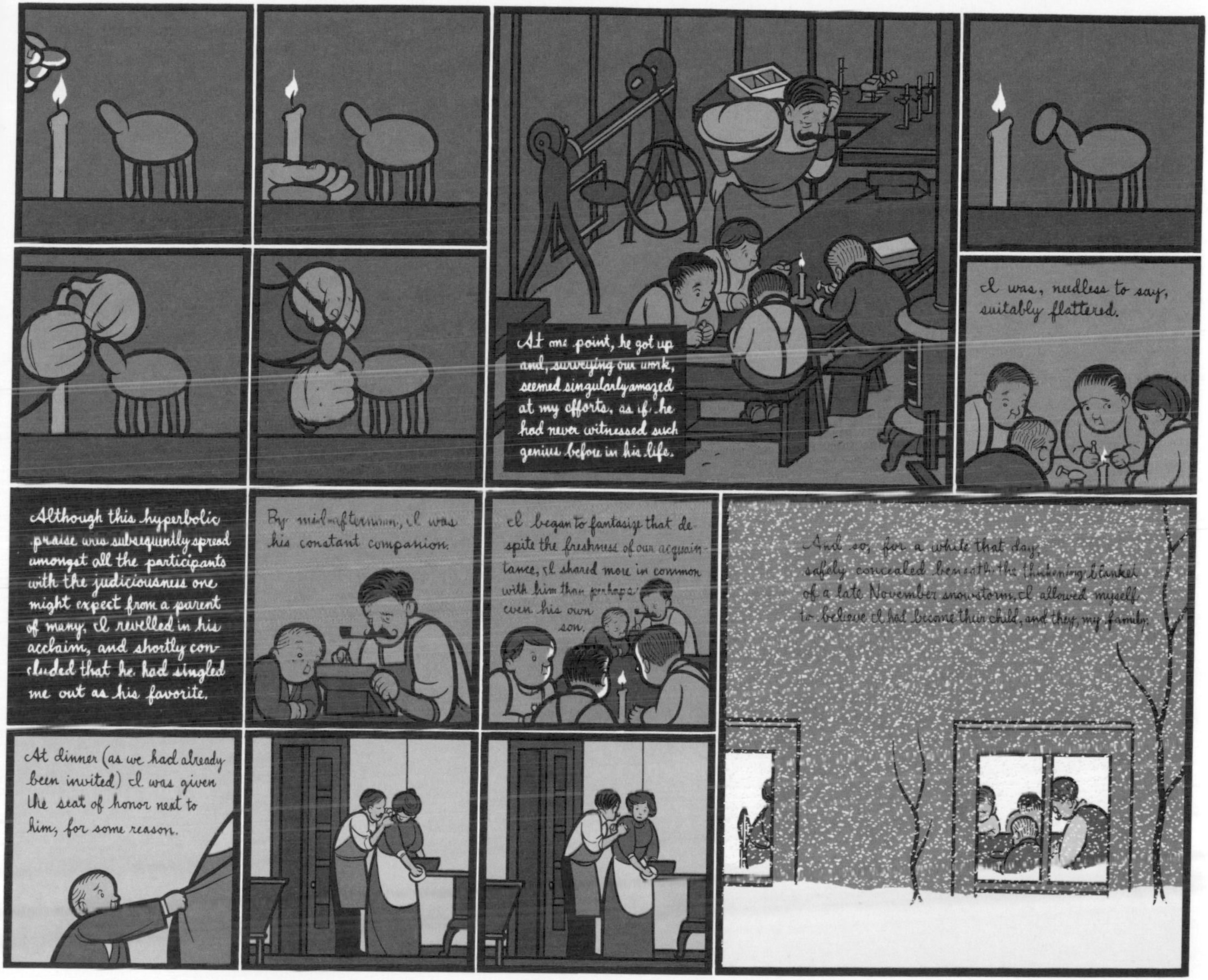
At one point, he got up and, surveying our work, seemed singularly amazed at my efforts, as if he had never witnessed such genius before in his life.
I was, needless to say, suitably flattered.
Although this hyperbolic praise was subsequently spread amongst all the participants with the judiciousness one might expect from a parent of many, I revelled in his acclaim, and shortly concluded that he had singled me out as his favorite.
By mid-afternoon, I was his constant companion.
I began to fantasize that despite the freshness of our acquaintance, I shared more in common with him than perhaps even his own son.
And so, for a while that day, safely concealed beneath the thickening blanket of a late November snowstorm, I allowed myself to believe I had become their child, and they, my family.
At dinner (as we had already been invited) I was given the seat of honor next to him, for some reason.

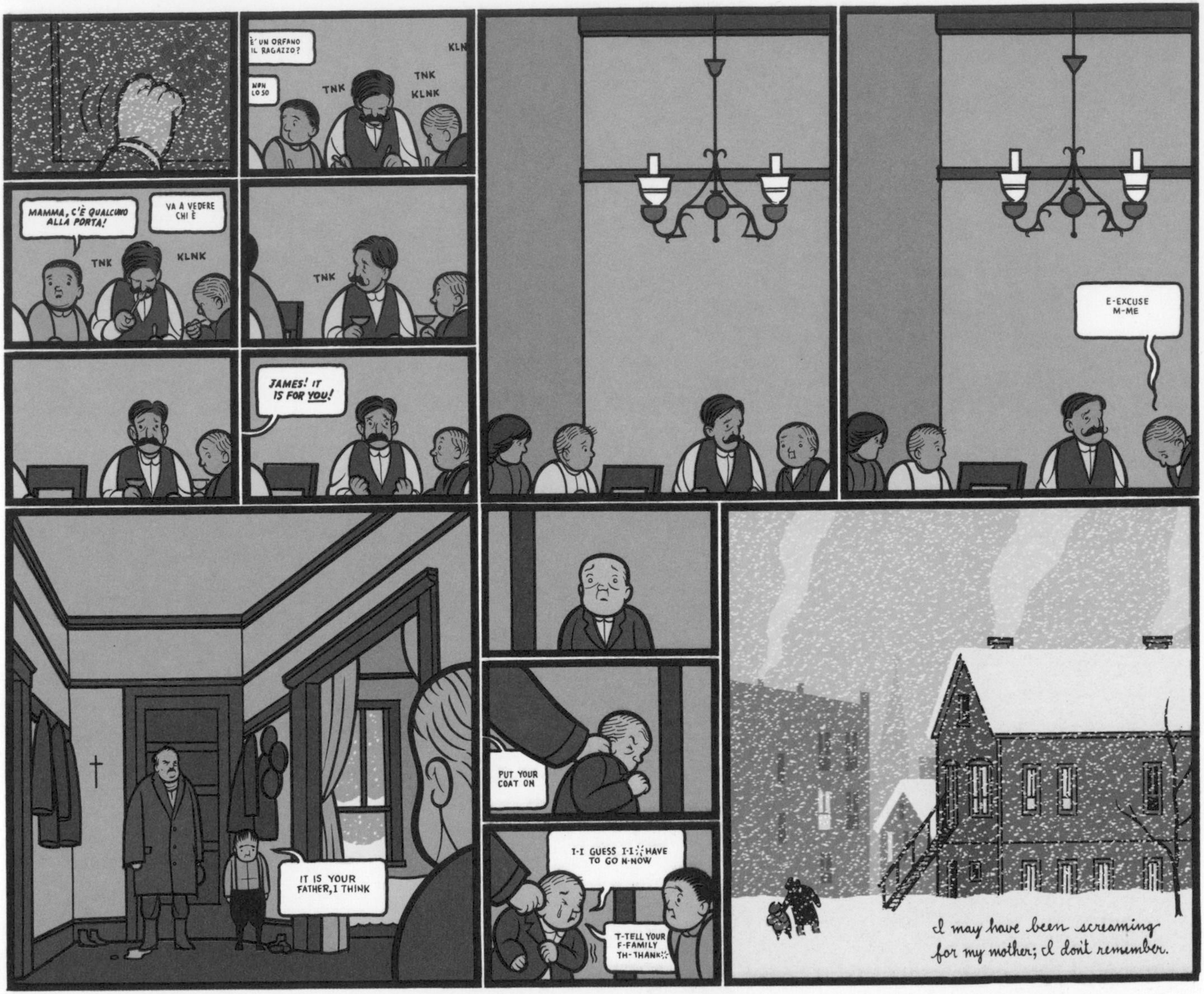
È UN ORFANO IL RAGAZZO?
NON LO SO
TNK
TNK
KLNK
KLN
MAMMA, C'È QUALCUNO ALLA PORTA!
VA A VEDERE CHI È
TNK
KLNK
TNK
JAMES! IT IS FOR YOU!
E-EXCUSE M-ME
IT IS YOUR FATHER, I THINK
PUT YOUR COAT ON
I-I GUESS I-I HAVE TO GO N-NOW
T-TELL YOUR F-FAMILY TH-THANK
I may have been screaming for my mother; I don't remember.

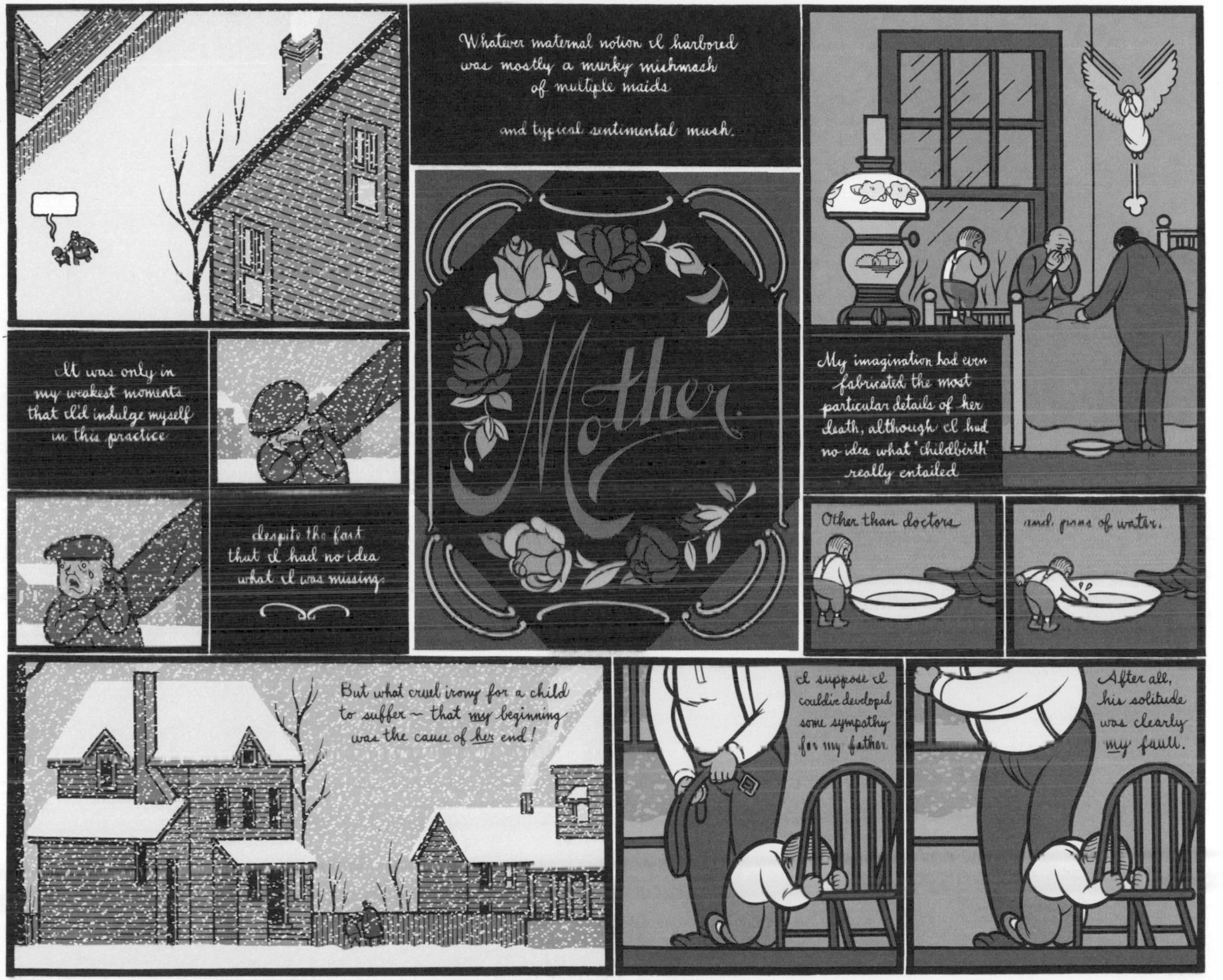
Whatever maternal notion I harbored was mostly a murky mishmash of multiple maids
and typical sentimental mush.
It was only in my weakest moments that I'd indulge myself in this practice
despite the fact that I had no idea what I was missing
Mother.
My imagination had even fabricated the most particular details of her death, although I had no idea what "childbirth" really entailed
Other than doctors
and pans of water.
But what cruel irony for a child to suffer ~ that my beginning was the cause of her end!
I suppose I could've developed some sympathy for my father
After all, his solitude was clearly my fault.

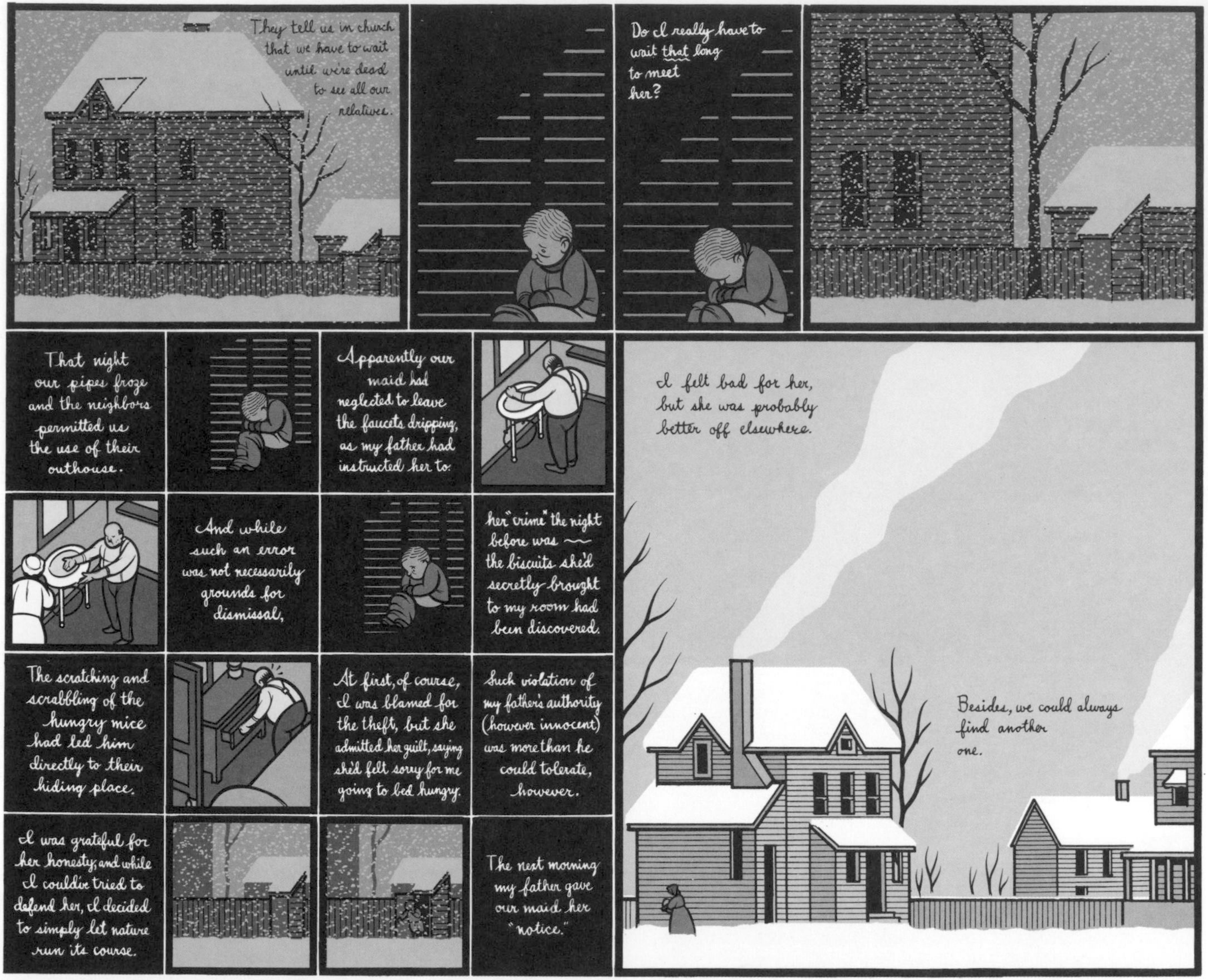

They tell us in church that we have to wait until we're dead to see all our relatives.
Do I really have to wait that long to meet her?
That night our pipes froze and the neighbors permitted us the use of their outhouse.
Apparently our maid had neglected to leave the faucets dripping, as my father had instructed her to.
And while such an error was not necessarily grounds for dismissal,
her "crime" the night before was — the biscuits she'd secretly brought to my room had been discovered.
The scratching and scrabbling of the hungry mice had led him directly to their hiding place.
At first, of course, I was blamed for the theft, but she admitted her guilt, saying she'd felt sorry for me going to bed hungry.
Such violation of my father's authority (however innocent) was more than he could tolerate, however.
I was grateful for her honesty, and while I could've tried to defend her, I decided to simply let nature run its course.
The next morning my father gave our maid her "notice."
I felt bad for her, but she was probably better off elsewhere.
Besides, we could always find another one.

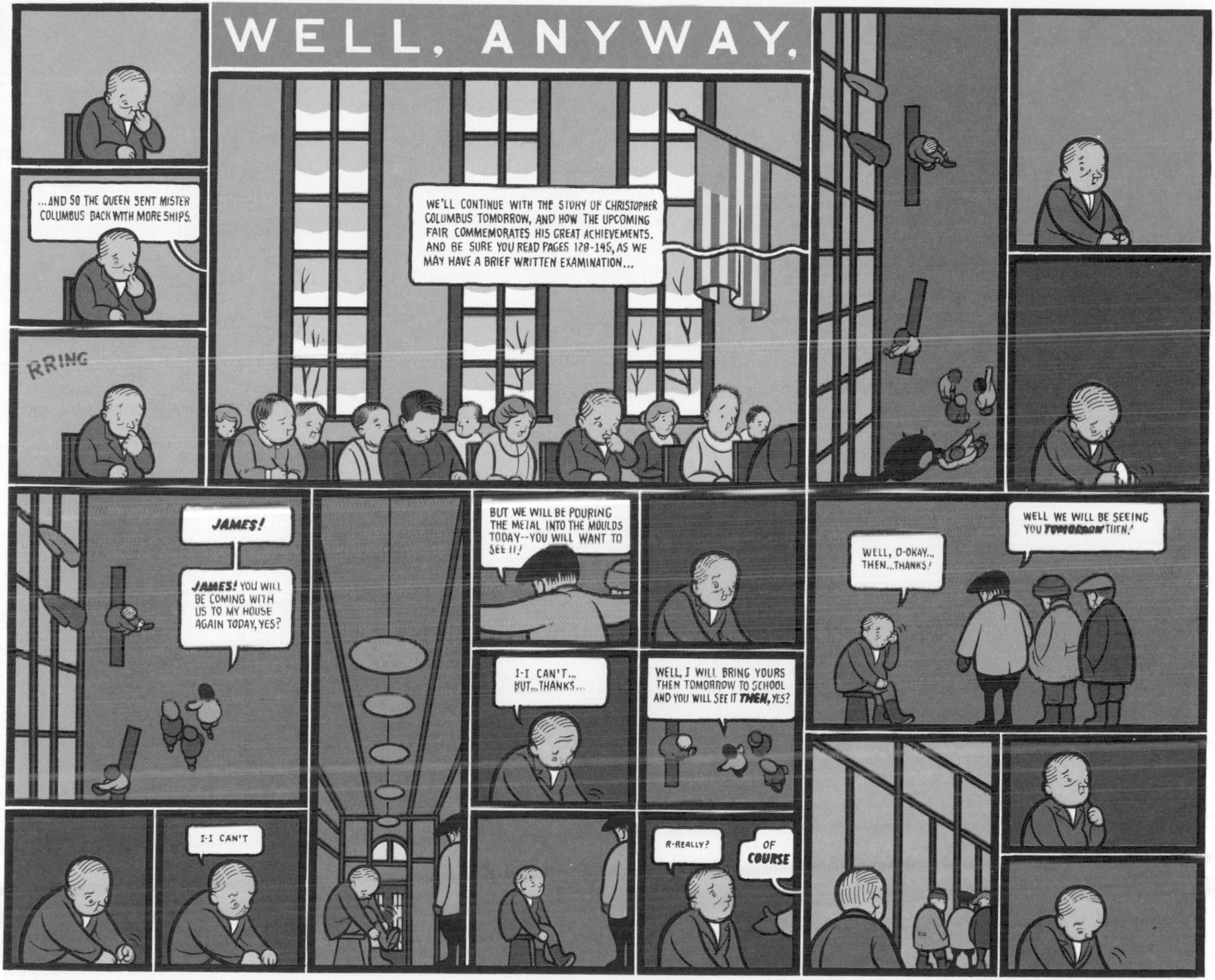
WELL, ANYWAY,
...AND SO THE QUEEN SENT MISTER COLUMBUS BACK WITH MORE SHIPS.
RRING
WE'LL CONTINUE WITH THE STORY OF CHRISTOPHER COLUMBUS TOMORROW, AND HOW THE UPCOMING FAIR COMMEMORATES HIS GREAT ACHIEVEMENTS. AND BE SURE YOU READ PAGES 128-145, AS WE MAY HAVE A BRIEF WRITTEN EXAMINATION...
JAMES!
JAMES! YOU WILL BE COMING WITH US TO MY HOUSE AGAIN TODAY, YES?
I-I CAN'T
BUT WE WILL BE POURING THE METAL INTO THE MOULDS TODAY--YOU WILL WANT TO SEE IT!
I-I CAN'T... BUT...THANKS...
WELL, I WILL BRING YOURS THEN TOMORROW TO SCHOOL AND YOU WILL SEE IT THEN, YES?
R-REALLY?
OF COURSE
WELL, O-OKAY... THEN...THANKS!
WELL WE WILL BE SEEING YOU TOMORROW THEN!

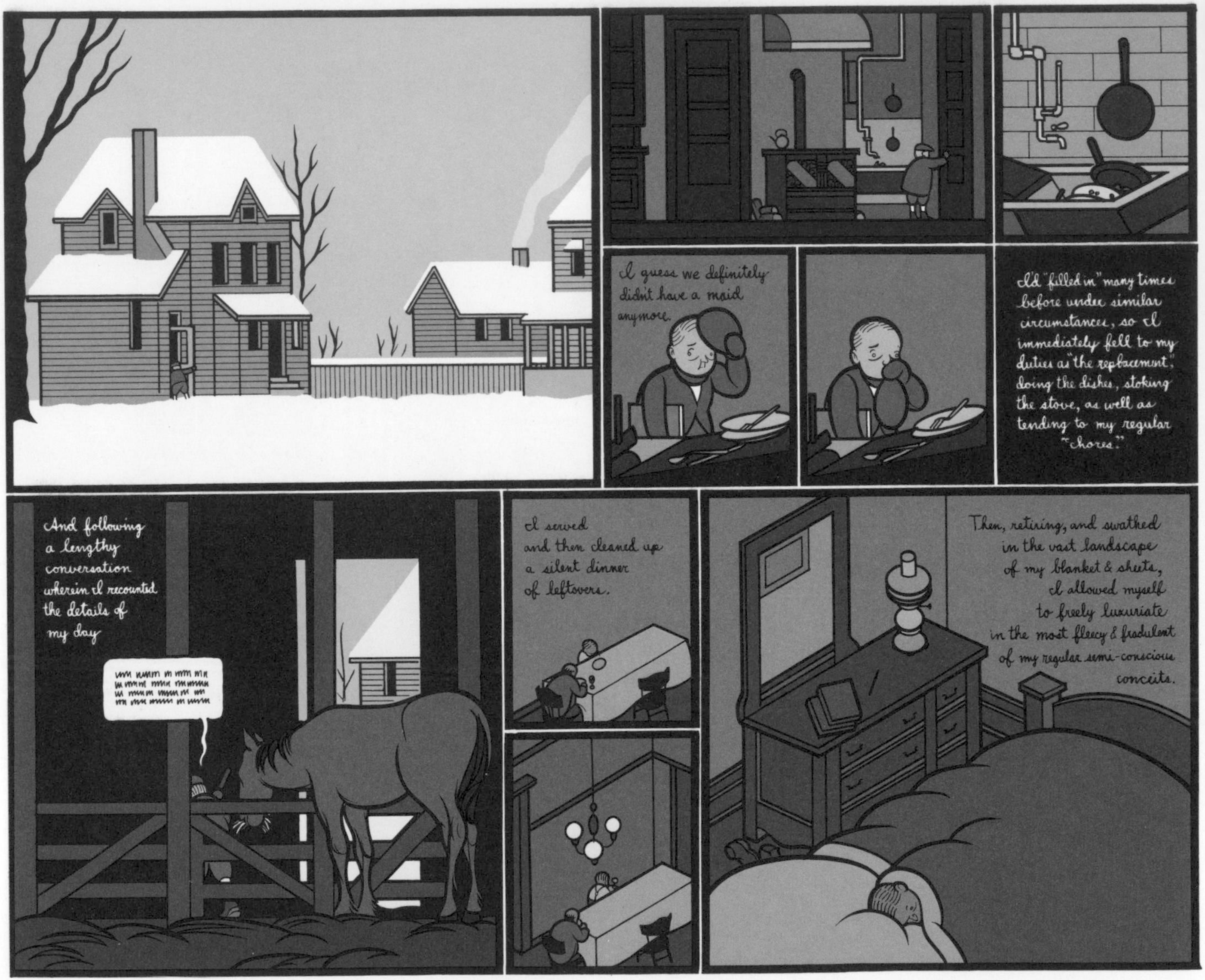
I guess we definitely didn't have a maid anymore.
I'd "filled in" many times before under similar circumstances, so I immediately fell to my duties as "the replacement," doing the dishes, stoking the stove, as well as tending to my regular "chores."
And following a lengthy conversation wherein I recounted the details of my day
I served and then cleaned up a silent dinner of leftovers.
Then, retiring, and swathed in the vast landscape of my blanket & sheets, I allowed myself to freely luxuriate in the most fleecy & fradulent of my regular semi-conscious conceits.

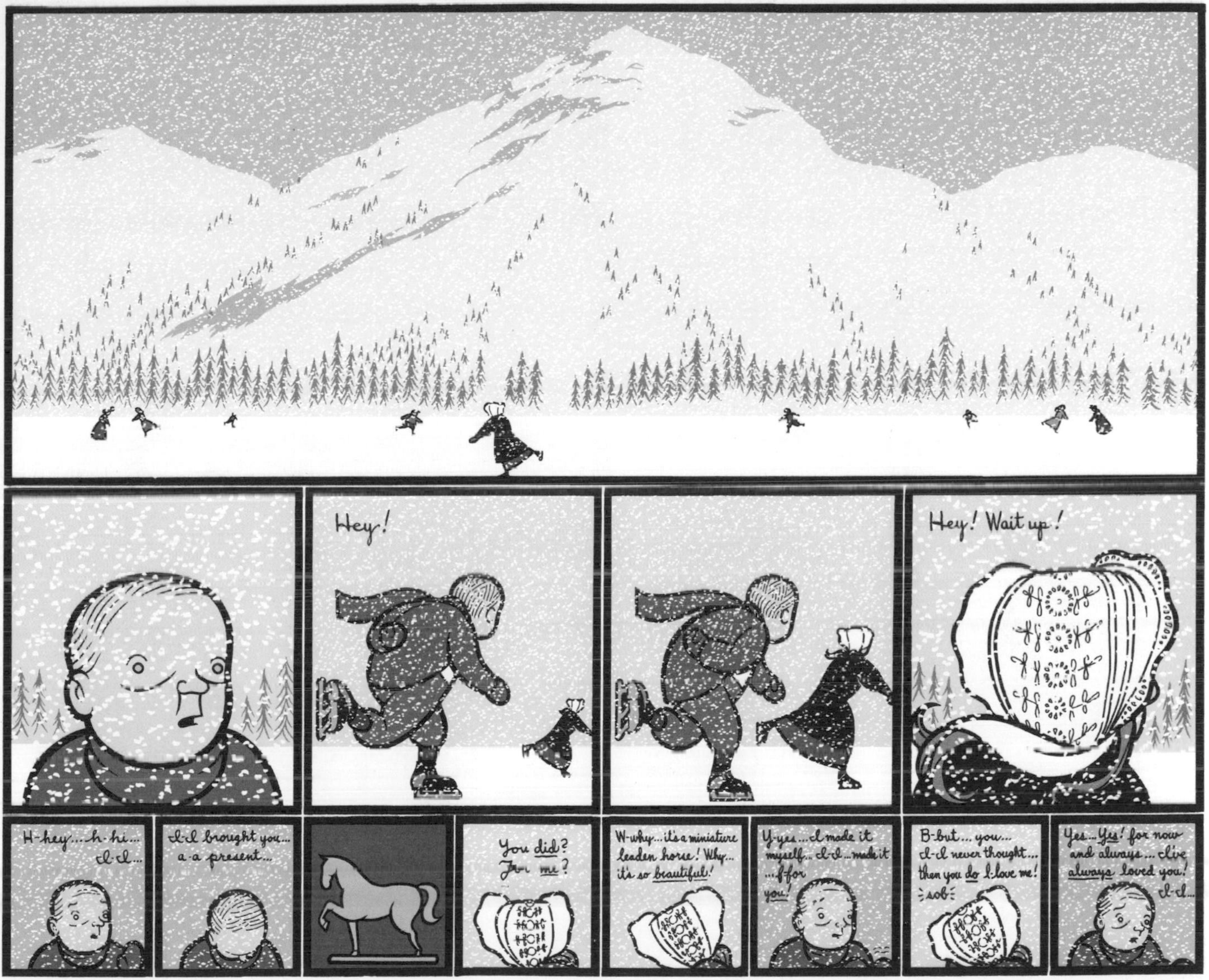
Hey!
Hey! Wait up!
H-hey... h-hi... I-I...
I-I brought you... a-a present...
You did? For me?
W-why... it's a miniature leaden horse! Why... it's so beautiful!
Y-yes... I made it myself... I-I... made it ...f-for you!
B-but... you... I-I never thought... then you do l-love me!
sob
Yes... Yes! for now and always... I've always loved you! I-I...

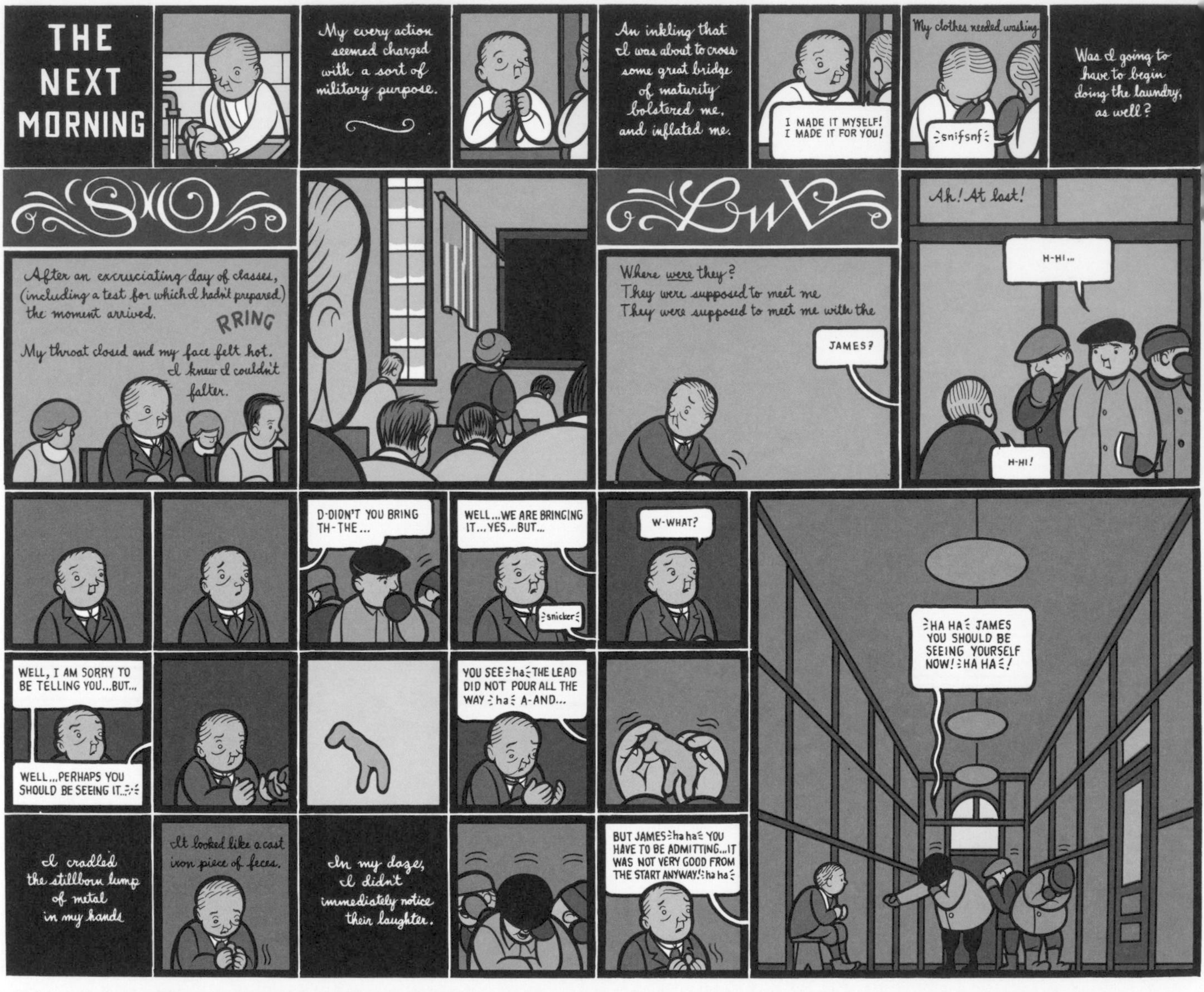

THE NEXT MORNING
My every action seemed charged with a sort of military purpose.
An inkling that I was about to cross some great bridge of maturity bolstered me, and inflated me.
I MADE IT MYSELF! I MADE IT FOR YOU!
My clothes needed washing
snifsnf
Was I going to have to begin doing the laundry, as well?
After an excruciating day of classes, (including a test for which I hadn't prepared) the moment arrived.
RRING
My throat closed and my face felt hot. I knew I couldn't falter.
Where were they? They were supposed to meet me They were supposed to meet me with the
JAMES?
Ah! At last!
H-HI...
H-HI!
D-DIDN'T YOU BRING TH-THE...
WELL... WE ARE BRINGING IT... YES... BUT...
snicker
W-WHAT?
WELL, I AM SORRY TO BE TELLING YOU... BUT...
WELL... PERHAPS YOU SHOULD BE SEEING IT...
YOU SEE ha THE LEAD DID NOT POUR ALL THE WAY ha A-AND...
I cradled the stillborn lump of metal in my hands
It looked like a cast iron piece of feces.
In my daze, I didn't immediately notice their laughter.
BUT JAMES ha ha YOU HAVE TO BE ADMITTING... IT WAS NOT VERY GOOD FROM THE START ANYWAY! ha ha
HA HA JAMES YOU SHOULD BE SEEING YOURSELF NOW! HA HA!

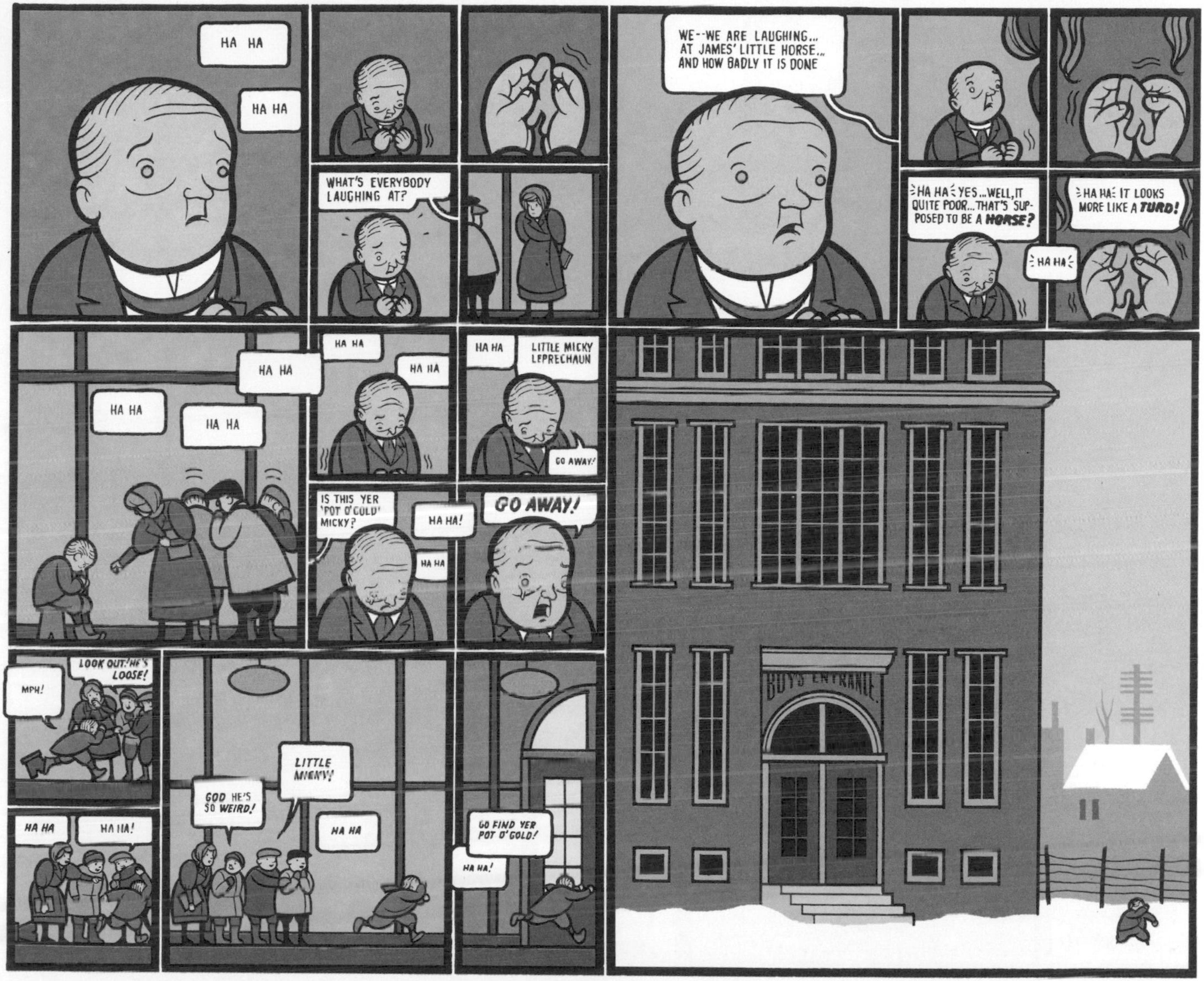

HA HA
HA HA
WHAT'S EVERYBODY LAUGHING AT?
WE--WE ARE LAUGHING... AT JAMES' LITTLE HORSE... AND HOW BADLY IT IS DONE
HA HA YES...WELL, IT QUITE POOR... THAT'S SUP-POSED TO BE A **HORSE?**
HA HA
HA HA IT LOOKS MORE LIKE A **TURD!**
HA HA
HA HA
HA HA
HA HA
HA HA
HA HA
HA HA
LITTLE MICKY LEPRECHAUN
GO AWAY!
IS THIS YER 'POT O' GOLD' MICKY?
HA HA!
HA HA
GO AWAY!
LOOK OUT! HE'S LOOSE!
MPH!
HA HA
HA HA!
GOD HE'S SO WEIRD!
LITTLE MICKY!
HA HA
GO FIND YER POT O' GOLD!
HA HA!
BOYS ENTRANCE

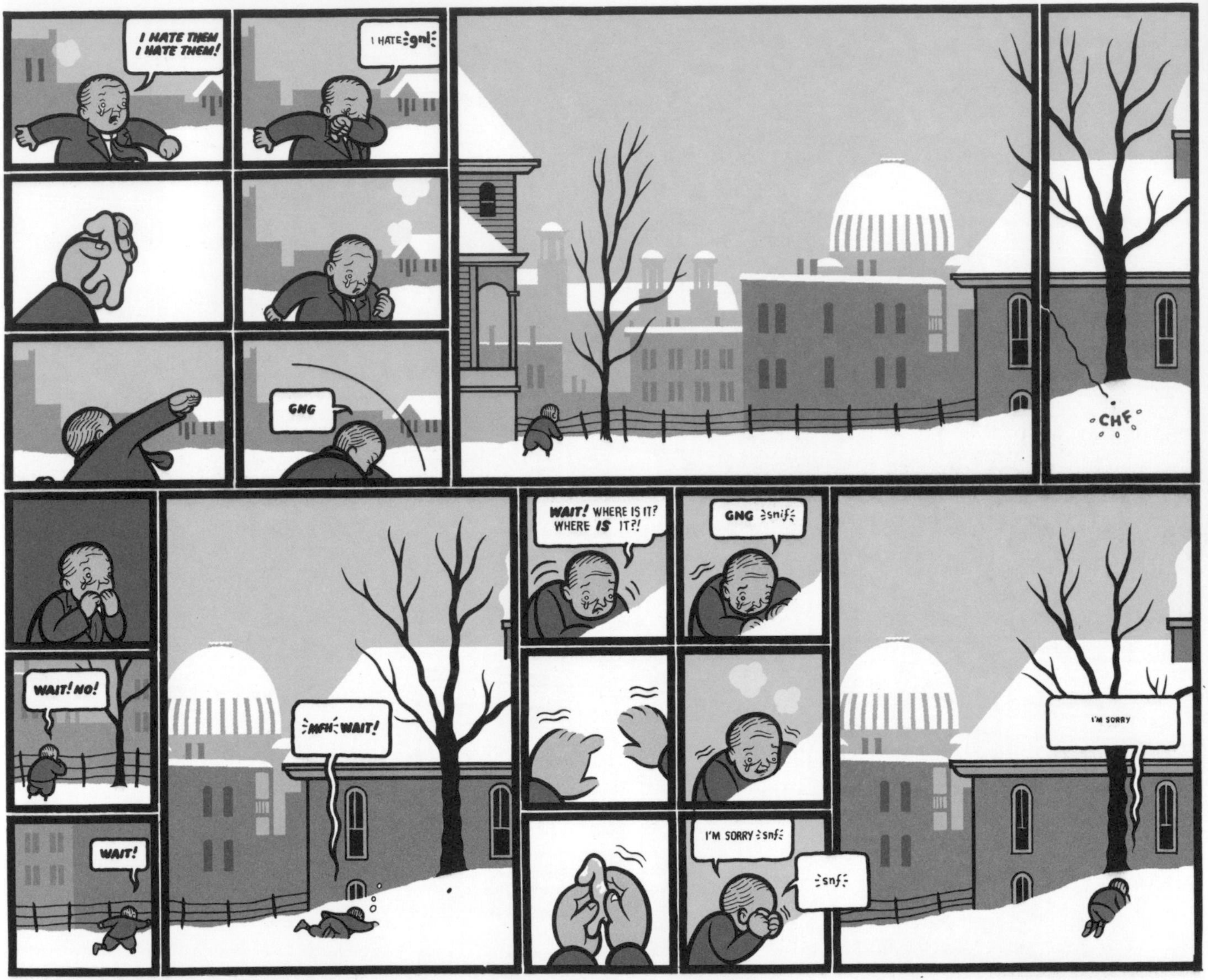
I HATE THEM
I HATE THEM!
I HATE gnl
GNG
CHF
WAIT! NO!
WAIT!
MFH WAIT!
WAIT! WHERE IS IT?
WHERE IS IT?!
GNG snif
I'M SORRY snf
snf
I'M SORRY

THE REMAINING WINTER

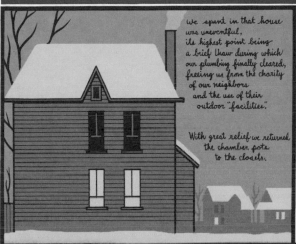

We spent in that house was uneventful, its highest point being a brief thaw during which our plumbing finally cleared, freeing us from the charity of our neighbors and the use of their outdoor "facilities".

With great relief we returned the chamber pots to the closets.

As well, my father hired a new servant, so that I was able once again to pursue my solitary interests.

These dual improvements in our living conditions did more to raise the general spirits than even the more traditional celebrations of Thanksgiving & Christmas, both of which passed without incident.

One event bears repeating, however.

One night in February, as I was disposing of the evening's refuse, I was startled by the sudden appearance of a Negro woman from behind our house.

Only after a moment did I recognize her as my grandmother's old maid, the one whom my father had fired some months before.

Since I'd remembered feeling that her dismissal had seemed somewhat unfair, I advanced a tentative greeting, but she retreated.

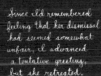

Y-YOUR FATHER AT HOME, JAMES?

Y-YES...OF COURSE... D-DO YOU WANT ME TO GO G-GET HIM?

Then I proceeded to the trash heap behind the old shack

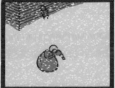

Running away from me, she seemed to be carrying some sort of burden, concealed at the waist of her coat— perhaps a bundle of clothes or a parcel, I thought.

I listened to her disappear into the snow

where I emptied the remains of our evening roast.

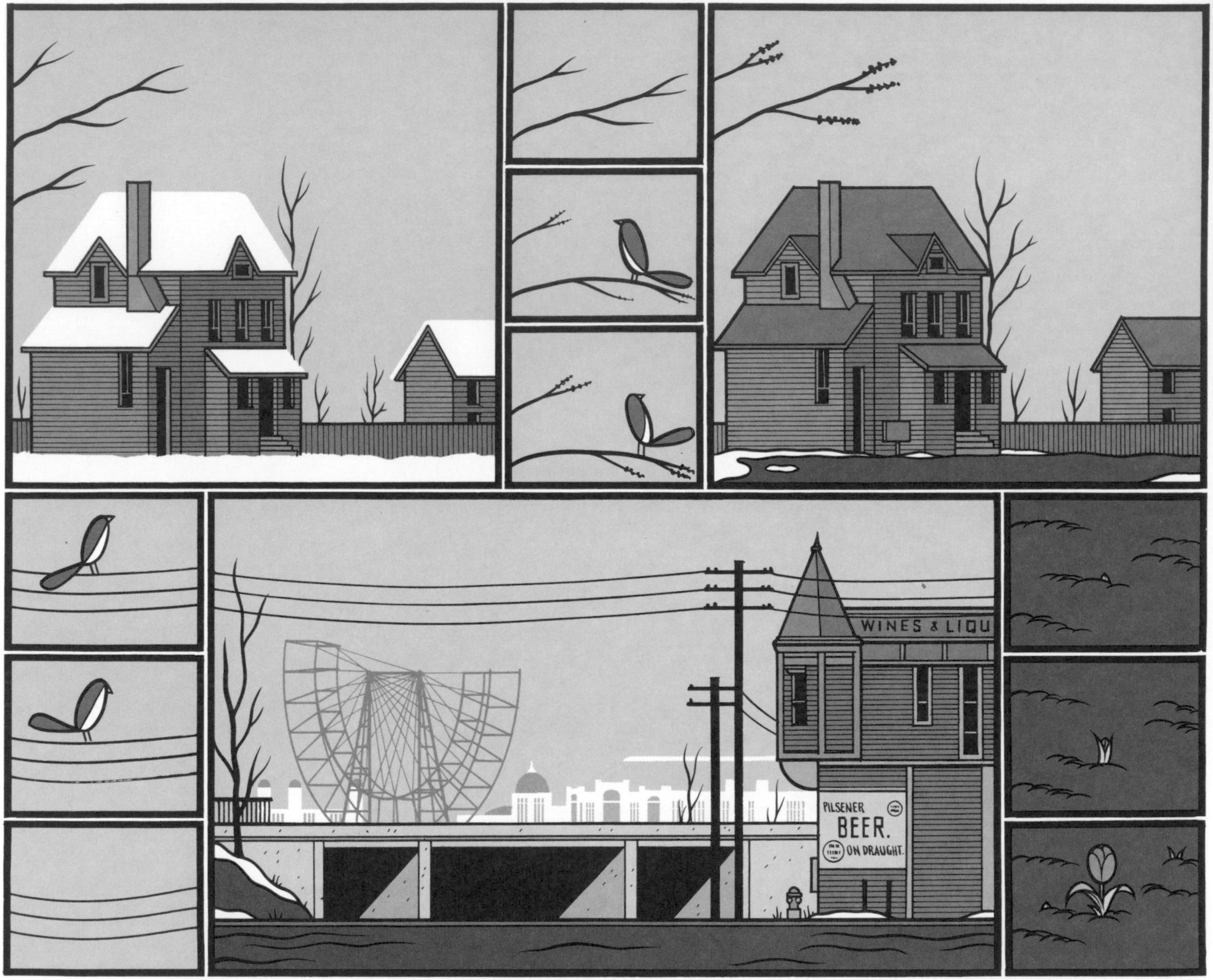
WINES & LIQU
PILSENER
BEER.
ON DRAUGHT.

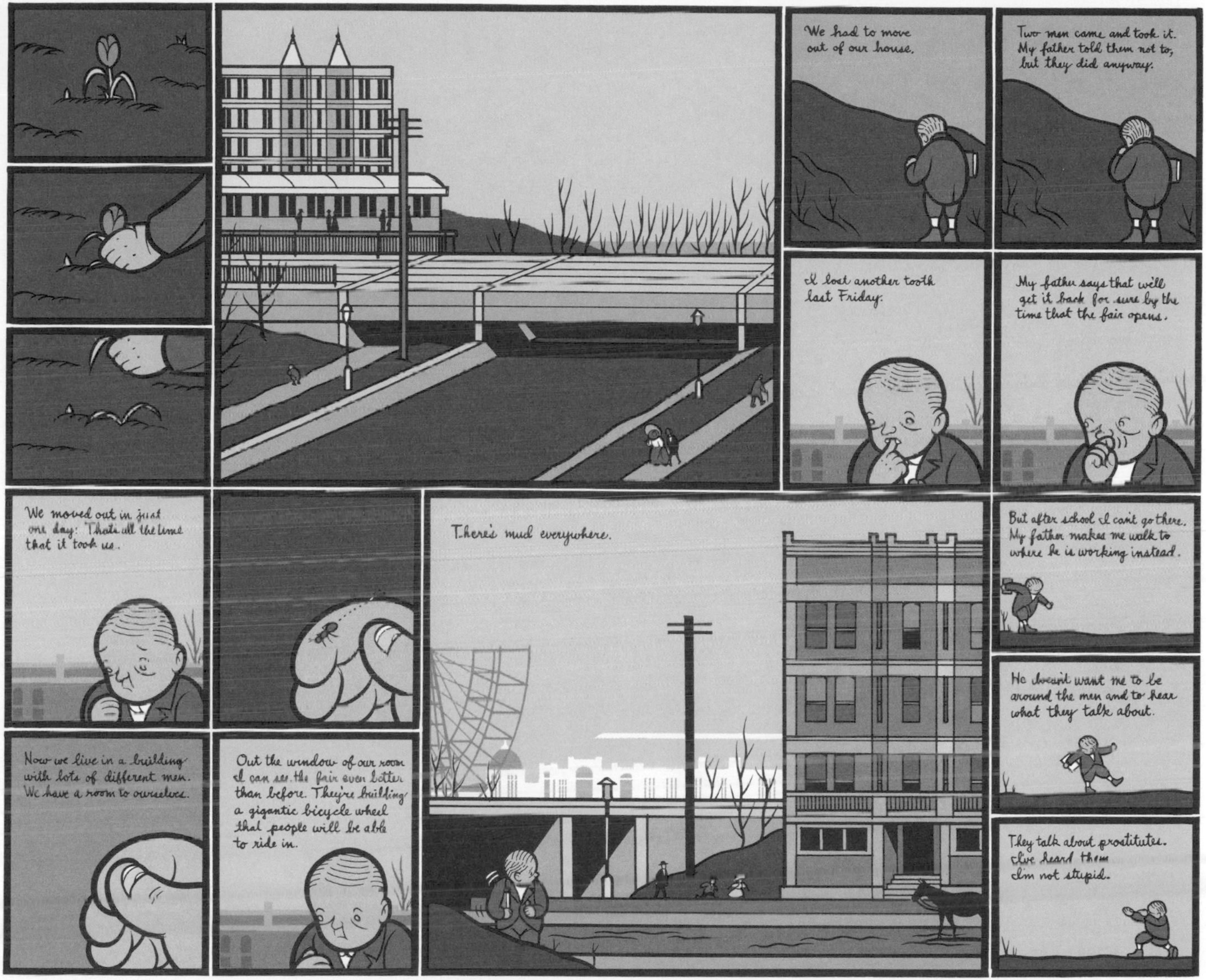
We had to move out of our house.
Two men came and took it. My father told them not to, but they did anyway.
I lost another tooth last Friday.
My father says that we'll get it back for sure by the time that the fair opens.
We moved out in just one day: That's all the time that it took us.
Now we live in a building with lots of different men. We have a room to ourselves.
Out the window of our room I can see the fair even better than before. They're building a gigantic bicycle wheel that people will be able to ride in.
There's mud everywhere.
But after school I can't go there. My father makes me walk to where he is working instead.
He doesn't want me to be around the men and to hear what they talk about.
They talk about prostitutes. I've heard them I'm not stupid.

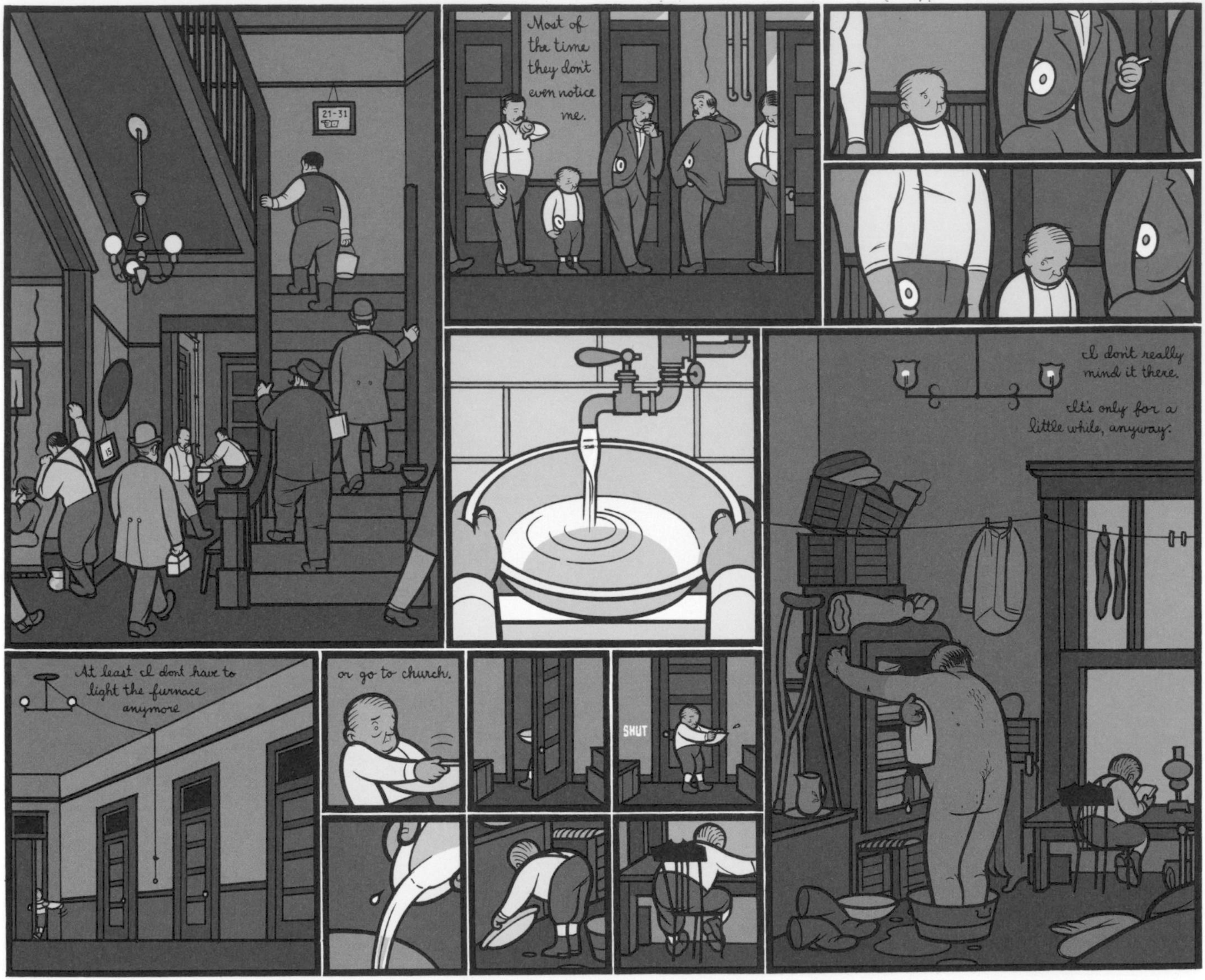
21-31
15
Most of the time they don't even notice me.
I don't really mind it there.
It's only for a little while, anyway.
At least I dont have to light the furnace anymore
or go to church.
SHUT

WE'RE COMING.
W.H. HAVERL MINSTREL
Every day there are more and more people.
WE'RE COMING.
W.H. HAVERLAND MINSTRELS
POSITIVELY NO SMOKING
everyday
everyday
everyday
DWELLINGS OF THE Cannibals.
DWELLINGS OF THE Cannibals.
My father is working here now.
He is building it for an Englishman.
ZOOPRAXOGRAPHICAL HALL.
GLAZIER
The Englishman is going to use it to show a machine that makes pictures dance.
SQUSH
SLSH
SQUSCH
HI MINNIE! LOOK... I BROUGHT YOU SOMETHING!
I met him once. He had bad breath.
HEY! DON'T EAT IT!
JAMES? JAMES IS THAT YOU?
JAMES COME IN HERE IMMEDIATELY
It's going to be my birthday soon.
SSSSHH
I'm going to be nine.

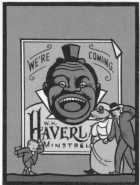

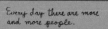

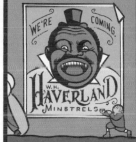

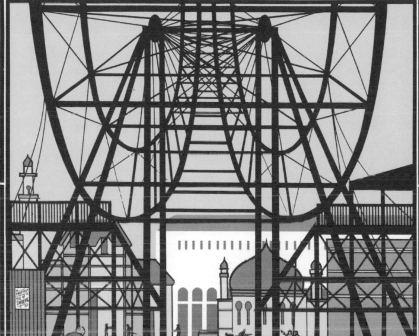

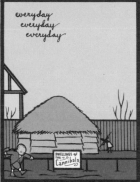

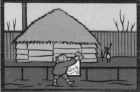

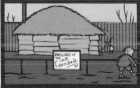

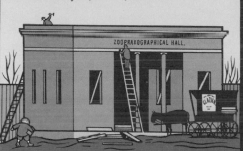

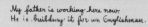

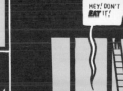

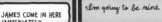

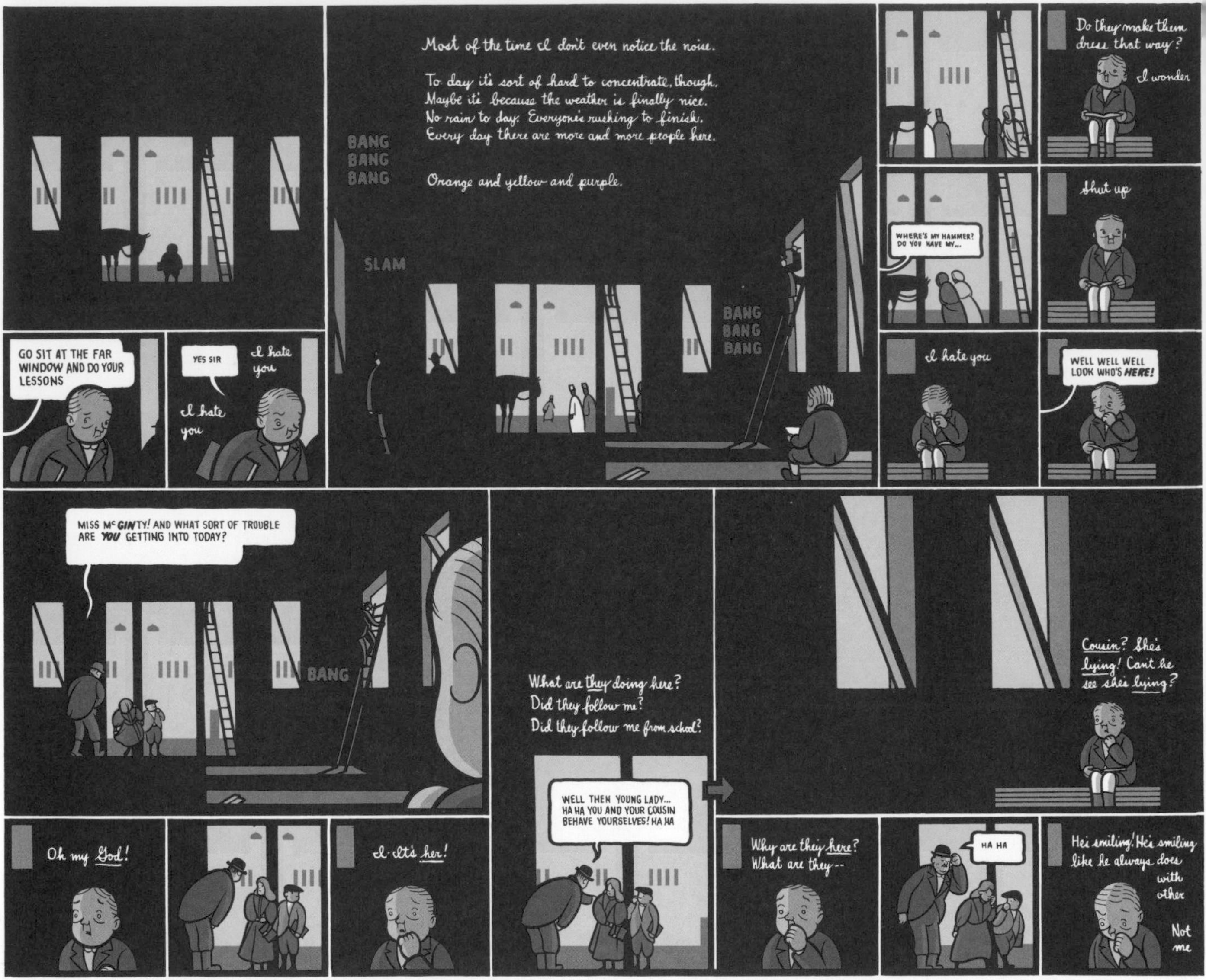
Most of the time I don't even notice the noise.
To day it's sort of hard to concentrate, though. Maybe it's because the weather is finally nice. No rain to day. Everyone's rushing to finish. Every day there are more and more people here.
Orange and yellow and purple.
BANG BANG BANG
SLAM
BANG BANG BANG
Do they make them dress that way?
I wonder
WHERE'S MY HAMMER? DO YOU HAVE MY...
Shut up
GO SIT AT THE FAR WINDOW AND DO YOUR LESSONS
YES SIR
I hate you
I hate you
I hate you
WELL WELL WELL LOOK WHO'S HERE!
MISS McGINTY! AND WHAT SORT OF TROUBLE ARE YOU GETTING INTO TODAY?
BANG
What are they doing here? Did they follow me? Did they follow me from school?
WELL THEN YOUNG LADY... HA HA YOU AND YOUR COUSIN BEHAVE YOURSELVES! HA HA
Cousin? She's lying! Can't he see she's lying?
Oh my God!
I-It's her!
Why are they here? What are they--
HA HA
He's smiling! He's smiling like he always does with other
Not me

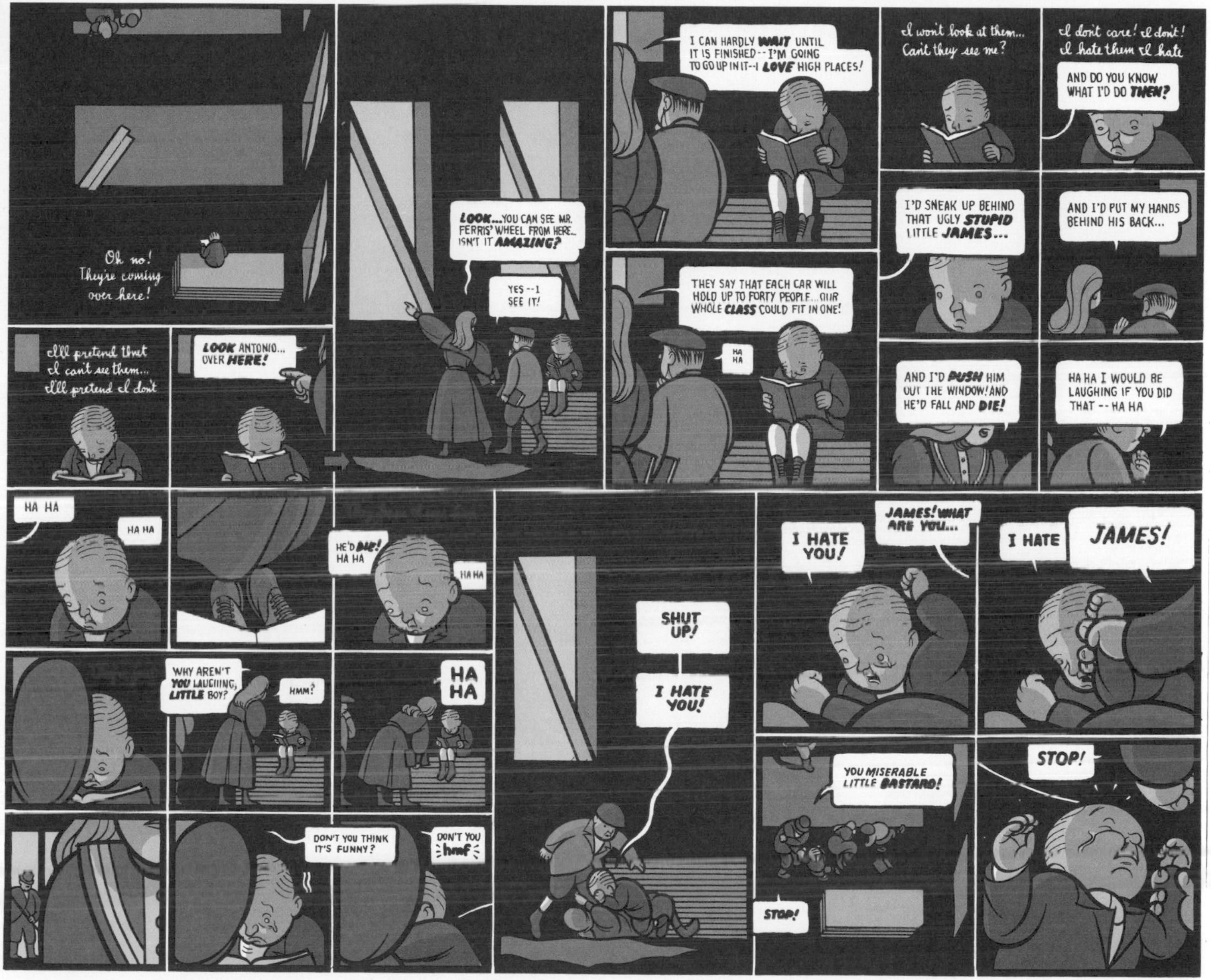
Oh no! They're coming over here!
I'll pretend that I can't see them... I'll pretend I don't
LOOK ANTONIO... OVER HERE!
LOOK... YOU CAN SEE MR. FERRIS' WHEEL FROM HERE... ISN'T IT AMAZING?
YES -- I SEE IT!
I CAN HARDLY WAIT UNTIL IT IS FINISHED -- I'M GOING TO GO UP IN IT -- I LOVE HIGH PLACES!
THEY SAY THAT EACH CAR WILL HOLD UP TO FORTY PEOPLE... OUR WHOLE CLASS COULD FIT IN ONE!
HA HA
I won't look at them... Can't they see me?
I don't care! I don't! I hate them I hate
AND DO YOU KNOW WHAT I'D DO THEN?
I'D SNEAK UP BEHIND THAT UGLY STUPID LITTLE JAMES...
AND I'D PUT MY HANDS BEHIND HIS BACK...
AND I'D PUSH HIM OUT THE WINDOW! AND HE'D FALL AND DIE!
HA HA I WOULD BE LAUGHING IF YOU DID THAT -- HA HA
HA HA
HA HA
HE'D DIE! HA HA
HA HA
WHY AREN'T YOU LAUGHING, LITTLE BOY?
HMM?
HA HA
DON'T YOU THINK IT'S FUNNY?
DON'T YOU hmf
SHUT UP!
I HATE YOU!
I HATE YOU!
JAMES! WHAT ARE YOU...
I HATE
JAMES!
YOU MISERABLE LITTLE BASTARD!
STOP!
STOP!

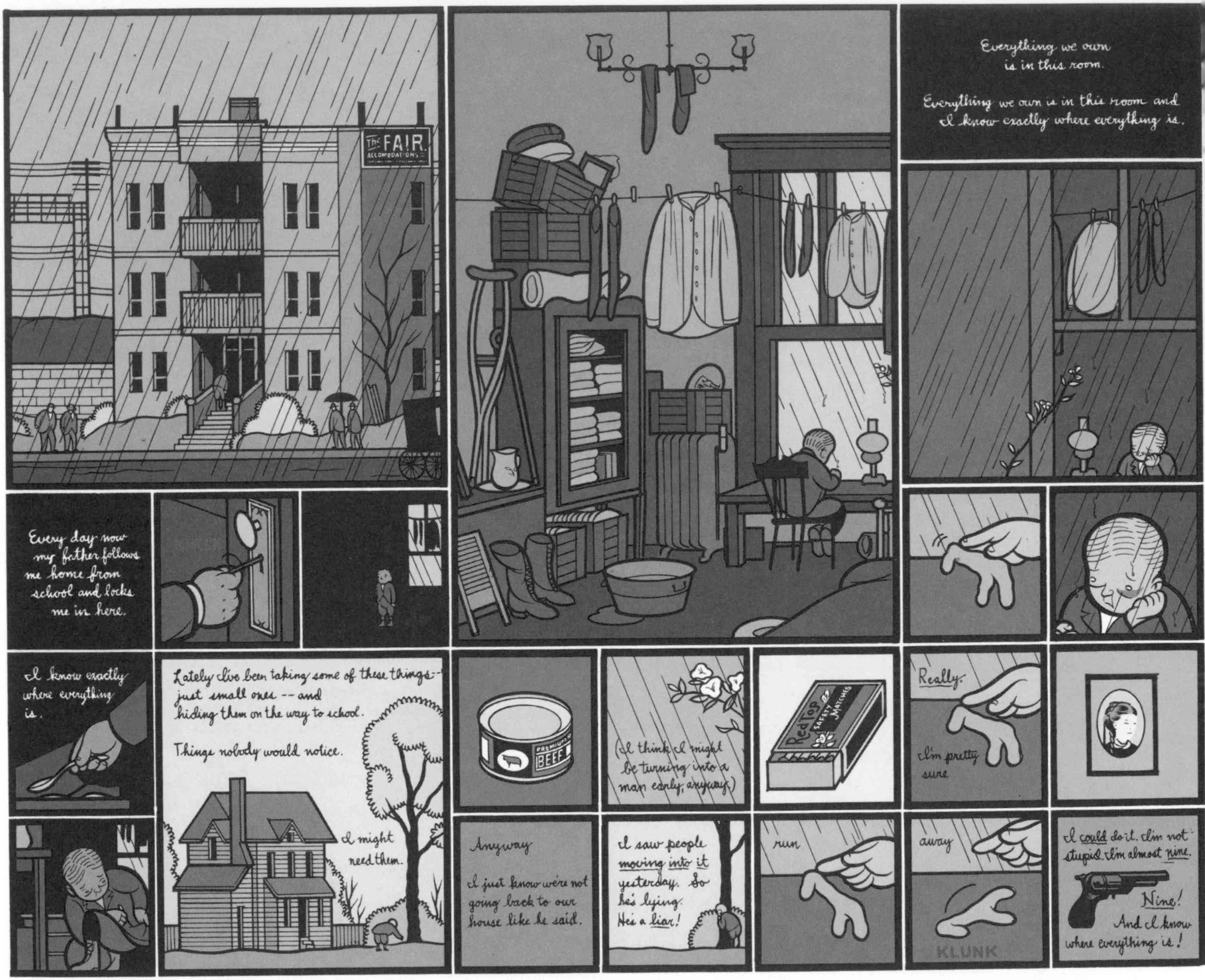

The FAIR.
ACCOMODATIONS
Everything we own is in this room.
Everything we own is in this room and I know exactly where everything is.
Every day now my father follows me home from school and locks me in here.
I know exactly where everything is.
Lately I've been taking some of these things-- just small ones -- and hiding them on the way to school.
Things nobody would notice.
I might need them.
PREMIUM BEEF
(I think I might be turning into a man early, anyway.)
RedTop SAFETY MATCHES
Really.
I'm pretty sure
Anyway
I just know we're not going back to our house like he said.
I saw people moving into it yesterday. So he's lying. He's a liar!
run
away
KLUNK
I could do it. I'm not stupid. I'm almost nine.
Nine!
And I know where everything is!

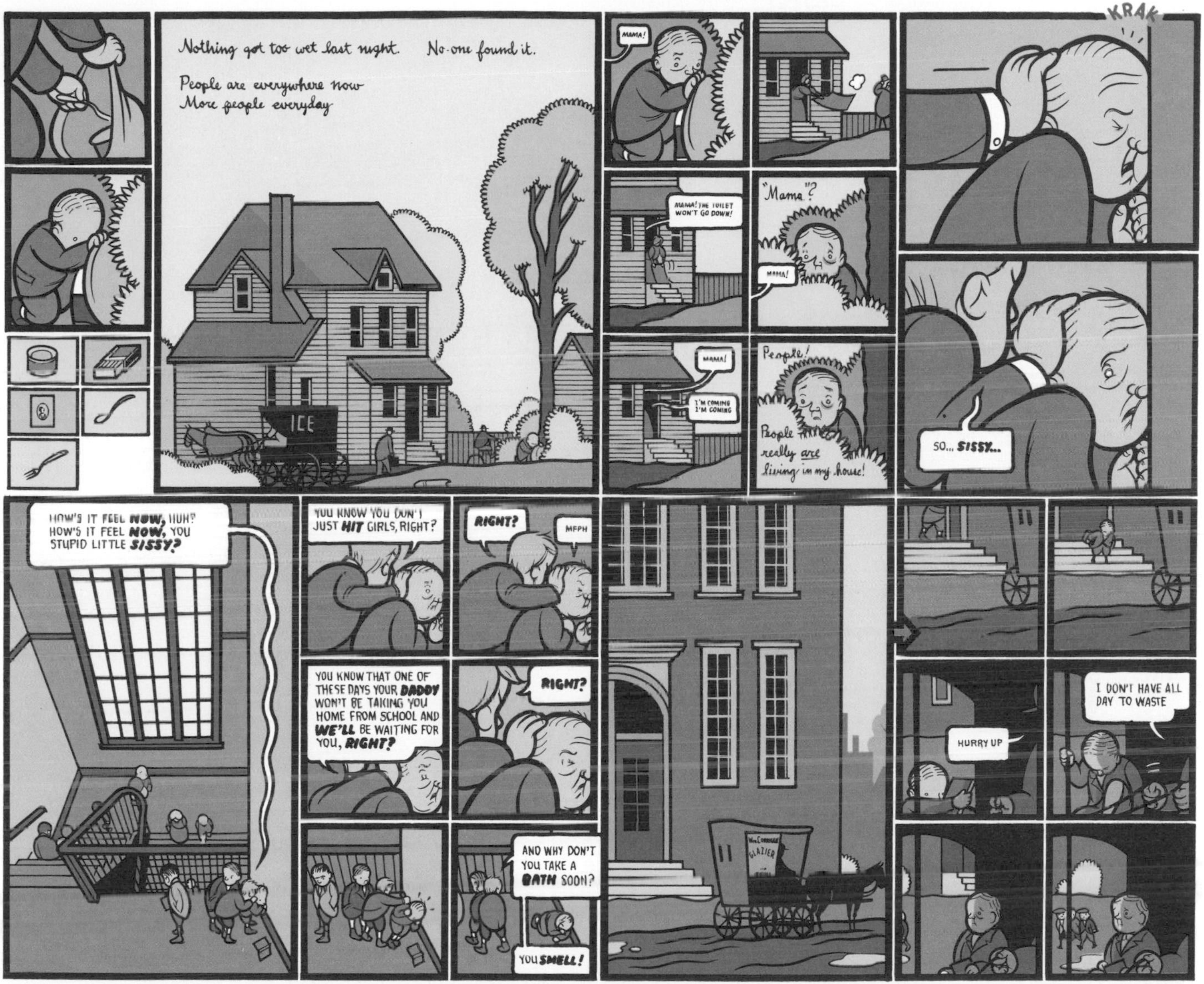
Nothing got too wet last night. No-one found it.
People are everywhere now
More people everyday
ICE
MAMA!
MAMA! THE TOILET WON'T GO DOWN!
MAMA!
I'M COMING I'M COMING
"Mama"?
MAMA!
People!
People really are living in my house!
KRAK
SO... SISSY...
HOW'S IT FEEL NOW, HUH? HOW'S IT FEEL NOW, YOU STUPID LITTLE SISSY?
YOU KNOW YOU DON'T JUST HIT GIRLS, RIGHT?
RIGHT?
MFPH
YOU KNOW THAT ONE OF THESE DAYS YOUR DADDY WON'T BE TAKING YOU HOME FROM SCHOOL AND WE'LL BE WAITING FOR YOU, RIGHT?
RIGHT?
AND WHY DON'T YOU TAKE A BATH SOON?
YOU SMELL!
GLAZIER
HURRY UP
I DON'T HAVE ALL DAY TO WASTE

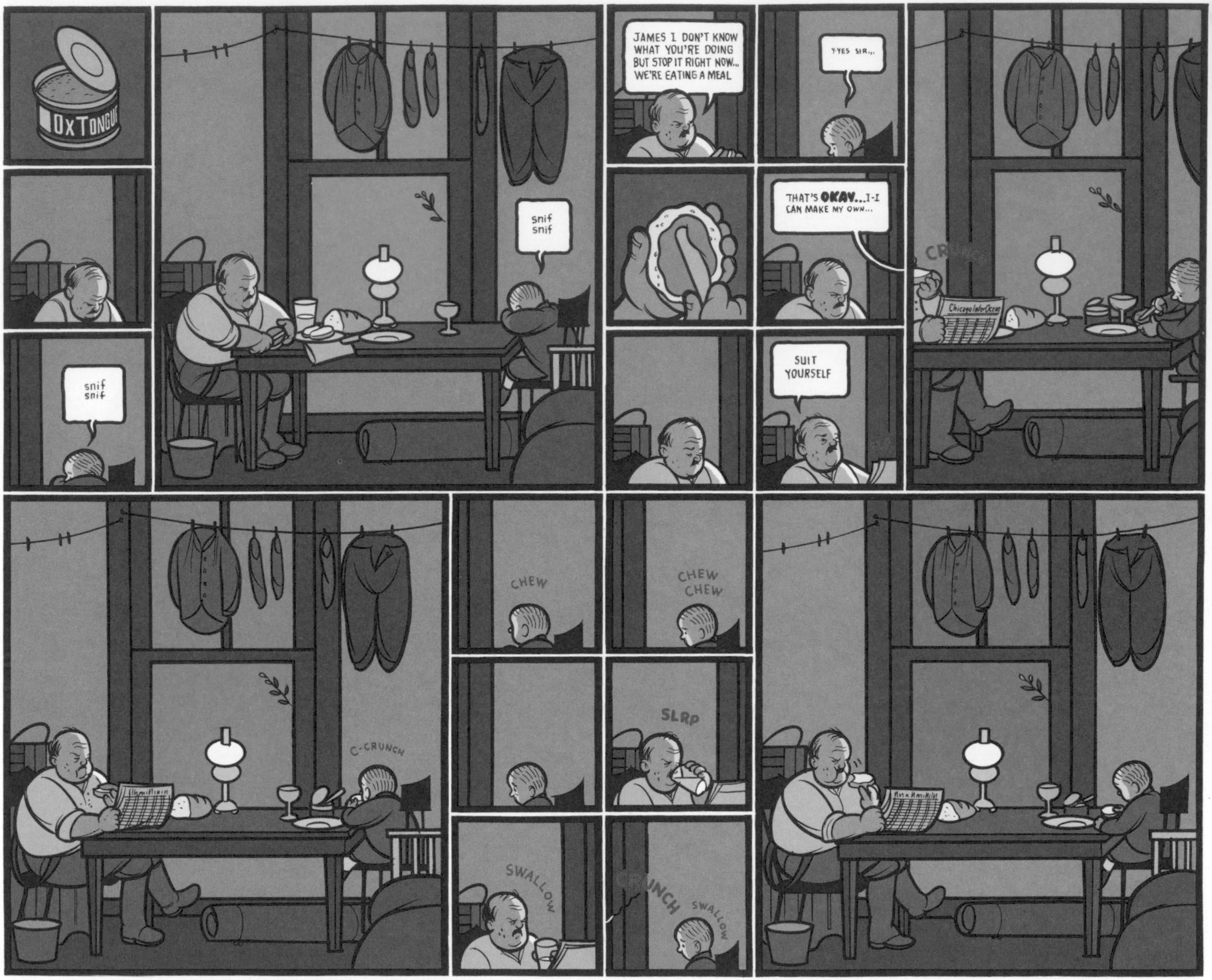

OxTongu
snif snif
snif snif
JAMES I DON'T KNOW WHAT YOU'RE DOING BUT STOP IT RIGHT NOW... WE'RE EATING A MEAL
Y-YES SIR...
THAT'S **OKAY**...I-I CAN MAKE MY OWN...
SUIT YOURSELF
CRUNCH
Chicago Inter Ocean
C-CRUNCH
CHEW
CHEW CHEW
SLRP
SWALLOW
CRUNCH
SWALLOW

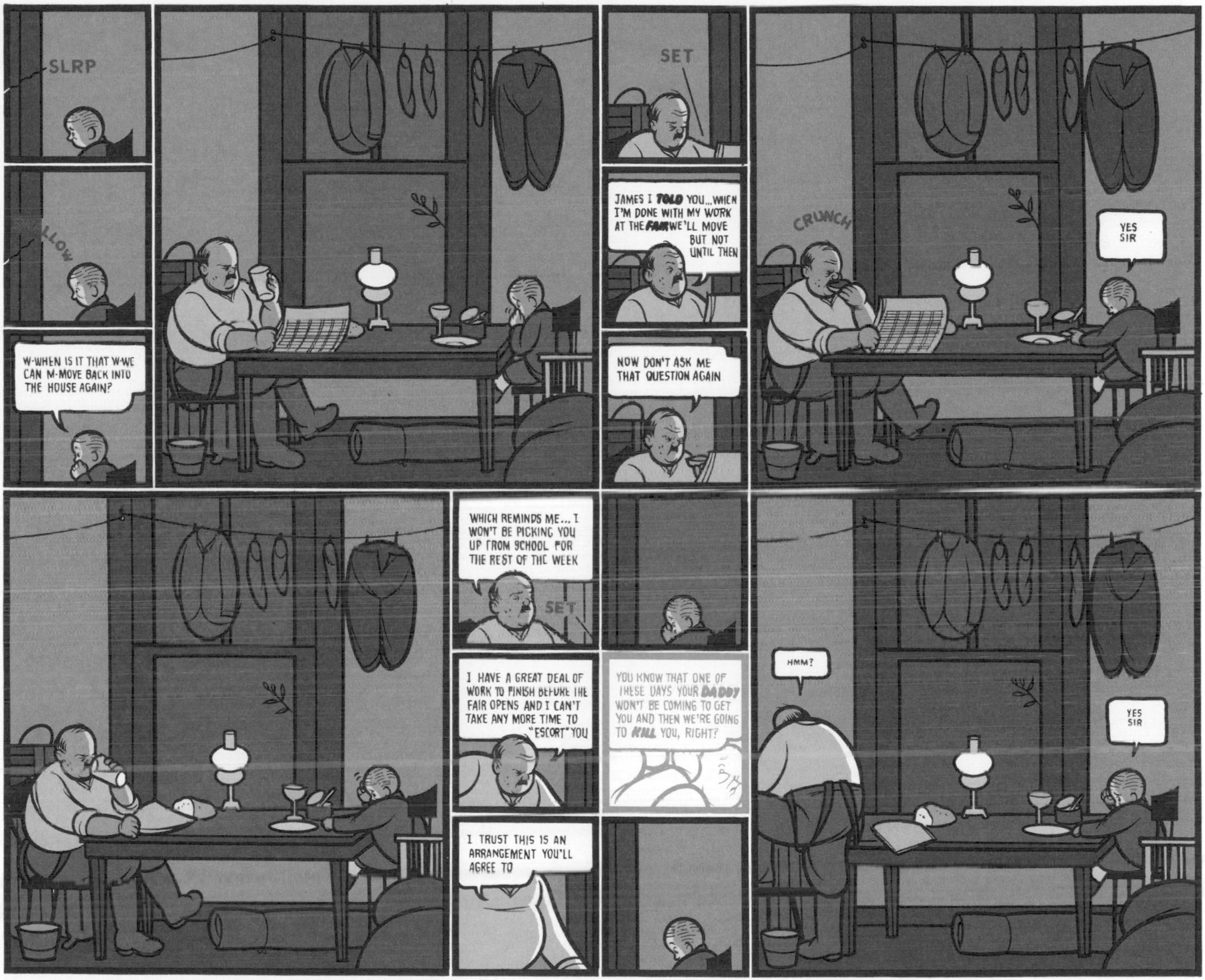
SLRP
LLOW
W-WHEN IS IT THAT W-WE CAN M-MOVE BACK INTO THE HOUSE AGAIN?
SET
JAMES I TOLD YOU... WHEN I'M DONE WITH MY WORK AT THE FAIR WE'LL MOVE BUT NOT UNTIL THEN
NOW DON'T ASK ME THAT QUESTION AGAIN
CRUNCH
YES SIR
WHICH REMINDS ME... I WON'T BE PICKING YOU UP FROM SCHOOL FOR THE REST OF THE WEEK
SET
I HAVE A GREAT DEAL OF WORK TO FINISH BEFORE THE FAIR OPENS AND I CAN'T TAKE ANY MORE TIME TO "ESCORT" YOU
YOU KNOW THAT ONE OF THESE DAYS YOUR DADDY WON'T BE COMING TO GET YOU AND THEN WE'RE GOING TO KILL YOU, RIGHT?
I TRUST THIS IS AN ARRANGEMENT YOU'LL AGREE TO
HMM?
YES SIR

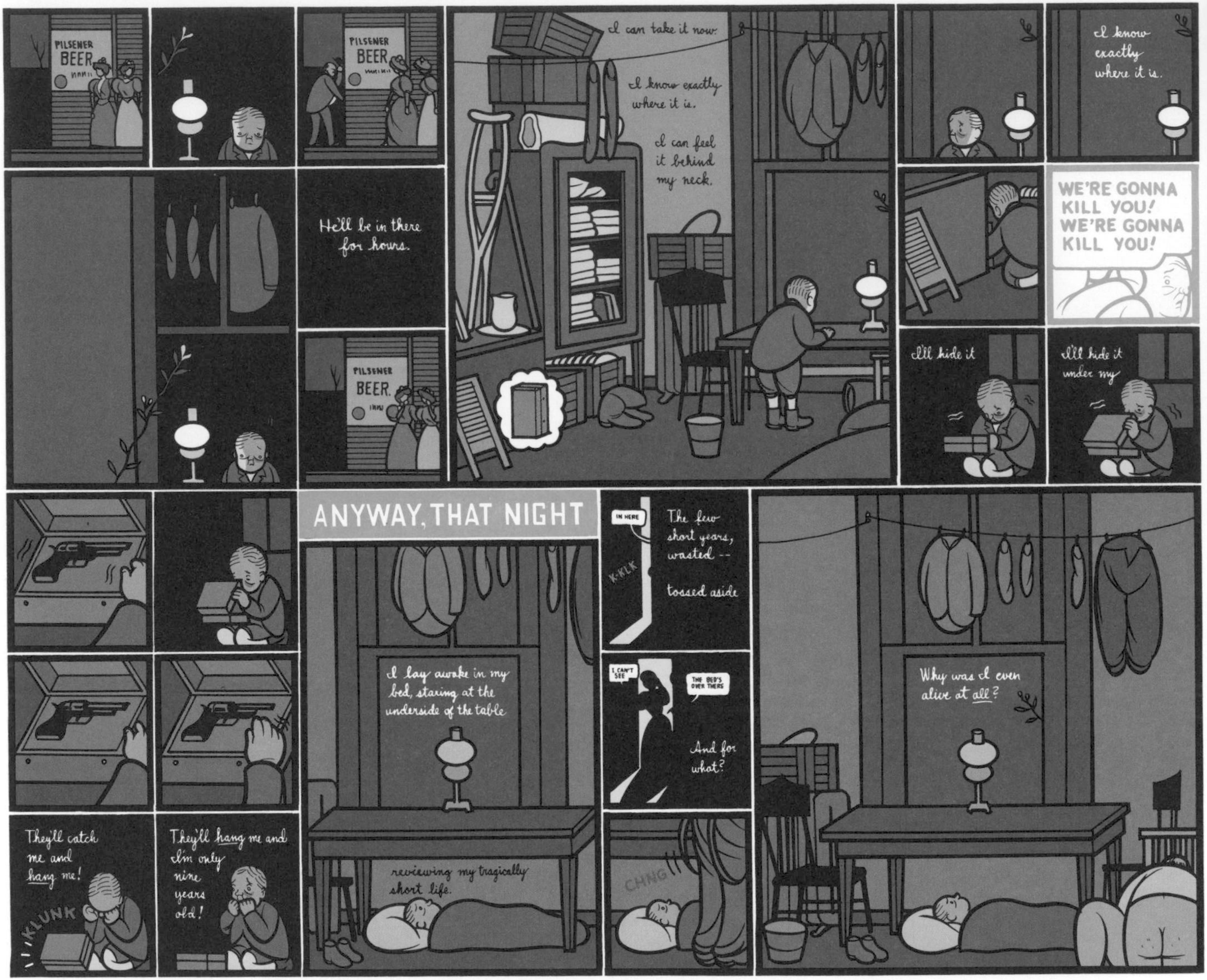

PILSENER BEER
PILSENER BEER
I can take it now.
I know exactly where it is.
I can feel it behind my neck.
I know exactly where it is.
He'll be in there for hours.
PILSENER BEER
WE'RE GONNA KILL YOU! WE'RE GONNA KILL YOU!
I'll hide it
I'll hide it under my
They'll catch me and hang me!
KLUNK
They'll hang me and I'm only nine years old!
ANYWAY, THAT NIGHT
I lay awake in my bed, staring at the underside of the table
reviewing my tragically short life.
IN HERE
K-KLK
The few short years, wasted --
tossed aside
I CAN'T SEE
THE BED'S OVER THERE
And for what?
CHNG
Why was I even alive at all?

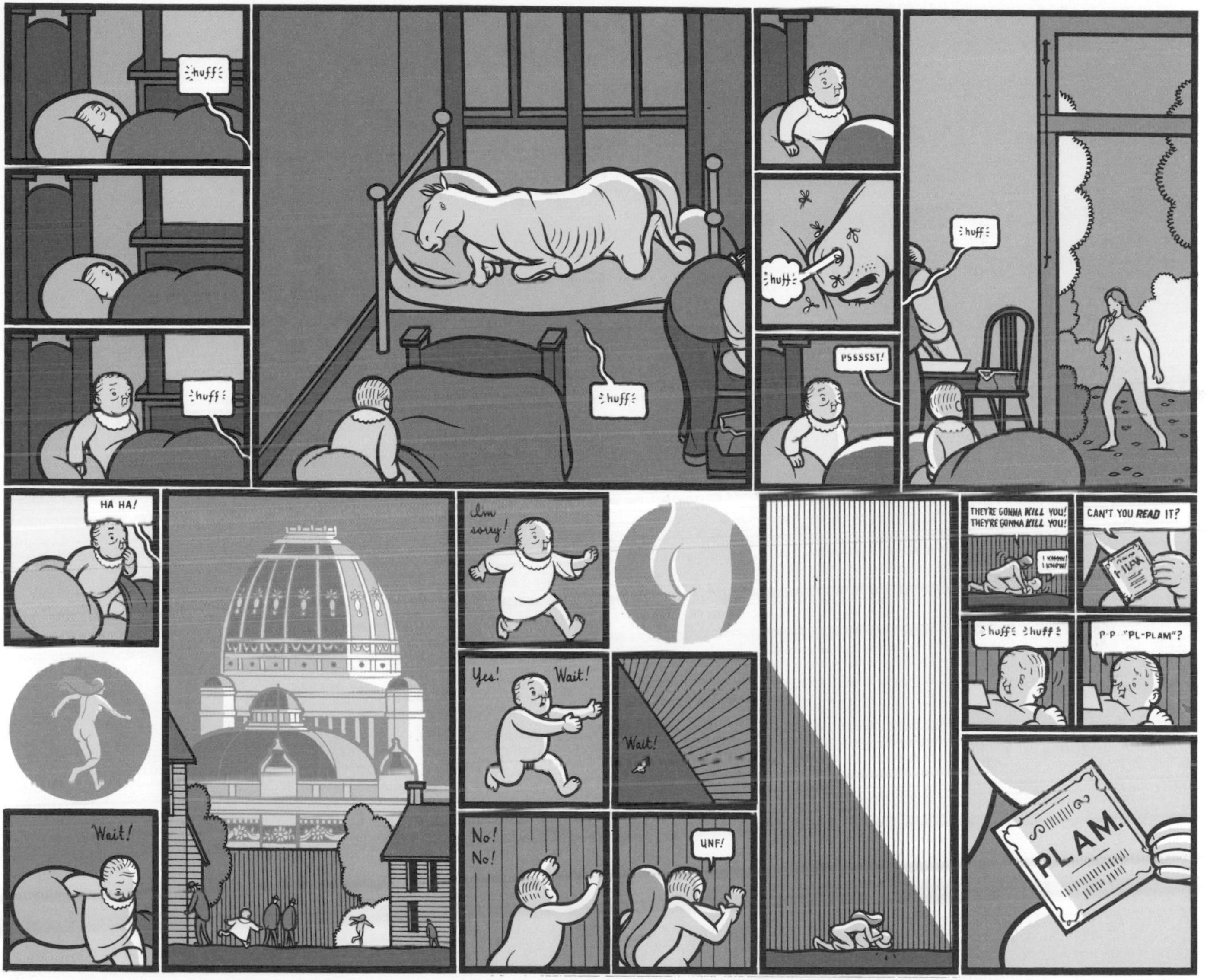
huff
huff
huff
huff
huff
PSSSSST!
huff
HA HA!
I'm sorry!
Yes! Wait!
Wait!
Wait!
No! No!
UNF!
THEY'RE GONNA **KILL** YOU! THEY'RE GONNA **KILL** YOU!
I KNOW! I KNOW!
CAN'T YOU **READ** IT?
huff huff
P-P... "PL-PLAM"?
PLAM.

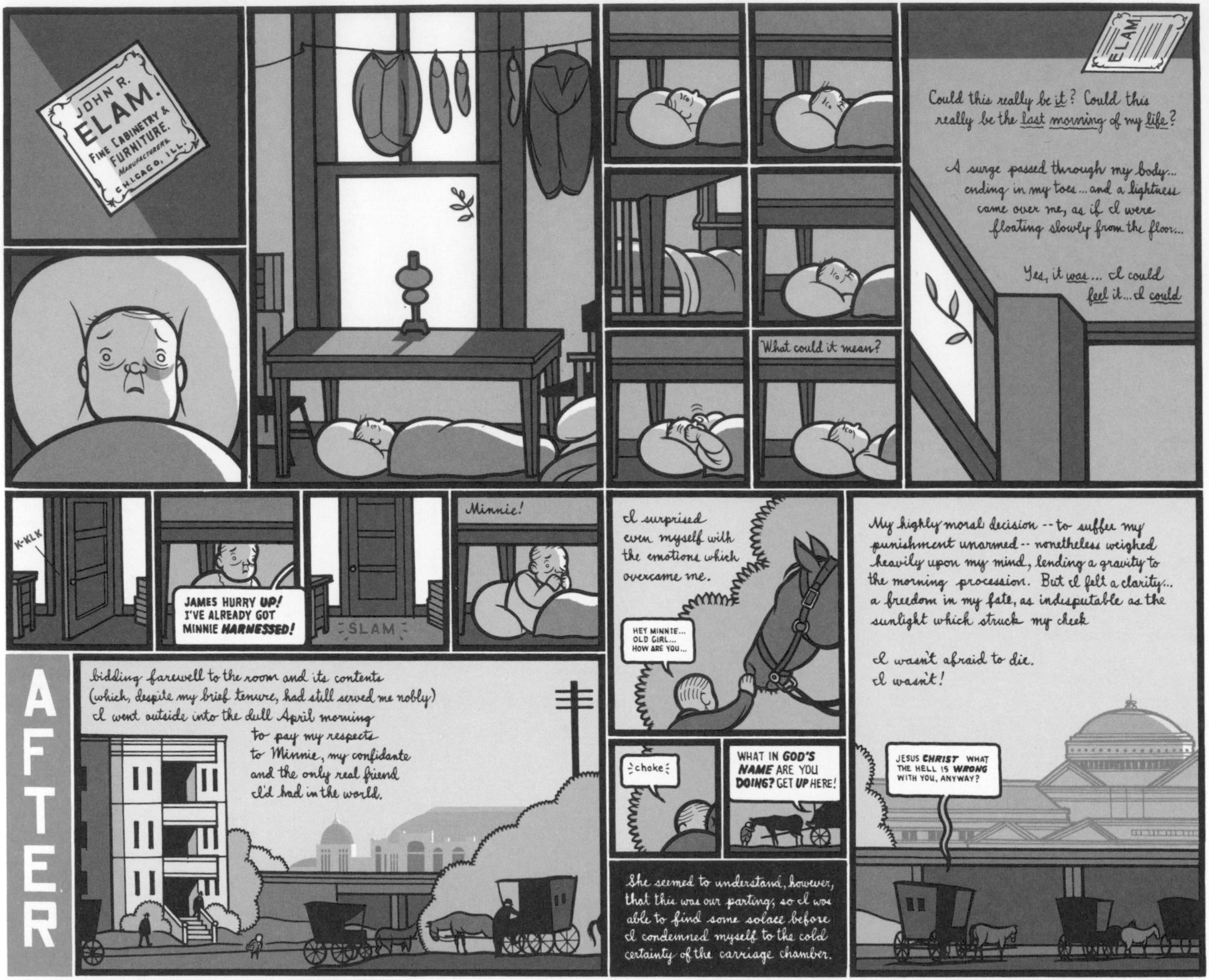
JOHN R. ELAM. FINE CABINETRY & FURNITURE. MANUFACTURERS. CHICAGO, ILL.
What could it mean?
ELAM
Could this really be it? Could this really be the last morning of my life?
A surge passed through my body... ending in my toes... and a lightness came over me, as if I were floating slowly from the floor...
Yes, it was... I could feel it... I could
K-KLK
JAMES HURRY UP! I'VE ALREADY GOT MINNIE HARNESSED!
SLAM
Minnie!
I surprised even myself with the emotions which overcame me.
HEY MINNIE... OLD GIRL... HOW ARE YOU...
My highly moral decision -- to suffer my punishment unarmed -- nonetheless weighed heavily upon my mind, lending a gravity to the morning procession. But I felt a clarity... a freedom in my fate, as indisputable as the sunlight which struck my cheek
I wasn't afraid to die.
I wasn't!
AFTER
bidding farewell to the room and its contents (which, despite my brief tenure, had still served me nobly) I went outside into the dull April morning to pay my respects to Minnie, my confidante and the only real friend I'd had in the world.
choke
WHAT IN GOD'S NAME ARE YOU DOING? GET UP HERE!
She seemed to understand, however, that this was our parting, so I was able to find some solace before I condemned myself to the cold certainty of the carriage chamber.
JESUS CHRIST WHAT THE HELL IS WRONG WITH YOU, ANYWAY?

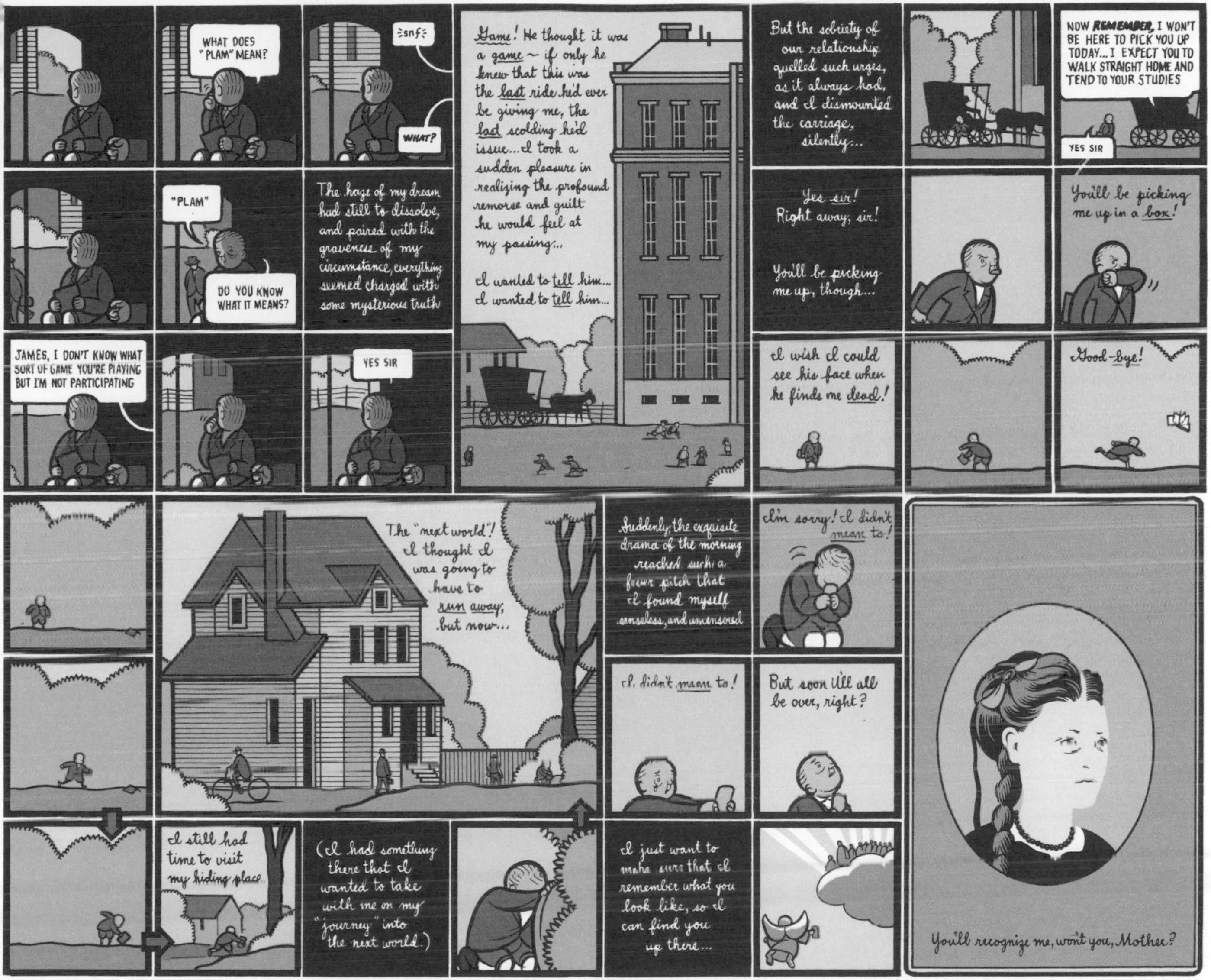
WHAT DOES "PLAM" MEAN?
snf
WHAT?
"PLAM"
DO YOU KNOW WHAT IT MEANS?
The haze of my dream had still to dissolve, and paired with the graveness of my circumstance, everything seemed charged with some mysterious truth
JAMES, I DON'T KNOW WHAT SORT OF GAME YOU'RE PLAYING BUT I'M NOT PARTICIPATING
YES SIR
Game! He thought it was a game ~ if only he knew that this was the last ride he'd ever be giving me, the last scolding he'd issue... I took a sudden pleasure in realizing the profound remorse and guilt he would feel at my passing...
I wanted to tell him... I wanted to tell him...
But the sobriety of our relationship quelled such urges, as it always had, and I dismounted the carriage, silently...
NOW REMEMBER, I WON'T BE HERE TO PICK YOU UP TODAY... I EXPECT YOU TO WALK STRAIGHT HOME AND TEND TO YOUR STUDIES
YES SIR
Yes sir! Right away, sir!
You'll be picking me up, though...
You'll be picking me up in a box!
I wish I could see his face when he finds me dead!
Good-bye!
The "next world"! I thought I was going to have to run away, but now...
Suddenly, the exquisite drama of the morning reached such a fever pitch that I found myself senseless, and uncensored
I'm sorry! I didn't mean to!
I didn't mean to!
But soon it'll all be over, right?
I still had time to visit my hiding place
(I had something there that I wanted to take with me on my "journey" into the next world.)
I just want to make sure that I remember what you look like, so I can find you up there...
You'll recognize me, won't you, Mother?

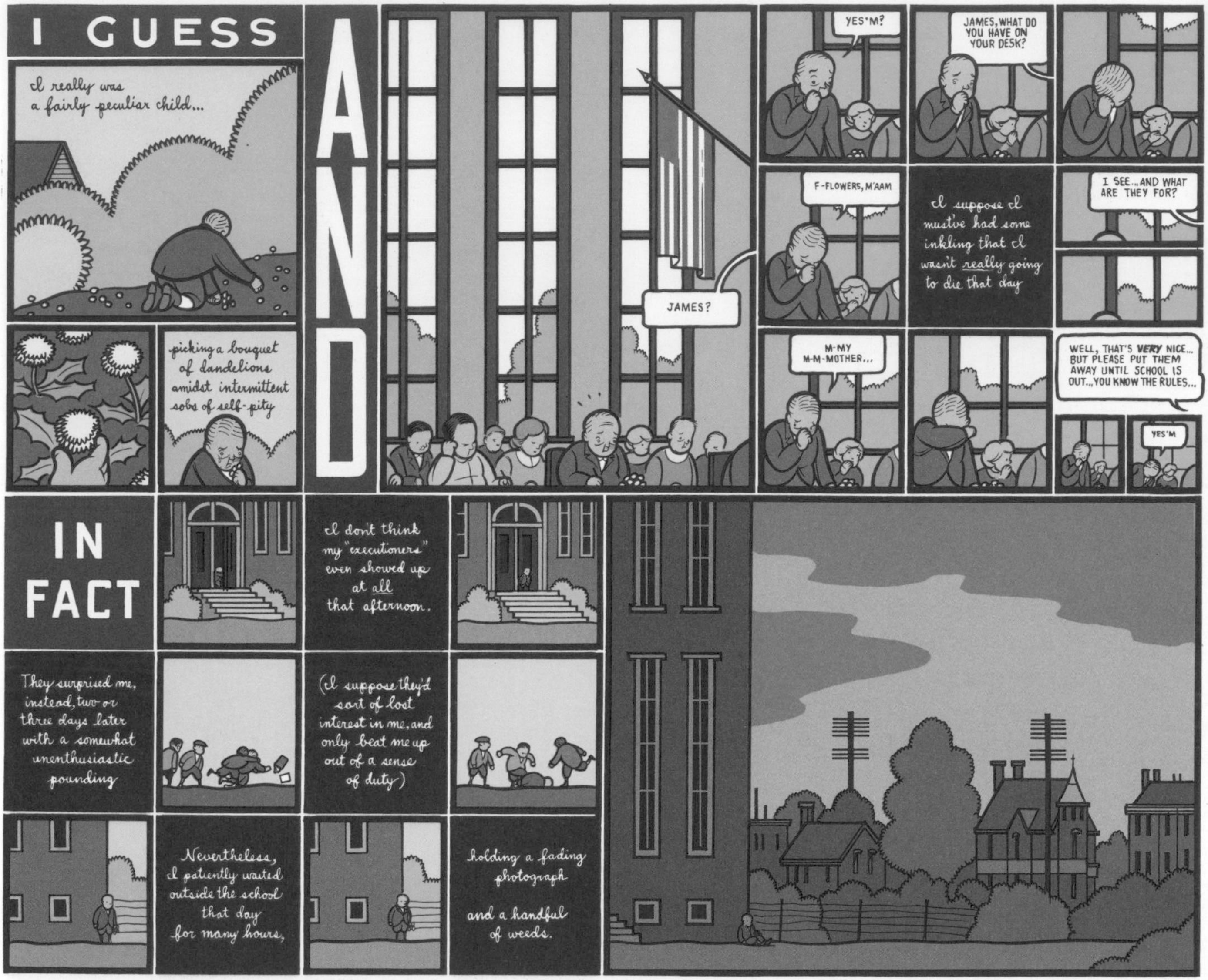
I GUESS
I really was a fairly peculiar child...
picking a bouquet of dandelions amidst intermittent sobs of self-pity
AND
JAMES?
YES'M?
JAMES, WHAT DO YOU HAVE ON YOUR DESK?
F-FLOWERS, M'AAM
I suppose I must've had some inkling that I wasn't really going to die that day
I SEE... AND WHAT ARE THEY FOR?
M-MY M-M-MOTHER...
WELL, THAT'S VERY NICE... BUT PLEASE PUT THEM AWAY UNTIL SCHOOL IS OUT... YOU KNOW THE RULES...
YES'M
IN FACT
I don't think my "executioners" even showed up at all that afternoon.
They surprised me, instead, two or three days later with a somewhat unenthusiastic pounding
(I suppose they'd sort of lost interest in me, and only beat me up out of a sense of duty)
Nevertheless, I patiently waited outside the school that day for many hours,
holding a fading photograph
and a handful of weeds.

That evening I returned home much later than I should have and I unlocked the door trepidaciously, anticipating punishment

But I was greeted by nothing more than an unoccupied room.

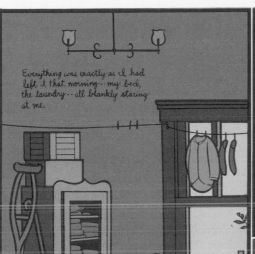

Everything was exactly as I had left it that morning -- my bed, the laundry -- all blankly staring at me.

I waited to feel some sense of relief at my good fortune; but none came.

Instead, I set about immediately arranging the room to appear as if I'd been "home" for hours

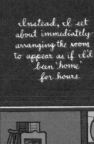

SHORTLY,

...however, I began to notice something odd...things... weren't as I'd left them that morning

Where, for instance

—were the crates of china, under the cabinet?

or the box of cutlery, atop the radiator?

On the gun case?

Oh no! Could we have been burglarized?

I must've left the door unlocked that morning... in my ridiculous state I could've done anything!

Stupid! Stupid! Stupid!

Sticking my head out into the hall, I expected to see some evidence of foul play, like footprints, or broken glass, but I found nothing.

How could it be possible?

How could such a terrible day have ended even more terribly? He'll kill me!

So I sat down (after locking the door) and chewed my fingers, awaiting my father's arrival, and cursing myself.

SO

When he did finally appear, I confessed myself to him in full, tearful detail. But, much to my surprise, he took little interest in my tale, dismissing me with a grunt.

Needless to say, I went to bed confused.

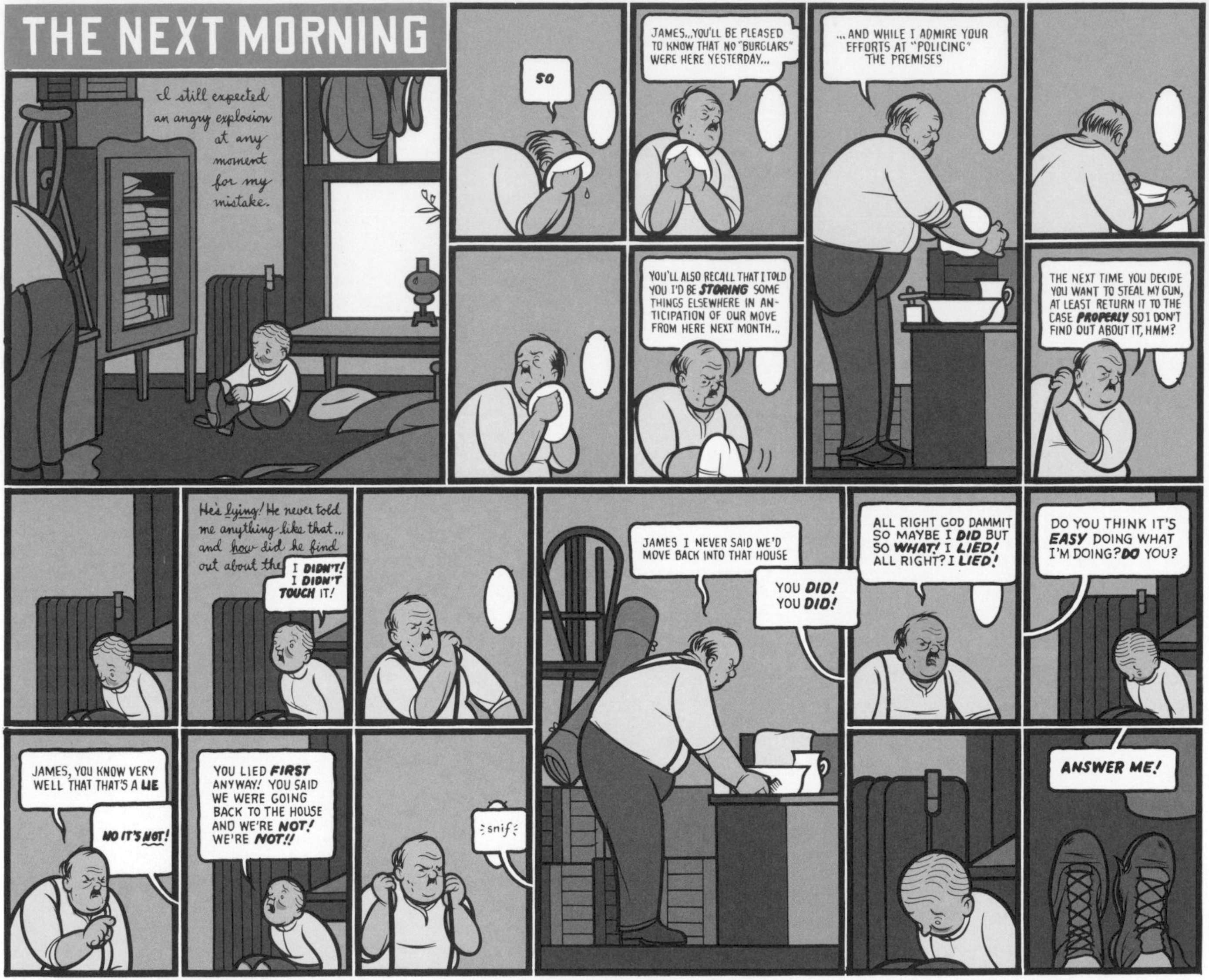
THE NEXT MORNING
I still expected an angry explosion at any moment for my mistake.
SO
JAMES... YOU'LL BE PLEASED TO KNOW THAT NO "BURGLARS" WERE HERE YESTERDAY...
YOU'LL ALSO RECALL THAT I TOLD YOU I'D BE STORING SOME THINGS ELSEWHERE IN ANTICIPATION OF OUR MOVE FROM HERE NEXT MONTH...
... AND WHILE I ADMIRE YOUR EFFORTS AT "POLICING" THE PREMISES
THE NEXT TIME YOU DECIDE YOU WANT TO STEAL MY GUN, AT LEAST RETURN IT TO THE CASE PROPERLY SO I DON'T FIND OUT ABOUT IT, HMM?
He's lying! He never told me anything like that... and how did he find out about the
I DIDN'T! I DIDN'T TOUCH IT!
JAMES, YOU KNOW VERY WELL THAT THAT'S A LIE
NO IT'S NOT!
YOU LIED FIRST ANYWAY! YOU SAID WE WERE GOING BACK TO THE HOUSE AND WE'RE NOT! WE'RE NOT!!
snif
JAMES I NEVER SAID WE'D MOVE BACK INTO THAT HOUSE
YOU DID! YOU DID!
ALL RIGHT GOD DAMMIT SO MAYBE I DID BUT SO WHAT! I LIED! ALL RIGHT? I LIED!
DO YOU THINK IT'S EASY DOING WHAT I'M DOING? DO YOU?
ANSWER ME!

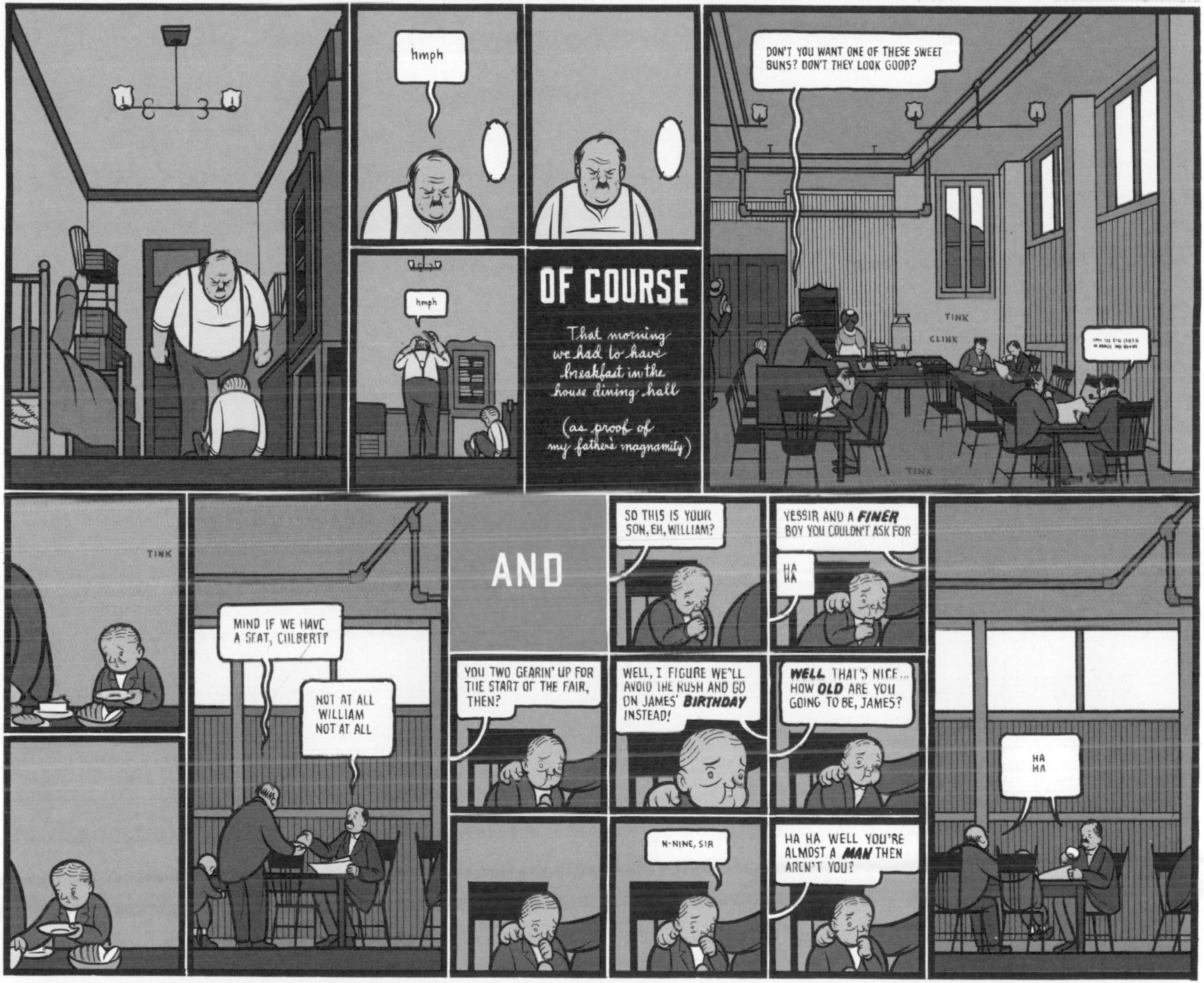

hmph
hmph
OF COURSE
That morning we had to have breakfast in the house dining hall
(as proof of my father's magnanimity)
DON'T YOU WANT ONE OF THESE SWEET BUNS? DON'T THEY LOOK GOOD?
TINK
CLINK
TINK
TINK
MIND IF WE HAVE A SEAT, CULBERT?
NOT AT ALL WILLIAM NOT AT ALL
AND
SO THIS IS YOUR SON, EH, WILLIAM?
YESSIR AND A **FINER** BOY YOU COULDN'T ASK FOR
HA HA
YOU TWO GEARIN' UP FOR THE START OF THE FAIR, THEN?
WELL, I FIGURE WE'LL AVOID THE RUSH AND GO ON JAMES' **BIRTHDAY** INSTEAD!
WELL THAT'S NICE... HOW **OLD** ARE YOU GOING TO BE, JAMES?
N-NINE, SIR
HA HA WELL YOU'RE ALMOST A **MAN** THEN AREN'T YOU?
HA HA

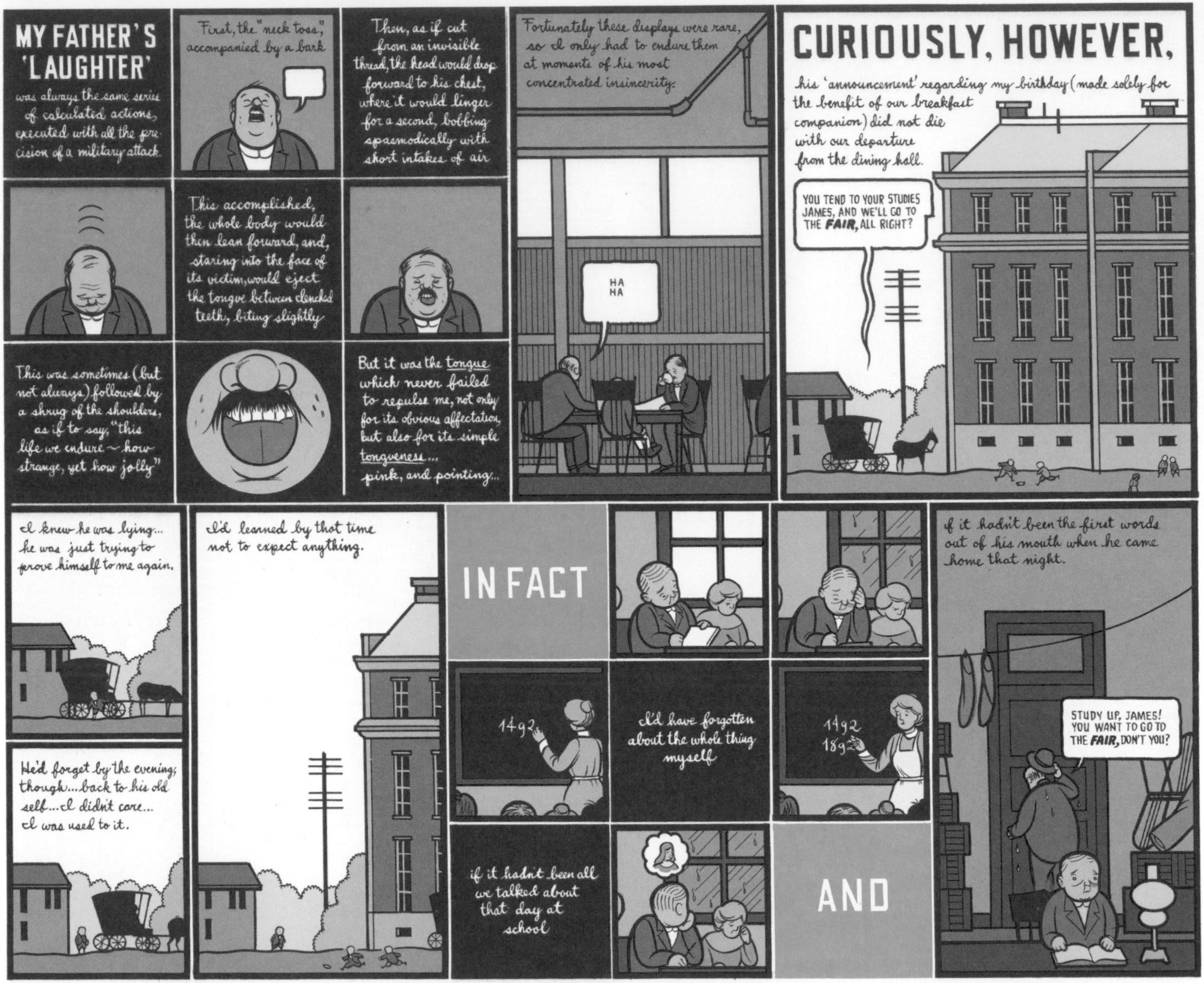
MY FATHER'S 'LAUGHTER'
was always the same series of calculated actions, executed with all the precision of a military attack.
First, the "neck toss," accompanied by a bark
Then, as if cut from an invisible thread, the head would drop forward to his chest, where it would linger for a second, bobbing spasmodically with short intakes of air
This accomplished, the whole body would then lean forward, and, staring into the face of its victim, would eject the tongue between clenched teeth, biting slightly
This was sometimes (but not always) followed by a shrug of the shoulders, as if to say, "this life we endure ~ how strange, yet how jolly"
But it was the tongue which never failed to repulse me, not only for its obvious affectation, but also for its simple tongueness... pink, and pointing...
Fortunately these displays were rare, so I only had to endure them at moments of his most concentrated insincerity.
HA HA
CURIOUSLY, HOWEVER,
his 'announcement' regarding my birthday (made solely for the benefit of our breakfast companion) did not die with our departure from the dining hall.
YOU TEND TO YOUR STUDIES JAMES, AND WE'LL GO TO THE FAIR, ALL RIGHT?
I knew he was lying... he was just trying to prove himself to me again.
He'd forget by the evening, though... back to his old self... I didn't care... I was used to it.
I'd learned by that time not to expect anything.
IN FACT
1492
I'd have forgotten about the whole thing myself
1492
1892
if it hadn't been all we talked about that day at school
AND
if it hadn't been the first words out of his mouth when he came home that night.
STUDY UP, JAMES! YOU WANT TO GO TO THE FAIR, DON'T YOU?

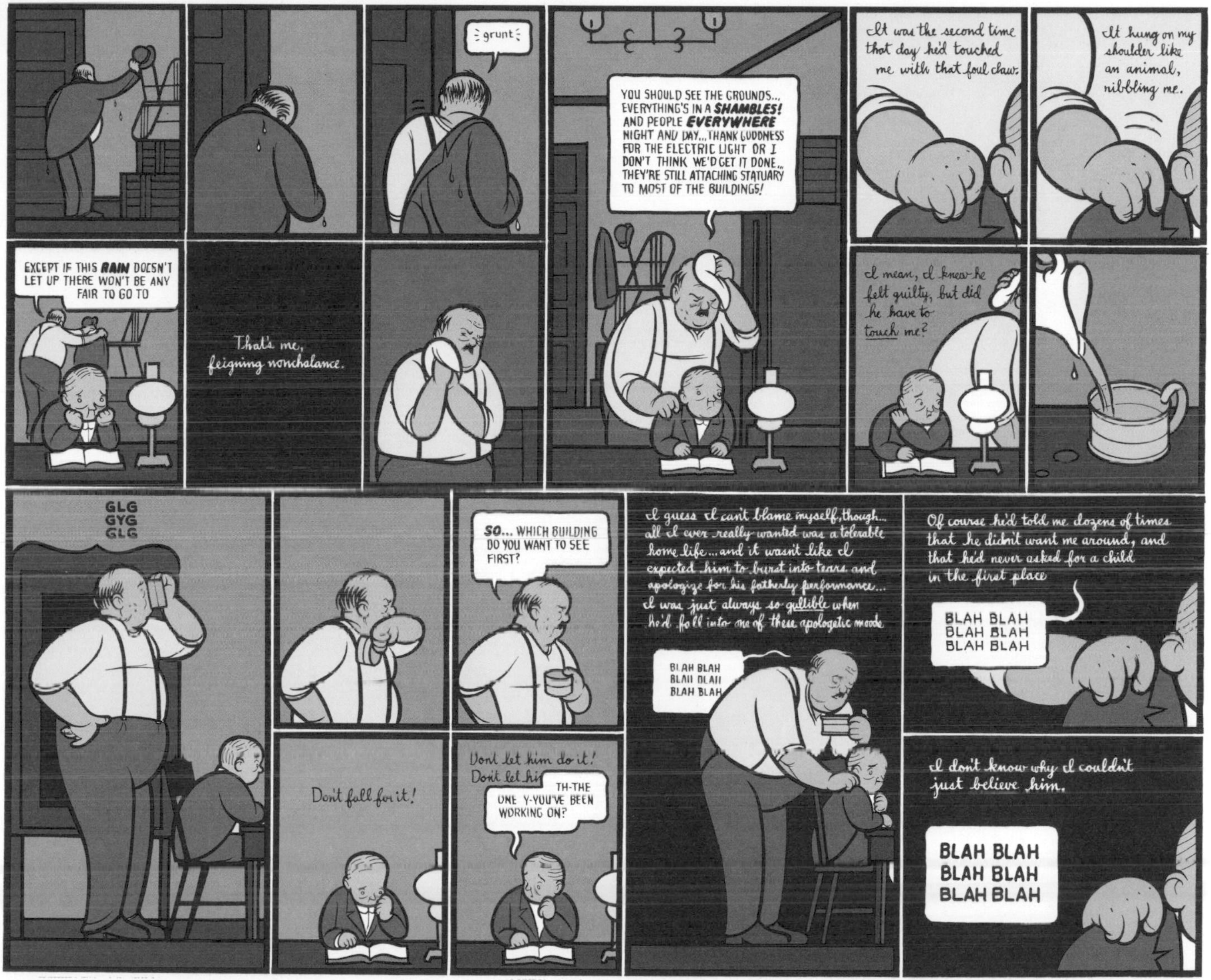
grunt
EXCEPT IF THIS RAIN DOESN'T LET UP THERE WON'T BE ANY FAIR TO GO TO
That's me, feigning nonchalance.
YOU SHOULD SEE THE GROUNDS... EVERYTHING'S IN A SHAMBLES! AND PEOPLE EVERYWHERE NIGHT AND DAY... THANK GOODNESS FOR THE ELECTRIC LIGHT OR I DON'T THINK WE'D GET IT DONE... THEY'RE STILL ATTACHING STATUARY TO MOST OF THE BUILDINGS!
It was the second time that day he'd touched me with that foul claw.
It hung on my shoulder like an animal, nibbling me.
I mean, I knew he felt guilty, but did he have to touch me?
GLG
GYG
GLG
SO... WHICH BUILDING DO YOU WANT TO SEE FIRST?
Don't fall for it!
Don't let him do it!
TH-THE ONE Y-YOU'VE BEEN WORKING ON?
I guess I can't blame myself, though... all I ever really wanted was a tolerable home life... and it wasn't like I expected him to burst into tears and apologize for his fatherly performance... I was just always so gullible when he'd fall into one of these apologetic moods
BLAH BLAH BLAH BLAH BLAH BLAH
Of course he'd told me dozens of times that he didn't want me around, and that he'd never asked for a child in the first place
BLAH BLAH BLAH BLAH BLAH BLAH
I don't know why I couldn't just believe him.
BLAH BLAH BLAH BLAH BLAH BLAH

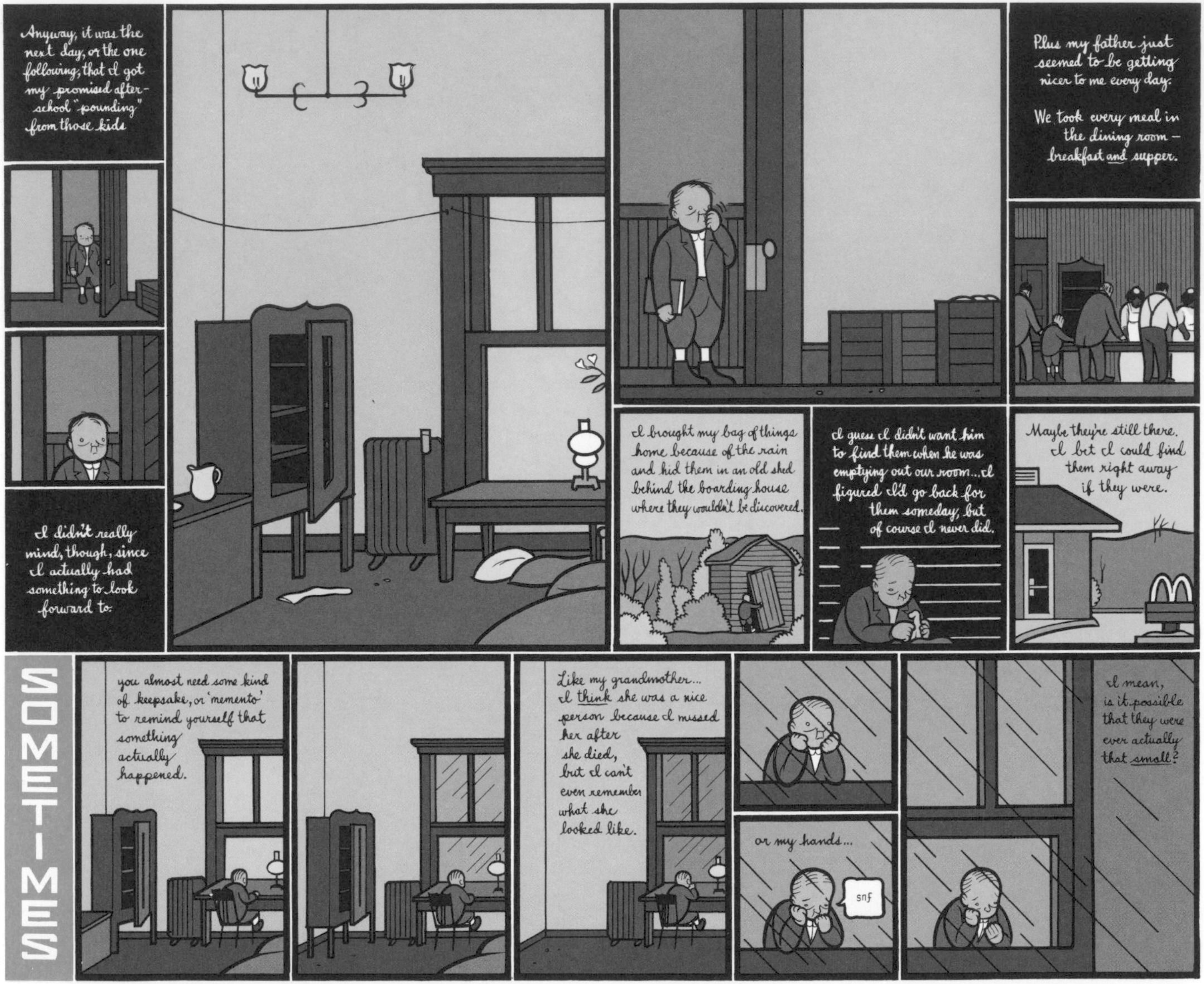
Anyway, it was the next day, or the one following, that I got my promised after-school "pounding" from those kids
I didn't really mind, though, since I actually had something to look forward to.
Plus my father just seemed to be getting nicer to me every day.
We took every meal in the dining room — breakfast and supper.
I brought my bag of things home because of the rain and hid them in an old shed behind the boarding house where they wouldn't be discovered.
I guess I didn't want him to find them when he was emptying out our room... I figured I'd go back for them someday, but of course I never did.
Maybe they're still there. I bet I could find them right away if they were.
SOMETIMES
you almost need some kind of keepsake, or 'memento' to remind yourself that something actually happened.
Like my grandmother... I think she was a nice person because I missed her after she died, but I can't even remember what she looked like.
or my hands...
snf
I mean, is it possible that they were ever actually that small?

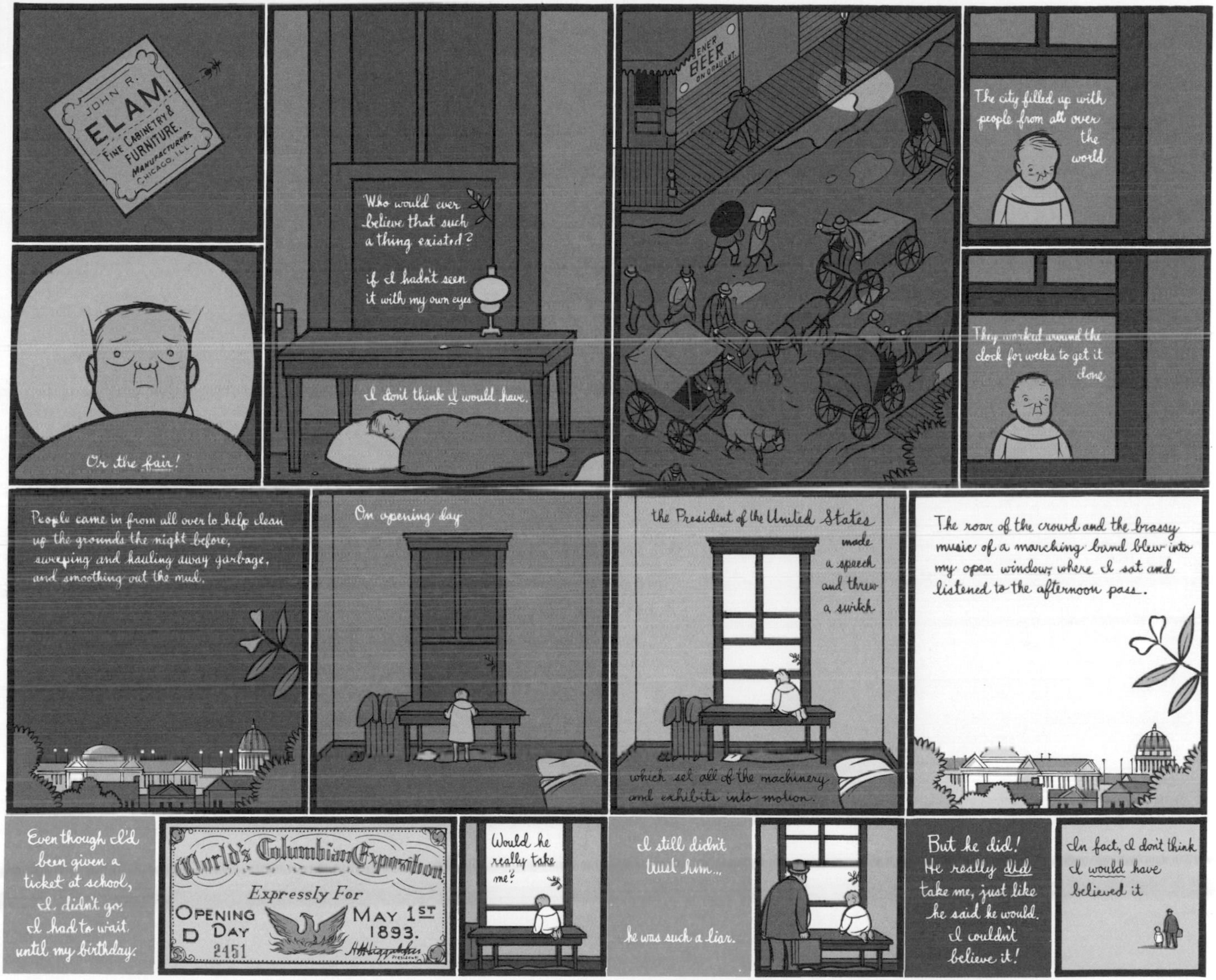
JOHN R. ELAM. FINE CABINETRY & FURNITURE. MANUFACTURERS. CHICAGO, ILL.
Who would ever believe that such a thing existed?
if I hadn't seen it with my own eyes
I don't think I would have.
BEER ON DRAUGHT
The city filled up with people from all over the world
Or the fair!
They worked around the clock for weeks to get it done
People came in from all over to help clean up the grounds the night before, sweeping and hauling away garbage, and smoothing out the mud.
On opening day
the President of the United States made a speech and threw a switch
which set all of the machinery and exhibits into motion.
The roar of the crowd and the brassy music of a marching band blew into my open window, where I sat and listened to the afternoon pass.
Even though I'd been given a ticket at school, I didn't go. I had to wait until my birthday.
World's Columbian Exposition
Expressly For
OPENING DAY
D
2451
MAY 1ST 1893.
Would he really take me?
I still didn't trust him...
he was such a liar.
But he did! He really did take me, just like he said he would. I couldn't believe it!
In fact, I don't think I would have believed it

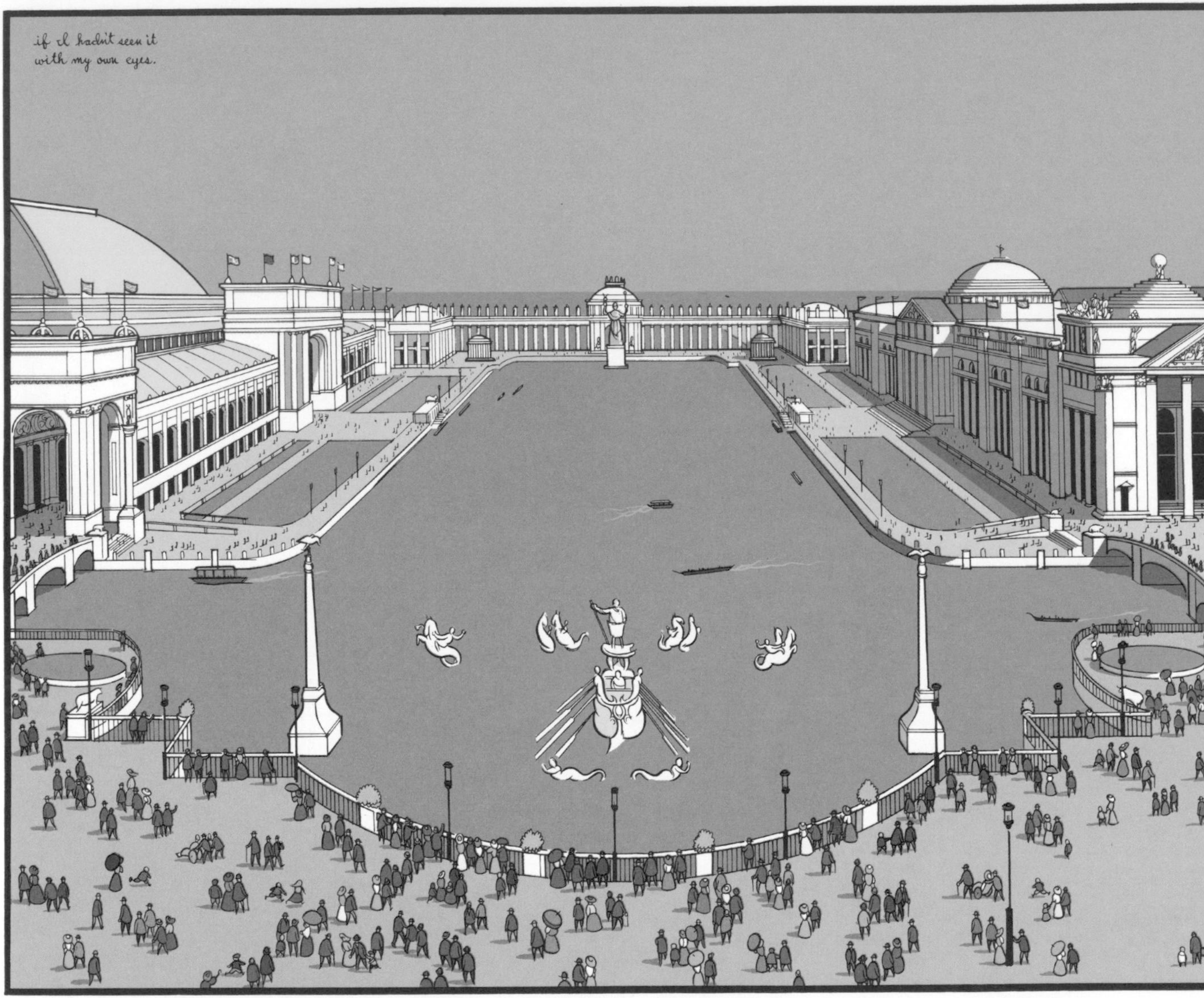
if I hadn't seen it
with my own eyes.

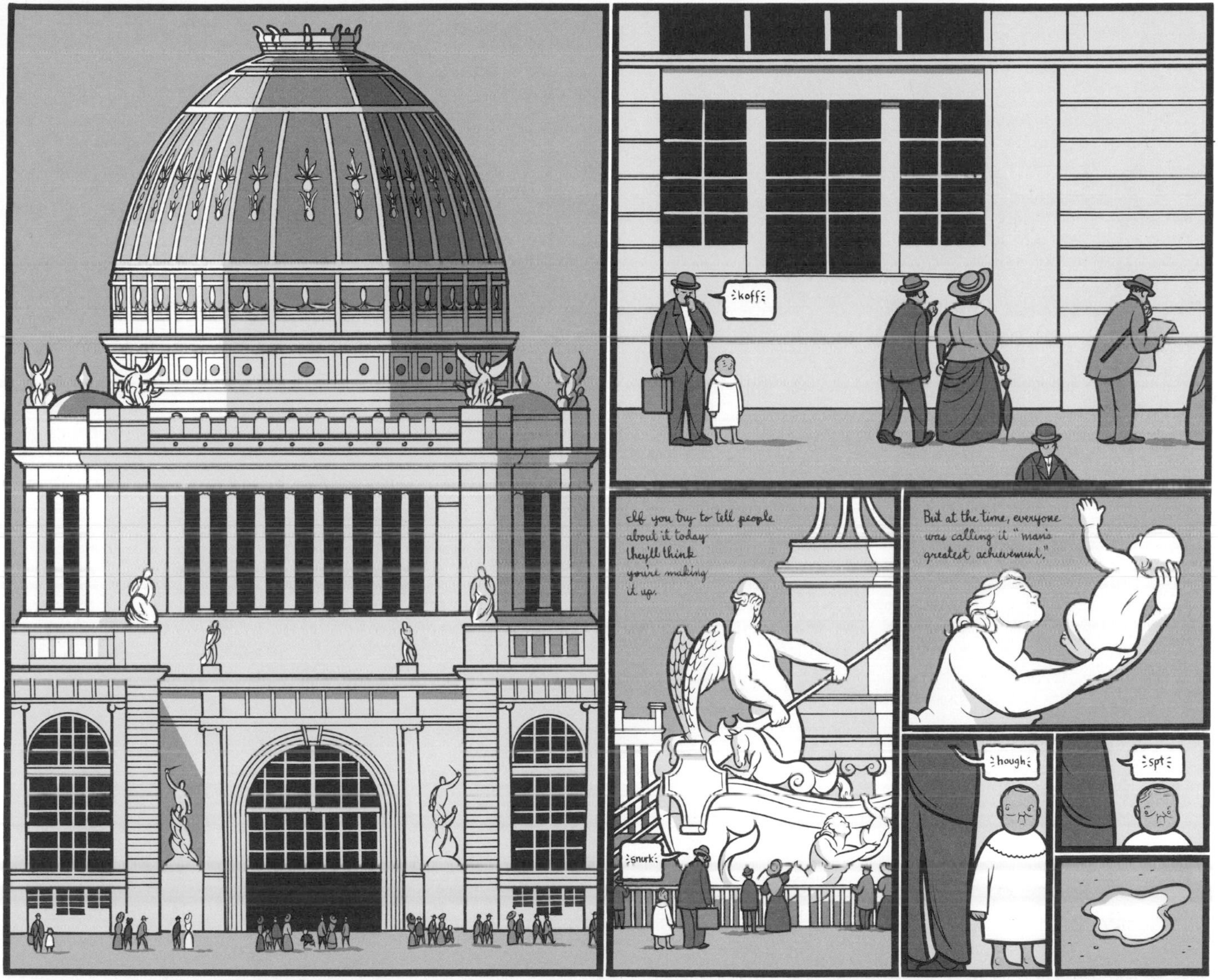
koff
If you try to tell people about it today they'll think you're making it up.
snurk
But at the time, everyone was calling it "man's greatest achievement."
hough
spt

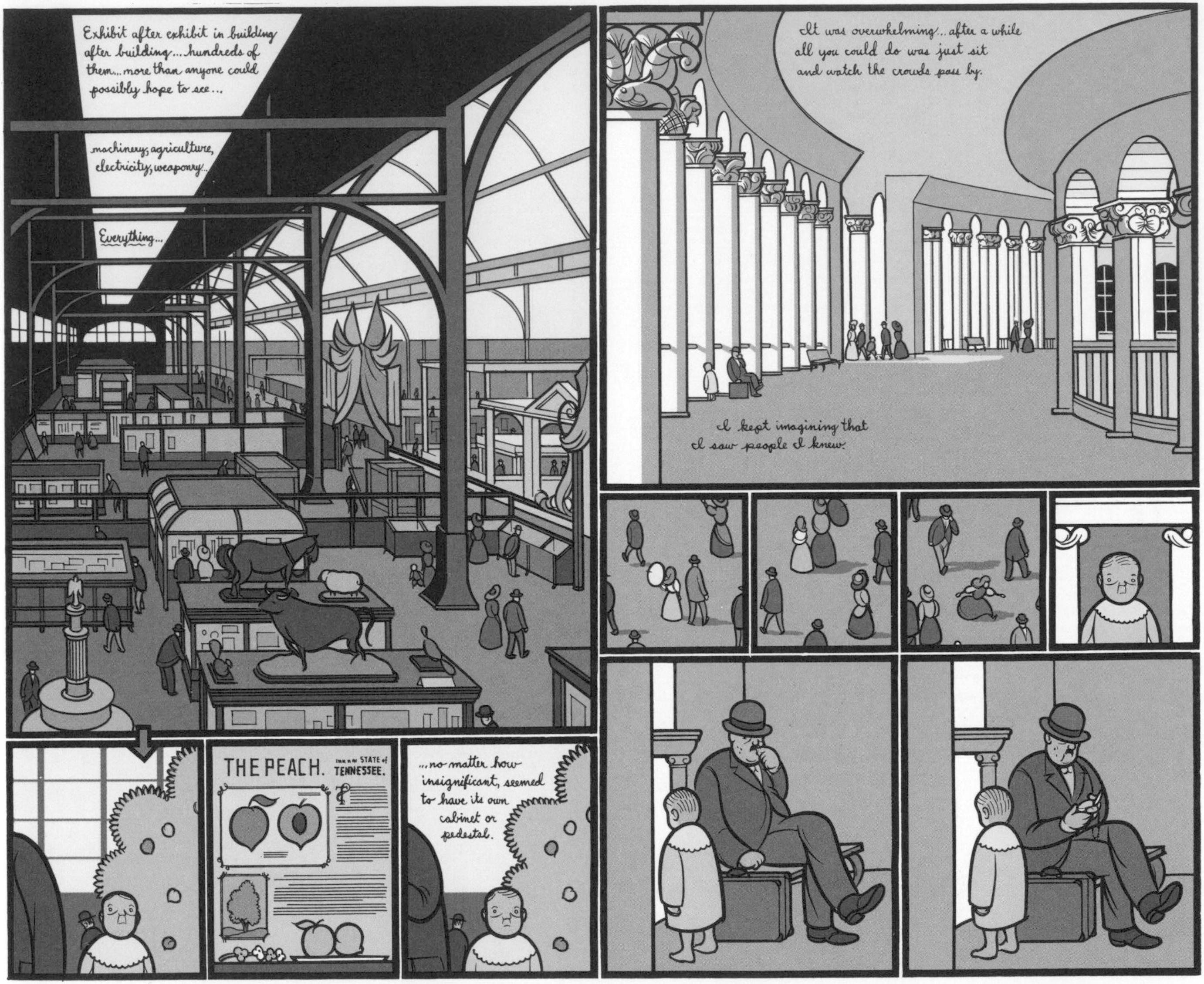
Exhibit after exhibit in building after building... hundreds of them... more than anyone could possibly hope to see...
machinery, agriculture, electricity, weaponry...
Everything...
THE PEACH. STATE of TENNESSEE.
...no matter how insignificant, seemed to have its own cabinet or pedestal.
It was overwhelming... after a while all you could do was just sit and watch the crowds pass by.
I kept imagining that I saw people I knew.

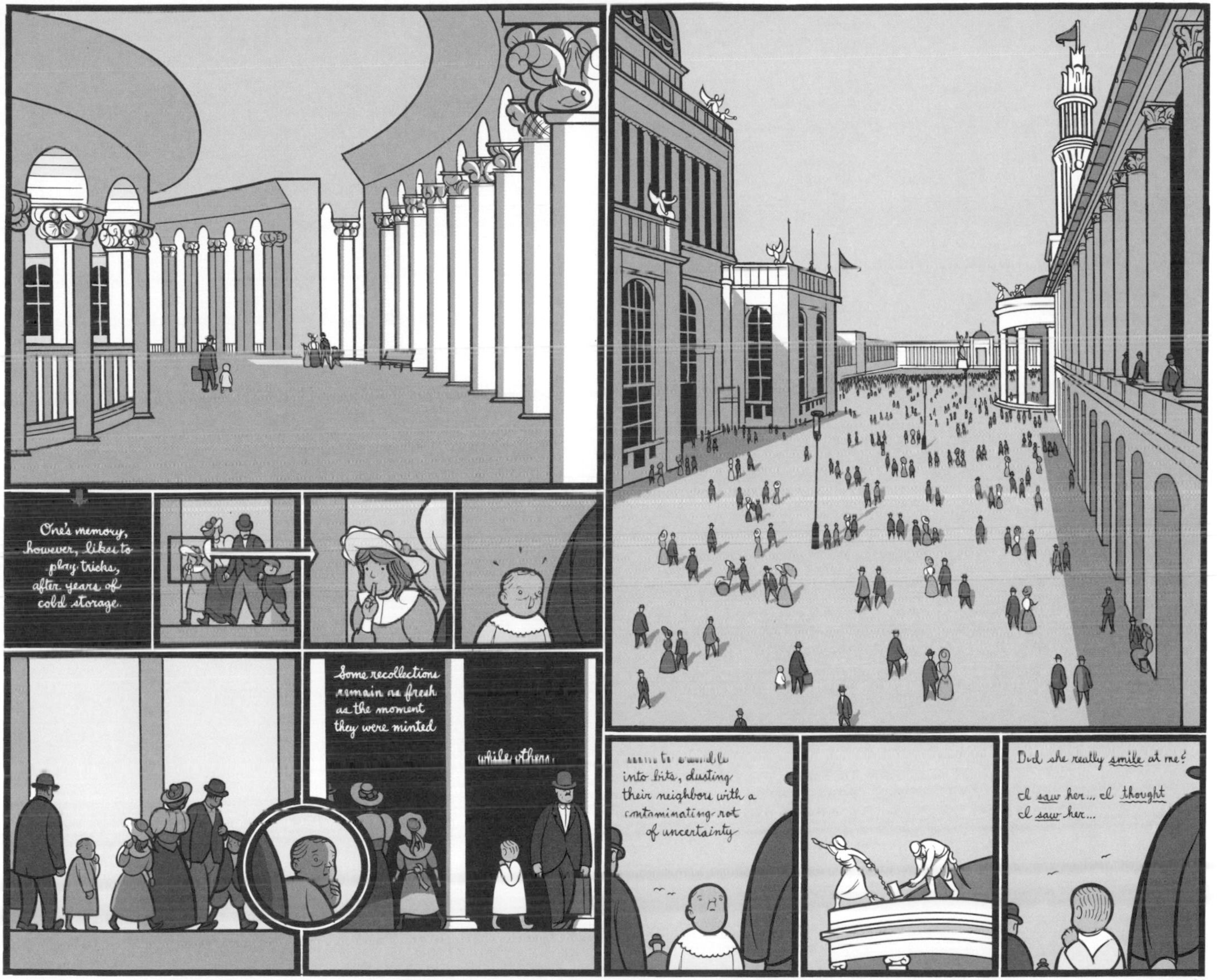

One's memory, however, likes to play tricks, after years of cold storage.
Some recollections remain as fresh as the moment they were minted
while others...
into bits, dusting their neighbors with a contaminating rot of uncertainty
Did she really smile at me?
I saw her... I thought I saw her...

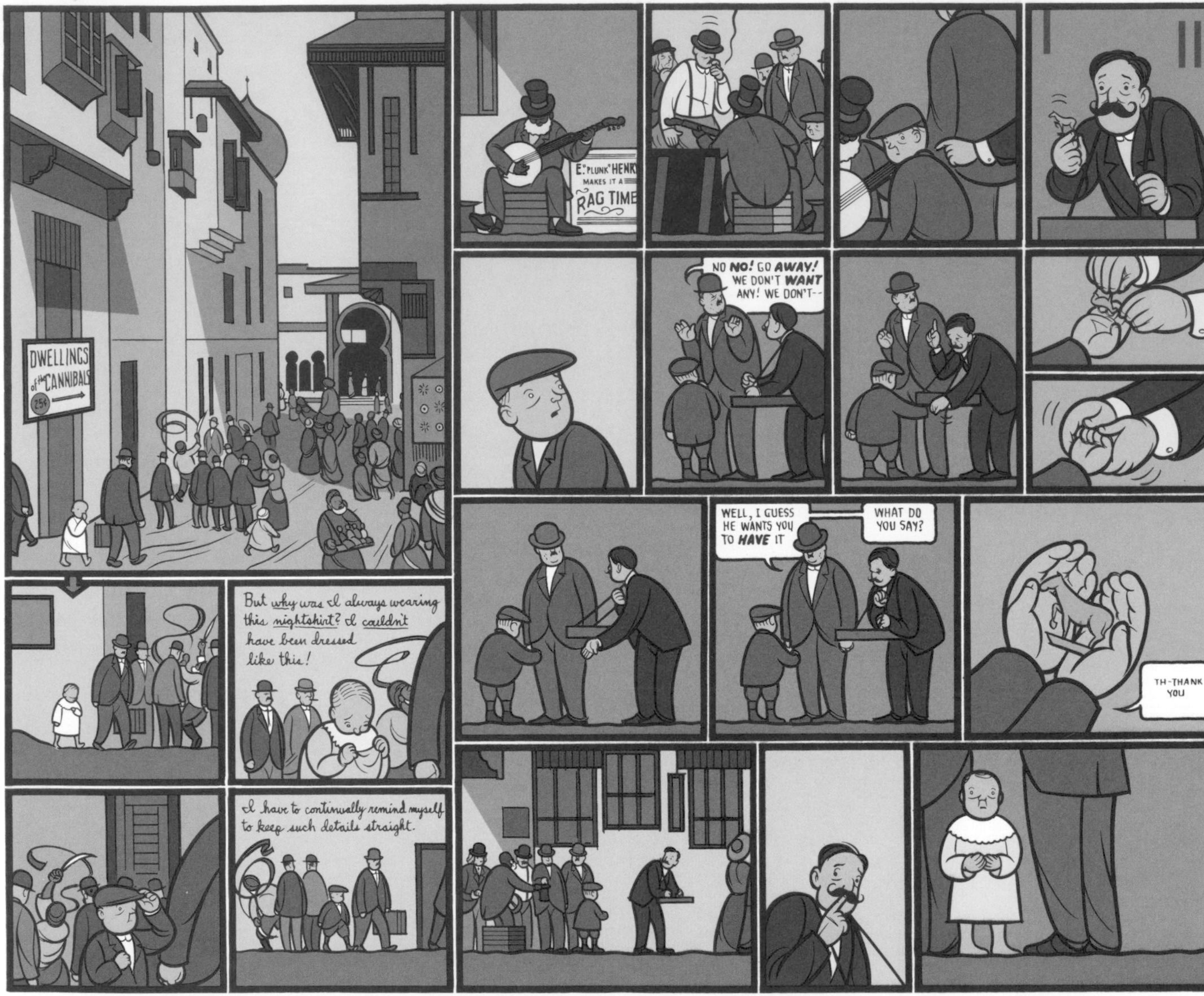
DWELLINGS of the CANNIBALS 25¢
E. "PLUNK" HENRY MAKES IT A RAG TIME
NO NO! GO AWAY! WE DON'T WANT ANY! WE DON'T--
But why was I always wearing this nightshirt? I couldn't have been dressed like this!
WELL, I GUESS HE WANTS YOU TO HAVE IT
WHAT DO YOU SAY?
TH-THANK YOU
I have to continually remind myself to keep such details straight.

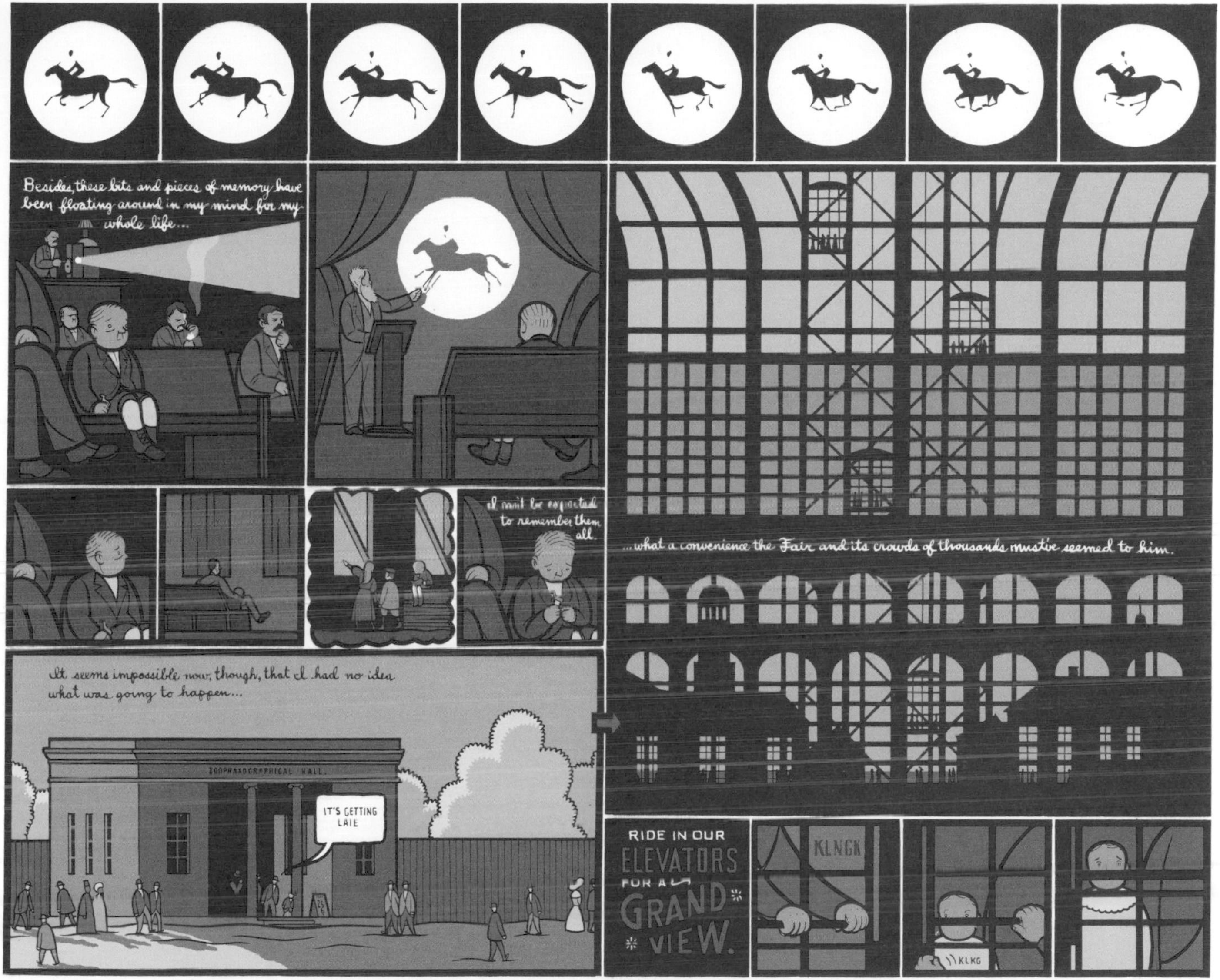
Besides, these bits and pieces of memory have been floating around in my mind for my whole life...
I can't be expected to remember them all.
It seems impossible now, though, that I had no idea what was going to happen...
ZOOPRAXOGRAPHICAL HALL.
IT'S GETTING LATE
...what a convenience the Fair and its crowds of thousands must've seemed to him.
RIDE IN OUR ELEVATORS FOR A GRAND VIEW.
KLNGK
KLKG

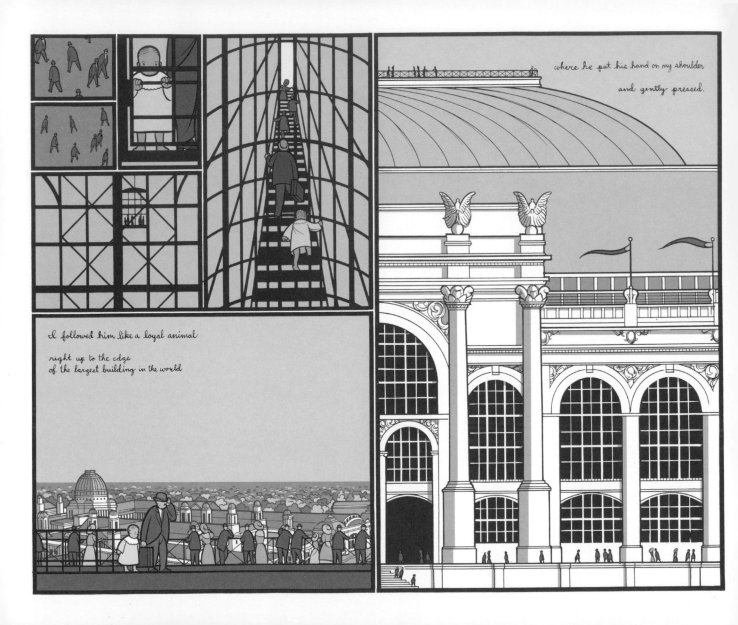

where he put his hand on my shoulder
and gently pressed.

I followed him like a loyal animal

right up to the edge
of the largest building in the world

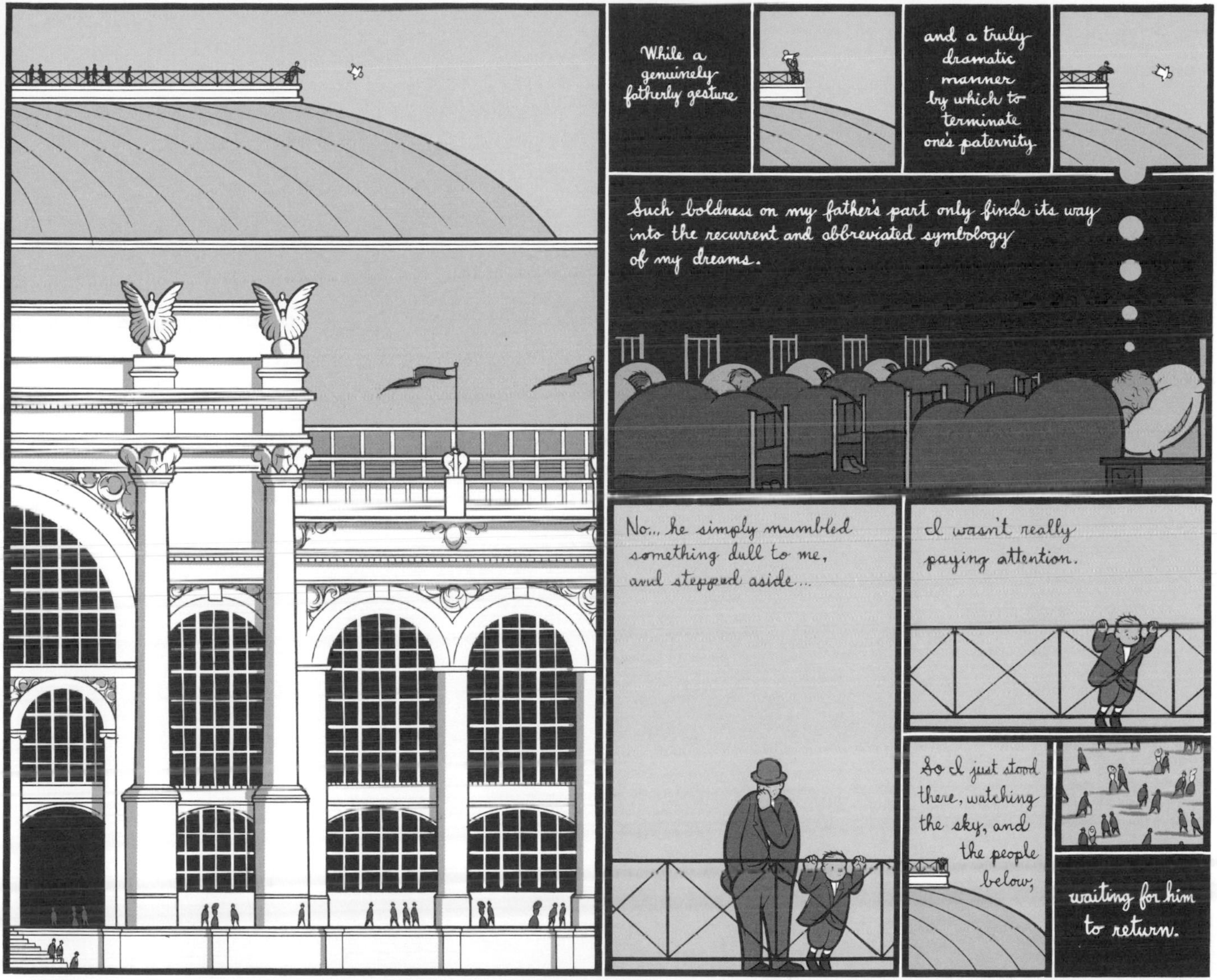

While a genuinely fatherly gesture
and a truly dramatic manner by which to terminate one's paternity
Such boldness on my father's part only finds its way into the recurrent and abbreviated symbology of my dreams.
No... he simply mumbled something dull to me, and stepped aside...
I wasn't really paying attention.
So I just stood there, watching the sky, and the people below,
waiting for him to return.

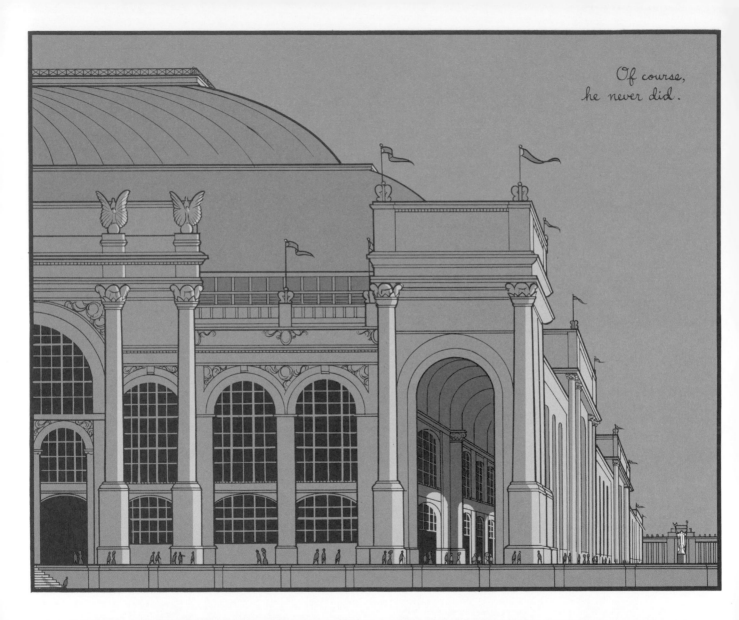

Of course,
he never did.

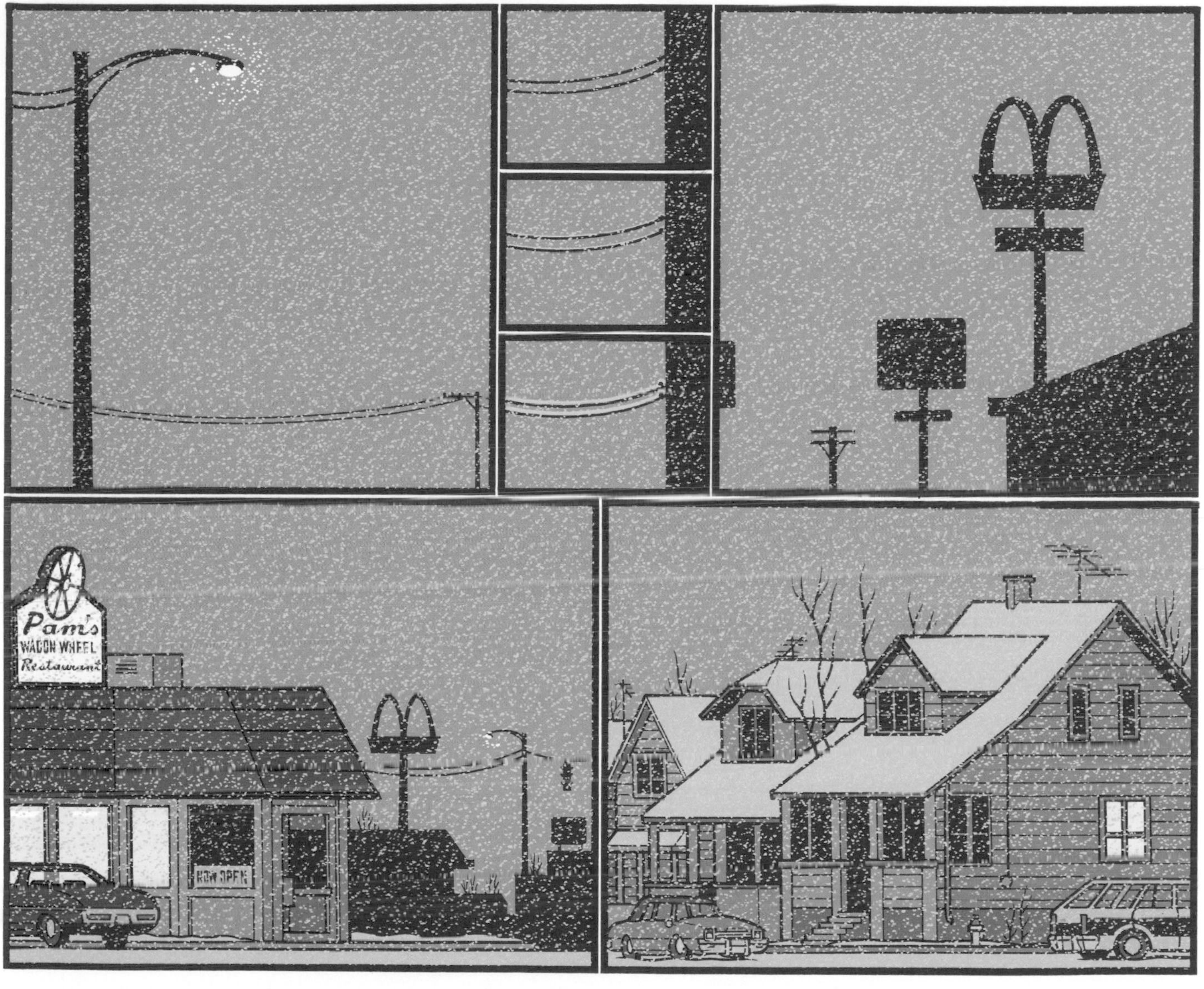
Pam's
WAGON WHEEL
Restaurant
NOW OPEN

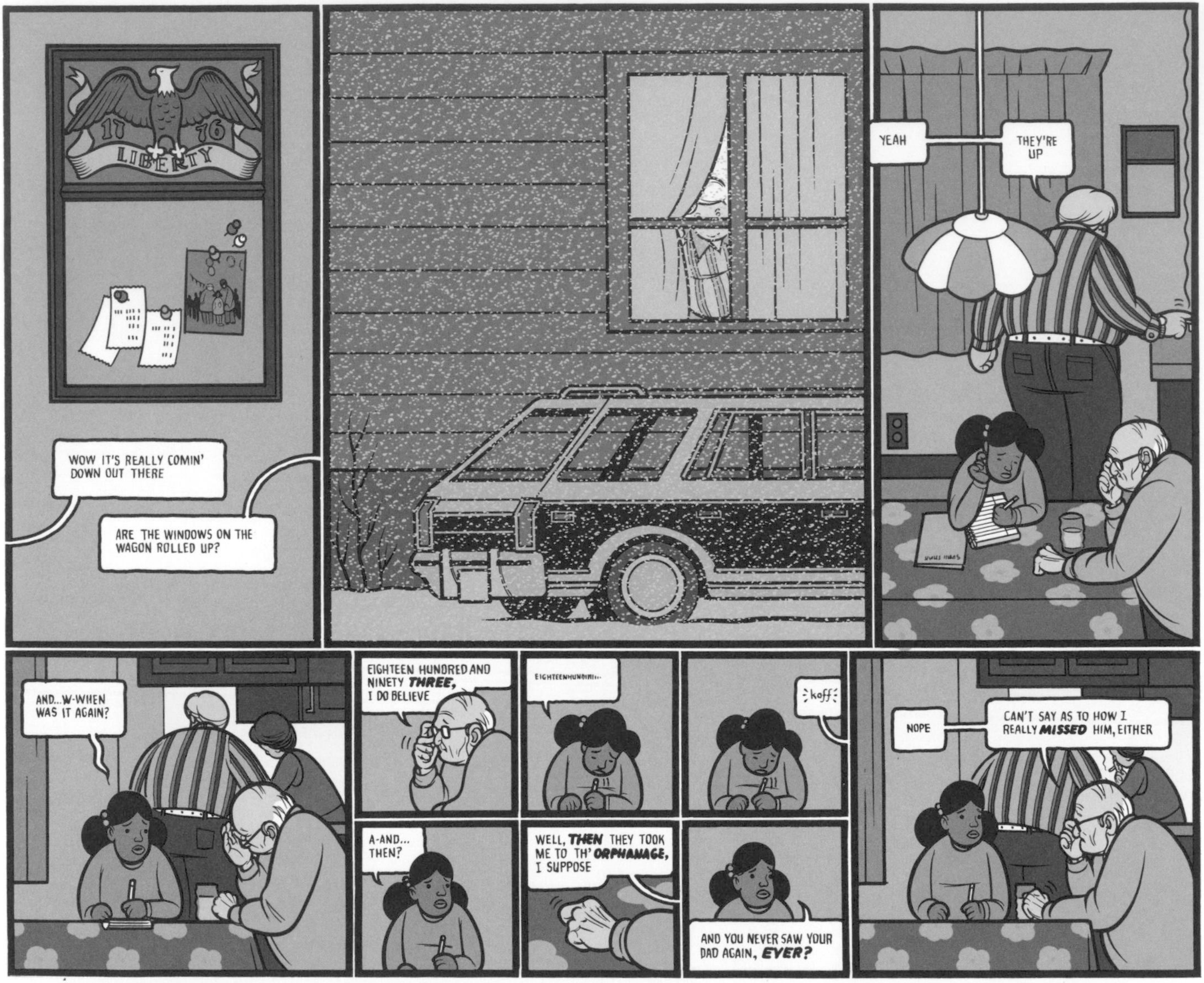
17 76
LIBERTY
WOW IT'S REALLY COMIN' DOWN OUT THERE
ARE THE WINDOWS ON THE WAGON ROLLED UP?
YEAH
THEY'RE UP
AND...W-WHEN WAS IT AGAIN?
EIGHTEEN HUNDRED AND NINETY **THREE,** I DO BELIEVE
EIGHTEENHUNDIHI...
koff
A-AND... THEN?
WELL, **THEN** THEY TOOK ME TO TH' **ORPHANAGE,** I SUPPOSE
AND YOU NEVER SAW YOUR DAD AGAIN, **EVER?**
NOPE
CAN'T SAY AS TO HOW I REALLY **MISSED** HIM, EITHER

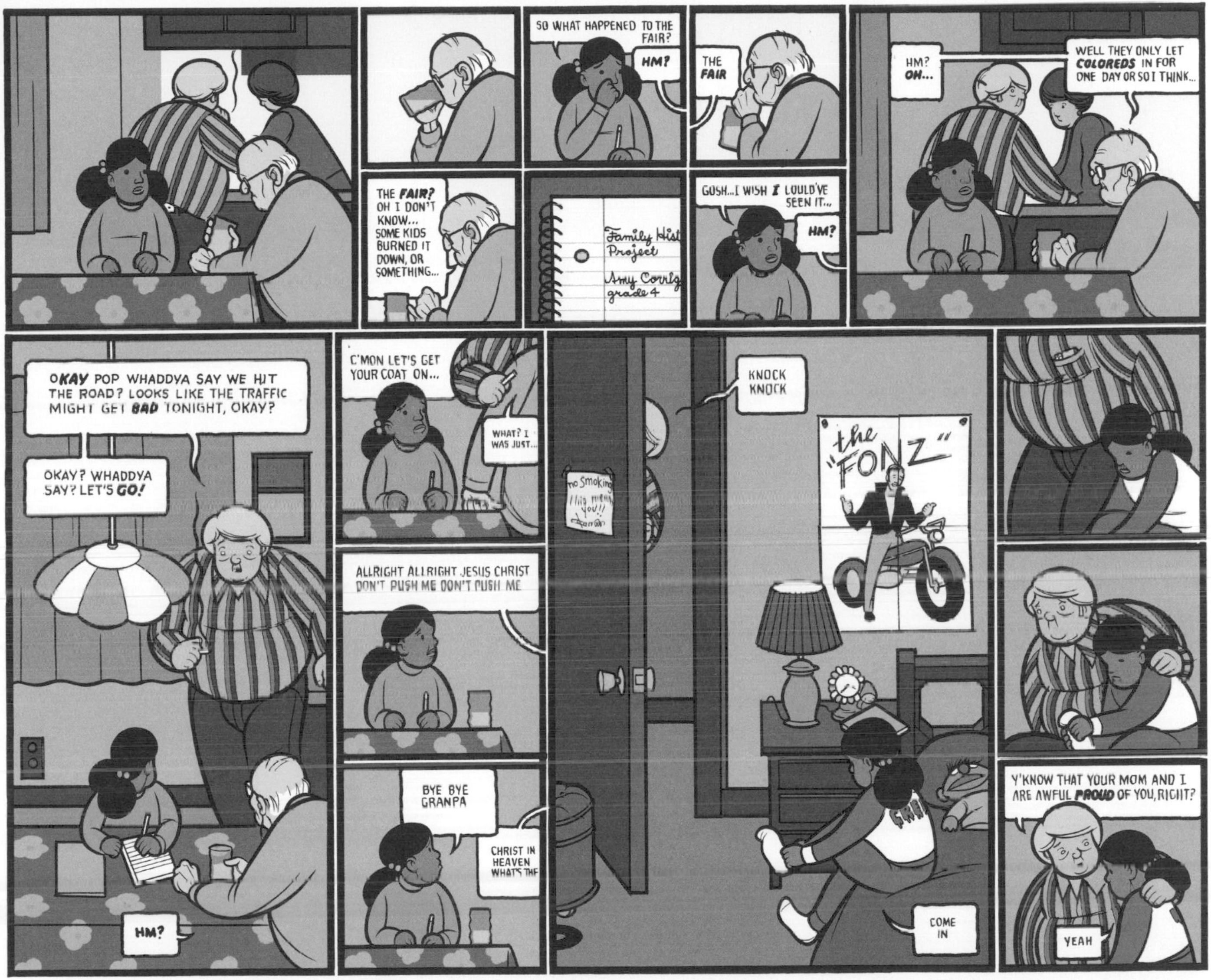
SO WHAT HAPPENED TO THE FAIR?
HM?
THE FAIR
HM? OH...
WELL THEY ONLY LET COLOREDS IN FOR ONE DAY OR SO I THINK...
THE FAIR? OH I DON'T KNOW... SOME KIDS BURNED IT DOWN, OR SOMETHING...
Family Hist Project
Amy Corrig grade 4
GOSH...I WISH I COULD'VE SEEN IT...
HM?
OKAY POP WHADDYA SAY WE HIT THE ROAD? LOOKS LIKE THE TRAFFIC MIGHT GET BAD TONIGHT, OKAY?
OKAY? WHADDYA SAY? LET'S GO!
HM?
C'MON LET'S GET YOUR COAT ON...
WHAT? I WAS JUST...
ALLRIGHT ALLRIGHT JESUS CHRIST DON'T PUSH ME DON'T PUSH ME
BYE BYE GRANPA
CHRIST IN HEAVEN WHAT'S THE
KNOCK KNOCK
no Smoking
the "FONZ"
COME IN
Y'KNOW THAT YOUR MOM AND I ARE AWFUL PROUD OF YOU, RIGHT?
YEAH

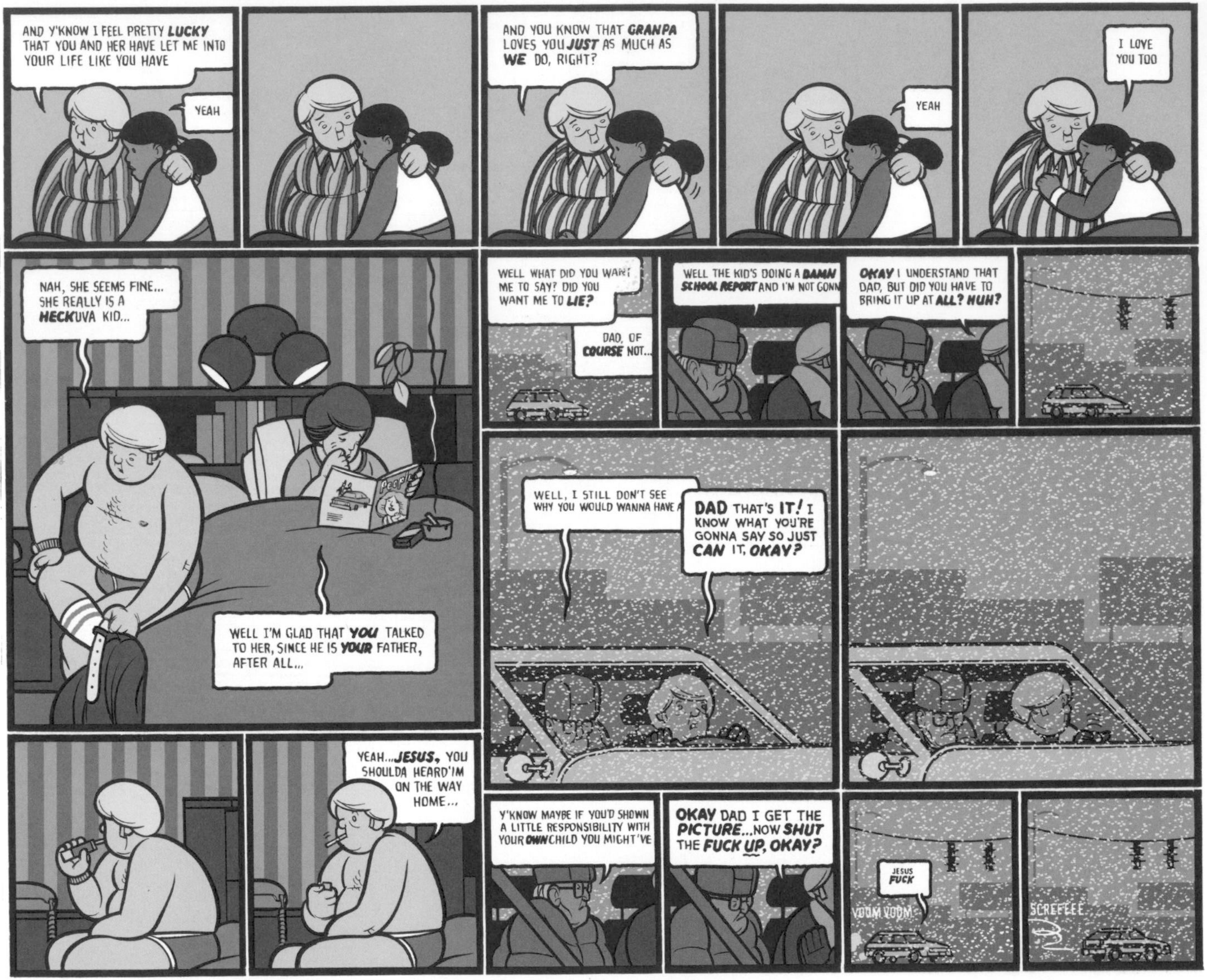

AND Y'KNOW I FEEL PRETTY **LUCKY** THAT YOU AND HER HAVE LET ME INTO YOUR LIFE LIKE YOU HAVE
YEAH
AND YOU KNOW THAT **GRANPA** LOVES YOU **JUST** AS MUCH AS **WE** DO, RIGHT?
YEAH
I LOVE YOU TOO
NAH, SHE SEEMS FINE... SHE REALLY IS A **HECK**UVA KID...
WELL I'M GLAD THAT **YOU** TALKED TO HER, SINCE HE IS **YOUR** FATHER, AFTER ALL...
YEAH... **JESUS,** YOU SHOULDA HEARD'IM ON THE WAY HOME...
WELL WHAT DID YOU WANT ME TO SAY? DID YOU WANT ME TO **LIE?**
DAD, OF **COURSE** NOT...
WELL THE KID'S DOING A **DAMN SCHOOL REPORT** AND I'M NOT GONN
OKAY I UNDERSTAND THAT DAD, BUT DID YOU HAVE TO BRING IT UP AT **ALL? HUH?**
WELL, I STILL DON'T SEE WHY YOU WOULD WANNA HAVE A
DAD THAT'S **IT!** I KNOW WHAT YOU'RE GONNA SAY SO JUST **CAN** IT, **OKAY?**
Y'KNOW MAYBE IF YOU'D SHOWN A LITTLE RESPONSIBILITY WITH YOUR **OWN** CHILD YOU MIGHT'VE
OKAY DAD I GET THE **PICTURE**...NOW **SHUT** THE **FUCK UP, OKAY?**
JESUS **FUCK**
VOOM VOOM
SCREEEEE

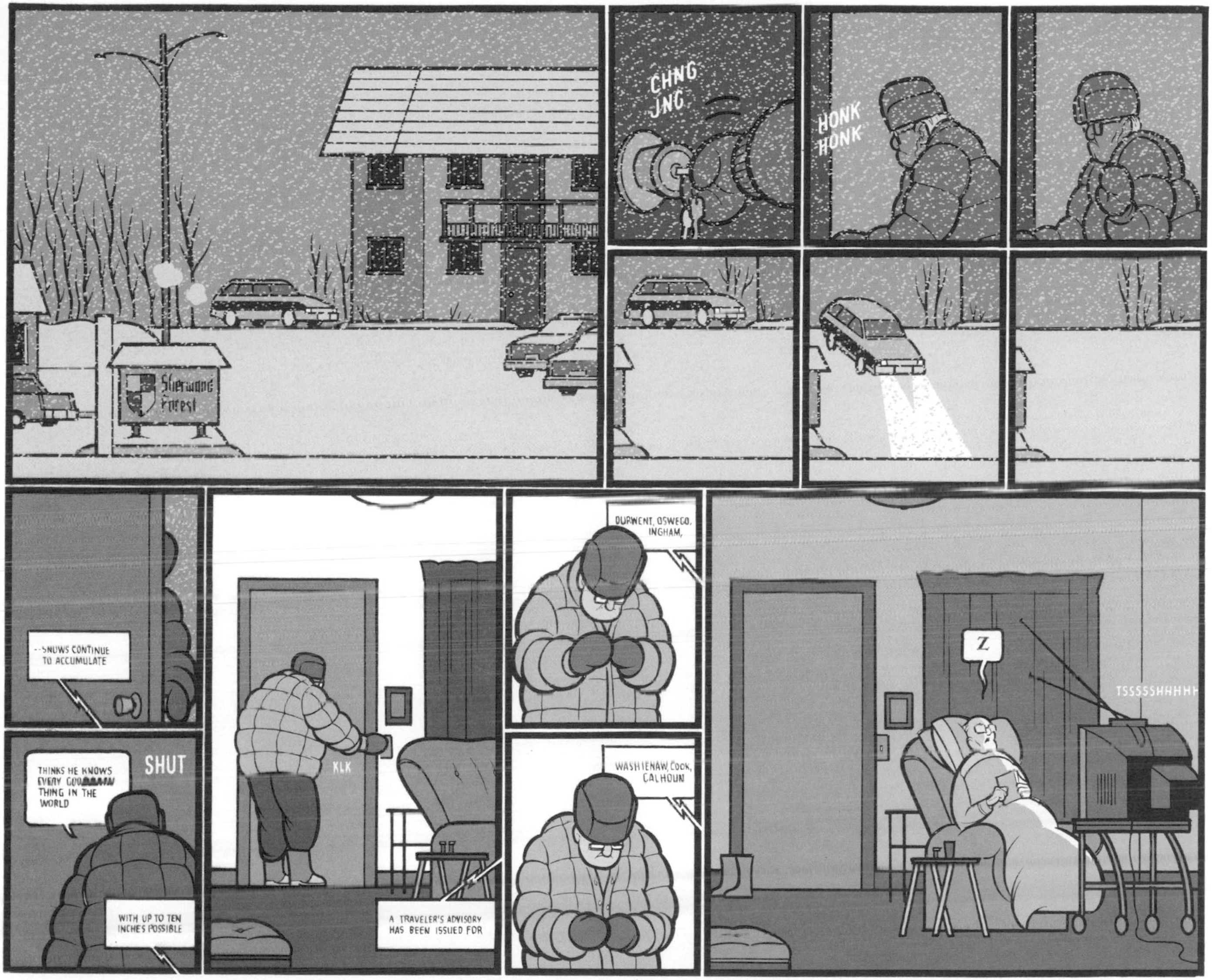
Sherwood Forest
CHNG JNG
HONK HONK
--SNOWS CONTINUE TO ACCUMULATE
SHUT
THINKS HE KNOWS EVERY GODDAMN THING IN THE WORLD
WITH UP TO TEN INCHES POSSIBLE
KLK
A TRAVELER'S ADVISORY HAS BEEN ISSUED FOR
DURWENT, OSWEGO, INGHAM,
WASHTENAW, COOK, CALHOUN
Z
TSSSSSHHHHH

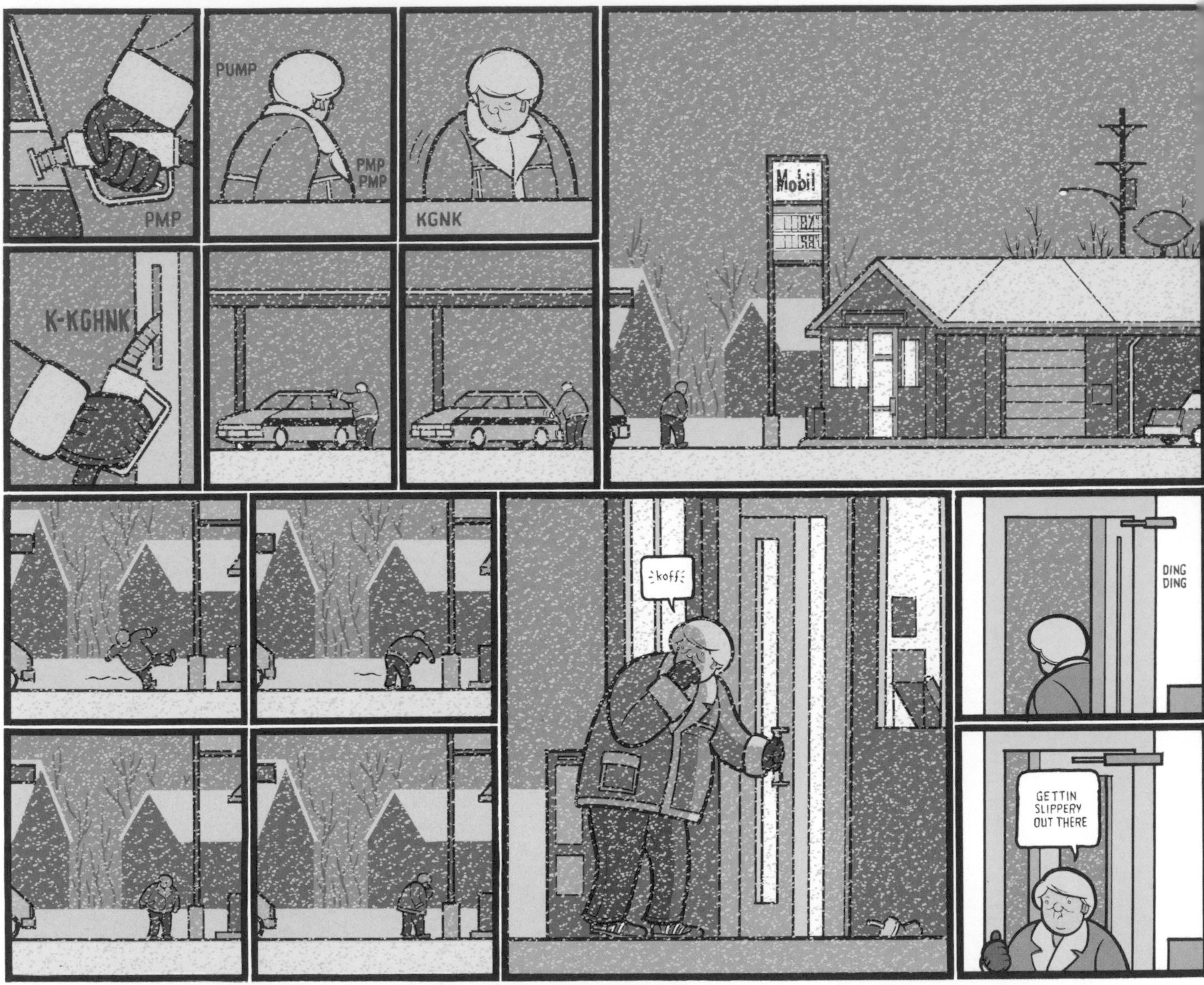
PMP
PUMP
PMP
PMP
KGNK
K-KGHNK
Mobil
koff
DING
DING
GETTIN SLIPPERY OUT THERE

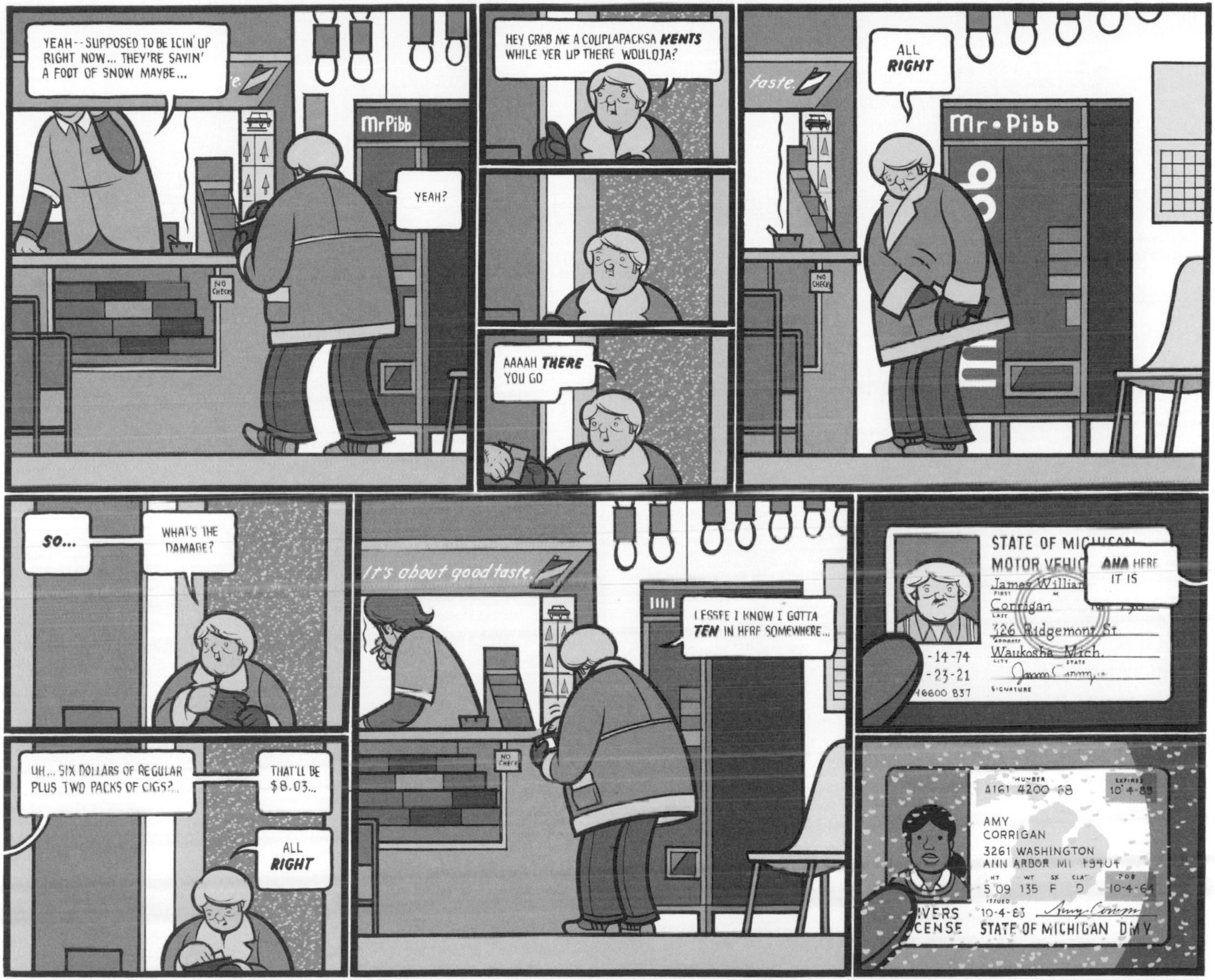

YEAH--SUPPOSED TO BE ICIN' UP RIGHT NOW... THEY'RE SAYIN' A FOOT OF SNOW MAYBE...
YEAH?
MrPibb
NO CHECKS
HEY GRAB ME A COUPLAPACKSA **KENTS** WHILE YER UP THERE WOULDJA?
AAAAH **THERE** YOU GO
taste.
ALL **RIGHT**
Mr•Pibb
NO CHECKS
SO...
WHAT'S THE DAMAGE?
UH... SIX DOLLARS OF REGULAR PLUS TWO PACKS OF CIGS?...
THAT'LL BE $8.03...
ALL **RIGHT**
It's about good taste.
NO CHECKS
LESSEE I KNOW I GOTTA **TEN** IN HERE SOMEWHERE...
STATE OF MIC
MOTOR VEHIC
James Willia
FIRST
Corrigan
LAST
326 Ridgemont St
ADDRESS
Waukosha Mich.
CITY STATE
SIGNATURE
-14-74
-23-21
46600 837
AHA HERE IT IS
NUMBER
A161 4200 68
EXPIRES
10-4-88
AMY
CORRIGAN
3261 WASHINGTON
ANN ARBOR MI
HT WT SX
5 09 135 F D
DOB
10-4-64
ISSUED
10-4-83
IVERS
CENSE
STATE OF MICHIGAN DMV

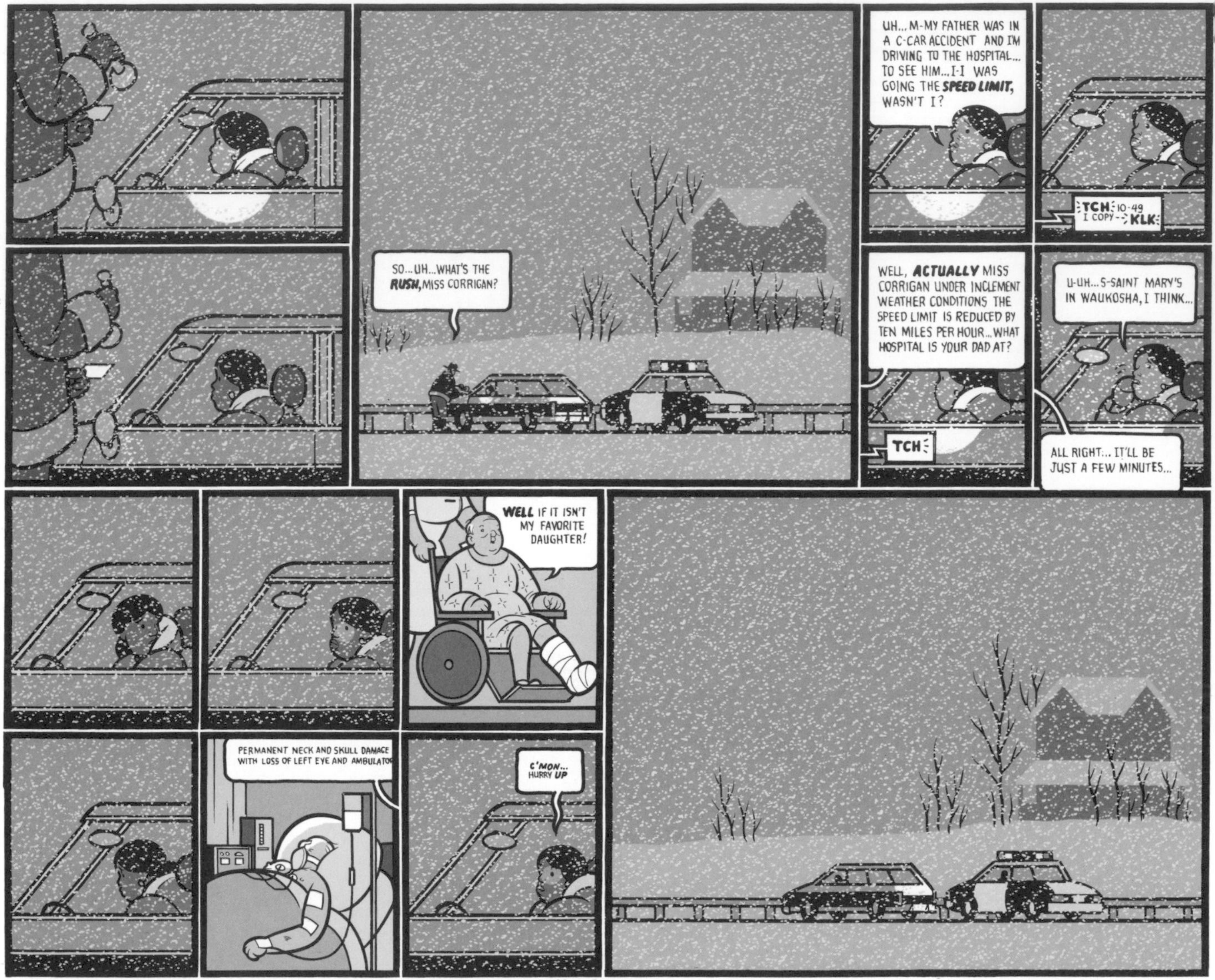

SO... UH... WHAT'S THE RUSH, MISS CORRIGAN?
UH... M-MY FATHER WAS IN A C-CAR ACCIDENT AND I'M DRIVING TO THE HOSPITAL... TO SEE HIM... I-I WAS GOING THE SPEED LIMIT, WASN'T I?
TCH 10-49 I COPY - KLK
WELL, ACTUALLY MISS CORRIGAN UNDER INCLEMENT WEATHER CONDITIONS THE SPEED LIMIT IS REDUCED BY TEN MILES PER HOUR... WHAT HOSPITAL IS YOUR DAD AT?
TCH
U-UH... S-SAINT MARY'S IN WAUKOSHA, I THINK...
ALL RIGHT... IT'LL BE JUST A FEW MINUTES...
WELL IF IT ISN'T MY FAVORITE DAUGHTER!
PERMANENT NECK AND SKULL DAMAGE WITH LOSS OF LEFT EYE AND AMBULATO
C'MON... HURRY UP

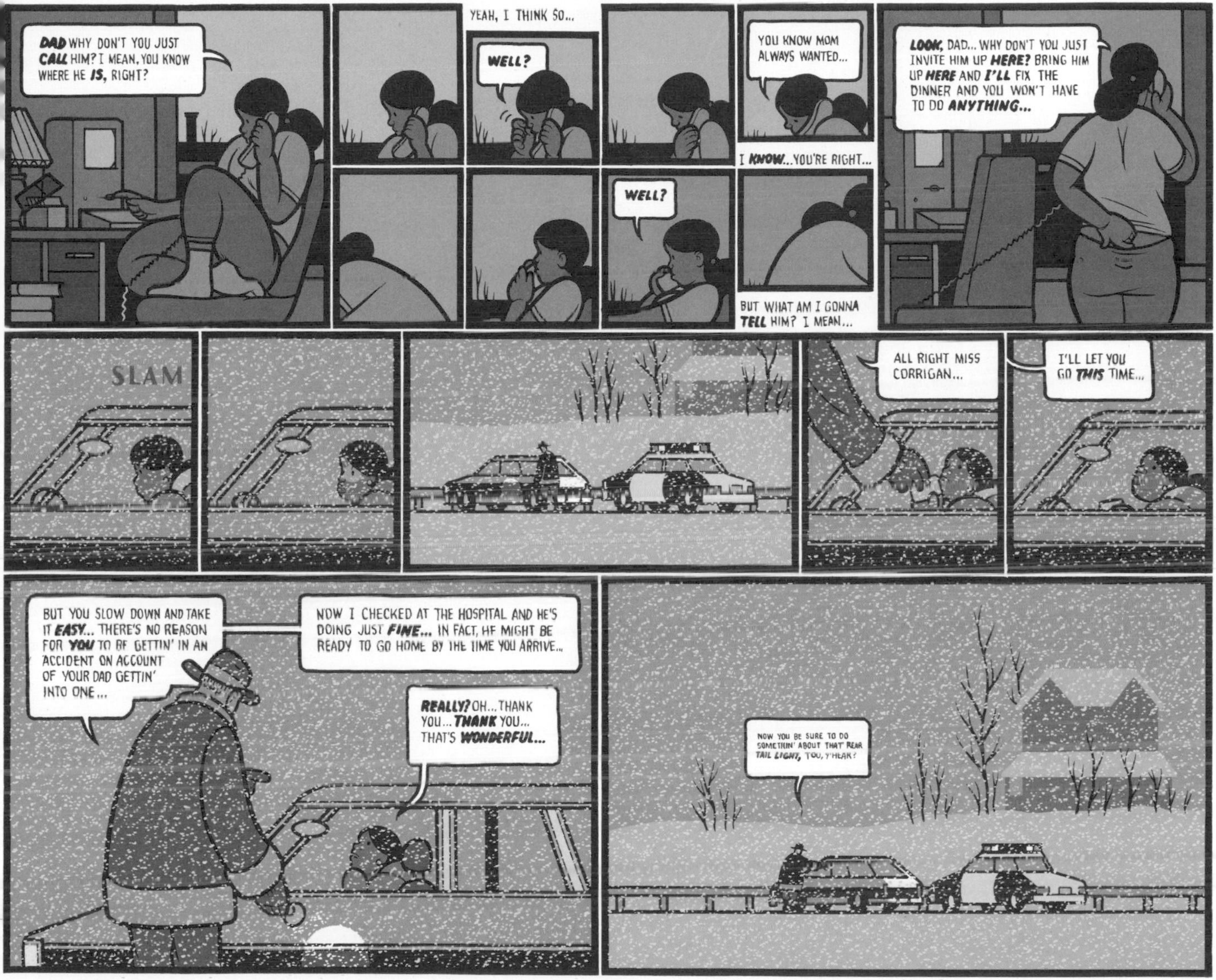
DAD WHY DON'T YOU JUST CALL HIM? I MEAN, YOU KNOW WHERE HE IS, RIGHT?
YEAH, I THINK SO...
WELL?
YOU KNOW MOM ALWAYS WANTED...
I KNOW...YOU'RE RIGHT...
WELL?
BUT WHAT AM I GONNA TELL HIM? I MEAN...
LOOK, DAD... WHY DON'T YOU JUST INVITE HIM UP HERE? BRING HIM UP HERE AND I'LL FIX THE DINNER AND YOU WON'T HAVE TO DO ANYTHING...
SLAM
ALL RIGHT MISS CORRIGAN...
I'LL LET YOU GO THIS TIME...
BUT YOU SLOW DOWN AND TAKE IT EASY... THERE'S NO REASON FOR YOU TO BE GETTIN' IN AN ACCIDENT ON ACCOUNT OF YOUR DAD GETTIN' INTO ONE...
NOW I CHECKED AT THE HOSPITAL AND HE'S DOING JUST FINE... IN FACT, HE MIGHT BE READY TO GO HOME BY THE TIME YOU ARRIVE...
REALLY? OH... THANK YOU... THANK YOU... THAT'S WONDERFUL...
NOW YOU BE SURE TO DO SOMETHIN' ABOUT THAT REAR TAIL LIGHT, TOO, Y'HEAR?

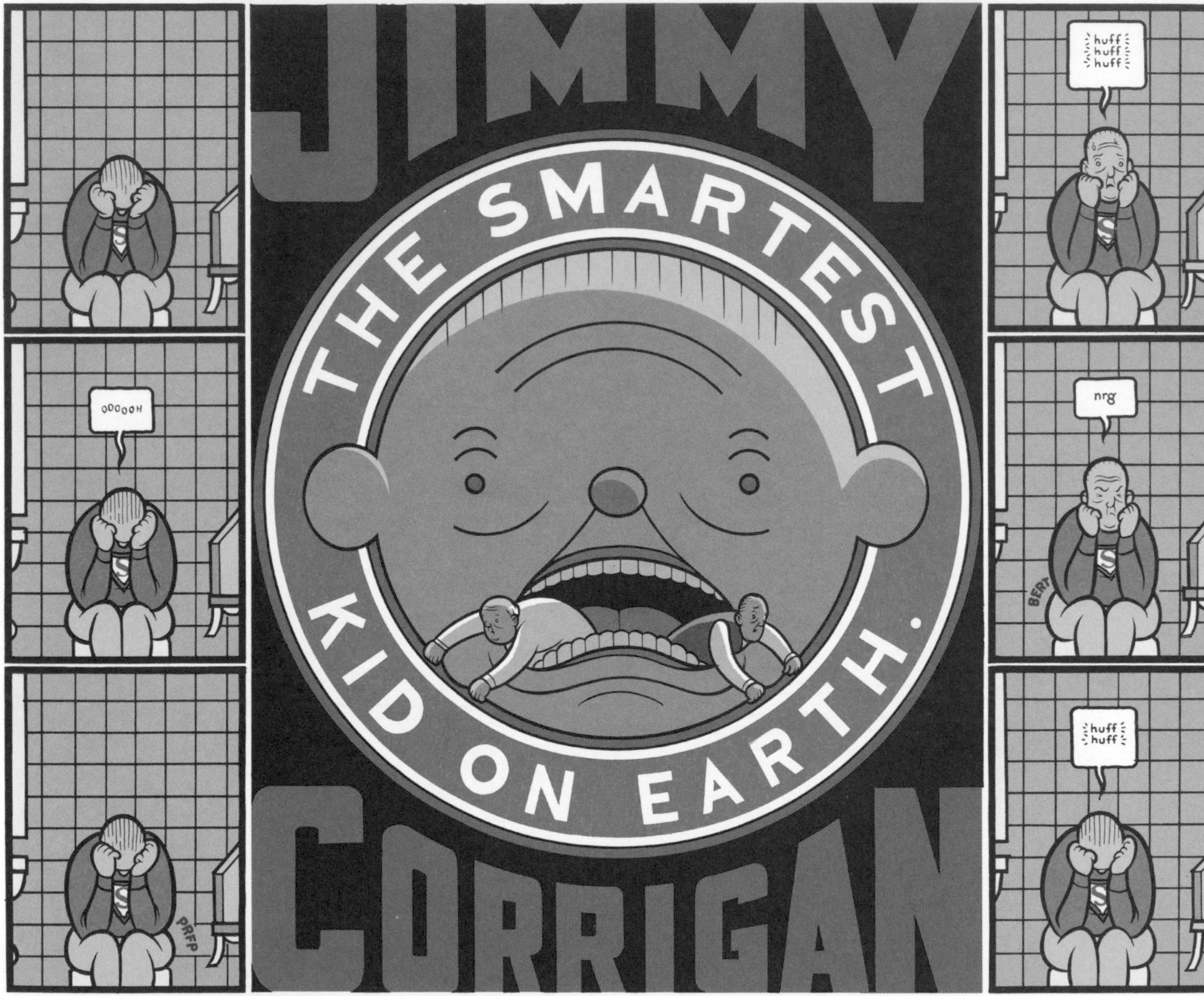
JIMMY
THE SMARTEST KID ON EARTH.
CORRIGAN
OOOOOH
PRFP
huff huff huff
nrg
BERT
huff huff

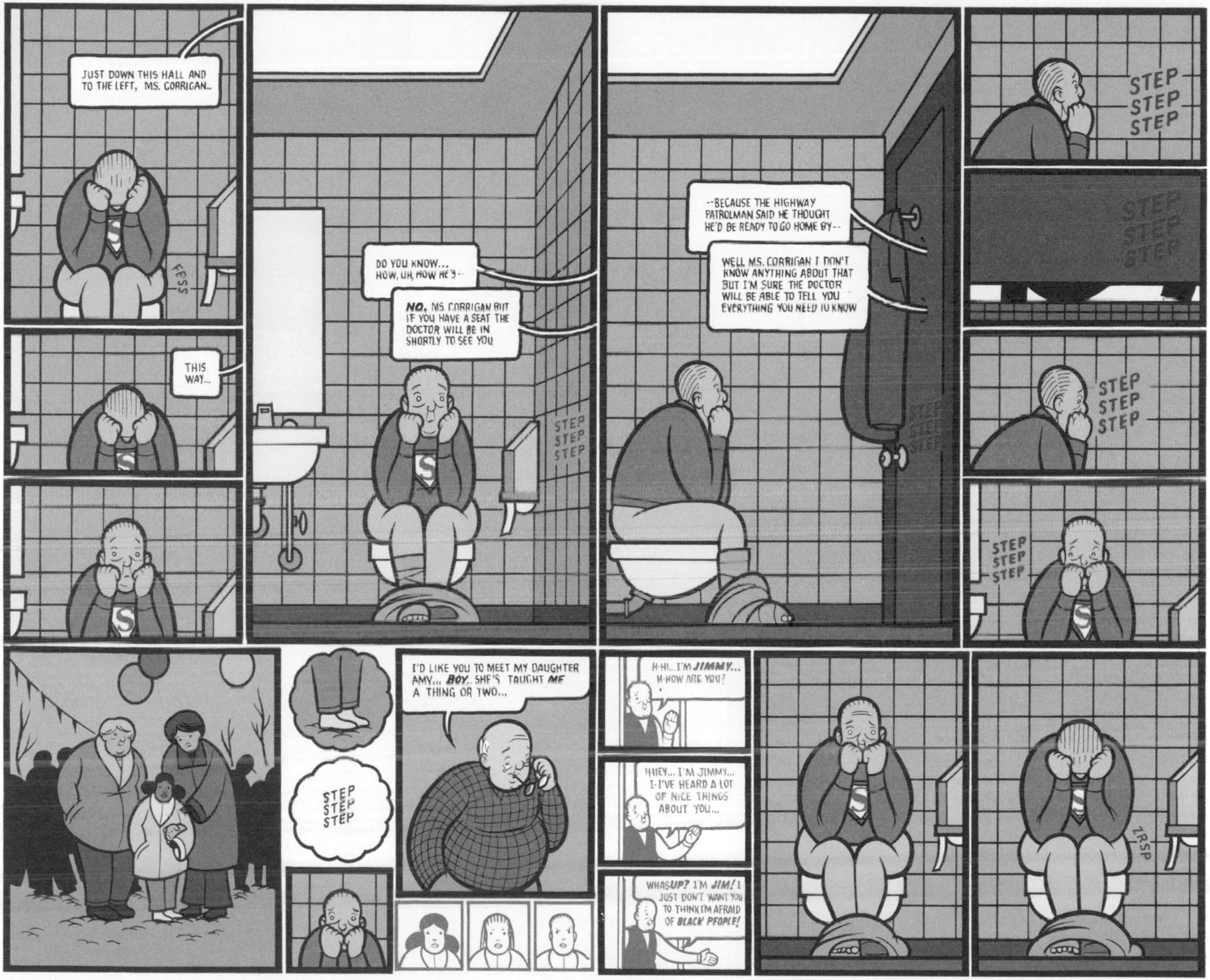

JUST DOWN THIS HALL AND TO THE LEFT, MS. CORRIGAN...
FESS
THIS WAY...
DO YOU KNOW... HOW, UH, HOW HE'S--
NO, MS. CORRIGAN BUT IF YOU HAVE A SEAT THE DOCTOR WILL BE IN SHORTLY TO SEE YOU
STEP STEP STEP
--BECAUSE THE HIGHWAY PATROLMAN SAID HE THOUGHT HE'D BE READY TO GO HOME BY--
WELL MS. CORRIGAN I DON'T KNOW ANYTHING ABOUT THAT BUT I'M SURE THE DOCTOR WILL BE ABLE TO TELL YOU EVERYTHING YOU NEED TO KNOW
STEP STEP STEP
STEP STEP STEP
STEP STEP STEP
STEP STEP STEP
STEP STEP STEP
STEP STEP STEP
I'D LIKE YOU TO MEET MY DAUGHTER AMY... BOY, SHE'S TAUGHT ME A THING OR TWO...
H-HI... I'M JIMMY... H-HOW ARE YOU?
H-HEY... I'M JIMMY... I-I'VE HEARD A LOT OF NICE THINGS ABOUT YOU...
WHASUP? I'M JIM! I JUST DON'T WANT YOU TO THINK I'M AFRAID OF BLACK PEOPLE!
ZRSP

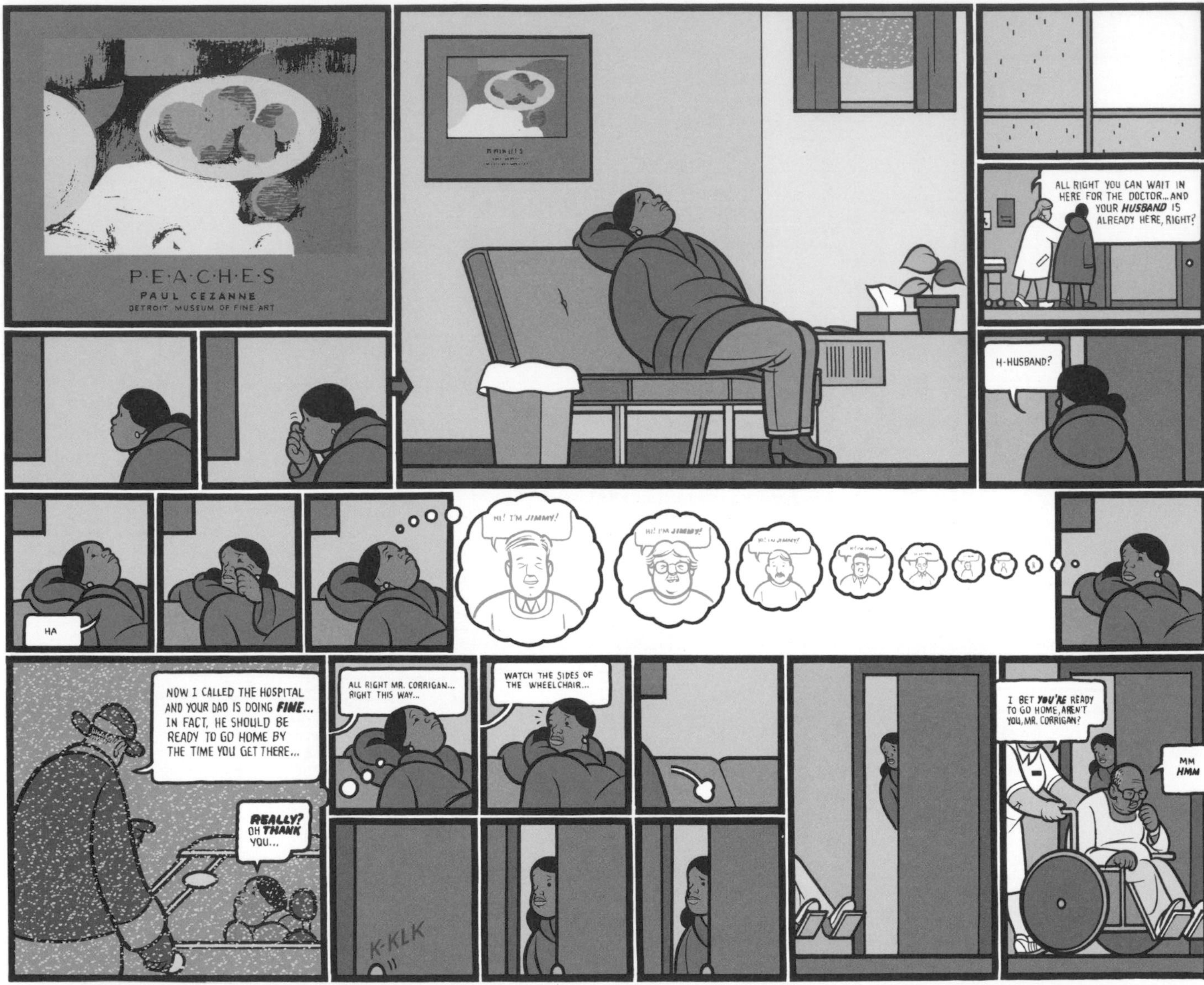

P·E·A·C·H·E·S
PAUL CEZANNE
DETROIT MUSEUM OF FINE ART
ALL RIGHT YOU CAN WAIT IN HERE FOR THE DOCTOR...AND YOUR **HUSBAND** IS ALREADY HERE, RIGHT?
H-HUSBAND?
HA
HI! I'M *JIMMY!*
HI! I'M *JIMMY!*
NOW I CALLED THE HOSPITAL AND YOUR DAD IS DOING **FINE...** IN FACT, HE SHOULD BE READY TO GO HOME BY THE TIME YOU GET THERE...
REALLY? OH **THANK** YOU...
ALL RIGHT MR. CORRIGAN... RIGHT THIS WAY...
WATCH THE SIDES OF THE WHEELCHAIR...
K-KLK
I BET **YOU'RE** READY TO GO HOME, AREN'T YOU, MR. CORRIGAN?
MM **HMM**

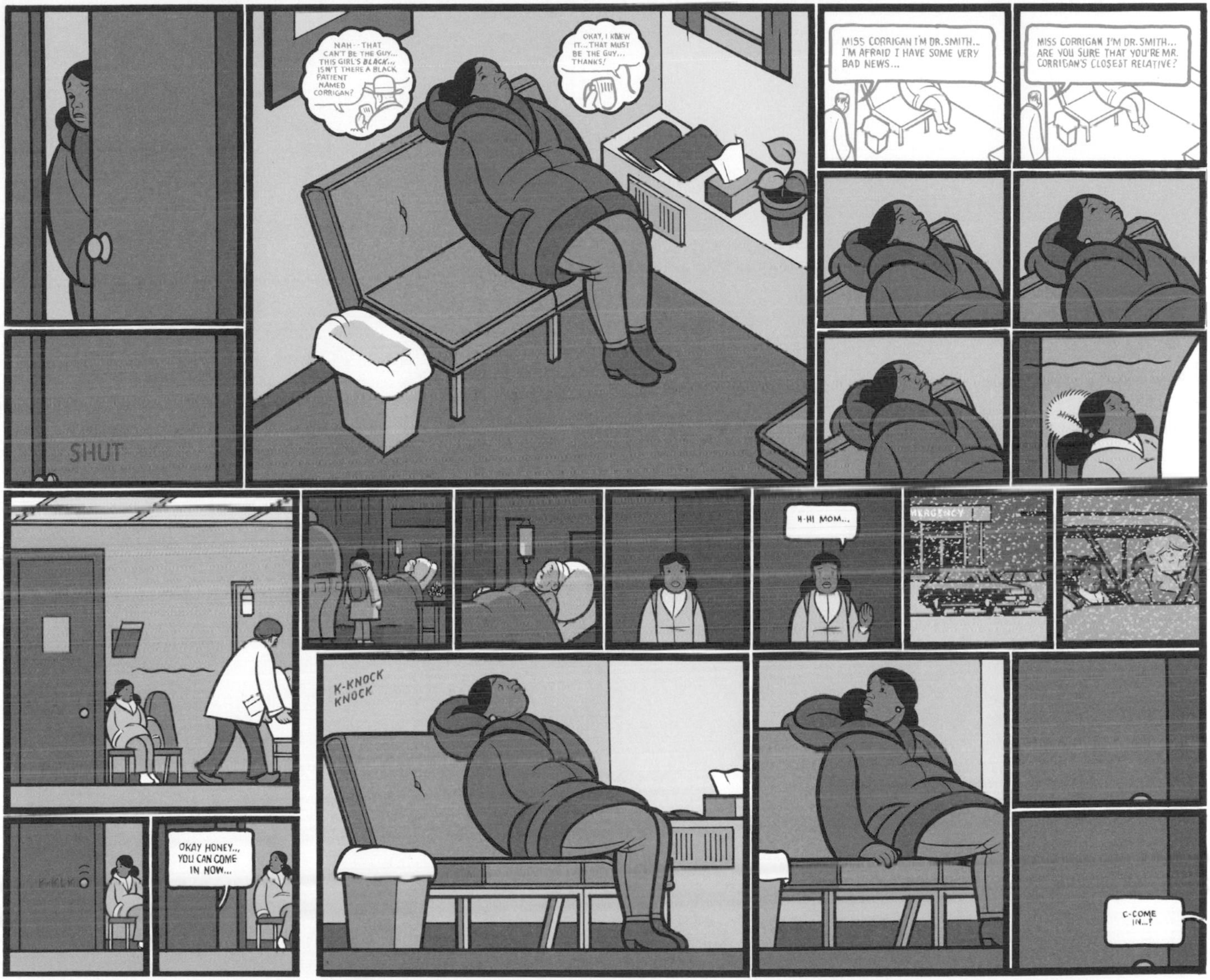
SHUT
NAH--THAT CAN'T BE THE GUY... THIS GIRL'S BLACK... ISN'T THERE A BLACK PATIENT NAMED CORRIGAN?
OKAY, I KNEW IT... THAT MUST BE THE GUY... THANKS!
MISS CORRIGAN I'M DR. SMITH... I'M AFRAID I HAVE SOME VERY BAD NEWS...
MISS CORRIGAN I'M DR. SMITH... ARE YOU SURE THAT YOU'RE MR. CORRIGAN'S CLOSEST RELATIVE?
OKAY HONEY... YOU CAN COME IN NOW...
H-HI MOM...
K-KNOCK KNOCK
C-COME IN...?

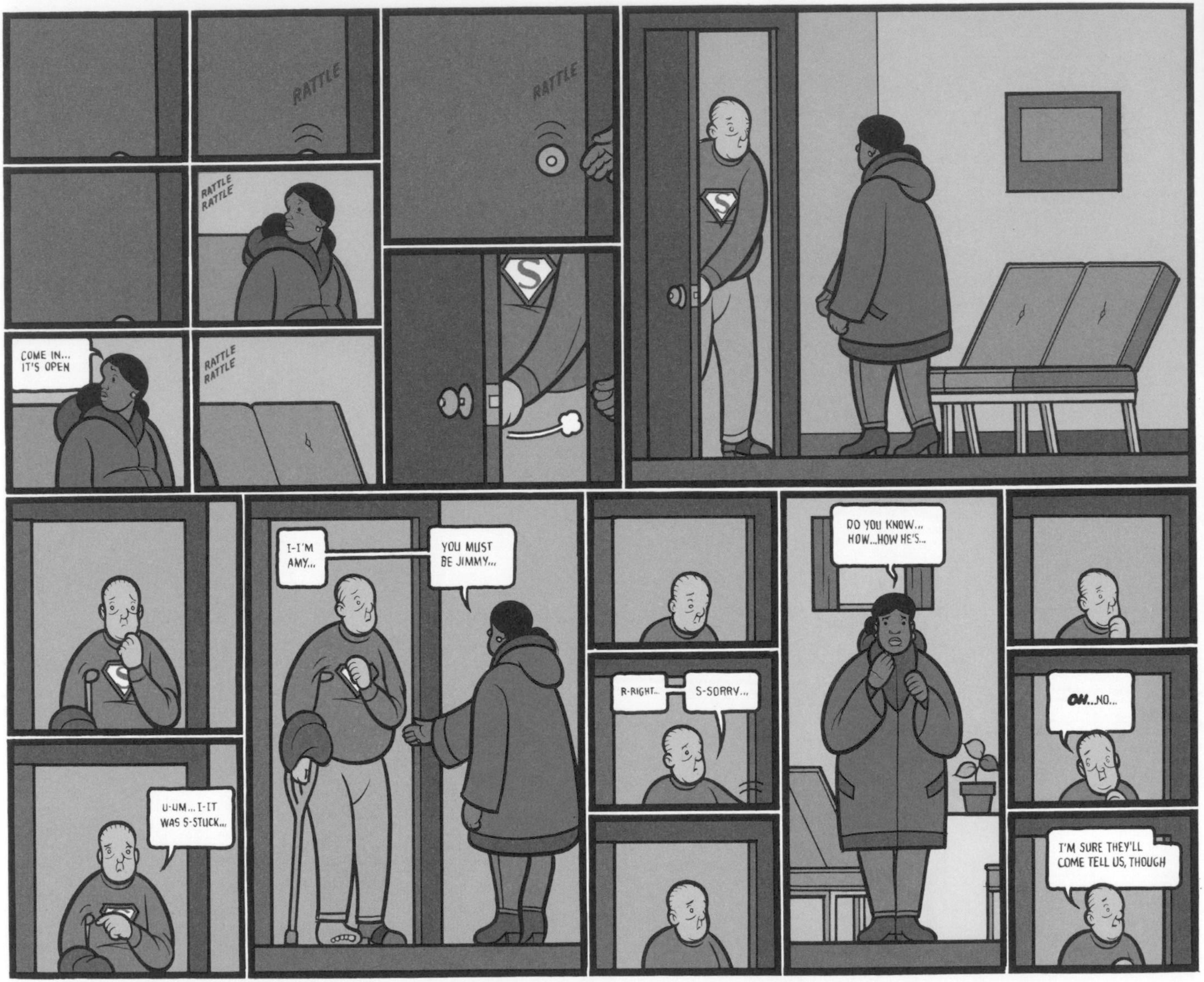
RATTLE
RATTLE
RATTLE RATTLE
COME IN... IT'S OPEN
RATTLE RATTLE
U-UM... I-IT WAS S-STUCK...
I-I'M AMY...
YOU MUST BE JIMMY...
R-RIGHT...
S-SORRY...
DO YOU KNOW... HOW...HOW HE'S...
OH...NO...
I'M SURE THEY'LL COME TELL US, THOUGH

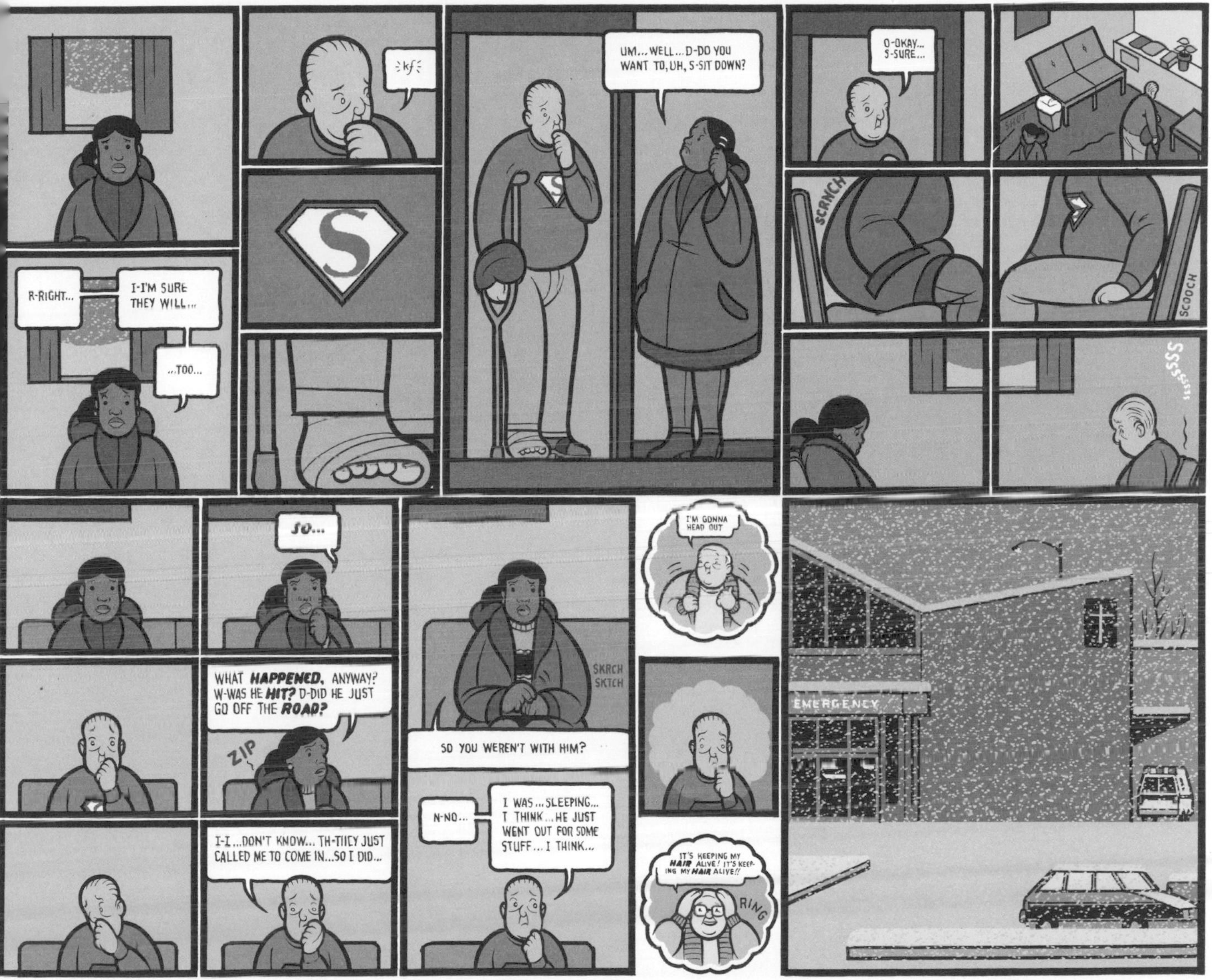

kf
R-RIGHT...
I-I'M SURE THEY WILL...
...TOO...
UM... WELL... D-DO YOU WANT TO, UH, S-SIT DOWN?
O-OKAY... S-SURE...
SHUT
SCRNCH
SCOOCH
SSSSSSSS
SO...
WHAT HAPPENED, ANYWAY? W-WAS HE HIT? D-DID HE JUST GO OFF THE ROAD?
ZIP
I-I... DON'T KNOW... TH-THEY JUST CALLED ME TO COME IN... SO I DID...
SKRCH SKTCH
SO YOU WEREN'T WITH HIM?
N-NO...
I WAS... SLEEPING... I THINK... HE JUST WENT OUT FOR SOME STUFF... I THINK...
I'M GONNA HEAD OUT
IT'S KEEPING MY HAIR ALIVE! IT'S KEEPING MY HAIR ALIVE!!
RING
EMERGENCY

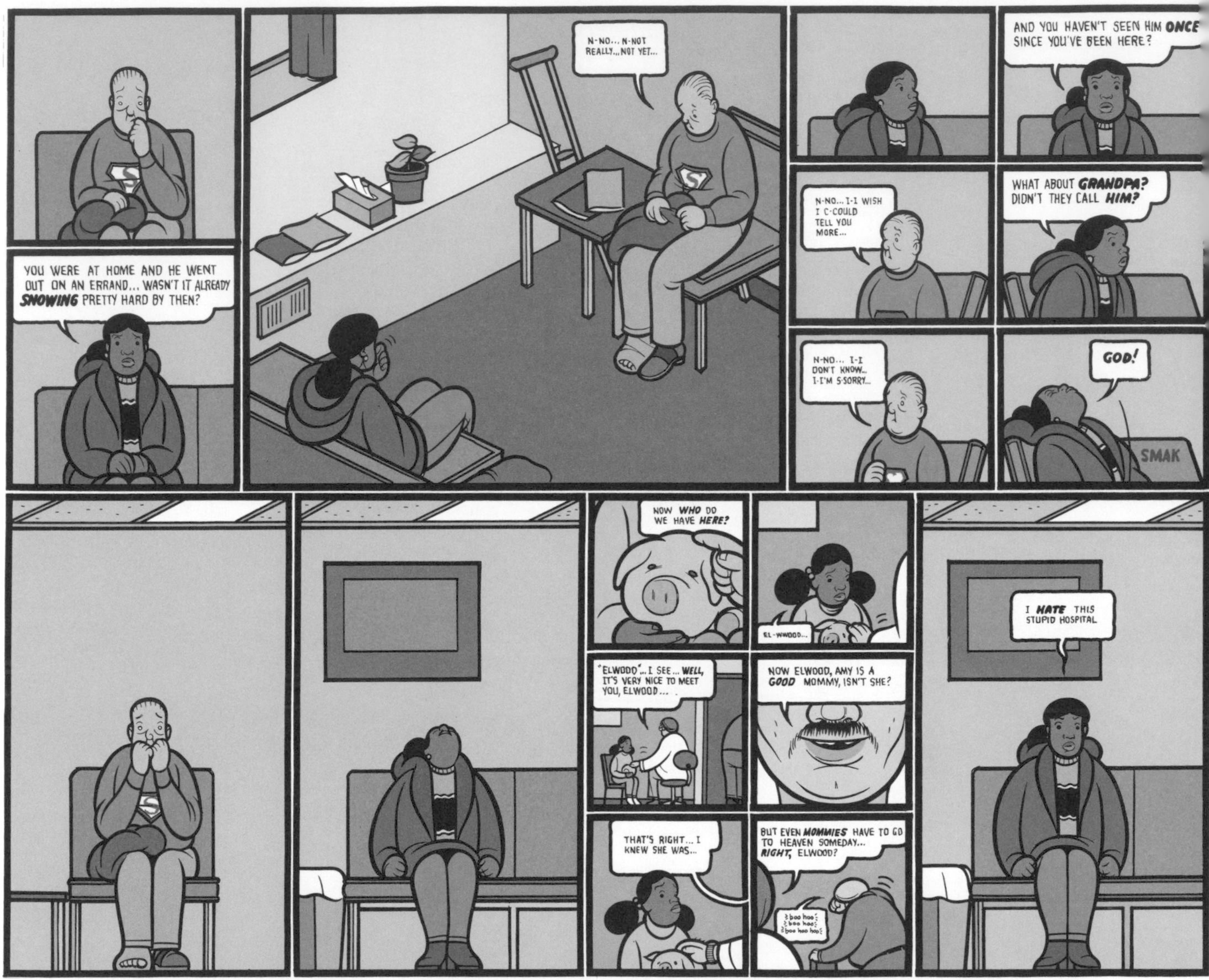
N-NO... N-NOT REALLY... NOT YET...
YOU WERE AT HOME AND HE WENT OUT ON AN ERRAND... WASN'T IT ALREADY **SNOWING** PRETTY HARD BY THEN?
AND YOU HAVEN'T SEEN HIM **ONCE** SINCE YOU'VE BEEN HERE?
N-NO... I-I WISH I C-COULD TELL YOU MORE...
WHAT ABOUT **GRANDPA?** DIDN'T THEY CALL **HIM?**
N-NO... I-I DON'T KNOW... I-I'M S-SORRY...
GOD!
SMAK
NOW **WHO** DO WE HAVE **HERE?**
EL-WWOOD...
"ELWOOD"... I SEE... **WELL,** IT'S VERY NICE TO MEET YOU, ELWOOD...
NOW ELWOOD, AMY IS A **GOOD** MOMMY, ISN'T SHE?
THAT'S RIGHT... I KNEW SHE WAS...
BUT EVEN **MOMMIES** HAVE TO GO TO HEAVEN SOMEDAY... **RIGHT,** ELWOOD?
boo hoo boo hoo boo hoo hoo
I **HATE** THIS STUPID HOSPITAL

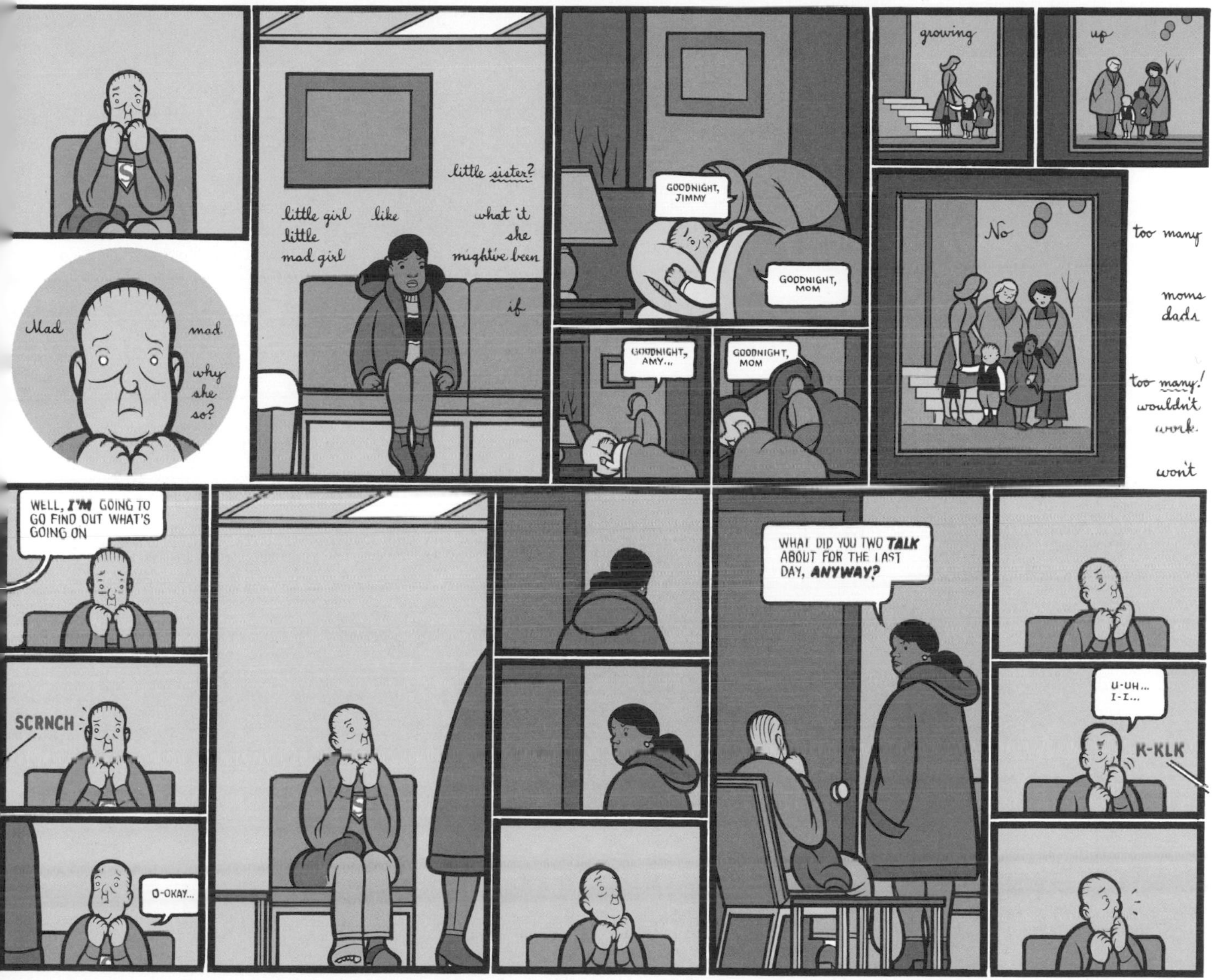

little sister?
little girl like
little
mad girl
what it
she
might've been
if
Mad
mad
why
she
so?
GOODNIGHT, JIMMY
GOODNIGHT, MOM
GOODNIGHT, AMY...
GOODNIGHT, MOM
growing
up
No
too many
moms
dads
too many!
wouldn't
work.
won't
WELL, I'M GOING TO GO FIND OUT WHAT'S GOING ON
SCRNCH
O-OKAY...
WHAT DID YOU TWO TALK ABOUT FOR THE LAST DAY, ANYWAY?
U-UH... I-I...
K-KLK

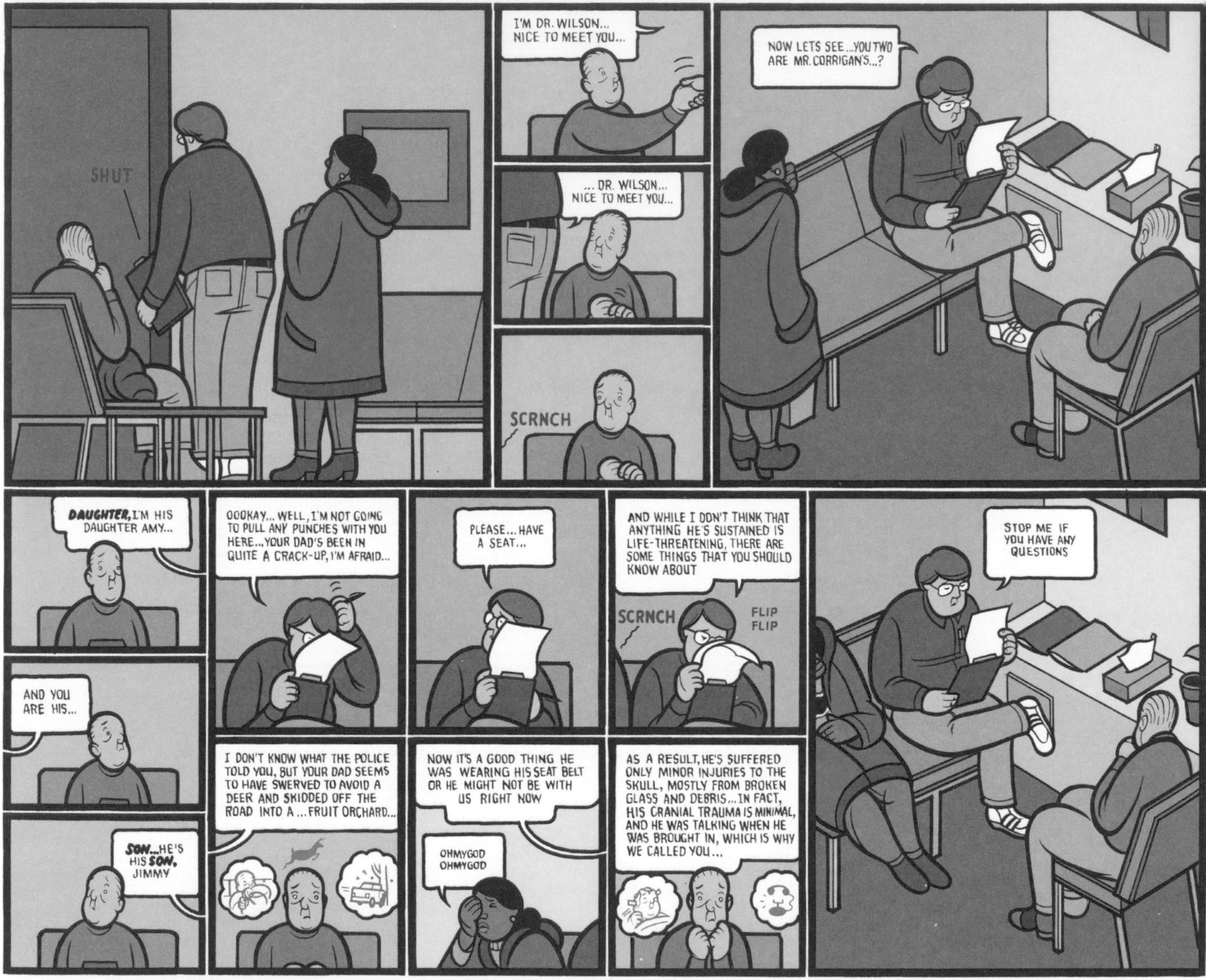
SHUT
I'M DR. WILSON... NICE TO MEET YOU...
... DR. WILSON... NICE TO MEET YOU...
SCRNCH
NOW LETS SEE...YOU TWO ARE MR. CORRIGAN'S...?
DAUGHTER, I'M HIS DAUGHTER AMY...
AND YOU ARE HIS...
SON...HE'S HIS SON, JIMMY
OOOKAY... WELL, I'M NOT GOING TO PULL ANY PUNCHES WITH YOU HERE...YOUR DAD'S BEEN IN QUITE A CRACK-UP, I'M AFRAID...
I DON'T KNOW WHAT THE POLICE TOLD YOU, BUT YOUR DAD SEEMS TO HAVE SWERVED TO AVOID A DEER AND SKIDDED OFF THE ROAD INTO A ... FRUIT ORCHARD...
PLEASE... HAVE A SEAT...
NOW IT'S A GOOD THING HE WAS WEARING HIS SEAT BELT OR HE MIGHT NOT BE WITH US RIGHT NOW
OHMYGOD OHMYGOD
AND WHILE I DON'T THINK THAT ANYTHING HE'S SUSTAINED IS LIFE-THREATENING, THERE ARE SOME THINGS THAT YOU SHOULD KNOW ABOUT
SCRNCH
FLIP FLIP
AS A RESULT, HE'S SUFFERED ONLY MINOR INJURIES TO THE SKULL, MOSTLY FROM BROKEN GLASS AND DEBRIS...IN FACT, HIS CRANIAL TRAUMA IS MINIMAL, AND HE WAS TALKING WHEN HE WAS BROUGHT IN, WHICH IS WHY WE CALLED YOU...
STOP ME IF YOU HAVE ANY QUESTIONS

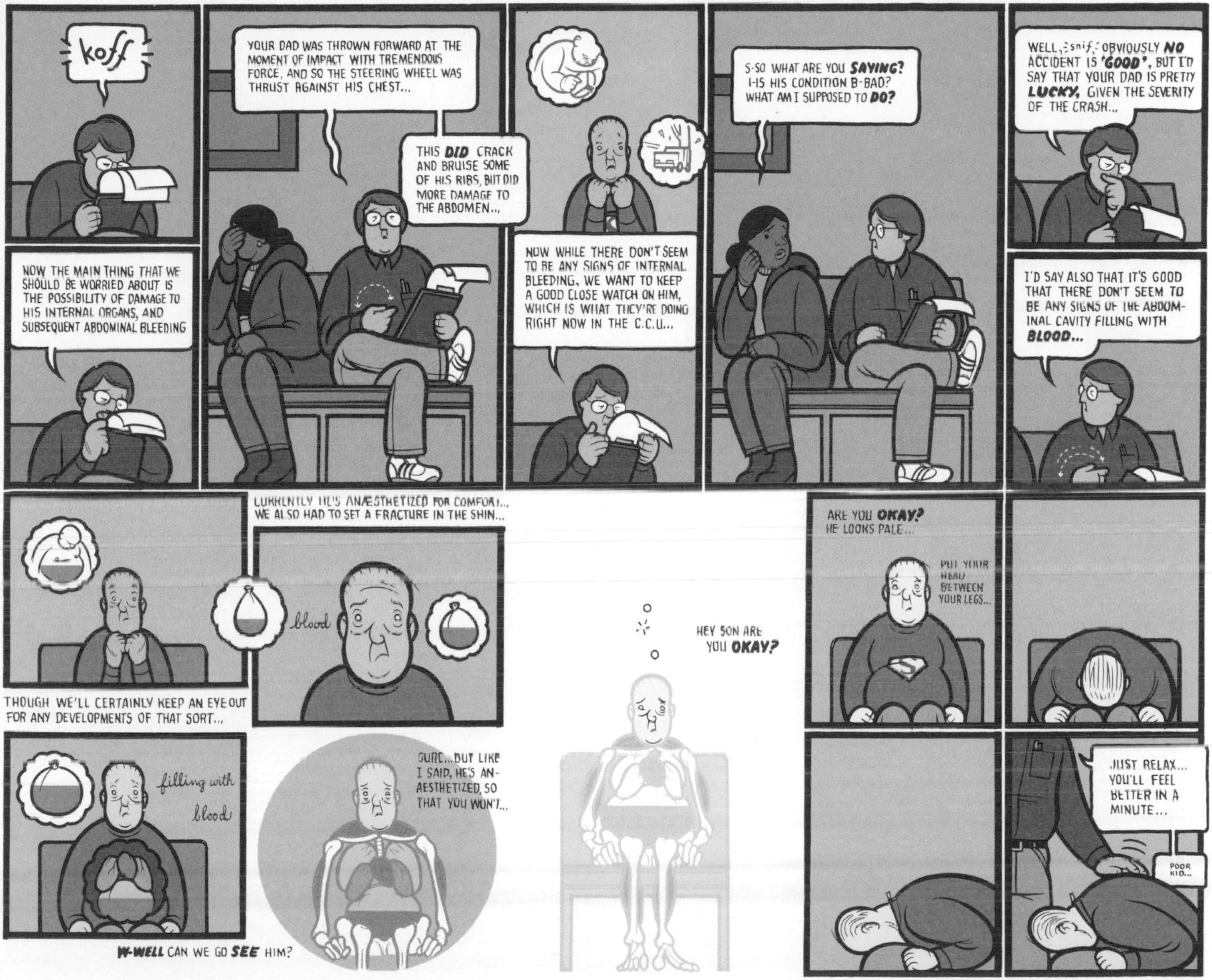
koff
YOUR DAD WAS THROWN FORWARD AT THE MOMENT OF IMPACT WITH TREMENDOUS FORCE, AND SO THE STEERING WHEEL WAS THRUST AGAINST HIS CHEST...
THIS DID CRACK AND BRUISE SOME OF HIS RIBS, BUT DID MORE DAMAGE TO THE ABDOMEN...
NOW WHILE THERE DON'T SEEM TO BE ANY SIGNS OF INTERNAL BLEEDING, WE WANT TO KEEP A GOOD CLOSE WATCH ON HIM, WHICH IS WHAT THEY'RE DOING RIGHT NOW IN THE C.C.U...
S-SO WHAT ARE YOU SAYING? I-IS HIS CONDITION B-BAD? WHAT AM I SUPPOSED TO DO?
WELL, snif, OBVIOUSLY NO ACCIDENT IS 'GOOD', BUT I'D SAY THAT YOUR DAD IS PRETTY LUCKY, GIVEN THE SEVERITY OF THE CRASH...
NOW THE MAIN THING THAT WE SHOULD BE WORRIED ABOUT IS THE POSSIBILITY OF DAMAGE TO HIS INTERNAL ORGANS, AND SUBSEQUENT ABDOMINAL BLEEDING
I'D SAY ALSO THAT IT'S GOOD THAT THERE DON'T SEEM TO BE ANY SIGNS OF THE ABDOMINAL CAVITY FILLING WITH BLOOD...
CURRENTLY HE'S ANÆSTHETIZED FOR COMFORT... WE ALSO HAD TO SET A FRACTURE IN THE SHIN...
blood
THOUGH WE'LL CERTAINLY KEEP AN EYE OUT FOR ANY DEVELOPMENTS OF THAT SORT...
filling with blood
SURE... BUT LIKE I SAID, HE'S ANAESTHETIZED, SO THAT YOU WON'T...
W-WELL CAN WE GO SEE HIM?
HEY SON ARE YOU OKAY?
ARE YOU OKAY? HE LOOKS PALE...
PUT YOUR HEAD BETWEEN YOUR LEGS...
JUST RELAX... YOU'LL FEEL BETTER IN A MINUTE...
POOR KID...

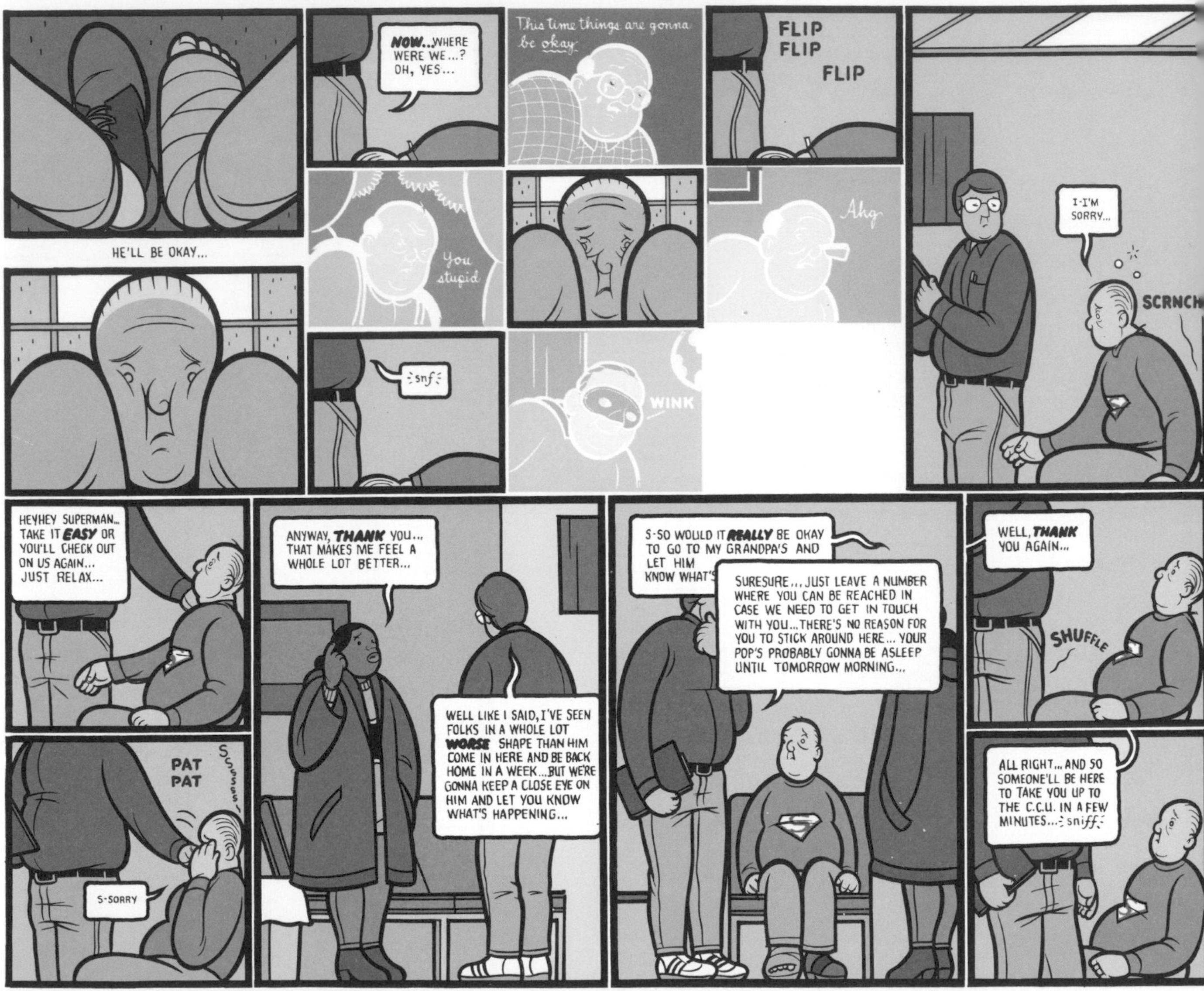

HE'LL BE OKAY...
NOW... WHERE WERE WE...? OH, YES...
This time things are gonna be okay
FLIP FLIP FLIP
You stupid
Ahg
snf
WINK
I-I'M SORRY...
SCRNCH
HEYHEY SUPERMAN... TAKE IT EASY OR YOU'LL CHECK OUT ON US AGAIN... JUST RELAX...
PAT PAT
Sssssss
S-SORRY
ANYWAY, THANK YOU... THAT MAKES ME FEEL A WHOLE LOT BETTER...
WELL LIKE I SAID, I'VE SEEN FOLKS IN A WHOLE LOT WORSE SHAPE THAN HIM COME IN HERE AND BE BACK HOME IN A WEEK... BUT WE'RE GONNA KEEP A CLOSE EYE ON HIM AND LET YOU KNOW WHAT'S HAPPENING...
S-SO WOULD IT REALLY BE OKAY TO GO TO MY GRANDPA'S AND LET HIM KNOW WHAT'S
SURESURE... JUST LEAVE A NUMBER WHERE YOU CAN BE REACHED IN CASE WE NEED TO GET IN TOUCH WITH YOU... THERE'S NO REASON FOR YOU TO STICK AROUND HERE... YOUR POP'S PROBABLY GONNA BE ASLEEP UNTIL TOMORROW MORNING...
WELL, THANK YOU AGAIN...
SHUFFLE
ALL RIGHT... AND SO SOMEONE'LL BE HERE TO TAKE YOU UP TO THE C.C.U. IN A FEW MINUTES... sniff

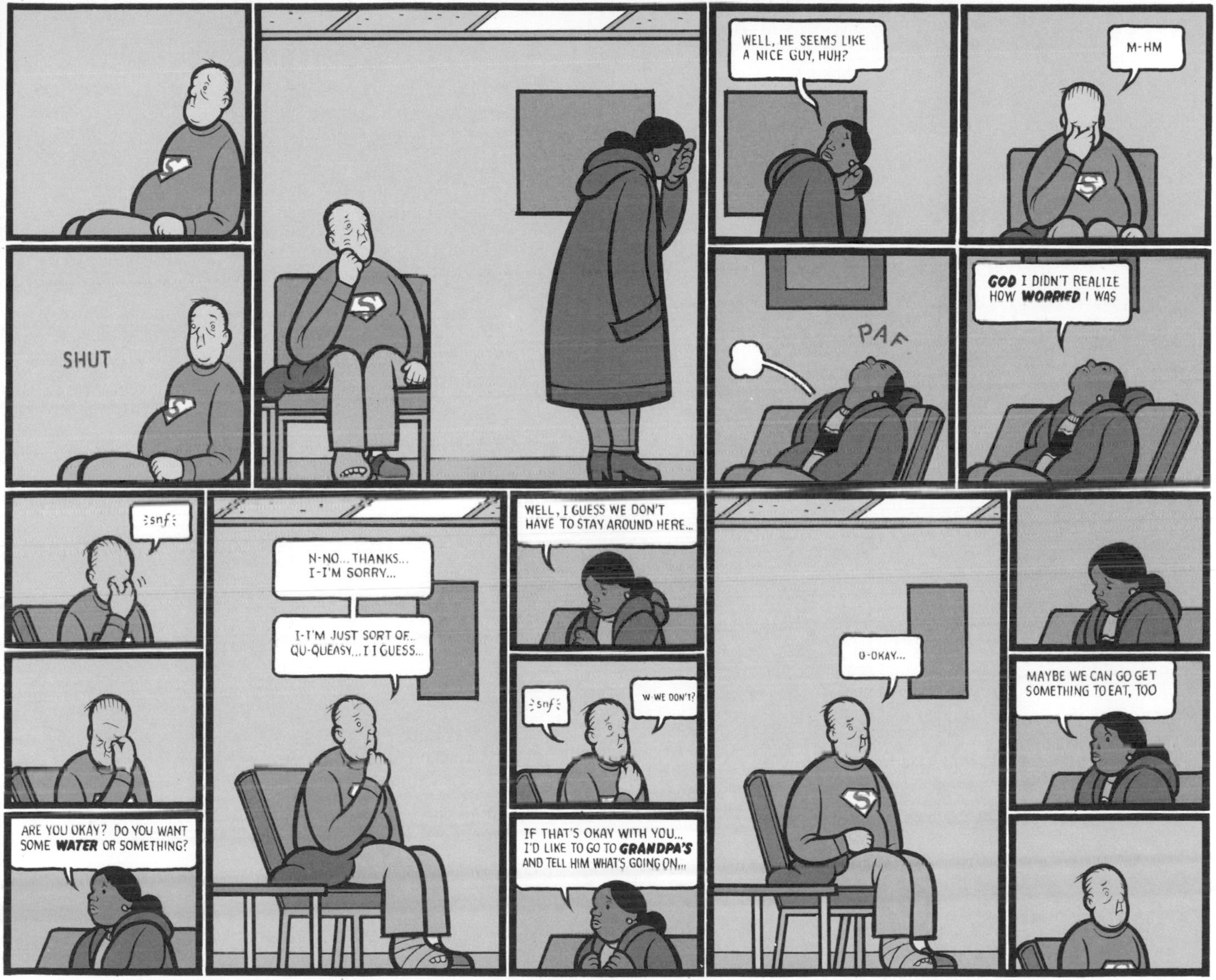
SHUT
WELL, HE SEEMS LIKE A NICE GUY, HUH?
M-HM
PAF
GOD I DIDN'T REALIZE HOW WORRIED I WAS
snf
ARE YOU OKAY? DO YOU WANT SOME WATER OR SOMETHING?
N-NO... THANKS... I-I'M SORRY...
I-I'M JUST SORT OF.. QU-QUEASY... I I GUESS...
WELL, I GUESS WE DON'T HAVE TO STAY AROUND HERE...
snf
W-WE DON'T?
IF THAT'S OKAY WITH YOU... I'D LIKE TO GO TO GRANDPA'S AND TELL HIM WHAT'S GOING ON...
O-OKAY...
MAYBE WE CAN GO GET SOMETHING TO EAT, TOO

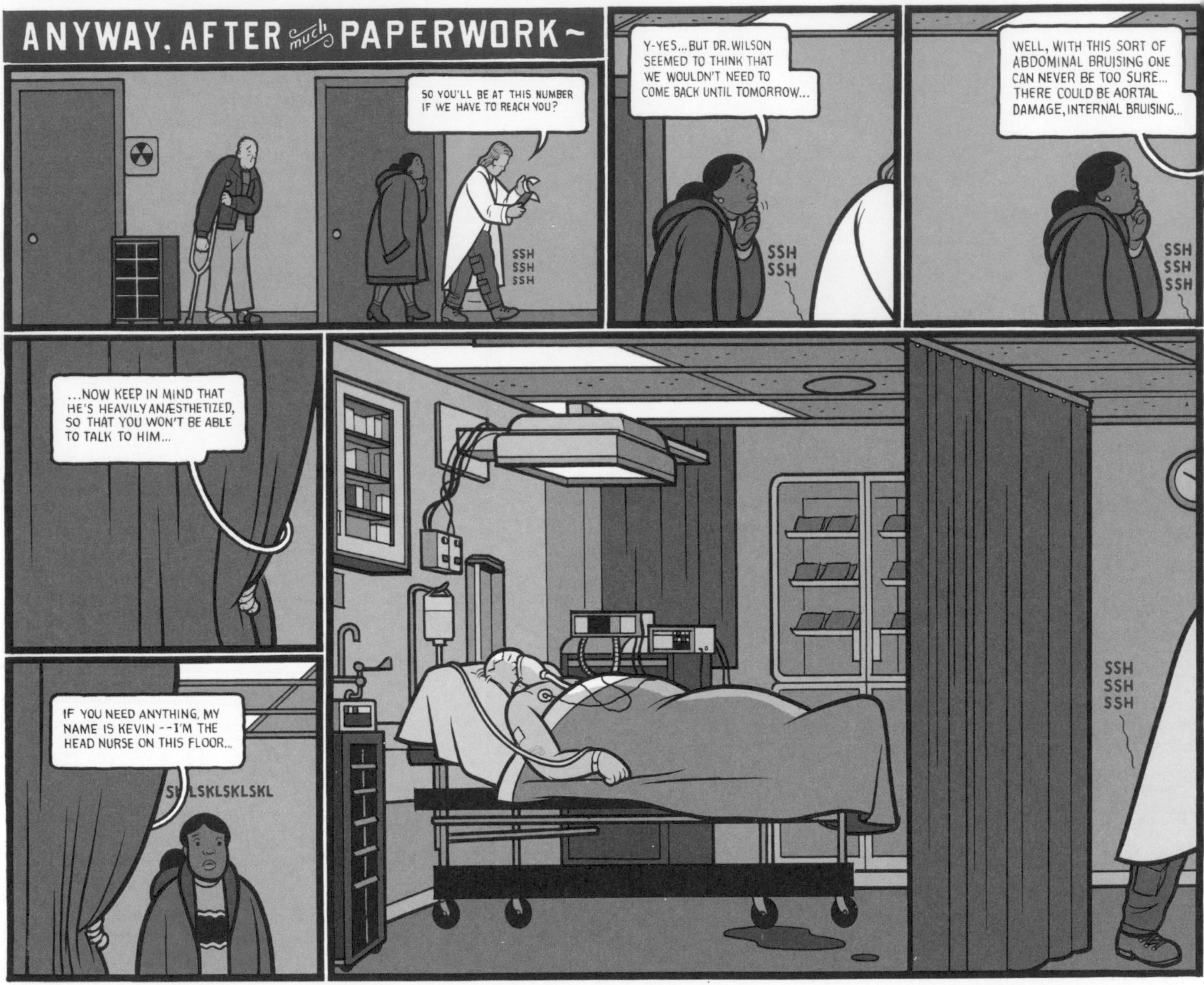
ANYWAY, AFTER much PAPERWORK~
SO YOU'LL BE AT THIS NUMBER IF WE HAVE TO REACH YOU?
SSH SSH SSH
Y-YES... BUT DR. WILSON SEEMED TO THINK THAT WE WOULDN'T NEED TO COME BACK UNTIL TOMORROW...
SSH SSH
WELL, WITH THIS SORT OF ABDOMINAL BRUISING ONE CAN NEVER BE TOO SURE... THERE COULD BE AORTAL DAMAGE, INTERNAL BRUISING...
SSH SSH SSH
...NOW KEEP IN MIND THAT HE'S HEAVILY ANÆSTHETIZED, SO THAT YOU WON'T BE ABLE TO TALK TO HIM...
IF YOU NEED ANYTHING, MY NAME IS KEVIN --I'M THE HEAD NURSE ON THIS FLOOR...
SSH SSH SSH

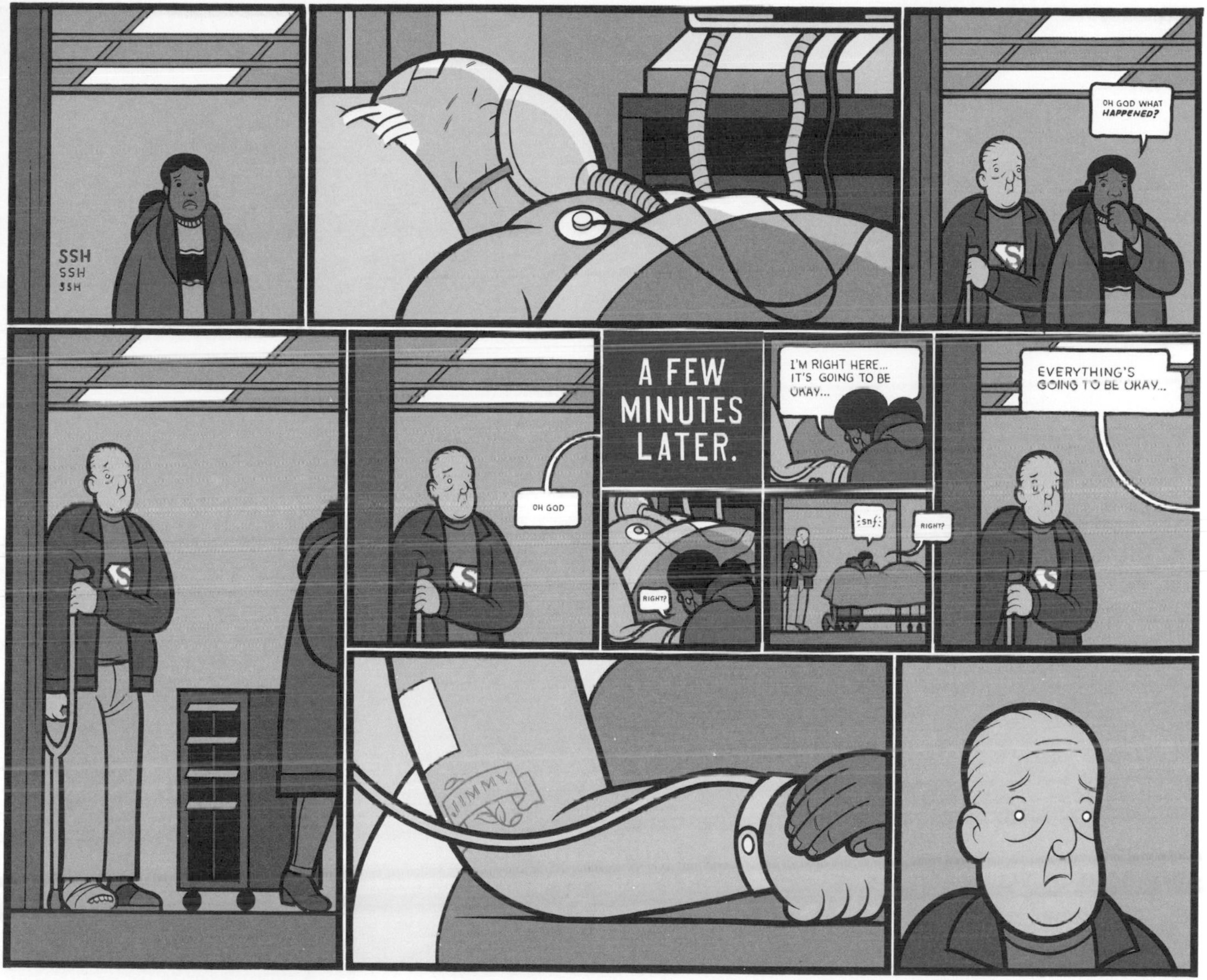
SSH
SSH
SSH
OH GOD WHAT HAPPENED?
OH GOD
A FEW MINUTES LATER.
I'M RIGHT HERE... IT'S GOING TO BE OKAY...
RIGHT?
snf
RIGHT?
EVERYTHING'S GOING TO BE OKAY...
JIMMY

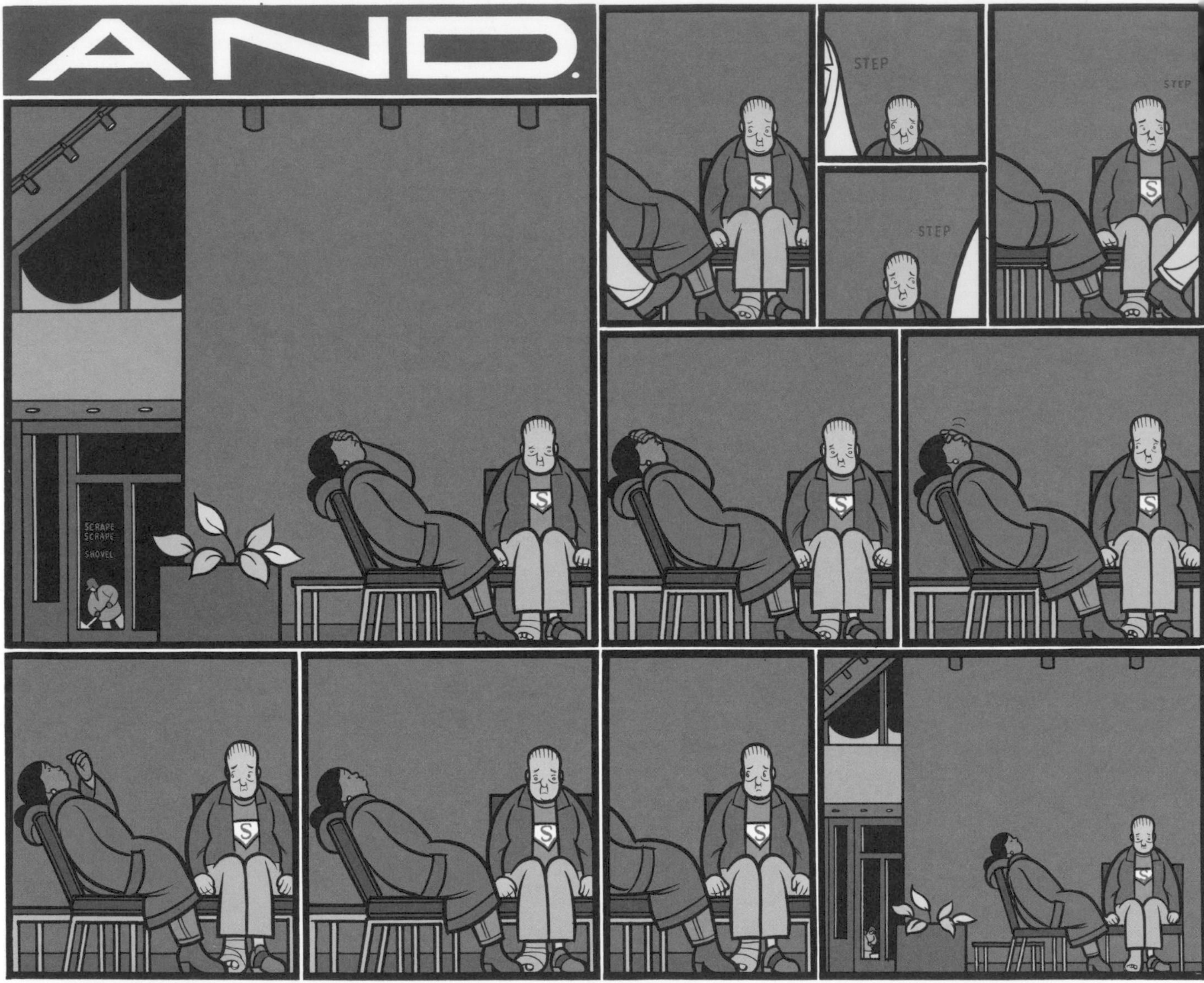

AND.
SCRAPE
SCRAPE
SHOVEL
STEP
STEP
STEP

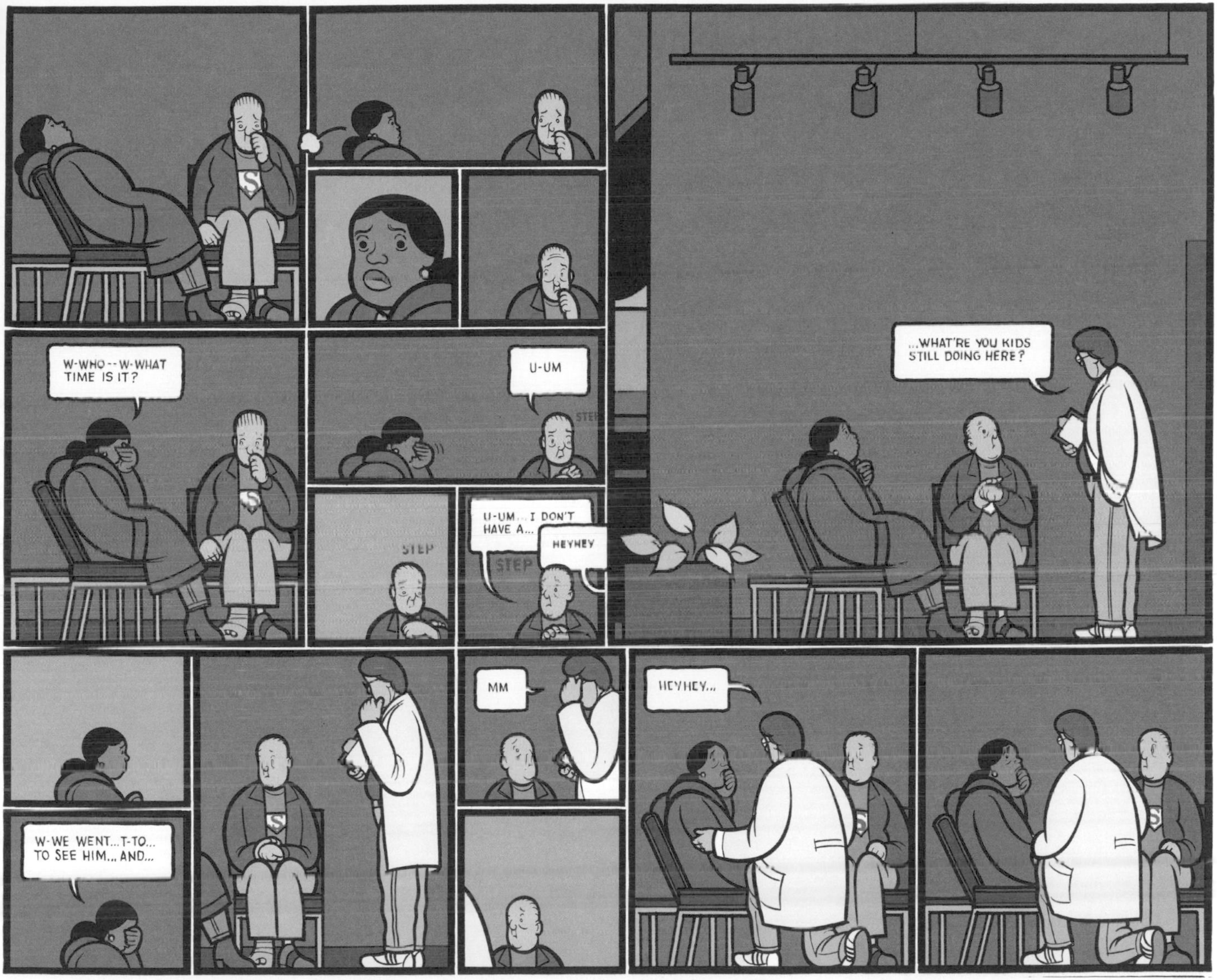
W-WHO--W-WHAT TIME IS IT?
U-UM
STEP
STEP
U-UM... I DON'T HAVE A...
STEP
HEYHEY
...WHAT'RE YOU KIDS STILL DOING HERE?
W-WE WENT...T-TO... TO SEE HIM... AND...
MM
HEYHEY...

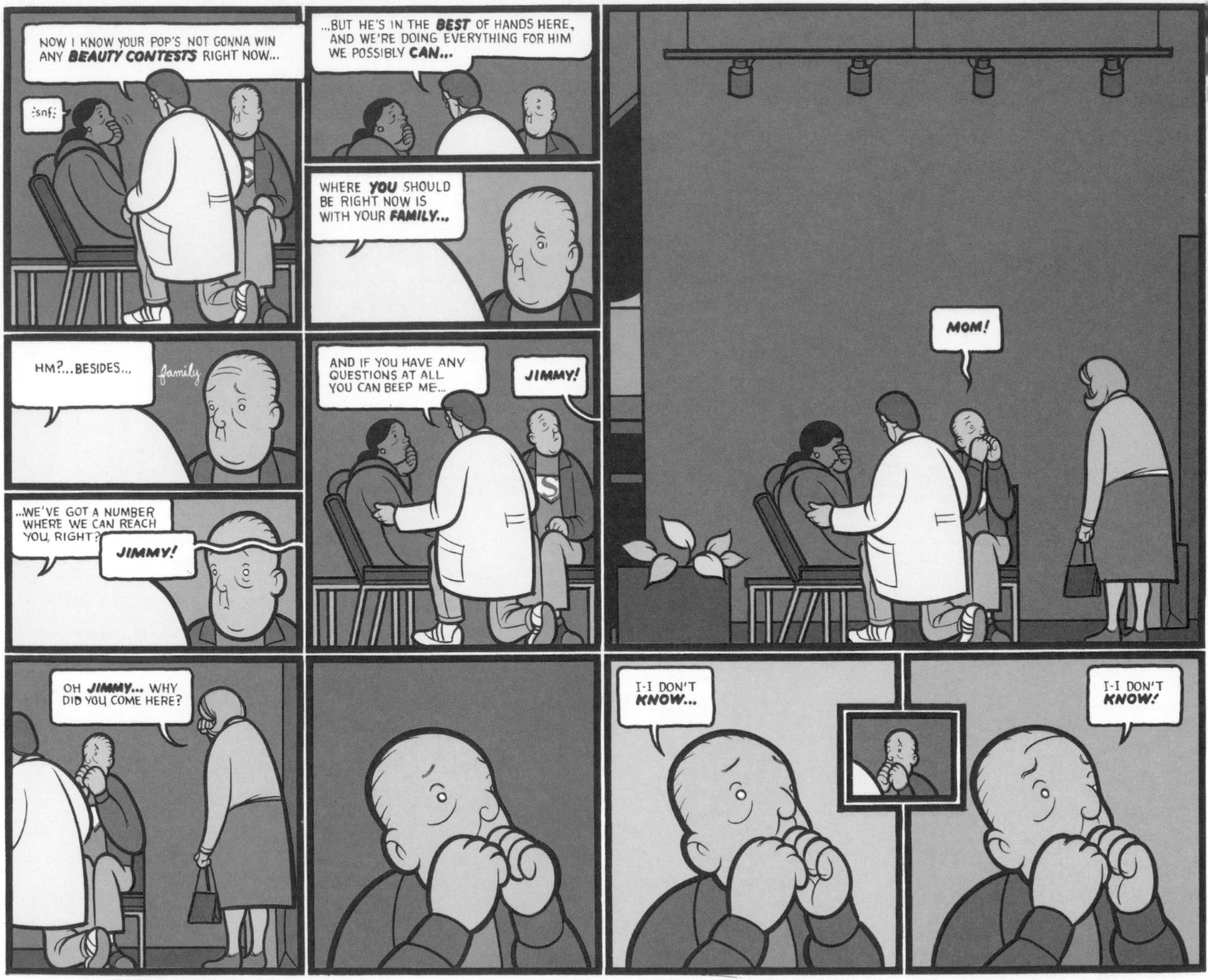
NOW I KNOW YOUR POP'S NOT GONNA WIN ANY BEAUTY CONTESTS RIGHT NOW...
snf
...BUT HE'S IN THE BEST OF HANDS HERE, AND WE'RE DOING EVERYTHING FOR HIM WE POSSIBLY CAN...
WHERE YOU SHOULD BE RIGHT NOW IS WITH YOUR FAMILY...
HM?...BESIDES...
family
...WE'VE GOT A NUMBER WHERE WE CAN REACH YOU, RIGHT?
JIMMY!
AND IF YOU HAVE ANY QUESTIONS AT ALL YOU CAN BEEP ME...
JIMMY!
MOM!
OH JIMMY... WHY DID YOU COME HERE?
I-I DON'T KNOW...
I-I DON'T KNOW!

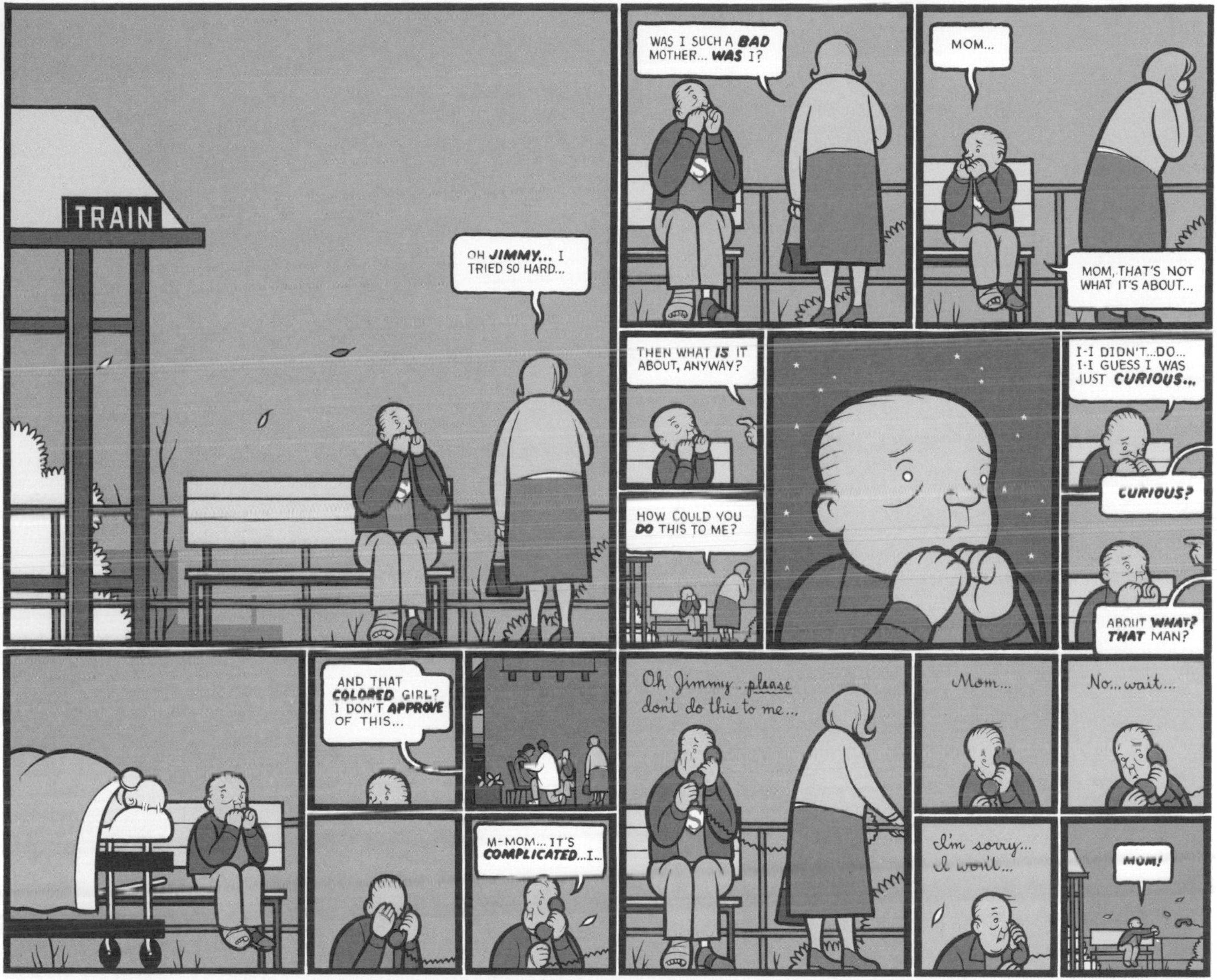
TRAIN
OH JIMMY... I TRIED SO HARD...
WAS I SUCH A BAD MOTHER... WAS I?
MOM...
MOM, THAT'S NOT WHAT IT'S ABOUT...
THEN WHAT IS IT ABOUT, ANYWAY?
HOW COULD YOU DO THIS TO ME?
I-I DIDN'T...DO... I-I GUESS I WAS JUST CURIOUS...
CURIOUS?
ABOUT WHAT? THAT MAN?
AND THAT COLORED GIRL? I DON'T APPROVE OF THIS...
M-MOM... IT'S COMPLICATED...I...
Oh Jimmy... please don't do this to me...
Mom...
No... wait...
I'm sorry... I won't...
MOM!

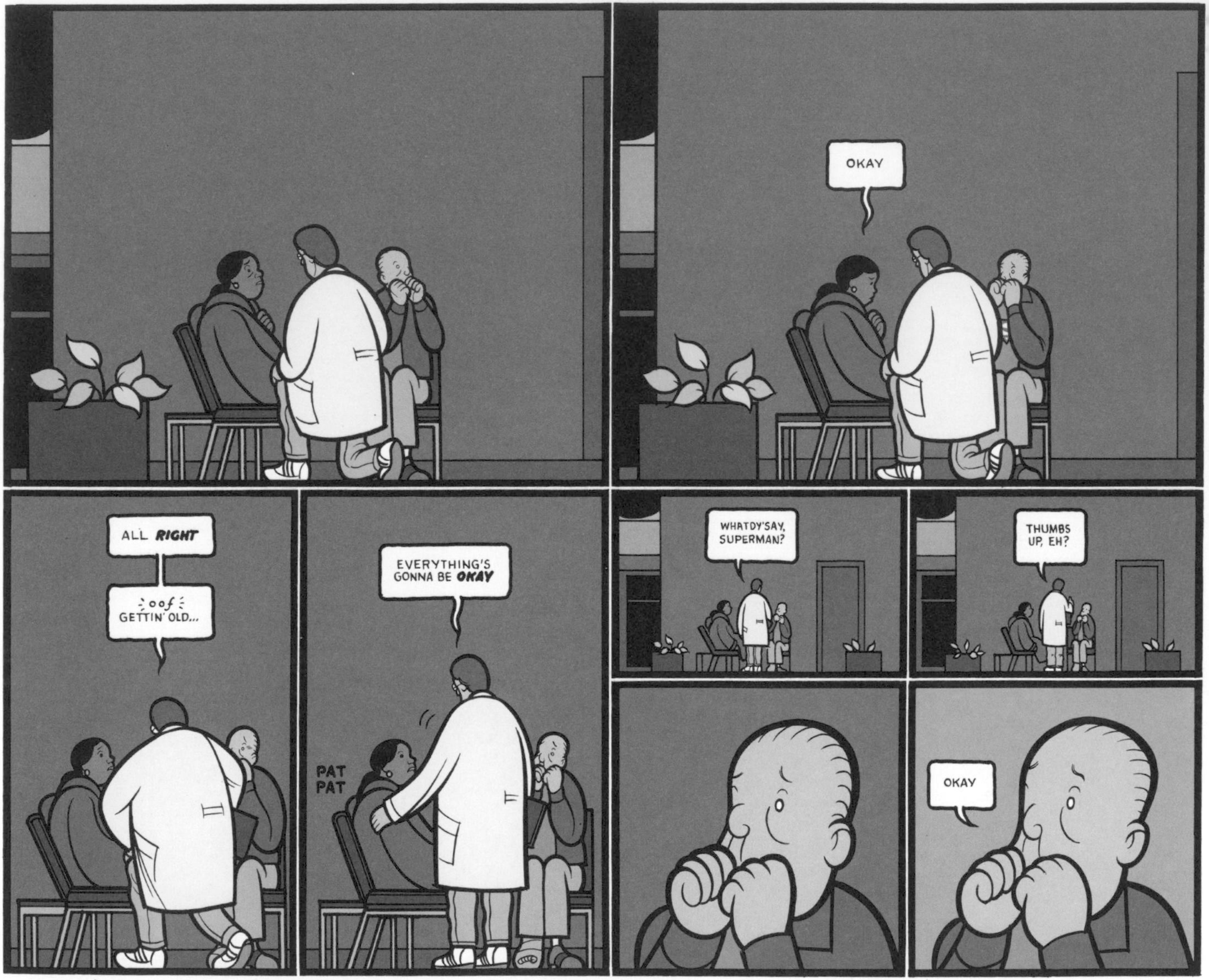
OKAY
ALL RIGHT
oof
GETTIN' OLD...
EVERYTHING'S GONNA BE OKAY
PAT PAT
WHATDY'SAY, SUPERMAN?
THUMBS UP, EH?
OKAY

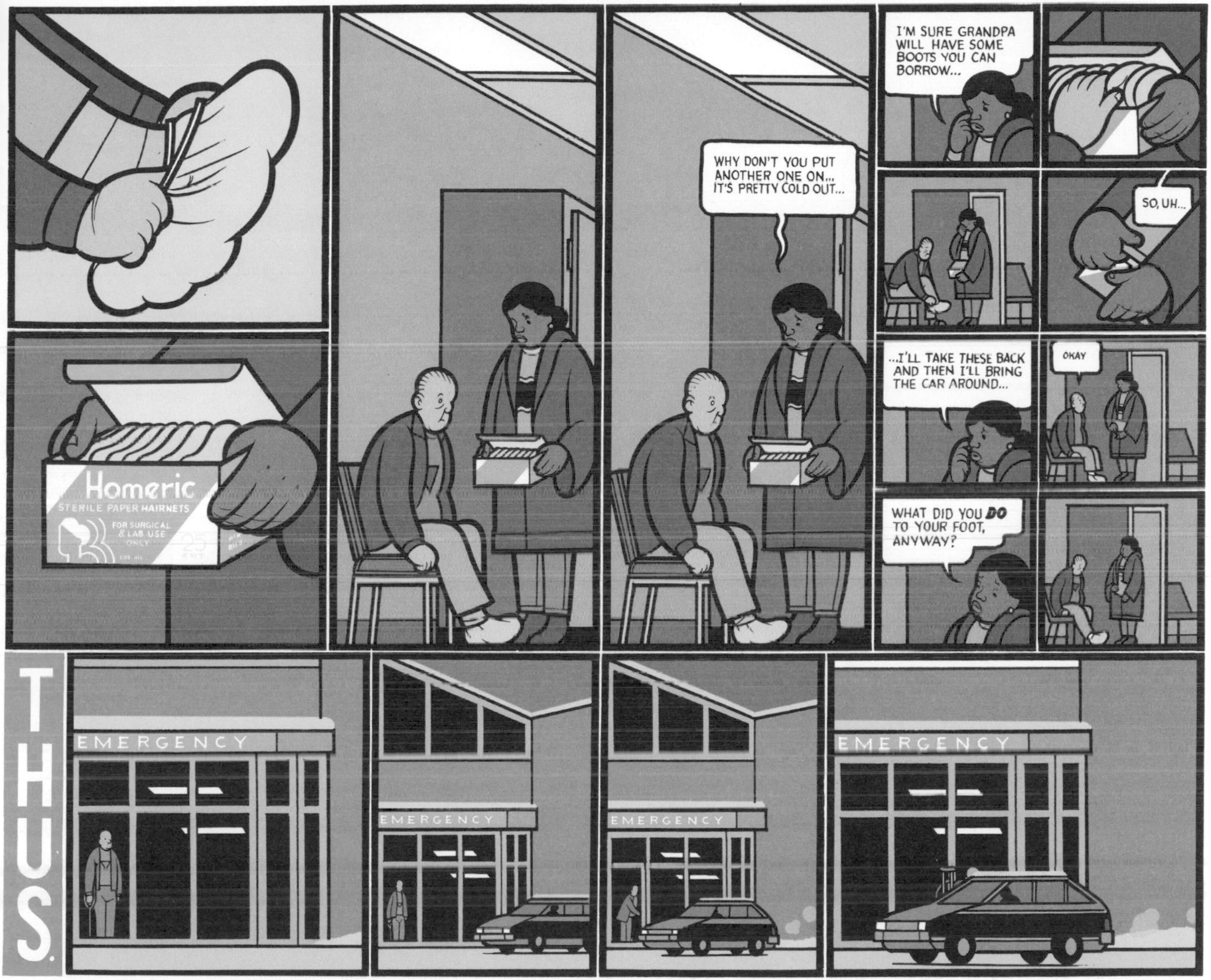
Homeric
STERILE PAPER HAIRNETS
FOR SURGICAL & LAB USE ONLY
WHY DON'T YOU PUT ANOTHER ONE ON... IT'S PRETTY COLD OUT...
I'M SURE GRANDPA WILL HAVE SOME BOOTS YOU CAN BORROW...
SO, UH...
...I'LL TAKE THESE BACK AND THEN I'LL BRING THE CAR AROUND...
OKAY
WHAT DID YOU DO TO YOUR FOOT, ANYWAY?
THUS.
EMERGENCY
EMERGENCY
EMERGENCY
EMERGENCY

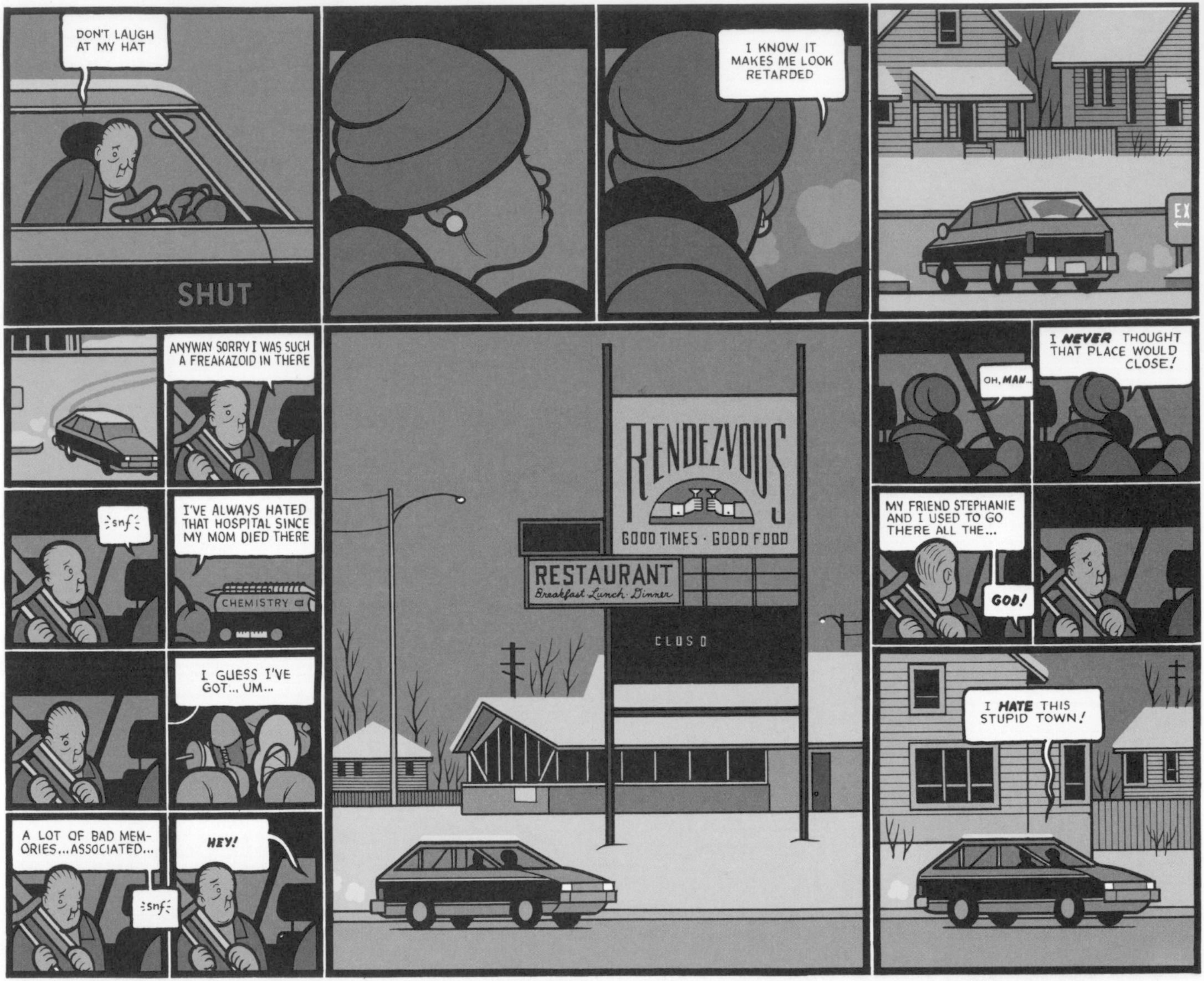
DON'T LAUGH AT MY HAT
SHUT
I KNOW IT MAKES ME LOOK RETARDED
EX
ANYWAY SORRY I WAS SUCH A FREAKAZOID IN THERE
snf
I'VE ALWAYS HATED THAT HOSPITAL SINCE MY MOM DIED THERE
CHEMISTRY
I GUESS I'VE GOT... UM...
A LOT OF BAD MEMORIES... ASSOCIATED...
snf
HEY!
RENDEZ-VOUS
GOOD TIMES · GOOD FOOD
RESTAURANT
Breakfast · Lunch · Dinner
OH, MAN...
I NEVER THOUGHT THAT PLACE WOULD CLOSE!
MY FRIEND STEPHANIE AND I USED TO GO THERE ALL THE...
GOD!
I HATE THIS STUPID TOWN!

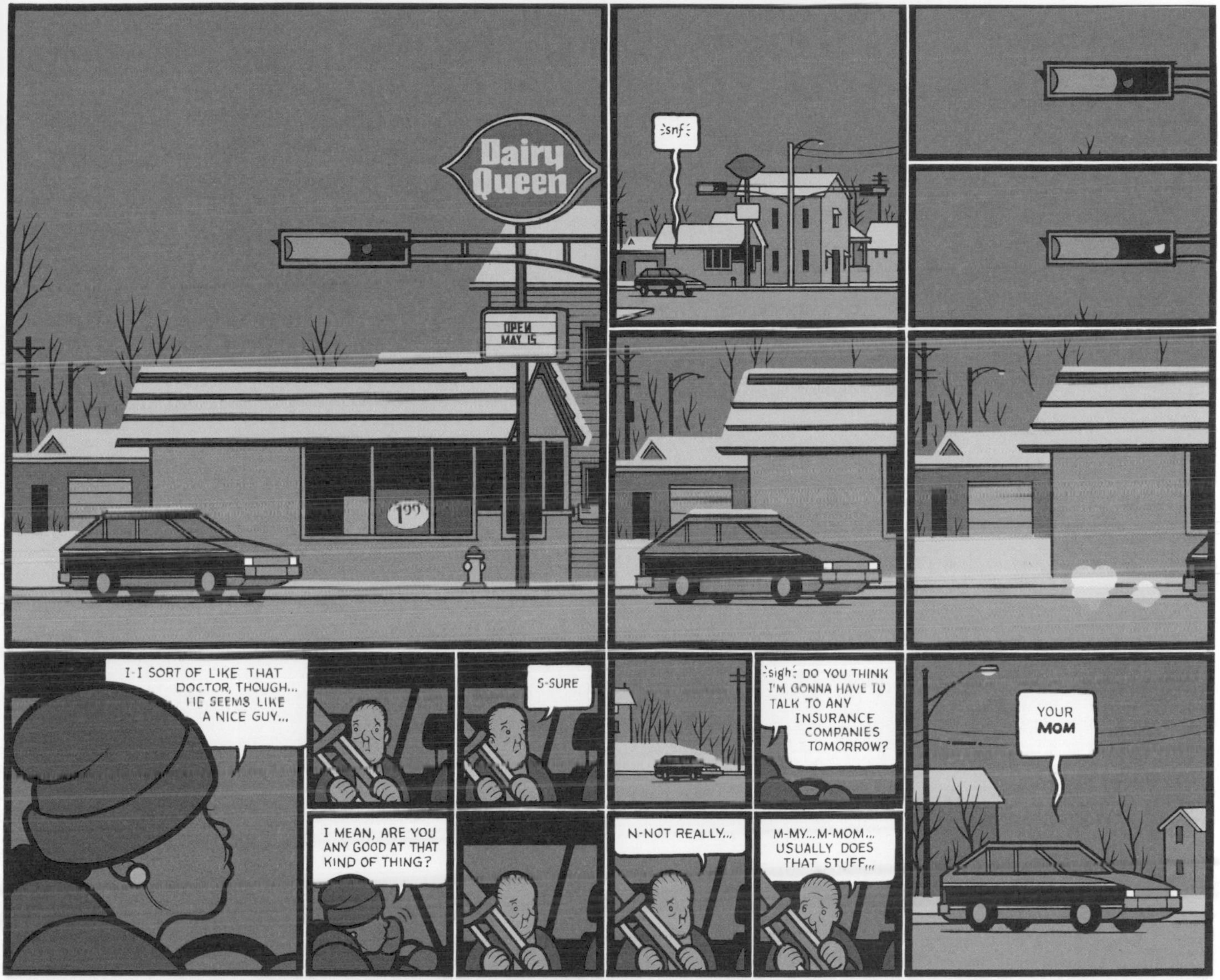
Dairy Queen
OPEN MAY 15
1.99
snf
I-I SORT OF LIKE THAT DOCTOR, THOUGH... HE SEEMS LIKE A NICE GUY...
I MEAN, ARE YOU ANY GOOD AT THAT KIND OF THING?
S-SURE
sigh DO YOU THINK I'M GONNA HAVE TO TALK TO ANY INSURANCE COMPANIES TOMORROW?
N-NOT REALLY...
M-MY...M-MOM... USUALLY DOES THAT STUFF...
YOUR MOM

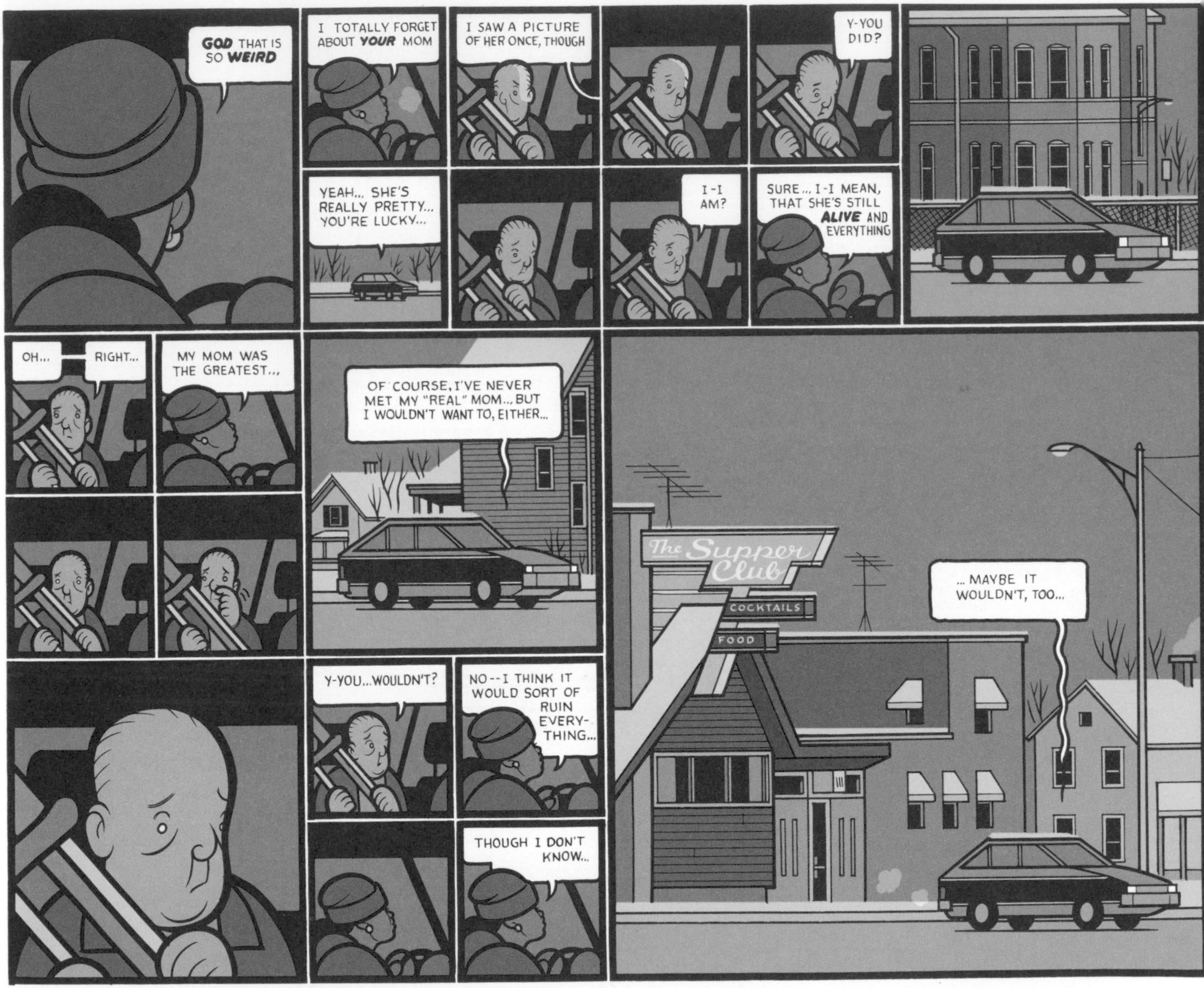

GOD THAT IS SO WEIRD
I TOTALLY FORGET ABOUT YOUR MOM
I SAW A PICTURE OF HER ONCE, THOUGH
Y-YOU DID?
YEAH... SHE'S REALLY PRETTY... YOU'RE LUCKY...
I-I AM?
SURE... I-I MEAN, THAT SHE'S STILL ALIVE AND EVERYTHING
OH...
RIGHT...
MY MOM WAS THE GREATEST...
OF COURSE, I'VE NEVER MET MY "REAL" MOM... BUT I WOULDN'T WANT TO, EITHER...
Y-YOU...WOULDN'T?
NO--I THINK IT WOULD SORT OF RUIN EVERY-THING...
THOUGH I DON'T KNOW...
The Supper Club
COCKTAILS
FOOD
... MAYBE IT WOULDN'T, TOO...

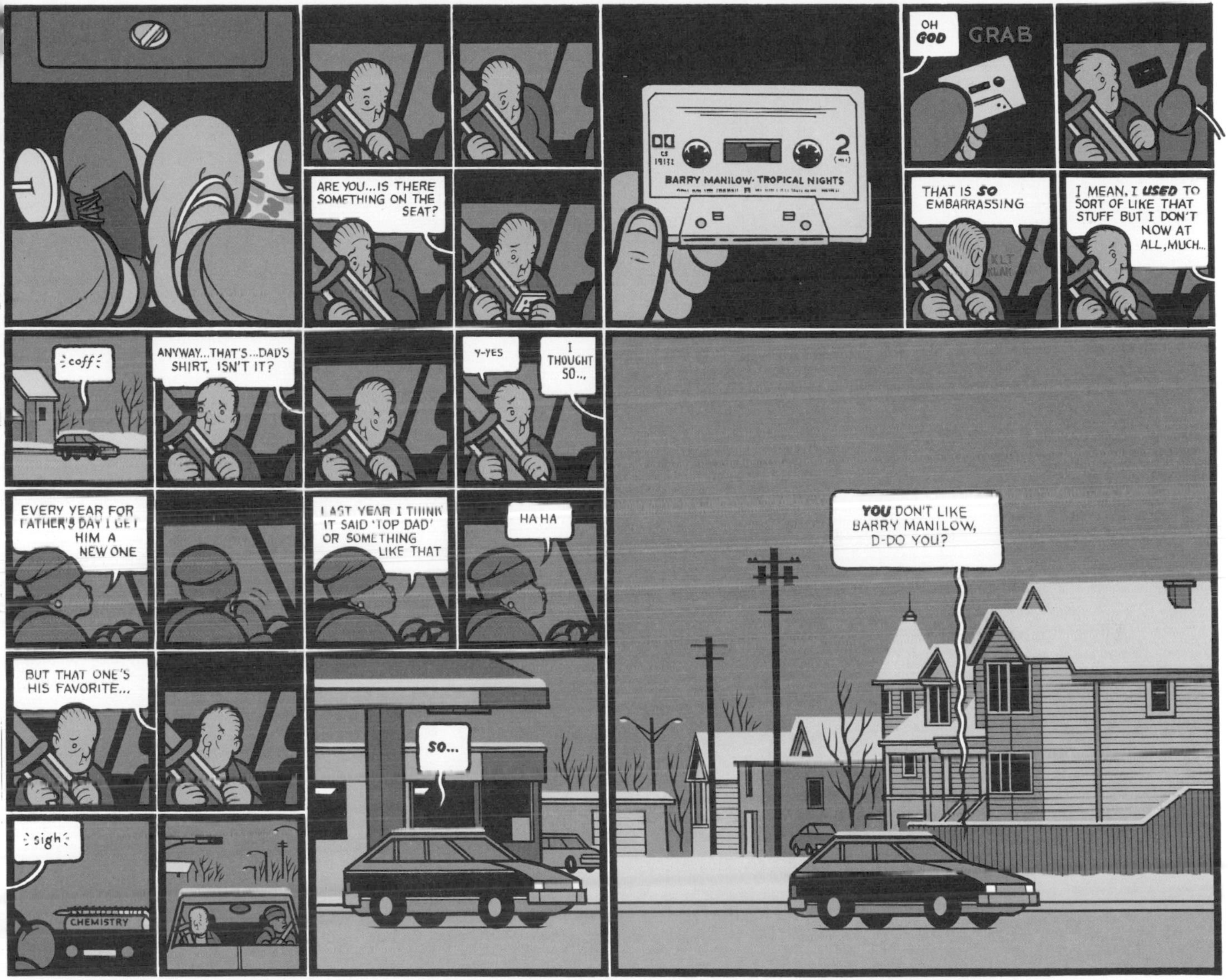
ARE YOU...IS THERE SOMETHING ON THE SEAT?
BARRY MANILOW · TROPICAL NIGHTS
OH GOD
GRAB
THAT IS SO EMBARRASSING
I MEAN, I USED TO SORT OF LIKE THAT STUFF BUT I DON'T NOW AT ALL, MUCH...
coff
ANYWAY...THAT'S...DAD'S SHIRT, ISN'T IT?
Y-YES
I THOUGHT SO...
EVERY YEAR FOR FATHER'S DAY I GET HIM A NEW ONE
LAST YEAR I THINK IT SAID 'TOP DAD' OR SOMETHING LIKE THAT
HA HA
BUT THAT ONE'S HIS FAVORITE...
SO...
sigh
CHEMISTRY
YOU DON'T LIKE BARRY MANILOW, D-DO YOU?

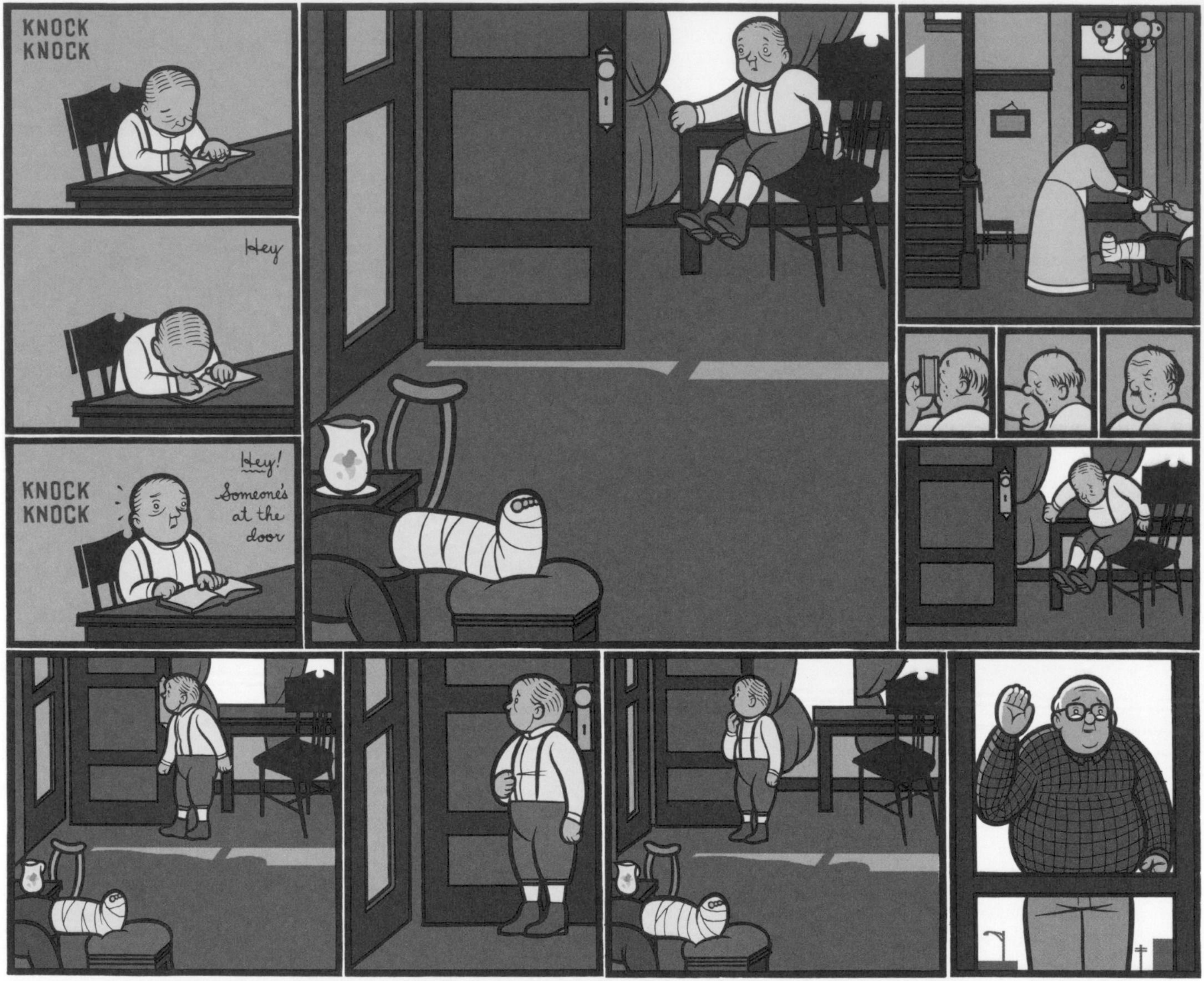
KNOCK KNOCK
Hey
Hey! Someone's at the door
KNOCK KNOCK

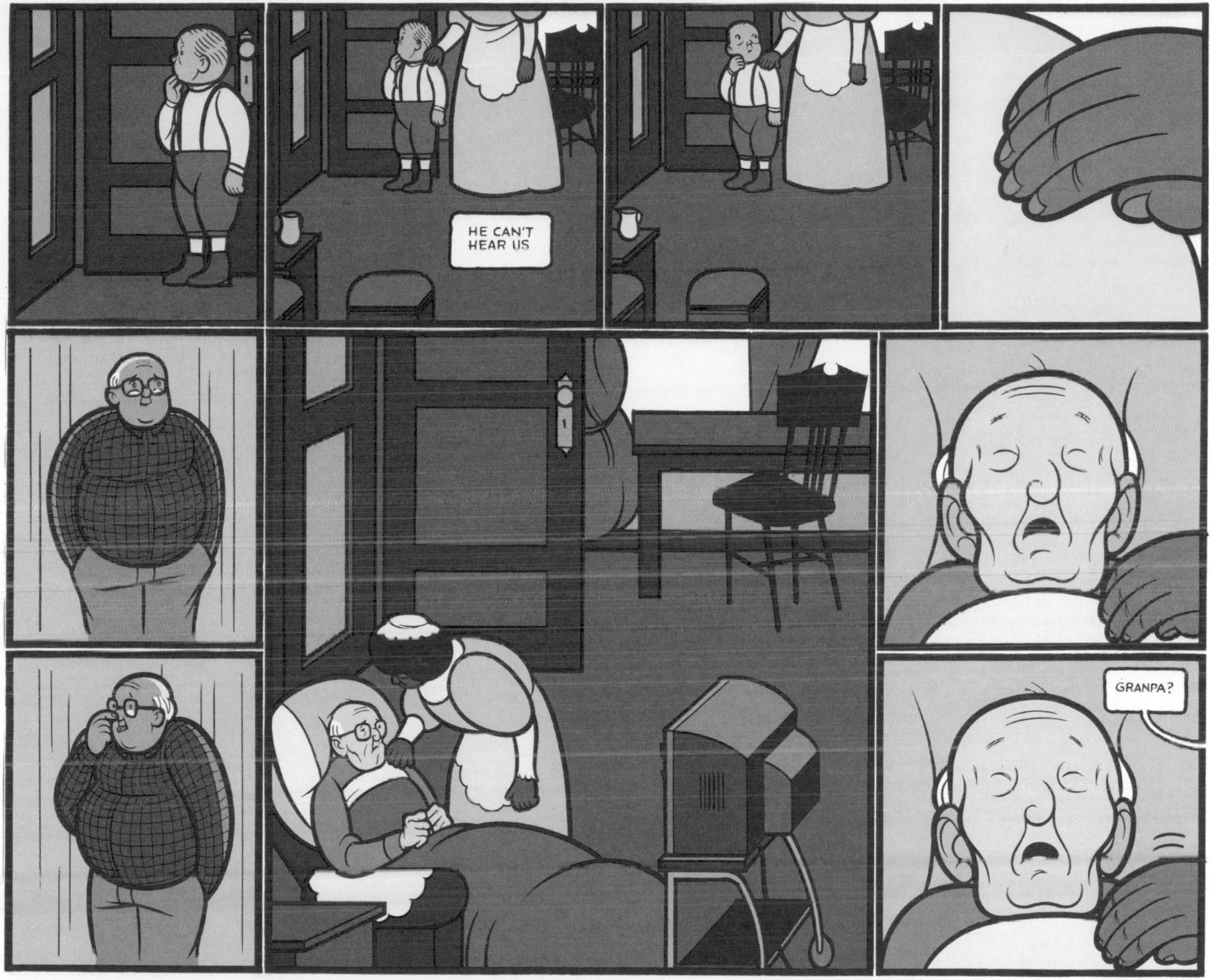
HE CAN'T HEAR US
GRANPA?

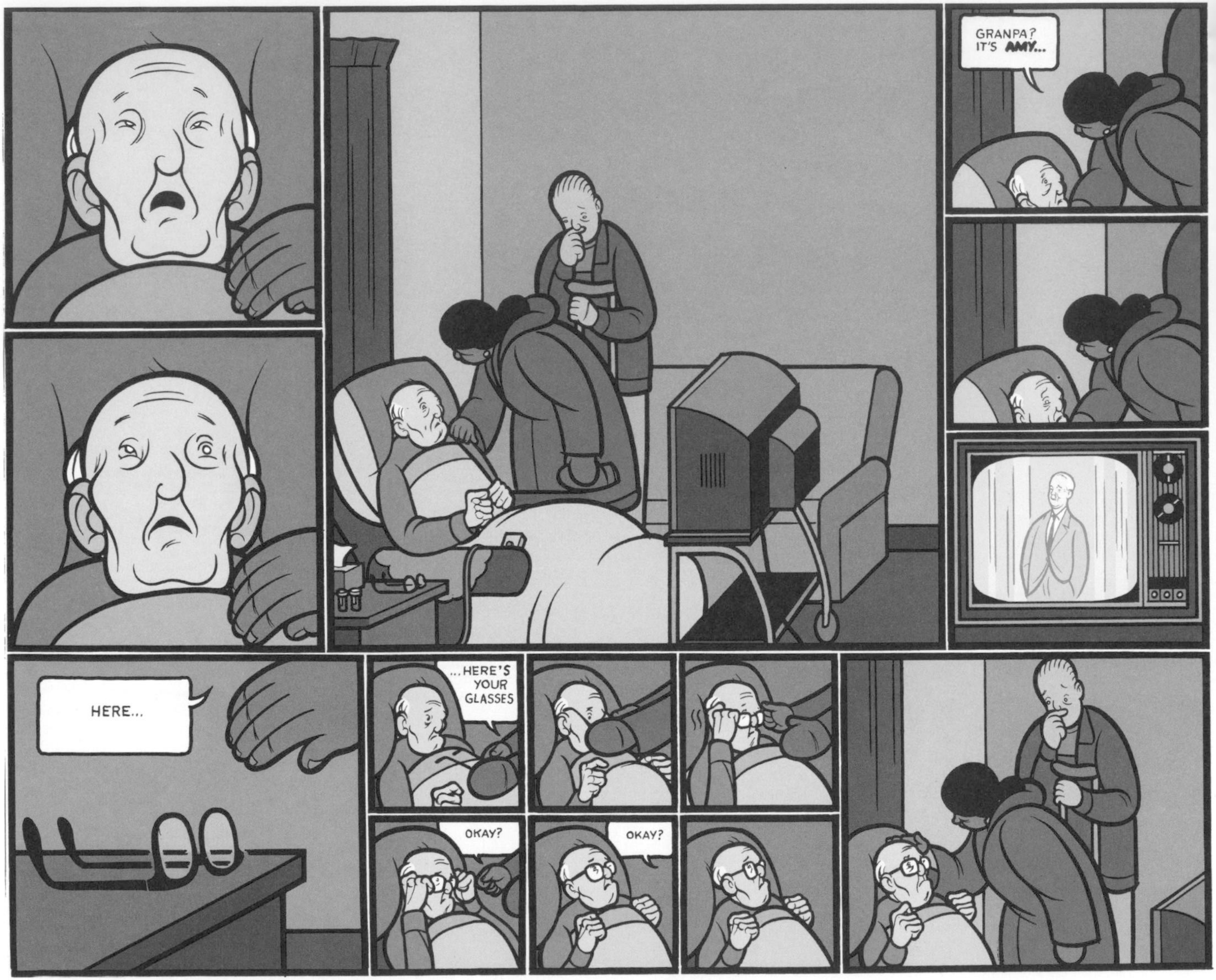

GRANPA? IT'S AMY...
HERE...
...HERE'S YOUR GLASSES
OKAY?
OKAY?

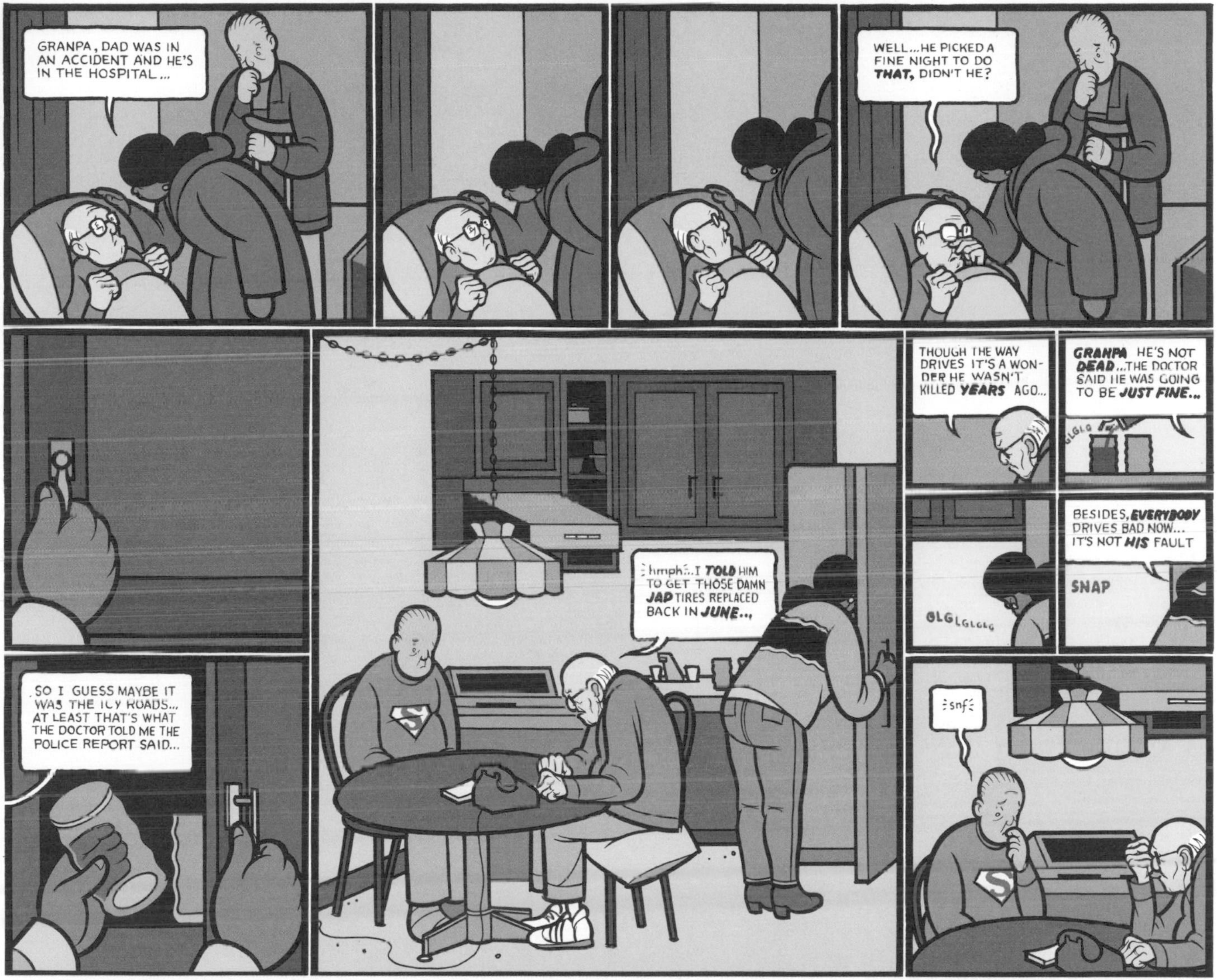
GRANPA, DAD WAS IN AN ACCIDENT AND HE'S IN THE HOSPITAL...
WELL... HE PICKED A FINE NIGHT TO DO **THAT,** DIDN'T HE?
SO I GUESS MAYBE IT WAS THE ICY ROADS... AT LEAST THAT'S WHAT THE DOCTOR TOLD ME THE POLICE REPORT SAID...
hmph... I **TOLD** HIM TO GET THOSE DAMN **JAD** TIRES REPLACED BACK IN **JUNE...**
THOUGH THE WAY DRIVES IT'S A WONDER HE WASN'T KILLED **YEARS** AGO...
GRANPA HE'S NOT **DEAD**...THE DOCTOR SAID HE WAS GOING TO BE **JUST FINE...**
GLGLG
BESIDES, **EVERYBODY** DRIVES BAD NOW... IT'S NOT **HIS** FAULT
SNAP
snf

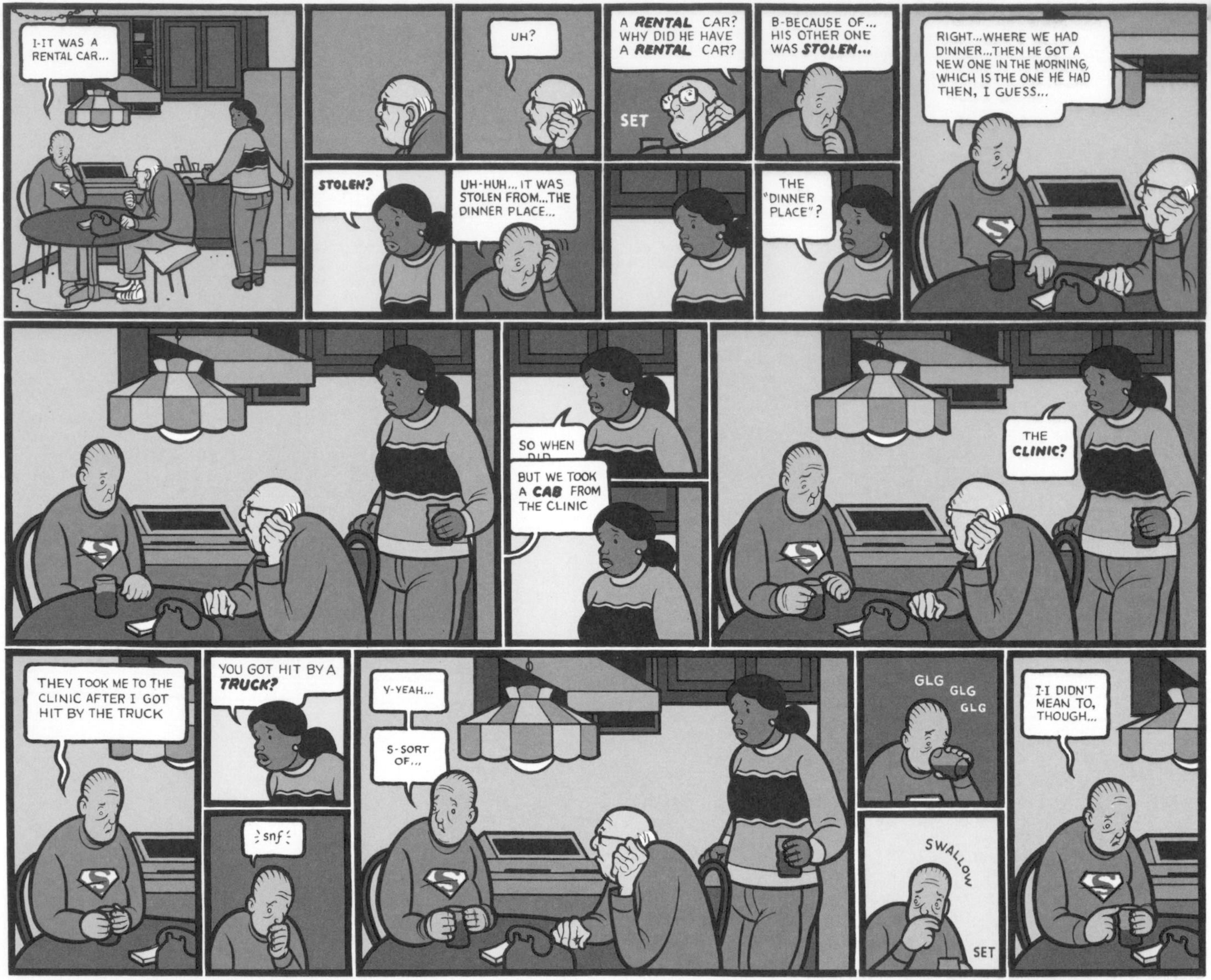
I-IT WAS A RENTAL CAR...
UH?
A RENTAL CAR? WHY DID HE HAVE A RENTAL CAR?
SET
B-BECAUSE OF... HIS OTHER ONE WAS STOLEN...
STOLEN?
UH-HUH... IT WAS STOLEN FROM...THE DINNER PLACE...
THE "DINNER PLACE"?
RIGHT...WHERE WE HAD DINNER...THEN HE GOT A NEW ONE IN THE MORNING, WHICH IS THE ONE HE HAD THEN, I GUESS...
SO WHEN
BUT WE TOOK A CAB FROM THE CLINIC
THE CLINIC?
THEY TOOK ME TO THE CLINIC AFTER I GOT HIT BY THE TRUCK
YOU GOT HIT BY A TRUCK?
snf
Y-YEAH...
S-SORT OF...
GLG GLG GLG
SWALLOW
SET
I-I DIDN'T MEAN TO, THOUGH...

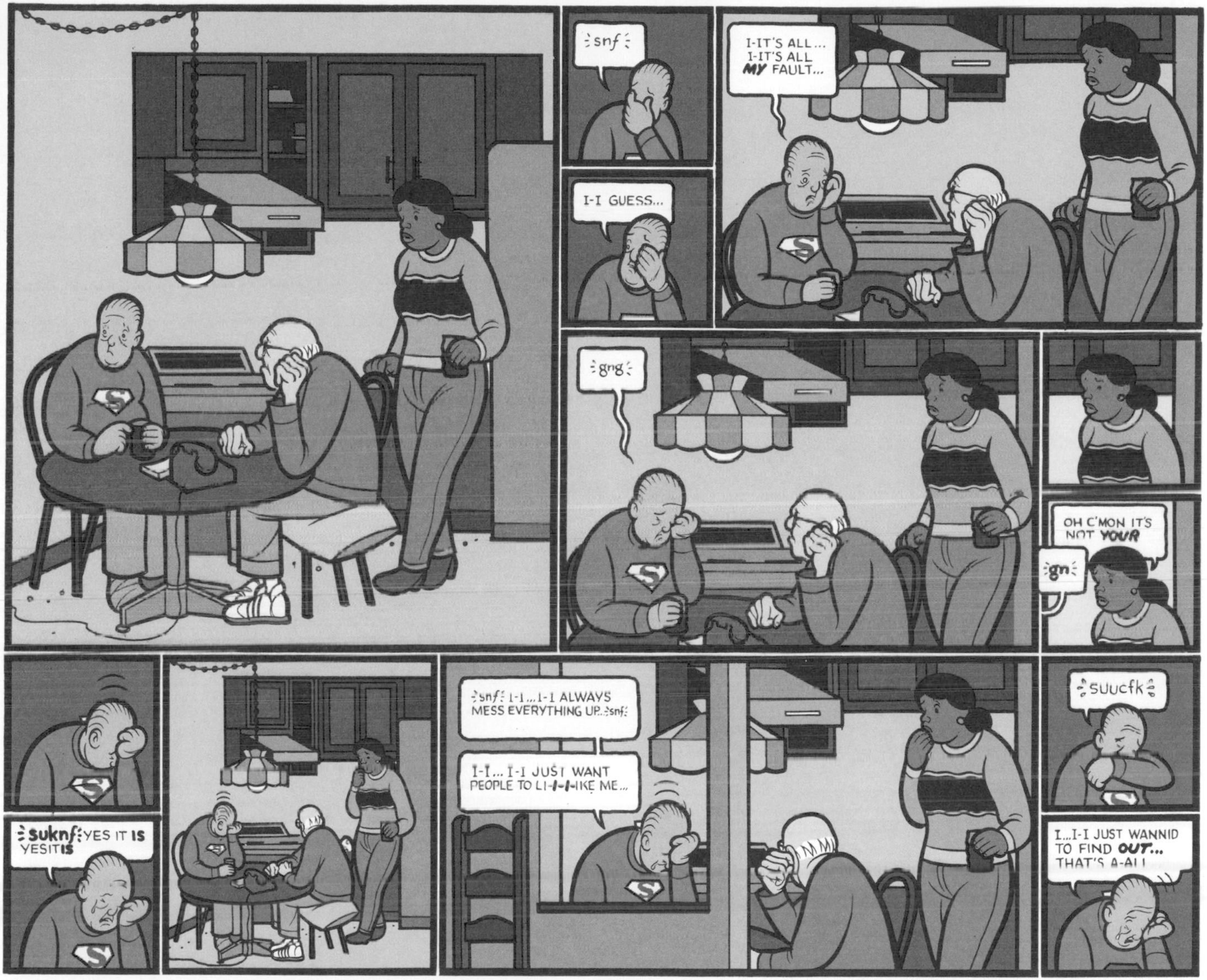
snf
I-I GUESS...
I-IT'S ALL... I-IT'S ALL MY FAULT...
gng
OH C'MON IT'S NOT YOUR
gn
suknf YES IT IS YESITIS
snf I-I...I-I ALWAYS MESS EVERYTHING UP...snf
I-I... I-I JUST WANT PEOPLE TO LI-I-I-IKE ME...
SUUCFK
I...I-I JUST WANNID TO FIND OUT... THAT'S A-ALL

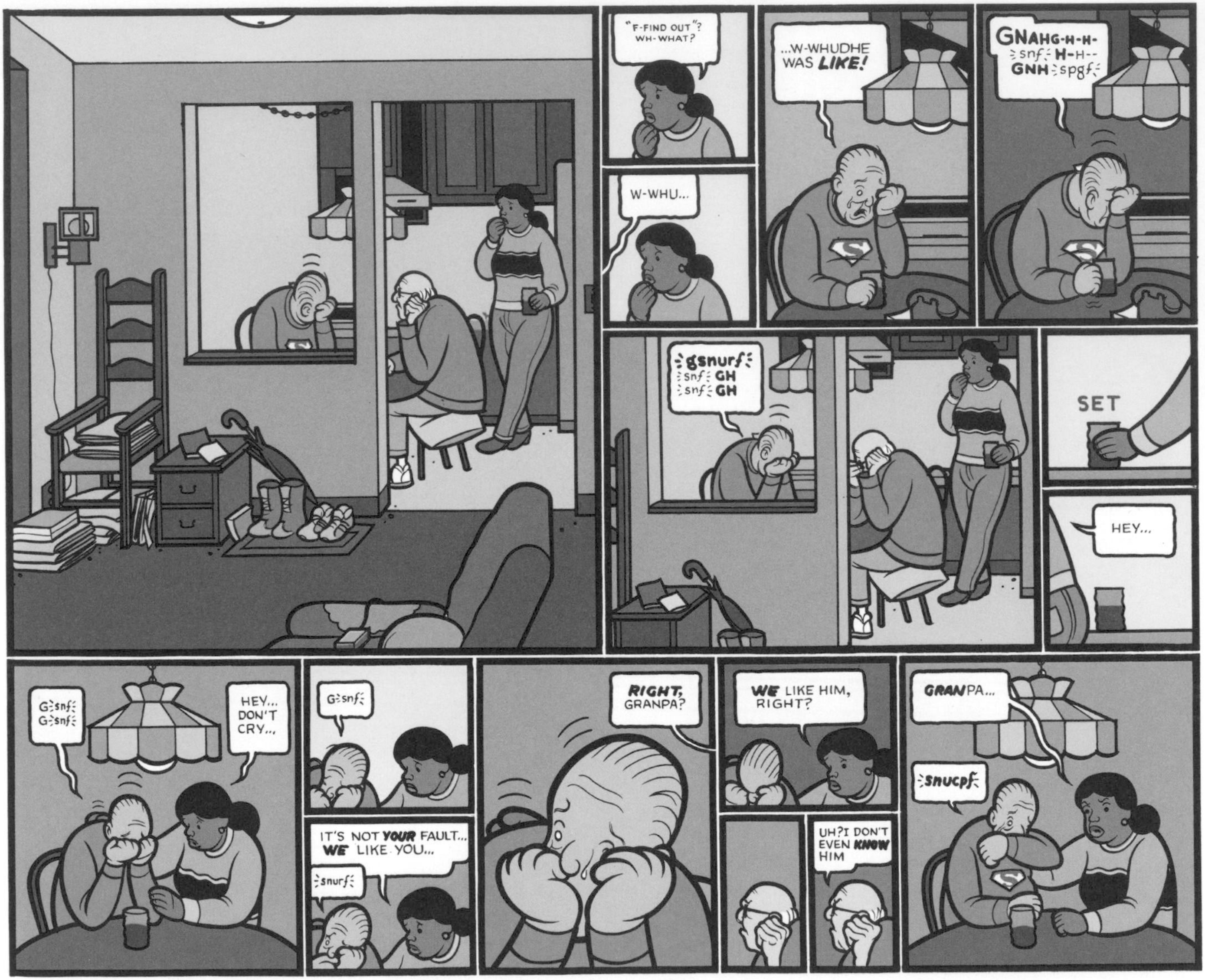
"F-FIND OUT"? WH-WHAT?
W-WHU...
...W-WHUDHE WAS LIKE!
GNAHG-H-H- snf H-H-- GNH spgf
gsnurf snf GH snf GH
SET
HEY...
G snf G snf
HEY... DON'T CRY...
G snf
IT'S NOT YOUR FAULT... WE LIKE YOU...
snurf
RIGHT, GRANPA?
WE LIKE HIM, RIGHT?
UH? I DON'T EVEN KNOW HIM
GRANPA...
snucpf

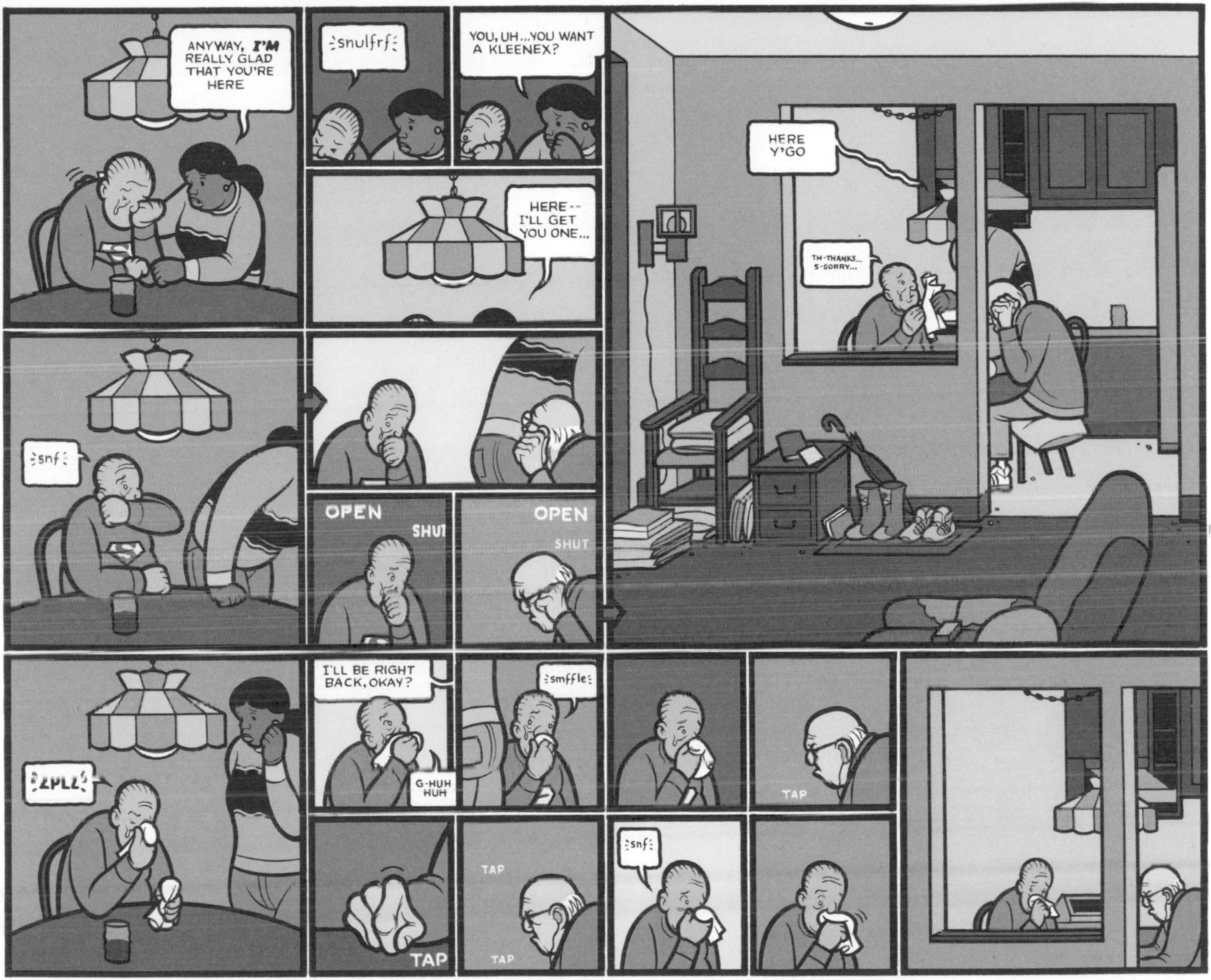
ANYWAY, I'M REALLY GLAD THAT YOU'RE HERE
snulfrf
YOU, UH...YOU WANT A KLEENEX?
HERE-- I'LL GET YOU ONE...
HERE Y'GO
TH-THANKS... S-SORRY...
snf
OPEN
SHUT
OPEN
SHUT
ZPLZ
I'LL BE RIGHT BACK, OKAY?
G-HUH HUH
smffle
TAP
TAP
TAP
TAP
snf

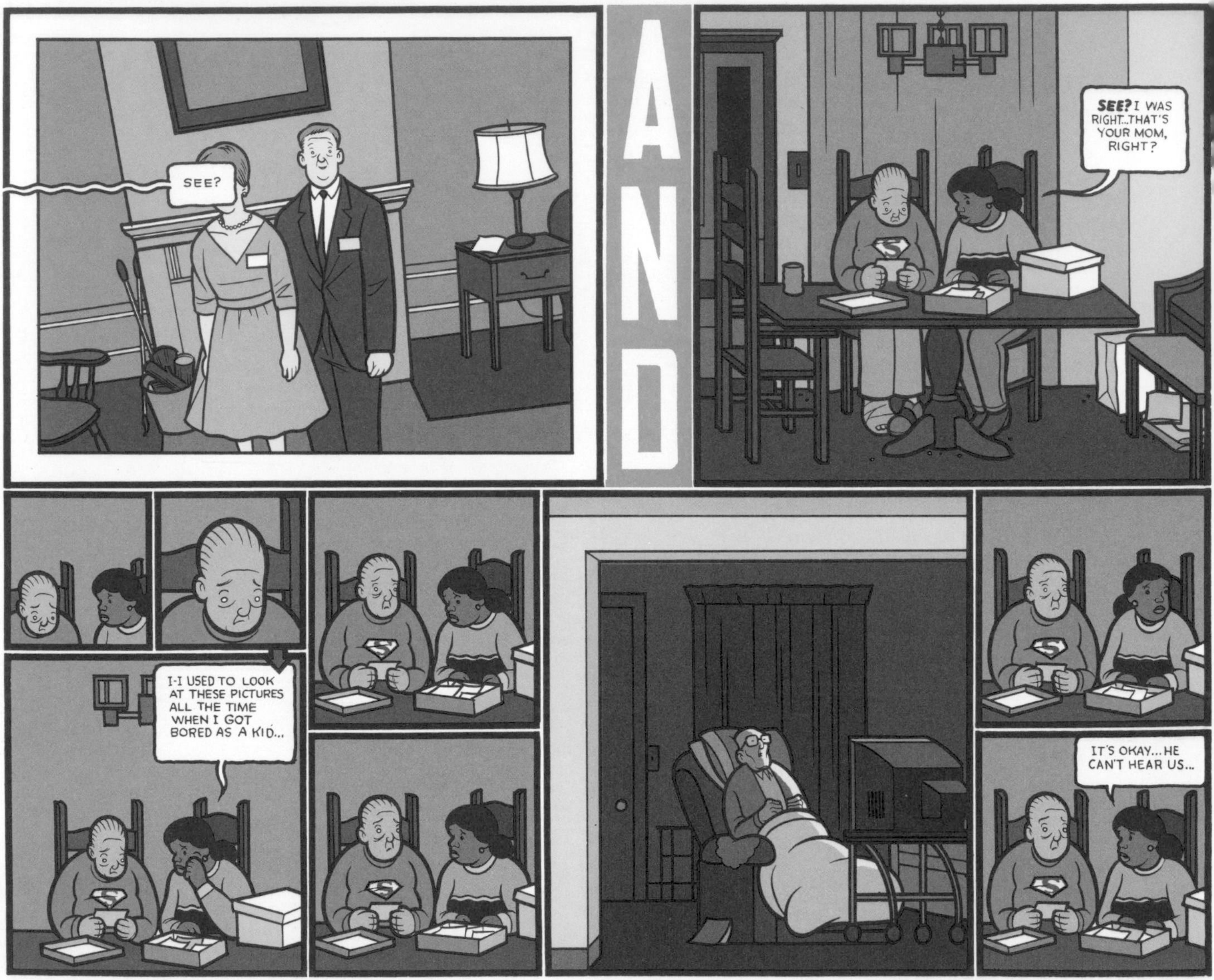
SEE?
AND
SEE? I WAS RIGHT...THAT'S YOUR MOM, RIGHT?
I-I USED TO LOOK AT THESE PICTURES ALL THE TIME WHEN I GOT BORED AS A KID...
IT'S OKAY... HE CAN'T HEAR US...

CHRISTMAS

I GOT A FRANKENSTEIN DOLL, I THINK... I LOVED MONSTERS...

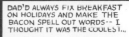

DAD'D ALWAYS FIX BREAKFAST ON HOLIDAYS AND MAKE THE BACON SPELL OUT WORDS-- I THOUGHT IT WAS THE COOLEST...

UM... HE BROUGHT A LOT OF THESE PICTURES OVER HERE AFTER MOM DIED CAUSE I GUESS HE DIDN'T WANT THEM AROUND ANYMORE...

HE STILL REALLY "BLAMES HIMSELF"

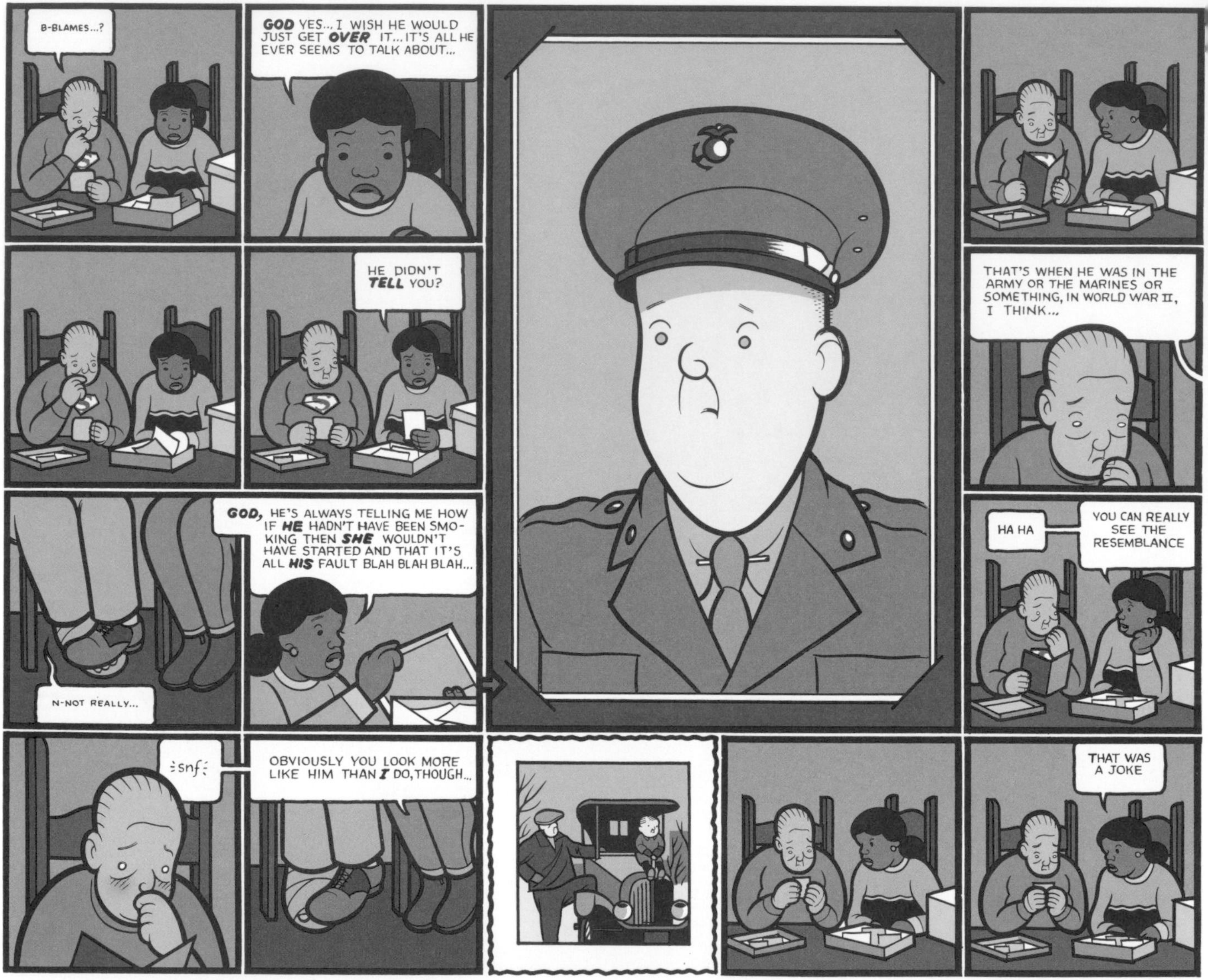
B-BLAMES...?
GOD YES... I WISH HE WOULD JUST GET OVER IT... IT'S ALL HE EVER SEEMS TO TALK ABOUT...
HE DIDN'T TELL YOU?
N-NOT REALLY...
GOD, HE'S ALWAYS TELLING ME HOW IF HE HADN'T HAVE BEEN SMOKING THEN SHE WOULDN'T HAVE STARTED AND THAT IT'S ALL HIS FAULT BLAH BLAH BLAH...
THAT'S WHEN HE WAS IN THE ARMY OR THE MARINES OR SOMETHING, IN WORLD WAR II, I THINK...
HA HA
YOU CAN REALLY SEE THE RESEMBLANCE
snf
OBVIOUSLY YOU LOOK MORE LIKE HIM THAN I DO, THOUGH...
THAT WAS A JOKE

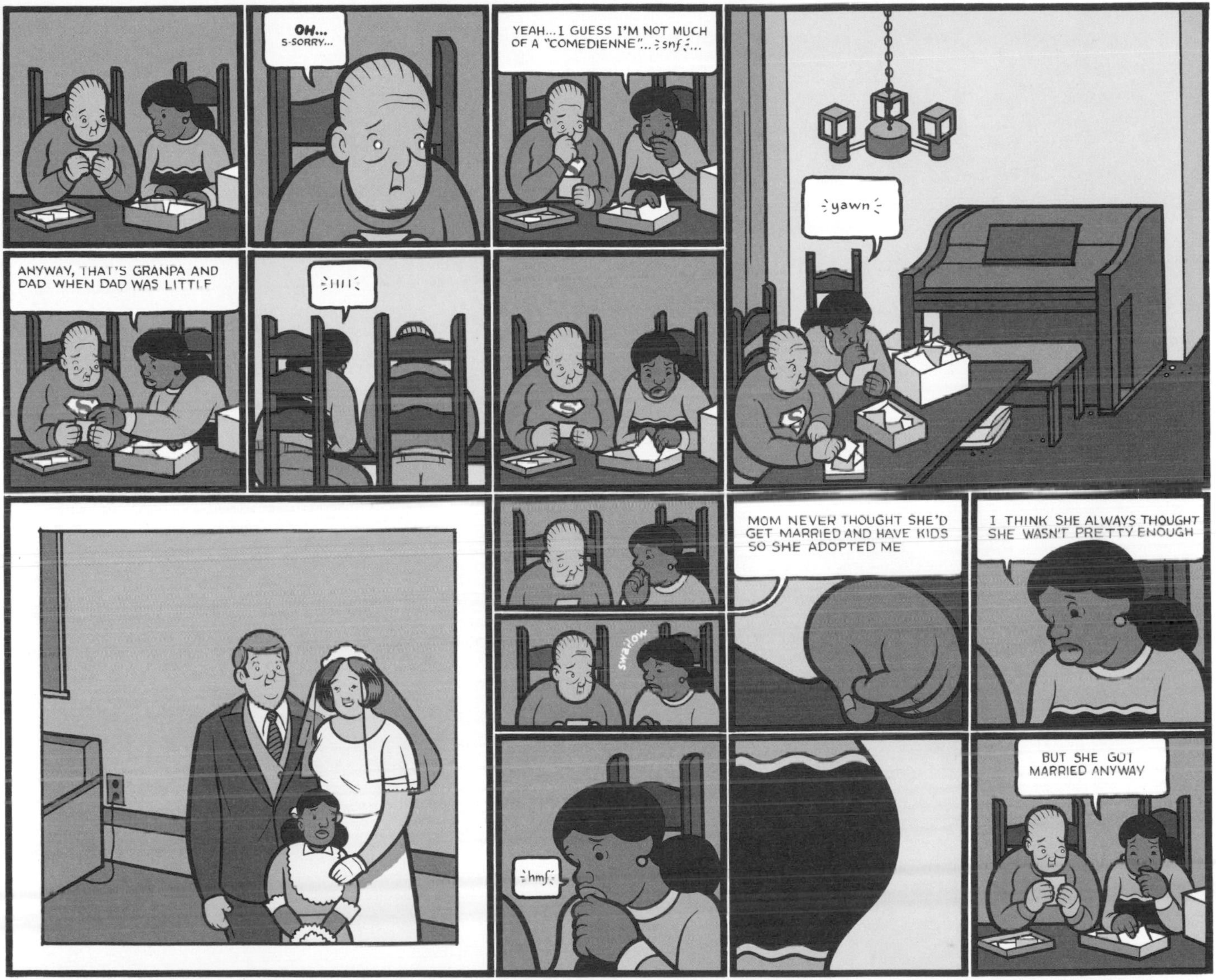
OH...
S-SORRY...
YEAH... I GUESS I'M NOT MUCH OF A "COMEDIENNE"... snf...
yawn
ANYWAY, THAT'S GRANPA AND DAD WHEN DAD WAS LITTLE
swallow
MOM NEVER THOUGHT SHE'D GET MARRIED AND HAVE KIDS SO SHE ADOPTED ME
I THINK SHE ALWAYS THOUGHT SHE WASN'T PRETTY ENOUGH
hmf
BUT SHE GOT MARRIED ANYWAY

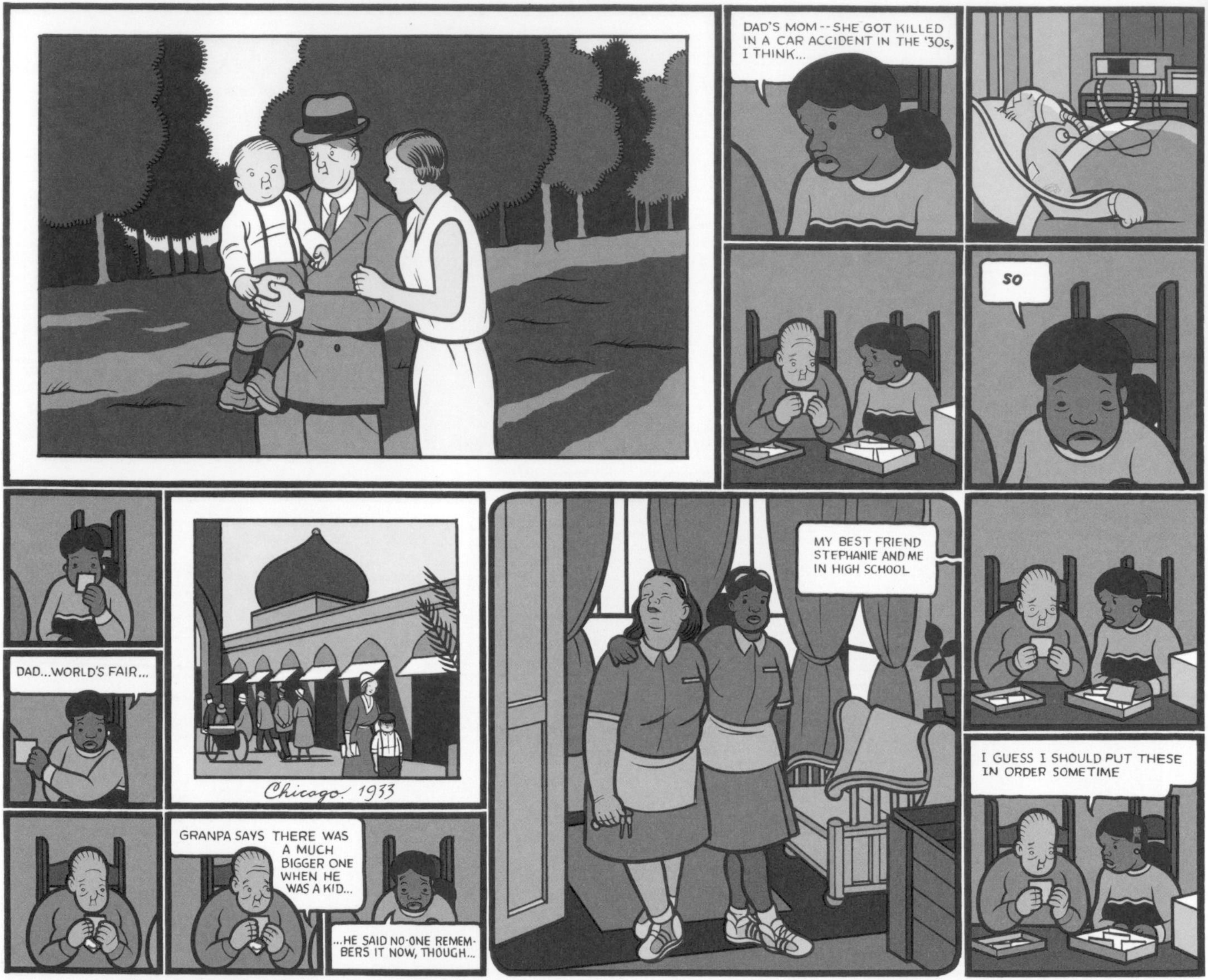
DAD'S MOM -- SHE GOT KILLED IN A CAR ACCIDENT IN THE '30s, I THINK...
SO
DAD...WORLD'S FAIR...
Chicago. 1933
GRANPA SAYS THERE WAS A MUCH BIGGER ONE WHEN HE WAS A KID...
...HE SAID NO-ONE REMEMBERS IT NOW, THOUGH...
MY BEST FRIEND STEPHANIE AND ME IN HIGH SCHOOL
I GUESS I SHOULD PUT THESE IN ORDER SOMETIME

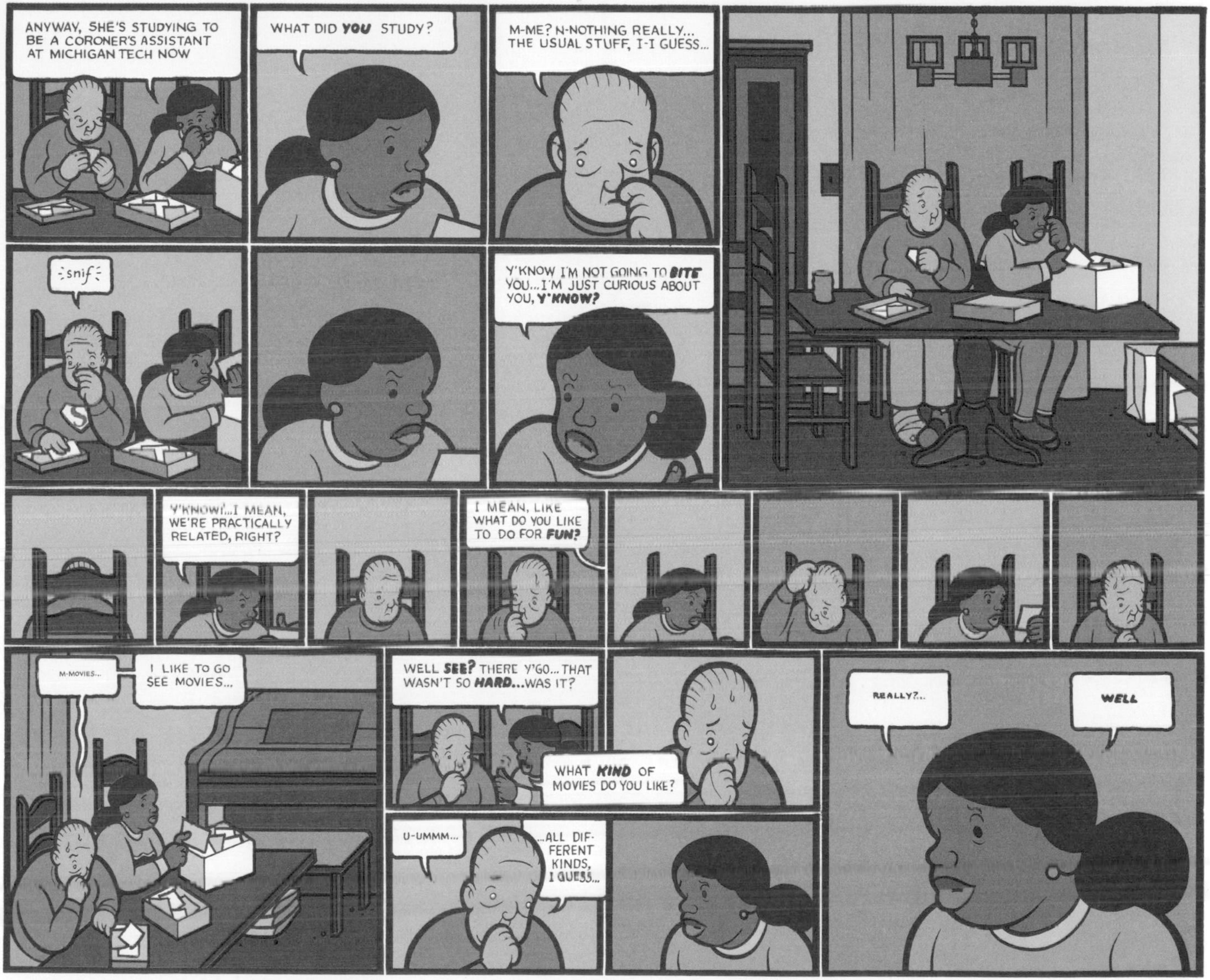
ANYWAY, SHE'S STUDYING TO BE A CORONER'S ASSISTANT AT MICHIGAN TECH NOW
WHAT DID YOU STUDY?
M-ME? N-NOTHING REALLY... THE USUAL STUFF, I-I GUESS...
snif
Y'KNOW I'M NOT GOING TO BITE YOU...I'M JUST CURIOUS ABOUT YOU, Y'KNOW?
Y'KNOW!...I MEAN, WE'RE PRACTICALLY RELATED, RIGHT?
I MEAN, LIKE WHAT DO YOU LIKE TO DO FOR FUN?
M-MOVIES...
I LIKE TO GO SEE MOVIES...
WELL SEE? THERE Y'GO...THAT WASN'T SO HARD...WAS IT?
WHAT KIND OF MOVIES DO YOU LIKE?
U-UMMM...
...ALL DIF-FERENT KINDS, I GUESS...
REALLY?...
WELL

B U U T.

I SAVE ALL OF MY MAGAZINES FOR THREE MONTHS, JUST IN CASE I HAVE TO LOOK UP SOMETHING IMPORTANT...

EXCEPT FOR MY NATIONAL GEOGRAPHICS... I NEVER THROW THOSE AWAY...

SINCE A SPACE SAVES SAVED SIXTY SNIFFS SLIPS IFS

:sniff:

I LIKE THE WAY THEY SHOW WHAT'S INSIDE ON THE OUTSIDE FLAT PART...

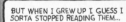

BUT WHEN I GREW UP I GUESS I SORTA STOPPED READING THEM...

I-I MEAN... I-I WOULDN'T R-REALLY R-READ THEM N-NOW... U-UNLESS THE ART WAS GOOD...

UH-HUH

NO, I TOTALLY AGREE WITH YOU

YOU'RE RIGHT ON THERE

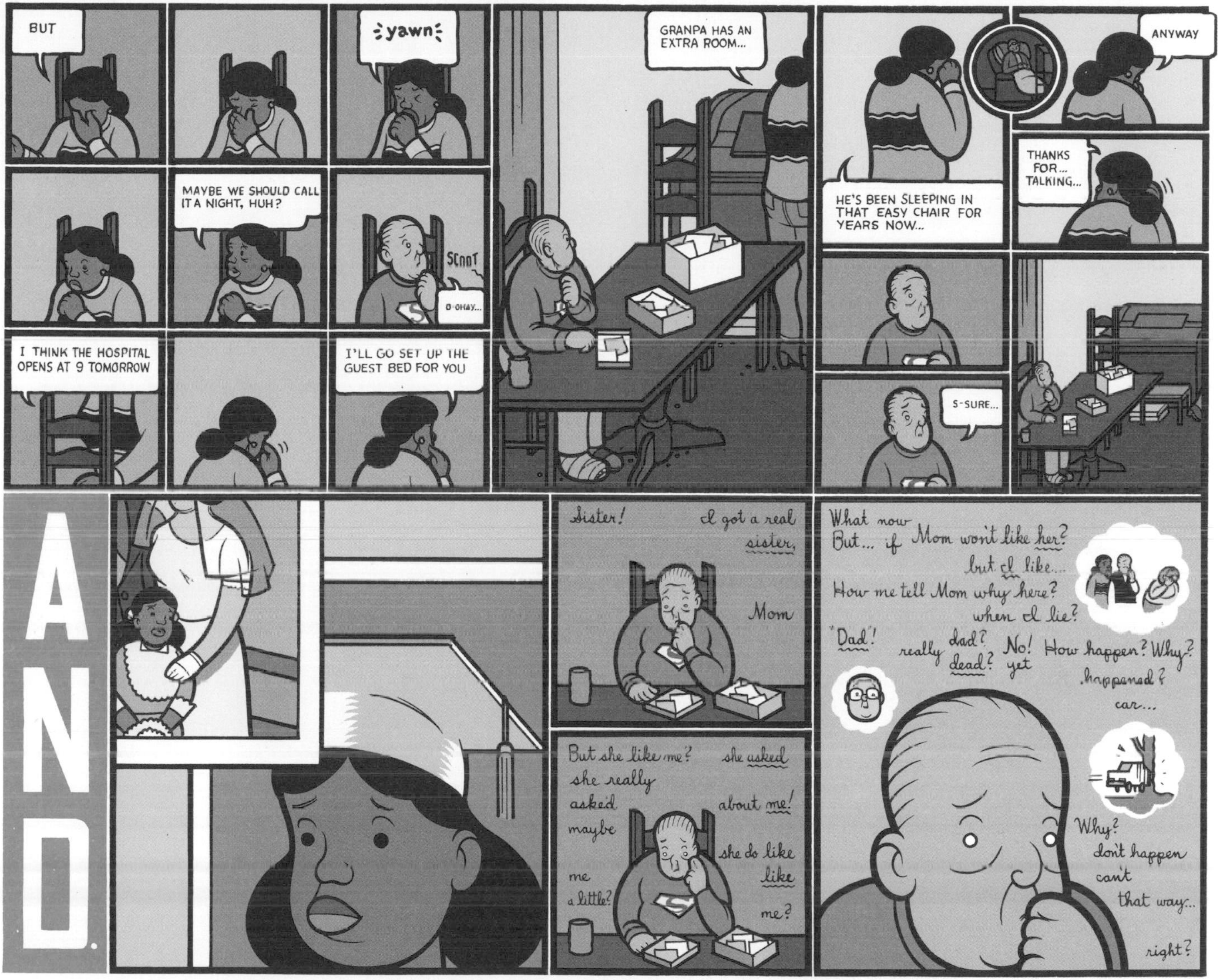
BUT
:yawn:
MAYBE WE SHOULD CALL IT A NIGHT, HUH?
SCNOT
O-OKAY...
I THINK THE HOSPITAL OPENS AT 9 TOMORROW
I'LL GO SET UP THE GUEST BED FOR YOU
GRANPA HAS AN EXTRA ROOM...
HE'S BEEN SLEEPING IN THAT EASY CHAIR FOR YEARS NOW...
ANYWAY
THANKS FOR... TALKING...
S-SURE...
AND.
Sister!
I got a real sister.
Mom
But she like me?
she really asked
she asked about me!
maybe she do like me a little?
like me?
What now
But... if Mom won't like her?
but I like...
How me tell Mom why here?
when I lie?
"Dad"!
really dad? dead?
No! yet
How happen? Why?
happened?
car...
Why?
don't happen
can't
that way...
right?

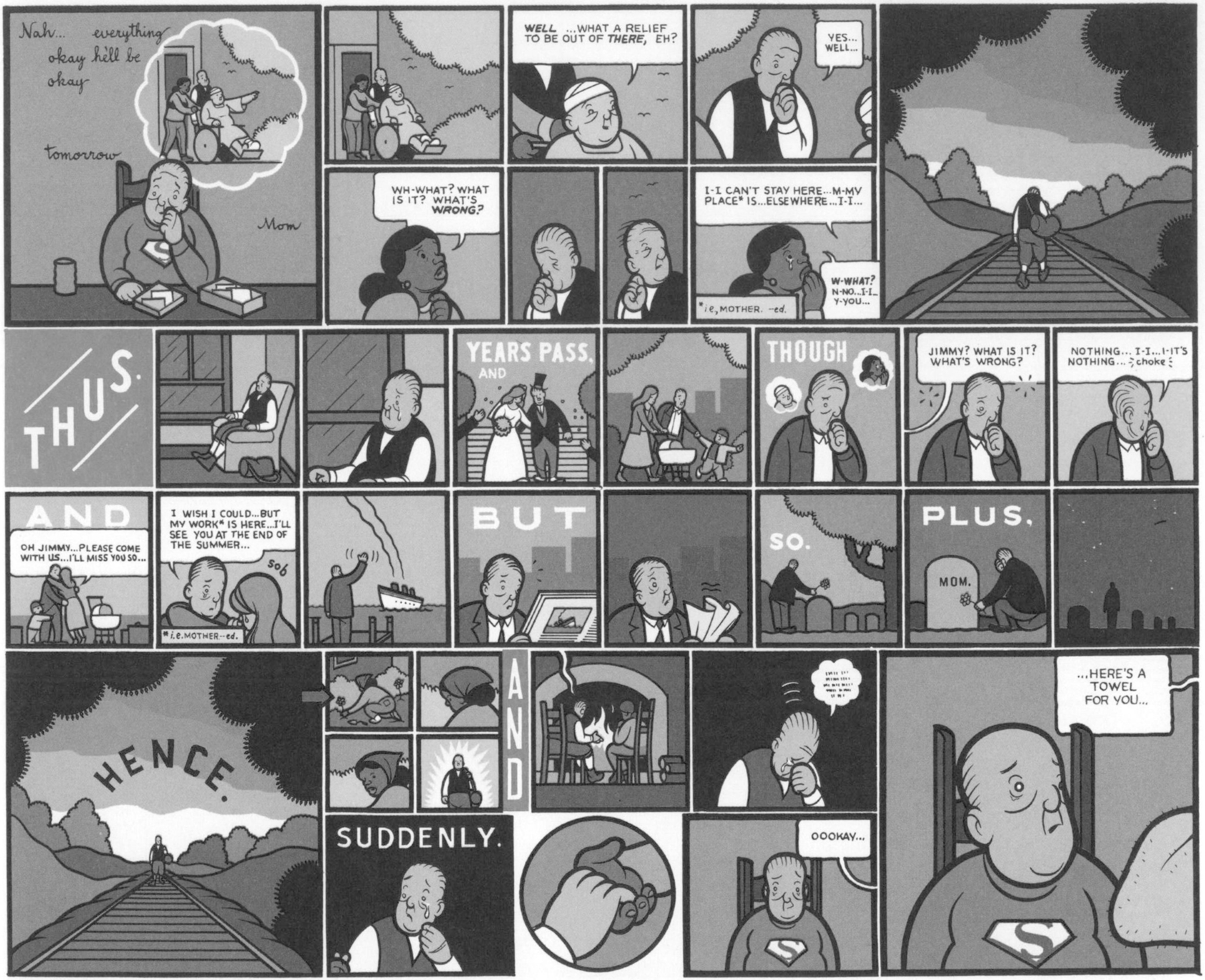
Nah... everything okay he'll be okay
tomorrow
Mom
WELL ...WHAT A RELIEF TO BE OUT OF THERE, EH?
YES... WELL...
WH-WHAT? WHAT IS IT? WHAT'S WRONG?
I-I CAN'T STAY HERE...M-MY PLACE* IS...ELSEWHERE...I-I...
W-WHAT? N-NO...I-I... Y-YOU...
*i.e, MOTHER. --ed.
THUS.
YEARS PASS, AND
THOUGH
JIMMY? WHAT IS IT? WHAT'S WRONG?
NOTHING... I-I...I-IT'S NOTHING... choke
AND
OH JIMMY...PLEASE COME WITH US...I'LL MISS YOU SO...
I WISH I COULD...BUT MY WORK* IS HERE...I'LL SEE YOU AT THE END OF THE SUMMER...
sob
*i.e. MOTHER--ed.
BUT
SO.
PLUS,
MOM.
HENCE.
AND
...HERE'S A TOWEL FOR YOU...
SUDDENLY.
OOOKAY...

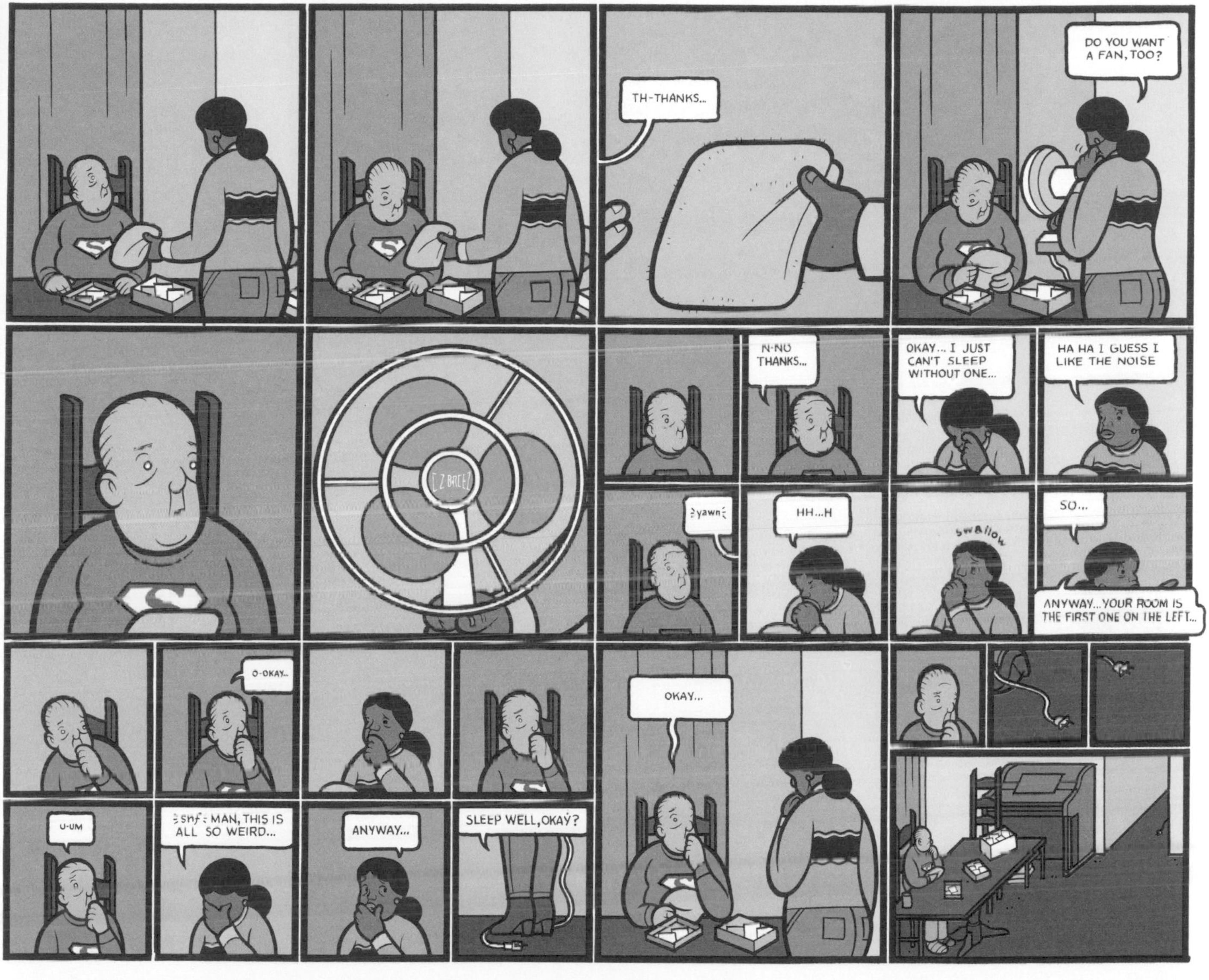
TH-THANKS...
DO YOU WANT A FAN, TOO?
N-NO THANKS...
OKAY... I JUST CAN'T SLEEP WITHOUT ONE...
HA HA I GUESS I LIKE THE NOISE
yawn
HH...H
swallow
SO...
ANYWAY... YOUR ROOM IS THE FIRST ONE ON THE LEFT...
O-OKAY...
U-UM
snf MAN, THIS IS ALL SO WEIRD...
ANYWAY...
SLEEP WELL, OKAY?
OKAY...

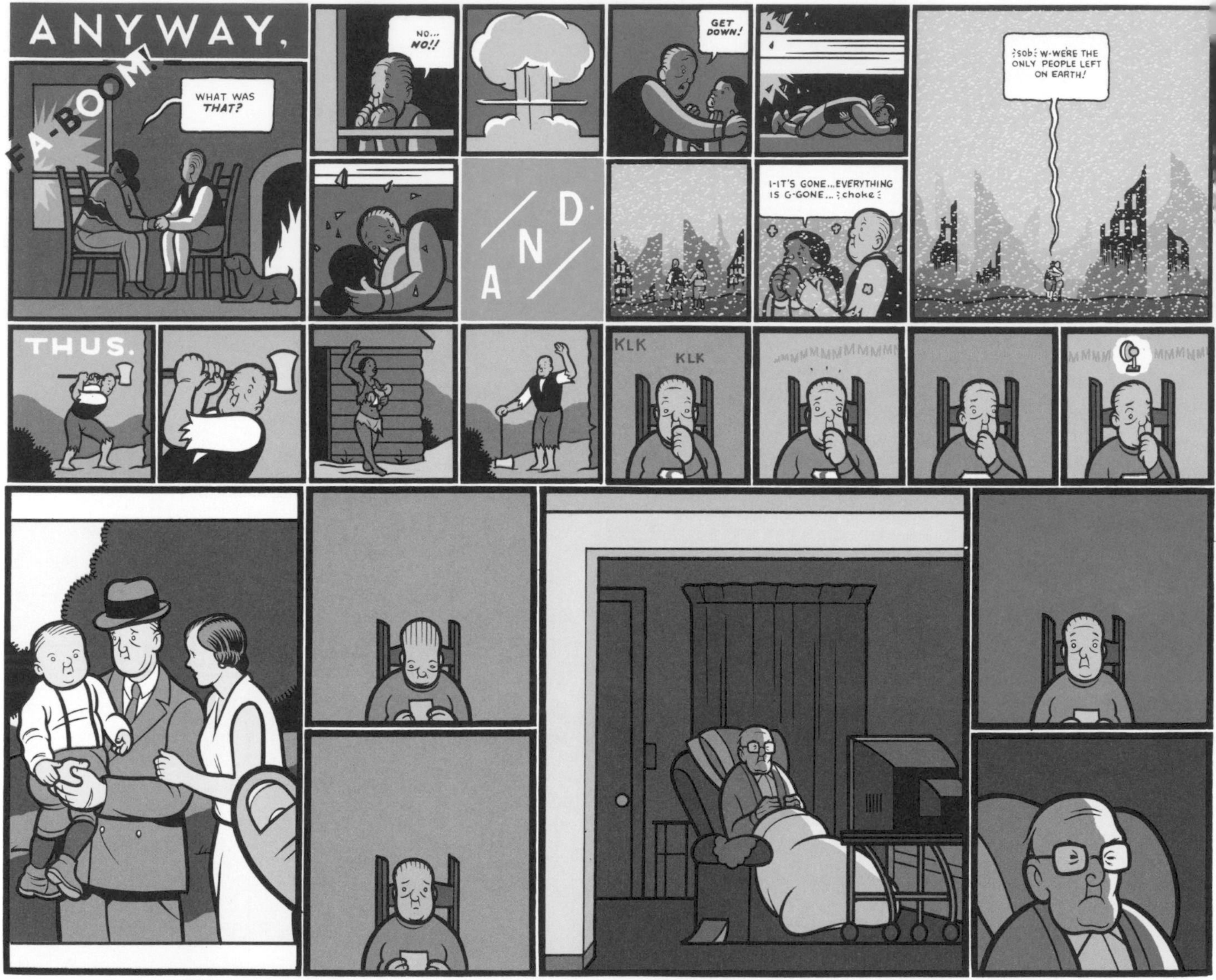
ANYWAY,
FA-BOOM!
WHAT WAS THAT?
NO... NO!!
GET DOWN!
AND
I-IT'S GONE... EVERYTHING IS G-GONE... ¦choke¦
¦sob¦ W-WE'RE THE ONLY PEOPLE LEFT ON EARTH!
THUS.
KLK
KLK

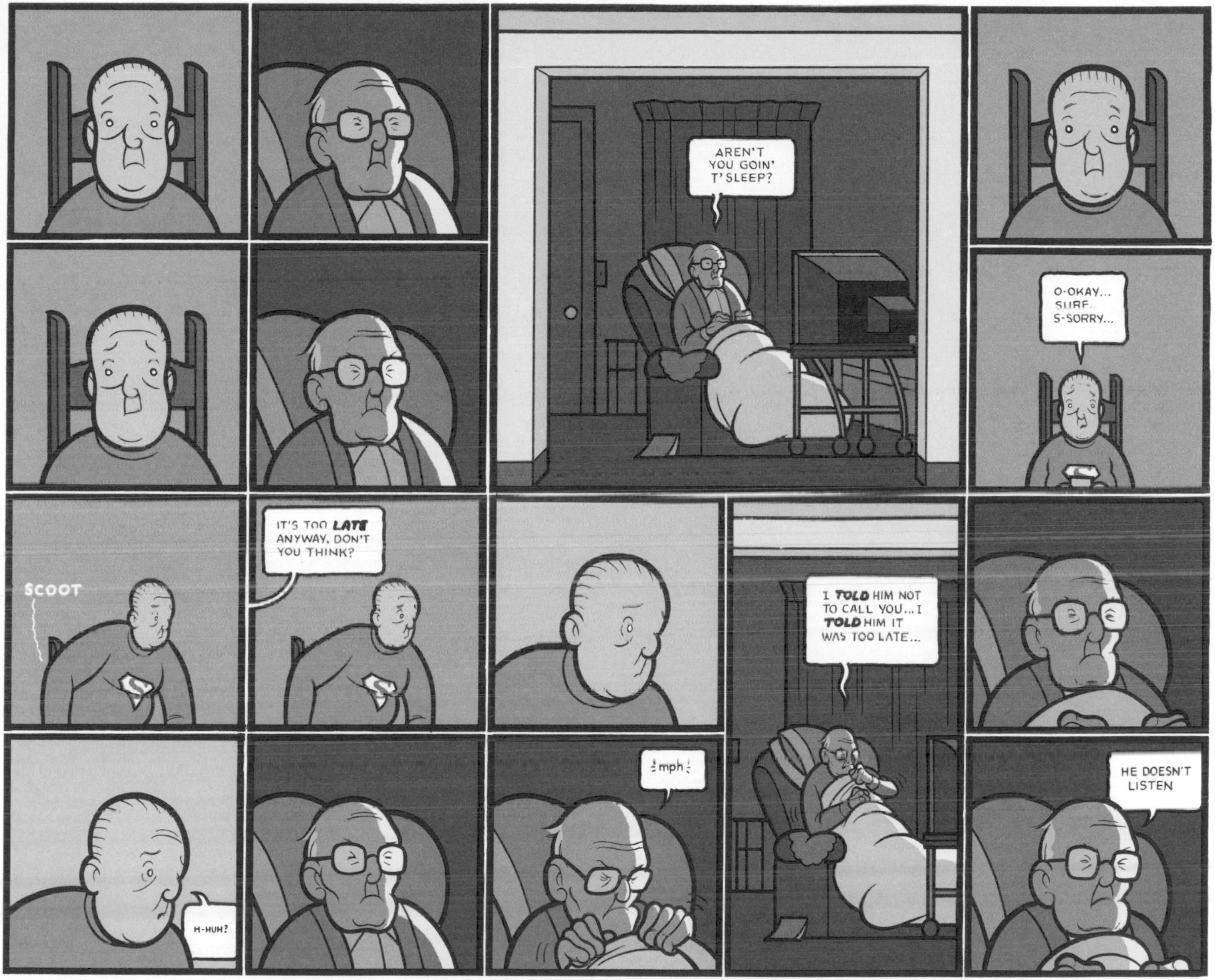
AREN'T YOU GOIN' T'SLEEP?
O-OKAY... SURE.. S-SORRY...
SCOOT
IT'S TOO LATE ANYWAY, DON'T YOU THINK?
I TOLD HIM NOT TO CALL YOU... I TOLD HIM IT WAS TOO LATE...
H-HUH?
mph
HE DOESN'T LISTEN

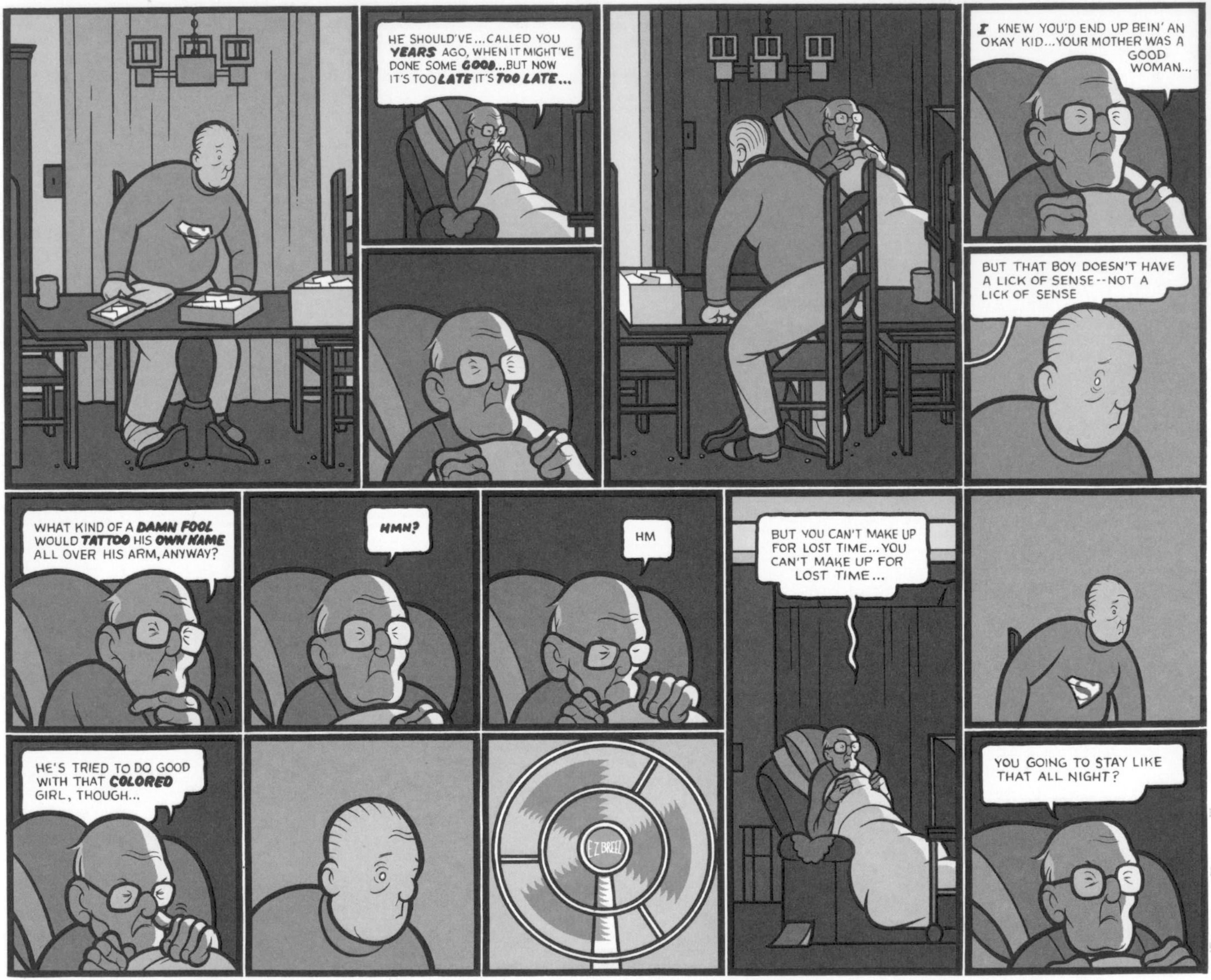

HE SHOULD'VE...CALLED YOU YEARS AGO, WHEN IT MIGHT'VE DONE SOME GOOD...BUT NOW IT'S TOO LATE IT'S TOO LATE...
I KNEW YOU'D END UP BEIN' AN OKAY KID...YOUR MOTHER WAS A GOOD WOMAN...
BUT THAT BOY DOESN'T HAVE A LICK OF SENSE--NOT A LICK OF SENSE
WHAT KIND OF A DAMN FOOL WOULD TATTOO HIS OWN NAME ALL OVER HIS ARM, ANYWAY?
HMN?
HM
BUT YOU CAN'T MAKE UP FOR LOST TIME...YOU CAN'T MAKE UP FOR LOST TIME...
HE'S TRIED TO DO GOOD WITH THAT COLORED GIRL, THOUGH...
EZ BREEZ
YOU GOING TO STAY LIKE THAT ALL NIGHT?

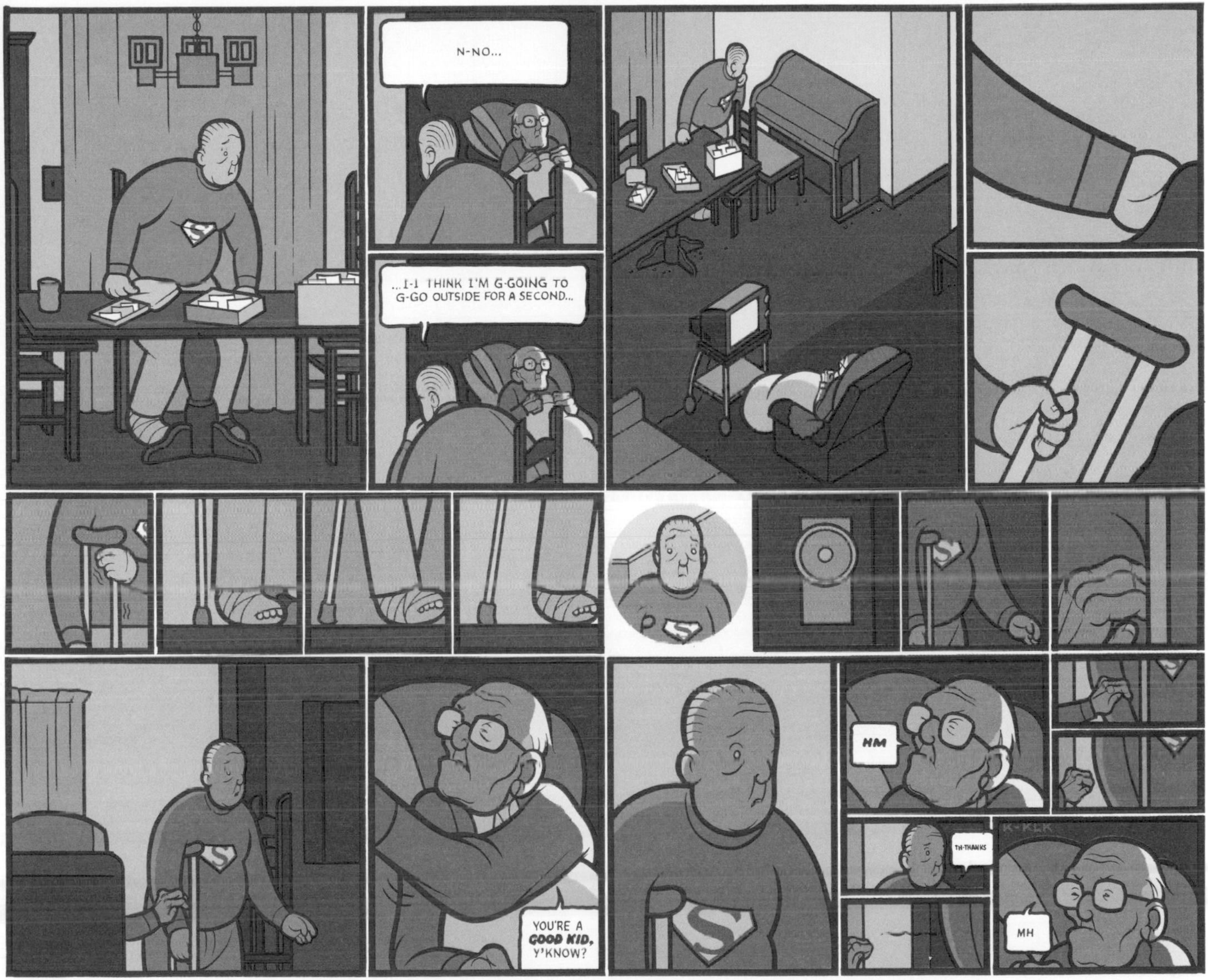
N-NO...
...I-I THINK I'M G-GOING TO G-GO OUTSIDE FOR A SECOND...
YOU'RE A **GOOD KID,** Y'KNOW?
HM
TH-THANKS
K-KLK
MH

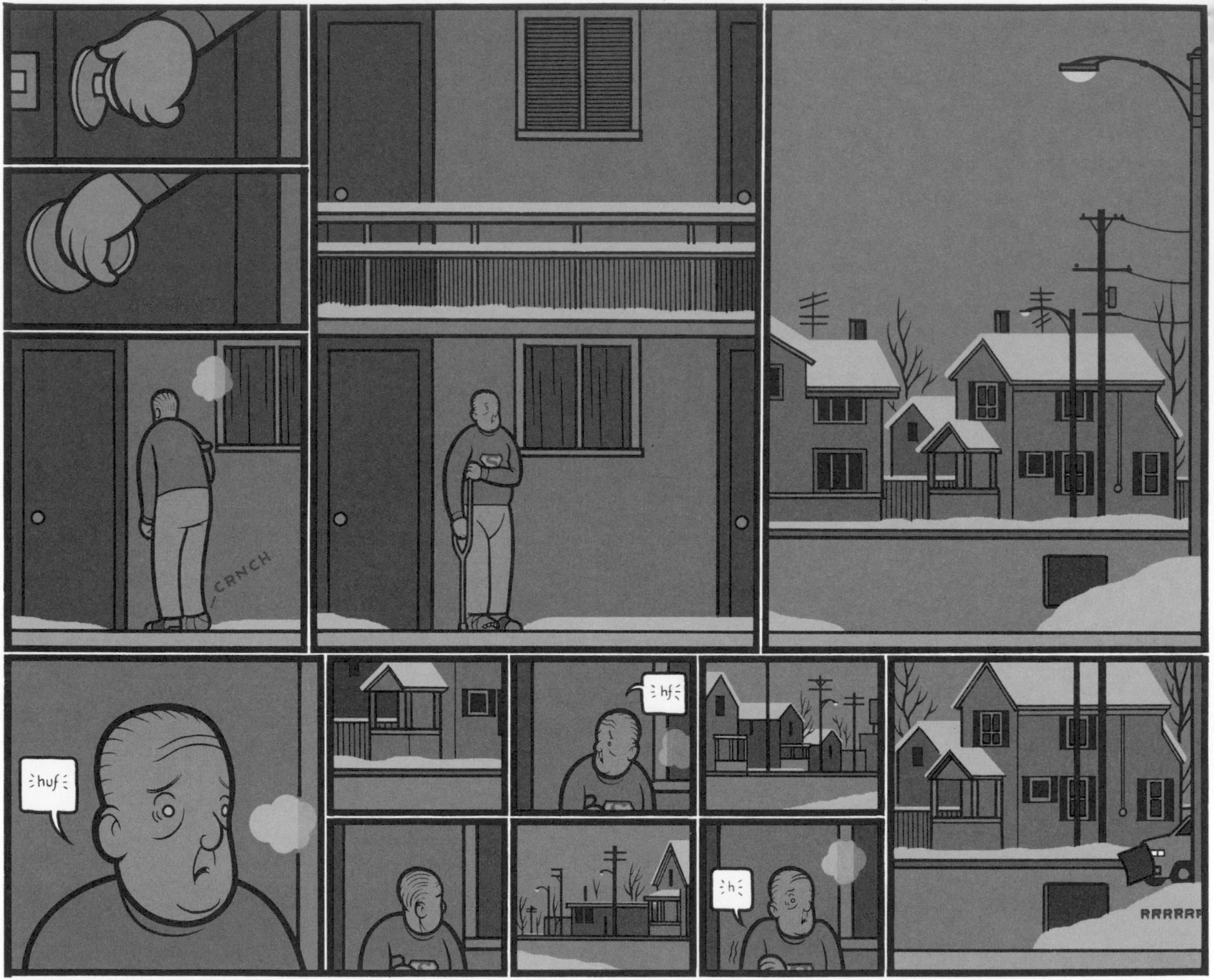
CRNCH
huf
hf
h
RRRRRR

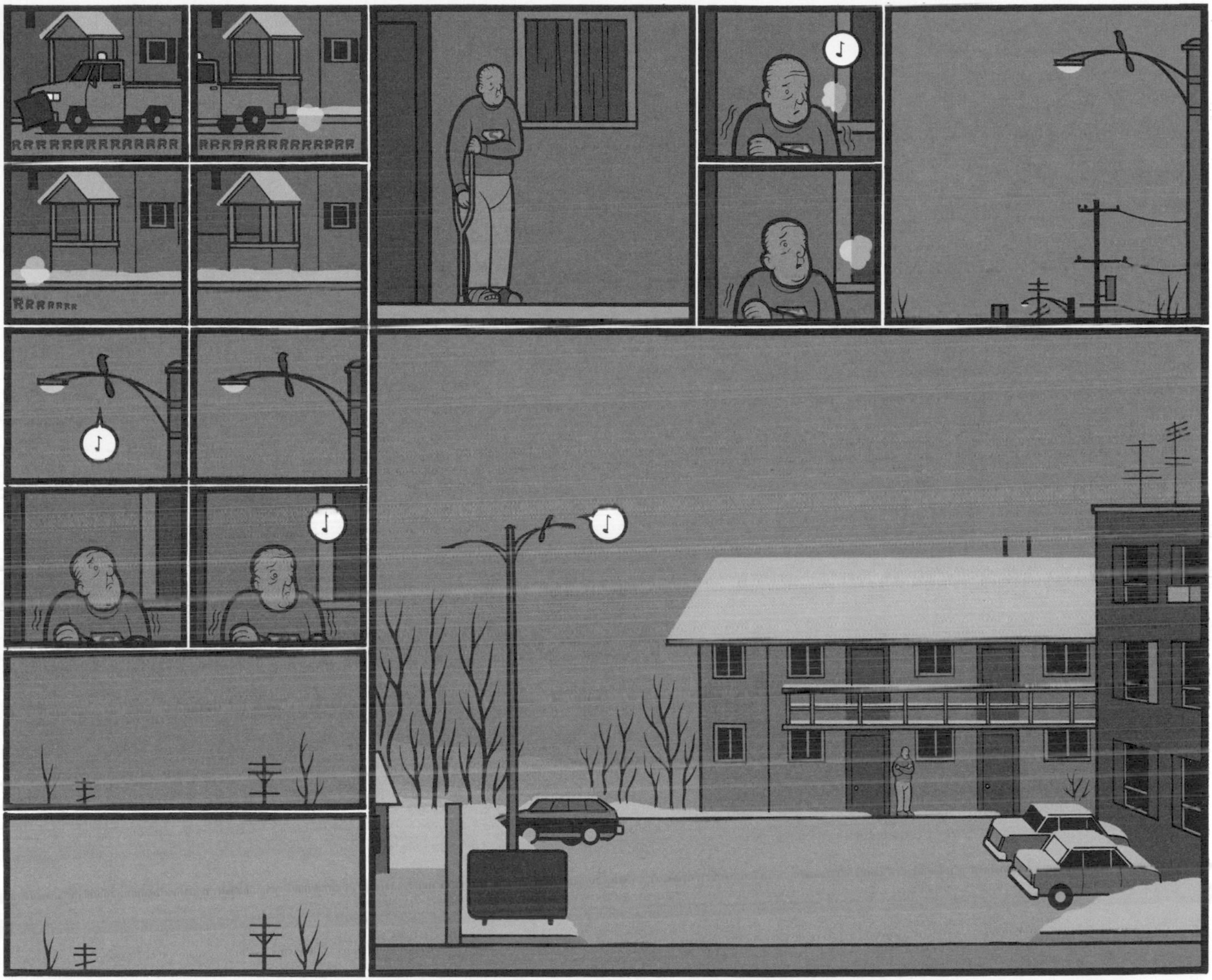

RRRRRRRRRRRRRR
RRRRRRRRRRRRRR
RRRRRRR
♪
♪
♪
♪

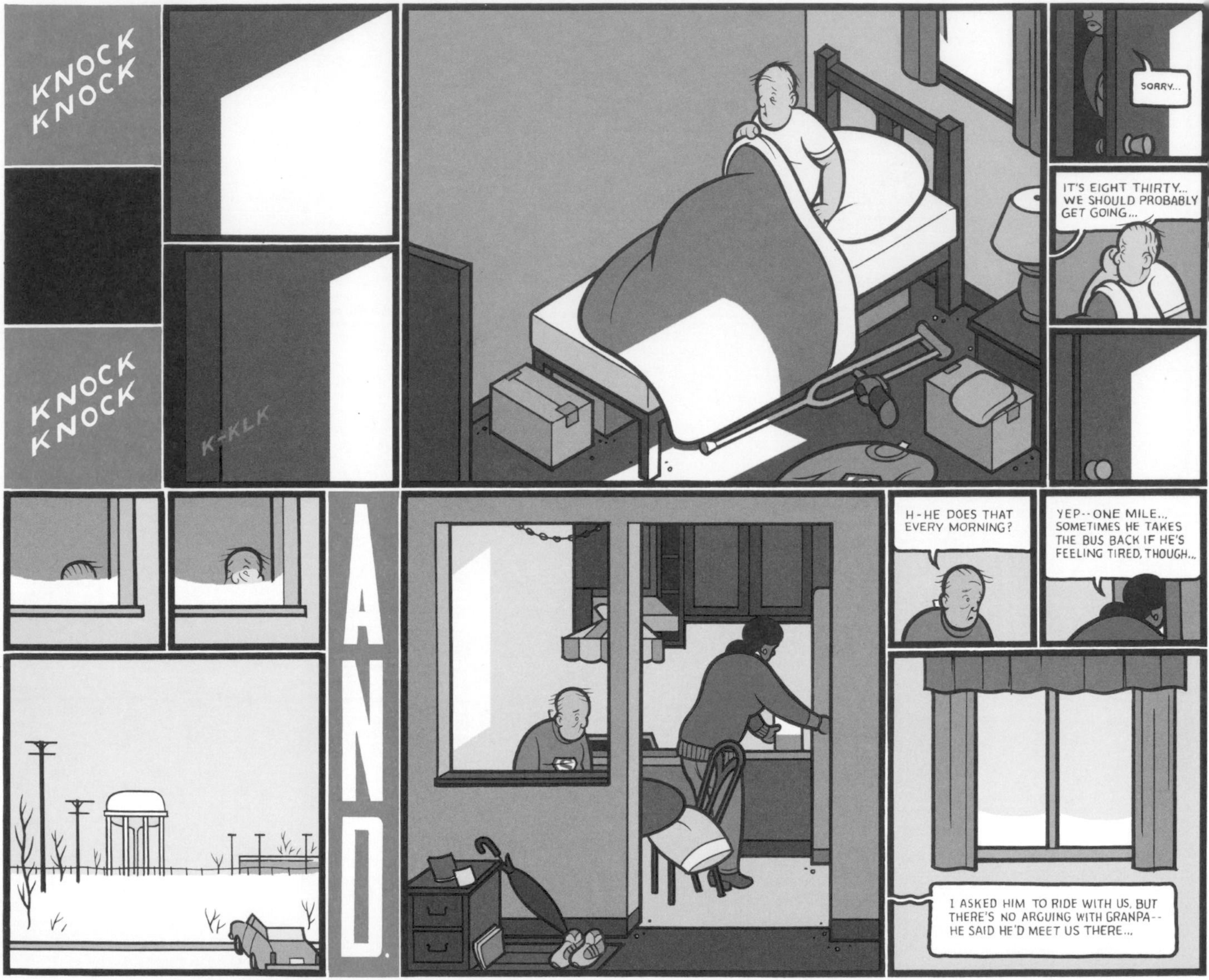
KNOCK KNOCK
KNOCK KNOCK
K-KLK
SORRY...
IT'S EIGHT THIRTY... WE SHOULD PROBABLY GET GOING...
AND.
H-HE DOES THAT EVERY MORNING?
YEP--ONE MILE... SOMETIMES HE TAKES THE BUS BACK IF HE'S FEELING TIRED, THOUGH...
I ASKED HIM TO RIDE WITH US, BUT THERE'S NO ARGUING WITH GRANPA-- HE SAID HE'D MEET US THERE...

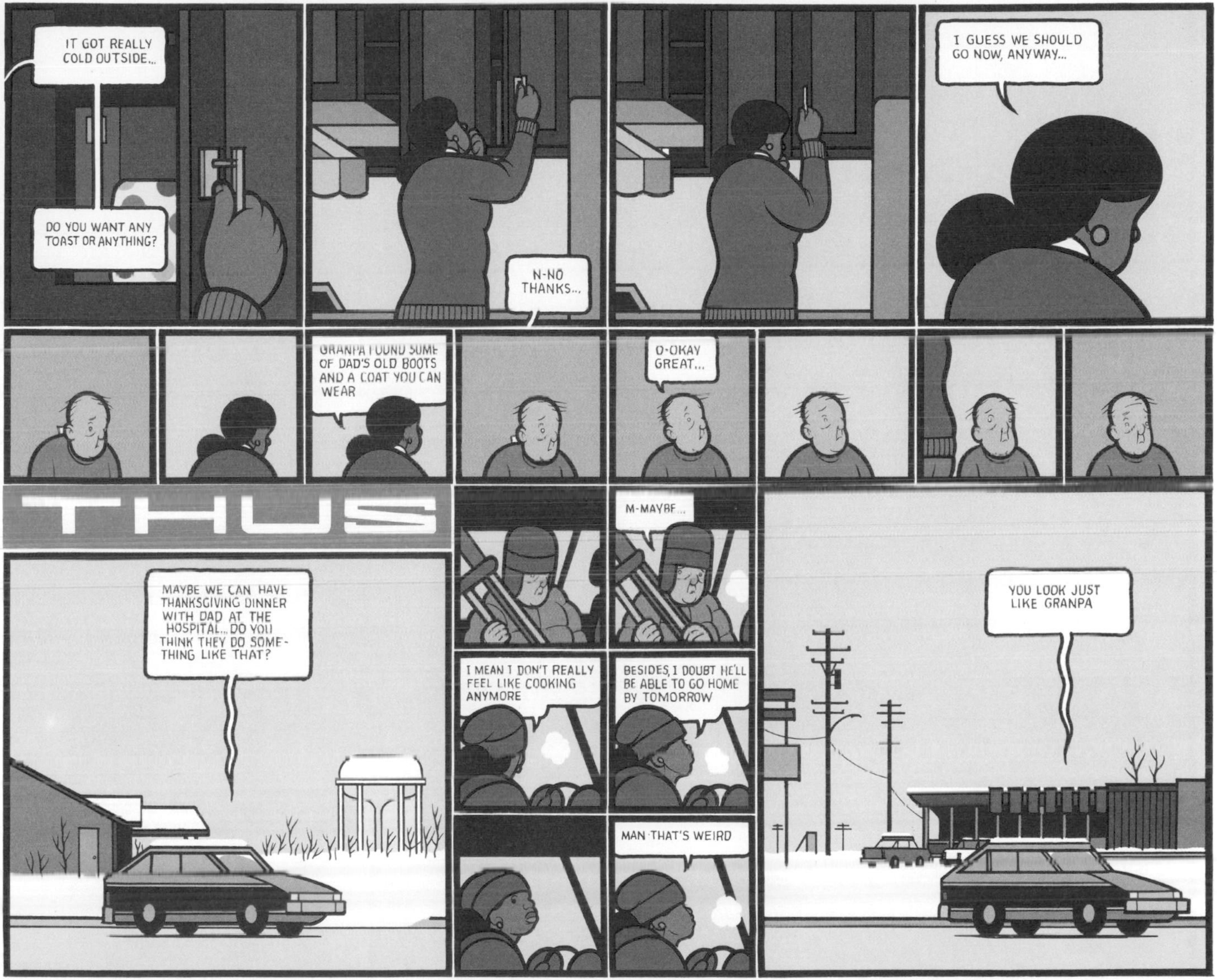
IT GOT REALLY COLD OUTSIDE...
DO YOU WANT ANY TOAST OR ANYTHING?
N-NO THANKS...
I GUESS WE SHOULD GO NOW, ANYWAY...
GRANPA FOUND SOME OF DAD'S OLD BOOTS AND A COAT YOU CAN WEAR
O-OKAY GREAT...
THUS
MAYBE WE CAN HAVE THANKSGIVING DINNER WITH DAD AT THE HOSPITAL... DO YOU THINK THEY DO SOMETHING LIKE THAT?
M-MAYBE...
I MEAN I DON'T REALLY FEEL LIKE COOKING ANYMORE
BESIDES, I DOUBT HE'LL BE ABLE TO GO HOME BY TOMORROW
MAN·THAT'S WEIRD
YOU LOOK JUST LIKE GRANPA

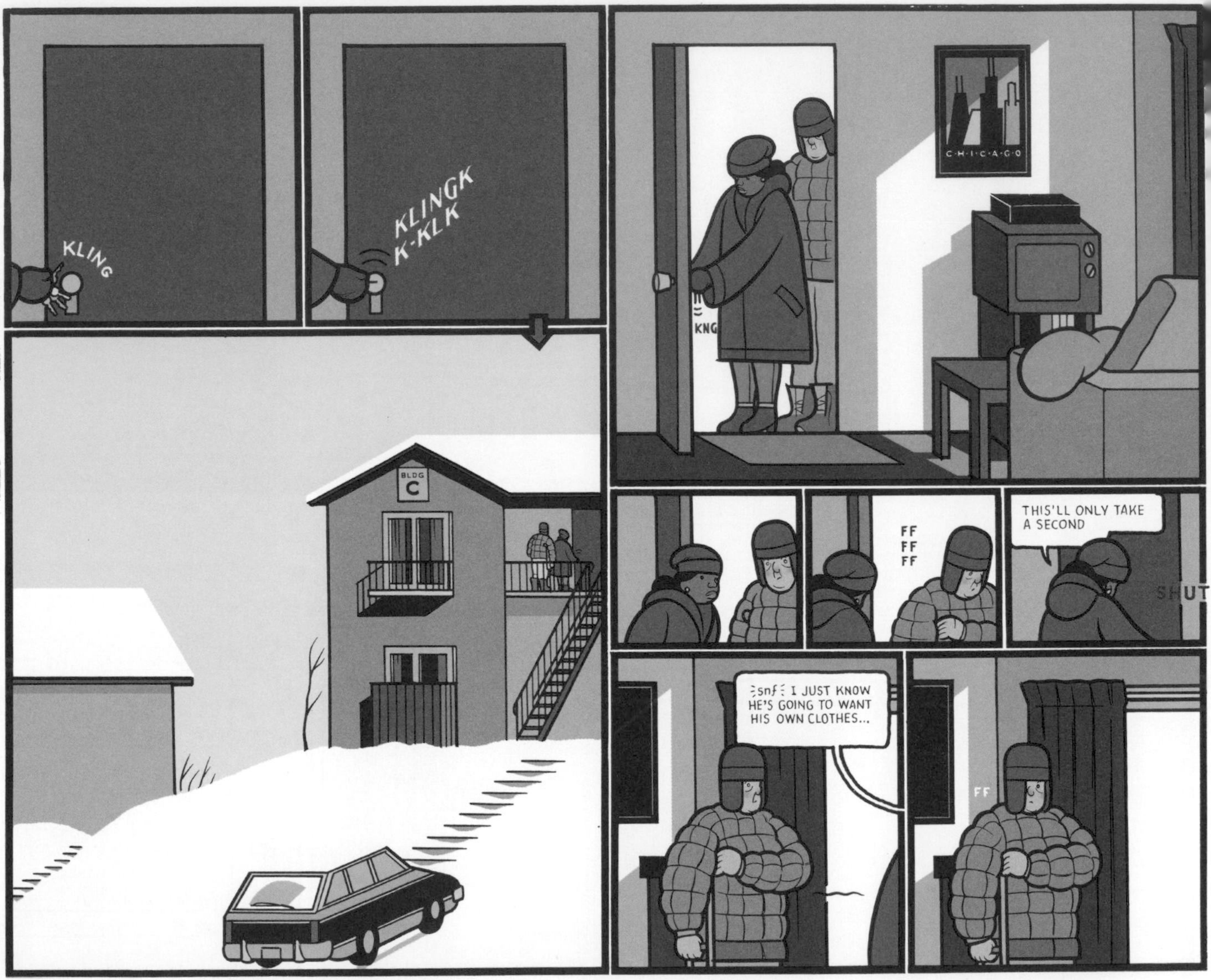

KLING
KLINGK K-KLK
BLDG C
C·H·I·C·A·G·O
KNG
FF FF FF
THIS'LL ONLY TAKE A SECOND
SHUT
snf I JUST KNOW HE'S GOING TO WANT HIS OWN CLOTHES...
FF

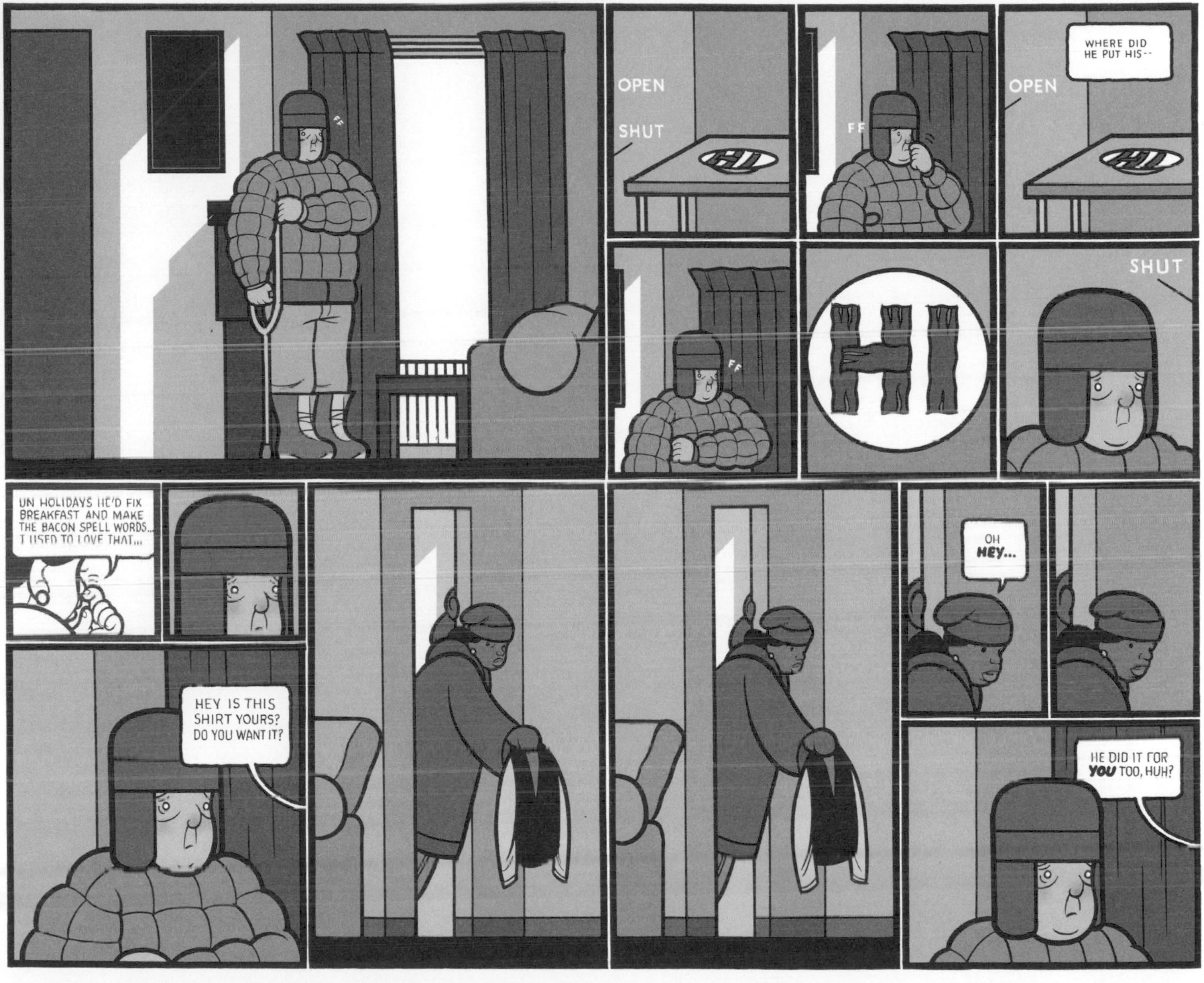

FF
OPEN
SHUT
HI
FF
HI
WHERE DID HE PUT HIS--
OPEN
FF
HI
SHUT
ON HOLIDAYS HE'D FIX BREAKFAST AND MAKE THE BACON SPELL WORDS... I USED TO LOVE THAT...
HEY IS THIS SHIRT YOURS? DO YOU WANT IT?
OH **HEY...**
HE DID IT FOR ***YOU*** TOO, HUH?

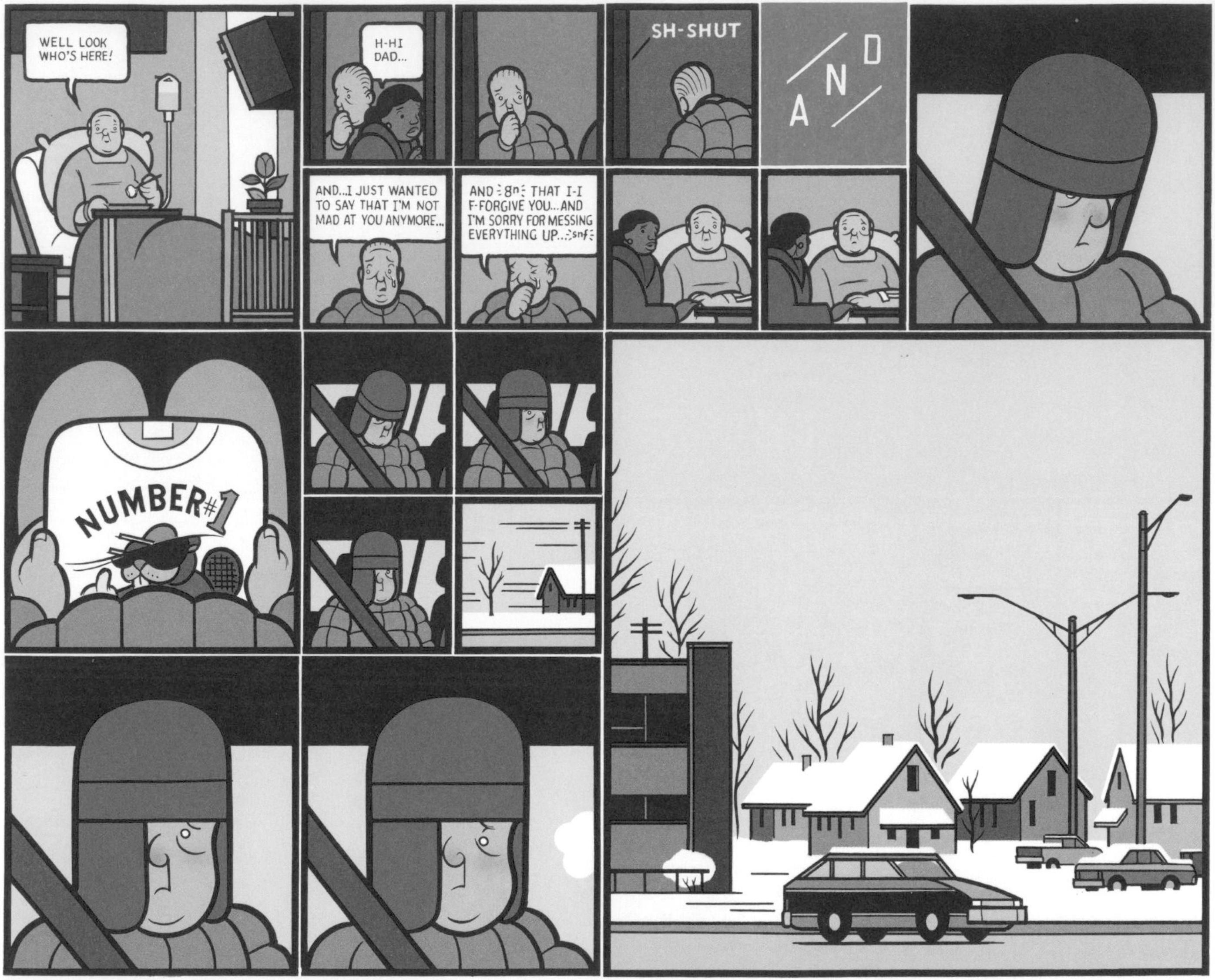
WELL LOOK WHO'S HERE!
H-HI DAD...
SH-SHUT
AND
AND...I JUST WANTED TO SAY THAT I'M NOT MAD AT YOU ANYMORE...
AND 8n THAT I-I F-FORGIVE YOU...AND I'M SORRY FOR MESSING EVERYTHING UP... snf
NUMBER#1

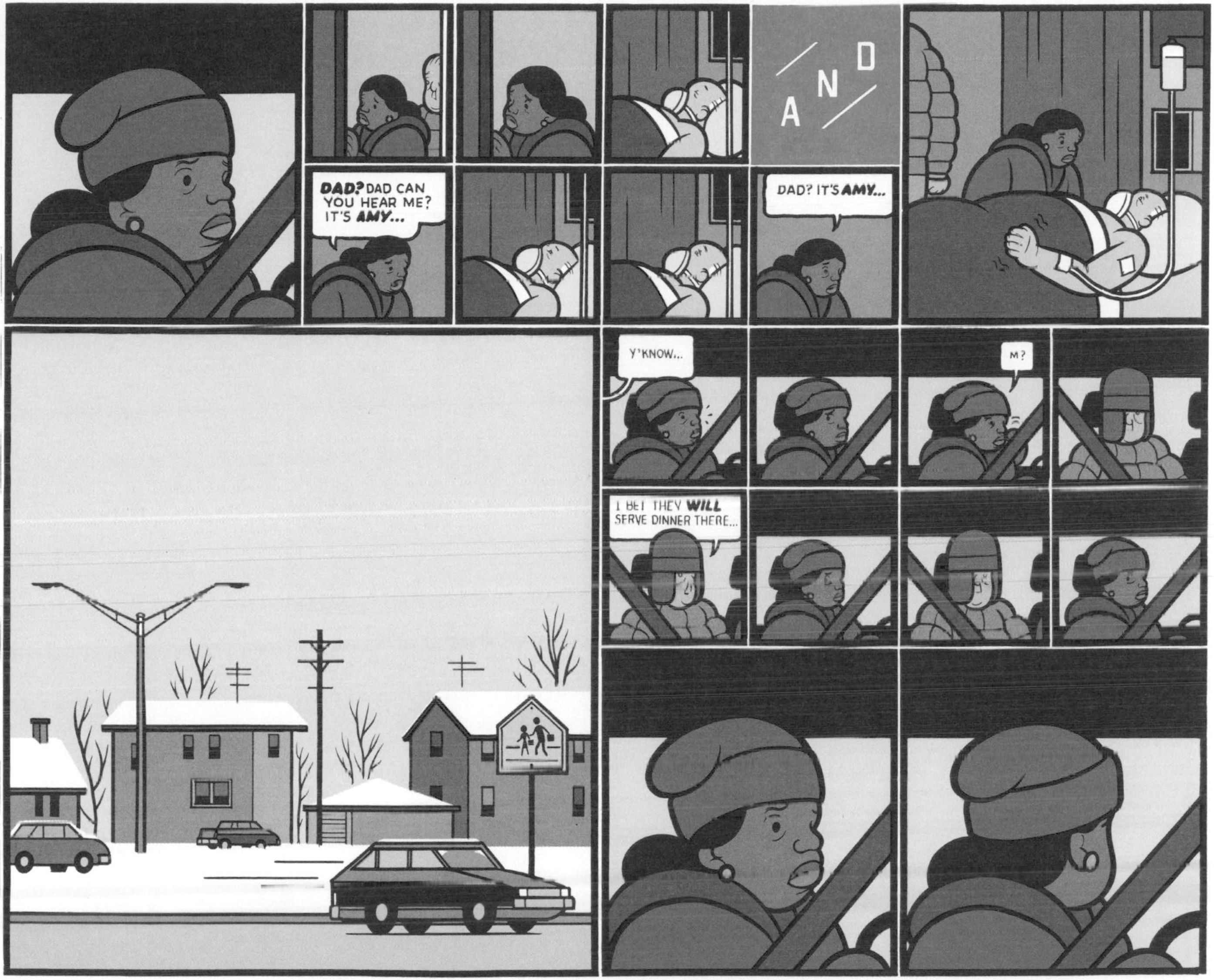
AND
DAD? DAD CAN YOU HEAR ME? IT'S AMY...
DAD? IT'S AMY...
Y'KNOW...
M?
I BET THEY WILL SERVE DINNER THERE...

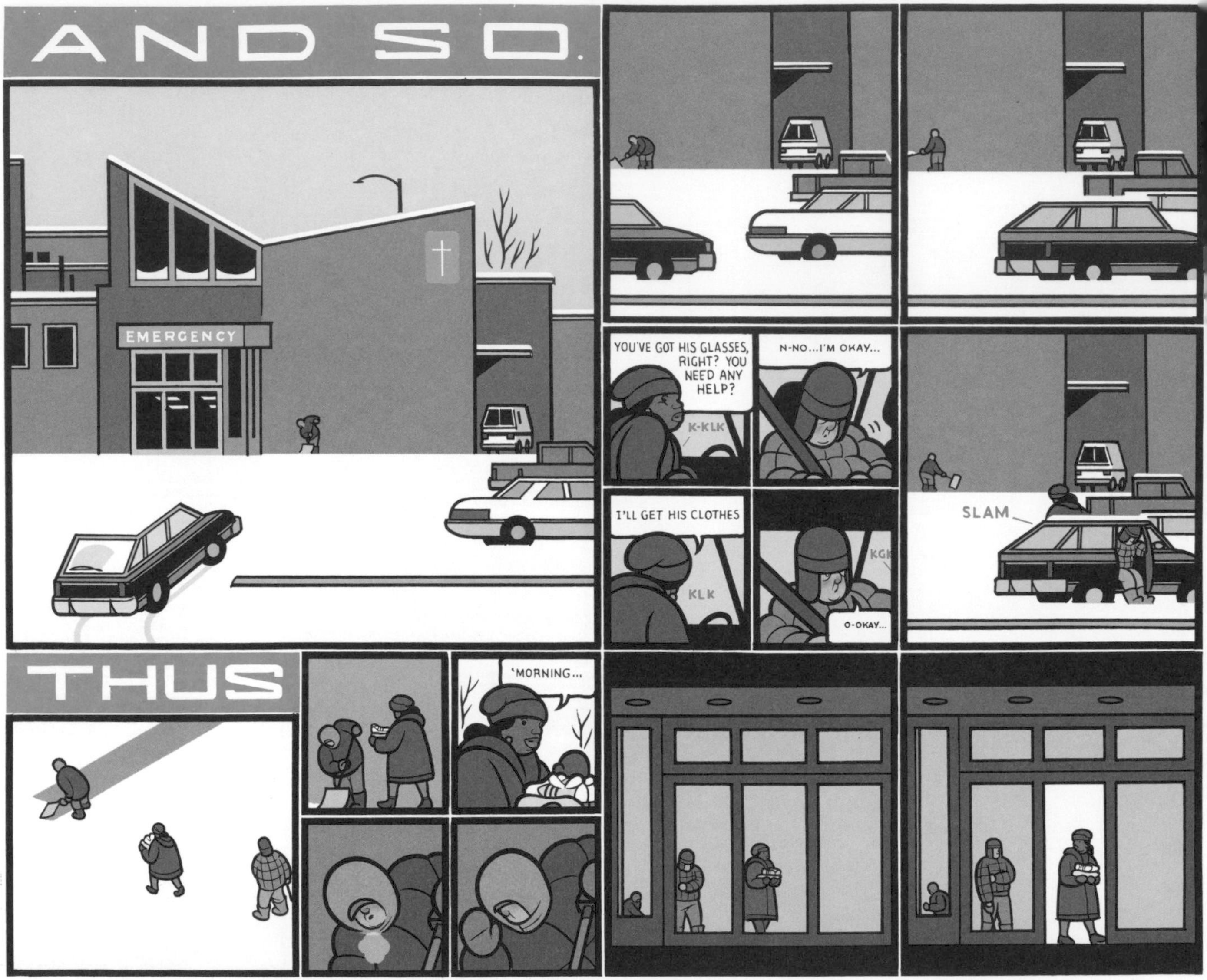
AND SO.
EMERGENCY
YOU'VE GOT HIS GLASSES, RIGHT? YOU NEED ANY HELP?
K-KLK
N-NO...I'M OKAY...
I'LL GET HIS CLOTHES
KLK
KGK
O-OKAY...
SLAM
THUS
'MORNING...

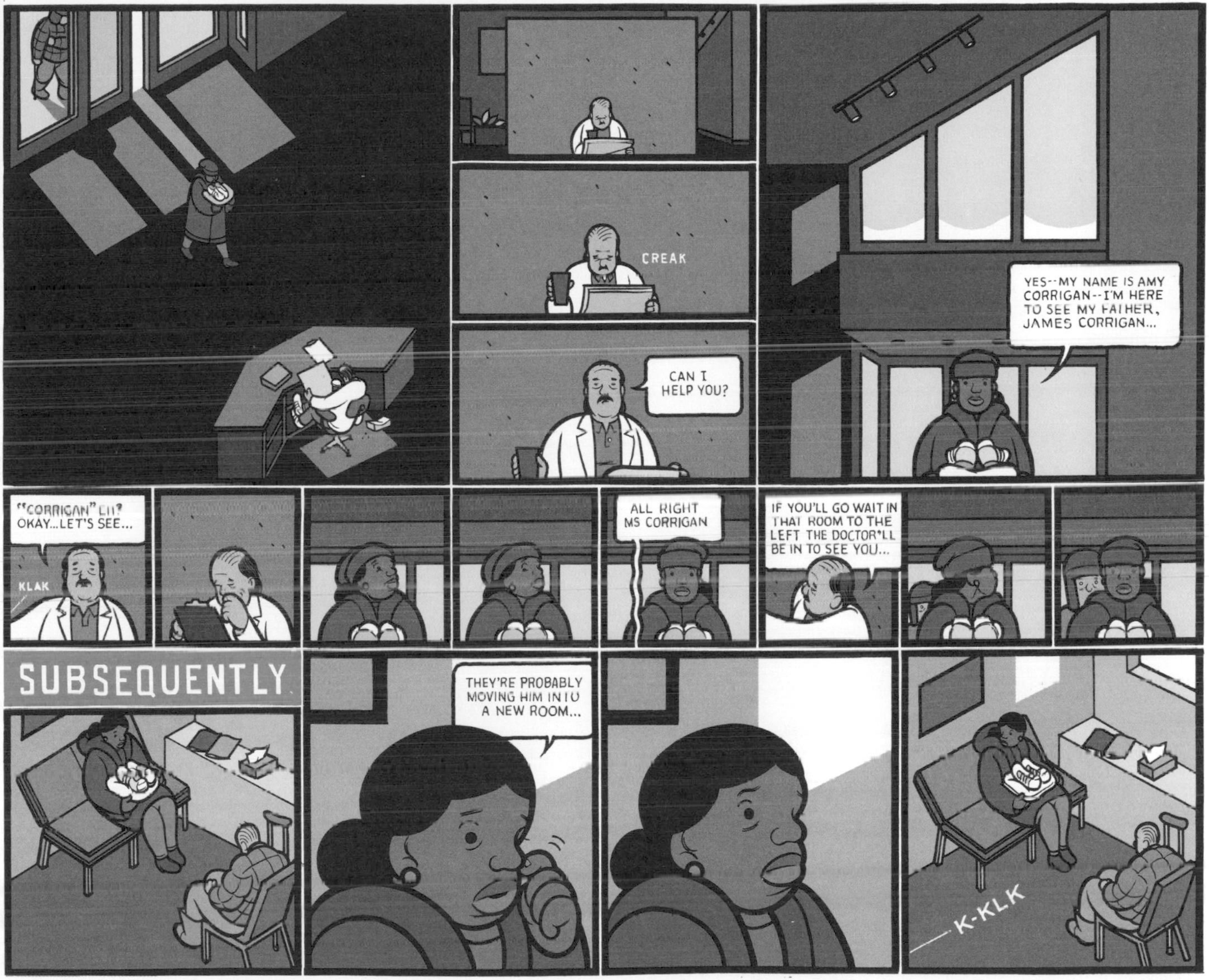
CREAK
CAN I HELP YOU?
YES--MY NAME IS AMY CORRIGAN--I'M HERE TO SEE MY FATHER, JAMES CORRIGAN...
"CORRIGAN" EH? OKAY...LET'S SEE...
KLAK
ALL RIGHT MS CORRIGAN
IF YOU'LL GO WAIT IN THAT ROOM TO THE LEFT THE DOCTOR'LL BE IN TO SEE YOU...
SUBSEQUENTLY
THEY'RE PROBABLY MOVING HIM INTO A NEW ROOM...
K-KLK

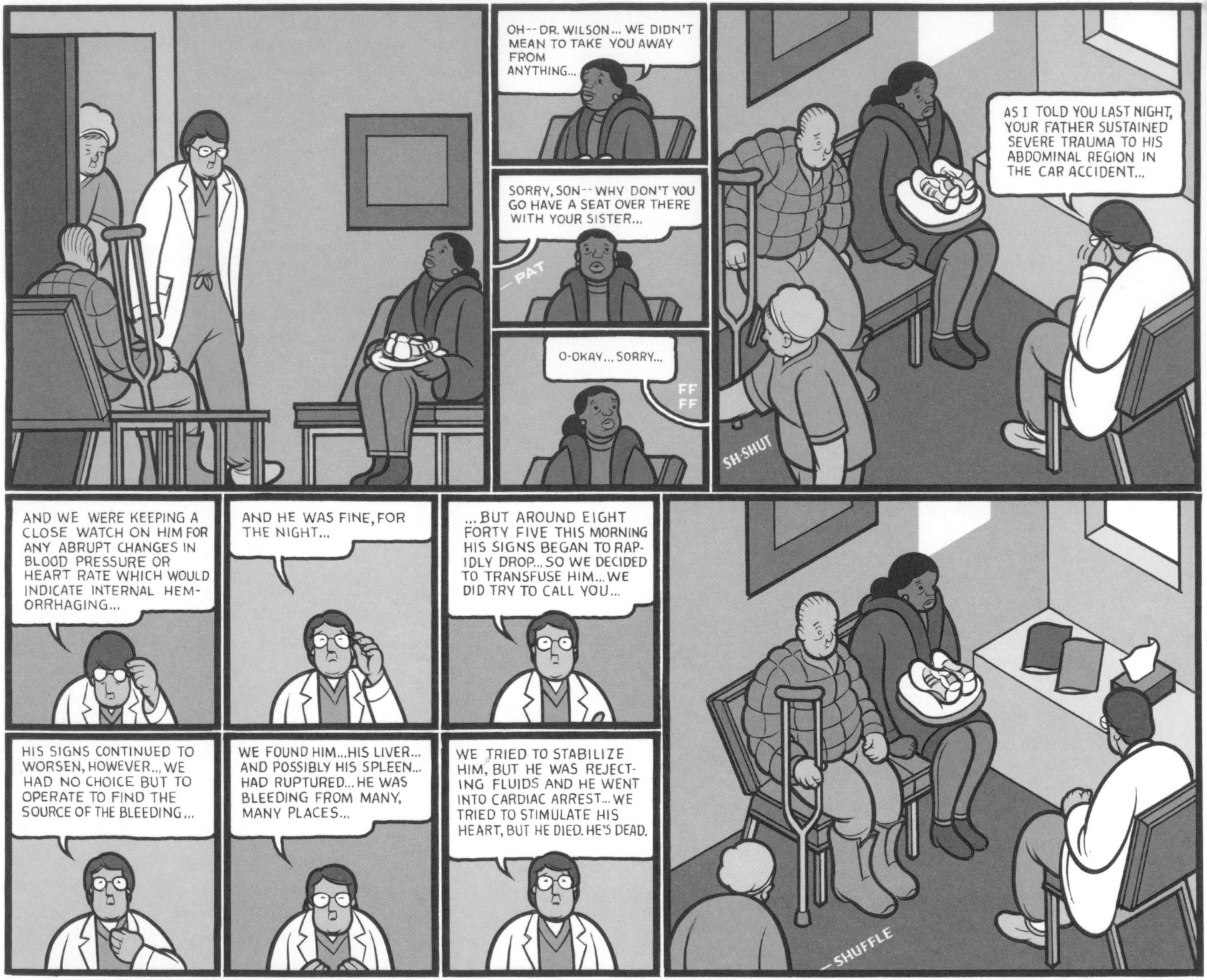
OH-- DR. WILSON... WE DIDN'T MEAN TO TAKE YOU AWAY FROM ANYTHING...
SORRY, SON-- WHY DON'T YOU GO HAVE A SEAT OVER THERE WITH YOUR SISTER...
PAT
O-OKAY... SORRY...
FF FF
AS I TOLD YOU LAST NIGHT, YOUR FATHER SUSTAINED SEVERE TRAUMA TO HIS ABDOMINAL REGION IN THE CAR ACCIDENT...
SH-SHUT
AND WE WERE KEEPING A CLOSE WATCH ON HIM FOR ANY ABRUPT CHANGES IN BLOOD PRESSURE OR HEART RATE WHICH WOULD INDICATE INTERNAL HEM-ORRHAGING...
AND HE WAS FINE, FOR THE NIGHT...
...BUT AROUND EIGHT FORTY FIVE THIS MORNING HIS SIGNS BEGAN TO RAP-IDLY DROP... SO WE DECIDED TO TRANSFUSE HIM... WE DID TRY TO CALL YOU...
HIS SIGNS CONTINUED TO WORSEN, HOWEVER... WE HAD NO CHOICE BUT TO OPERATE TO FIND THE SOURCE OF THE BLEEDING...
WE FOUND HIM...HIS LIVER... AND POSSIBLY HIS SPLEEN... HAD RUPTURED... HE WAS BLEEDING FROM MANY, MANY PLACES...
WE TRIED TO STABILIZE HIM, BUT HE WAS REJECT-ING FLUIDS AND HE WENT INTO CARDIAC ARREST... WE TRIED TO STIMULATE HIS HEART, BUT HE DIED. HE'S DEAD.
SHUFFLE

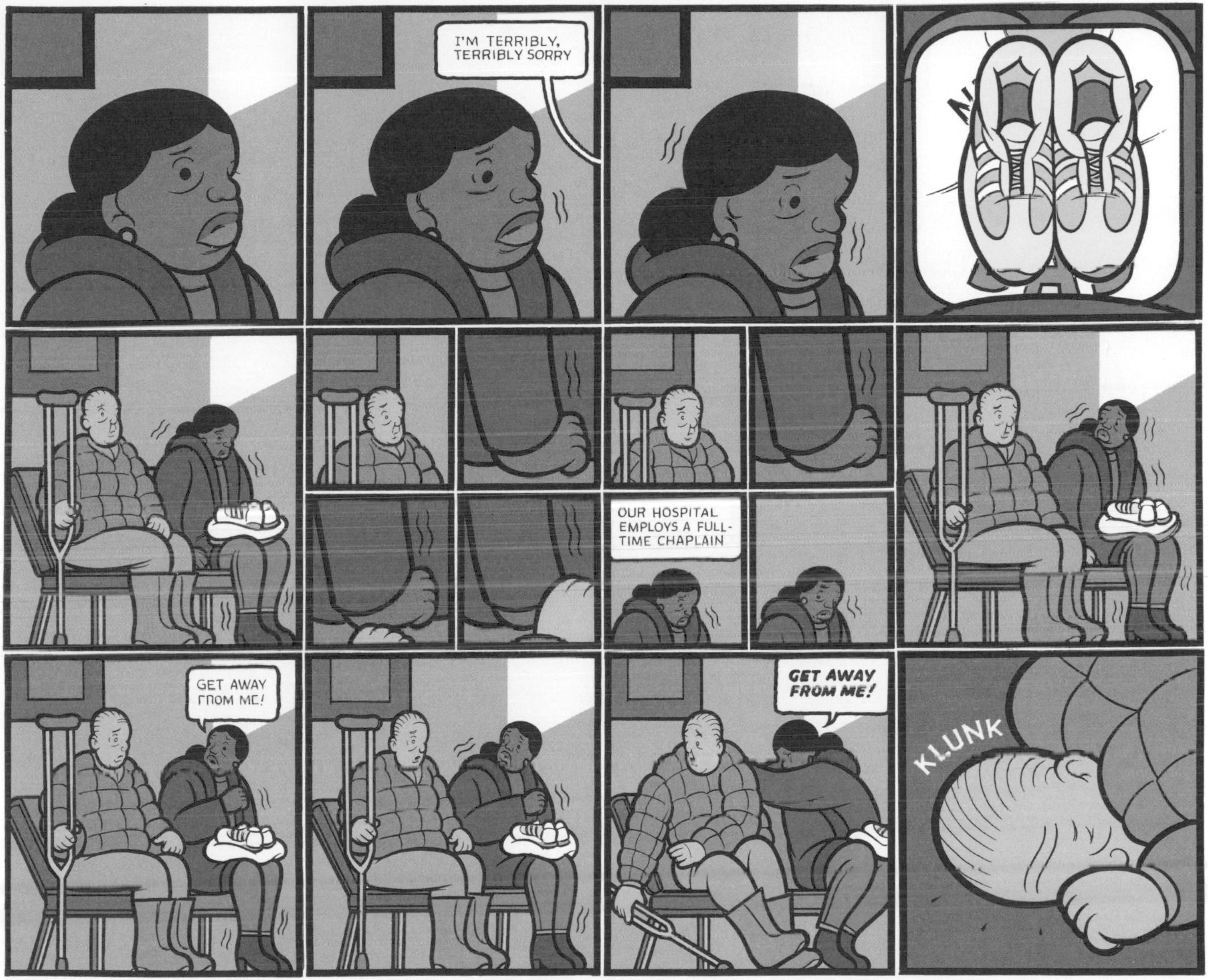

I'M TERRIBLY, TERRIBLY SORRY
OUR HOSPITAL EMPLOYS A FULL-TIME CHAPLAIN
GET AWAY FROM ME!
GET AWAY FROM ME!
KLUNK

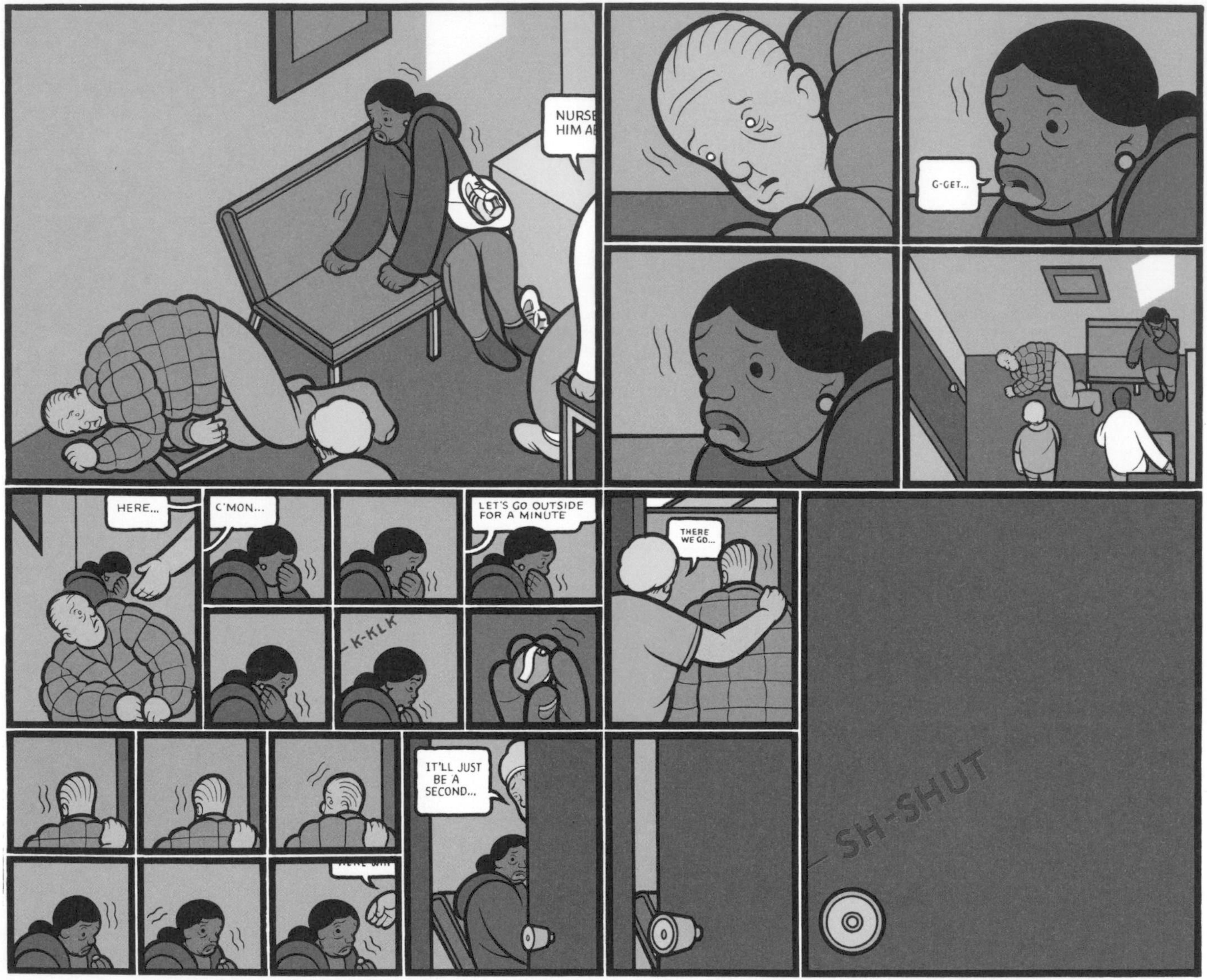
NURSE
HIM
G-GET...
HERE...
C'MON...
LET'S GO OUTSIDE FOR A MINUTE
K-KLK
THERE WE GO...
IT'LL JUST BE A SECOND...
SH-SHUT

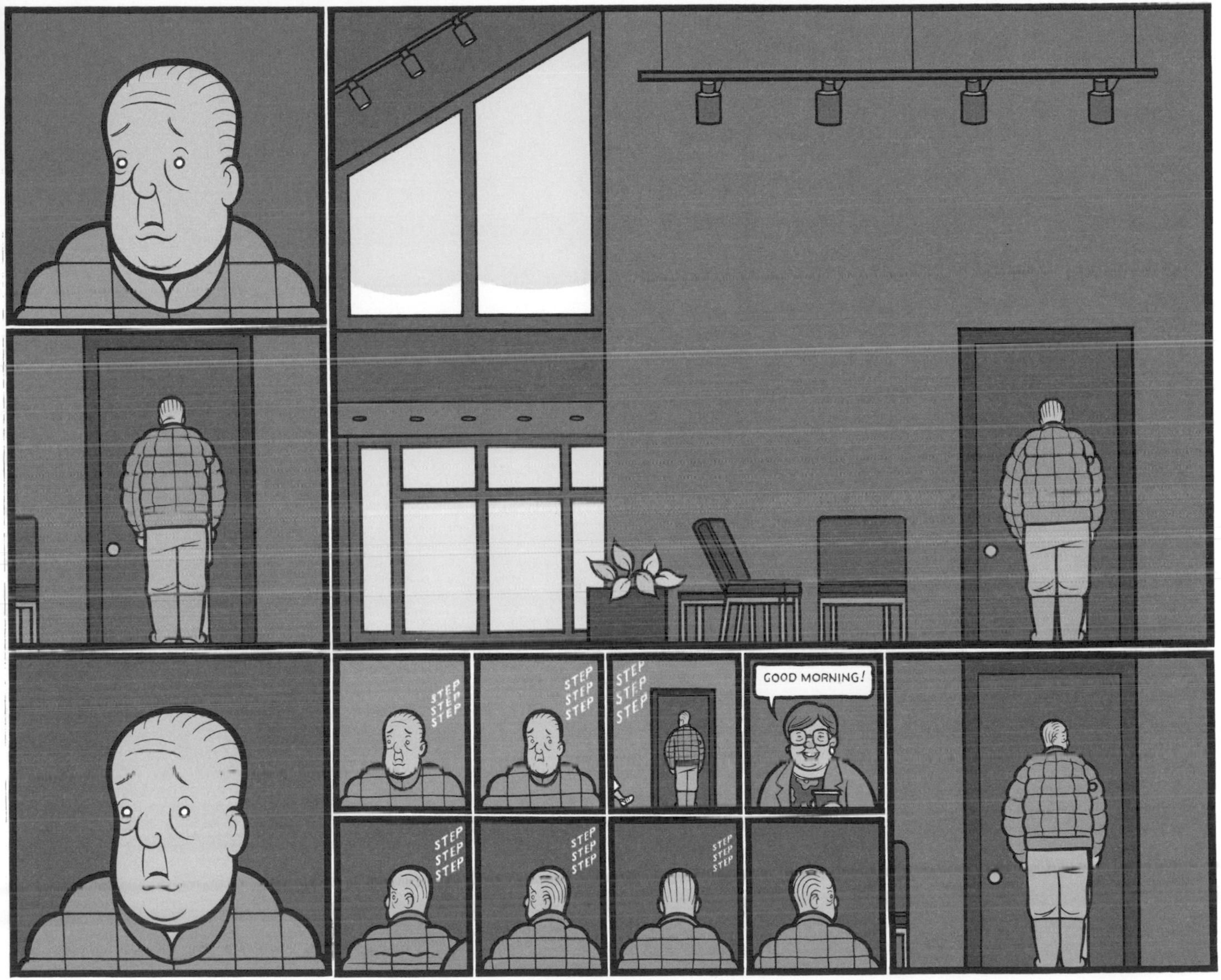

STEP STEP STEP
STEP STEP STEP
STEP STEP STEP
GOOD MORNING!
STEP STEP STEP
STEP STEP STEP
STEP STEP STEP

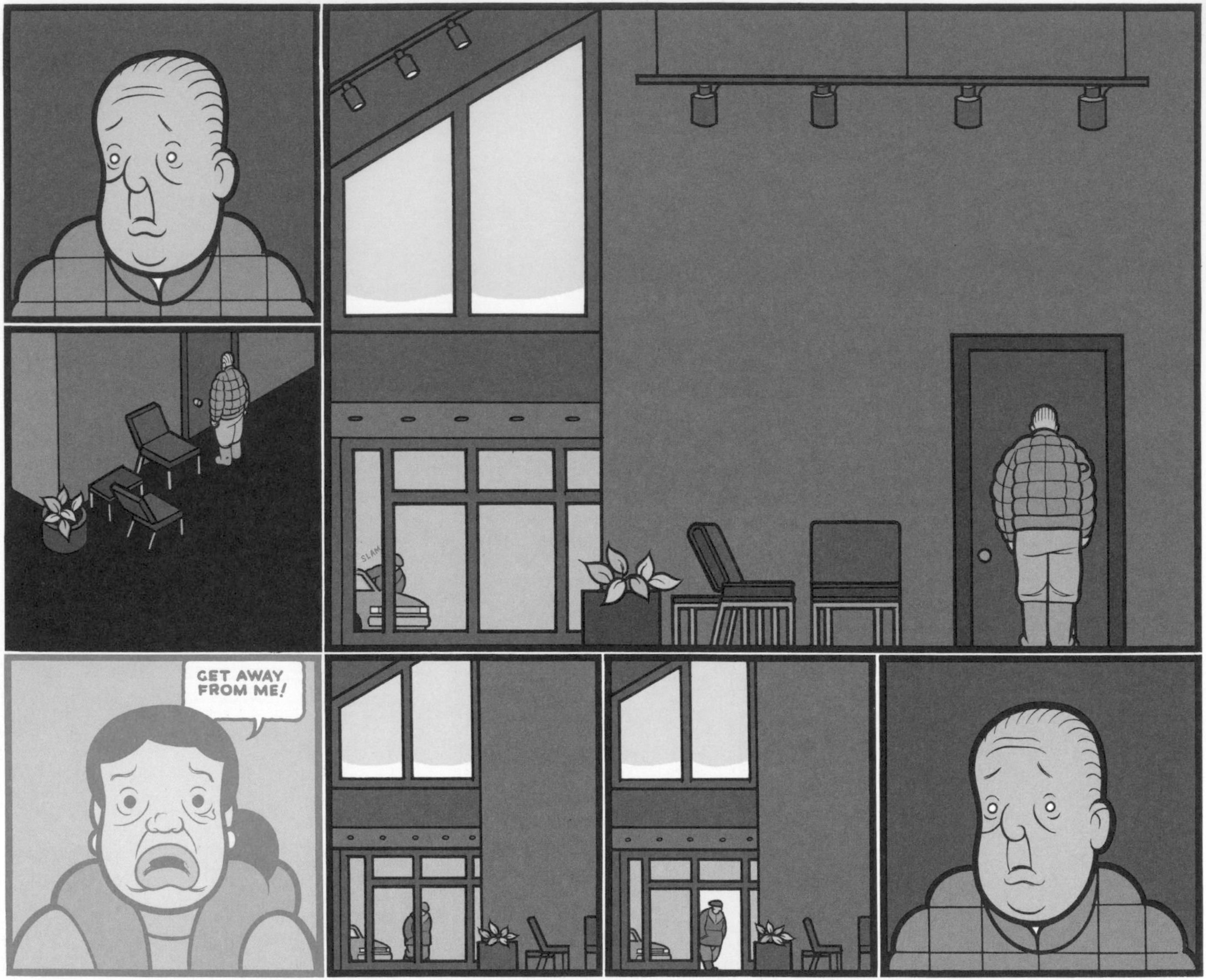
SLAM
GET AWAY FROM ME!

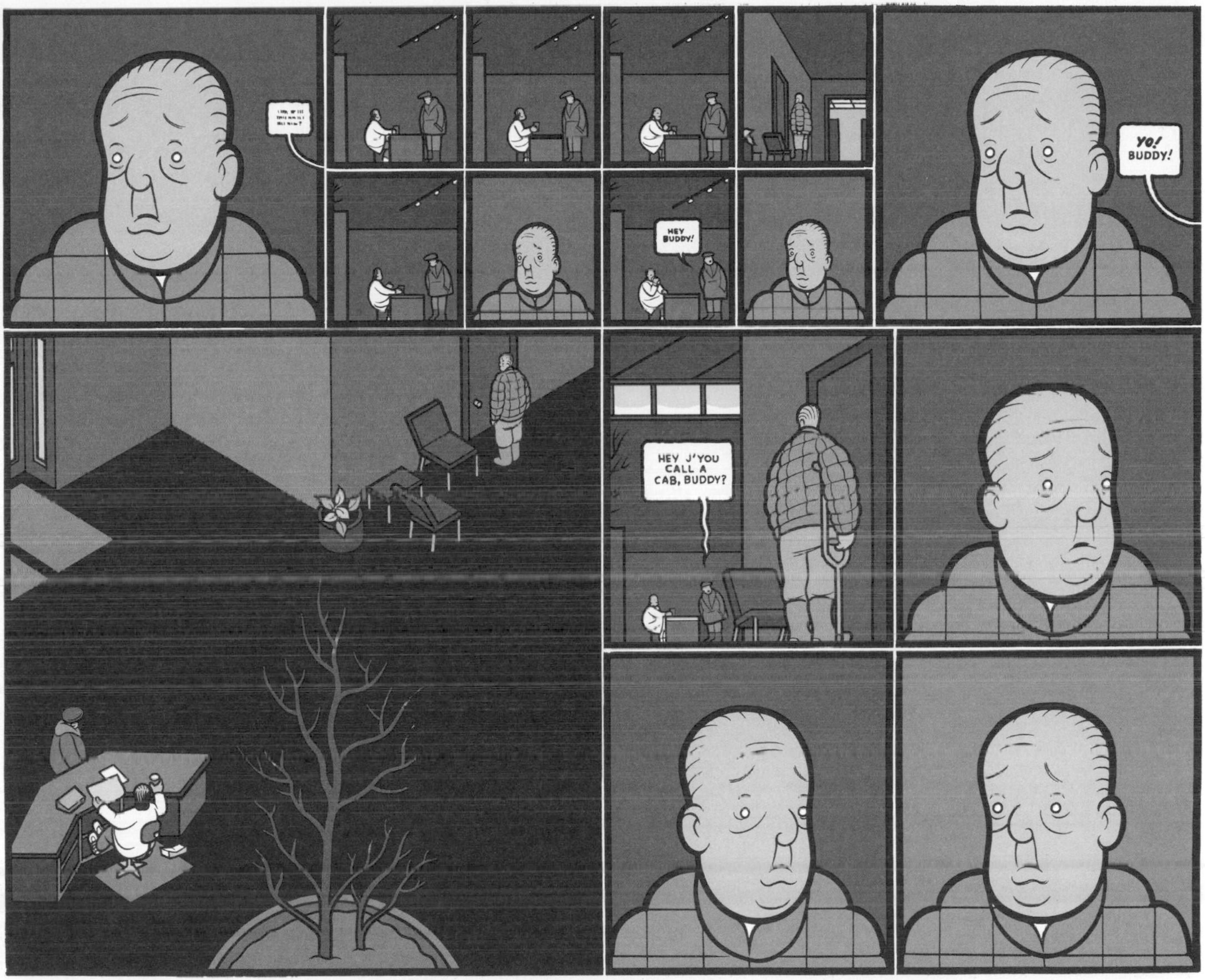
HEY BUDDY!
YO! BUDDY!
HEY J'YOU CALL A CAB, BUDDY?

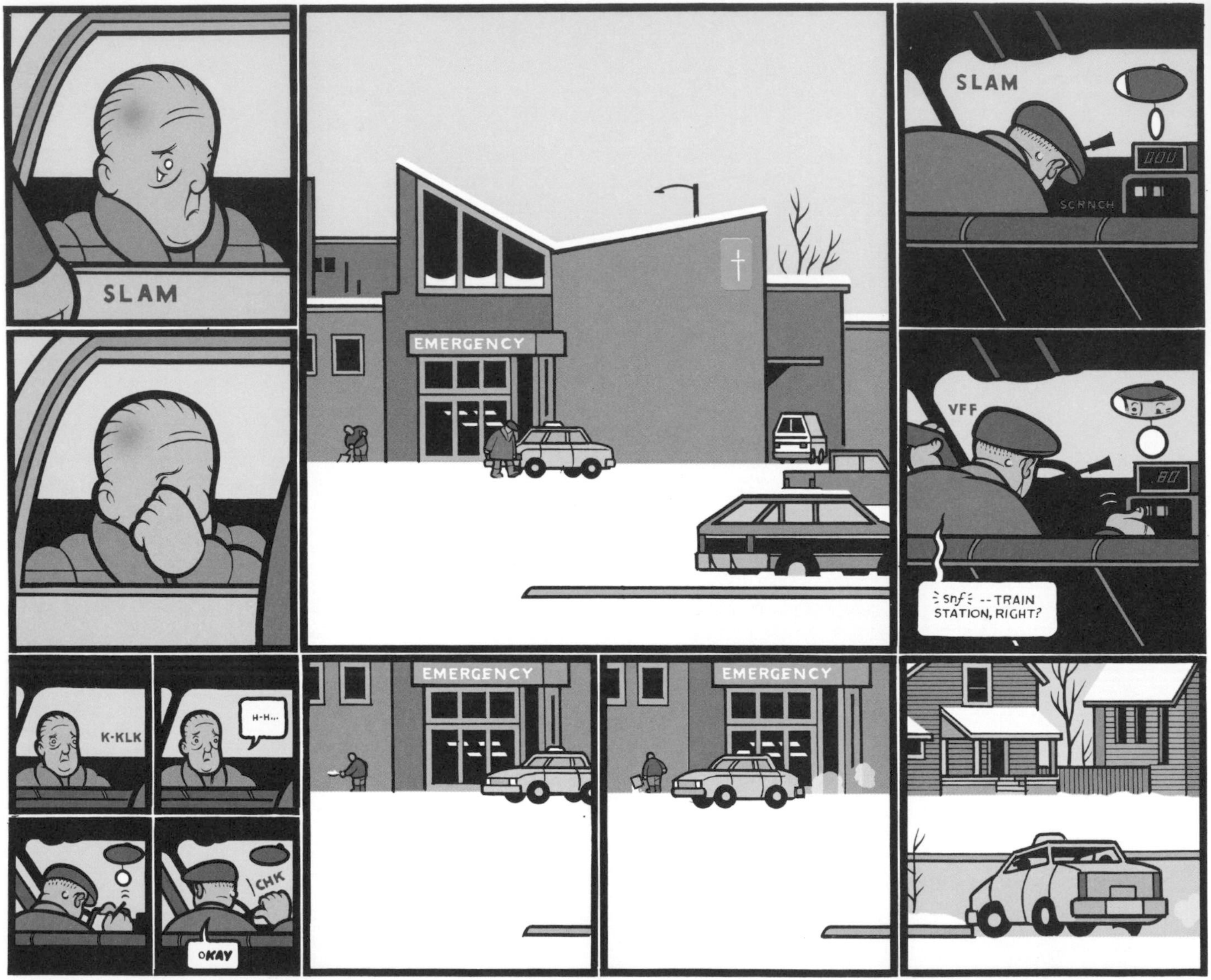

SLAM
EMERGENCY
SLAM
SCRNCH
VFF
snf --TRAIN STATION, RIGHT?
K-KLK
H-H...
CHK
OKAY
EMERGENCY
EMERGENCY

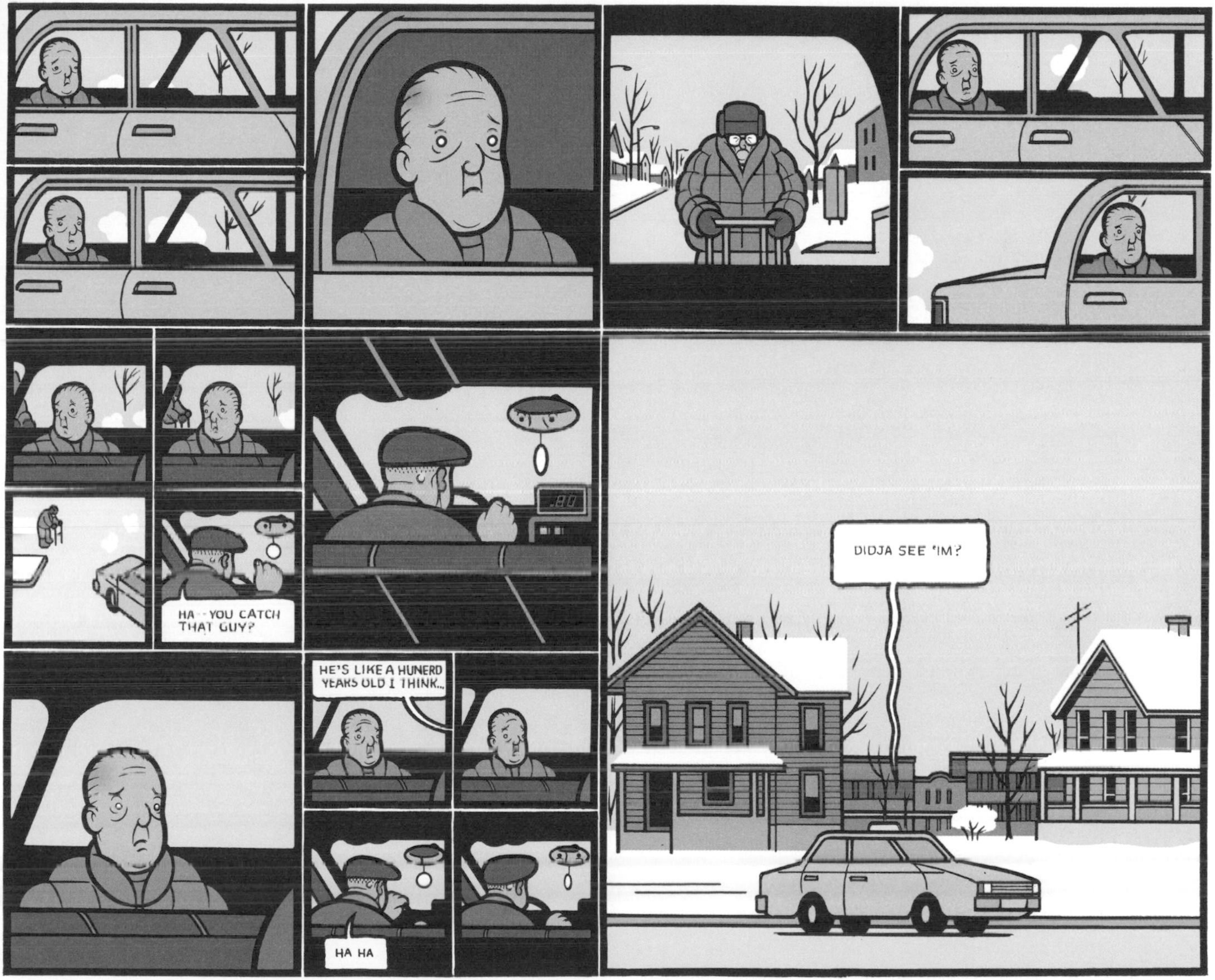
HA--YOU CATCH THAT GUY?
HE'S LIKE A HUNERD YEARS OLD I THINK...
HA HA
DIDJA SEE 'IM?

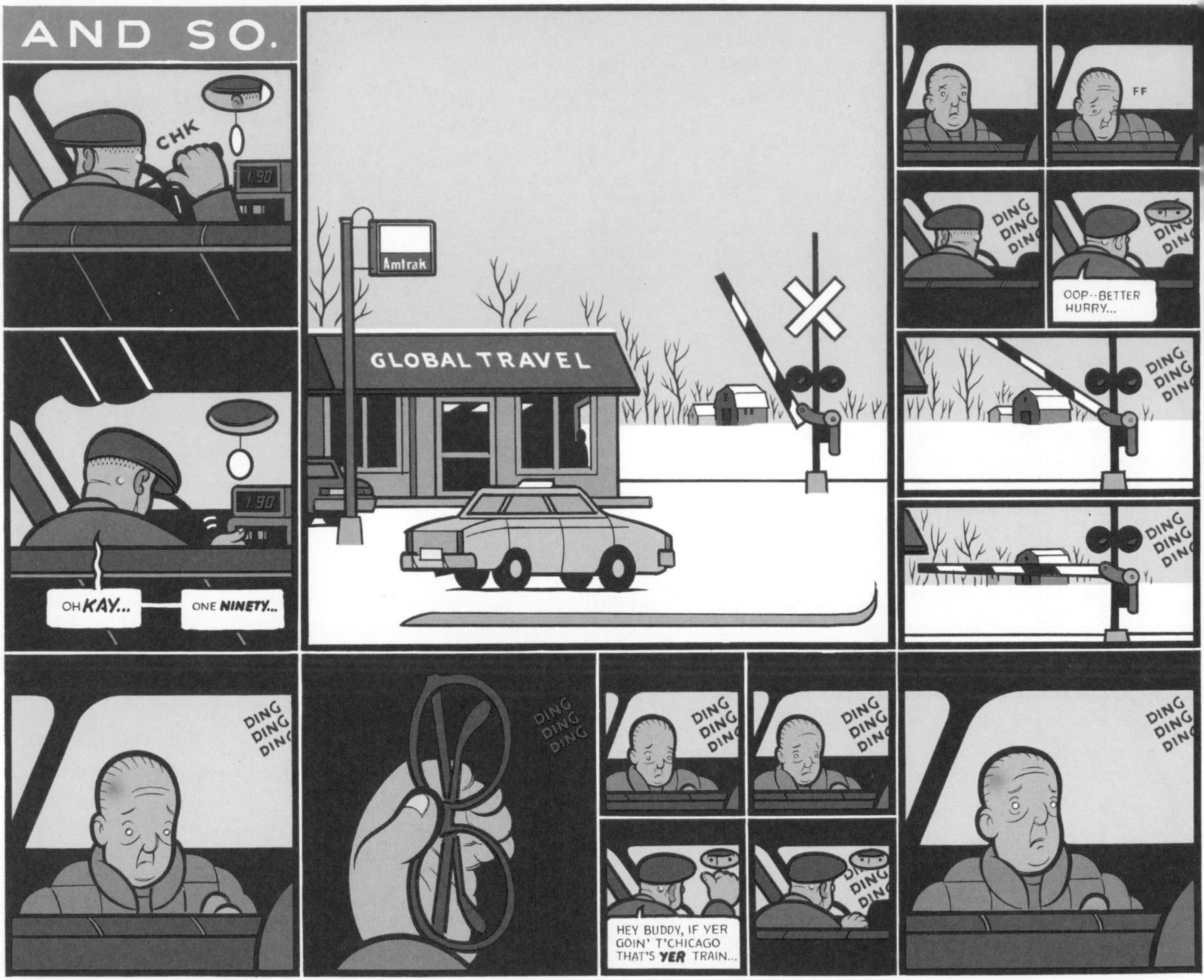

AND SO.
CHK
1.90
1.90
OH KAY...
ONE NINETY...
Amtrak
GLOBAL TRAVEL
FF
DING DING DING
OOP--BETTER HURRY...
DING DING DING
DING DING DING
DING DING DING
DING DING DING
DING DING DING
DING DING DING
HEY BUDDY, IF YER GOIN' T'CHICAGO THAT'S YER TRAIN...
DING DING
DING DING DING

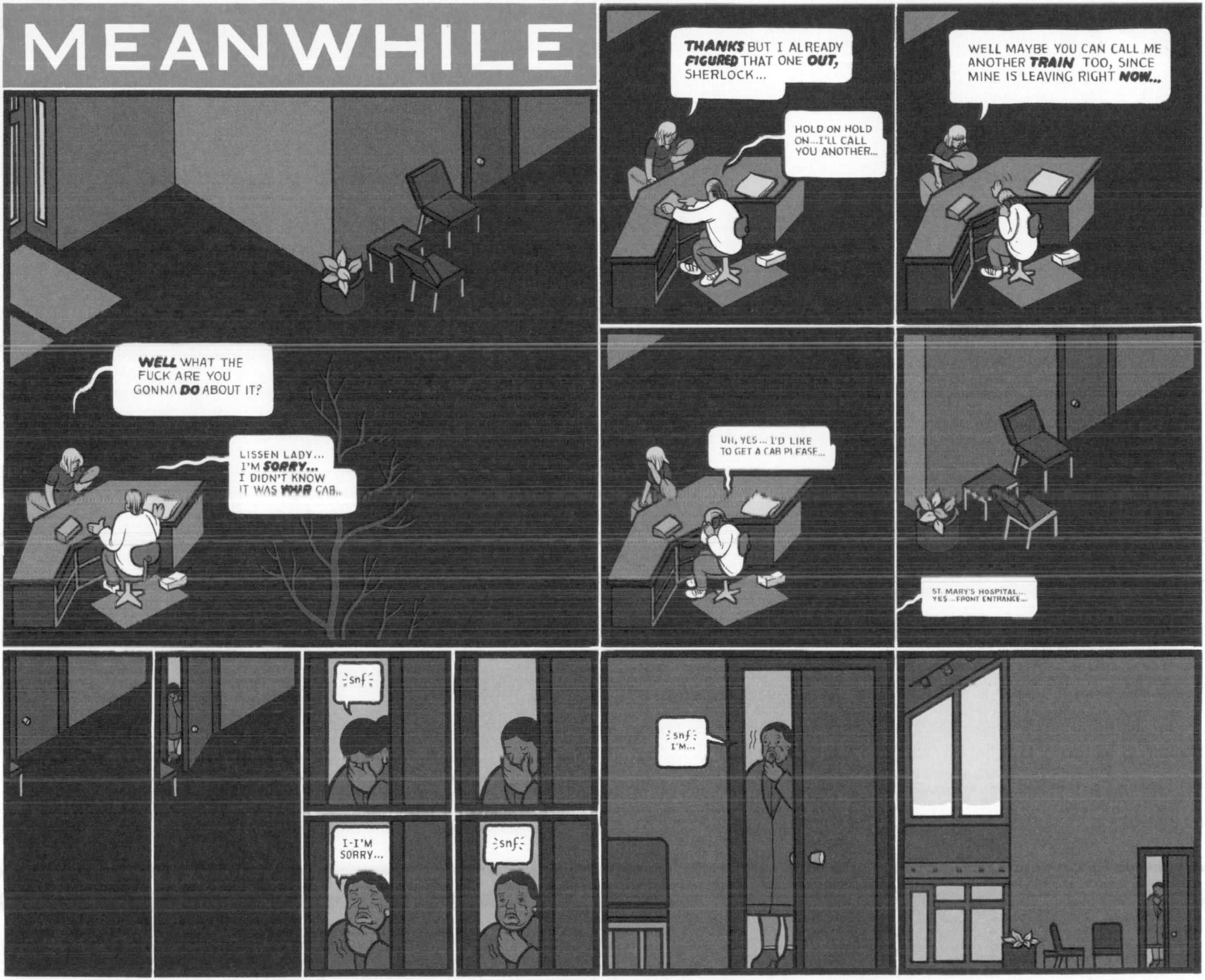
MEANWHILE
THANKS BUT I ALREADY FIGURED THAT ONE OUT, SHERLOCK...
HOLD ON HOLD ON...I'LL CALL YOU ANOTHER...
WELL MAYBE YOU CAN CALL ME ANOTHER TRAIN TOO, SINCE MINE IS LEAVING RIGHT NOW...
WELL WHAT THE FUCK ARE YOU GONNA DO ABOUT IT?
LISSEN LADY... I'M SORRY... I DIDN'T KNOW IT WAS YOUR CAB...
UH, YES... I'D LIKE TO GET A CAB PLEASE...
ST. MARY'S HOSPITAL... YES... FRONT ENTRANCE...
snf
I-I'M SORRY...
snf
snf I'M...

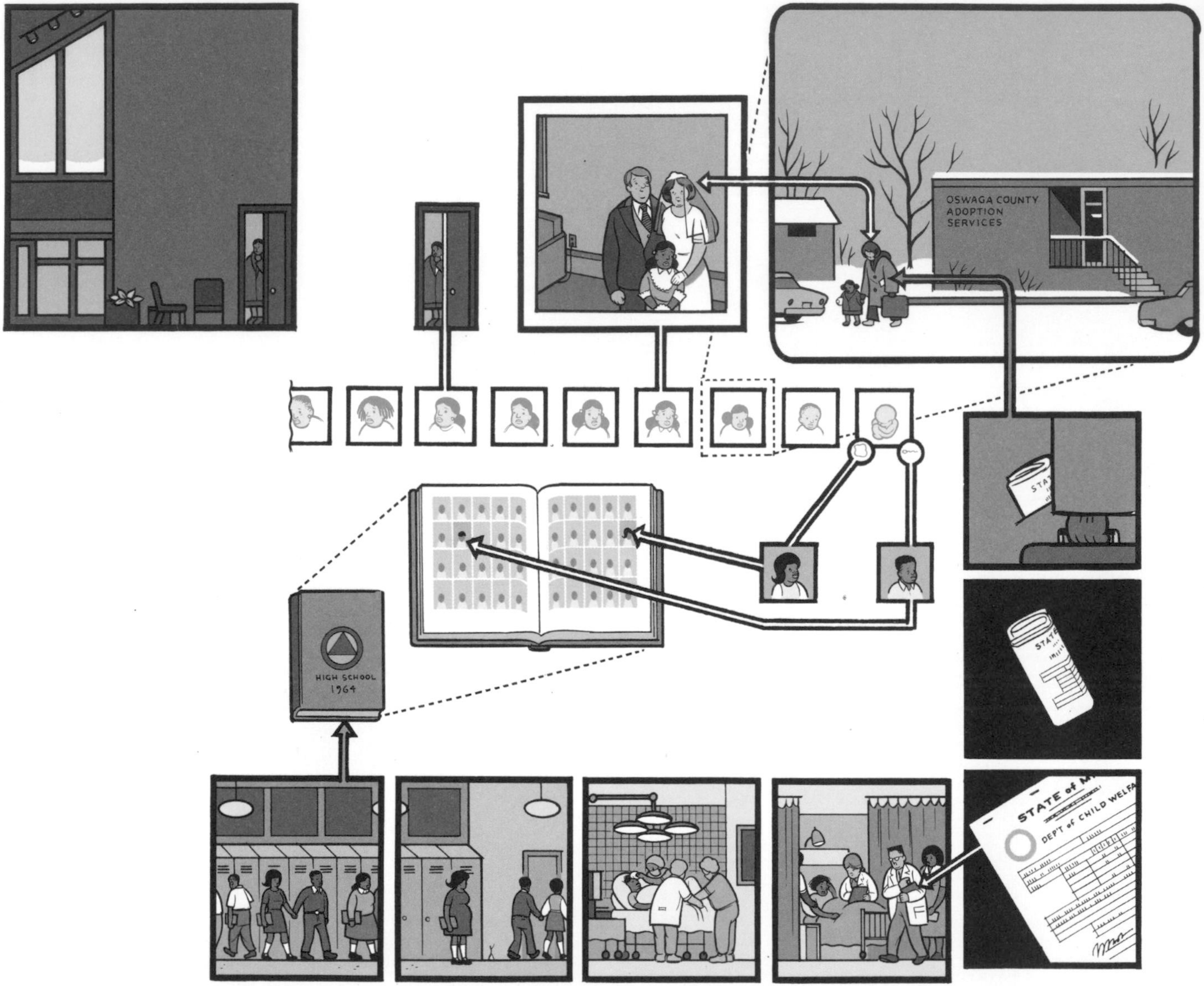
OSWAGA COUNTY
ADOPTION
SERVICES
HIGH SCHOOL
1964
DEP'T of CHILD WELFA

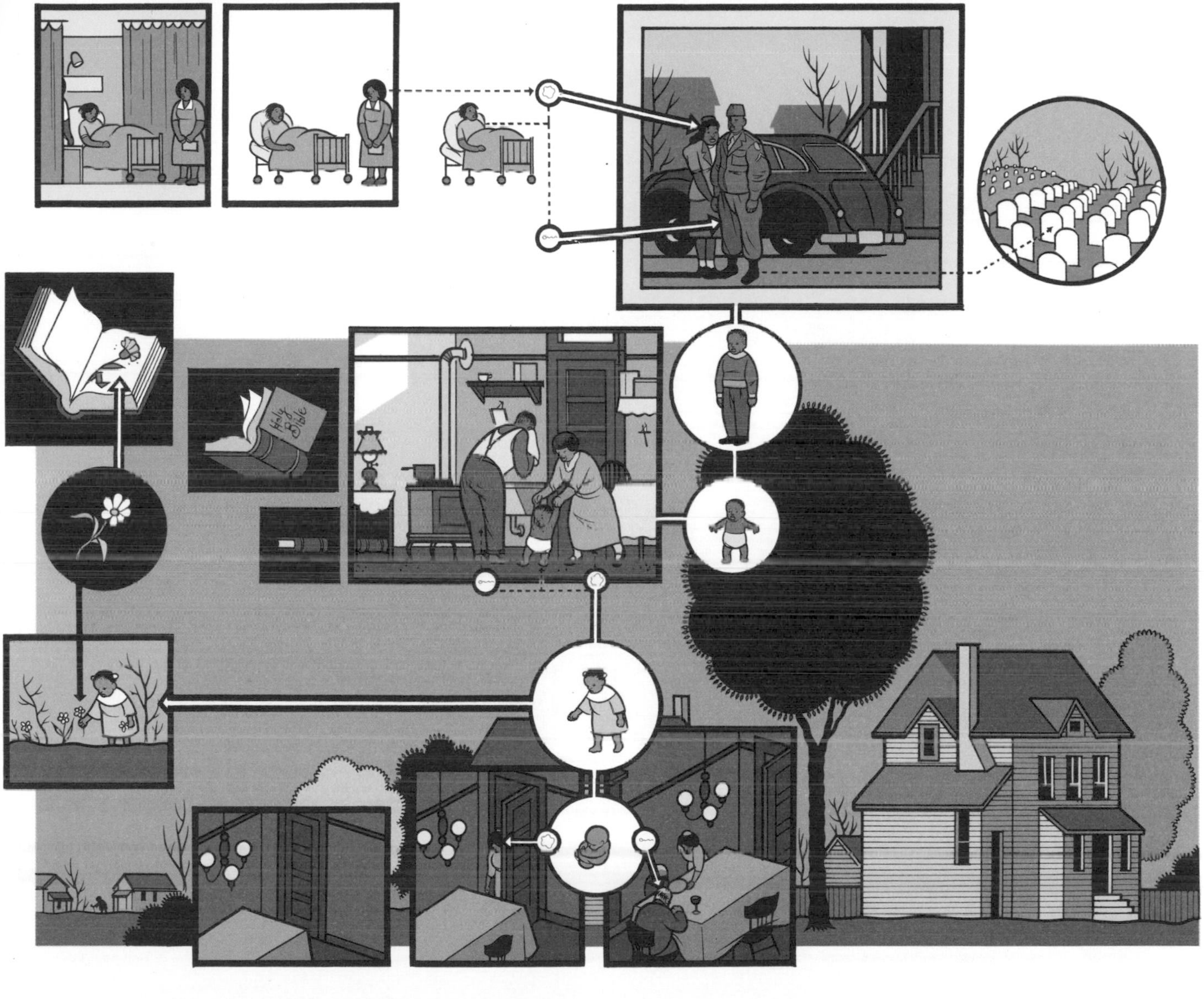
Holy Bible

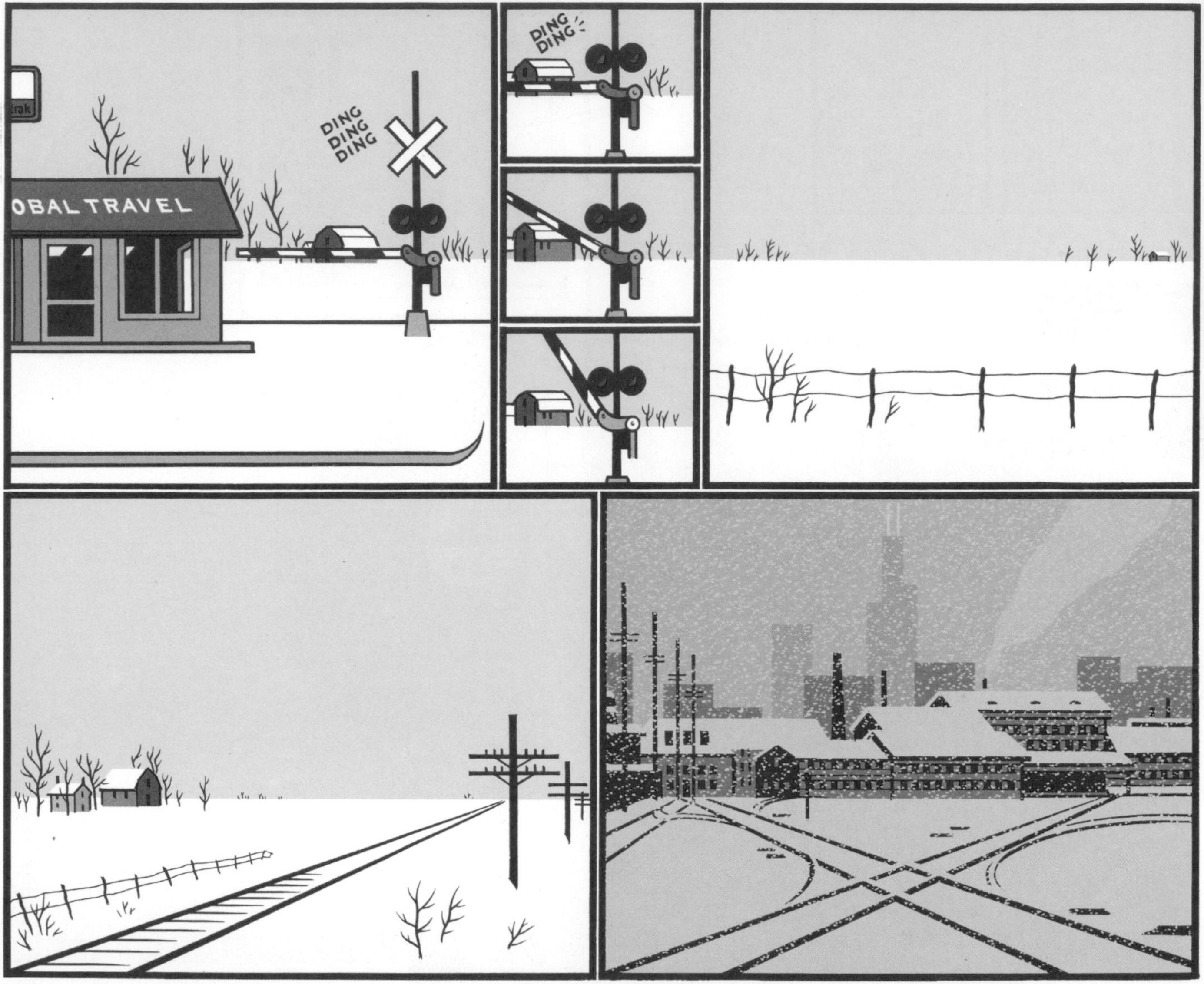
OBAL TRAVEL
DING
DING
DING
DING
DING

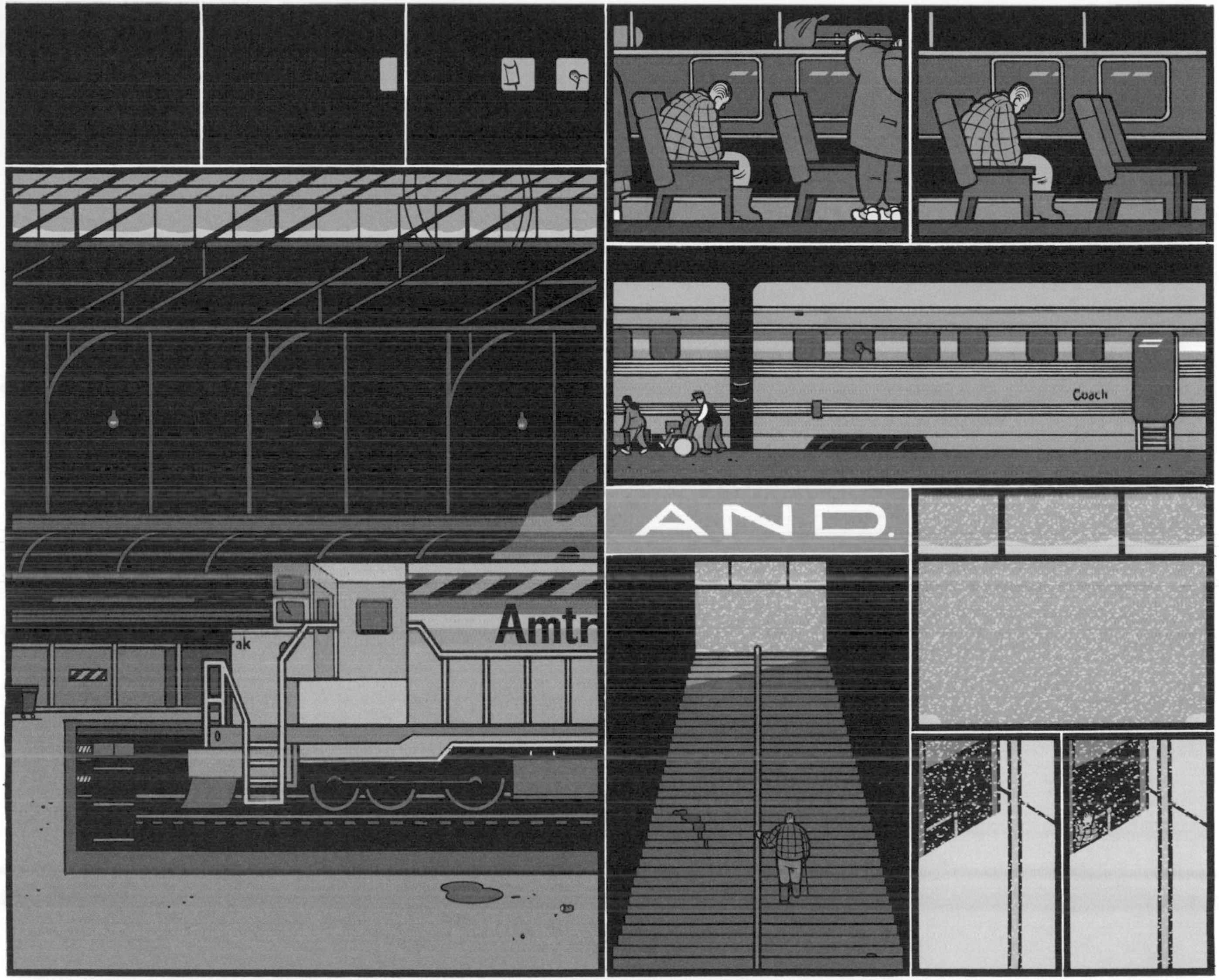
Coach
AND.
Amtr
rak

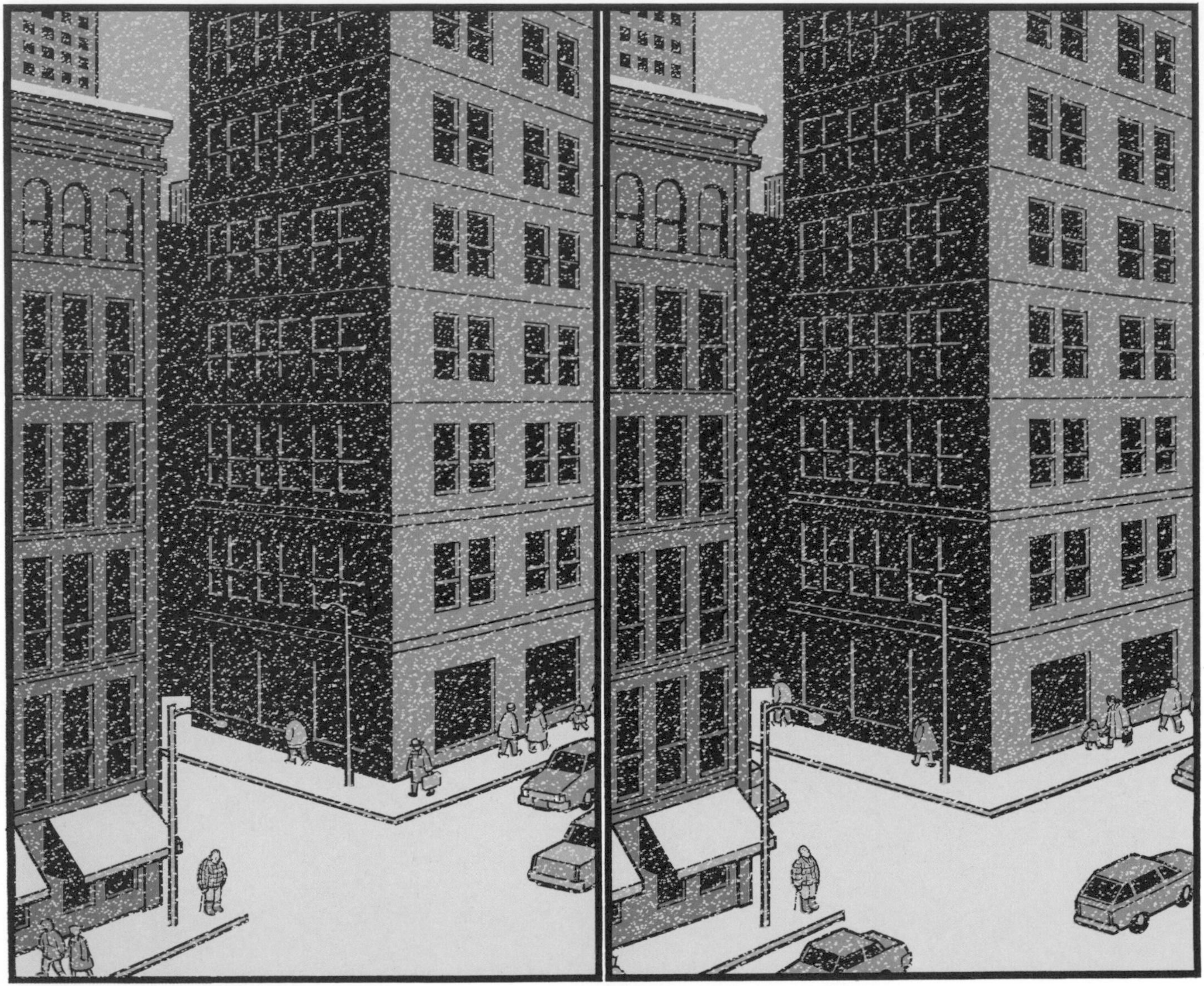

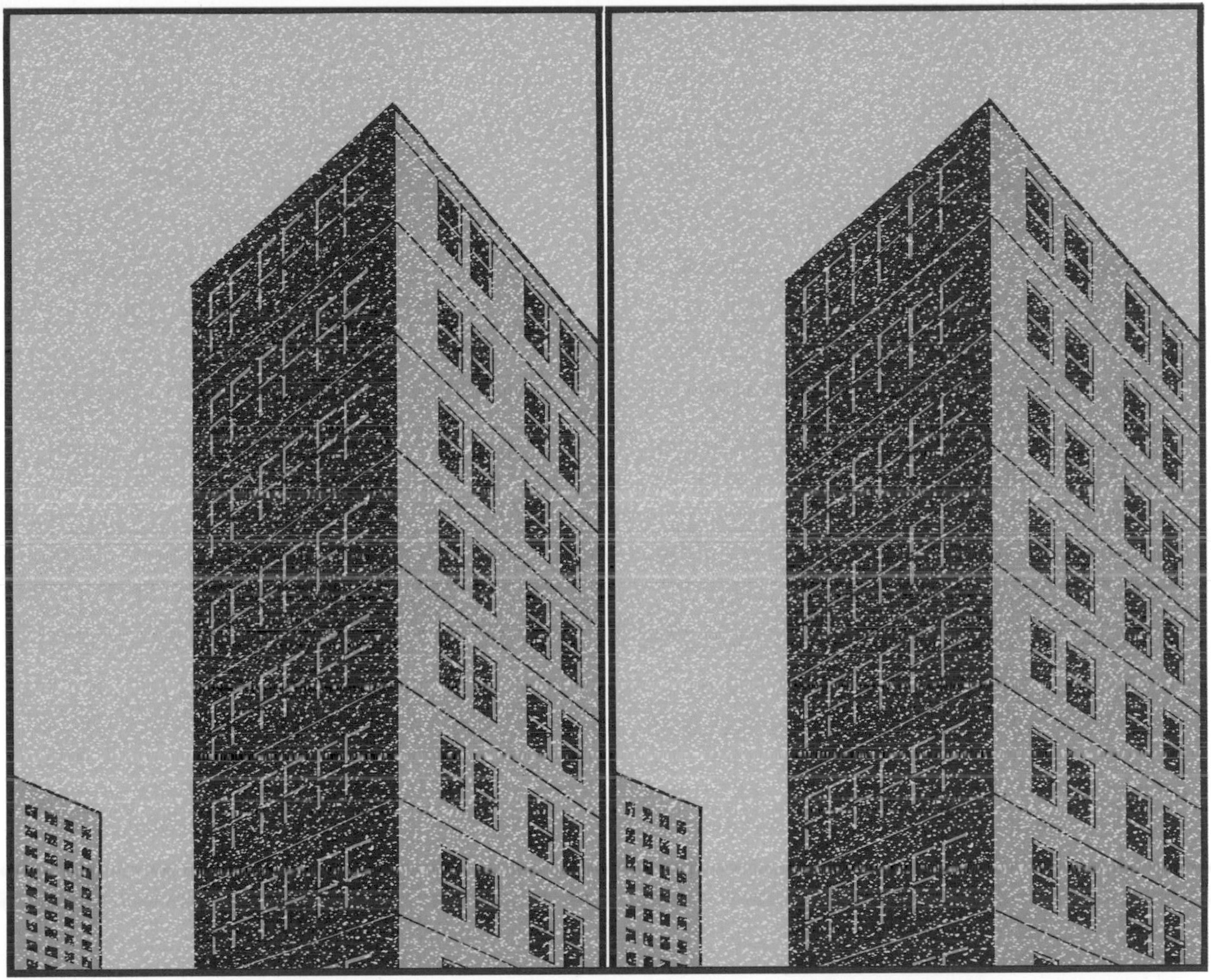

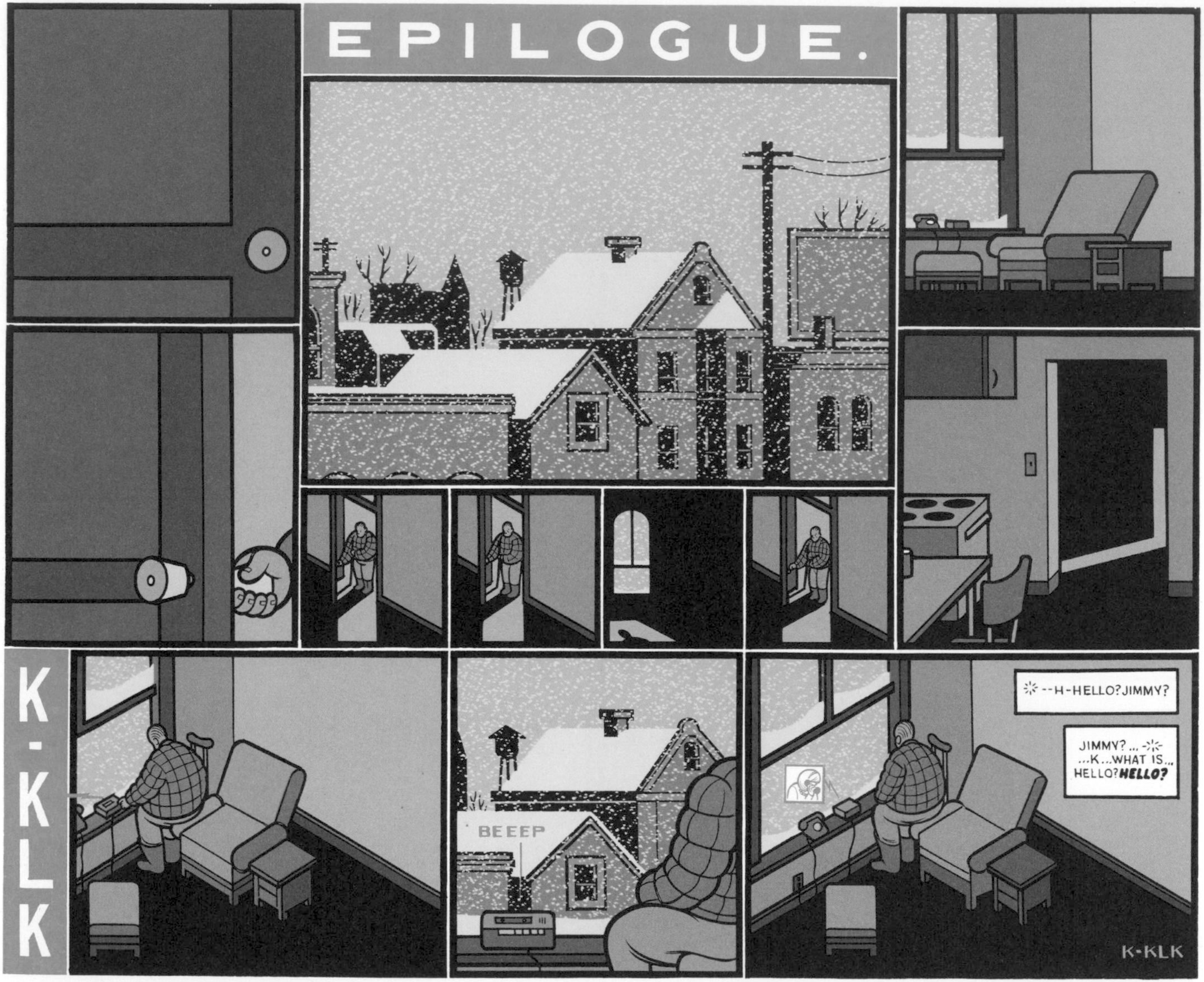
EPILOGUE.
K-KLK
BEEEP
--H-HELLO? JIMMY?
JIMMY? ... ...K... WHAT IS... HELLO? HELLO?
K-KLK

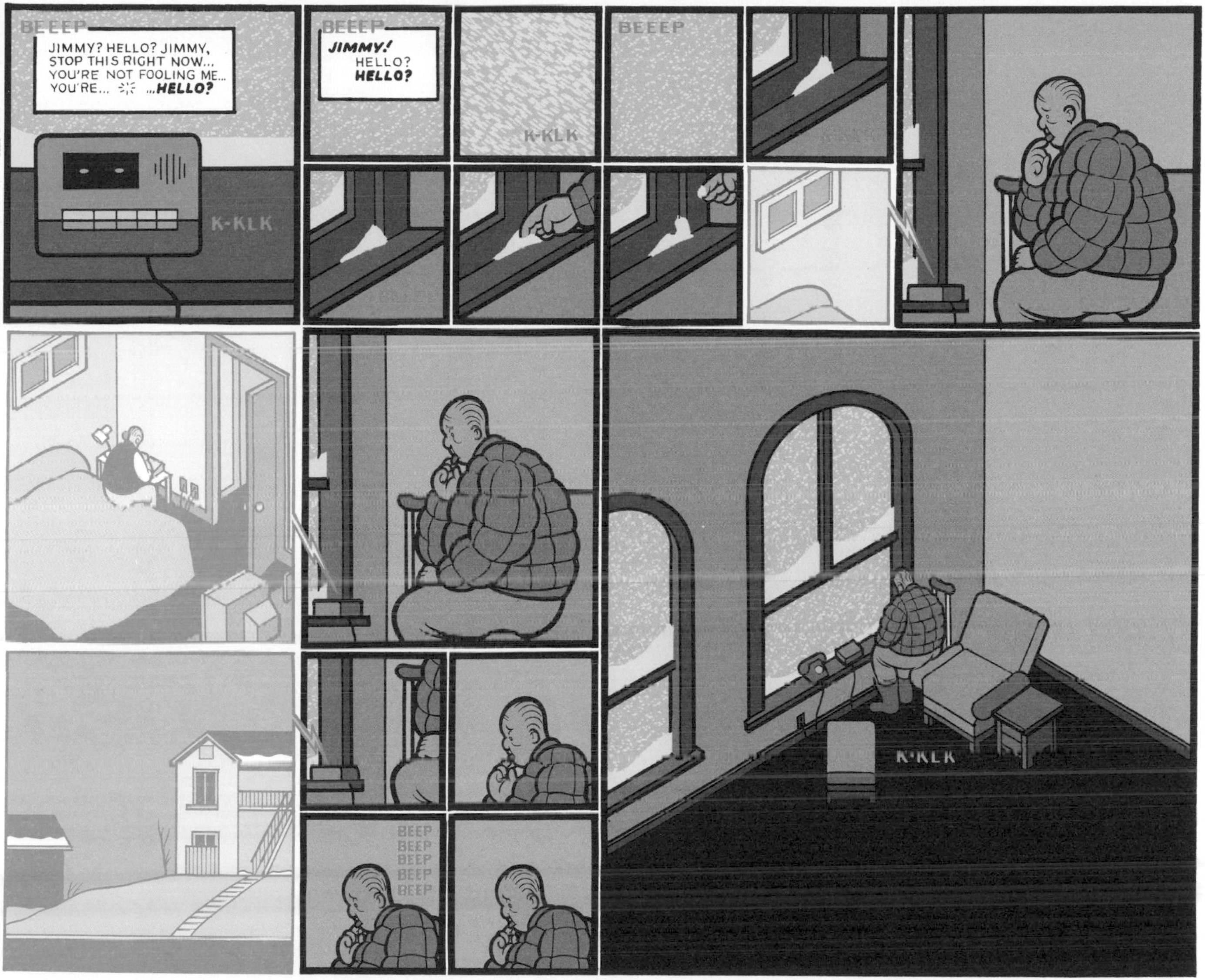
BEEEP
JIMMY? HELLO? JIMMY, STOP THIS RIGHT NOW... YOU'RE NOT FOOLING ME... YOU'RE... ...HELLO?
K-KLK
BEEEP
JIMMY! HELLO? HELLO?
K-KLK
BEEEP
K'KLK
BEEP
BEEP
BEEP
BEEP
BEEP

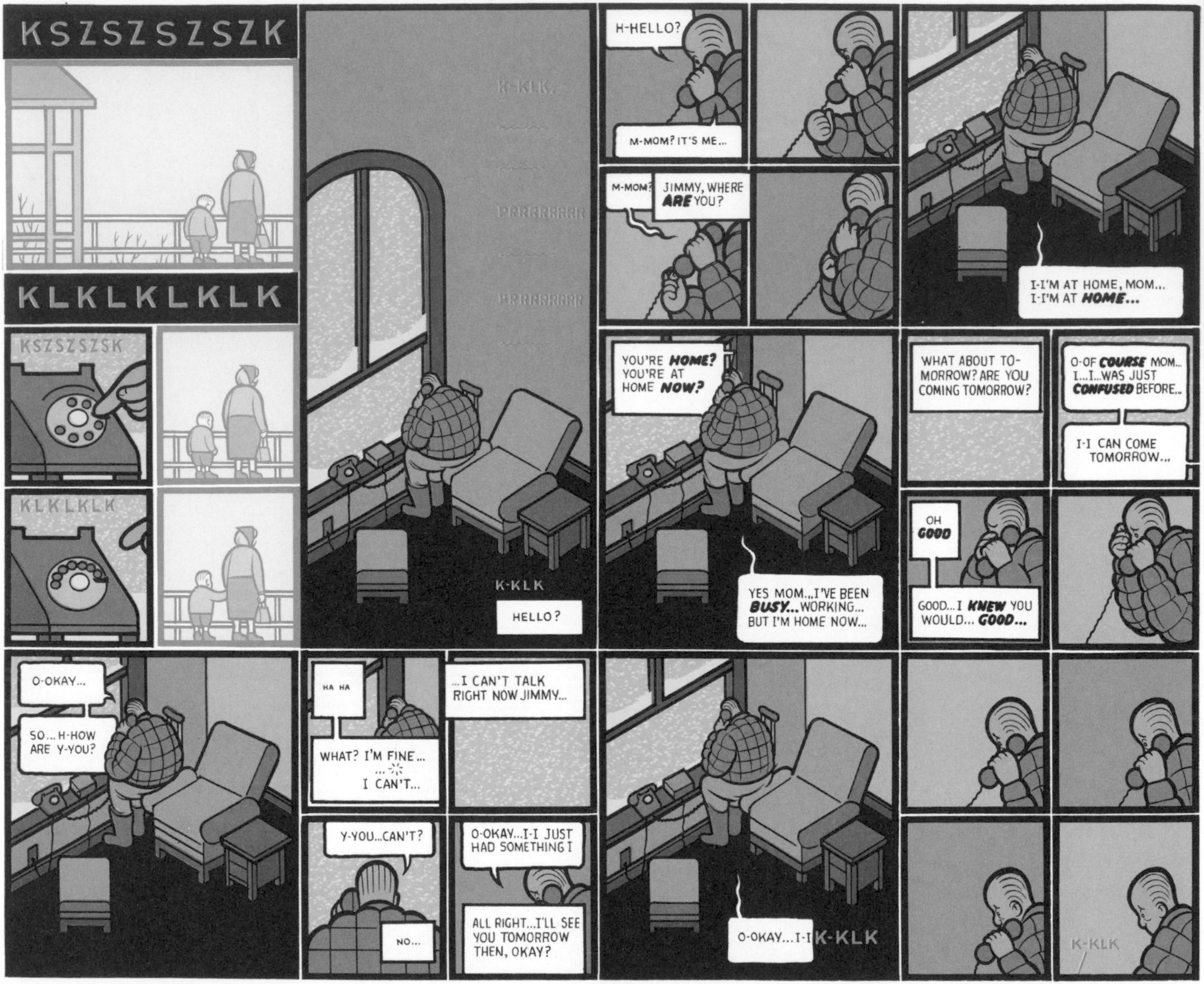
KSZSZSZSZK
KLKLKLKLK
KSZSZSZSK
KLKLKLK
K-KLK.
PRRRRRRRR
PRRRRRRRR
K-KLK
HELLO?
H-HELLO?
M-MOM? IT'S ME...
M-MOM?
JIMMY, WHERE ARE YOU?
I-I'M AT HOME, MOM... I-I'M AT HOME...
YOU'RE HOME? YOU'RE AT HOME NOW?
YES MOM...I'VE BEEN BUSY...WORKING... BUT I'M HOME NOW...
WHAT ABOUT TO-MORROW? ARE YOU COMING TOMORROW?
O-OF COURSE MOM... I...I...WAS JUST CONFUSED BEFORE...
I-I CAN COME TOMORROW...
OH GOOD
GOOD...I KNEW YOU WOULD... GOOD...
O-OKAY...
SO... H-HOW ARE Y-YOU?
HA HA
WHAT? I'M FINE... ... I CAN'T...
...I CAN'T TALK RIGHT NOW JIMMY...
Y-YOU...CAN'T?
NO...
O-OKAY...I-I JUST HAD SOMETHING I
ALL RIGHT...I'LL SEE YOU TOMORROW THEN, OKAY?
O-OKAY...I-I
K-KLK
K-KLK

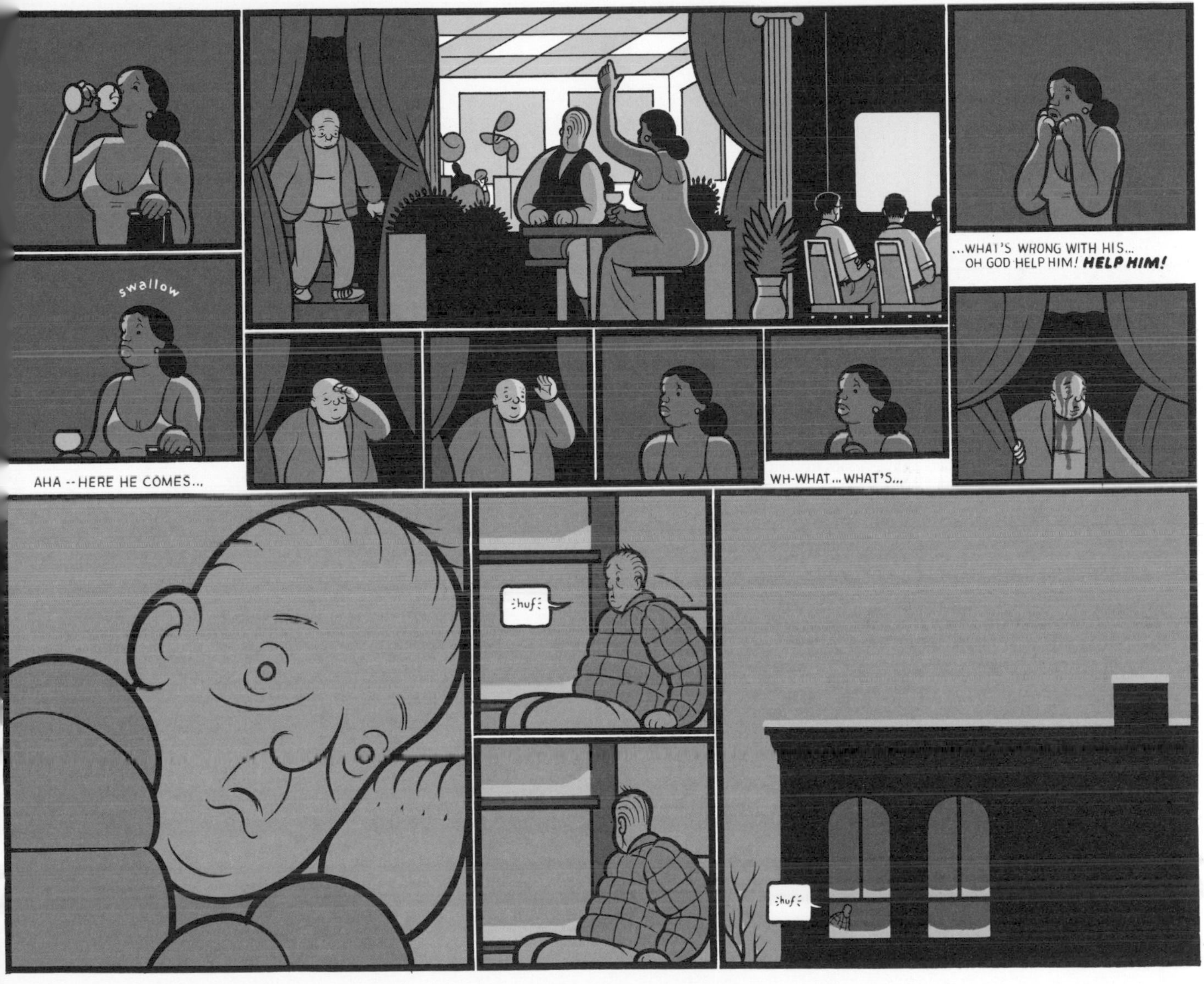
swallow
AHA -- HERE HE COMES...
WH-WHAT... WHAT'S...
...WHAT'S WRONG WITH HIS...
OH GOD HELP HIM! HELP HIM!
huf
huf

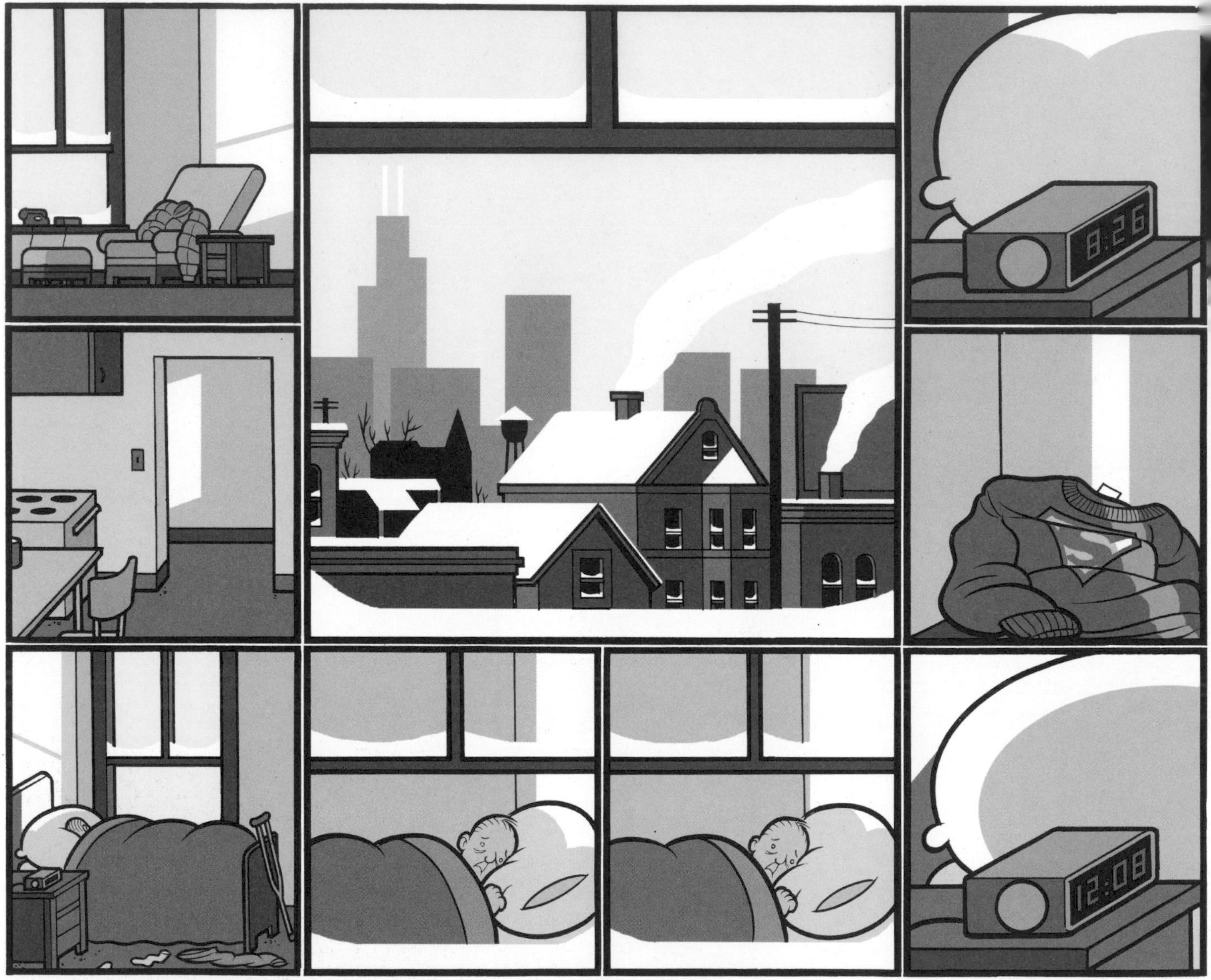
8:26
12:08

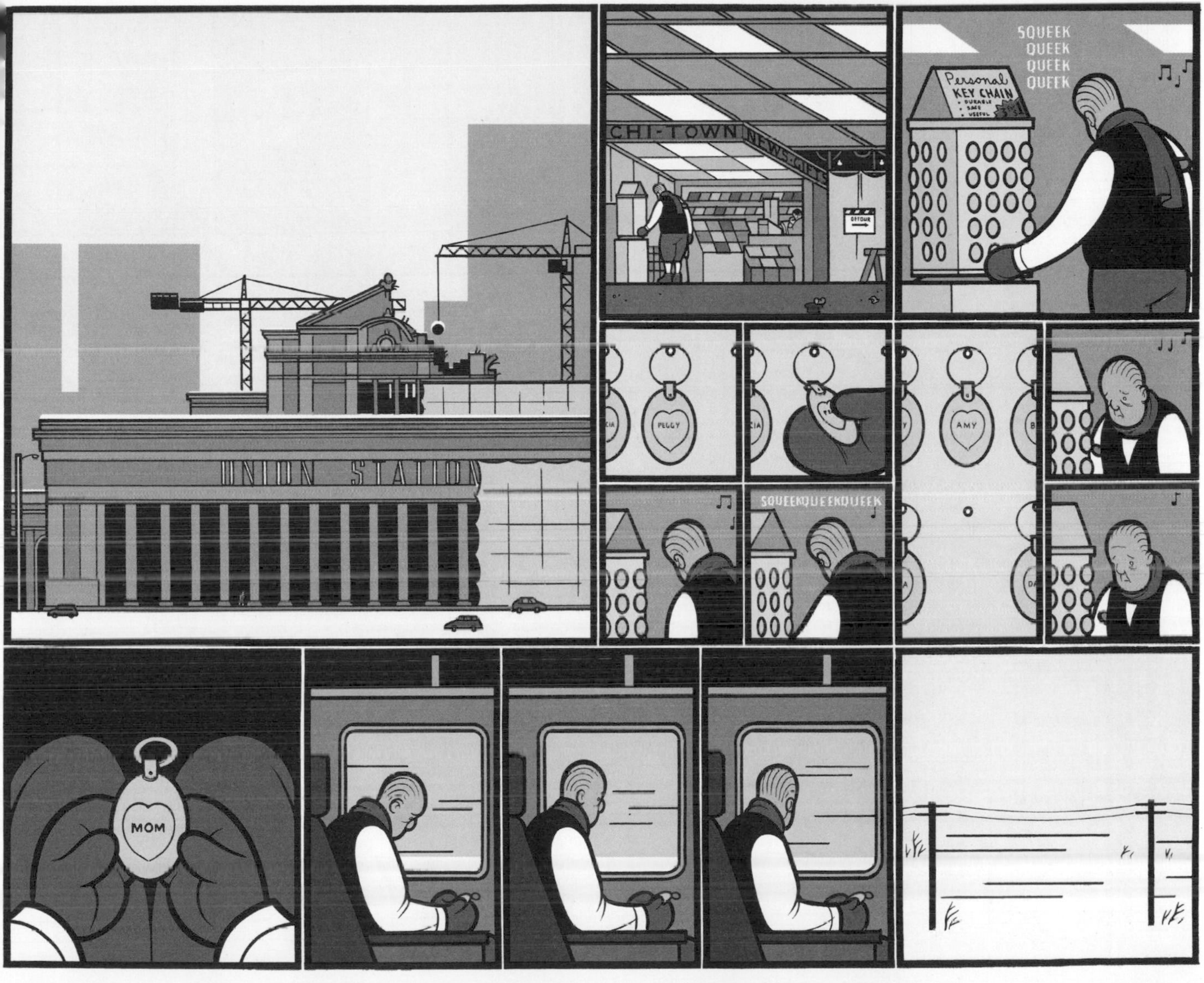
UNION STATION
CHI-TOWN NEWS-GIFTS
DETOUR
SQUEEK
QUEEK
QUEEK
QUEEK
Personal
KEY CHAIN
• DURABLE
• SAFE
• USEFUL
PEGGY
AMY
SQUEEKQUEEKQUEEK
MOM

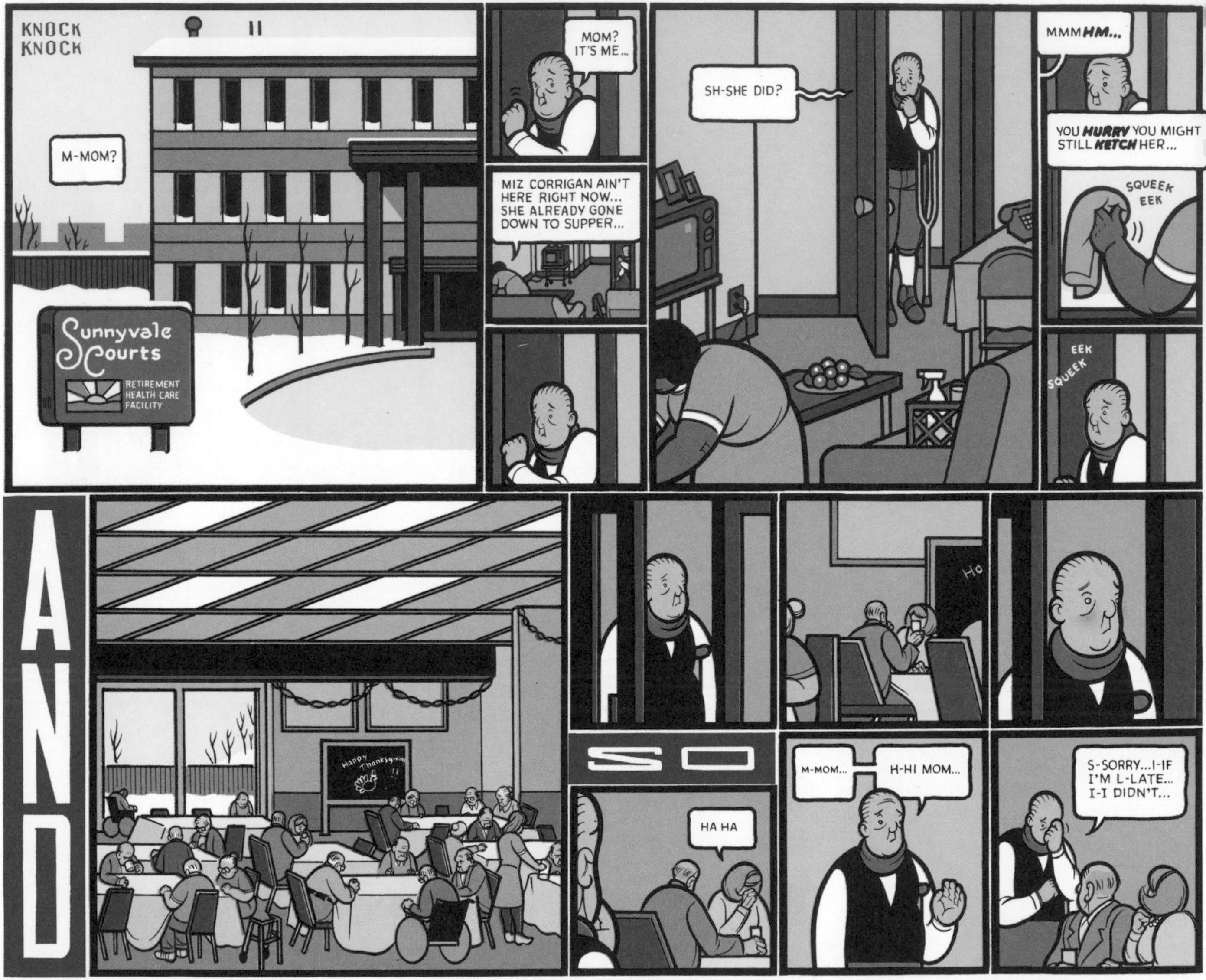
KNOCK KNOCK
M-MOM?
Sunnyvale Courts
RETIREMENT HEALTH CARE FACILITY
MOM? IT'S ME...
MIZ CORRIGAN AIN'T HERE RIGHT NOW... SHE ALREADY GONE DOWN TO SUPPER...
SH-SHE DID?
MMMHM...
YOU HURRY YOU MIGHT STILL KETCH HER...
SQUEEK EEK
EEK SQUEEK
AND
Happy Thanksgiving
SO
HA HA
M-MOM...
H-HI MOM...
S-SORRY...I-IF I'M L-LATE... I-I DIDN'T...

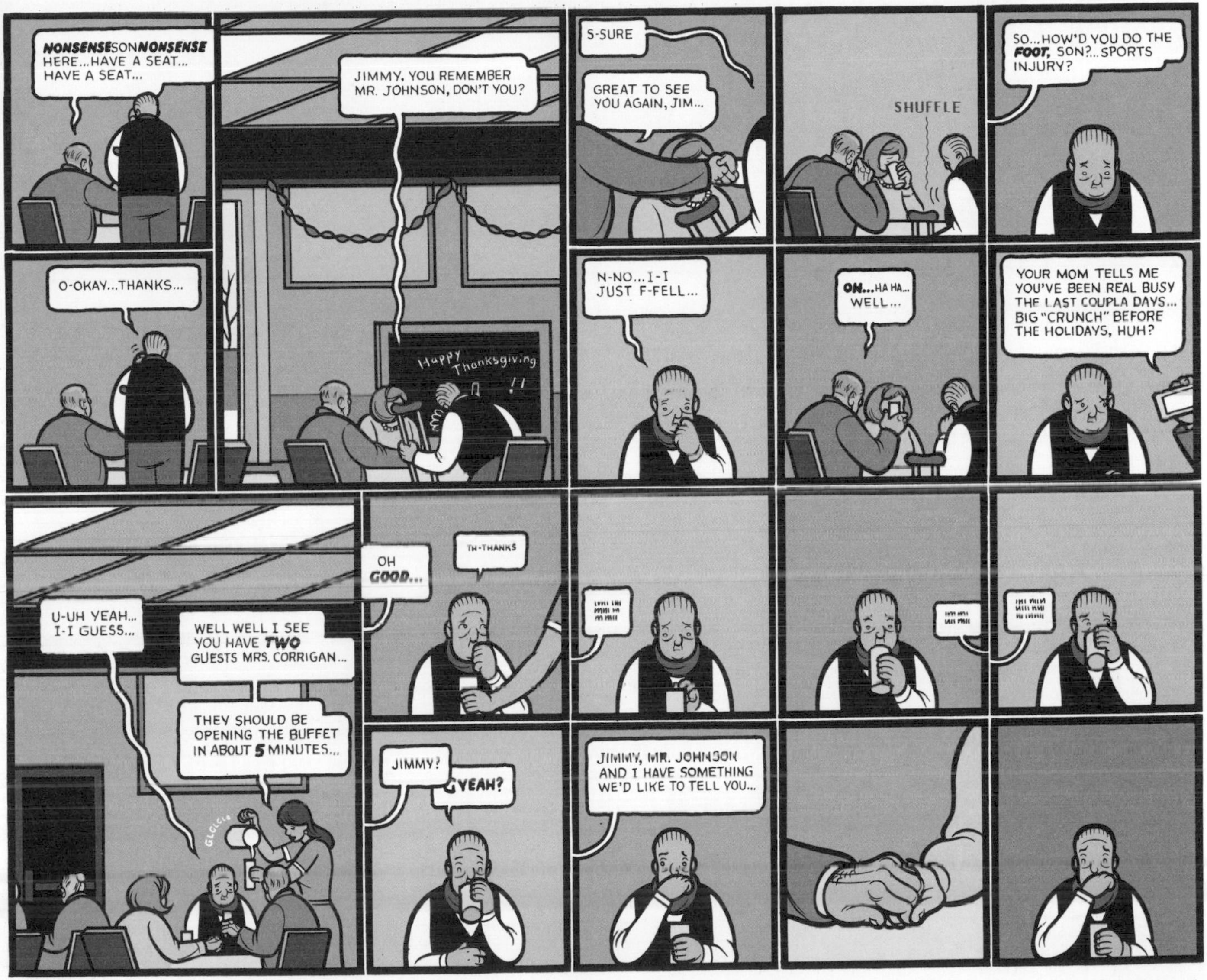

NONSENSE SON NONSENSE HERE...HAVE A SEAT... HAVE A SEAT...
JIMMY, YOU REMEMBER MR. JOHNSON, DON'T YOU?
S-SURE
GREAT TO SEE YOU AGAIN, JIM...
SHUFFLE
SO...HOW'D YOU DO THE FOOT, SON?...SPORTS INJURY?
O-OKAY...THANKS...
Happy Thanksgiving
N-NO...I-I JUST F-FELL...
OH...HA HA... WELL...
YOUR MOM TELLS ME YOU'VE BEEN REAL BUSY THE LAST COUPLA DAYS... BIG "CRUNCH" BEFORE THE HOLIDAYS, HUH?
U-UH YEAH... I-I GUESS...
WELL WELL I SEE YOU HAVE TWO GUESTS MRS. CORRIGAN...
THEY SHOULD BE OPENING THE BUFFET IN ABOUT 5 MINUTES...
GLGLGL
OH GOOD...
TH-THANKS
JIMMY?
YEAH?
JIMMY, MR. JOHNSON AND I HAVE SOMETHING WE'D LIKE TO TELL YOU...

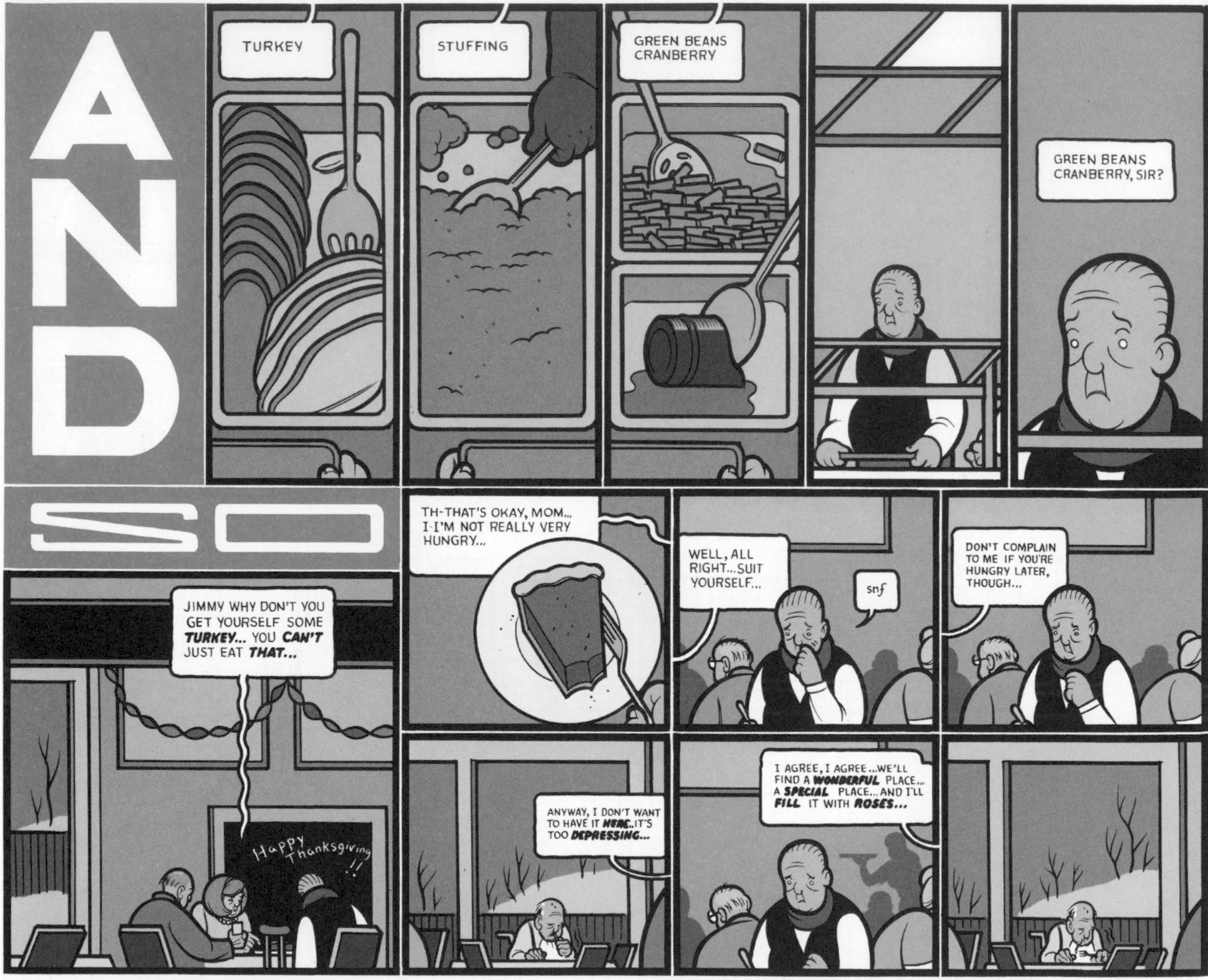
AND
TURKEY
STUFFING
GREEN BEANS CRANBERRY
GREEN BEANS CRANBERRY, SIR?
SO
JIMMY WHY DON'T YOU GET YOURSELF SOME TURKEY... YOU CAN'T JUST EAT THAT...
Happy Thanksgiving !!
TH-THAT'S OKAY, MOM... I-I'M NOT REALLY VERY HUNGRY...
WELL, ALL RIGHT...SUIT YOURSELF...
snf
DON'T COMPLAIN TO ME IF YOU'RE HUNGRY LATER, THOUGH...
ANYWAY, I DON'T WANT TO HAVE IT HERE..IT'S TOO DEPRESSING...
I AGREE, I AGREE...WE'LL FIND A WONDERFUL PLACE... A SPECIAL PLACE... AND I'LL FILL IT WITH ROSES...

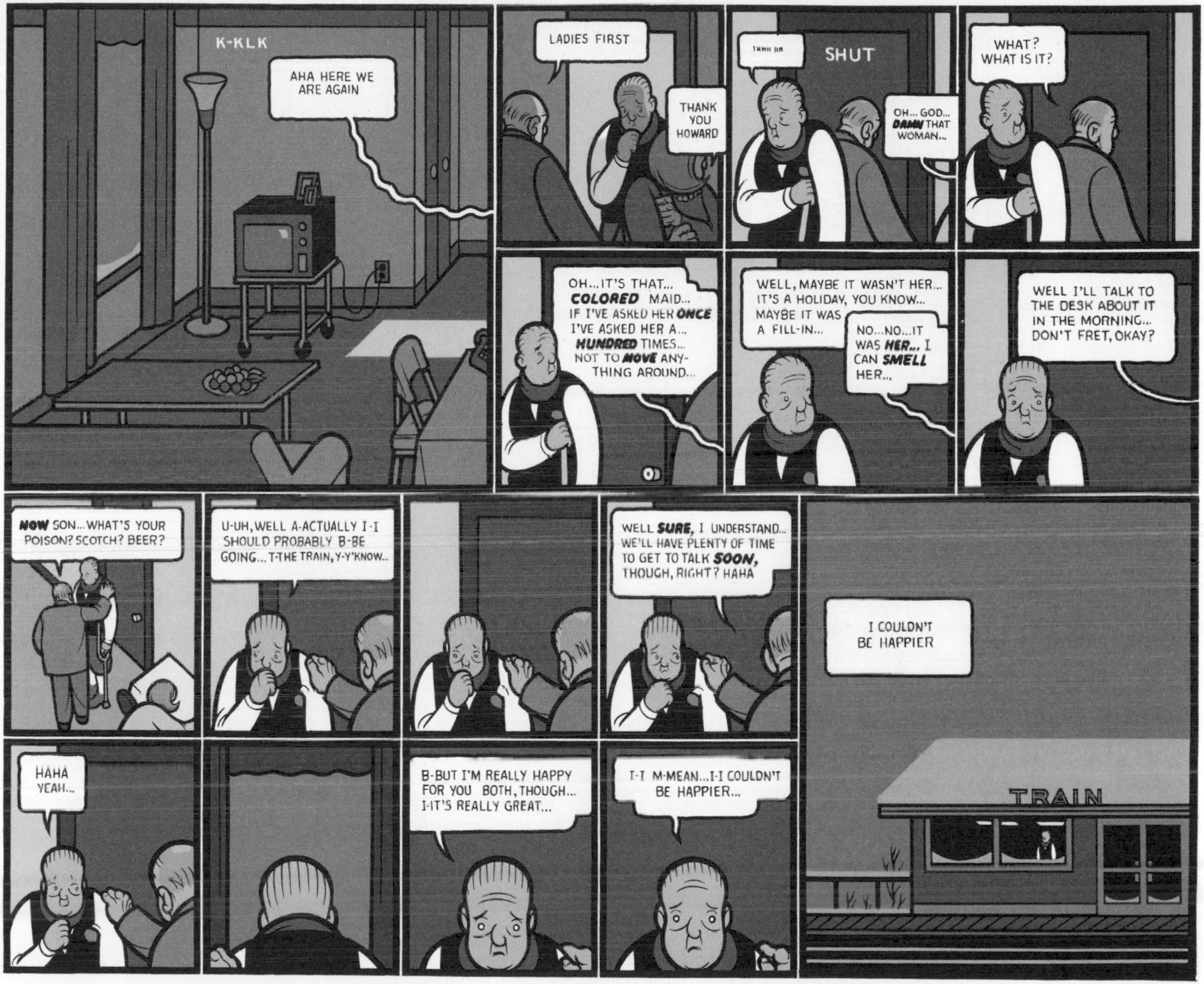
K-KLK
AHA HERE WE ARE AGAIN
LADIES FIRST
THANK YOU HOWARD
SHUT
OH... GOD... DAMN THAT WOMAN...
WHAT? WHAT IS IT?
OH... IT'S THAT... COLORED MAID... IF I'VE ASKED HER ONCE I'VE ASKED HER A... HUNDRED TIMES... NOT TO MOVE ANY-THING AROUND...
WELL, MAYBE IT WASN'T HER... IT'S A HOLIDAY, YOU KNOW... MAYBE IT WAS A FILL-IN...
NO... NO... IT WAS HER... I CAN SMELL HER...
WELL I'LL TALK TO THE DESK ABOUT IT IN THE MORNING... DON'T FRET, OKAY?
NOW SON... WHAT'S YOUR POISON? SCOTCH? BEER?
U-UH, WELL A-ACTUALLY I-I SHOULD PROBABLY B-BE GOING... T-THE TRAIN, Y-Y'KNOW...
WELL SURE, I UNDERSTAND... WE'LL HAVE PLENTY OF TIME TO GET TO TALK SOON, THOUGH, RIGHT? HAHA
HAHA YEAH...
B-BUT I'M REALLY HAPPY FOR YOU BOTH, THOUGH... I-IT'S REALLY GREAT...
I-I M-MEAN... I-I COULDN'T BE HAPPIER...
I COULDN'T BE HAPPIER
TRAIN

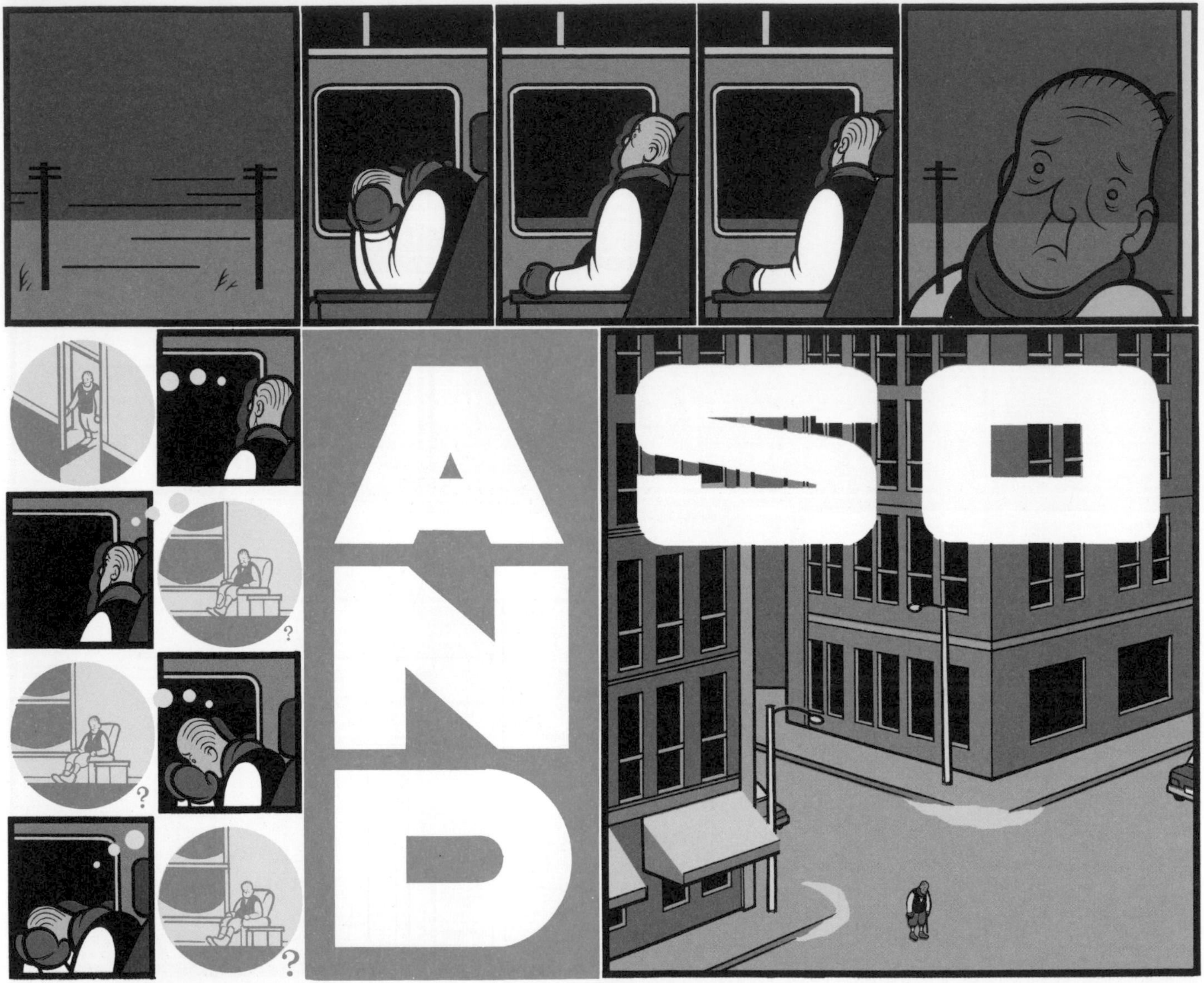
?
?
?
AND
SO

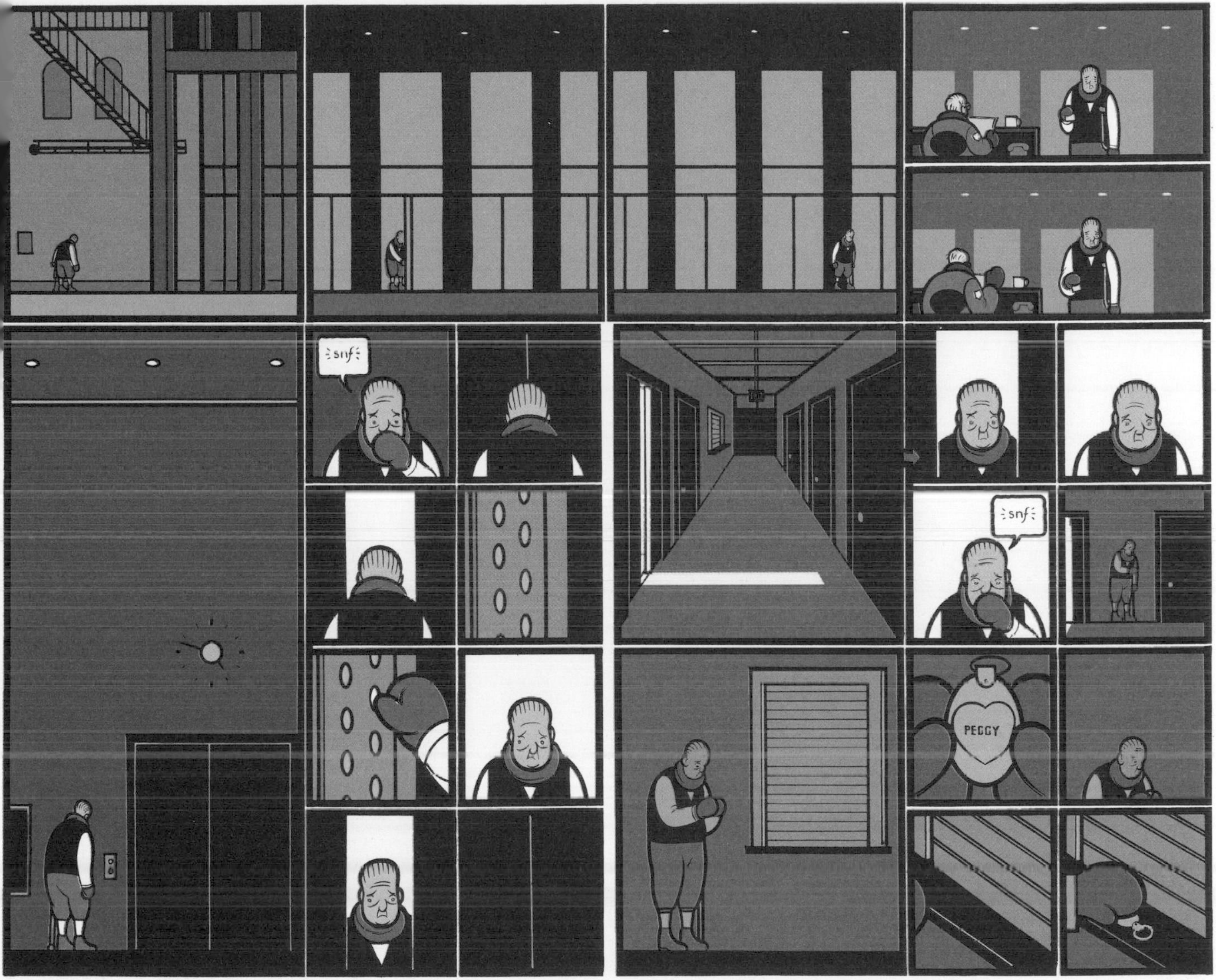
snf
snf
PEGGY

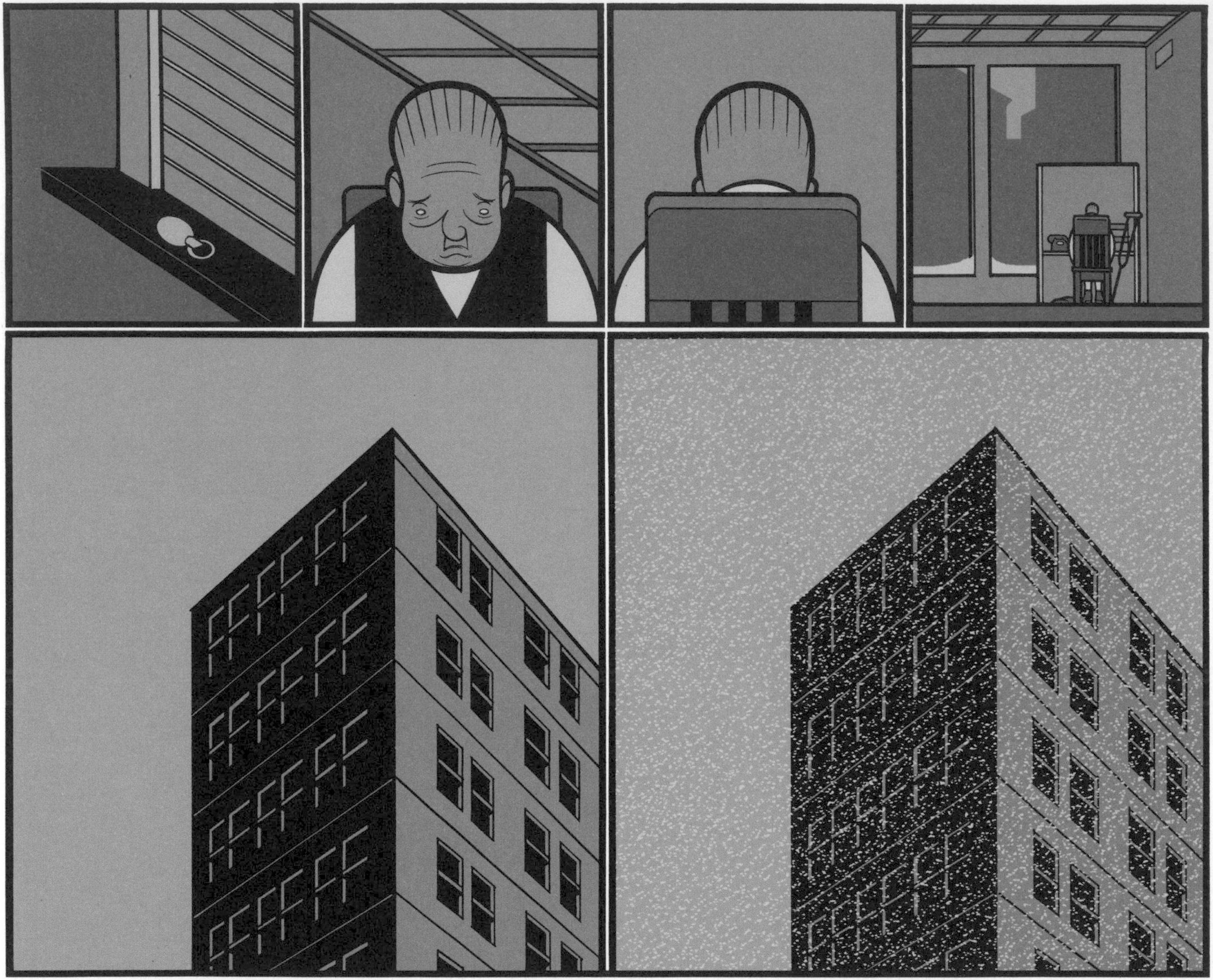

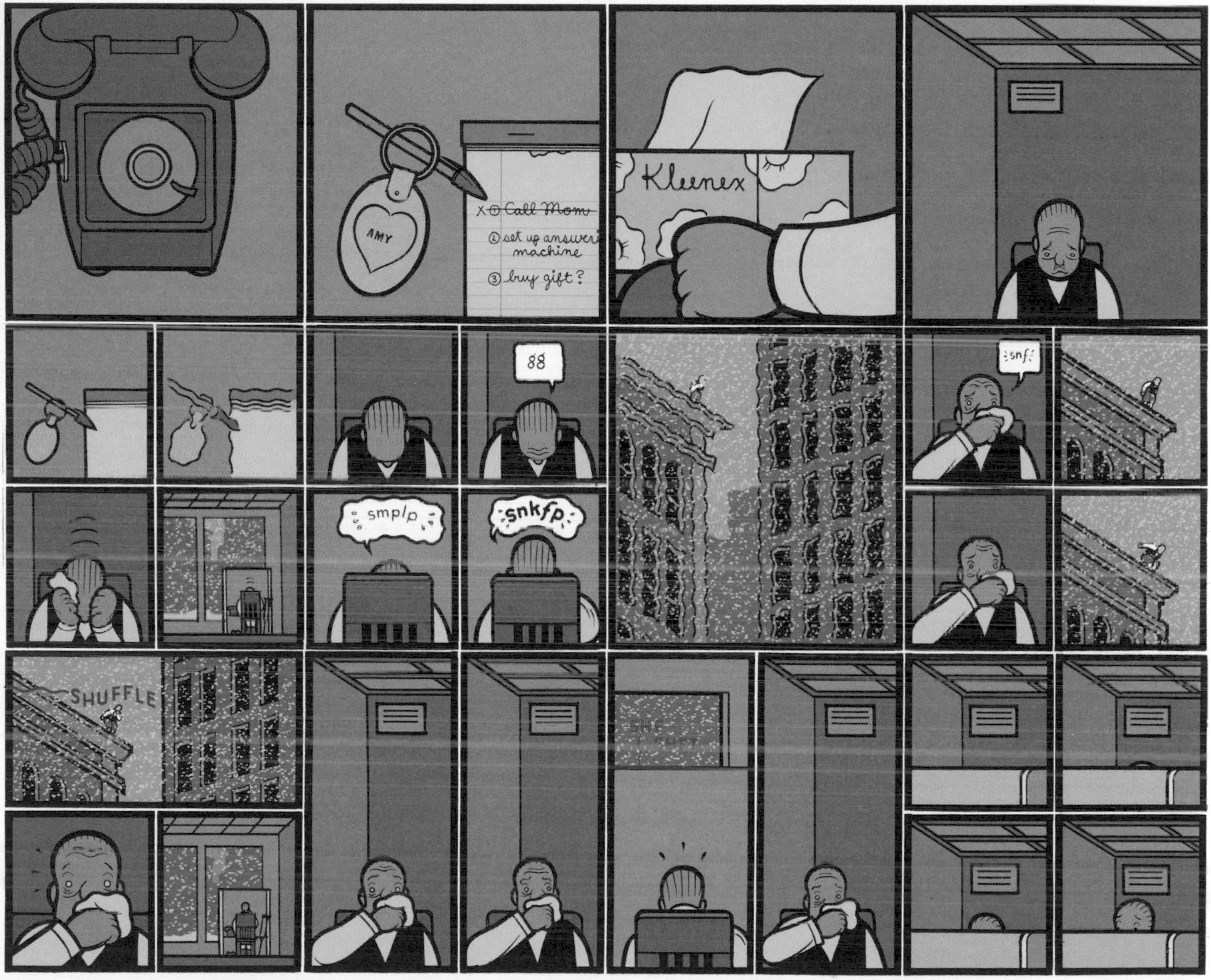
AMY
x ① ~~Call Mom~~
② set up answeri machine
③ buy gift?
Kleenex
88
snf
smplp
snkfp
SHUFFLE

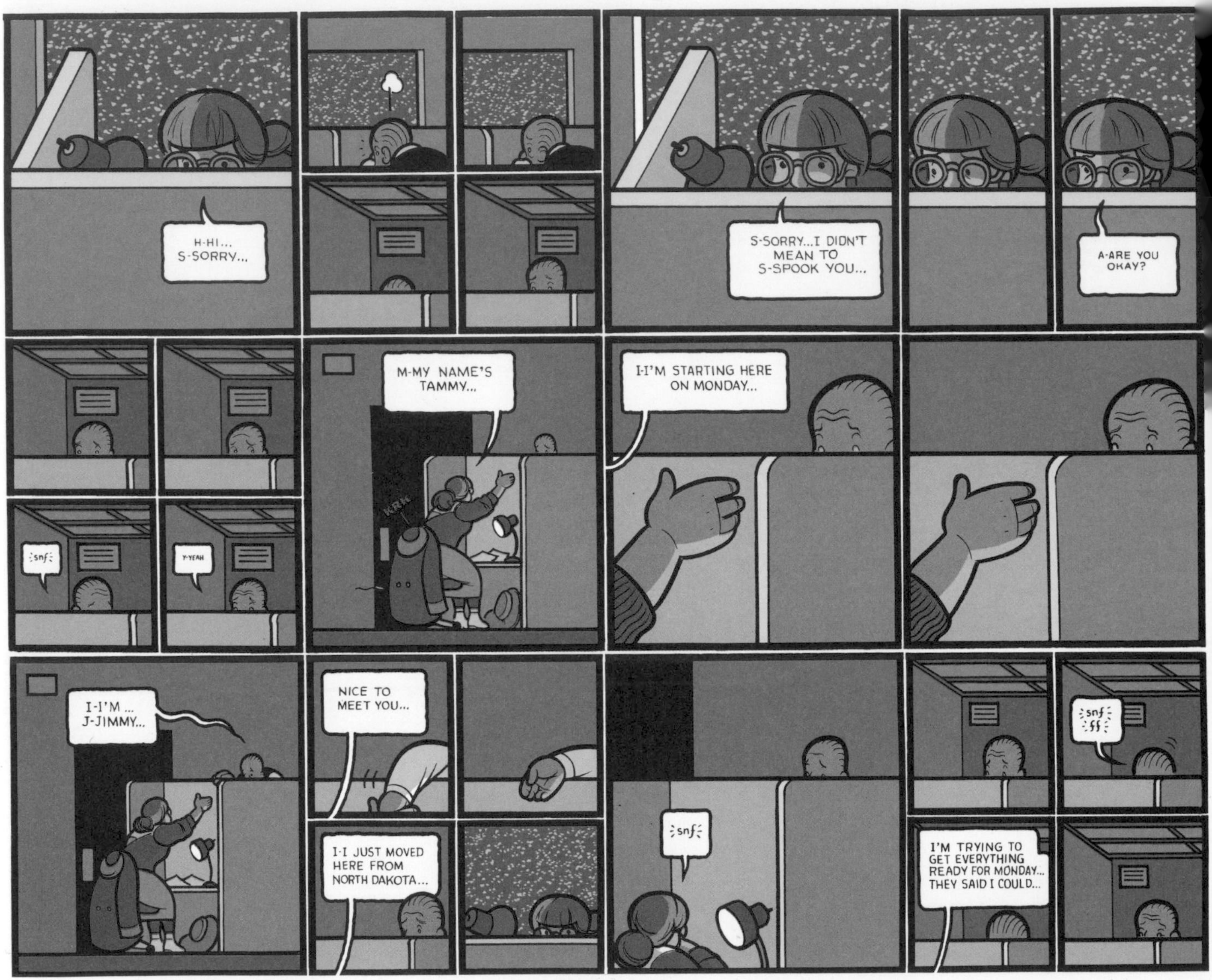
H-HI... S-SORRY...
S-SORRY...I DIDN'T MEAN TO S-SPOOK YOU...
A-ARE YOU OKAY?
snf
Y-YEAH
KRK
M-MY NAME'S TAMMY...
I-I'M STARTING HERE ON MONDAY...
I-I'M ... J-JIMMY...
NICE TO MEET YOU...
I-I JUST MOVED HERE FROM NORTH DAKOTA...
snf
I'M TRYING TO GET EVERYTHING READY FOR MONDAY... THEY SAID I COULD...
snf ff

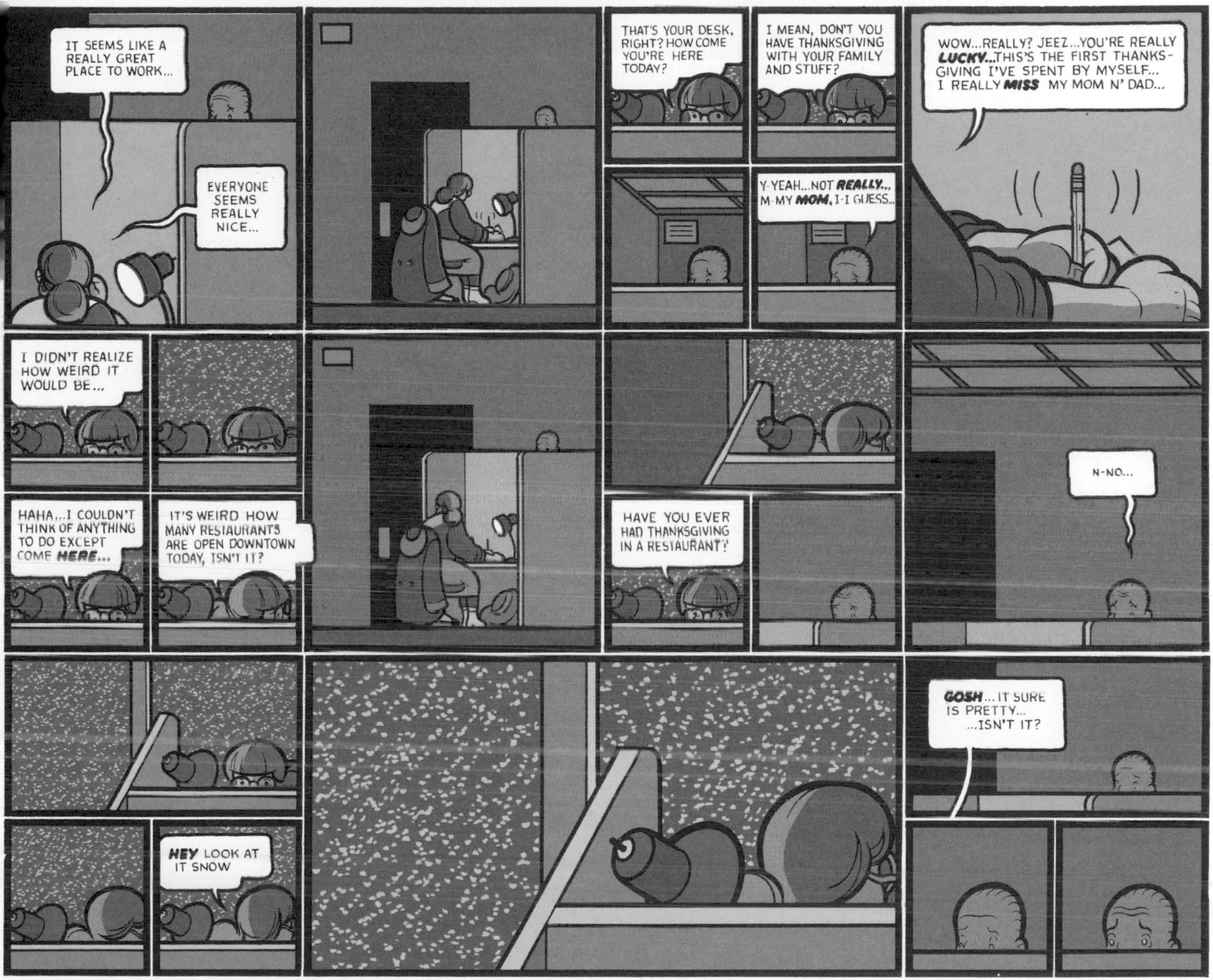
IT SEEMS LIKE A REALLY GREAT PLACE TO WORK...
EVERYONE SEEMS REALLY NICE...
THAT'S YOUR DESK, RIGHT? HOW COME YOU'RE HERE TODAY?
I MEAN, DON'T YOU HAVE THANKSGIVING WITH YOUR FAMILY AND STUFF?
Y-YEAH...NOT REALLY... M-MY MOM, I-I GUESS...
WOW...REALLY? JEEZ...YOU'RE REALLY LUCKY...THIS'S THE FIRST THANKSGIVING I'VE SPENT BY MYSELF... I REALLY MISS MY MOM N' DAD...
I DIDN'T REALIZE HOW WEIRD IT WOULD BE...
HAHA...I COULDN'T THINK OF ANYTHING TO DO EXCEPT COME HERE...
IT'S WEIRD HOW MANY RESTAURANTS ARE OPEN DOWNTOWN TODAY, ISN'T IT?
HAVE YOU EVER HAD THANKSGIVING IN A RESTAURANT?
N-NO...
HEY LOOK AT IT SNOW
GOSH... IT SURE IS PRETTY... ...ISN'T IT?

The End

CORRIGENDA

(kə̄rə-jĕn′də) n. pl. A LIST OF ERRORS WITH THEIR CORRECTIONS, IN A BOOK. [LATIN, gerundive of CORRIGERE, to CORRECT.] ARRANGED ALPHABETICALLY.

APOLOGY

(ə-pŏl′ə-jē) n. ALSO **POSTSCRIPT.**

I BEGAN THIS STORY IN 1993 AS A WEEKLY COMIC STRIP IN A VERY TOLERANT AND FORGIVING CHICAGO NEWSPAPER, "NEW CITY." IT WAS PLANNED PURELY AS AN IMPROVISATORY EXERCISE, TO TAKE NO MORE THAN A SUMMER TO COMPLETE, AND TO HOPEFULLY PROVIDE A SEMI-AUTOBIOGRAPHICAL SETTING IN WHICH I COULD "WORK OUT" SOME OF THE MORE EMBARRASSING PROBLEMS OF CONFIDENCE AND EMOTIONAL TRUTHFULNESS I WAS EXPERIENCING AS A VERY IMMATURE, AND NOT TERRIBLY FACILE, CARTOONIST. I'D POKED INTO THE SUBJECT BEFORE—THAT OF MEETING AN ESTRANGED PARENT — BUT I WANTED TO TRY A MORE RESPECTABLE "STAB," BY SHOVING MY HAPLESS AND POORLY-WRITTEN "ALTER EGO" OF THE MOMENT, "JIMMY CORRIGAN," THROUGH THE STARTING GATES FIRST. I HAD SPENT MY ENTIRE LIFE AVOIDING CONTACT WITH MY OWN FATHER, AND I GUESS I THOUGHT THAT ONCE THIS STORY WAS FINISHED, I WOULD SOMEHOW HAVE 'PREPARED' MYSELF TO MEET THE REAL MAN, AND THEN BE ABLE TO GET ON WITH MY LIFE. OF COURSE, REAL LIFE IS MUCH MORE BADLY PLOTTED THAN THAT.

ROUGHLY FIVE YEARS LATER, AFTER THOROUGHLY MIRING MYSELF IN THE SWAMPY MUCK OF A "STORY" WHICH NOW SEEMED TO HAVE NO END IN SIGHT, AND, EVEN WORSE, LIKELY NO POINT TO THE POOR MOVIEGOERS AND "SWM"S WHO HAD TO WADE AROUND IT EVERY WEEK TO SWIM IN THE FRESHER WATERS OF THE FILM REVIEWS AND PERSONAL ADS, I RECEIVED A TELEPHONE CALL, WITHOUT WARNING, FROM A MAN CLAIMING TO BE MY FATHER. AT FIRST I THOUGHT IT A JOKE, PERPETRATED BY A DISGRUNTLED OR MEAN-SPIRITED NEWSPAPER READER, BUT THE SHAKY, DECISIVE, RIDICULOUSLY UNFAMILIAR VOICE TOLD ME THAT HE WASN'T TRYING TO BE FUNNY. I WILL NOT CATALOG OUR CONVERSATION HERE, NOR WILL I DETAIL HOW HE LOCATED ME, NOR WILL I TRY TO DESCRIBE THE EMBARRASSING SENSE OF FRUSTRATION AND OUTRAGE THAT I FELT BY HIS BREAKING OUR THIRTY YEAR SILENCE, INSTANTLY LAYING TO REST THE SELF-PITYING IDENTITY I'D UNCONSCIOUSLY CULTURED AND INVESTED INTO A STORY THAT I WASN'T EVEN DONE WITH YET. IN OUR TWENTY MINUTES OF TALK, HOWEVER, I WAS SURPRISED TO DISCOVER THAT, AT LEAST COMPARED TO THIS MAN WHO HAD SUDDENLY STEPPED FORWARD TO CLAIM MY CO-AUTHORSHIP, I WAS THE BETTER WRITER, FOR THE PAINFULLY AWKWARD AND INAPPROPRIATELY FAMILIAR PHRASES WITH WHICH HE TRIED TO LIGHTEN HIS MONOLOGUE WERE MUCH MORE ILL-CONSIDERED AND NONPLUSSED THAN ANYTHING I HAD EVER PUT INTO JIMMY'S DAD'S MOUTH.

HE CALLED ME TWO OR THREE MORE TIMES OVER THE NEXT YEAR, ALWAYS SUGGESTING THAT WE "GET TOGETHER SOMETIME," I ALWAYS VAGUELY AGREEING WITHOUT COMMITTING TO ANY TIME OR PLACE. I DIDN'T LIKE HIS INSISTENCE, AND I WASN'T SURE IF I EVEN WANTED TO MEET WITH HIM YET. WHY, I DON'T KNOW. BUT ONE DAY, ABOUT A YEAR AFTER OUR FIRST "CONTACT," HE CALLED TO SAY THAT HE'D BE VISITING CHICAGO SOON AND ASKED IF I WOULD CONSIDER MEETING HIM AND HIS WIFE AT A RESTAURANT FOR DINNER — NO PRESSURE — JUST DINNER. MY WIFE, WHO HAD UNDERGONE A SIMILAR EXPERIENCE YEARS BEFORE, RIGHTFULLY ENCOURAGED ME. I AGREED. WHAT ELSE WAS I SUPPOSED TO DO?

I DREADED THE DAY, HAVING ATTRIBUTED SO MUCH IMPORTANCE TO IT FOR NEARLY MY ENTIRE LIFE. FUNDAMENTALLY, I GUESS I WAS JUST AFRAID--THE WORST FEAR OF ALL-- THAT HE SIMPLY WOULDN'T LIKE ME. BUT IT WAS EASY: WE MET. I SAW HIM FROM ACROSS THE RESTAURANT: A SMALL, LARGE-HEADED MAN WHOM I WOULDN'T HAVE EVER PICKED OUT OF A CRIMINAL LINE-UP OF A THOUSAND FATHERS. HE WAS PLEASANT, AND SEEMED AS HUMBLED BY MY PRESENCE AS I WAS BY HIS. WE TALKED, OR TRIED TO — I WAS RELIEVED, AT THE VERY LEAST, TO GLEAN FROM HIS REMARKS THAT HE'D NEVER SEEN MY STUFF, THE INVISIBLE AND UNIVERSALLY UNFASHIONABLE WORLD OF THE COMIC STRIP HAVING LEFT ME THANKFULLY UNREAD. GRADUALLY, THE SUBLIME OUTRAGEOUSNESS OF OUR EVENING ERODED INTO TWO PEOPLE SIMPLY RUNNING OUT OF THINGS TO SAY TO EACH OTHER. WE WEREN'T FATHER AND SON ANYMORE, JUST A PAIR OF REGRETFUL MEN. AFTER ABOUT THREE HOURS, WE SAID GOODBYE, SOMEWHAT AFFABLY AGREED TO MEET AGAIN, AND GOT ON WITH OUR LIVES.

THAT CHRISTMAS, I FINALLY WORKED UP THE NON-COURAGE TO CALL HIM AND WISH HIM A HAPPY HOLIDAY, THOUGH HIS ANSWERING MACHINE WAS BARELY AUDIBLE SO I WASN'T SURE IF THE CONNECTION WAS GOOD. I LEFT A MESSAGE ANYWAY. I DIDN'T HEAR FROM HIM AGAIN UNTIL THE FOLLOWING SPRING; HE SAID HE'D BE IN TOWN AGAIN, AND AGAIN ASKED IF I WOULD LIKE TO GET TOGETHER, AND SO I AGAIN AGREED, MARKING THE DATE ON MY CALENDAR SOMEWHAT RELUCTANTLY. HE SAID HE'D CALL WHEN HE GOT INTO TOWN. THE DAY CAME, AND WENT, AND THE TELEPHONE NEVER RANG.

IN THE ENSUING MONTHS I "FINISHED" THE STORY, SHINING IT UP TO THE BEST OF MY ABILITY, GENUINELY SURPRISED THAT IT MIGHT GRADUATE FROM THE EXILE OF NEWSWEEKLIES AND COMIC BOOKS INTO THE "REAL WORLD" OF BOOKSTORES, REMAINDERED TABLES, AND RUMMAGE SALES, DESPITE ITS AWFUL FLAWS. I RESOLVED THAT ONCE IT WAS PUBLISHED AS A BOOK I WOULD PRESENT IT TO FATHER, FOR BETTER OR WORSE; AT LEAST IT WOULD BE MORE PREFERABLE MEANS OF DISCOVERY FOR HIM THAN A GARAGE SALE, OR IN A NURSING HOME LIBRARY. UNFORTUNATELY, HOWEVER, I WILL NOT HAVE THAT OPPORTUNITY, AS HE DIED OF A HEART ATTACK IN JANUARY. I MENTION NONE OF THIS TO TRY AND ALIGN MYSELF WITH THE SEEMINGLY UNSTOPPABLE SWARM OF PERSON MEMOIRISTS WHO POPULATE THE EXTRA-CURRICULAR BOOK LISTS OF MULTIPLE SELF-HELP PROGRAMS, BUT TO ADMIT THE CHASM WHICH GAPES BETWEEN THE RIDICULOUS, ARTLESS, DUMBFOUNDEDLY MEANINGLESS COINCIDENCE OF "REAL" LIFE AND MY WEAK FICTION -- NOT TO MENTION INABILITY AT KNITTING THEM TOGETHER. IN OTHER WORDS, I WISH I COULD'VE DONE A BETTER JOB. MAYBE I SHOULD'VE JUST TRIED TO BE A MEMOIRIST, OR, MORE EFFECTIVELY, SIMPLY KEPT MY INK BOTTLE CAPPED.

REGARDLESS, IN RACING THROUGH THIS STORY FOR ITS FINAL "EDIT," SKIDDING PAST ALL THESE ERRORS, OMISSIONS, AND MISTAKES, IT OCCURRED TO ME UPON CLOSING THE "MANUSCRIPT" THAT THE FOUR OR FIVE HOURS IT TOOK TO READ IS ALMOST EXACTLY THE TOTAL TIME I EVER SPENT WITH MY FATHER, EITHER IN PERSON OR ON THE TELEPHONE. ADDITIONALLY, AND AT RISK OF SOUNDING MELODRAMATIC, ITS FINAL PRINTED SIZE SEEMS NEARLY EQUAL IN VOLUME TO THE LITTLE BLACK BOX, OR URN, BEFORE WHICH I BRIEFLY STOOD THIS JANUARY BENEATH A COLOR PHOTO OF THE MAN ITS LABEL CLAIMED TO CONTAIN.

— C. WARE, CHICAGO, MARCH, 20

CRUTCH

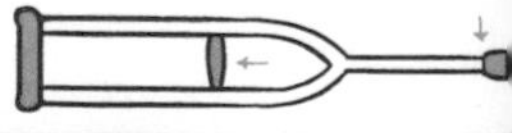

A SUPPORT, USED BY THE LAME OR INFIRM AS A WALKING AID, esp. FOLLOWING A LOCOMOTIVE INJURY, viz:

DEDICATION

(dĕd′ə-kā′shən) n.

IN THIS SEMI-AUTOBIOGRAPHICAL WORK OF FICTION, I FEAR I MAY HAVE POTENTIALLY IMPUGNED (AT LEAST, PERHAPS, IN A CARELESS READER'S COMPREHENSION OF THE BOOK) SOME "REAL-LIFE" ALTER-EGOS, MOST NOTABLE OF WHOM MIGHT BE MY MOTHER, WHO, BEING A THOUGHTFUL, INTELLIGENT, AND SUPPORTIVE WOMAN THUS BEARS NO RESEMBLANCE WHATSOEVER TO THE MISERABLE WRETCH WHO DOMINATES POOR JIMMY. AS SUCH, THIS BOOK IS DEDICATED TO HER, ESPECIALLY AS IT IS WHOLLY CHARACTERIZED BY HER ABSENCE.

DRAFT RIOTS

(drăft' ri'ots) n. pl. THE "CIVIL WAR DRAFT RIOTS" OCCURRED IN NEW YORK CITY, BOSTON, AND OTHER LARGE METROPOLITAN CENTERS IN JULY 1863. AT THAT TIME, PERSONS WHO WERE ABLE TO PAY A $300 "SUBSTITUTION FEE" (i.e. THE RICHER CLASSES) WERE FREED FROM THE RESPONSIBILITY OF UNION ARMY SERVICE, LEAVING THE POOR CLASSES (PARTICULARLY IRISH IMMIGRANTS) ESPECIALLY VUNERABLE TO THE DRAFT. AFRO-AMERICANS WERE, IRONICALLY, INELLIGIBLE FOR ACTIVE ARMY SERVICE, AND SO BY DEFAULT WERE POSITIONED TO TAKE OVER THE MOSTLY MENIAL JOBS WHICH WOULD BE VACATED BY THE IRISH. ANGRY MOBS, REPORTEDLY COMPOSED OF PRIMARILY IRISH CITIZENS MURDERED NEARLY ONE THOUSAND AFRO-AMERICANS AND CAUSED OVER TWO MILLION DOLLARS WORTH OF PROPERTY DAMAGE OVER A PERIOD OF FOUR DAYS.

EXPOSITION

(ĕk'spə-zĭsh'ən) n. THE MAIN BODY OF A WORK, esp. THAT WHICH EXPLICATES A MAIN THEME, OR INTRODUCES A FUNDAMENTAL MOTIF.

FINGER

(fĭng'gər) n. ONE OF THE FIVE DIGITS OF THE HAND, ESPECIALLY, ONE OTHER THAN THE THUMB. slang. TO DOMINATE OR HANDLE SOMETHING POSSESSIVELY. slang. A GREETING, INVOLVING SINGULAR EXTENSION of THE MIDDLE DIGIT, AND BESTOWING A WISH of COPULATION UPON THE RECIPIENT; SEE **HELLO**.

GLASSES

HELLO

(hě-lō', hə-) interj. ALSO **HULLO**. AN INFORMAL EXPRESSION, UTILIZED AS A GREETING, IN ANSWER OF A TELE-PHONE, OR AS A MEANS OF SUMMONING ATTENTION. IT WAS PROBABLY NOT IN COMMON USAGE BEFORE THE TWENTI-ETH CENTURY, AND SO ITS CAVALIER EMPLOYMENT IN SECTIONS OF THIS BOOK SET IN THE AMERICAN 1890s MAY BE ENTIRELY UNJUSTIFIED.

LONELY

(lŏn'lē) adj. ALONE, OR BY ONE-SELF. THE PERMANENT STATE OF BEING FOR ALL HUMANS, DESPITE ANY EFFORTS TO THE CONTRARY. CAN BE SOOTHED OR SUBDUED IN A VARIETY OF WAYS, viz. MARRIAGE, SEXUAL INTERCOURSE, BOARD GAMES, LITERATURE, MUSIC, POETRY, TELEVISION, PARTY HATS, PASTRIES, ETC., BUT CANNOT BE SOLVED.

METAPHOR

(mĕt'ə-fôr(-fər) n. A TIGHTLY FITTING SUIT OF METAL, GENERALLY TIN, WHICH ENTIRELY ENCLOSES THE WEARER, BOTH IMPEDING FREE MOVEMENT AND PRE-VENTING EMOTIONAL EXPRESSION AND/OR SOCIAL CONTACT.

PEACH

(pēch) n. A SOFT, SINGLE-SEEDED STONE FRUIT, WITH A PINKISH, RED-TINTED DOWNY SKIN, AND MOIST, DEWY FLESH; THE TREE, *PRUNUS PERSICA*, IS NATIVE TO CHINA, BUT HAS BEEN WIDELY CULTIVATED THROUGHOUT THE WORLD, HAVING BEEN SPREAD BY THE ROMANS AND THEN BROUGHT BY THE SPANISH TO AMERICA. see **SYMBOL**.

REPRODUCE

(rē'prə-doos) v.tr. TO PRODUCE A COUNTERPART, IMAGE, OR COPY OF, OR, TO BRING TO MIND AGAIN, AS IN A MEMORY. —intr. TO GENERATE OFFSPRING, OR, TO UNDERGO COPYING. PRINTING. TO PRINT, OR TO PUBLISH. ART. TO MAKE VALUELESS.

SIMPLETON

(sĭm'pəl-tən) n. A STUPID PERSON; A FOOL, OR, ONE WHO DEVOTES ONE-SELF TO STUPID OR FOOLISH THINGS; ex: "Billy is a simpleton; he reads comic books." MANY OF THE ORIGINAL COMIC BOOKS IN WHICH THIS BOOK WAS SERIALIZED ARE STILL AVAILABLE; CONSULT www.fantagraphics.com ON YOUR HOME TERMINAL FOR PRICES AND AVAILABILITY, OR TELEPHONE 800 657 1100.

SYMBOL

(sĭm'bəl) n. SOMETHING THAT REPRESENTS SOMETHING ELSE, esp. COMMON IN BAD LITERATURE. ALSO, A PRINTED OR WRITTEN SIGN USED TO REPRESENT AN UNDERSTOOD CORRESPONDING ASPECT OF EXPERIENCE, GENERALLY READ, AND NOT AP-PRECIATED AS AN ESTHETIC FORM IN AND OF ITSELF.

THANKS

(thăngks) pl. n. TO THOSE EDITORS WHO SHOWED GREAT FOOLHARDINESS BY PUBLISHING THIS WORK IN ONE FORM OR ANOTHER: BRIAN HIEGGELKE; KIM THOMPSON & GARY GROTH; DAN FRANK & CHARLES I. KIDD. AS WELL, FOR GUIDANCE: R. KEANE, R. LOESCHER, & A. SPIEGELMAN, APRIL & ERIC WILSON, DR. D. McCALL, AND MRS. MARNIE WARE.

WARE, C.

(wâr, sē) n. AMERICAN CAR-TOONIST, b. 1967, OMAHA, NEB-RASKA, CURRENTLY RESIDING CHICAGO, ILLINOIS. AUTHOR AND CREATOR OF THE BELOVED "ACME NOVELTY LIBRARY" SERIES OF CHILDREN'S GUIDE-BOOKS, GAME PAMPHLETS, AND PICNIC SONGSHEETS, IRREGULAR ORGANS THROUGH WHICH THE BULK OF THIS WORK FIRST PASSED. MR. WARE IS MARRIED, YET HAS NOT REPRODUCED.

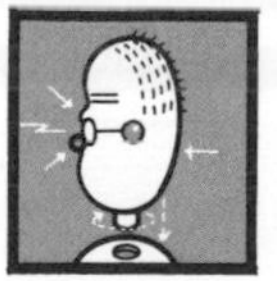

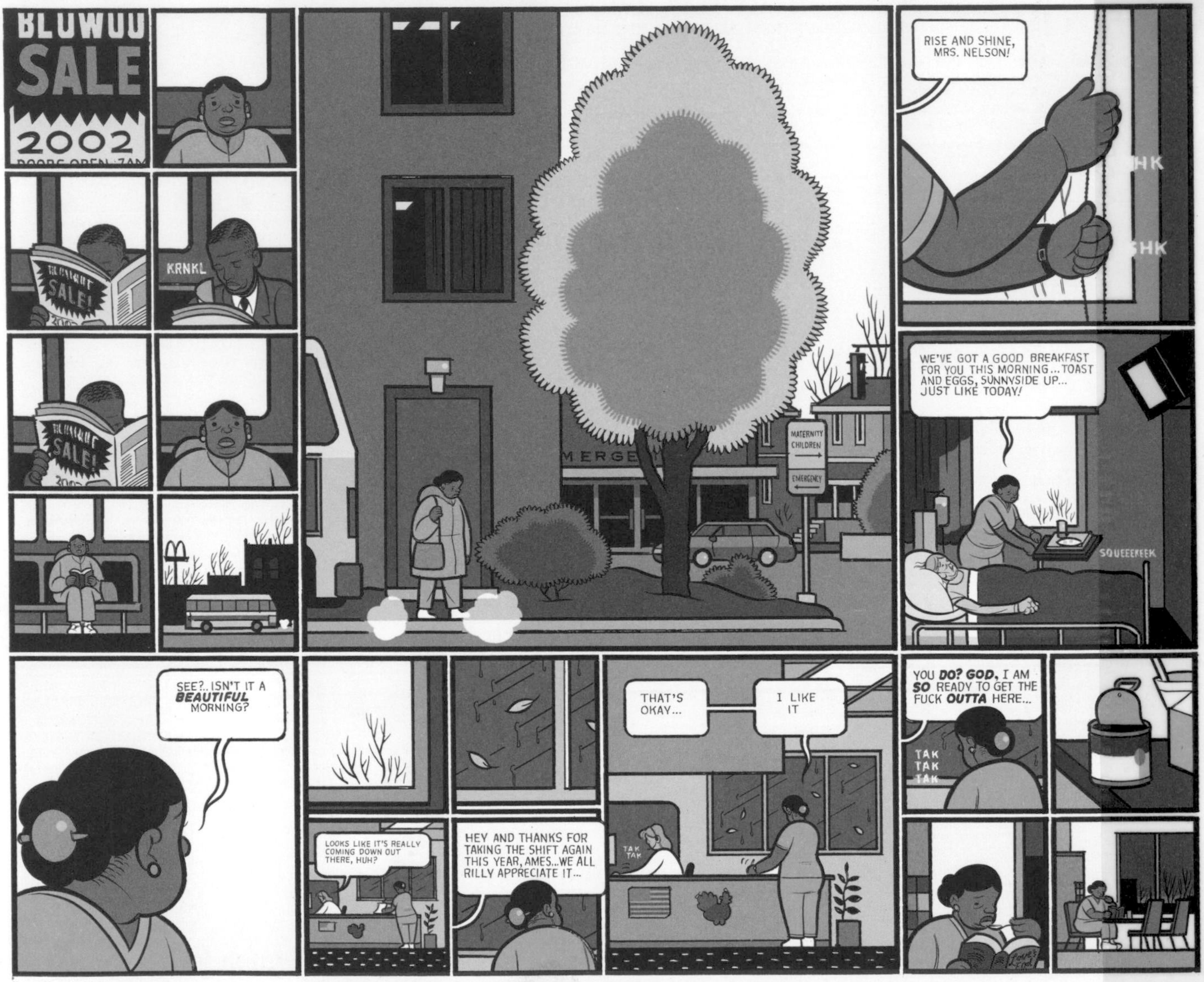
SALE
2002
KRNKL
SALE!
SALE!
MATERNITY
CHILDREN
EMERGENCY
RISE AND SHINE, MRS. NELSON!
SHK
SHK
WE'VE GOT A GOOD BREAKFAST FOR YOU THIS MORNING... TOAST AND EGGS, SUNNYSIDE UP... JUST LIKE TODAY!
SQUEEEEEEK
SEE?.. ISN'T IT A BEAUTIFUL MORNING?
LOOKS LIKE IT'S REALLY COMING DOWN OUT THERE, HUH?
HEY AND THANKS FOR TAKING THE SHIFT AGAIN THIS YEAR, AMES... WE ALL RILLY APPRECIATE IT...
THAT'S OKAY...
I LIKE IT
TAK TAK
YOU DO? GOD, I AM SO READY TO GET THE FUCK OUTTA HERE...
TAK
TAK
TAK

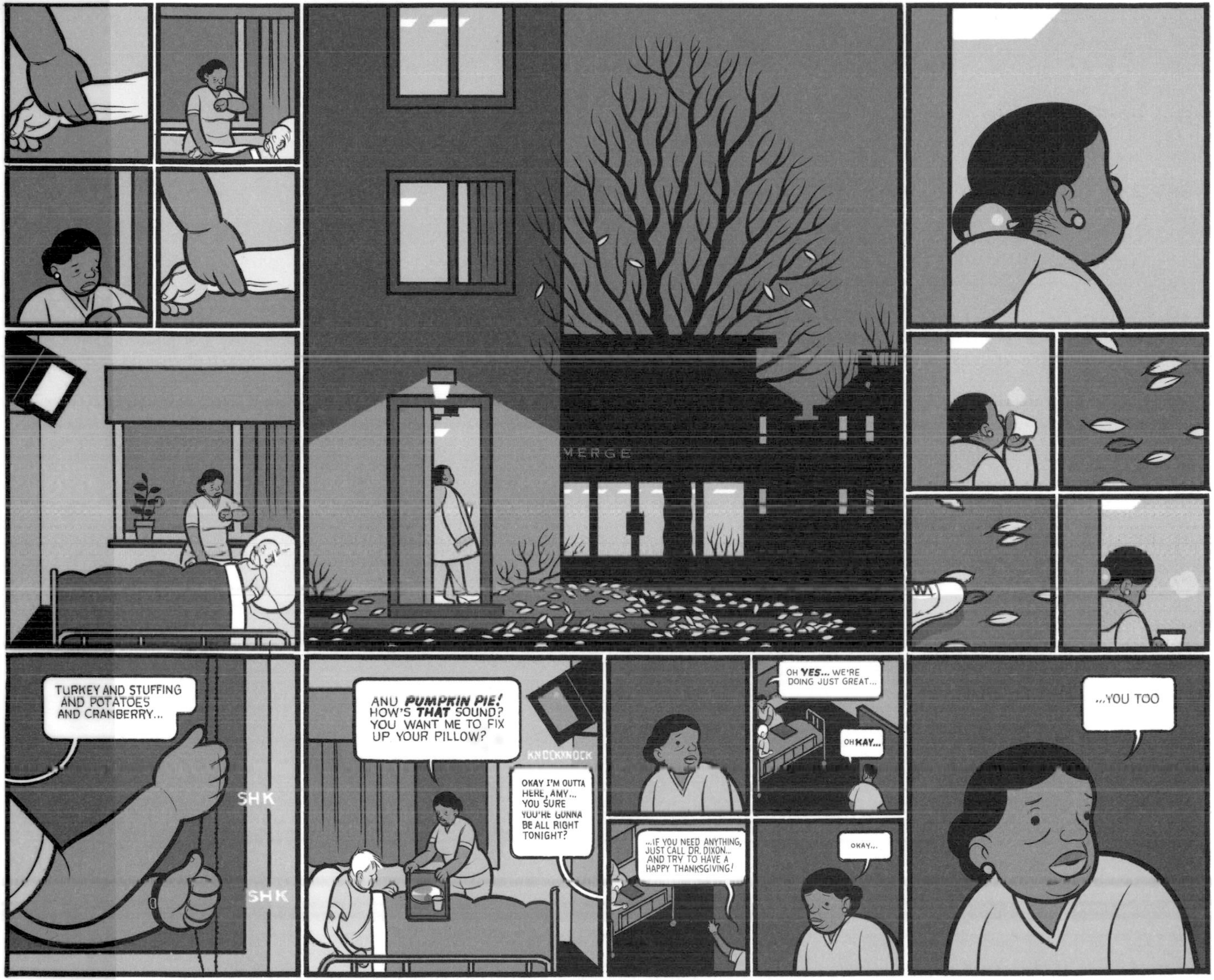
MERGE
TURKEY AND STUFFING AND POTATOES AND CRANBERRY...
SHK
SHK
AND PUMPKIN PIE! HOW'S THAT SOUND? YOU WANT ME TO FIX UP YOUR PILLOW?
KNOCKKNOCK
OKAY I'M OUTTA HERE, AMY... YOU SURE YOU'RE GONNA BE ALL RIGHT TONIGHT?
OH YES... WE'RE DOING JUST GREAT...
OHKAY...
...IF YOU NEED ANYTHING, JUST CALL DR. DIXON... AND TRY TO HAVE A HAPPY THANKSGIVING!
OKAY...
...YOU TOO

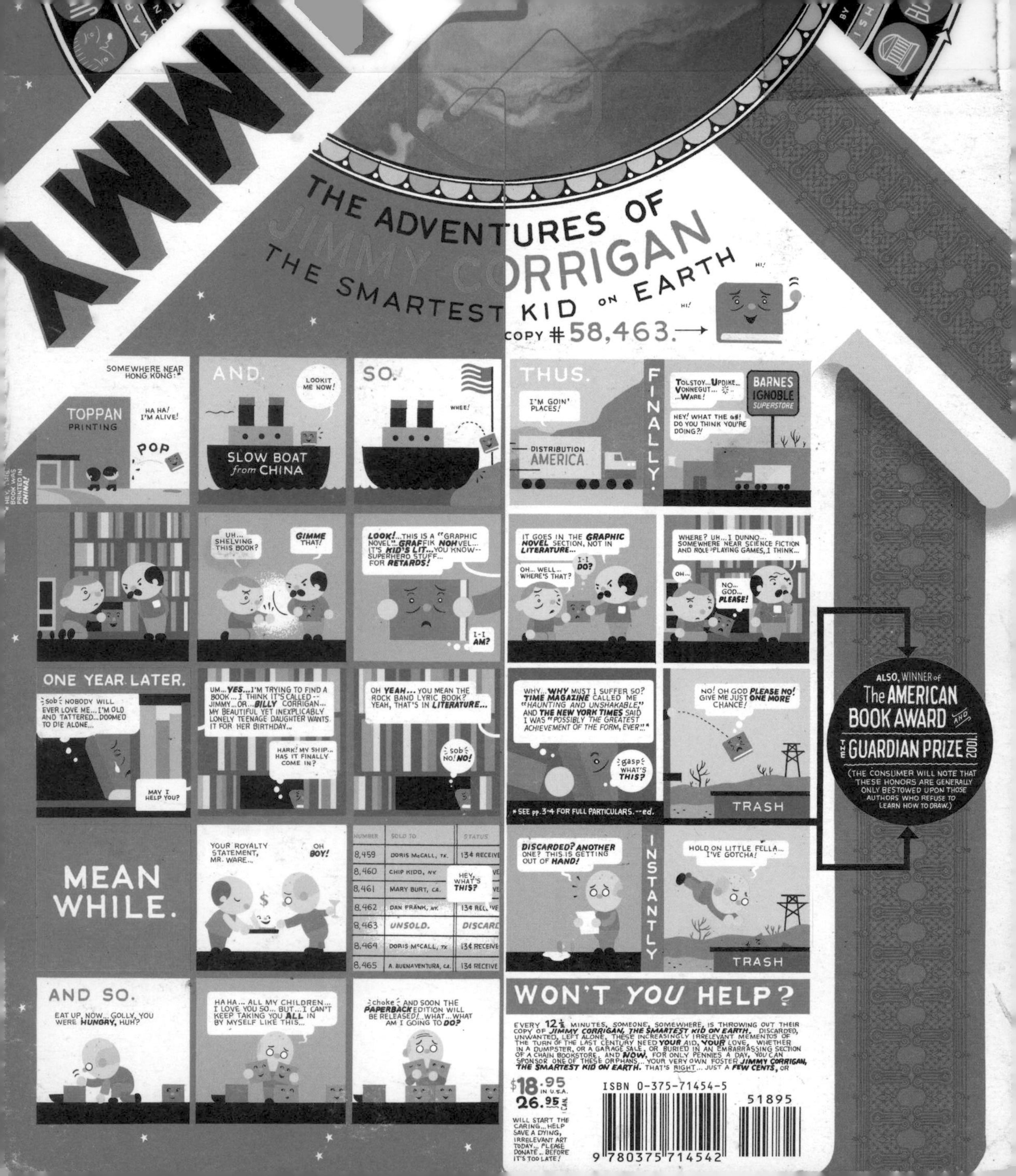
THE ADVENTURES OF
JIMMY CORRIGAN
THE SMARTEST KID ON EARTH
COPY #58,463.
HI!
HI!
HEY, THIS BOOK WAS PRINTED IN CHINA!
SOMEWHERE NEAR HONG KONG:*
TOPPAN PRINTING
HA HA! I'M ALIVE!
POP
AND.
LOOKIT ME NOW!
SLOW BOAT from CHINA
SO.
WHEE!
THUS.
I'M GOIN' PLACES!
DISTRIBUTION AMERICA
FINALLY.
TOLSTOY...UPDIKE... VONNEGUT... ...WARE!
BARNES IGNOBLE SUPERSTORE
HEY! WHAT THE @#! DO YOU THINK YOU'RE DOING?!
UH... SHELVING THIS BOOK?
GIMME THAT!
LOOK!...THIS IS A "GRAPHIC NOVEL"...GRAFFIK NOHVEL... IT'S KID'S LIT...YOU KNOW-- SUPERHERO STUFF... FOR RETARDS!
I-I AM?
IT GOES IN THE GRAPHIC NOVEL SECTION, NOT IN LITERATURE...
OH... WELL... WHERE'S THAT?
I-I DO?
WHERE? UH...I DUNNO... SOMEWHERE NEAR SCIENCE FICTION AND ROLE-PLAYING GAMES, I THINK...
OH...
NO... GOD... PLEASE!
ONE YEAR LATER.
sob NOBODY WILL EVER LOVE ME...I'M OLD AND TATTERED...DOOMED TO DIE ALONE...
MAY I HELP YOU?
UM...YES...I'M TRYING TO FIND A BOOK...I THINK IT'S CALLED-- JIMMY...OR...BILLY CORRIGAN... MY BEAUTIFUL YET INEXPLICABLY LONELY TEENAGE DAUGHTER WANTS IT FOR HER BIRTHDAY...
HARK! MY SHIP... HAS IT FINALLY COME IN?
OH YEAH... YOU MEAN THE ROCK BAND LYRIC BOOK? YEAH, THAT'S IN LITERATURE...
sob NO! NO!
WHY...WHY MUST I SUFFER SO? TIME MAGAZINE CALLED ME "HAUNTING AND UNSHAKABLE," AND THE NEW YORK TIMES SAID I WAS "POSSIBLY THE GREATEST ACHIEVEMENT OF THE FORM, EVER!"*
gasp WHAT'S THIS?
* SEE pp. 3-4 FOR FULL PARTICULARS.--ed.
NO! OH GOD PLEASE NO! GIVE ME JUST ONE MORE CHANCE!
TRASH
MEAN WHILE.
YOUR ROYALTY STATEMENT, MR. WARE...
OH BOY!
NUMBER | SOLD TO | STATUS
8,459 | DORIS McCALL, TX. | 13¢ RECEIVE
8,460 | CHIP KIDD, NY. | VE
8,461 | MARY BURT, CA. | VE
8,462 | DAN FRANK, NY. | 13¢ REC VE
8,463 | UNSOLD. | DISCARD
8,464 | DORIS McCALL, TX | 13¢ RECEIVE
8,465 | A. BUENAVENTURA, CA. | 13¢ RECEIVE
HEY, WHAT'S THIS?
DISCARDED? ANOTHER ONE? THIS IS GETTING OUT OF HAND!
INSTANTLY
HOLD ON LITTLE FELLA... I'VE GOTCHA!
TRASH
ALSO, WINNER of The AMERICAN BOOK AWARD AND THE GUARDIAN PRIZE 2001.
(THE CONSUMER WILL NOTE THAT THESE HONORS ARE GENERALLY ONLY BESTOWED UPON THOSE AUTHORS WHO REFUSE TO LEARN HOW TO DRAW.)
AND SO.
EAT UP, NOW... GOLLY, YOU WERE HUNGRY, HUH?
HA HA... ALL MY CHILDREN... I LOVE YOU SO... BUT... I CAN'T KEEP TAKING YOU ALL IN BY MYSELF LIKE THIS...
choke AND SOON THE PAPERBACK EDITION WILL BE RELEASED!...WHAT...WHAT AM I GOING TO DO?
WON'T YOU HELP?
EVERY 12½ MINUTES, SOMEONE, SOMEWHERE, IS THROWING OUT THEIR COPY OF JIMMY CORRIGAN, THE SMARTEST KID ON EARTH. DISCARDED, UNWANTED, LEFT ALONE, THESE INCREASINGLY IRRELEVANT MEMENTOS OF THE TURN OF THE LAST CENTURY NEED YOUR AID, YOUR LOVE. WHETHER IN A DUMPSTER, OR A GARAGE SALE, OR BURIED IN AN EMBARRASSING SECTION OF A CHAIN BOOKSTORE, AND NOW, FOR ONLY PENNIES A DAY, YOU CAN SPONSOR ONE OF THESE ORPHANS... YOUR VERY OWN FOSTER JIMMY CORRIGAN, THE SMARTEST KID ON EARTH. THAT'S RIGHT... JUST A FEW CENTS, OR
$18.95 IN U.S.A.
26.95 CAN.
WILL START THE CARING... HELP SAVE A DYING, IRRELEVANT ART TODAY... PLEASE DONATE... BEFORE IT'S TOO LATE!
ISBN 0-375-71454-5
51895
9 780375 714542